Debating the Law, Creating Gender

Women and Gender

THE MIDDLE EAST AND THE ISLAMIC WORLD

VOLUME 18

The titles published in this series are listed at *brill.com/wg*

Debating the Law, Creating Gender

Sharia and Lawmaking in Palestine, 2012–2018

By

Irene Schneider

BRILL

LEIDEN | BOSTON

Cover illustration: Palestinian Legislative Council, Ramallah/Palestine. The permission was given by Wafa, Palestine News & Info Agency, thanks to Khoulud Assaf.

Library of Congress Cataloging-in-Publication Data

Names: Schneider, Irene (Professor of Islamic studies), author.
Title: Debating the law, creating gender : Sharia and lawmaking in Palestine, 2012–2018 / by Irene Schneider.
Description: Leiden, The Netherlands : Koninklijke Brill NV, [2021] | Series: Women and gender, 1570–7628 ; 18 | Includes bibliographical references and index.
Identifiers: LCCN 2020034023 (print) | LCCN 2020034024 (ebook) | ISBN 9789004442306 (hardback) | ISBN 9789004442313 (ebook)
Subjects: LCSH: Divorce—Law and legislation—Palestine. | Women—Legal status, laws, etc.—Palestine. | Legislation (Islamic law)—Palestine—History. | Divorce (Islamic law) | Khulʿ (Islamic law) | Conflict of laws (Islamic law) | Conflict of laws—Divorce--Gaza Strip—Gaza. | Convention on the Elimination of All Forms of Discrimination against Women (1979 December 18)
Classification: LCC KMK577 .S36 2021 (print) | LCC KMK577 (ebook) | DDC 346.5694/20166—dc23
LC record available at https://lccn.loc.gov/2020034023
LC ebook record available at https://lccn.loc.gov/2020034024

Typeface for the Latin, Greek, and Cyrillic scripts: "Brill". See and download: brill.com/brill-typeface.

ISSN 1570-7628
ISBN 978-90-04-44230-6 (hardback)
ISBN 978-90-04-44231-3 (e-book)

This book is printed on acid-free paper and produced in a sustainable manner.

Contents

Preface

When I arrived in Palestine in the fall of 2013 to spend my sabbatical at Birzeit University, I did not know that I was going to be drawn into a fascinating societal and intellectual debate that would captivate me for the next seven years or so. My research interest, continuing my previous fieldwork in Iran (2009), was about "law in context." What I found was a country – under occupation and thus functioning under very difficult conditions – with a vibrant civil society, a state that despite the struggle over its territory established itself with all available means, and a Sharia establishment that reflected the full range and variety of different interpretations of what is normally called "Islamic law" or Sharia.

I stepped into the middle of a hot discussion about *khulʿ* (divorce) and more generally about women's extended access to divorce, which had already begun in 2012 before the issuing of the new ruling, the Supreme Judge's 2012 *taʿmīm*. *Khulʿ* continued to be debated in the public sphere even after the implementation of the ruling in the Sharia Courts. I decided to take up the topic in my book because looking through this lens enabled me to grasp what interests me most: how different societies, including my own, create and deal with gender roles, gender clichés, gendered rights, and hierarchies, as well as how politics and law interact. I returned to Palestine in 2014, 2017, 2018, and 2019. Since 2014, the debate about *khulʿ* was slowly replaced by a new aspect that became more dominant by 2017 and 2018: the perspective of international law. The question was brought up, and as always in Palestine, controversially discussed: how to reconcile the requirement of gender equality and equal rights for men and women entailed by international law with the existing outdated national legislation in the West Bank and Gaza. Whereas at first my idea had been to keep the focus on the *khulʿ* debate, I decided to take this shift in the public debate as an opportunity to broaden my understanding of public discourse in Palestine, to understand the interaction between the Sharia establishment, civil society, and the state with regard to family law and the construction of gender and gender roles.

My first and most deeply felt gratitude is to the Palestinians, those academics and non-academics who always welcomed and were open to my questions, who gave of their time patiently answering my questions, and who invested a lot of effort in explaining to me their opinions and points of view with regard to the legal discussions, especially on the legal position of women and women's rights under the extremely difficult political situation. I sincerely thank my old friend Nazmi Jubeh, Professor of History and Archaeology at Birzeit University, who was always ready to listen, explain, and help. Palestine was new to me after my work in Iran in the preceding years. I owe him much in terms of understanding Palestine, the country, its history, and its present situation. I am also grateful to Helga Baumgarten, who at that time was a Professor of Political Sciences at Birzeit University. She introduced me into the Palestinian academic field and helped me better understand the academic system as well as the political background in the West Bank and Gaza. I profited much from her profound knowledge of the Palestinian political system. In both of them I always had friends I could consult and rely upon in what I experienced as sometimes difficult situations. I also thank Jamal Juda, Professor of History at Nablus University, who introduced me to colleagues at his university and arranged fascinating meetings with them. I thank Asem Khalil and Jamil Salim, professors at Birzeit University for the time they took to listen to my research questions and Professor Mudar Qasis who accepted me as a visiting professor at the Muwatin Institute for Democracy and Human Rights in 2018. At Al-Quds University, I am grateful to Professor Mustafa Abu Sway in the Theology Department, Professor Munir Nuseibeh in the Law Department, and Professor Amne Badran in the Department of Political Sciences. Bärbel Stark at the office of International Relations did a great job connecting me to many colleagues.

In the West Bank, I met with and talked to many people who left great impressions on me. I name only some of them: I am very grateful to Sheikh Yusuf Id'is, at that time Supreme Judge in Ramallah who allowed me in 2013 to attend his class at Birzeit University and gave me an interview. I was deeply impressed by his scholarly personality and his openness and engagement with his students but also with me. I was and I still am very impressed by all the women and men in Palestinian society who struggle to improve the legal and social conditions for women. First and foremost, I am indebted to Sumud al-Damiri, Judge of the Sharia Appeal Court and Head of Prosecution in Family Law. She is not only a very engaged jurist with a high degree of professionality but also an open-minded woman with clear visions and ideas for the development of her society and a sharp analytical understanding of what could be the solution to many of the current problems. I thank Laila Abed-Rabho who put me in contact with three female judges in the West Bank and enabled me to interview them. Of civil society actors, I want to thank the late Nihaya Muhammad (d. 2015) for two long interviews that opened my eyes to the position of civil society. I also thank the late Maha Abu Dayyah (d. 2015), Randa Siniora, and many others for long talks and much information about not only the positions of their organizations but also different projects and strategies. Basma Khatib, working at the German Representative Office in Ramallah, gave me invaluable advice for my research and connected me to very interesting people. I owe much to her in-depth knowledge of legal and social debates in Palestine, and

I thank her for our long talks. Juman Qunays introduced me to the media in Palestine and her program *Lāzim Naḥkī*. With regard to the State of Palestine, I thank Hasan al-ʻUri, legal advisor to the president, for two long interviews; I also thank many employees of the Ministries of Justice and Women's Affairs. I am grateful to Dr. Haifa Agha, former Minister of Women's Affairs who took time to have a long talk with me, and Omar Iwadallah of the Ministry of Foreign Affairs for an inspiring interview about the future of international law in Palestine.

I am grateful to Bettina Marx, Head of the Heinrich-Böll-Office (Ramallah) and Reham Alhelsi, who enabled me to travel finally to Gaza in April 2019 to evaluate one of Heinrich-Böll-Foundation's projects about the *khulʿ* law in Gaza. With their help, I was able to have interviews with Zaynab al-Ghunaymi of the civil society, Hasan al-Juju from the Sharia establishment, and Huda Naim, a state representative. I was impressed by the cooperation between these three very different personalities, and their joint effort to improve the legal status of women. This very short (due to travel restrictions) field trip to Gaza considerably deepened my understanding of the legal debate in Gaza and helped to reconsider my former results, which I had gained from watching TV programs and reading the news and announcements of different participants of the debate.

I could not have written this book without the invaluable gift of time provided by relief from my university duties. Therefore, I thank the Käthe-Hamburger-Kolleg in Bonn that granted me a stipend for three months in the summer of 2014. From 2016 to 2019, I had the chance to be part of an European Union project "Understanding Sharia: Past Perfect/Imperfect Present," which led me, together with my esteemed colleagues Robert Gleave (Exeter), Knut Vikør (Bergen), Léon Buskens (Leiden), and our postdocs Nijmi Edres, Mahmood Kooria, Omar Anchassi, and Eirik Hovden, to discuss in depth questions of how the past was used in current debates. It sharpened my perception of this aspect and of the arguments used in Palestine in the family law debates. Our meetings were always incredibly stimulating and their comments invaluable to me.

Finally, I want to thank the Wissenschaftskolleg in Berlin that accepted me as a fellow in the academic year 2018/19. This was a great opportunity for me to finish this book. The Wissenschaftskolleg provided an inspiring environment for me to meet many colleagues from different disciplinary backgrounds and benefit from their views.

I am especially thankful to all who read and commented on my book or parts of it: Amr Hamzawy (Stanford) and Christoph Möllers (Berlin) as well as Fritz Schulze (Göttingen).

I relied on a great team assisting me at Göttingen University. I thank Lara-Lauren Goudarzi-Gereke who was extremely helpful and quick in finding new articles and websites, and tracing information online. I am indebted to Ghada Issa who transliterated many of the recorded audio and TV programs and also the *Qāḍī al-Quḍāt*'s course at Birzeit University with patience and accuracy, discussing with me the pitfalls of the Palestinian dialect. I am thankful to Judith Koschorke and Bettina von Linde-Suden for their help. I also thank Claudia Winter for proofreading the text in her usual, absolutely reliable and very precise way. I thank Judith Tucker and Susanne Dahlgren, the editors of the series "Women and Gender. The Middle East and the Islamic World" for including my book in their series. I thank Nienke Brienen-Moolenaar for coordinating the publication process, Ilana Brown for excellent editing and Dinah Rapliza for the layout, and Brill for publishing it. Any shortcomings are mine.

As always, I owe much to the love and support of my family, my husband Kamran and my sons Daniel and Jonas. I thank them for their interest in the topic, for reading and engaging in sometimes quite lively and controversial discussions with me about the questions within this book and many others.

Berlin, June 17, 2020

Figures and Tables

Figures

Tables

1 See: Registered Divorces [sic] Cases 2017.

Abbreviations

BL	Basic Law/*al-Qānūn al-Asāsī*
HSCC	Higher Sharia Court Council/*al-Majlis al-Aʿlā lil-Qaḍāʾ al-Sharʿī* [Gaza]
ICHR	Independent Commission for Human Rights/*al-Hayʾa al-Mustaqilla li-Ḥuqūq al-Insān*
ICNL	International Center for Not-For-Profit-Law
LHC	Legislation Harmonization Committee/*Lajnat Muwāʾamat al-Tashrīʿāt*
MoWA	Ministry of Women's Affairs/*Wizārat Shuʾūn al-Marʾa*
NCFL	National Committee of the Family Law/*al-Lajna al-Waṭaniyya li-Qānūn al-Usra*
PA	Palestinian Authority/*al-Sulṭa al-Filasṭīniyya*
PLC	Palestinian Legislative Council/*Al-Majlis al-Tashrīʿī al-Filasṭīnī* [Gaza]
PLC	Palestinian Legislative Council/*al-Majlis al-Tashrīʿī al-Filasṭīnī* [West Bank]
PSL	Personal Status Law/*Qānūn al-Aḥwāl al-Shakhṣiyya*
SCC	Supreme Constitutional Court/*al-Maḥkama al-Dustūriyya al-ʿUlyā*
SCHC	[West Bank] Sharia Court High Council/*al-Majlis al-Aʿlā li-l-Qaḍāʾ al-Sharʿī*

Notes on Transliteration

The system of transliteration I use in this book is IJMES (International Journal for Middle Eastern Studies).

Consonants

’	(hamza)	ض	ḍ
ب	b	ط	ṭ
ت	t	ظ	ẓ
ث	th	ع	‘
ج	j	غ	gh
ح	ḥ	ف	f
خ	kh	ق	q
د	d	ك	k
ذ	dh	ل	l
ر	r	م	m
ز	z	ن	n
س	s	ه	h
ش	sh	و	w
ص	ṣ	ي	y

Vowels

Long Vowels

ا or ’	ā
و	ū
ي	ī

Doubled

ي	i yy (final form ī)
و	uww (final form ū)

Diphthongs

و	au or aw

Short

- - -	a
	u
	i

CHAPTER 1

Introduction

1.1 Research Design

1.1.1 *Prelude: Palestinian-Style Divorce*

On August 20, 2012, the Supreme Judge Department of the Sharia Court High Council (SCHC) (*Dīwān Qāḍī al-Quḍāt, al-Majlis al-Aʿlā li-l-Qaḍāʾ al-Sharʿī*) in Ramallah/West Bank under the chairmanship of the *Qāḍī al-Quḍāt,* the Supreme Judge Yūsuf Idʿīs, issued a ruling (*taʿmīm* 59/2012) regarding *khulʿ* (divorce) on the basis of financial compensation. From that day on, Palestinian women in the West Bank could get a divorce against their husband's will prior to the consummation of the marriage (*qabla al-dukhūl*) or to the provision of privacy (*khalwa*) that could have enabled the couple to have intercourse. This "Palestinian-style Divorce" had been hotly debated in Palestinian society and in the media for several months, and it continued to be debated over the following years. In Gaza, women's organizations campaigned to be granted the same version of *khulʿ* but without success (as of April 2019). The ruling, according to which women pay back their dower or another sum to get their freedom, was in fact not as unique as it might seem at first glance: a precedent had been set in Jordan, where a similar version of *khulʿ* was discussed and legislated in 2010.[1]

In a letter written by the Supreme Judge addressing this ruling, he advised his Sharia judges in the West Bank to apply this new form of divorce, which was also called "judicial *khulʿ*" and which he based on the Islamic past, in their courts. With this letter and this ruling, he factually revised the Jordanian Law of Personal Status (JLPS) of 1976, which applies in the West Bank and according to which this kind of divorce was permitted only on the basis of mutual consent between the spouses and not against the husband's wishes. Article 102 of the JLPS reflects this "classical" understanding of *khulʿ*. Yūsuf Idʿīs was criticized for this *ijtihād* (independent legal opinion) from different political quarters, for example by Ḥasan al-ʿŪrī, the legal advisor to Palestinian President Mahmoud Abbas,[2] and by Judge Ḥasan al-Jūjū, the head of the Higher Sharia Court Council (HSCC) (*Raʾīs al-Majlis al-Aʿlā li-l-Qaḍāʾ al-Sharʿī*) in Gaza.[3] Both

1 Hughes 2016; Engelcke 2017a: 24.

2 Ḥasan al-ʿŪrī, interview on October 13, 2014.

3 Lāzim Naḥkī 2013.

 | DOI:10.1163/9789004442313_002

argued that there should be "proper legislation" and that such a reform should go through constitutional channels, i.e., the Palestinian Legislative Council (PLC).[4] Yūsuf Idʿīs justified his decision to enact this ruling on the grounds that the parliament in Ramallah had not met since the 2007 split between Fatah and Hamas, and that there was only an old law that ignored the special social problems faced by what were mostly very young women. He stressed that it was his emphatic wish to help this group of young women resist "blackmailing" (*ibtizāz*) by young men.

What had happened? A social problem had arisen that caused a political and social uproar in Palestine and was finally resolved by the Supreme Judge's ruling. According to Palestinian custom, young women and men sign a marriage contract at the time of their engagement. With their signatures their marriage is already established under law (JLPS, Articles 14–16) and can only be ended by a divorce. However, the social perception is different. As long as the marriage ceremony, including the wedding night (*laylat al-dukhla*) and the consummation of the marriage, has not occurred, society does not consider the couple properly married, only "engaged." During the interim period between "engagement" and consummation of the marriage, an increasing number of engaged women realized that they and their fiancés were not a good match and consequently did not want to stay with them. However, their fiancés refused to dissolve the "marriage" through repudiation (*ṭalāq*), which is still a male prerogative, and used their leverage to claim money spent on gifts and dinner invitations as well as other alleged costs. The amounts demanded by the not-yet-real husbands were usually high and far exceeded the incurred costs. It was in this context that Idʿīs used the expression "blackmailing" (*ibtizāz*). Women, he argued, were trapped because they were unable to pay such large sums. As a consequence, they were socially and legally tied to their husbands (not-) to-be, who, having the option of taking a second and third wife or leaving the country and disappearing, left the young women in the status of "inbetweeners" (*muʿallaqāt*). This problem raised hot debates in Palestinian society. How could this situation be satisfactorily resolved in a not-yet state that had had no working parliament since 2007 and was subject to the authority of two different governments with different ideological backgrounds and two heads of the Sharia Councils, Ḥasan al-Jūjū in Gaza and Yūsuf Idʿīs in Ramallah? What could be done in a situation where, according to Article 43 of the Basic Law, President Abbas had the right to issue a presidential decree, but did not do so? It was in this politically, socially, and legally complex situation

4 PLC, the Palestinian Legislative Council (*Al-Majlis al-Tashrīʿī al-Filasṭīnī*), is currently meeting only in Gaza, see chapter 9, but not in Ramallah.

that the Sharia judges under Idʿīs' chairmanship found the above-mentioned solution in Islamic law and the SCHC in Ramallah issued the new ruling, which was soon applied in the Sharia courts of the West Bank.[5] Can the Supreme Judge therefore be called a quasi-legislator?

The legal situation in Palestine is special in the sense that there is as yet no Palestinian family law. Old versions of the Jordanian law (JLPS of 1976) and the Egyptian Family Rights Law (EFRL of 1954) are applicable in the West Bank and Gaza, but both are outdated and seen as no longer adequate by policy-makers and society at large. Across Palestinian society, from state representatives to civil society organizations and representatives of the Sharia establishment in both Gaza and the West Bank, there is broad agreement that a new unified Palestinian family law is required. However, the different actors disagree on what this law should entail. Should it be compatible with international law? Should it be more secular or religious, and, if based on Islamic law, which interpretation of Islamic law should prevail? Should it be a more moderate and modern version oriented toward gender equality and therefore more in accordance with international law or a more conservative version in keeping with what is still a traditional society, preserving male privilege and curtailing women's rights, for example in questions of divorce? When in 2014 President Abbas signed the UN convention CEDAW (Convention on the Elimination of All Forms of Discrimination against Women) without any reservations, when in 2017 the Supreme Constitutional Court (SCC) issued a judgment that could be seen as putting international law above national law, and when in 2018 a Palestinian delegation travelled to Geneva to present its first state report on CEDAW to the UN Committee, the question of gender equality in general and specifically with regard to divorce came under more intense scrutiny. As the signature to international treaties includes the obligations of the signatories to adapt the existing law to international standards, discussions in the West Bank and Gaza now began to focus on the relationship of national law to international law and Islamic law and their general (in)compatibility.

This book deals with law in contexts and focuses on the process of the vehement public debates about *khulʿ* in the first phase and the relation between national and international law in the second phase. It puts forward the hypothesis that public debates cannot be properly understood without taking into consideration the linguistic aspect. Such a connection of discourse analysis with detailed linguistic analysis is new in empirical research on the Middle East. It seems, however, to fit perfectly into the definition of what Seyla Benhabib calls "iterations": "Democratic iterations are such linguistic, legal, cultural,

5 Schneider 2016b: 45–47.

and political repetitions-in-transformation, invocations which are also revocations. They not only change established understandings but also transform what passes as the valid or established view of an authoritative precedent."[6]

In a broader sense, iterations are thus "complex processes of public argument, deliberation and exchange"[7] through which rights claims "… are contested and contextualized, invoked and revoked, posited and positioned throughout legal and political institutions as well as in the associations of civil society."[8] Those iterations may lead, Benhabib argues, to jurisgenerative politics.[9] In the case of the abovementioned example, one could see the *khulʿ* ruling of 2012, even though it was not issued by the parliament, as such a jurisgenerative effect, because it was applied after 2012 in the Sharia courts. But what of the developments in 2014–2018 that were obviously triggered by President Abbas' signature to CEDAW but were not followed – as of the time this research was concluded (April 2019) – by a draft law taking the requirements of this international convention into account? Here, obviously, no jurisgenerative result is in evidence. In Gaza a draft law was accepted by the Gaza Parliament but was not put into force.

To understand these processes, the shifts in the debates and their connections with practices such as the *taʿmīm*, an action undertaken by the Supreme Sharia Judge, but also the signature to CEDAW, an action undertaken by the highest political authority in the person of the president, it is important to take, as Benhabib points out, both levels of iterations into account, the social and the linguistic one.

1.1.2 *Aim of the Study and Research Questions*

The study aims to understand the way gendered legal concepts, gender relations, and gender hierarchies were reflected in debates on law. Law is interpreted as law in context and for this reason the analysis draws on not only law texts in the narrow sense of the word but also draft laws, *taʿmīmāt*, debates in the media, minutes of meetings, and university lectures – in short – texts and iterations, debates and practices. I was interested in how the actors shaped and presented their arguments and the way they (re)constructed and (re)defined gender roles in society and law with the help of a range of different sources, including classical Islamic sources ("uses of the past"), modern interpretations of Islamic law, national legislation, and international law but also arguments

6 Benhabib 2004: 180.
7 Benhabib 2004: 19; Benhabib 2010: 6.
8 Benhabib 2004: 19.
9 Benhabib 2004: 181.

concerning society and politics. This study is thus an examination of how law adapts and changes through discourses with regard to content and wording. It interprets law and legal debates as ongoing processes, as negotiations to which different parts of Palestinian society contributed. It considers law, last but not least, as the result of a power struggle between different positions in Palestinian society.

Why was the debate on *khulʿ* chosen as a starting point? The debate around *khulʿ* as part of divorce law reflects one of the many collision points between a conservative interpretation of Islamic law and modern international law, or more explicitly between interpretations entailing hierarchical or egalitarian gender relations. As mentioned above, the right of the husband to almost unrestricted *ṭalāq* (repudiation) is still enshrined in the applicable laws in Palestine. There is no obligation on the husband to take the matter before a court; he merely has to register his repudiation after he uttered it – with or without the wife's knowledge or presence. The applicable laws (JLPS, EFRL) are outdated and do not reflect recent reforms in other codifications in the Muslim world, among which are those undertaken in neighboring countries Egypt (2000) and Jordan (2010),[10] but also in Morocco (2004), which is often referred to in Palestine.[11] Collision points that are often the subject of public debate include, among many others, the necessity of a male guardian for a woman to conclude a marriage contract (*wilāyat al-nikāḥ*), polygyny (*taʿaddud al-zawjāt*), child custody and male guardianship for the children (*ḥaḍāna/wilāya*), and inheritance (*irth*) as well as other legal fields. There were several reasons for using the case of *khulʿ* as a starting point for this analysis. First, prior to and after the ruling in 2012, this controversial debate arose throughout Palestinian society because of the special social situation described above; it started before the issuing of the *taʿmīm* and continued to dominate the iterations until around 2014. This debate was a frequent subject of media and television reports and a focus topic of civil society organizations. Second, a factual change of the applicable law (JLPS) was seen as not only possible but in fact took place, was accepted by society, and the new ruling was finally applied in the Sharia courts. Third, the 2012 *khulʿ* ruling permeated, as will be shown, not only the iterations on international law but also Palestine's state report on CEDAW. However, in the second phase between 2014 and 2018 another topic gained dominance: the more general question of how international law and especially CEDAW could be brought into harmony with national legislation. Divorce rulings were only part of this more general discourse, but an important one. It became the focus

10 There is a new Jordanian law of 2019, which has not been analyzed.

11 See Schneider 2014: 58–75.

of public attention in Palestine not so much when President Abbas signed international treaties, among them CEDAW, but when a Palestinian delegation travelled to Geneva and presented the first Palestinian report in July 2018 to the CEDAW Committee.

In general, in Europe as well as in the Arab and Muslim states, family law and gender relations are of special importance for national identities and cultural authenticity. Family law debates, gender relations, gender roles, social and legal duties, rights and obligations of men and women toward each other and in the family, the construction of the family as the core and kernel of society, and culturally developed concepts of femininity and masculinity can be described as powerful markers of national identities and an important expression of cultural authenticities, in short as "pillars and weak points in the construction of identity."[12] Gender relations are thus a highly sensitive and central topic of social debates – or, in Yassir Arafat's words – family law is a "wasps' nest" (*ʿushsh al-dabābīr*).[13]

So what can the outcome of the linguistic and social analysis of iterations concerning the "*khulʿ* case" in connection with the debate on international law tell us about Palestinian society and its position on gender hierarchy and gender equality? Surely it does not allow a prediction of what a later family law in a future Palestinian state will look like. But it can provide us with some clues as to how these debates around a future Palestinian law may develop, who the different and main actors are in this debate, and what their position is with regard to gender relations and gender equality as well as the power and influence they exercise in society and politics and, of course, in the iterations. According to Michel Foucault, discourses are not only always interwoven with practices but also intrinsically connected with power relations.[14] Following these iterations over the course of seven years allows us to see different developments and configurations and perceive power shifts in these iterations, which might reflect the influence of one or the other group. It enables us to better understand which of these iterations were or became dominant or even led to jurisgenerative practices at one time or another; to understand how debates and practices – the *khulʿ* ruling but also draft-laws, the signing of CEDAW, the SCC judgment etc. – were interwoven; which gender relations were negotiated by whom; and, linguistically, how this was justified by referring to other

12 Hélie-Lucas 1994: 393; Moors 1999: 150; Buskens 2003. Hammami 2004: 125 describes a fracture in 1990s Palestine between "a legacy of secular nationalism and a newer resistance identity that was nationalist but based in narrower ethnic and religious terms."

13 The saying attributed to Arafat was quoted on the television program *Ḥārisāt Nārinā* (April 9, 2017) by the host.

14 Hall 1997: 47–50.

Islamic or non-Islamic legal terms. What it does not allow us to assume is a more or less automatic development toward gender equality as reflected in theories of modernity and depicted in some approaches to international law according to which the signature of international treaties sets forth a process of norm-adaption that ends more or less automatically in the complete implementation of international law. The process is much more complicated, as this research will reveal.[15] Looking at the *khulʿ* case can function as a magnifying glass that helps us to understand more general debates and negotations on how gender roles are constructed, argued, and defended by different actors in society. But not in which direction these debates will go in the future.

The central question is: Who leads this debate and steers this process of legislation toward a specific goal? Or, in the words of Ḥasan al-ʿŪrī, legal advisor to the president drawing on a famous Arab proverb: Who will bell the cat?[16] The state, he said, must "bell the cat." But did it do so?

My research questions regarding iterations as a social phenomenon are:

1. Who participates in the iterations? Who can "bell the cat"? Who can influence or even steer these iterations in a certain direction? Can Islamic law be called a *doxa*?[17] How do iterations turn "jurisgenerative"?

On the linguistic level the questions would be:

2. What are the terms, the counter terms, and key concepts used in these iterations? Are the terms equally applicable for men and women or do they reveal a gendered meaning, i.e., a meaning that is different for men and women? How are they (re)interpreted? How is the Islamic past "used" and transferred to the present? How is international law "translated" into national law and/or the national debate on law?

With regard to the first phase of the iteration around *khulʿ* and how the past is used to remedy the present the questions would be:

3. What are the regulations of the codified laws, the draft laws and the *taʿmīmāt* (chapters 2 and 4) with regard to *khulʿ*? Which gender roles, gendered rights and duties, and gender hierarchies do these texts reflect?

---

15 See chapter 8.

16 In Arabic: *man yuʿalliq al-jaras?*, literally: Who hangs the bell [around the neck of the cat]? This saying is based on a fable: mice who want to protect themselves decided (and in the end, succeeded) in hanging a bell around the neck of a cat so that they can hear her coming and run away. "Who Will Bell the Cat?" https://www.youtube.com/watch?v=gz7wHiFfbRo, accessed April 1, 2019. The fable is often attributed to Aesop but seems to be of later origin. It means "to attempt, or agree to perform, an impossibly difficult task," see "Belling the cat" in https://en.wikipedia.org/wiki/Belling_the_Cat, accessed April 1, 2019. In this context, Ḥasan al-Ūrī meant the task of steering the process of legislation.

17 This term refers to Bourdieu, see below pp. 9–10.

4. How did the participants in the iteration – civil society, the State of Palestine, and the Sharia establishment – debate the subject of *khulʿ* and what special role do universities and university teaching play in these iterations (chapters 5 and 6)? Which "uses of the past" were made?

With regard to the second phase of the Palestinian legal iterations between 2014 and 2018 the questions are:

5. How did the State of Palestine respond to the challenge of gender equality as laid down in CEDAW? How was global international law "translated" into local legal iterations? How was it discussed in civil society and the media (chapter 7)?

While most of the research was done in the West Bank, the situation in Gaza will be addressed in a final chapter and it will be asked:

6. How was *khulʿ* and international law discussed in Gaza (chapter 9) in comparison to the West Bank?

In order to observe and present iterations and dominant discourses in terms of their developments over a certain time, the book has for the most part been structured chronologically. After the introduction to the research design and the research literature (chapter 1), the Palestinian legal system is introduced in chapter 2, presenting the Basic Law (BL) of 2003 (2.1.1), Palestine's basic institutions, such as the Palestinian Legislative Council (PLC), the Sharia Court High Council (SCHC) (2.1.2) and the Supreme Constitutional Court (SCC) (2.1.3); the current applicable legislation in the West Bank and Gaza is described (2.2). As there is no new Palestinian family law as yet, different draft laws gain importance and are analyzed in more detail (2.2.2); an important meeting that took place in the president's residence in Ramallah, the *Muqāṭaʿa*, in November 2013, where I was present, will be dealt with because it brought together all the important players in society and seemed for a moment to put a new Palestinian family law within reach (2.2.3). In chapter 3, the main actors will be presented: the state, the civil society, the Sharia establishment. In chapter 4, the Supreme Judge's ruling in 2012 on *khulʿ* is analyzed in detail, legally and linguistically. Chapter 5 presents the way the Supreme Judge taught *khulʿ* to his students at Birzeit University (BZU), one of the most prominent universities in the West Bank. Universities are undoubtedly an important sector of the public space and a highly productive, but still underresearched arena of iterations in which the future legal elite is trained. The topic will be tackled from two sides: the actual class the Supreme Judge taught (5.3) is contrasted with an analysis of the university textbook the students were supposed to read (5.4). Chapter 6 takes these iterations into the whole society and looks at the way civil society (6.1), the state (6.2) and the Sharia establishment (6.3) discussed this ruling. As iterations shifted with the presidential signature to CEDAW, chapter 7 looks at the state report delivered by the State of Palestine (7.1) and the following exchange with the UN committee (7.2). However, civil society was active in this context, too, and delivered shadow reports (7.3). In addition, the way the delegation presented itself in Geneva is examined (7.4). In chapter 8, the highly controversial and revealing iterations this state report triggered in Palestine are analyzed. Generally, the controversial debates that took place in the media were compelling, open, and very critical, and this applied to both the West Bank and Gaza. Chapter 9 draws attention to Gaza, which has its own story to tell, not only with regard to its different legal background (9.1) but also with regard to legal development (9.2) and the iterations that were as intense as in the West Bank but different and did produce a surprising result (9.3). In chapter 10, I present my overall conclusions.

1.1.3 *Theoretical Framework*

1.1.3.1 Islamic Law as a Repertoire and/or as *Doxa?*

Examining the complex social and political processes of how codifications of law were "produced" in Palestine in the transitionary period of 1994–2000, Lynn Welchman argues that "Islamic repertoires" played an important role. A repertoire is a "cluster of formal resources around legitimizing principles."[18] Welchman characterizes the situation in Palestine as follows:

> The understanding of what can or should be represented as "the Islamic sharia" may differ insofar as it is actually defined, but it remains the dominant repertoire in discussions of personal status while the production of a set of rules from within this framework is being conditioned by the dynamic engagement of differently positioned social and institutional actors.[19]

The result of this research will corroborate Welchman's classification. But is this also true for the concept of *doxa*, which has been used especially in the Palestinian context? Rema Hammami, a researcher at Birzeit University, called Islamic law the *doxa* of Palestinian society,[20] referring to Pierre Bourdieu's concept. Bordieu uses *doxa* for a very small set of beliefs and practices that appear in the "extreme case" of a "quasi-perfect correspondence between the objective order and the subjective principles of organization (as in ancient societies)." It is – and this is the important aspect of the definition – something "taken for

18 Dupret 1999: 34.
19 Welchman 2003: 69.
20 Welchman 2009: 143; Hammami 2004: 134.

granted."[21] It is "unaware of the very question of legitimacy."[22] *Doxa* becomes orthodoxy when it is no longer taken for granted and accepted unconsciously but recognized as being, at least in part, arbitrarily constructed and in competition with other beliefs.[23]

Hammami puts this into concrete terms, arguing:

> While for some social groups the centrality of shari'a in regulating gender relations is taken for granted, and beyond question, for others shari'a has become a central concept within a larger political project that attempts to replace the present set of social and political arrangements. The goal of this orthodoxy is an attempt to reassert shari'a's central and "natural" role in regulating all aspects of life.[24]

Hammami would thus herself restrict the concept of *doxa* to "some social groups," arguing that it is necessary to differentiate between "*doxic* attitudes" in relation to Sharia and the personal status law and "newer orthodox attitudes," which conceive of Sharia as having a much wider purpose.[25] Dörthe Engelcke argues with regard to Jordan that the assumption that family law is Islamic law constitutes not *doxa* but *orthodoxy* in Jordan.[26] The question – which will not be dealt with here – remains of whether Hammami's concept is still in keeping with Bourdieu's definition of *doxa*? We are also left with the question of what this means for the greater context of legal iterations in Palestine in the years 2012–2018?

1.1.3.2 Iterations – Unrestricted or Chained?

Discourses as understood and defined by Foucault are the production of meaningful statements and a way of representing knowledge, and thus the production of knowledge through language. They comprise sayings and practices that mutually influence each other.[27] In a discourse, there are certain rules that govern the way an object can meaningfully be talked about. Just as discourse "rules in," as Stuart Hall puts it, certain ways of talking about a topic, it also "rules out," limits and restricts other ways of talking or constructing knowledge

21 Bourdieu 1972: 168.
22 Bourdieu 1972: 168.
23 Bourdieu 1972: 164.
24 Hammami 2004: 134.
25 Hammami 2004: 134.
26 Engelcke 2017a: 6.
27 Hall 1997: 44.

about it and creates "taboo-topics," things that cannot be said.[28] This concept of discourse was further developed by Benhabib into the already-mentioned concept of "iterations," which she used in her book *Rights of Others* (2004) to discuss the legal status of migrants in Europe and their relation to international law and human rights.[29] The application of her concept of iterations in the West Bank, to a Muslim and non-Western state, needs justification.

Iterations are not restricted to debates about international norms and rights. The term covers all socio-legal debates in society, which would eventually lead to a reinterpretation of the law, or, as Benhabib puts it, to a "reappropriation and reinterpretation of guiding norms and principles." When a public discussion in the West Bank and Gaza takes place and in the end de facto (even if not de jure) the law is changed and a new ruling for divorce is implemented in the Sharia courts, this, I argue, can be called a "jurisgenerative" process emerging out of social and political iterations around this legal topic. These iterations are connected to global discourses insofar as Palestine has signed CEDAW without reservation and thus has accepted the obligation to adapt national legislation to international law – a fact that is reflected in the national debate especially after 2014. What Benhabib describes is the "normal" process of debating new legal developments in a society. The opposite would be a law imposed from above, an act not observable in Palestine with regard to family law. Any iteration transforms meaning, adds to it, and enriches it. The antecedent is reposited and resignified. In Palestine, as in the majority of the other Muslim states, family law is discussed at first on the basis of the (re)interpretation of Islamic norms and rulings and thereby draws heavily on "uses of the past," i.e., Quranic verses, sayings of the Prophet, rulings of the schools of law, etc. Are also terms and concepts taken from international law? The intersection of these discourses is new and one of the crucial questions that can only be answered by a detailed analysis of the linguistic aspect of the iterations, i.e., the terminology in the texts, reports, and interviews.

Because Benhabib uses the analytical instrument of iterations for democratic societies mainly in Europe and takes examples from the European context, such as the headscarf debate in France, the question arises if her concept can be applied to Palestine without examining whether the existing Palestinian state is "democratic."

28 Hall 1997: 44–45.

29 Benhabib 2004: 1.

Benhabib writes:

> If democratic iterations are necessary in order for us to judge the legitimacy of a range of variation in the interpretation of a right claim how can we assess whether democratic iterations have taken place rather than demagogic processes of manipulation or authoritarian indoctrination? Must not democratic iterations themselves presuppose some standards of rights to be properly evaluated?[30]

She refers here to Jürgen Habermas, according to whom only those states may claim legitimacy that can meet with the assent (*Zustimmung*) of all citizens.

> The "legal constitution of a discursive procedure of legislation" is possible only in a society that institutionalizes a communicative framework through which individuals as citizens or residents can participate in opinion- and will-formation regarding the laws which are to regulate their lives in common.[31]

At first glance, there seems to be no doubt that such a process of "opinion- and will-formation" took place in Palestine with regard to the *khulʿ* issue. The *khulʿ* iterations as well as iterations about the role of international law and its relation to Sharia reveal a discoursive process in which different layers of society took part. Particular emphasis needs to be placed on the role of the media in lending a platform to different and contradictory positions in Palestine. The emerging question is, of course, the extent this concrete iteration is independent of or connected to the state and/or another actor, for example, the Sharia institutions such as the SCHC (in the West Bank) or HSCC (in Gaza). Did state institutions or the SCHC or even the civil society try to steer and channel it or enhance and encourage it? Did the state interfere, promote, or impede these iterations? Was it a truly open discursive process? Was a large part of the population involved? When the new ruling was issued, were different parts of society given the chance to speak out and did the new ruling meet the *Zustimmung* of the (majority of the) population? These questions will be dealt with following a thorough analysis of these discourses in the West Bank and to a lesser extent in Gaza. But even in case the answer to the question if Benhabib's concept can be applied to Palestine was "yes," this would not say anything about the general political context in Palestine, the functioning (or currently, in the West Bank,

30 Benhabib 2010: 6.

31 Quoted in Benhabib 2010: 6.

non-functioning) of legislation as well as other state organs, the reduced separation of powers and the (non)functioning of the rule of law, and many other important factors that are deemed necessary for a working democracy.[32] The question of whether or not the State of Palestine is a democratic state cannot be debated here as it would need a completely different research design, starting with an in-depth analysis of the constitution and legal structure, the rule of law as well as the actual political and legal application of laws in what the Birzeit professor of law Asem Khalil called a "state in waiting."[33] This "state in waiting" is currently under Israeli occupation and faces a tremendous problem resulting from the political, ideological, and geographical divisions between Fatah and Hamas. It is economically and politically heavily dependent on the EU and the United States making the situation even more complicated.

This research therefore takes as a point of departure and focuses on the iterations around the new ruling on *khulʿ* and on the question of whether the applicable law can be "harmonized" with international law only in a restricted sense, i.e., iterations that were observable and obviously influenced legal policy and led to jurisgenerative actions in the West Bank (chapter 6) and in Gaza (chapter 9). One highly innovative aspect of this research besides the focus on iterations as social and linguistic approaches lies in the fact that it looks at not only the media and what is normally called the "public sphere," but also a special part of this public sphere: university teaching. University teaching frames the education of a future Palestinian legal elite (chapter 5). It also focuses on a broader and more controversial debate about the role of Sharia and international law generally (chapter 7). The Palestinian media play an important role in this context, as will become evident, by providing a platform for these discussions.

Iterations generally take place in a public sphere, and here Muhammad Khalid Masud's definition of the "public" is useful, because it takes as a point of reference the public space in a Muslim state, in his case Pakistan. He defines the public sphere "as a space that the modern media and mass education have helped to create and where public debates on issues of common concern are taking place."[34] For him this space has at least two characteristics of publicness: a plurality of voices and a fragmentation of traditional authority. It is for Masud the site where debates on religion and Sharia are increasingly taking place and which the traditional scholars, the *ʿulamāʾ*, have to share with "lay"

32 For the critique of civil society with regard to these points, see the Shadow Reports to the CEDAW Committee (chapter 7.3).

33 Khalil 2012: 587.

34 Masud 2005: 155; see also Eickelman/Anderson 1999: 1–2.

members of society who publicly discuss Sharia.[35] The framing of this debate is religious, he concedes, "However, while it is not a secular critique, it is certainly not led or dominated by the religious 'orthodoxy' either."[36]

This is reflected in the Palestinian media and TV programs, where discussions normally included representatives of the Sharia establishment and civil society, and to a lesser extent of the state. Masud argues that the secularity of publicness predominant in many definitions is specific to Europe and that excluding religion from the public sphere is not acceptable in a Muslim country. He considers Habermas's theory of communicative action as relevant, as it lays a primary stress on the autonomy of the self and on the open and rational character of public discourse.[37] As in my own research, Masud's focus is on how individuals – and organizations – communicate on the basis of their interests: "The norms created by this discourse in the public sphere reflect an ongoing consensus based on the reflexive self-positioning of individuals. These norms are assumed to faithfully mirror pluralism and autonomy, which are very basic to modern life."[38] The result, particularly in legal debates, is what Masud calls the "social construction of Shari'a," which is the outcome of a social process rather than state action. He does not see this as an essentially modern phenomenon, but the emerging public sphere defined above has, in his view, made it more transparent.[39]

There have been different studies about these processes of socio-legal debate, that, while not referring explicitly to Benhabib's concept, outline the form and consequences of these debates for jurisgenerative politics, however, not with the intense connection to a linguistic analysis as is done in this research. In his analysis of the process that led to the new codification in Morocco in 2004, Léon Buskens deals with questions very similar to the ones asked here with regard to Palestine.[40] The setting is different, especially because of the prominent role of the king in the field of women's rights. In Morocco, the struggle for women's rights was already linked to the struggle for human rights in the 1980s.[41] *Ijtihād* claimed as a right by the king played a special and

35 Masud 2005: 155–156.

36 Masud 2005: 156.

37 Masud 2005: 156.

38 Masud 2005: 156.

39 Masud 2005: 158.

40 Buskens 2003: 7; for similar analyses of public discussions, see Moors 2003 as a general overview. Welchman 2000 and 2003 and Shehada 2011 focus on Palestine, Schneider 2016a on Iran; for Jordan, see Engelcke 2017a, for a comparison between Jordan and Morocco, see Engelcke 2019.

41 Buskens 2003: 78.

prominent role and had to be defended against Islamists' claims.[42] Important scholars opposed the proposed changes as being against Islamic law.[43] Liberal politicians and journalists as well as women's and human rights groups reacted strongly and challenged Muslim scholars' exclusive right to interpret sacred texts, arguing that *ijtihād* should be a right of every believer.[44] Buskens writes:

> Despite the wide differences in opinion, most parties share certain key concepts. All refer to Islam and the Sharīʿa as the source for their ideas and ideals. No debate about family law seems to be possible outside the limits of an Islamic discourse. In 1990 representatives of women's organizations explained to me unambiguously that the demands for secular family law were unacceptable and therefore impossible in Morocco, and this situation has not changed in the intervening years.[45]

He argues that the intensity of the debate, the strong language that was used and included accusations of apostasy, heresy, obscurantism, barbarism, and treason, "show that powerful symbols and fundamental values are at stake."[46] In the end, a new law was implemented in 2004 after a process very much pushed forward and steered by the king.[47] Buskens points to the fragility of this emerging public sphere. "To what extent do parties agree to disagree?" he asks.[48] This situation of a strong king willing to reform family law and actively intervening in the discussion, even steering it, is very different from the Palestinian situation. It also differs from the Jordanian situation in which the Supreme Judge Department has played a more active role in the process of family law reform of 2010 than the king.[49]

With regard to Egypt, Hendrik Denker and Nadia Sonneveld have analyzed the context of the disputes about *khulʿ* and the development of law reform in 2000.[50] Both Denker and Sonneveld come to the same conclusion as Buskens does for Egypt and point to the fact that the debate is framed by the language of Islam.[51] Sonneveld writes:

42 Buskens 2003: 83.
43 Buskens 2003: 90–91.
44 Buskens 2003: 92.
45 Buskens 2003: 120.
46 Buskens 2003: 121.
47 Schneider 2014: 63–75.
48 Buskens 2003: 123.
49 Engelcke 2017a: 16–18; see also Engelcke 2019.
50 Denker 2004; Sonneveld 2012.
51 Denker 2004: 176.

> Despite the complexities of the debate, there is one thing that stands beyond doubt: all parties resorted to the language of Islam in order to present their particular point of view as the true understanding of Islam. For this reason, we can speak of the emergence of a public sphere which is characterized by the inclusion of a wider range of participants, who all claim that they have the right to interpret the principles of Islam in an authoritative manner.[52]

She adds, that this does not necessarily mean that the issues at stake are religiously motivated.[53]

Iterations, as fascinating as they are, are not easy to grasp. They include public debates on television and in other media as well as the statements and opinions of the main actors in these public debates: the state itself, civil society, and the Sharia establishment.[54] One particularly interesting aspect of public debate in this research that is normally ignored but has been included is university teaching. Teaching in universities is a process of training future academics as well as practitioners in the field of law, in this case future lawyers, judges, prosecutors etc. as well as future scholars of law. Universities can be defined as public spaces and as a privileged site for both scholarly and political action because they stand at the intersection of many disciplines and at the same time are a platform for political discussions.[55] The focus on the way in which *khulʿ* was taught in Birzeit University reveals new and surprising insights into the public discourse (chapter 5). Palestinian universities have faculties of Sharia and faculties of law and centers for gender studies with very different curricula and methodological approaches. Generally, before the backdrop of the political situation in Palestine they can be described as political hot spots where many political debates take place as well as demonstrations and strikes. The Supreme Judge's special way of presenting the development of "his" new ruling on the *khulʿ-taʿmīm* to the students of the law faculty raises the general question of the influence of education and more specifically university education on a culture of discussion. It is especially here, in university teaching, where much about the "uses of the past" and *Begriffsgeschichte* can be learned and about how "linguistic, legal, cultural, and political repetitions-in-transformation"

---

52 Sonneveld 2012: 56.

53 Sonneveld 2012: 56.

54 I will define in detail what exactly is meant by these categories. They are not monolithic and intersect at many points, see chapter 3.

55 Ambrozas 1998.

are shaped, used, corrected, and (re)constructed and become part of social debates.

1.1.3.3 Linguistic "Repetitions-in-Transformation" – Koselleck's *Begriffsgeschichte* and the Concept of "Translation" – How Do They Relate?

The focus on the linguistic aspect of iterations is twofold. With regard to the "uses of the past," in which classical legal terms and concepts are transported into the twenty-first-century legal debate, Reinhart Koselleck's *Begriffsgeschichte* is used. Koselleck developed *Begriffsgeschichte* with a diachronical and a synchronical dimension and used it especially for analyzing the adaption of terms of the German political history to the nineteenth century.[56] His use is thus intracultural and diachronic, looking at semantic changes of words and terms as well as concepts over time. But it reflects on a general level the history terms have. The second approach is "translation," a methodological tool mainly, but not exclusively, developed by Dipesh Chakrabarty, with a focus on cross-cultural use; for our context this is the "translation" of international law into the national, Palestinian, context. Both the "uses of the past" and "translation from the global to the local" will turn out to play an important role in the iterations under discussion here, in debates on *khulʿ* and in the general question of a possibility to harmonize Sharia and international law.

To start with the intra-cultural aspect, Koselleck describes the history of terms (*Begriffsgeschichte*) as follows:

> Such a procedure has of necessity to translate[57] words of the past and their meanings into our present understanding. Each history of word or concept leads from a determination of past meanings to a specification of these meanings for us. Insofar as this procedure is reflected in the method of *Begriffsgeschichte*, the synchronic analysis of the past is supplemented diachronically. Diachrony has the methodological obligation of scientifically defining anew the inventory of past meanings of words.[58]

Applied to the present context this means: focusing on the use of the terms in the debate of 2012–2018 and taking into consideration how the "use of the

56 Koselleck 2004: 76. My focus here is on Koselleck's *Begriffsgeschichte* and not on his broader methodological approach to historical developments, especially not his use of the term and concept of *Sattelzeit*.

57 In the English version, Koselleck himself uses the word "translate" and in the German version the German equivalent *übersetzen*. Koselleck 2013: 115.

58 Koselleck 2004: 81–82.

past" relates to these terms in this context, i.e., how the terms with their deep legal history are constructed in present day use of the language of Islamic law to justify the (re)definition of gender rights and gender roles. In today's Muslim societies the "uses of the past" in the context of family law and gender relations is very obvious, as mentioned earlier, and a prominent feature of debates: Quran verses are quoted in TV discussions, members of human rights organizations refer to the different rulings issued by the schools of law in the eighth century, and the Prophet's normative behavior is omnipresent. A complete diachronical analysis of the classical meanings and development of the term – e.g., *khulʿ* through the centuries and in different sources – is not and cannot be the topic of this book.[59] Thankfully, we have Denker's seminal article on *khulʿ*[60] along with other research on the topic to refer to. The question guiding this research is which classical sources and terms ("uses of the past") are quoted in today's iteration processes and how are they quoted? To what extent has the intentional substance of one and the same word – *khulʿ* – remained the same? Has it changed with the passage of time; has a historical transformation reconstructed the sense of the concept?[61] According to Koselleck, concepts can be arranged into three groups: (1) concepts whose meanings have persisted and, even under modern conditions, retained an empirical validity, (2) concepts that have changed radically such that the word itself remains only "a shell," and (3) neologisms.[62] Can *khulʿ* be seen as a "traditional concept" that retains an empirical validity? Or has it changed its meaning radically despite still being named *khulʿ*?

To understand the (re)defined meaning, it is necessary to look for semantic fields, parallel concepts, and counterconcepts.[63] Counterconcepts for *khulʿ* are, for example, the different terms for separation, such as *ṭalāq* (repudiation), *tafrīq* (separation), and *faskh* (dissolution of marriage). *Iftidāʾ* (redemption), a parallel concept that has a slightly different meaning, always comes up in iterations and is used widely and in a special way sometimes even replacing *khulʿ*, as will be outlined.

Whereas Koselleck focuses on *Begriffsgeschichte*, thereby limiting his approach to the diachronical and synchronical study of terms and concepts within the framework of one cultural context, in newer research the concept

59 Guth 2011 has demonstrated this brilliantly using the example of *riwāya*, whose meaning changed from "transmission" (mostly of poems and sayings of the Prophet, i.e., *aḥādīth*) to "novel" in the nineteenth and twentieth centuries.

60 Denker 2004.

61 Koselleck 2004: 82.

62 Koselleck 2004: 83.

63 Koselleck 2004: 78, 88; see Guth 2011: 158, Schneider 2018b.

of “translation” has been applied to the transcultural context, and more precisely to the “translation” of international – not only legal – terms and contexts to a national culture or law. Why use such a metaphor? Lena Foljanty argues that on an etymological level the term “translation” – which simply adds another metaphor to a list that includes “travel,” “transplant,” “migration,” and “transfer” – will not provide any strikingly new insight. However, she argues, the more important point is if the “contemporary use offers the potential to shift research questions in a fruitful manner.” It is here that “translation” enables a “deeper understanding of processes of legal transfer by addressing aspects of the processes that are not sufficiently illuminated by most studies in the field of comparative law.”[64]

Chakrabarty's approach is important not so much in terms of its application to the field of law – which is not his field – but as a general, thought-provoking attempt to transcend European epistemology. He argues that, in order to avoid Europeanizing methodological and theoretical approaches in the scholarly investigation of non-European countries and cultures, Europe has to be “provincialized.”[65] Notions such as “civilization,” “modernity,” “development,” “evolution,” and “progress” allowed Western, as well as non-Western, elites to measure the temporal distance between non-Western societies and the standard of Western democracy and modernity. Chakrabarty's translation theory, Wolf Schäfer argues, elevates the “translational processes of modernity”[66] in non-Western cultures and lifeworlds. It stipulates that postcolonial modernization cannot be understood with the “colonial translations” of the area-studies glossary, but requires delving deep into a “non-European language,” which would be Bengali in Chakrabarty's case, to provide “plural or conjoined genealogies” for European categories.[67] Setting the linguistic bar high is, as Schäfer argues, a welcome challenge of the translational agenda for area studies specialists with intimate knowledge of languages other than English. As Chakrabarty puts it:

> The point is not to reject social science categories but to release into the space occupied by particular European histories sedimented in them other normative and theoretical thought enshrined in other existing life practices and their archives.[68]

64 Foljanty 2015: 6.

65 Chakrabarty 2008; 2014. For a continuation of this debate, see Pernau 2016.

66 Chakrabarty 2008: 17; Schäfer 2014: 166.

67 Schäfer 2014: 166.

68 Chakrabarty 2008: 20.

Chakrabarty's approach is useful because it points toward a focus on emic terms and concepts such as the ones which will be debated in this book.

"Translation" has become, Foljanty argues, a key term in describing what happens in intercultural encounters.[69] To make the concept useful for the legal context she points to negotiations that take place in this process, focusing not so much on the result as on processuality, thereby taking into account the "bridgeheads," i.e., persons and institutions in the culture into which the term is "translated".[70] She argues:

> The metaphor invites us to look at the actors, their perspectives, their understandings, their patterns of thinking, and their decisions, not to mention at the processuality of the transfer process itself. It offers an approach enabling us to not only gain an understanding of the complexity of transfer processes, but also for us to grasp how this process is shaped by the interplay of active decisions, subtle shifts, and internal dynamics. It makes it possible for us to point out the contradictions and fault lines inherent in the process as well as to examine their effects on law and on its role in society. In the end, all of these insights enable us to ascertain how the process of transfer is inscribed into the newly implemented law.[71]

Sally Merry, concentrating on international laws against gender violence, adds an important aspect of this "translation":[72]

> In order for human rights ideas to be effective, however, they need to be translated into local terms and situated within local contexts of power and meaning. They need, in other words, to be remade in the vernacular. How does this happen?[73]

She admits, like Foljanty, that "remaking" human rights in what she calls the "vernacular" "is difficult."[74] This might be the reason for the fact that the topic has hitherto not been approached – at least in the legal area – on the basis of empirical research. Nor, to the best of my knowledge, has use been made of the combination of *Begriffsgeschichte* and "translation from the global to the local"

69 Foljanty 2015: 8.
70 Foljanty 2015: 15–16.
71 Foljanty 2015: 16.
72 Merry 2006: 1; see also Bachmann-Medick 2009.
73 Merry 2006: 1.
74 Merry 2006: 1; Foljanty 2015: 18.

in the context of the Middle East or the realm of Islamic law. The reason may be that those engaging with the topic so far have been jurists with training in European or Western law or social science scholars but not researchers rooted in the cultures and languages which are – according to the traditional view – seen as "recipients" of these "legal transplants," i.e., translations. This situation recalls the approach of "Orientalism," i.e., looking at the "Orient" instead of taking entanglement into account. It is for this reason that the focus here is on the "contact zone," the "entangled sphere," and what Foljanty calls "bridgeheads": the Palestinian state, civil society, and the Sharia establishment and the way they negotiate law, taking *khulʿ* and international law as an example.

1.1.3.4 Gender as a Crosscutting Category and Its Connection to Law

With regard to the connection of gender and law it might be enlightening to take a quick comparative look at the situation in German law and legislation. Article 3 of the German Basic Law of 1949 reads:

> Article 3 [Equality before the law]
> (1) All persons shall be equal before the law.
> (2) Men and women shall have equal rights. The state shall promote the actual implementation of equal rights for women and men and take steps to eliminate disadvantages that now exist.
> (3) No person shall be favoured or disfavoured because of sex, parentage, race, language, homeland and origin, faith, or religious or political opinions. No person shall be disfavoured because of disability.[75]

This article roots gender equality in the constitution. However, as Christine Langenfeld outlines, in 1957 the German legislator still defined the so-called housewife-marriage as a model. In this form of marriage the woman had to stay at home and take care of the children whereas the husband was the breadwinner. Even though the above constitutional article existed at the time, this situation persisted, as Langenfeld shows, until the German family law was amended in 1957 and 1977. Until 1977, a wife was only allowed to take up a professional job as long as it was considered compatible with her duties in the household and family, and the husband agreed. The wife needed the husband's consent to sign an employment contract.[76] A "biological" division of the genders was still considered normal, according to which the women's role was to give birth to children and rear and educate them while the public space belonged to men.

75 See Basic Law for the Federal Republic of Germany (1949).
76 Langenfeld 2016: 33–34.

Gender constructions differ with cultural contexts, develop through time, are closely connected to the establishment of national identities, are reflected in national legislation and constitutions, and represent the nation's perception on a global and local level.[77] Suad Joseph argues convincingly that citizenship has been gendered from the beginning, in the Middle East and elsewhere,[78] including Europe as demonstrated by the example of Germany. Joseph points to problems such as the right to vote – which was always given first to men then to women – to own a business, to travel without the permission of the father or husband,[79] and the right to pass on one's citizenship to one's children.[80] Gendered citizenship issues, she argues, result from the political privileging of the family as a unit and the legal privileging within families of males over females. And some gender issues arise from the entrenchment of religious communities and the legal authority of religious leaders over their members.[81] Often, and this is the case for Palestine too, women have been seen as crucial in establishing and maintaining the boundaries of nations and have been made into the symbolic markers of the nation itself.[82] One reason, Joseph argues, that citizenship is often dependent on familial membership is that patriarchy still weaves together civil society, state, market, and family subverting the separations and boundaries that Western theorists argue are necessary for democracy.[83] This is reflected in all (with the exception of Tunisia and Turkey) Middle Eastern legislation and personal status codes based on different interpretations of Islamic law, which subject women to the patriarchal control of male relatives[84] or to the control of a still patriarchally influenced personal status law.

How will gender relations be constructed in a future Palestinian state? What will the future Palestinian family law look like? These questions cannot be answered yet, of course. But an analysis of the debates and iterations characterizing the period 2012–2018 can be instructive. Gender is a central concept in this analysis and the approach used here reflects that of Joanne Conaghan. She argues – like Langenfeld for the German context – that law took its modern form not under conditions of gender-neutrality but in the context of a legally

77 Hélie-Lucas 1994.
78 Joseph 2005: 47.
79 Joseph 2005: 47.
80 Joseph 2005: 48.
81 Joseph 2005: 49.
82 Joseph 2005: 50.
83 Joseph 2005: 51.
84 Joseph 2005: 52.

sanctioned gender hierarchy.[85] Taking the UK as an example she adds: "In the jurisprudential imagination, law occupies a self-consciously artificial and gender-devoid world in which the individual legal subject is presumed to be without gender, although as feminist analysis has shown, 'he' is generally male by default."[86] By the late 1970s and early 1980s, the biological and essentialist perception of gender had been overcome and it had become commonplace in feminist scholarship to understand gender as a social and cultural construct in contrast to sex, which was seen as a biological essence.[87] As a social construct it became obvious that these gender roles belonged to specific times and places and changed with the transformation of society. This scientific approach is today accepted throughout all disciplines. With social development, women, who became increasingly educated and took up professions, were no longer seen as only housewives but were considered able to act in the public sphere like men. They were no longer confined to the kitchen and their role in life was no longer seen as restricted to bringing up children. In particular, the idea that women had to be protected by men has been abandoned. It is this idea of protection, however, that is still contained in what can be called the model of Islamic marriage based on the husband's payment of a dower (*mahr*) and maintenance and the wife's obligation to obey. This has, in short, been termed the "maintenance-obedience relation."[88]

On the epistemological level, this meant – in the developing field of gender studies – separating biology from the social environment as a first step. Whereas there were still men and women, it was argued, in what can be called heterosexual normativity, women's rights were socially adapted to their advancing positions in society. Whereas women remained biologically clearly identifiable, there was no obvious reason why they should not become active in all parts of the society. One result of this realization was the change from a family model in which the man was the head of the family and the breadwinner to a family model based on partnership between husband and wife. The following years saw the development of the argument that not only gender but also sex was subject to processes of social and cultural construction, an argument that cannot be followed up at this point and is not widely discussed in the Middle East. In addition, if the constructivist approach is followed to its logical conclusion, what will become of the materiality and the embodied context, which would then be seen as only a discursive product? Without ignoring

85 Conaghan 2013: 4.
86 Conaghan 2013: 5.
87 Conaghan 2013: 19.
88 See, for example, Sonneveld 2012 in many places.

this epistemic problem, Conaghan argues that nature and nurture are not as easily disentangled as the sex/gender distinction would imply[89] but concludes for her approach:

> The point here is not to suggest that sex is purely the product of social and cultural construction or that real differences between men and women's bodies do not exist. Rather it is to emphasize that how we know or apprehend bodies and the differences between them is inevitably socially and culturally mediated.[90]

Her approach "is to take gender as a category of analysis, that is, as a conceptual tool with which to probe and interrogate understandings of law and legal phenomena."[91] This is the approach that is also taken here.

1.1.4 *Sources*

The sources used here are textual sources, interviews and participant observations in classes at the Faculty of Law at Birzeit University. For the most part, the sources can be divided into the following categories:

a) Legal texts such as laws, draft laws, rulings (*taʿmīmāt*), *fatāwā* and decrees (*qarārāt*). Many legal texts, but not all, can be found in the database Muqtafi,[92] provided by Birzeit University, which generally contains legislation, legal texts but also some judgments, and can be accessed often both in English and Arabic versions.
b) Texts of websites of the state, the Sharia establishment and civil society organizations.
c) The textbook of Birzeit University for analyzing the Supreme Judge's teaching was especially prepared for the course "Personal Status Law" in the winter semester 2013.
d) Recordings of the Supreme Judge's class in October – December 2013. Combining the textbook and the recording helps generate an integral view of the way students are taught "the law." Participant observation in the Supreme Judge's classes provided additional insight into the intellectual and university discourse around the topic.

89 Conaghan 2013: 21.
90 Conaghan 2013: 21.
91 Conaghan 2013: 23.
92 http://muqtafi.birzeit.edu/en/, accessed January 11, 2018.

e) Television and other media reports (e.g., the already mentioned *Lāzim Naḥkī*, which can be accessed via Youtube and/or Facebook) are used to analyze the socio-legal iterations in society.
f) Expert interviews have been conducted with representatives of the state, civil society, and the Sharia establishment.

1.1.5 *Methods*

1.1.5.1 Texts

The textual sources as well as the recordings of the class and media reports are analyzed on the basis of close critical reading, and the above-mentioned set of questions. Critical reflection on this material is informed by the theoretical approaches outlined above. Whereas the focus on iterations in a more general sense follows the development of the debates and their topics between 2012 and 2018 and the analysis identifies the debates that dominated the public sphere and media, on the linguistic level a close reading will reveal the processes of (re)structuring, or changing of terms and concepts used. The two levels are also analyzed in relation to one another. No analysis of social and political debates can do without the question of power that permeates and steers the discourse and determines the order of importance of the topics, the time of their launching and the way they are talked about. Foucault's concept of power as an ubiquitous category structuring all social life and going far beyond simple top-down rule by the state forms an underlying concept for this research especially before the backdrop of the weak state of Palestine.[93] Obviously, the question "who bells the cat" cannot be answered without taking the power relations in Palestinian society into consideration.

1.1.5.2 Field Work, Participant Observation

I visited Palestine, the West Bank, five times between 2013 and 2019: October 3 to December 21, 2013; September 29 to October 14, 2014; November 15 to December 13, 2017; February 18 to March 7, 2018; and April 9 to 17, 2019. In April 2019, I was also able to enter Gaza and conduct interviews but only for a short period (April 10–11). In 2018, I had the official status of visiting professor at Birzeit University.

Not being an anthropologist by training and having a different agenda, I used "participant observation" especially in the Supreme Judge's class in a modified way: with more emphasis on observation and less on participation.[94] "Participant" observation can refer to a spectrum of different forms of "being

93 Hall 1997: 41–67.
94 Hauser-Schäublin 2003: 34.

engaged" with the society or groups the researcher is studying. Physical presence surely is one of the important prerequisites for this kind of research.[95] If I had, however, engaged in the debates in the class by asking questions or offering remarks, this would have interrupted the teaching process. I therefore chose a more distanced version, staying in the background. The leading assumption of participant observation is that through face-to-face participation, immediate and direct experience of situations and aspects of actions are possible, and aspects of these acts become observable, which would not have been otherwise observable.[96] This was of special importance in the class where I could "feel" the atmosphere of exchange between the Supreme Judge and his students as well as mood swings – students laughing about the Supreme Judge's jokes, starting to discuss among themselves when they were obviously irritated or bored by what he had said, etc. Staying in the background enabled me to follow what seemed to me the quite normal flow of the classes, the discussions, questions, and answers, etc.

This method of observation enabled me to not only follow the discussion but also concentrate on the subtext – the (re)construction of law and gender in a twenty-first century Islamic framework. Being well-acquainted with the classical literature of law and procedure, I was impressed by how much traditional knowledge – "uses of the past" – was taught by the Supreme Judge.[97]

1.1.5.3 Interviews

I conducted only expert interviews with around forty persons, with some of them I spoke twice or even three times. These interviews were a special form of semi-structured interview and focused on expertise in a certain field. They started for many of my interview partners with the same questions around *khulʿ*; their opinion of the new ruling; their opinion with regard to international law, Islamic law, and the roles of men and women in the law; their opinion

95 Hauser-Schäublin 2003: 34.

96 Lüders 2003: 151.

97 Coming from an academic background in Germany where language and talking about gender and gender roles is a sensitive issue and many terms are considered insulting, it was not easy for me to adapt to a terminology and language that seemed to me problematic and even disrespectful. It was, however, considered by the Supreme Judge and the students as the normal legal language. One example may suffice here. Talking about a married woman as *madkhūl bihā* was normal and is the official language of marriage and especially divorce documents. It means literally "penetrated" and refers to the alleged active-passive constellation of man and woman in the sexual act. Men penetrate, women are penetrated. Connected to the perception of men as actors not being divorced but divorcing and women as passive, which played a role in the debates about *khulʿ* (see especially Chapter 6), this seemed to me a pejorative term for a married woman but was not meant as such, at least not in this context of teaching.

with regard to a new Palestinian law and what it should look like. The questions were adapted to the position and knowledge of the interviewed person. However, the interviews developed very differently. Some of my interview partners answered my questions easily and explained much about the legal background, thus providing me a lot of insight into their legal thinking and the legal background of the West Bank; others gave only short answers and I had to actively ask more.

I interviewed the Supreme Judge in Ramallah, Yūsuf Idʿīs, in 2013 and his successor since 2014, Maḥmūd al-Habbāsh, as well as their colleague, the Supreme Judge in East Jersualem, Wāṣif al-Bakrī and Ḥasan al-Jūjū in Gaza. Furthermore, I interviewed representatives of the ministries, women's organizations, and the Sharia establishment. Of special importance was and is one of the female judges in the West Bank, Ṣumūd al-Ḍamīrī, Head of Family Prosecution, whom I had the honor to receive as a visiting fellow of the HERA-project in Göttingen in June 2018[98] and who provided me with invaluable insights into the legal situation of women in the West Bank from her perspective as a Sharia court judge.

All my interview subjects thus had a high degree of skill and knowledge in their respective domains because of their education and long years of experience; their skills and knowledge also provided them with status, power to act and decision-making opportunities.[99] I was surprised at and I am thankful for the level of access I was given, the openness and friendliness with which I was received, and the patience with which my questions were answered.

1.2 Research Literature

Research literature will be discussed according to the different themes dealt with in this research, i.e., law, gender, and university teaching.

1.2.1 *Law*

An important source for the study of law in Palestine is the al-Muqtafī database[100] created by the Law Faculty of Birzeit University (BZU). It is a source for the historical and relevant legislation in the area, as well as for presidential

98 As outlined in the preface, this project provided a framework for my work on this book and gave me valuable input especially with regard to the lens of "uses of the past." See http://www.usppip.eu/, accessed February 26, 2019.

99 Belting 2008: 1; Marotzki 2003: 153–154.

100 http://muqtafi.birzeit.edu. It is free of charge but an account has to be created. This is why it is only quoted here as such. For anyone interested in the historical and present legal system of Palestine, this database is highly recommended.

decrees and court judgments. The offices of the Sharia jurisdiction as well as the ministries and civil society organizations can be accessed through their websites, but they often also have Facebook pages.[101]

Feras Milhem[102] has dealt with the history and current state of the Palestinian legal system in his extremely rich and detailed study *The Origins and Evolution of the Palestinian Sources of Law* (2004). Starting from the Ottoman Empire and describing the British legal colonization, the time of the mandate, Jordan's annexation of the West Bank, the Egyptian administration of the Gaza strip, the Israeli occupation, and the role of the Palestinian Authority, he analyzes in detail and with accuracy legal structures and the system of legislation, with a focus on the period since the creation of the Palestinian Authority after the Oslo treaties. He especially deals with the Basic Law. In the last part of his book, he puts Palestinian legal development into a comparative global perspective. Another internationally known Palestinian jurist is Asem Khalil,[103] professor in the faculty of law at BZU. With regard to the topic of this book, he has published widely on the constitution and constitutional policy,[104] dealt with the legal fragmentation of Palestine and Israel[105] and with formal and informal justice, meaning tribal courts in the framework of what can be called a special Palestinian blend of legal pluralism.[106] In 2017, he and his colleagues commented critically on the judgment of the SCC, which in general terms stated that international law is above national legislation.[107] He considered it not well argued. Mutaz Qafisheh, professor of law at Hebron University, has published on a range of topics, including family law. His perspective on the discrepancy between international law, i.e., CEDAW, and existing legislation as well as his suggestions as to how to overcome these divisions[108] could, if accepted in the public sphere, serve as a basis for a future discussion of the family law.

With regard to the history of family law, Judith Tucker's groundbreaking work *In the House of the Law* (1998) and her analysis of *fatāwā*, legal opinions of the Ottoman Courts in Syria and Palestine in the seventeenth and eighteenth centuries should be mentioned. Her general result is that the muftis and judges supported hierarchical gender relations, but they also, in a certain sense,

101 See the references.
102 Milhem 2004.
103 Khalil 2012; 2013.
104 Khalil 2009a; 2012; 2013.
105 Khalil and del Sarto 2015.
106 Khalil 2009b.
107 Khalil 2017.
108 Qafisheh 2018.

took care of women by preventing men from abusing their rights.[109] Whereas Ottoman jurists could act with a certain degree of flexibility, Tucker has reservations with regard to codification which according to her reduced the scope of action for women's interests in law.[110] This stimulated a discussion about the general usefulness of codification for empowering women and women's rights. Aharon Layish[111] provides an overview of the approaches of Western scholars who are divided as to whether the codification of Sharia and a wide range of methods and mechanisms designed for its application since the middle of the nineteenth century should be assessed in terms of development "within" or "outside" Sharia. Some scholars maintain that this development is an expression of Sharia's vitality and ability to reform or renew itself to internalize Western inspiration and to adapt itself to changing conditions. Layish would rather see codification as detached from Sharia and even as "secularization."[112] Thomas Bauer, a scholar of Arabic medieval literature, labels the process of codification as a *Pervertierung*, i.e., perversion of the classical Islamic law.[113] Such an assessment seems simplistic and does not do justice to the complex and not yet fully researched relationship between legislation, jurisdiction, jurisprudence, and legal practice and the developments they have undergone in the last one hundred years in the Middle East.[114] Nahda Shehada rejects the critical view of codification in her research on courts in Gaza around the year 2000, stating that codification is not synonymous with the end of the traditional flexibility and fluidity of Islamic jurisprudence, which she sees preserved in the work of the Sharia courts.[115] Generally no family law is made for all time. Amendments are discussed in public, legal regulations are challenged, and reforms are discussed, decided upon, and introduced as this publication shows in detail. I argue that a detailed analysis of the changes to the family laws in the Middle East in the last twenty years or so shows a slow but perceivable development toward more gender-equal rights. These results are, however, no automatism, and they can be debated and are open to challenge; thus

109 Tucker 1998: 180.

110 Tucker 1998: 184.

111 Layish 2004: 91.

112 Layish 2004: 92; Engelcke argues that Muslim jurists in Jordan did not lose their monopoly and they have not ceded their authority to lawyers. The Ottoman reform process did not instigate a process of secularization that would ultimately bring about the slow demise of Sharia courts, see Engelcke 2017a: 32–33.

113 Bauer 2011: 181, for a review see Schneider 2012.

114 Schneider 2014: 63–75.

115 Shehada 2005: 323.

each draft and each law has to be analyzed in detail with regard to the gender concept it is based on.[116]

With regard to Sharia "within" and "outside," my position would be that as long as Muslim states include Sharia in whichever version – conservative or more modern, i.e., more in accordance with traditional gender roles based on a gender hierarchy or with international law and gender equality – Sharia is obviously part of the legal and legislative system of these states. There is no doubt, that Sharia – in Palestine, it is mostly this term used in the public debate rather than "jurisprudence" (*fiqh*) – is an important part of the iterations in many Muslim countries.

With regard to the more recent history of family law in Palestine, Lynn Welchman has done groundbreaking research. In *Beyond the Code* (2000), she meticiously analyzes the legal norms of all areas of family law and their rootedness in classical – mostly Hanafi – jurisprudence. She also looks at all areas of family law from engagement to divorce as defined in the applicable laws in the West Bank and Gaza and adds an analysis of court judgments from the 1990s. Focusing on what she calls the "interim" or "transitional period," i.e., the period after Oslo from 1994 until 2000, during which there was still hope that an independent Palestinian state would soon be created, she analyzes the "political processes of how codifications of laws are produced"[117] and touches on very similar questions to those examined in this book. Acknowledging that the task of unifying legislation in Palestine has to be seen as an enormous challenge for the Palestinian Authority,[118] she investigates the interaction between women's organizations, focusing on the so-called Model Parliament created by civil society and women's organizations and the Sharia system.[119] She provides an overview of the creation of the position of Supreme Judge in 1994,[120] his subsequently important role in the debate, and his rulings from 1995 onwards.[121] Perceiving Sharia at that time as "the dominant repertoire in discussions of personal status,"[122] as outlined earlier, she generates insights into a certain discoursive openness of the Sharia establishment for some of the women's arguments.[123]

116 Schneider 2014: 63–75.
117 Welchman 2003: 35.
118 Welchman 2003: 41.
119 Welchman 2003: 42–44; for the Model Parliament, see also Shehada 2011.
120 Welchman 2003: 52.
121 Welchman 2003: 43, 57–58.
122 Welchman 2003: 69.
123 Welchman 200: 57–69.

Since then important developments have taken place. The original vision of a Palestinian state-in-waiting during the post-Oslo years has given way to a position of resignation on the political level, especially since the political split between Hamas and Fatah in 2007 and the subsequent absence of any parliamentary session outside of Gaza. The Supreme Judge stepped into this vacuum of legislation and continued to issue from his powerful position rulings such as the *taʿmīm* on *khulʿ* divorce. Delineating the extent to which he was able to manipulate the process of iterations is one of the aims of this research.[124] In 2014, President Abbas signed CEDAW, and in 2017, the newly created SCC issued a ruling that could be understood as saying that international law is above national law. And in 2018, the Palestinian delegation went to Geneva to submit the first CEDAW report along with shadow reports by civil society organizations. The question "who bells the cat?" was thus put on the table with a completely new constellation of actors, one of them now being international law.

With regard to family law and the legal situation in the territories, especially the situation of women, a large amount of grey literature exists, mostly published by civil society organizations, often in cooperation with international donors. Examples of such literature maintaining a high scientific standard are publications by Ashraf Abu Hayyeh[125] and Reem Al-Botmeh,[126] the latter being a text edited by UNDP (United Nations Development Program). In particular, the organization WCLAC (Women's Centre for Legal Aid and Counselling) has published many booklets and papers in the area of family law and women's rights and has cooperated with such distinguished scholars as Lynn Welchman[127] – the result in this latter case being a useful little booklet on the most important rulings imposed by family law in the West Bank and Gaza.

The Palestinian population's opinion of family law was a focus of empirical research based on a quantitative approach examining gender roles and family law questions in the Palestinian context conducted by Rema Hammami (2004) and Rema Hammami and Penny Johnson (2013),[128] and the Institute of Women's Studies at Birzeit University with the support of the United Nations Development Program (UNDP). The results reveal different positions among citizens of the West Bank and Gaza with regard to the rights of women generally, the rights of women to divorce (including *khulʿ*) and the role of legislative institutions, i.e., the parliament as well as the Sharia courts, which are useful

124 For an equally important role of the Supreme Judge Department in Jordan, see Engelcke 2017a.

125 Abu Hayyeh 2011.

126 Al-Botmeh 2012.

127 Welchman 1999.

128 Johnson and Hammami 2013.

for this research. Regrettably, to my knowledge, there has not been any direct survey or poll regarding the *khulʿ*-ruling or the question of how international law could or should be integrated into national legislation.

Research into Sharia courts and their practices is interesting but only marginally relevant for this research. Welchman[129] and Shehada have worked on this topic.[130] Shehada's main focus is on the work of Gaza courts and she looks at the way these courts negotiate the legal rights of women.[131] She argues that Sharia judges are far more flexible, pragmatic, and dynamic than expected, to some extent echoing Tucker's conclusions regarding the pre-modern era.[132] Like Tucker in her work on historical Islam,[133] she argues that judges acted as "protectors" of women.[134] In a similar way to Sonneveld, Shehada takes into account the "diverse perspectives of ordinary people" and provides a different perspective on mainstream representations. In terms of legal theory, she tackles the question of who can claim the right to interpret the sources of law[135] and also the clash between the reinforcement of equal citizenship and religious specificities.[136] The debate itself is described by her as both "open and controlled."[137] In the period under examination, she argues, religious authorities to some extent excluded "experts" from the debate and transferred it from the social to the political domain.[138] The women's movement was, according to her research, less successful in shifting the discourse and more inclined to use a religious idiom in the West Bank and the women's movement in Gaza was denied access to the public (mosques, public meetings, television).[139] This changed in the time of my research and the Sharia establishment met with civil society on TV talk shows.[140]

With regard to "uses of the past" and the analysis of the debate on *khulʿ* in a neighboring country, i.e., Egypt, Denker's[141] seminal article has already been mentioned. He has produced a very valuable overview of the development of the concept of *khulʿ* from classical to modern law especially focusing

129 Welchman 2000.
130 Shehada 2005.
131 Shehada 2005: 317.
132 Shehada 2005: 110, 147.
133 Tucker 1998.
134 Shehada 2005: 323; for further research on courts, see Giunchi 2014.
135 Shehada 2005: 319.
136 Shehada 2005: 319.
137 Shehada 2005: 319.
138 Shehada 2005: 319.
139 Shehada 2005: 320.
140 See chapter 9.
141 Denker 2004.

on aspects of "uses of the past" in these debates and arguing that the debate in Egypt did not go into depth in what concerns the "uses of the past."[142] The participants in these debates took "the easy way out" – they did not refer to the texts to the expected extent. This "use of the past" in Egypt will have to be compared to its use in Palestine. A more recent publication by Sonneveld looks at *khulʿ* in Egypt in the context of social debates and its reflection in films and caricatures.[143] Sonneveld, who does not seem to have been aware of Denker's article, approaches *khulʿ* as a legal solution for an Egyptian woman, Nūra, and women in her situation, considering the everyday experience of women before the courts. She argues that not only wealthy women[144] – as sometimes stated in the public discourse – but also very poor women could and did use this form of divorce.[145] Again the question arises: how high is the percentage of women using this form of divorce? Sonneveld's research on how *khulʿ* was represented in cartoons and films reveals many clichés and preconceptions of gender roles and women's position in society, which are very similar to that found in Palestine.

Finally, an important aspect of the Palestinian judiciary is the plurality of laws that are applied – JLPS (Jordanian Law of Personal Status) in the West Bank, EFRL (Egyptian Family Rights Law) in Gaza, tribal laws, etc. In socio-legal studies legal pluralism means a plurality of social fields, of producers of norms in partial interaction with each other: a perspective depriving the state of its function as the sole social actor and the monopolist of legal production.[146] Baudouin Dupret, Maurits Berger, and Laila Al-Zwaini define legal pluralism as a "handy tool" and as a model of analysis that needs modification for each specific case.[147] Surely, it is of great importance to be aware of the interaction, intersection, and interferences of different sets of laws and how these situations impact citizens. In his article Khalil discusses legal pluralism in Palestine in the field of tribal law, focusing on tribal conciliation and alternative dispute settlement in the penal law area of what he calls "customary law."[148] He argues that there are serious grounds for believing that the Palestinian Authority had encouraged tribal law, not only by backing the actors of informal justice, but also through the whole system of government.[149] This interesting aspect is,

142 Denker 2004: 176.
143 Sonneveld 2012.
144 Sonneveld 2012: 7, 84, 87ff.
145 Sonneveld 2012: 5.
146 Dupret, Berger and Al-Zwaini 1999: XI.
147 Dupret, Berger and Al-Zwaini 1999: XII.
148 Khalil 2009b.
149 Khalil 2009b: 176.

however, not dealt with much in this research because in family-law matters the Sharia courts are responsible and obviously also approached by Palestinian women. A plurality of legal settings could offer a choice, as Ido Shahar argues, in his conceptualization of "forum-shopping."[150] According to his research the legal situation in Jerusalem offers a wide variety of different courts that Muslims can use, as the Jordanian Sharia courts operate alongside the Israeli Sharia court system and the Israeli civil court system. Again, this fascinating topic of the legal situation of Jerusalem would need a book in itself.

1.2.2 *Gender*

The general theoretical approach toward gender has been outlined above. The family structure and the unequal rights for men and women point to a gender hierarchy with males at the top. I use the term "patriarchal" for this hierarchical organization of family based on male dominance over subordinate women and children. As Buskens argues, this male dominance is expressed in norms about gender concepts, decent behavior of women, obedience, sexuality and very concretely in gendered legal regulations with regard to marriage, divorce and child custody.[151] According to Deniz Kandiyoti there is no doubt that patriarchy is a "powerful cultural ideal," even given the fact that the material bases of classic patriarchy crumble under the impact of new market forces and capital penetration in rural areas.[152] Criticizing an uncritical and wide use of this term, Kandiyoti argues that her more narrow definition of "patriarchy" offers better prospects for a detailed analysis of processes of transformation.[153] Aiming to stress woman's agency, she develops her concept of "bargaining strategies" and points to the fact that these patriarchal bargains are not timeless or immutable entities, but are susceptible to historical transformations that open up new areas of struggle and renegotiation of the relations between women and men.[154] It is not always the case, she argues, that women opt for

150 Shahar 2013.

151 See Buskens 2003: 75, fn. 5. I do agree with Buskens that this term may mask differences in regional and temporal versions of patriarchy. For the difference of the Islamic conept of patriarchy in contrast to the Roman concept see Schneider 2007: 369–373.

152 Kandiyoti 1991: 107.

153 Kandiyoti 1991: 105; 114; Kandiyoti differentiates between the liberal use of the term by "radical feminists," applying it to virtually any form or instance of domination by men, whereas socialist feminists have restricted themselves to analyzing the relationships between patriarchy and class under capitalism, see Kandiyoti 1991: 104.

154 Kandiyoti 1991: 104; see also Schneider 2015 giving an Iranian example of two female jurists with opposite perceptions of the (in)compatability of Islamic law with international law.

"equality" or "more equal" rights.[155] Instead, women in what Kandiyoti calls "classic patriarchy"[156] often use their bargaining options to adhere as long as possible to the status quo as a means of gaining "protection."[157] Patriarchal bargains do not merely inform women's rational choices, she argues, but also shape the more unconscious aspects of their gendered subjectivity, because they permeate the content of their early socialization as well as their adult cultural milieu.[158]

As Kandiyoti has outlined, a systematic analysis of women's strategies and coping mechanisms with regard to these gender-unequal laws and customs can help capture the nature of patriarchal systems in their cultural, class-specific, and temporal concreteness and reveal how men and women resist, accommodate, adapt, and come into conflict with each other over resources, rights, and responsibilities.[159] Following this approach it may turn out that men consider their acting to be to the benefit of women, whereas women themselves have another point of view. Suggestions made to improve women's situation as in the *taʿmīm* have to be analyzed precisely with regard to the effects they have, which might differ from their intentions. Furthermore, following Kandiyoti, iterations need to be seen as a process of negotiations and it will become clear that this process is at different times influenced by different actors. To quote Kandiyoti: "A better understanding of the short- and medium-term strategies of women in different social locations could provide a corrective influence to ethnocentric or class-bound definitions of what constitutes a feminist consciousness."[160]

James Norman Dalrymple Anderson, who bases his research on the analysis of classical jurisprudential literature and the comparison with modern codification, is attacked harshly by Annelies Moors[161] because he characterizes pre-modern Islamic family law as "patriarchal."[162] According to Anderson, modern codifications have restricted male supremacy to some extent but not extinguished it. I can see no reason why this labeling of Islamic classical family law should be regarded as unjust, especially as Anderson is well aware of the problematic term "patriarchal" and defines it with special reference to Islamic

155 Schneider 2015.
156 For a definition of what she calls "classic patriarchy" and a conceptualization of its ideal type, see Kandiyoti 1991: 108–109.
157 Kandiyoti 1991: 109.
158 Kandiyoti 1991: 114.
159 Kandiyoti 1991: 114.
160 Kandiyoti 1991: 115.
161 Moors 1999: 142ff.
162 Anderson 1968.

classical law.[163] It is correct that classical *fiqh* (jurisprudence) books contain a wide range of different legal opinions, some of which can be interpreted to be oriented more toward gender equality than others from the present point of view. The abundance of opinions and *ikhtilāf* (diversity of opinions) in classical *fiqh* literature, which Anderson is of course well aware of, served as a basis for the selection of the legal codification at the beginning of and during the twentieth century via *takhayyur* (selection of opinions from different schools of law) and *talfīq* (combination of opinions). The general feature of Islamic marriage – man pays and woman obeys – however, has never been done away with, not even in modern law. Dower (*mahr*) plays an important role today as a way of stabilizing this marriage system, although the "house of obedience" (*bayt al-ṭāʿa*), i.e., bringing back women who left their home without their husband's permission,[164] has been abolished in some legal systems and seems to be slowly disappearing in others. However, it is still the case that a woman not paying attention to her husband or disobeying him runs the risk of losing her financial support. This is what Sonneveld calls the "maintenance-obedience" relationship,[165] which gives the genders different obligations, rights, and duties.

The approach taken by this book therefore entails a meticulous analysis of gender relations as delineated in texts and statements in the media and in interviews. A gendered approach to law also has to include men, construction of masculinities, and male rights as well as behavior. In his seminal article "Conceiving the Masculine: Gender and Palestinian Nationalism," Joseph Massad analyzes masculinity from the political point of view as a colonial model that figured in nationalist discourse through a case study of Palestinian nationalism.[166] Looking at the charters of the PLO, he is able to show in a close and critical reading how gender is defined in the framework of the nationalist project. The "Zionist enemy" is seen as masculine, the occupation seen as "rape of the land," thus feminizing the land and creating a gender hierarchy. This is a discourse that echoes well-known Orientalist discourses and Massad is aware of this. This discourse is later replaced by another discourse on paternity. Accordingly, being born to a Palestinian father is now the main prerequisite for Palestinianness. Again gender hierarchy and patriarchal family structures are dominant. This perception or categorization is connected intimately to the gendered concept of "honor," which has to be preserved by males since females

163 Anderson 1968: 221–222.
164 Shaham 2018.
165 Sonneveld 2012.
166 Massad 1995.

are, as he puts it, "only the soil."[167] It was in the Intifada in 1987, Massad argues, that these gendered notions and the hierarchy they imply slowly started to change. Gender and citizenship have been dealt with by different authors[168] and the prevalent concepts of femininity and masculinity have also been researched, by authors such as Julie Peteet and Daniel Monterescu.[169] The role of the women's movement has been researched by Peteet, Rabab Abdulhadi, and Islah Jad.[170] These studies can be seen as a prelude to the research on civil society organizations, especially the women's organizations that concern us here.[171]

Civil society is dealt with in this book mainly with a focus on women's and human rights organizations. As discussed in detail in chapter 3 the question of how to define civil society is a complex one, and even the European context in which this term was coined has not yielded a universally accepted definition.[172] The question of whether or not the concept of "civil society" can and should be applied to Muslim societies is a question on a more theoretical level and will not be tackled in this research.[173] With regard especially to Palestinian women's organizations Islah Jad[174] has done important research, as has Karin Gerster,[175] who consider the international influence on the civil society organizations as highly problematic because of the influence of international donors.[176]

1.2.3 *Teaching the Law*

There is not yet much research on the topic of university teaching as part of public iteration that influences the new generation of lawyers, judges, and legal scholars. In chapter 5, this study breaks new ground and analyzes the Supreme Judge's teaching at BZU and especially his class on the introduction of the *khulʿ* ruling has been analyzed in detail. Before the backdrop of the textbook,[177] it is revealing to look at the textbook as a special category of texts. John Issitt's research on textbooks is a useful starting point, as will be outlined

167 Massad 1995: 474.
168 Abdo 1999; Shalhoub-Kevorkian 2010.
169 Massad 1995; Peteet 2005; Monterescu 2006.
170 Peteet and Harlow 1991; R. Abdulhadi 1998; Jad 2004.
171 Shalhoub-Kevorkian 2012.
172 Reese-Schäfer 2007.
173 But see Hamzawy 2003; Albrecht 2005; Fathi and Karolewski 2015.
174 Jad 2004.
175 Gerster 2011.
176 Gerster 2011.
177 Schneider 2018b.

in the fifth chapter.[178] The analysis of the teaching process as such requires a special methodology, already partly outlined above in the elucidation of the version of participant observation. It is based on established methods of conducting research in school classes, because as yet there has been little research on university teaching and university education in the field of law, and none to the best of my knowledge conducted about and in Palestine. Monique Cardinal has investigated teaching in the area of Islamic legal theory (*uṣūl al-fiqh*) in some contemporary Arab universities – comparing Tunisia, Morocco, Egypt, Syria, and Jordan.[179] She argues that judges, court officials, and lawyers are no longer required to know the substantive law of Islamic legal tradition because their reference point is foreign-inspired modern law. As a consequence, Islamic legal theory is taught but only in a simplified and reformulated manner. Unlike the present study, she confines herself to the analysis of textbooks and does not take the actual teaching process into consideration.

To the best of my knowledge, there is no research available on the didactic method and communication in academic teaching in connection with the analysis of the textbook and even the connected research of the teaching process at schools is still in its infancy. There is surely no simple toolbox that could help delineate a methodological approach to this topic. Matthias Proske and Wolfgang Meseth have described (school-)teaching as a special form of communication with a high degree of communicative dynamic.[180] This approach is useful when applied to the *Qāḍī al-Quḍāt*'s classes at BZU with some slight adaptations because of the special conditions prevailing at universities in comparison to schools. Ignas Kalpokas warns that being present in class means that the researcher can only analyze the communication in the class and that he or she cannot say anything about the process of acquiring knowledge, i.e., about what the students think or learn.[181] This surely would have been an exaggerated expectation in the context of the present publication. However, as I hope will become evident, the pure communication of the Supreme Judge's narrative to his mostly female students and the way he constructed his arguments and developed his justification for factually amending the existing law provides a fascinating insight into a lively, controversial, and sometimes highly emotional debate.

178 Issitt 2004.

179 Cardinal 2005.

180 Proske and Meseth 2006.

181 Kalpokas 2012.

CHAPTER 2

Palestinian Legal System

Two main aspects have to be pointed out at the beginning of this chapter: the question of Palestinian statehood and the general role of Islamic law in the legislation of Palestine.

The names given to this territory range from Palestine, State of Palestine, Palestinian Territories to the geographical names, i.e., West Bank and Gaza (more exactly the Gaza Strip). The question of statehood of Palestine and how it developed in a long process of struggle culminating in the Oslo Accords in 1993–1999, the outstanding role of the Palestinian Liberation Organization (PLO) and its role after the creation of the Palestinian Authority (PA/*al-sulṭa al-filasṭīniyya*), as well as the position of the PA after the Oslo Accords are complicated legal and political topics that cannot be dealt with here in detail.[1] It is evident that in the 2010s, Palestine, its government, and its people consider themselves a state operating under severe restrictions of the Israeli occupation. This is reflected in the laws and decrees issued bearing the title of the "State of Palestine" (*Dawlat Filasṭīn*). Palestine possesses state-like structures, including a government, ministries, and an administration in Ramallah and the Palestinian Authority exercises its authority through legislative, executive, and judicial powers.[2] Since 2007, Hamas established itself in the Gaza Strip with a parallel administration and government in Gaza City.

Is Palestine a state? From an international perspective, the debate over statehood is dominated by two competing theories: the declaratory and the constitutive. The constitutive theory provides that a state is only a state upon the political act of recognition by other states. The declaratory theory determines that recognition is merely acknowledgement of the existing statehood status, and that the act of recognition does not by itself confer status. Rather, statehood is acquired when certain objective criteria are satisfied.[3] Although many international law jurists stick to one or the other theory as being confirmed by practice, William Thomas Worster argues the record bears neither of these contentions out; neither of these two theories satisfactorily describes the state of the law on the matter. To date, Palestine is recognized as a state by

1 But see Milhem 2004; Khalil 2009a.

2 Khalil 2013: 34–41.

3 Worster 2009: 118.

 | DOI:10.1163/9789004442313_003

137 of 193 member states of the UN[4] but not by the United States, Israel, and most EU-states, with the exception of Sweden, Poland, Slovakia, and the Czech Republic. Worster describes Palestine as a state whose supposed nationality with a claim to independence is widely ignored.[5]

One reason is, according to the Conflict Risk Assessment Report 2018,[6] the inability of the PA to determine sovereignty over the Palestinian territories, i.e., Gaza, West Bank, and East Jerusalem. As is well known, the situation is characterized by a history of armed conflicts, fragile governments, and high levels of political instability. The Gaza Strip is, since 2018, "nearing total collapse."[7] Chances for a peaceful agreement between Hamas and Fatah are not high. In early 2019, what can be called a "unity government" of technocrats acknowleged by Fatah and Hamas resigned.[8] The Israeli occupation has, according to this report, steadily been intensified, thereby reducing the potential for a peaceful solution. Youth bulge, a high unemployment rate, stagnating GDP growth, inconsistent direct foreign investments, and political decisions, such as the one taken by US President Donald Trump to move the US Embassy from Tel Aviv to Jerusalem in May 2018,[9] have left the Palestinian territories in a state of fragility and further diminished prospects for a peaceful solution.[10]

According to the Oslo Accords, control over civilian and security affairs were given to the Palestinian Authority in the so-called Area A, which includes the urban centers of Ramallah, Nablus, Hebron, and Jericho. Area B is only under civil control of the PA, Area C, around 60 percent of the West Bank, is completely controlled by Israel, Area A comprises around 18 percent of the area of which was originally seen as the territory of a Palestinian state. Most of Area C has been used to build Israeli settlements.[11] The Office for the Coordination for Humanitarian Affairs of the UN in the occupied territories of Palestine, i.e., West Bank and Gaza, states in its report in 2018:

> This [Israeli control of Area C][12] impedes the development of adequate housing, infrastructure and livelihoods in Palestinian communities,

4 Vesey-Byrne 2017.
5 Worster 2009: 153.
6 Laborce, Malcolm et al. 2018.
7 Laborce, Malcolm et al. 2018: 1.
8 Kershner 2019.
9 Usher 2018.
10 Laborce, Malcolm et al. 2018: 1.
11 OCHA 2018.
12 Arabic terms or the English translations are always added in ( ); in direct quotes comments and explanations are given in [ ]. If something is left out, this is indicated by....

> and has significant consequences for the entire West Bank population. Structures built without permits are regularly served with demolition orders, creating chronic uncertainty and threat, and encouraging people to leave. Where the orders are implemented, they have resulted in displacement and disruption of livelihoods, the entrenchment of poverty and increased aid dependency. The humanitarian community has faced a range of difficulties in providing aid in Area C, including the demolition and confiscation of assistance by the Israeli authorities.[13]

High risk for intensification of the conflict is seen in the policy of settlements but also the aggression of Hamas and other Islamist groups. Furthermore, the PA's postponement of the elections due in 2016 was considered a shift toward a more authoritarian regime.[14] With regard to citizenship, the question of the Palestinian refugees is not yet solved. They represented almost a quarter of the global refugee population in 2017[15] and are spread out mostly in the main refugee camps all over the neighboring states but also outside the Middle East. There is a substantial Palestinian minority living in Israel who possesses Israeli citizenship.[16]

In 1974, the UN General Assembly Resolution 3236 recognized the right of the Palestinian people to self-determination and the PLO as the sole legitimate representative of the Palestinian people. In September 2011, President Mahmoud Abbas submitted an application for membership in the UN. On November 29, 2012, the General Assembly of the United Nations granted Palestine non-member observer status with Resolution 67/19 and on December 17, 2012, the General Assembly decided that "the designation 'State of Palestine' shall be used in all official United Nations documents."[17]

The second aspect concerns Palestine's legal system. The Islamic legacy has been strong in the legal area, especially but not exclusively in the area of family law. With the decree of May 20, 1994, President Yassir Arafat regulated that all Sharia courts, the courts for family law, in Palestine should continue to function. He appointed Muḥammad Abū Sardāna at first as deputy to the Minister of Justice in the PA, and shortly afterward promoted him to the position of Supreme Judge (*Qāḍī al-Quḍāt*),[18] giving him the rank of a minister.[19]

13 OCHA 2018.
14 Laborce, Malcolm et al. 2018: 1–2.
15 Laborce, Malcolm et al. 2018: 2.
16 Khalil and del Sarto 2015.
17 Gharib 2012. This designation is thus used in this book.
18 Welchman 2000: 89, 92.
19 Welchman 2000: 92.

There is thus a continuity for the legal system in Palestine to be influenced by Islamic law especially in the area of private law. Hilmar Krüger confirms that Palestinian courts have been active since 1994[20] and argues that whether or not a state is internationally recognized does not matter when looking at the family law and the jurisdictional structure. Islamic law is mentioned, also as usual in most Muslim states,[21] in the constitution, the Basic Law (BL).

This book does not deal with the "regular" or "secular" legal system, the civil jurisdictional system, as it does not play a role in family law. The focus lies on debates in Islamic law and thus on the Sharia court system, the Islamic "religious" jurisdictional system, but with one exception. Beside the Sharia Court High Council (SCHC) there is one important – non-religious – institution which has to be mentioned: the Supreme Constitutional Court (SCC) whose duty it is, according to the BL, to interpret the BL and Palestinian legislation.[22] The SCC delivered an important judgment in November 2017 regarding the role of international law and a second one in March 2018 and therefore took a position in the debates about the future direction of personal status law in Palestine.

In the first part of this chapter (2.1), the Basic Law will be presented (2.1.1), as will be the Sharia Court High Council (2.1.2) and the Supreme Constitutional Court (2.1.3). In the second part of the chapter (2.2), the legislation in the realm of family law is dealt with: the applicable family laws in the West Bank and Gaza (2.2.1) and developments toward a Palestinian personal status law as can be traced in the draft laws (2.2.2). In the final section (2.2.3), the meeting of the National Committee of the Family Law (NCFL) (*al-Lajna al-Waṭaniyya li-Qānūn al-Usra*) in the president's seat in November 2013 is described and analyzed as an introduction into the legal debates in the West Bank in 2013.

2.1 Basic Law, Sharia Court High Council, and Supreme Constitutional Court

2.1.1 *Basic Law (BL): Legislation, Basic Rights, and the Role of Islam*

The legal situation in Palestine generally and with regard to family law can be named as legally plural. Palestine has a rich legal history, today combining Ottoman, Jordanian, Egyptian, and Palestinian law, Israeli military law, and international law as applicable laws – as well as custom. The actual codes in force

20 Krüger 2014: 1110–1111.
21 Schneider 2008.
22 See Article 103 1 (b).

in personal status law in the West Bank is the Jordanian Law of Personal Status (JLPS) of 1976, in Gaza it is the Egyptian Family Rights Law (EFRL) of 1954. Especially in the case of personal status law, the basis of the law are Islamic regulations that are constantly reconstructed and discussed and changed, as in the *khulʿ* ruling of 2012, thus reflecting the Islamic law in its different interpretations. Islamic law can thus be called "plural" in itself. Legal pluralism in the sense that the state or the legislature recognizes the existence of a multiplicity of legal sources is thus confirmed for Palestine.[23] According to the Basic Law (Article 4, [2]), the principles of Islamic Sharia "shall be a principal source of legislation."[24] According to Article 10 (2) the Palestinian National Authority shall "work without delay to become a party to regional and international declarations and covenants." There was a decisive step taken toward this when in 2014 Palestine signed CEDAW (Convention on the Elimination of all Forms of Discrimination against Women) and other international treaties. Thus there is an inherent tension between the influence of Islamic law, which is codified in old versions of family law and is debated differently, and international law stimulating debates about more "secular" versions of the personal status law.

In 1968, the Palestine Liberation Organization (PLO) issued the Palestinian National Charter, which remains formally in force.[25] On November 15, 1988, the National Council of the PLO declared the independent Palestinian state.[26] According to this Declaration of Independence, a democratic government and a constitution would govern Palestine. These provisions were not fulfilled since the PLO was still in exile and had no access to the land.[27] In 1993, the Oslo Accords prompted the PLO legal committee to start drafting a Basic Law to govern the interim self-government even before signing the Interim Agreement.[28] In 1994, the year of the implementation of the PA, there were three constitutional instruments applicable in the West Bank and Gaza. Those were the Jordanian Constitution of 1952 in the West Bank, the Constitutional Declaration of 1962 in Gaza insofar as it did not contradict the Palestine Order-in-Council of 1922, and the Israeli Military Orders, which had constitutional effects according to Milhem.[29] Following the first legislative and presidential elections

23 Dupret, Berger, and Al-Zwaini 1999: XI. The anthropological definition of legal pluralism is left out here.

24 See https://www.palestinianbasiclaw.org/basic-law/2003-amended-basic-law, accessed September 26, 2018, see also Muqtafi.

25 See Palestinian National Charter 1968.

26 See Palestinian Declaration of Independence 1988.

27 Milhem 2004: 183; Khalil 2009a: 5.

28 Milhem 2004: 183.

29 Milhem 2004: 182.

in 1996, changes needed to be made to the draft BL. The legal committee of the Palestinian Legislation Council (PLC), the parliament, had taken a central role in shaping the final version of the draft BL that was approved, almost unanimously, by the PLC in its third reading on October 2, 1997. Five years later, the president endorsed the BL (on May 29, 2002) which came into force on July 7, 2002. Different reasons are given for this delay.[30] The official reason given by President Arafat was that the adoption of a BL was a matter for all Palestinians to consider and not only the PLC.[31] The BL remains legally binding, including its amendment in 2005.[32] According to its own provision, the BL shall only apply during the interim period and may be extended until a new constitution of the State of Palestine is enforced.[33] The procedure for amendment of the BL is by a two-thirds majority vote in the parliament.[34] Furthermore, in 1994 a decree was issued according to which all laws, regulations, and decisions that were in force in the occupied territories, i.e., West Bank and Gaza, remain in force until they were amended or repealed.[35]

Within the establishment of the PA, several shifts and conflicts took place, as Khalil argues: first, a shift in Palestinian political life from "outside" (i.e., abroad) to Palestine; second, a growing conflict between the formulae governing Palestinian politics in exile and those appropriate to the new situation inside; third, a shift in the goal of demanding the right to a state on all of historic Palestine to the goal of recovering territory occupied by the Israelis since 1967; and fourth, the end of the "revolutionary" stage of the national liberation struggle of the PLO and the political structures that accompanied it.[36] The political split between Hamas and Fatah in 2007 after Hamas won the elections had a major influence. Since then, parliament has not met in Ramallah, but it has in Gaza City.

Taking into account the provisions of the BL and limitations of the Oslo Accords helps indirectly to understand, Khalil argues, what a future State of Palestine would look like. The establishment of a Palestinian state would not

30 Khalil 2009a: 6.

31 Khalil 2009a: 6.

32 Khalil 2013: 40, see https://www.palestinianbasiclaw.org/basic-law/2003-amended-basic-law, accessed September 20, 2018; see also Muqtafi.

33 BL Article 115; Khalil 2009a: 6.

34 BL Article 120; Khalil 2009a: 16; Milhem 2004: 180–181. Milhem has dealt extensively with the development of the constitution in his book: Milhem 2004: 180–217.

35 BL Articles 118–119; Milhem 2004: 180–181.

36 Khalil 2009a: 11.

imply "divine-like" creation *ex nihilo*.[37] This applies accordingly, as argued in the introduction, to the future family law.

Feras Milhem describes the BL of 2003 as follows:

> Its provisions are rich with significant sources of law, particularily in respect to human rights and basic freedoms as well as social and cultural rights, which would be eventually incorporated in the prospective legislation. These provisions are not merely general statements to be adopted by the legislature; they are also superior formal sources to be applied and protected by the judicial system.[38]

International scholars such as Brown saw its strength and potential: "The final draft of the Basic Law is perhaps the most carefully crafted and liberal constitutional document in Arab history."[39] Generally, the structure of the State of Palestine is based on the separation of powers. The BL lays down provisions for human rights and general freedoms.[40] Human rights are to be considered a formal source.[41] Furthermore, it is the duty of courts to guarantee their respect by individuals and the executive, pointing escpecially to Article 10 as being crucial.[42] Khalil, in describing the most important aspects of the constitution, not only summarizes the existing rules and regulation in the BL but also sheds light on the debate of scholars and lawyers accompanying the emergence of this BL thus putting it in the context of the legal and also political iterations around the BL. He shows the wide range of different approaches to the analysis of the constitution and the wide range of views with regard to central questions for a future Palestinian state – e.g., with regard of the question of the relation between state and religion.

There had been different opinions with regard to the time of establishing a democratic state. Some expressed severe doubts that a democratic state could be implemented before the end of the occupation, whereas others argued that transition to democracy does not need to wait for statehood, it can accompany the liberation process and democracy can be achieved under conditions of occupation, or can even bring it to an end.[43] The BL defines the political system

37 Khalil 2013: 40.

38 Milhem 2004: 216.

39 Brown 2000: 25. Brown expressed this high regard of the Palestinian BL in 2000, two years before ratification, see Milhem 2004: 187.

40 Milhem 2004: 191.

41 Milhem 2004: 191.

42 Milhem 2004: 191.

43 Khalil 2009a: 10.

as a "representative democracy."[44] It has elements of both a parliamentary system, in the form of a government that is answerable to the parliament, and a presidential system, whereby the elected president enjoys wide-ranging executive authority but is not answerable to the parliament.

The legislative power is with the parliament[45] but the president has the right to issue decree-laws (*qarārāt*) under certain circumstances[46] – e.g., in a state of emergency – and the power to endorse or return a draft-law to the parliament.[47] Normally, drafting of legislations goes through the channel of the Legislation and Advisory Bureau (LAB/*Dīwān al-Fatwā wa-l-Tashrīʿ*), which is tasked to prepare and draft laws. In the final stage, after the draft laws have been accepted by the parliament, the Legislation and Advisory Bureau prepares them for the publication in the Official Gazette.[48] According to Khalil, the legal and regulatory framework has been the object of numerous studies, and certain gaps and shortcomings have been identified.[49] He discusses differing opinions on the general "secular-religious" orientation the Palestinian state has or should have:

> According to the BL and DPC [Draft Palestinian Constitution] the principals of *shari'a* (Islamic law), are a primary source of legislation in Palestine. Indeed, Islam is the official state religion and for that reason, *shari'a* principles should be considered one of the most important legal foundations of the "state-in-waiting."[50]

Conversely, the PLO, with Fatah as its leading member, has always been a secular organization, and consequently its various declarations were oriented toward the establishment of a secular state. However, as Khalil points out, these declarations were never intended to be anti-religion.[51] Article 4 states as follows:

1. Islam is the official religion in Palestine. Respect for the sanctity of all other divine religions shall be maintained.
2. The principles of Islamic Shari'a shall be a principal source of legislation.
3. Arabic shall be the official language.

---

44 BL Article 5.
45 BL Article 47.
46 BL Article 43.
47 Khalil 2009a: 24.
48 *Dīwān al-fatwā wa-l-tashrīʿ* (Legislation & Advisory Bureau): http://www.lab.pna.ps/ar_new/index.php?p=home, accessed January 17, 2018.
49 Khalil 2009a: 23–25.
50 Khalil 2009a: 31.
51 Khalil 2009a: 31; see also Abusada 2010.

Khalil points out that there are two main groups in Palestinian society: those who believe that religion has a role to play and those who think the state and religion should be separated.[52] Article 4 has accordingly been interpreted by some as the end of secularism, which seemed to be expressed in many PLO declarations and as a reflection of reality regarding the majority of people being religious by others. In this article, Sharia is construed as *a* principal source of legislation, not *the* source as in the 1980 Constitution of Egypt. Qualifying it as "a" source, some argued – and still argue, as we will see in the context of the implementation of international law – would leave room for other sources of the law, too.

Milhem suggests a comparative study between Islamic jurisprudence and laws of other legal systems. But "the matter is not simple," he concedes, as any person may bring the question of constitutionality of any provision before the SCC.[53] The question yet to be answered is what is exactly meant by the "principles of Islamic Shari'a"? Milhem here gives the example of the Egyptian SCC, according to which these principles are universal rules embodied in the Quran.[54] Khalil directs attention to a group who argues that Sharia enjoys a high degree of credibility in Palestinian society: "For this group, *shari'a* takes priority even over international law and conventions."[55] Hamas's political manifesto for the elections of 2006 included a change of the text of the constitution moving Sharia from *a* to *the* source.[56] The position that Sharia takes priority over international law is also held by the present *Qāḍī al-Quḍāt* Maḥmūd al-Habbāsh.[57] Asked, who should prepare the draft of a new Palestinian family law, he pointed to the office of the *Qāḍī al-Quḍāt* but added that this should happen in cooperation with society. There is, furthermore, a suggestion that a Sharia judge should become judge of the Supreme Constitutional Court (SCC) and judges of the Constitutional Court should use Sharia as a reference.[58]

On the other hand, there are those who want to remove the Sharia reference from the constitution. In the committee drafting the BL it was agreed that references to Islam and Sharia take into account the reality of Palestinian society, so Christian communities were consulted and agreed to this version of the BL.[59]

---

52 Khalil 2009a: 32.
53 Milhem 2004: 196–197.
54 Milhem 2004: 197.
55 Khalil 2009a: 33.
56 Khalil 2009a: 33.
57 Maḥmūd al-Habbāsh, interview on December 9, 2017; see also Wattan, June 21, 2018.
58 Khalil 2009a: 34.
59 Khalil 2009a: 34–35.

According to Article 9 of the BL: "Palestinians shall be equal before the law and the judiciary, without distinction based upon race, sex, color, religion, political views or disability." The existing legislation, i.e., JLPS of 1976 and EFRL of 1954, is not in accordance with either the BL or international law, CEDAW, signed by President Abbas.[60] On the other hand, there is an obligation resulting from the signing of CEDAW after it has been published in the Official Gazette that leads to the question: how can these tensions be resolved? International law is mentioned in the constitution:

> Article 10
> 1. Basic human rights and liberties shall be protected and respected.
> 2. The Palestinian National Authority shall work without delay to become a party to regional and international declarations and covenants that protect human rights.

There are generally two different approaches of states with regard to the question of how international law and international treaties have to be integrated legally into the national legal system. Monistic states follow the idea that international law becomes effective automatically with the state's ratification of these international treaties, whereas dualistic states require enactment via the legislative body.[61] Milhem argues, that this sole reference to international law in Article 10 does not explicitly rule that international rules have a direct effect on domestic law. According to his interpretation, the legislature has intended to make the international treaties binding upon the domestic law but without direct effect: "As a result, the PA must first ratify these treaties."[62] According to Article 103, a High Constitutional Court (HCC)/Supreme Constitutional Court (SCC)[63] should be created to ratify international treaties. However, this had not happened until 2016. Before its establishment, the High Court acted according to Article 104 as a constitutional court.

When the SCC finally came into existence in April 2016, it was accompanied, as expected and usual in Palestine, by hot and controversial debates of

60 Qafisheh 2018.
61 Motala 1995: 342f.
62 Interview Feras Milhem, November 28, 2017; see also Khalil 2009a: 39.
63 In the English version of the BL, Art. 103, it is called "High Constitutional Court." In the discussions of 2016 after this court was created, it is most often called "Supreme Constitutional Court" (SCC) – see al-Haq 2016 etc. I will choose the second version because it was the normal version used in the discussions after the judgment of the status of international law.

Palestinian jurists, lawyers and civil society organizations in the West Bank and Gaza especially with regard to its judgment on international law (see 2.1.3).

2.1.2 *The Sharia Court High Council (SCHC) and the Supreme Judge Department*

The independence of the judiciary is ensured in the BL Articles 97–99 and the Judicial Authority Law of 2002.[64] The creation and position of the Sharia Court High Council (*al-Majlis al-Aʿlā li-l-Qaḍāʾ al-Sharʿī*) is not anchored in the BL. It came into existence with Arafat nominating Abū Sardāna first deputy to the Minister of Justice and then *Qāḍī al-Quḍāt* in 1994, as described above.[65] From then on, the Supreme Judges slowly expanded the system of religious court organs and Khalil points to the duality of jurisdiction between religious/*sharʿī* and regular courts as an "inevitable adoption" ensuring the independence of (recognized) religious communities.[66]

> The independence of religious communities in regulating their own personal status issues, and the jurisdiction of their courts to decide on cases involving members of their communities, was confirmed by the Article on Islam [Art. 4] delineating it as the official religion of the state. In other words, the autonomy of religious communities to decide and legislate on personal issues is considered to be part of the solution rather than the problem.[67]

As already mentioned above, the SCHC controlled[68] and still controls drafting laws, at least in family law matters. This organ therefore will now be described in detail. According to the Basic Law, Article 4 (1) and (2) given above, Islam is the official religion in Palestine, while the principles of Islamic Sharia are also *a* principal source of legislation. Article 101 (1) says: "Matters governed by *Shari'a* law and matters of personal status, shall come under the jurisdiction of *Shari'a* and religious courts, in accordance with the law."

Of the SCHC, to date two versions exist: the one in Ramallah and the one in Gaza – in addition to the *Qāḍī al-Quḍāt* in Jerusalem who is invested by Jordan. The structure of the Sharia Judiciary in Ramallah, which will be explained below, is shown in the following diagram:

64 Khalil 2009a: 24; Milhem 2004: 267. For the problem of independence before the backdrop of occupation and special fragmentation, see Khalil 2009a: 24.

65 Welchman 2000: 89, 92.

66 Khalil 2009a: 25.

67 Khalil 2009a: 25.

68 Welchman 2000: 458–483.

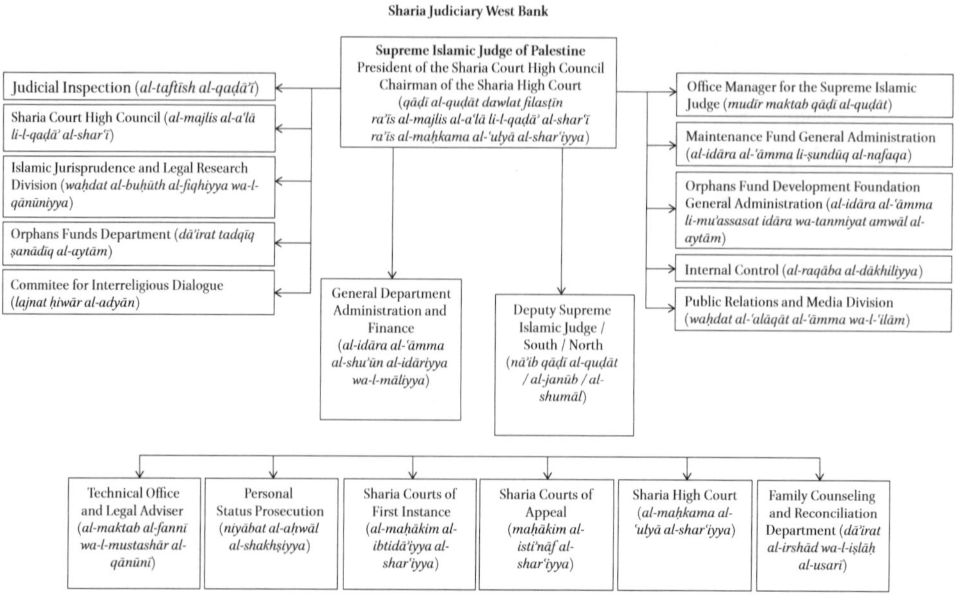

FIGURE 2.1 Structure of the Sharia Judiciary in Ramallah

The Ramallah branch of the head of the SCHC was headed by the Supreme Judge (*Qāḍī al-Quḍāt*), i.e., Yūsuf Idʿīs from 2012 to 2014 and since then Maḥmūd al-Habbāsh. In Gaza, his counterpart, Ḥasan al-Jūjū (since 2008)[69] does not bear the title "Supreme Judge"; he is named only as the Head of Higher Sharia Court Council (HSCC), the Gaza version of the SCHC. Both institutions in Ramallah and Gaza control the "Sharia courts" and their different instances, both have departments for "Islamic Jurisprudence and Legal Research" and both supervise "Family Counselling and Reconciliation." Both also have an office of "Internal Control." The Ramallah SCHC seems to be more extensive, having, according to the website, an additional "Committee for Interreligious Dialogue" as well as a "Public Relations and Media Division."

The Sharia judiciary in Gaza has a slightly different structure as is shown in the following diagram:

69 President Abbas dismissed him as as Judge of the Court of Appeals, see Alaqsavoice (February 19, 2008), see chapter 9.

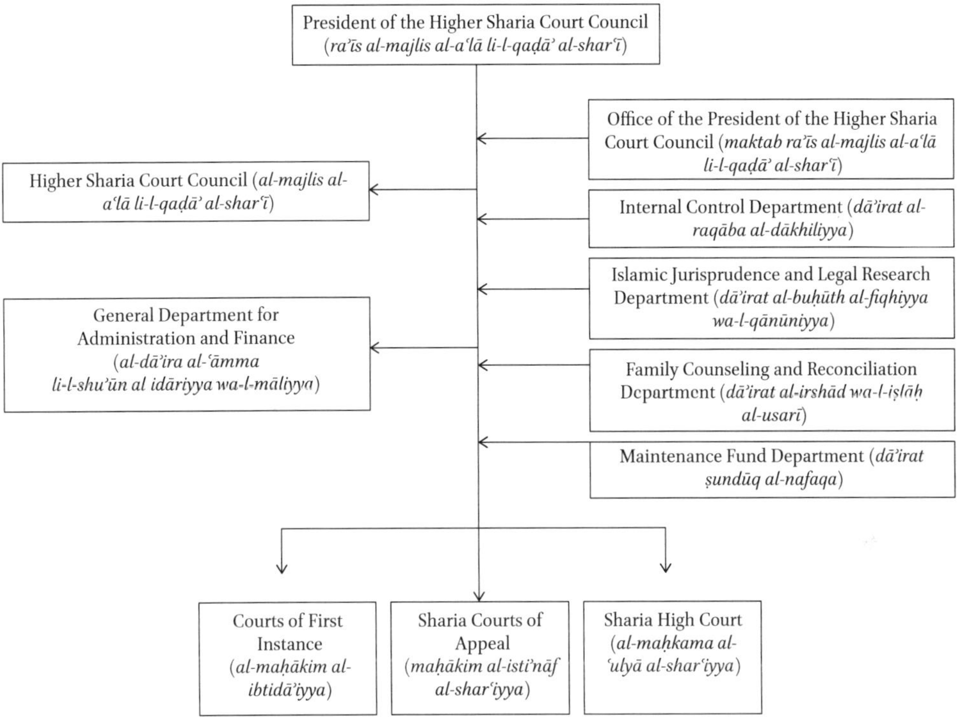

FIGURE 2.2 Structure of the Sharia Judiciary in Gaza

In East Jerusalem since 2016, Wāṣif al-Bakrī is Supreme Judge invested by Jordan, since Jordan still controls the Old City and the Sharia court system in Jerusalem.[70]

The Supreme Judge Department in Ramallah with the *Qāḍī al-Quḍāt* at its head was created as a governmental organization (*mu'assasa ḥukūmiyya*) linked directly to the president. The establishment is based on Arafat's already mentioned Decree 1/1994, which provides that legislation and laws that were effective before June 5, 1967, in the West Bank and Gaza Strip would remain in effect.[71] When Arafat appointed Muḥammad Abū Sardāna as first Supreme

70 Not much information is available on him, see http://sjd.gov.jo/Pages/viewpage.aspx?pageID=154, accessed February 5, 2018. Generally, Jerusalem is not dealt with in this book because it would require a special analysis of the pluralistic legal structure and context of this city. The parallel structure of Israeli and Jordanian Sharia courts and how they are used, researched under the aspect of "forum-shopping" are only one aspect of this, see Shahar 2013.

71 All information here is taken from the website:
Arabic: http://kudah.pna.ps/ar_page.aspx?id=keYhnpa1896843729akeYhnp;

Judge in the West Bank and the Gaza Strip, he implemented, as Welchman described, a number of administrative rulings in the Sharia courts, e.g., raising the age of marriage for men and women in Gaza to be the same as in the West Bank. He also constituted a committee mandated to unify the personal status legislation, which he chaired during his term of office. He intended to introduce necessary modifications after examination of past applications of these laws,[72] drawing for this purpose on a range of sources. He argued that those were matters of interpretation (*ijtihād*) and that among the views of the schools of law and jurists that view should be taken, that best takes into consideration the interest of the Palestinians.[73]

The Supreme Judge/*Qāḍī al-Quḍāt* has the rank of a minister, according to Arafat's decree and to the decree-law 3/2012,[74] and his department has administrative and financial independence. In addition, the Supreme Judge can change, cancel, or merge any department in his house according to work interest (see figure 2.1).[75] According to the Law of the Formation of the Sharia Courts of 1972,[76] the SCHC's responsibilities and duties are to appoint Sharia judges, promote them, transfer them outside judicial work, accept their resignations, refer them to retirement, discipline them, and try them. All the council decisions will be brought to the Supreme Judge for approval.[77] According to the Supreme Judge Department's ruling number 12\2012 on May 29, 2012, the position of the General Secretariat of the council was created with the responsibilities to prepare council meetings and notify the council board, to

Engl: http://kudah.pna.ps/page.aspx?id=nPP4Dwa1934913849anPP4Dw, both accessed on September 17, 2018; for the history and the structure of the SCHC, see also Jabʿītī 2012.

72 Welchman 1999: 21.

73 Welchman 1999: 21.

74 See Muqtafi.

75 See: Arabic: http://kudah.pna.ps/ar_page.aspx?id=Z2Bmiwa1904457753aZ2Bmiw; Engl: http://kudah.pna.ps/page.aspx?id=vmNnbFa1945383132avmNnbF, both accessed September 11, 2018. The presidential decree of 3/2012 organized the relation between the Sharia Judiciary, Supreme Judge, and Judicial Council confirming again that the Supreme Judge is appointed with the rank of a minister. He is allowed to act on all the tasks, duties, and powers given to him according to the law and this Presidential Decree will be presented to the PLC in the first session convened for approval. This is a normal stipulation in the absence of regular sessions of the parliament. For a detailed description of the applicable laws, the structure, and also deficiencies, see Jabʿītī 2012.

76 *Qānūn Tashkīl al-Maḥākim al-Sharʿiyya* 19/1972: http://muqtafi.birzeit.edu, accessed September 18, 2018.

77 Arabic: http://kudah.pna.ps/ar_page.aspx?id=Z2Bmiwa1904457753aZ2Bmiw. Engl: http://kudah.pna.ps/page.aspx?id=vmNnbFa1945383132avmNnbF.

implement and codify the council's decisions and to keep the records.[78] The Ramallah SCHC does not recognize the independence of the Gaza Higher Sharia Court Council (HSCC).[79]

Sharia courts of first instance[80] have the authority to settle disputes and the right of judiciary, according to the Law of the Formation of the Sharia Courts. These courts deal with the following matters: personal status of Muslims, Islamic endowments (*waqf*), blood money issues, if both sides are Muslims or non-Muslims and both sides accept litigation in Sharia courts. In personal status matters, they deal with marriage contracts, orphans' funds management, divorce cases, inheritance issues and registration of wills; they solve disputes arising from inheritance, alimony issues, documenting power of attorney, lawsuits concerning death and donations. Among the thirty judges in 2018, three were female: Asmahān al-Waḥīdī in Ḥalḥūl/Hebron, Khulūd al-Faqīh in Birzeit/Ramallah, and Ṣumūd al-Ḍamīrī as Head of the Personal Status Prosecution. In 2019, there was an additional female judge appointed with, Sīrīn ʿAynbūsī.[81]

The Sharia Courts of Appeal (*Maḥkamat al-Istiʾnāf al-Sharʿiyya*)[82] are considered courts of second instance. The judges take into consideration issues coming from first instance courts, under Articles 135–152 of the Law of the Procedure for Sharia Courts/*Qānūn Uṣūl al-Muḥākamāt al-Sharʿiyya* 31/1959,[83] and applicable under Presidential Decree 1/1994 issued by Yassir Arafat. Ṣumūd al-Ḍamīrī in Ramallah was promoted as the first and only woman to the Sharia Court of Appeal in November 2018, besides acting as Head of Personal Status Prosecution. The Sharia High Court/Sharia Supreme Court (*al-Maḥkama al-ʿUlyā al-Sharʿiyya*)[84] was formed on September 19, 2003, according to a Presidential Decree from President Yassir Arafat. The formation of the

78 Arabic: http://kudah.pna.ps/ar_page.aspx?id=XVNUoGa1904457753aXVNUoG, accessed March 2, 2019.
Engl: http://kudah.pna.ps/page.aspx?id=vmNnbFa1945383132avmNnbF

79 See chapter 9.

80 Arabic: http://kudah.pna.ps/ar_page.aspx?id=FQwBE9a1913023530aFQwBE9; accessed September 11, 2018.
Engl: http://kudah.pna.ps/page.aspx?id=6Gf4vwa1956804168a6Gf4vw, accessed September 11, 2018.

81 Information of Judge al-Ḍamīrī of May 5, 2019. I could not trace her on the internet.

82 Arabic: http://kudah.pna.ps/ar_page.aspx?id=Tkg3sYa1912071777aTkg3sY;
Engl: http://kudah.pna.ps/page.aspx?id=HhCirVa1955852415aHhCirV, both accessed January 17, 2018.

83 See Muqtafi.

84 Arabic: http://kudah.pna.ps/ar_page.aspx?id=uZ7Giva1911120024auZ7Giv;
Engl: http://kudah.pna.ps/page.aspx?id=wP8m2La1954900662awP8m2L, both accessed January 17, 2018. In the English version, both names are given.

Supreme Court in Palestine created the third instance of litigation in addition to primary and appeals courts. The Sharia Supreme Court is a court of law like the cassation court in the regular court system. It is considered the top of the pyramid for Sharia judiciary.

An important department is the Personal Status Prosecution[85] that deals with claims on behalf of the public right of Sharia. The prosecutor sets up the lawsuit and investigates family law matters concerning the right of God (*ḥaqq Allāh*) in divorce, marriage, and paternity. Personal Status Prosecution has been created according to a Presidential Decree from President Arafat on April 30, 2004, under the organizational structure of the Supreme Judge Department. Personal Status Prosecution exercises its work in the entire West Bank but not in Gaza because of the current political and legal separation. The Personal Status Prosecution Team is headed by Judge Ṣumūd al-Ḍamīrī. There are at least three other women in this body: Rīm al-Shanṭī, Fāṭimaʿ Ayyād, Nabīla Ḥurūb.[86]

One further important department is Family Counselling and Reconciliation (*Dā'irat al-Irshād wa-l-Iṣlāḥ al-Usarī*).[87] Its offices exercise their work in all Sharia courts distributed in provinces of the country and, according to the website, help to strengthen family ties and reduce community conflicts. The department achieved according to the website, good results in reducing marital disputes and divorce. The Family Counselling and Reconciliation Department is directly controlled by the office of the Supreme Judge.

The legal bases for the Supreme Judge Department are the different laws of procedure as well as the personal status laws.[88] The Courts' inspector is responsible for all the Sharia courts; he or she is appointed by the Supreme Judge. According to Article 18 of the Law of the Formation of the Sharia Courts of 1972, the Supreme Judge has the right to supervise and manage all judges

---

85 Arabic: http://kudah.pna.ps/ar_page.aspx?id=hMCuLfa1909216518ahMCuLf; Engl: http://kudah.pna.ps/page.aspx?id=WTuvsMa1951093650aWTuvsM, both accessed January 17, 2018; see Damiri 2018: 114–115.

86 Arabic: http://kudah.pna.ps/ar_page.aspx?id=hMCuLfa1909216518ahMCuLf; Engl: http://kudah.pna.ps/page.aspx?id=WTuvsMa1951093650aWTuvsM, both accessed January 17, 2018.

87 Arabic: http://kudah.pna.ps/ar_page.aspx?id=GSxnBca1916830542aGSxnBc; Engl: http://kudah.pna.ps/page.aspx?id=x1CQk0a1962514686ax1CQk0, both accessed January 17, 2018.

88 Law of the Procedure for Sharia Courts 31/1959 (*Qānūn Uṣūl al-Muḥākamāt al-Sharʿiyya*); Law of the Procedure for Sharia Courts 12/1965; JLPS 61/1976 in the West Bank and EFRL 69/1954 for Gaza. Furthermore, the Law of Sharia Lawyers 12/1952 (*Qānūn al-muḥāmīna al-sharʿiyyīn*); as well as the Law of the Formation of the Sharia Courts (*Qānūn Tashkīl al-Maḥākim al-Sharʿiyya* of 19/1972). See al-Muqtafī.

and Sharia courts. The Sharia supervisor helps the Supreme Judge monitor and control Sharia courts.[89]

This short overview demonstrates that the SCHC is a highly complex and comprehensive body. However, there is no hint in the BL that the SCHC can act as a legislative body. According to Asem Khalil, the authors of the BL "avoided taking a position" and decided instead to leave many things as they were.[90]

Being an impressive and powerful body, the Supreme Judge and his department were reportedly trying to expand and strengthen their position in the time of this research.[91] In a highly laudatory media report of the Palestinian news agency Maan news of February 2012, the Sharia jurisdiction is praised as being among the most important parts of justice that "represents the state in family law matters."[92] With regard to the importance for the societal security and family and religious security, the SCHC works with all available legal means to help to improve the legal system and protects the independence of its system. The Supreme Judge Idʿīs is quoted explaining that he worked with *taʿmīmāt* (rulings) and *qarārāt* (decisions) since there was no legislation. One important aim was to prevent secret marriages (*zījāt sirriyya*). When a married man wants to marry again, his wife is informed.[93] The Supreme Judge also mentioned another *taʿmīm* dealing with registration of division of inheritance only four months after the death of the testator (*takhāruj*), which is considered to help women who are often put under pressure to renounce their share of inheritance. There is also another *taʿmīm* that foresees disciplinary sanctions (*farḍ ʿuqūba taʿzīriyya*) for any divorce that does not take place in court.[94]

The Supreme Judge also announced in this report in February that there would be a *taʿmīm* with regard to *khulʿ* – the one which was finally issued on August 20, 2012. At the time of the report,[95] matters had already been transferred to the Special Fiqh Committee (*al-Lajna al-Fiqhiyya al-Khāṣṣa*) in the *Dīwān* to study these points and to develop recommendations to pass the "law" ([*sic!*] *qānūn*).

89 See al-Muqtafī; see also Jabʿītī 2012: 2–3.

90 Asem Khalil, interview on November 21, 2017.

91 For the "transitional period," Welchman observed the same tendency, see Welchman 2003: 51–53.

92 Maannews, February 21, 2012; the Supreme Judge praised the development of the Sharia court system under the PA, see Paltoday, January 19, 2012.

93 A short information about this *taʿmīm* can be found on the official website of the *Dīwān*, see http://kudah.pna.ps/ar_page.aspx?id=tj6TbDa1921589307atj6TbD, accessed September 8, 2017.

94 Maannews, February 21, 2012; Paltoday, January 19, 2012. These rulings cannot be found on the website, as far as I can see.

95 Maannews, February 21, 2012.

The Supreme Judge intended to provide publications for raising awareness and guidance. Furthermore, he demanded money for renovation of old buildings, for new computers, etc. and a piece of land to erect buildings for the Sharia Judiciary. Ṣumūd al-Ḍamīrī complained that the workload of the Sharia courts had increased considerably, by 48 percent, from 62,000 cases in 2010 to 92,000 cases in 2011.[96]

The comparatively independent position of the SCHC has provoked strong criticism in the media, too.[97] ʿAnān Jabʿītī, in her analysis written for the civil society organization Amān,[98] criticized many shortcomings and weaknesses.[99] Basically, analyzing the lack of integrity, accountability, and transparency of the SCHC and the Supreme Judge Department, she pointed to the direct nomination of the Supreme Judge by the president according to Article 1 of the decree-law 3/2012,[100] and his rank as a minister. Jabʿītī refers to the organizational structure and the development plan of the Supreme Judge Department validated by the cabinet on November 29, 2005, that it should be a "governmental organization connected to the President" seeing a contradiction because principally governmental organizations are connected to the cabinet and not to the president.[101] A second argument concerns the independent structure of the SCHC. Generally, in the neighboring states, two main systems of structuring the Sharia courts exist, she argues. They are either independent from the civil court system – as in Jordan and Palestine – or integrated into one administrative unit with the civil court system as in Kuwait and the UAE. The second version is preferred by Jabʿītī because it is better suited for judicial independence and enforcement of judgments, which happens in the same place and makes the institution more accessible to citizens.[102] With regard to accountability, Jabʿītī makes a strong argument for better education and training for the judges – a topic that will be dealt with in chapter 5 in which university teaching is analyzed. According to Article 3[103] of the Law of the Formation of the Sharia Courts, the candidate must have Jordanian citizenship (Article 3[a]) – as it is a Jordanian law – and be at least twenty-two years old (Article 3[b]). Besides, the candidate should hold a "Certificate of

96 Maannews, February 21, 2012; Paltoday, January 19, 2012.

97 Abū Taʿīma June 23, 2013; Jabʿītī 2012.

98 See Aman Transparency Palestine, an NGO: https://www.aman-palestine.org/en/about-aman/about-organization, accessed September 21, 2018.

99 Jabʿītī 2012.

100 See Muqtafi.

101 Jabʿītī 2012: 2–3.

102 Jabʿītī 2012: 3.

103 Qānūn Tashkīl al-Maḥākim al-Sharʿiyya of 19/1972, see Muqtafi.

Sharia judiciary (*ijāza al-qaḍāʾ al-sharʿī*) by a Faculty of Sharia of any Arab or Muslim country or have worked as a Sharia judge or alternatively he should hold a 'Certificate in law' (*shahāda fī al-qānūn*)" (Article 3[c]). Jabʿītī argues that candidates should have additional knowledge or even a certificate from the other law: the candidate with a Sharia certificate should have a certificate in civil law (*qānūn*) and the candidate with civil law certificate should have one in Sharia.[104]

With regard to the control of finances, the *Dīwān* is accused of not having transferred the special fees it had received for marriage contracts to the state administration. This had been admonished in a report of the Board of Financial and Administrative Control (*Dīwān al-Raqāba al-Māliyya wa-l-Idāriyya*) of 2010 and 2011.[105] The absence of operationalization of the unit of internal control despite its being mentioned in the organizational structure[106] is criticized as well as the fact that the director of the internal control unit is at the same time responsible for the executive functions.[107] Jabʿītī sees a conflict of interest in cases where judges have other jobs beside their judgeship. There is no regulation to restrain political activities of judges[108] and no "code of conduct" (*mudawwana sulūk*), neither for judges nor for the rest of the staff working in the Sharia courts.[109]

With regard to transparency, it is criticized that there is no clarification of the procedures and especially that the rulings (*taʿmīmāt*) are not shown on the website. The website thus does not contain the important information about the functioning and the output of the *Dīwān*.[110] The disciplinary accountability is described as weak. Also, the *Qāḍī ul-Quḍāt* did not submit regular reports to the president.[111] Jabʿītī in her report sums up that there should be integration of the Sharia courts into the civil court system. If this was not attainable then there should be a law regulating the functioning of the Sharia courts, periodical reports to the president of Palestine, regulation of judicial training in Sharia and law (*qānūn*), a code of conduct and more information to the public: in short, more transparency.[112]

104 Jabʿītī 2012: 4.
105 Jabʿītī 2012: 4–5; see also Abū Taʿīma 2013.
106 See p. 50: *al-Raqāba al-Dākhiliyya*.
107 Jabʿītī 2012: 5.
108 Jabʿītī 2012: 6.
109 Jabʿītī 2012: 6.
110 Jabʿītī 2012: 7.
111 Jabʿītī 2012: 8. This has happened in between as the report of, e.g., 2015, is on the Internet.
112 Jabʿītī 2012: 9–10.

The activity of the SCHC of issuing *taʿmīmāt* has already been mentioned, taking the example of the *khulʿ* ruling. But how is it rooted in the laws? The Jordanian law, applicable in the West Bank, regulates "independent legal opinion" (*ijtihād*) according to Article 150 (Law of the Procedure for Sharia Courts 31/1959) (*Qānūn Uṣūl al-Muḥākamāt al-Sharʿiyya*). Where there are contrasting Appeal Court rulings on the matters in question or where it seems appropriate to issue a ruling contrary to all previous rulings, the court considering the case shall consist of a panel of five rather than the usual three judges. The judicial exercise of independent legal opinion (*ijtihād*) is thus carefully regulated, as Lynn Welchman states: it is the task of the legislature, in drawing up the codes of family law on which all but the rarest rulings will be based. The Appeal Court deals with points arising in practice only, he has to confirm or reject the *ijtihād* exercised of necessity by the individual judge in the first instance court in those cases in which he is faced with a novel situation not covered by the texts and without previous Appeal Court decisions to guide him or when he considers it might be time to challenge an established practice. Such occasions are rare, according to Welchman's research.[113]

In his master's thesis submitted to Nablus University in 2014 with the title "Studies about the Situation of the Sharia Courts and the Development of the Applied Laws in Palestine" (*Dirāsat ʿan Wāqiʿ al-Maḥākim al-Sharʿiyya wa-Taṭawwur al-Qawānīn al-Maʿmūl bi-hā fī Filasṭīn*), ʿAbdalkarīm Jabr ʿAlī Ṭuwāfisha argues that personal status law is a highly important topic because it deals with central issues of people's life and that the Islamic jurisprudence (*fiqh*) has always been applied. He connects the personal status law to the the *fiqh*,[114] and coins the term "personal status *fiqh*" (*fiqh al-aḥwāl al-shakhṣiyya*)[115] being well aware that *al-aḥwāl al-shakhṣiyya*/personal status law is a modern Western-inspired term that was first used by Muḥammad Qadrī Pasha.[116] He provides an overview of the history of legislation and legal institutions in Palestine since Ottoman times with all its developments, including the *taʿmīmāt* and the Supreme Judge's much-discussed Draft of 2013,[117] which he discusses at some length.[118] He considers the *taʿmīmāt* a cure for the lack of legislation in the country and for the fact that different laws are applied in

113 In practice, Welchman stated for the time of her research, i.e., the 1960s–1990s, the majority of appeals submitted by West Bank litigants to the Sharia Court of Appeal in the case material of this study were based on procedural matters. Welchman 2000: 35.

114 Ṭuwāfisha 2014: 1.

115 Ṭuwāfisha 2014: 1.

116 Ṭuwāfisha 2014: 240.

117 See chapter 2.2.2.

118 Ṭuwāfisha 2014: 198–239.

the West Bank and Gaza – Jordanian and Egyptian laws respectively.[119] In his final statements and recommendations,[120] Ṭuwāfisha calls the *Qāḍī al-Quḍāt* the "highest religious and political power" in the *Dīwān* and the SCHC the administrative head of the Sharia judiciary and stresses the fact that he has the rank of a minister, equal to the position of the Minister of Justice.[121] He complains that the Israeli occupation undermines the Sharia court system, forgetting to mention that the split between Hamas and Fatah is also one of the decisive factors. His proposed solution is to apply Sharia in all legal fields, i.e., not to confine it to personal status law and to create on this basis a unified legislation. He recommends the approval of the draft law drawn up by the Supreme Judge in 2013 and supports the need for special buildings for the Sharia courts and the creation of a special institute for the qualification and training of Sharia judges and other employees as well as an increase in the number of Sharia-judges.[122] Ṭuwāfisha's thesis reflects an academic approach in the Faculty of Islamic Law and Legislation (*Kulliyyat al-Fiqh wa-l-Tashrīʿ*) in Nablus University, which advocates a return to classical Islamic jurisprudence, ignoring, suppressing, or even replacing secular jurisdiction or other realms of law with the aim of placing them under the umbrella of Islamic law. He also does ignore international law. His research is based on Arabic sources only and does not take English sources or any English-language research into consideration. To a certain extent this scientific piece of work reflects what can be called a deep split in society and science in Palestine between traditional Muslim scholarship writing and discussing in Arabic and focusing on Arabic sources and classical Islamic methodology only and modern Western scholarship that is published mostly in English and takes international research as well as new legal methods into consideration. Both parts of academia, I would argue, often do not take notice of each other.

The SCHS and the Supreme Judge Department have a powerful and more secular institutional counterpart, the SCC.

2.1.3 *Supreme Constitutional Court (SCC)*

Article 103 of the BL requires the creation of a High Constitutional Court (HCC)[123] (*Maḥkama Dustūriyya ʿUlyā*):

119 Ṭuwāfisha 2014: 242.
120 Ṭuwāfisha 2014: 240–244.
121 Ṭuwāfisha 2014: 242.
122 Ṭuwāfisha 2014: 243. As we will see later, the Sharia establishment strongly demands the improvement of its working conditions (see 2.2.2.2).
123 [*Sic*] in the English version of the BL, but in the discussion: Supreme Constitutional Court, SCC.

1. A High Constitutional Court shall be established by law to consider:
   a) The constitutionality of laws, regulations, and other enacted rules.
   b) The interpretation of the Basic Law and legislation.
   c) Settlement of jurisdictional disputes which might arise between judicial entities and administrative entities having judicial jurisdiction.
2. The law shall specify the manner in which the High Constitutional Court is formed and structured, the operating procedures it will follow and the effects resulting from its rulings.[124]

The creation of the SCC finally in 2016 garnered much criticism as fear was widespread that the SCC would replace the parliament as the highest legislative authority, especially because the PLC was not sitting and all the judges were named by the president.[125] Hamas criticized this decision, of course, since Abbas had not consulted them.[126] Politically this step was considered especially by independent jurists and civil society as an attempt to monopolize all political decisions[127] and several social and political bodies expressed their concern about this development.[128] Muḥammad ʿAbdalghanī al-Ḥājj Qāsim became the Head of the SCC[129] and Ḥasan al-ʿŪrī tried to defend this appointment and the implementation of the court in an interview with *Al-Monitor*:

> The consultations preceding the establishment of this Court started in 2006, but the Palestinian division in 2007 between the West Bank and the Gaza Strip after Hamas took over Gaza delayed the process. Today, President Abbas had to rise to the challenge for two main reasons: first, the difficulty of examining the appeals and constitutional issues that require decisions and legislations – brought before the High Court – which acted as a temporary constitutional court according to Article 104 of the Palestinian Basic Law, which stipulates that the temporary High Court shall handle all cases brought before the administrative courts and the Supreme Constitutional Court until they are formed; and second, the implementation of Article 103 of the Palestinian Basic Law.[130]

124 BL, Article 103.
125 Nazzal 2016; Qatrawi 2016.
126 Qatrawi 2016.
127 Qatrawi 2016.
128 Qatrawi 2016.
129 Shasha News April 20, 2016.
130 Qatrawi 2016.

The NGOs al-Haq[131] and Musawa, which describes itself on its website as the "Palestinian Center for the Independence of the Judiciary and the Legal Profession" and claims to be a "neutral, unpartisan and independent Palestinian civil society organization,"[132] issued a statement demanding that Abbas withdraw the constitutional court formation. Two written memos (April 3 and April 12, 2016) were sent to President Abbas demanding that the formation of the SCC should take place slowly and only after all the necessary constitutional requirements are available with national reconciliation being at the forefront.[133] But these demands were not heard.

2.1.3.1 An Important Judgment?

The SCC issued a judgment on November 19, 2017 (4/2017), in a legal case the court of first instance of Jenin referred to it. The Jenin decision from March 28 (decision 487/2016) concerned an employee of an international organization (UNRWA) and disputed immunity. The Jenin court asked "a constitutional question with regard to the definition of the position of international treaties agreed upon in relation to the national Palestinian legislation with explaining the instruments to the implementation in the national Palestinian legislation to become binding."[134] The SCC answered generally with regard to human rights and this answer was about to stir up the iterations among jurists and legal scholars as well as civil society organizations in the West Bank with regard to the role of international law and Islamic law and their intersection in Palestine, taking into consideration the special importance of Article 10 (1) that basic human rights shall be protected and respected (Article 10 [1]) and that the Palestinian Authority shall work "without delay" to become a party to regional and international declarations and covenants that protect human rights (Article 10 [2]).

The important sentence in the SCC's answer to this question is the following:

> The Court ruled in its majority in answering the constitutional question which was the topic of the referral stating that international treaties are *above* (*sumūw*) national legislation in such a manner as international treaties stand above national legislation *so far as they are in harmony*

131 Al-Haq, December 27, 2016.

132 See http://www.musawa.ps/about/about-us.html, accessed October 30, 2018.

133 Musawa, May 17, 2016.

134 See Muqtafi.

> *(muwā'ama) with the national, religious, and cultural identity (huwiyya) of the Arabic Palestinian people.*[135]

In the judgment, the SCC argued that the BL is silent on the definition of the position of the international treaties with the exception of Article 10, which confirms that human rights are obligatory and have to be respected, but the BL does not have any instruments to integrate the enforcement of international treaties into the national legislature system. The Court also argued that signing international treaties generally means that the state waives a part of its sovereignty, it being evident that the Palestinian state in its legal development pays respect to international treaties. International law and jurisdiction (*al-fiqh*[136] *wa-l-qaḍā' al-duwaliyyayni*) are established on the principle of the superiority of international treaties over national law. Palestine has according to this judgment an international legal personality (*al-shakhṣiyya al-qānūniyya al-dawliyya*) and as such has signed many treaties in recent years, which express its waiving of parts of its sovereignty. It has thus shown its positive exchange with the international body besides respecting the national, religious, and cultural identity of the Palestinian people. One dissenting opinion disagrees not with the result, but with one aspect: international treaties are above national law but below the constitution.

The judgment was welcomed by many because it seemed to confirm generally, that international treaties were above national legislation. There was hope in the West Bank that the JLPS, which contradicts several regulations in international law and was now outdated and no longer applicable,[137] could be reformed, or a Palestinian family law would be created based on this judgment. Milhem welcomed the judgment[138] and explained that it was the SCC's task to shed light on this issue and that now judges could use it. Negative in his opinion are only the "conditions" that are much too vague and leave too much room ("identity," "culture") to serve as a basis for any judgment.

Khalil, on the other hand, called the judgment a shame because of its faulty arguments.[139] The Constitutional Law Unit at Birzeit University, including Khalil and others, published a harshly critical Position Paper in 2017. The SCC was not seen as qualified to give such a decision, it transgressed its constitutional and legal competence, and infringed upon the responsibility of the

135 See Muqtafi, emphasis added.

136 Interestingly, here for international law the term *fiqh*, referring normally only to Islamic jurisprudence, is used.

137 Qafisheh 2018.

138 Feras Milhem, interview on February 28, 2018.

139 Asem Khalil, interview on February 20, 2018; see also Dahīdī, December 13, 2017.

legislature.[140] It would have been the task of the PLC to decide the question of how to integrate international law into the national legislation. The argument was that the constituent power is the only competent body to determine the position of international treaties.[141] The silence of the constituent power on defining the place of international treaties in no way means that the SCC can take over this task of defining.[142] Second, the SCC is criticized for its reference to the rules connected to diplomatic immunity and privileges as a firm "customary international law," which is inconsistent as well as the reference to the international treaties (the other source of international law, besides custom) being higher than the national legislation.[143] The jurists point to the lack of regulations for incorporation of international law into national law and complain that despite this lack, many international treaties are signed. They ask provocatively whether the SCC should give the president complete power to sign international treaties.[144] Third, the jurists criticize, as Milhem, the ambiguity in the wording of the judgment, when it says that "international treaties are superior to (*sumūw*) national legislation" only when they are in harmony (*muwāʾama*) "with the national, religious and cultural identity of the Arab Palestinian people." They complain that this is "ambiguous and doubtful" and argue that these formulations approach reservations that some states apply to international treaties upon ratification.[145] They also point to the fact that reservations happen before or during the accession to a convention.[146] The jurists point out that normally judgments of the SCC are binding and that it is not allowed for the courts to apply law that the SCC has deemed non-constitutional. But the analysis and conclusion used by the SCC in this case, they went on, cannot be called a source for a legal ruling or, as in this case, a new constitutionality. The ruling that international treaties have superiority over national legislation is thus not a binding constitutional regulation for the courts.[147] There is a difference between "international declarations and covenants" (Article 10 [2]) and human rights in a general way.

On March 12, 2018, the SCC rendered a further decision on the Constitutional Appeal No. 5/2017 regarding the interpretation of Article 10 of the Basic Law. In this decision, the Court highlighted the "duality of legal norms" without

140 Constitutional Law Unit at Birzeit University (12/2017): 2.
141 Constitutional Law Unit at Birzeit University (12/2017): 2.
142 Constitutional Law Unit at Birzeit University (12/2017): 2–3.
143 Constitutional Law Unit at Birzeit University (12/2017): 3.
144 Constitutional Law Unit at Birzeit University (12/2017): 4.
145 Constitutional Law Unit at Birzeit University (12/2017): 4.
146 Constitutional Law Unit at Birzeit University (12/2017): 4.
147 Constitutional Law Unit at Birzeit University (12/2017): 5–6.

a constitutional or legal basis. The Court held that "international treaties and conventions are not considered by themselves as a law to be applied to Palestine. To be enforced, these must possess power by passing through the formal stages to be fulfilled for the enactment of a particular domestic law."[148] This means that the enforcement of international conventions would need to be domestically approved in accordance with the mechanisms for approving and publishing laws in the Official Gazette. According to this decision, the Court reiterated its general "reservation" to the applicability of international conventions "without prejudice to the religious and cultural identity of the Palestinian people." The civil society organization Al-Haq pointed to these two SCC judgments in its letter to the CEDAW Committee and drew the attention of the CEDAW Committee to the fact that the SCC had been created by the president without the involvement of the PLC.[149]

The international treaties have to be published in the Official Gazette to be domestically approved – a step that has not yet been taken (May 2020) for the conventions signed by President Abbas including CEDAW.

2.2 The Jordanian Law of Personal Status (JLPS) of 1976, Applicable in the West Bank and the Egyptian Family Rights Law (EFRL) of 1954, Applicable in Gaza

2.2.1 *The Applicable Family Laws in the West Bank and Gaza*

Palestine, i.e., the West Bank and Gaza, are governed by different and complex bodies of law that reflect the political history of Palestine: Ottoman, Jordanian, Egyptian, Palestinian, and Israeli law. Until the twentieth century, Islamic law on personal status matters was applied by Sharia courts that acted on the basis of classical sources of the four Sunni schools.[150] The Ottomans gave precedence to the Hanafi law that was the basis for the first codification of the Ottoman Law of Family Rights (OLFR) of 1917. In Palestine, the OLFR was implemented by the British Mandate authorities and remained in force until 1948, when the State of Israel was founded[151] and the West Bank came under Jordanian rule and Gaza under Egyptian rule.[152] The British Mandate

148 See Muqtafi.

149 Al-Haq, June 2018: 3. See also https://tbinternet.ohchr.org/Treaties/CEDAW/Shared%20 Documents/PSE/INT_CEDAW_NGO_PSE_31670_E.pdf, accessed July 6, 2018.

150 Tucker 1996.

151 In Israel, it is still the basis of the Sharia court decisions, see Edres, Lindbekk and Schneider 2018: 20.

152 Welchman 1999: 18.

authorities (1922–1948) decided to apply the OLFR to all Muslim citizens and to cancel the provisions of the OLFR that applied to non-Muslims, who were allowed to continue to apply their own personal status laws.[153] The Ottoman law of 1917, besides setting a precedent for the codification of Sharia rules, also set an example by introducing rules from non-Hanafi sources on the basis of public interest (*maṣlaḥa*). This process of selection from various opinions provided the legislature with a certain flexibility in approaching core areas of family law, particularly as they affected women, in light of the changing role of women in society.[154] In the 1950s, a number of newly independent Arab states issued laws of personal status, which included rules drawn from all four Sunni schools, from minority and individual juristic opinions, and, in certain cases, from independent legal opinion (*ijtihad*) based on the interpretation of the primary legal sources of the Quran and Sunna. The first such code was the Jordanian Law of Family Rights 1951, followed by Syria, Tunisia, Morocco, and Iraq.[155]

Today, the Sharia courts in the West Bank apply the Jordanian Law of Personal Status (JLPS) of 1976, which replaced the 1951 Jordanian Law of Family Rights[156] and the courts in Gaza apply the EFRL of 1954.[157] EFRL was issued as Order No. 303 by the Governor of the Gaza Strip when it was under Egyptian administration. This law abrogated the Ottoman Law of Family Rights (OLFR) of 1917 but if there is no applicable text in the EFRL, the judges have to go back to the OLFR.[158] There was one amendment in 2009 changing the age of the children who could stay in their mother's care (*ḥaḍāna*): it changed from seven to nine for boys and for girls from nine to eleven, if it was in the best interest (*maṣlaḥa*) of the child.[159] In 1999, a civil status law was issued (2/1999) for all Palestine that regulated the registration of births, deaths, marriages, and

153 Engelcke 2017b: 123.

154 Welchman 1999: 19.

155 Welchman 1999: 19.

156 Welchman points to the fact that Sharia courts in the West Bank (including East Jerusalem) applying legislation issued in Jordan after the 1967 Israeli occupation is an anomaly, since in all other areas the law was "frozen" in its pre-occupation state of 1967 and Israeli military orders took the place of legislation. This was a result, Welchman writes, of the position of non-recognition of the Israeli occupation by the Sharia courts in the area, sparked by the Israeli annexation of East Jerusalem and Israel's refusal to recognize the validity of rulings from Sharia courts there. See Welchman 1999: 18.

157 The exact regulations in these laws with regard to *khulʿ* will be dealt with in chapter 4, see 4.2.

158 Ṭuwāfisha 2014: 175. See chapter 9.

159 Ṭuwāfisha 2014: 175.

divorces. Article 17 permits either parent to register his/her children, a change from prevailing Jordanian law.[160]

The West Bank did not introduce the newest amendment in the Jordanian law, the JLPS of 2010, as Gaza did not introduce new Egyptian legislation, although several reforms in Islamic family law have been implemented in Cairo since that time. The reason was Arafat's decision mentioned above to leave the legislation as it was and the hope that there would soon be a Palestinian family law. Among the amendments in the neighboring countries is the influential *khulʿ* law of 2004 in Egypt, which for the first time in the Middle East gave women before and after consummation the right to end a marriage without having to give a reason.[161]

Like the Ottoman law, there is a provision in both applicable laws – the JLPS of 1976 and the EFRL of 1954 – that in the absence of any specific text addressing the subject being dealt with by the courts, reference is to be made to the dominant opinion of the Hanafi school.[162]

In 1998, the issue of personal status law in Palestine was – as Welchman describes it – "propelled into the forefront of public debate" by the work of the Model Parliament: Woman and Legislation. This project was pushed forward by a civil society seeking to identify in all areas of the law provisions that discriminated against women's rights and aimed to draft, debate, and build consensus on proposed amendments to those provisions.[163] The debate raised issues related to the place of Islam and Islamic law in the cultural heritage of Palestine, the meaning of democracy and pluralism, women's rights. Welchman describes a vehemence of the reaction from certain quarters against the questions being raised, and concludes that this vehemence "shows that many of these debates have a long way to run."[164] As a direct response to the activities of the Model Parliament, the Supreme Judge, Taysīr al-Tamīmī, Supreme Judge of Palestine until 2012 announced the establishment of a committee to draft a personal status law as a matter of priority. Where does the debate stand more than twenty years later, in 2012–2018? And why is there no progress toward a Palestinian family law?

160 Johnson 2004a: 123; it is not, as in the text, law no. 1 but law no. 2, see also Muqtafi.

161 Denker 2004.

162 Welchman 1999: 19. Welchman shows in her book that frequent reference is made to the standard compilation of Hanafi rulings on issues of personal status compiled by Muḥammad Qadrī Pasha, see Welchman 1999: 19.

163 Welchman 1999: 21.

164 Quoted in Welchman 1999: 21.

2.2.2 *Toward a Palestinian Law of Personal Status (2010–2018): The Drafts*

As outlined above, the need to have a Palestinian family law was already seen in the 1990s,[165] but it had always been considered a sensitive topic and in Yassir Arafat's terms, a "wasps' nest" (*ʿushsh al-dabābīr*).[166] Ṣabāḥ Salāma, Coordinator of the Palestinian Nongovernmental Organisation against Domestic Violence against Women al-Muntada (*Muntadā al-Munaẓẓamāt al-Ahliyya al-Filasṭiniyya li-Munāhaḍa al-ʿUnf ḍidda al-Marʾa*),[167] confirmed the importance of this law for civil society and women's organizations but did not see the law to be more a wasps' nest than other laws concerning women.[168]

Several draft laws are mentioned in the literature for 2001, 2003, 2005/06, 2007, and 2008.[169] The parliamentary deadlock and the political split further diminished the chances for a unified law. The question of whether a unified family law should be introduced by presidential decree was raised. According to Ashraf Abū Ḥayyah, in 2007 the Minister for Women's Affairs in cooperation with the Head of SCHC forwarded a draft that was prepared by the presidential committee to President Abbas. Civil society, however, intervened and prevented the draft from being passed pointing to a lack of consensus between civil society groups and state institutions regarding family law. They argued that civil society groups must have a chance to comment on the draft.[170] In 2008, the General Union of Palestinian Women (GUPW), i.e., the women's organization of the PLO, the Ministry of Women's Affairs (MoWA), and civil society groups issued the Charter of the Rights of the Palestinian Woman (*Wathīqat Ḥuqūq al-Marʾa al-Filasṭīniyya*) with basic rights for women which is, however, not a draft law.[171] In 2010, a group of women activists met with Prime Minister Salām Fayyāḍ to discuss the issue. The Prime Minister asked them to provide him with a memo mentioning the articles they thought should be amended. Abū Ḥayyah states in his article published in 2011 that the memo was not sent.[172]

There were two draft laws under examination at the time available to me, one from 2010 drafted by the civil society, slightly before the time of this research but important because it was still quoted especially by members of the

165 Welchman 1999; 2003; 2009.

166 *Ḥārisāt Nārinā*, April 9, 2017.

167 See http://www.almuntada-pal.ps/?p=329.

168 *Hārisāt Nārinā*, April 9, 2017.

169 For the 1990s, Welchman states that the draft laws were always drawn up by the Sharia establishment, see 1995 and 1998, see Welchman 2004: 108–109; Welchman 2009: 132; Polfus 2014: 51; Goudarzi-Gereke 2018: 51–53.

170 Abu Hayyeh 2011.

171 Wathīqat 2008.

172 Abu Hayyeh 2011.

civil society, and one by the Office of the *Qāḍī al-Quḍāt* of 2013. In 2017, when asked what civil society had done to promote a Palestinian family law, Ṣabāḥ Salāma mentioned various drafts that had been presented on the policy and also the work of civil society to raise awareness of women's rights.[173] Ṣumūd al-Ḍamīrī, Sharia Judge and Head of Personal Status Prosecution, had a different view on this and argued that there had been a committee for preparing the law but that even civil society had not reached a consensus within itself.[174]

2.2.2.1 Draft of the National Committee of Family Law (NCFL), 2010[175]

In preparation for a new family law, the National Committee of the Family Law (NCFL, *al-Lajna al-Waṭaniyya li-Qānūn al-Usra*) had been created. It was overseen by Ḥasan al-ʿŪrī who brought together representatives of the Sharia establishment; the state, especially the Ministries of Justice and Women's Affairs; and civil society.[176] The idea had been to invite experts from different parts of society to discuss and draft the Palestinian family law, which could be accepted by all of Palestinian society. The result had been the 2010 Draft Law.

Gender equality is the aim of this Draft according to the title drawn up by the NCFL as a body. Many Islamic concepts are missing, for example, repudiation (*ṭalāq*). The marriage contract is not defined in the classical Islamic way but as a contract between a man and a woman, adults with legal capacity, equal in rights and obligations.[177] The marriage age for both sexes is eighteen solar years. In Article 2 (4), under the heading of "engagement" (*khiṭba*), it is said that in case the marriage contract (*ʿaqd*, [*sic!*]) is dissolved before consummation, the woman will be referred to as "unmarried" in official documents. This regulation was later adopted by the *taʿmīm* of 2012, giving young women the chance to be divorced before the consummation of marriage without being referred to as divorcées in their documents.

Article 13 states that every person who has reached the marriage age can enter into a marriage contract by himself/herself thus doing away with the legal guardian for marriage (*walī*) who is again made obligatory in the 2013 Draft Law. Instead, the 2010 Draft makes it voluntary for a person to have a legal guardian,[178] but the language is gender neutral, "the person" may chose a representative. According to Article 14 of the Draft, the judge has to confirm the benefit (*maṣlaḥa*) and consent of a woman to a marriage to a man who is older

173 *Ḥārisāt Nārinā*, April 9, 2017.
174 *Ḥārisāt Nārinā*, April 9, 2017.
175 Palestinian Women and Security (2012), 156–167.
176 Ḥasan al-ʿŪrī, interview on October 13, 2014.
177 Article 3 of the Draft.
178 Article 13 (2).

than she is by fifteen years or more. According to Article 15, marriage with more than one person is only allowed after permission of the court. According to Article 58, marriage ends with death or divorce (*taṭlīq*),[179] and there is no divorce outside of a special court.[180] Both spouses can file for divorce[181] and both or their proxies have to be present.[182] In Article 59, the "classical" reasons for judicial divorce are stated, such as "dispute and discord" (*al-nizāʿ wa-l-shiqāq*) (59 [5]) or nonpayment of maintenance (59 [3]) (*ʿadam al-infāq*). Under Article 59 (6), there is a new rubric called "violence in all forms" (*al-ʿunf bi-kāffat ashkālihā*). Article 60 is quite innovative: there can be no divorce out of court, and second, that the court can separate a couple on the basis of (a) mutual consent as well as based on the divorce application of (b) the husband or (c) the wife. The term used is "ending the marital relation" (*inhāʾ al-ʿalāqa al-zawjiyya*). The term *khulʿ* is not mentioned in the document.

2.2.2.2 Meeting in Al-Quds University November 2, 2013: The Sharia Establishment Hits Back

This 2010 Draft was discussed and rejected by the Sharia establishment in a meeting that took place on November 2, 2013. A group of Sharia scholars published on that day a final communiqué of a meeting with regard to the 2010 NCFL Draft[183] under the title "Communiqué of the Special Day of Study for the Discussion of the Draft of the Personal Status Law Proposed by the National Committee for the Family Law (NCFL)" (*Al-Bayān al-Khitāmī, Bayān al-Yawm al-Dirāsī al-Mukhaṣṣaṣ li-Munāqashat Mashrūʿ Qānūn al-Aḥwāl al-Shakhṣiyya al-Muqtaraḥ min al-Lajna al-Waṭaniyya li-Qānūn al-Usra*).[184]

The meeting was headed by Dr. Ḥamza Dhīb, Dean of both Faculties of "Mission and Principles of Religion" and "Quran and Islamic Studies" of al-Quds University with the participation of a great number of Sharia judges,

179 Article 58 (1).
180 Article 58 (2).
181 Article 58 (3).
182 Article 58 (4).
183 Bayān al-Khitāmī, al- (November 2, 2013). All in all there were five judges present, fourteen university lecturers and professors, and one Sharia lawyer.
184 A similar incident happened in 1998 when the Model Parliament met to discuss family law matters. Welchman describes that a memorandum was submitted to the speaker and members of the parliament, signed by over a dozen Sharia court judges and others associated with the Sharia establishment such as Sharia college instructors, deans of university departments, and imams appealing to the Model Parliamant to reject the "personal status law draft prepared and supervised by women of the 'Model Parliament'" on the grounds that "most of the provisions of this draft are in explicit violation of God's book and the Prophet's *Sunna* and the consensus (*ijmāʿ*) of the Muslims." (Welchman 2003: 52–53).

among them the *Qāḍī al-Quḍāt* Yūsuf Idʿīs and Tawfīq Abū al-Hāshim, a judge in the Sharia High Court, with university professors, including ʿAlī al-Sarṭāwī of Najāh-University in Nablus and scholars especially from al-Quds University, but also from Hebron University. All of them were males, not a single woman was on the list, which is remarkable because there were at that time three female judges in Sharia courts and the topic was family law.

After a long discussion the participants presented the following statements and recommendations:[185]

1. To stress the importance of the functional jurisdiction of the Sharia judiciary for implementing its full competence and that the competent authority in proposing any law or claims to reform it in connection to the personal status law is the *Dīwān Qāḍī al-Quḍāt*. This is seen in accordance with the BL, which provides for the necessity of respecting the judicial authority and confirms the principle of separation of powers.
2. The implementation of bodies for interfering with the work of the Sharia courts without competent authority is against the laws in force and therefore it was not opportune of the committee [meaning the NCFL] to submit the Draft of 2010.
3. The Draft contains infringements of Sharia in regulations and principles of Islamic Sharia and it has fallacies and conceptual confusions. For example, giving the woman financial competence is absolutely not necessary, there are effects given to contracts that are void (*bāṭil*), and incompatible scenarios are given to end conjugal life.
4. The 2010 Draft does not address many main Sharia regulations that are connected with Islamic jurisprudence of the family (*fiqh al-usra*) and must be addressed.
5. The organizations and associations presenting the drafts and laws of PSL went beyond Sharia regulations claiming to fight discrimination against women. They want "absolute equality" (*musāwāh muṭlaqa*) between man and woman. This appears to be an unjust claim (*iddiʿāʾ ẓālim*), since Islamic Sharia does justice to women (*anṣafat al-marʾa*), preserves their rights (*ḥuqūq*) and dignity (*karāma*), and ensures security, maintenance (*nafaqa*), and protection (*riʿāya*), and guarantees rights in inheritance and other matters.
6. The Draft goes beyond Sharia in many articles and marginalizes the role of family in social relations. It ignores the role of guardians in marriage contracts and has a negative impact on the structure of the family, which has to be protected according to the laws.

185 What follows is a summary, not a translation.

7. Confirmation of the positive role of the organs of the Sharia judiciary for the family and the endowments (*awqāf*) is necessary.
8. The Draft submitted by the committee is excessive, especially with the backdrop of a draft issued by the Technical Bureau of the Supreme Judge Department.
9. There is need to create a consultative Sharia body composed of Sharia professors of the Palestinian universities for the provision of scientific well-founded advice to inform the Sharia judiciary.
10. There should be a bar association for Sharia lawyers to support their efforts and guard their rights.
11. Media campaigns have to inform the people about the jurisdiction of family law based on Islamic rulings and to eliminate suspicions levelled against it.

The text of the Communiqué is in many aspects vague, and does not even quote the articles of the 2010 Draft that were criticized. Still, several points can be affirmed from it:

- The only organ justified to develop and present a draft of a family law is the *Qāḍī al-Quḍāt*'s Department. No one else has the right to make a draft. Not even the NCFL.
- The basis of family law is Islamic law.
- The interpretation of Islamic law is to be determined by the "Sharia establishment," which is here described as consisting of the office of the *Qāḍī al-Quḍāt* and a "consultative Sharia body," which will have Sharia scholars, especially professors from universities.[186]
- This "Sharia establishment" is to be strengthened by the creation of additional bodies, such as the bar association of Sharia lawyers and the consultative Sharia body.
- There are several severe problems concerning special regulations of the 2010 Draft that regard equal access to divorce, abolition of the marriage guardians, as well as what is called the women's organizations demand for "absolute equality."

This conservative Position Paper can be read as a very distinct and clear answer to the NCFL Draft of 2010. In many points and in its language, it went several steps back to traditional and hierarchical gender concepts. For example the paper argues that "giving the woman financial competence is absolutely not necessary" and it is stated that the marriage guardian must be preserved ignoring the fact that according to Hanafi law a woman of age can marry

186 At that time, all professors at Palestinian universities in the faculties of Sharia were men. There was no female professor in a Sharia faculty.

without a guardian. Equality (*musāwāh*) is explicitly named and rejected, it comes from "them" and is called an "unjust claim, since Islamic Sharia does "justice" to women." This Islamic justice and the preservation of woman's dignity are defined to be enclosed in the right of the woman to maintenance (*nafaqa*) and "protection" (*riʿāya*). The "maintenance-obedience model" with maintenance as a pillar of the Islamic family system and the wife's obedience toward the husband is thus not only confirmed to be in conformity with Islamic law but it is also described as "justice." The demand for equality, even "absolute equality" is turned into a demand for justice as defined in a conservative Islamic gender unequal understanding. "They," i.e., the women's organizations, are described as claiming "to fight discrimination against women," a formulation that is a hint to CEDAW, the Convention on the Elimination of all Forms of Discrimination against Women, as "discrimination" is not a legal term in Islamic law. There are no attempts to approach the problems of women in twenty-first-century Palestine, to reform Islamic law, or to adapt "equality" from international law to Islamic law.[187] The Communiqué can be read as a clear rejection of international law. The chance to deal with "equality," the term used in CEDAW Articles 2 and 16, and to "translate" it into the Palestinian context is not used, instead the old hierarchical gender model is confirmed with the reference to security, maintenance, and protection. *Riʿāya* (protection) can be read as a hint to Quran 4:34 in which men "standing above women" is often translated as the man protecting the woman, not as a relation of equality.[188] The Communiqué is even more conservative than the *taʿmīm*, as will become evident in the analysis of the *taʿmīm*. Especially in its wording, it can be seen, as I have argued elsewhere, as a strategy of "othering," of excluding the women's organizations from the iterations arguing that they are incapable of writing such a draft.[189] This informal meeting of Muslim scholars at a university not only rejects the NCFL's proposal and therefore a committee that had been commissioned by President Abbas to draw up a law but also wants only the SCHC to be responsible for drawing up family law.

2.2.2.3 Draft of 2013

The answer to the 2010 NCFL's Draft was the Supreme Judge's Draft of 2013, which would become the basis for any further public discussion. The Draft

187 See the *taʿmīm*, chapter 4.3 but also in the Gaza Draft Law, see chapter 9.2.

188 See different translations, see Quran: https://www.islamawakened.com/quran/4/34/default.htm, accessed June 14, 2019. Arberry translates it as "men are managers of the affairs of women." The Arabic wording *al-rijāl qawwamūna ʿalā al-nisāʾ* can be translated literally "men are standing above women", expressing a gender hierarchy.

189 Schneider: forthcoming.

prepared under Yūsuf Idʿīs comprises nine subdivided parts.[190] It covers marriage, divorce, maintenance, guardianship, custody, and inheritance. Article 291 stipulates that where the law is silent, the Hanafi school of law is to be followed.[191]

Marriage is generally defined in the traditional way, it is, according to Article 5, "a contract between a man and a woman who is permissible for him according to Sharia" and not, as in the 2010 Draft: "a contract between a man and a woman, adult and with legal capacity equal with rights and obligations."[192] Lara-Lauren Goudarzi-Gereke points to two additional important points and compares the Draft also with the JLPS of 2010. One important difference between the JLPS 1976 and the 2013 Draft is to be found in Article 10. Whereas the minimum age for marriage in the Draft is raised from sixteen to eighteen years for men and from fifteen to sixteen years for women, the JLPS 2010 determines eighteen solar years for both male and female as the minimum age for marriage. Goudarzi-Gereke observes that by raising the minimum marriage age for women by one lunar year, the 2013 Draft falls short of demands made, not only by women's rights groups, but also by an earlier draft prepared by the Supreme Judge Department.[193] The other point concerns Article 15, which states that there should be "no marriage without a guardian" (*lā zawāj illā bi-walī*). Goudarzi-Gereke explains that this provision, being a quotation of a *ḥadīth*, is much more explicit than the former and the current JLPS and stresses that, in most cases, a woman needs the participation or even consent of a male relative to enter into marriage. The third section of part four of the Draft (dissolution of the marriage contract) is titled "consensual *khulʿ*" (*al-khulʿ al-riḍāʾī*) and "*ṭalāq* based on money" (*ṭalāq ʿalā māl*).[194]

The consensual *khulʿ* is defined in Article 102 of the Draft as "the husband's *ṭalāq* against his wife for compensation (*ʿiwaḍ*) on which both parties agree through the term *al-khulʿ* or *al-talaq* or *al-mubāraʾa* or whatever (else) this meaning has." The exact same wording is found in Article 102 of the JLPS 2010 but is not, as Goudarzi-Gereke shows, included in the 1976 Jordanian Law. Also, the terminology is slightly different in the 1976 Law, where *khulʿ* is mostly called

190 For a detailed discussion, see Goudarzi-Gereke 2018 and Ṭuwāfisha 2014: 198–239. This paragraph is mainly based on Goudarzi-Gereke's very elaborate analysis and conclusions with a focus on some general questions and the regulation of *khulʿ*.

191 Goudarzi-Gereke 2018: 53.

192 Article 3 of the Draft.

193 Goudarzi-Gereke 2018: 54; Welchman 2009: 125–138.

194 To all the forms of *khulʿ*, *ṭalāq ʿalā al-māl, iftidāʾ*, *mubāraʾa* etc. see Goudarzi-Gereke 2018: 56–64.

mukhālaʿa and compensation (*badal*),[195] which, however, does not change the meaning. According to the Draft, *khulʿ* requires the husband's competence to perform repudiation (*ṭalāq*) and his wife's subjugation to it as well as her ability to fulfill the obligation of compensation.[196] *Khulʿ* divorce leads to the waiver of all claims to dower (*mahr*) and maintenance.[197] If both parties declare their rejection of any compensation, the divorce is considered a revocable *ṭalāq* (as long as it is not the third *ṭalāq* or takes place before consummation). The difference between *khulʿ* and *ṭalāq* for payment (*ṭalāq ʿalā māl*) is not explained in the Draft. Goudarzi-Gereke notes that if for *khulʿ* divorce the usage of the word *ṭalāq* is possible, it is not clear how *khulʿ* and *ṭalāq ʿalā māl* can be distinguished on the basis of the pronouncement.[198]

As the 2013 Draft does not differ from the JLPS 1976 where mention is made of *ṭalāq ʿalā māl*, it seems safe to assume, Goudarzi-Gereke argues, that the Draft maintains the same understanding of *ṭalāq ʿalā māl* as the JLPS 1976 does. She points to a general uncertainty in the understanding of what constitutes the difference between *khulʿ* and *ṭalāq ʿalā māl*.[199]

Section four of this part of the Draft deals with judicial divorce.[200] The first form of judicial divorce is "divorce by redemption" (*tafrīq li-l-iftidāʾ*) and is laid down in Article 104 of the Draft. This form of divorce is applicable only before consummation of the marriage. The wife may file for divorce and has to declare to give back the dower and other gifts she received as well as further expenses for the marriage the husband has had. If the husband rejects, the court works toward reconciliation between the couple. If reconciliation cannot be reached, the court refers the issue to two arbitrators, who undertake another attempt at reconciliation. They have a period of three months, after which, in the case of failure, the court dissolves the marriage contract after the wife has made the payment. This regulation therefore is in accordance with *taʿmīm* 59/2012.[201]

Even though the Draft deals with "divorce by redemption" (*tafrīq li-l-iftidāʾ*) in a different section, it can, as Goudarzi-Gereke argues, also be considered a form of *khulʿ* for a number of reasons. This expression of "redemption" is also used in the Egyptian *khulʿ* law of 2000[202] (*iftadat nafsahā*). *Iftidāʾ* in a stricter sense denominates one aspect of *khulʿ* divorce, which is the paying or giving

195 Article 102 of the Draft.

196 Article 103.

197 Articles 106, 107.

198 Goudarzi-Gereke 2018: 57.

199 Goudarzi-Gereke 2018: 58.

200 Goudarzi-Geeke 2018: 59–64.

201 See in detail, chapter 4.

202 Egyptian Law No. 1/2000.

back by the wife, but the term is also used synonymously with *khulʿ* according to Denker.[203] Goudarzi-Gereke points to the fact that in the Jordanian context, where *iftidāʾ* is included in the section on judicial divorce as well,[204] media reports reflect a somewhat unclear distinction between *khulʿ* and *iftidāʾ* by calling the introduction of *iftidāʾ* a "change of name from *khulʿ* to *iftidāʾ*."[205] This, Goudarzi-Gereke rightly argues, does not correctly express the legal development, as the consensual *khulʿ* divorce remains the same and the judicial *iftidāʾ* divorce is additionally introduced (first in 2001).[206]

Differently from the *Qāḍī al-Quḍāt*'s Draft, the JLPS 2010 allows for *iftidāʾ* also after the marriage is consummated. In this case, however, just as in the Egyptian law and the 2012 ruling, further conditions come into play that must be fulfilled, namely: the wife's declaration that she detests life with her husband, that there is no possibility to continue marital life, and that she fears crossing the limits set by God. According to the JLPS 2010, for *iftidāʾ* after consummation of the marriage, the woman has to give up all her claims against her husband.[207] Judicial *khulʿ*, first introduced in Jordan in 2001, already included the distinction between "before" and "after" consummation (*qabla* and *baʿda al-dukhūl*), but did not use the term *iftidāʾ*. This differentiation between *khulʿ* and *iftidāʾ* apparently, as Goudarzi-Gereke argues convincingly, aims to provide a clear distinction between classical *khulʿ*, which requires the husband's consent and remains untouched, and judicial *khulʿ*, which is an innovation that has been highly debated in Palestine as well as in Jordan.[208]

More ambiguities concerning *khulʿ* in Palestine are found with regard to *mubāraʾa*. This term is included in the definition of (consensual) *khulʿ* in Article 102 of the Draft. *Mubāraʾa* is sometimes explained to be a synonym of *khulʿ*, while, like *iftidāʾ*, it can also be understood in a more restricted sense as one aspect of *khulʿ*, namely the wife's or both spouses' renunciation of all claims deriving from the marriage.[209] In the Palestinian context, Welchman holds *khulʿ* and *mubāraʾa* to be different forms of divorce. Based on records of the Sharia courts in the West Bank from the 1960s to the 1990s, she states that while *khulʿ* requires the wife to pay back the dower she already received,

203 Denker 2004: 134, fn. 16.

204 JLPS 2010 Article 114.

205 Goudarzi-Gereke 2018: 59.

206 Goudarzi-Gereke 2018: 59.

207 JLPS 2010 Article 114.

208 Goudarzi-Gereke 2018: 61. This is Goudarzi-Gereke's argument and it is plausible. However, as we will see, there may also be other reasons, see p. 160.

209 Denker 2004: 134, fn. 16.

mubāraʾa includes only her renunciation of outstanding rights.[210] This differentiation noted by Welchman, however, is reflected neither in the 2013 Draft nor in any of the Jordanian or even the Egyptian laws on *khulʿ*. Oftentimes, both payment and renunciation go hand in hand under the title of *khulʿ*.[211]

To sum up, concerning the ambiguity of terms related to *khulʿ* divorce in the 2013 Draft, Goudarzi-Gereke concludes that these sometimes overlap, are sometimes synonymous, and sometimes denominate different forms of divorce. The *Qāḍī al-Quḍāt*'s Draft adopts the Jordanian model without providing more clarification in some points, which might have increased women's options. Divorce proceedings and options for women would, according to the Draft, remain not restricted, but complex and often difficult to realize for women.[212] The judicial *khulʿ* included under the title of *iftidāʾ* offers an additional option for women to terminate their marriages, but in a more restricted way than the JLPS 2010 by only enabling women to obtain this kind of divorce before the marriage consummation. This restriction is in accordance with the *Qāḍī al-Quḍāt*'s ruling from 2012.

2.2.3 *Meeting in the* Muqāṭaʿa *November 20, 2013*

When the meeting of the NCFL in the president's seat in Ramallah, the *Muqāṭaʿa*, took place on November 20, 2013, it turned out that the 2013 Draft of the *Qāḍī al-Quḍāt*'s office served as basis for the discussion and not, as the women's organizations had hoped, the 2010 Draft. The civil society representatives were surprised. In an interview with me, Nihāya Muḥammad complained about the Presidential Bureau's decision, which had, according to her, been taken by the Bureau without informing the civil society.[213] It, of course, makes a difference, she argued, whether a draft based on international law or one based on a conservative interpretation of Islamic law should serve as point of reference (*marjaʿiyya*) and as starting point of the debates.[214]

The meeting in the *Muqāṭaʿa* reflects an important but ultimately failed step in the history of drawing up Palestinian family law. Organized by the president's legal advisor, Ḥasan al-ʿŪrī, the state again, after having formed the NCFL, took matters in hand and brought together the legal experts of the NCFL

---

210 Welchman 2007: 112.

211 Goudarzi-Gereke 2018: 62.

212 Goudarzi-Gereke 2018: 63.

213 Nihāya Muḥammad, interview on November 24, 2013.

214 The prerogative of Islamic law had been claimed by the Supreme Judge before, as Welchman outlined. In the debate with the so-called Model Parliament in the late 1990s, *Shaykh* al-Tamīmī stated that even the individual Sharia judge can be seen as "the highest Islamic authority in the area of his jurisdiction" (quoted in Welchman 2003: 54).

to negotiate the substance of a future Palestinian law. It was the aim of the state not to decide but first to consult with the different experts and parts of society. This means that in late 2013, the drafting of a new family law was on the top of the legislative agenda and a new draft law was seen to be within reach by the government.

I had been invited and intended to arrive with a representative of the Sharia court who was supposed to pick me up at the meeting point in front of the Sharia court in Ramallah. The meeting itself was scheduled from 11:00 am to 1:00 pm at the *Muqāṭaʿa*. But due to some organizational misunderstanding, I waited in vain at our meeting point. When I finally arrived in the meeting around noon, the session had already started and I dropped into the middle of a controversial and loud discussion.[215] Ḥasan al-ʿŪrī'[216] was not present due to some engagement abroad, but was represented by his assistant Muḥammad al-Hindāwī, who moderated the discussion. Present at the meeting were representatives of the Ministries of Justice and Women's Affairs, the Sharia establishment, and civil society. I counted fourteen people, nine men and five women. At least three of the men were Sharia scholars, among them, as I learned later, because I did not know him yet, ʿAlī al-Sarṭāwī, professor at Nablus University. From the Ministry of Women's Affairs Wafāʾ al-Aʿraj and from the Ministry of Justice Rīm Abū al-Rubb and ʿAbdalrazzāq Mūsā attended the meeting. Of civil society, Ashraf Abū Ḥayyah (WCLAC) and Nihāya Muḥammad (General Union of Palestinian Women/GUPW) were present. When I entered the room the debate was in full swing, and there were obviously two different parties: the Islamic scholars and the civil society sitting more or less opposite each other. The debate was about Articles 2 and 3 and touched upon Article 4 of the 2013 Draft, the provisions regulating engagement. Article 1 contains only the title: "This law is called the 'law of personal status' of the year…." Article 2 states that engagement is the offer or promise of marriage. According to Article 3, marriage is not concluded by engagement, recitation of the first Surat of the Quran, Surat al-Fātiḥa, receipt of anything for dower, nor by the acceptance of a gift. These regulations in Articles 2 and 3 of the Draft are identical with Article 3 of the JLPS 1976. Article 4 states that both parties can desist from the engagement and that presents have to be restituted. The background of the discussion was the awareness that in practice in Palestine the marriage contract was signed already with the engagement. In the end, it was decided more or less unanimously to leave Articles 1–4 as they were.

215 I was not allowed to tape the discussion nor was I introduced to the persons present or informed about the discussion I stumbled into.

216 Ḥasan al-ʿŪrī, interview on October 13, 2014.

As I had missed a substantial part of the discussion and was thus not able to connect to all arguments, I held interviews with some of the persons present in the meeting, thereby choosing representatives from all sides, the state, civil society and also the Sharia establishment to roughly reconstruct what the discussion had been about.

There had been a meeting before, I was told. Nihāya Muḥammad (died June 29, 2015),[217] then vice-president of GUPW, in an interview with me later[218] explained that the question "What are the points of reference (*Ma hiya al-marjaʿiyya*)?" had been left open and that they had agreed to argue about every single article (*faṣl faṣl*), whereas ʿAbdalrazzāq Mūsā,[219] a jurist from the Ministry of Justice, as well as ʿAlī al-Sarṭāwī[220] conversely stated that they had agreed to take the Supreme Judge's Draft as a basis of discussion. Both were generally in agreement with it. Mūsā saw necessary improvements in the details,[221] whereas Muḥammad, on the other hand, recognized a fundamental problem in this Draft with the definition of marriage. Marriage should be "a contract between a man and woman, of age … for building a family on the basis of equality," she outlined.[222] The Sharia establishment defined it classically in the 2013 Draft as a "contract between a man and a woman permitting (*taḥillu lahu*) the woman to the man legally (*sharʿan*)"[223] thus repeating the classical Islamic legal definition. The women's organizations generally and GUPW especially argued that this reduced women to mere objects and thus was not acceptable. Other controversial topics she was sure would be discussed in the upcoming meetings were the age of marriage, polygyny, child care, and guardianship etc.[224]

In the meeting, Nihāya Muḥammad, as representative of the GUPW, suggested to define the time of engagement period as a time in which the couple could come to know each other, so that there would be no repudiation (*ṭalāq*) before first marital sex (*dukhūl*). There should be something like a preparatory contract (*ʿaqd ibtidāʾī*) or a "probationary period" (*fatra tajribiyya*). She rejected a classification in the identity card and the passport that would immediately

217 Karamapress, July 2, 2015.

218 Nihāya Muḥammad, interview on November 24, 2013. I remember her as a lovely person and at the same time an extremely experienced fighter for women's rights who took much time to introduce me to the problem of the discussion and the work of her organization. I am grateful to her.

219 ʿAbdalrazzāq Mūsā, interview on November 24, 2013.

220 ʿAlī al-Sarṭāwī, interview on December 3, 2013.

221 ʿAbdalrazzāq Mūsā, interview on November 24, 2013.

222 Karamapress, July 2, 2015.

223 Article 5 of the Supreme Judge's Draft.

224 Nihāya Muḥammad, interview on November 24, 2013.

reveal the women to be "divorced" if divorce took place before consummation. As divorce is still frowned upon in Palestine, this would make the life of young women difficult. The representatives of the Sharia establishment and of the ministries rejected these ideas in the meeting.

Rīm Abū al-Rubb[225] and ʿAbdalrazzāq Mūsā[226] agreed with the opinion of Muḥammad that it was a "custom and tradition" to sign the marriage contract already with the engagement. But they made no suggestion to change this but opted to leave the Articles as they were.

What would be the procedure? Abū Ḥayyah, lawyer of WCLAC, expressed his expectation[227] that there would soon be another meeting. Mūsā estimated that it would take three months[228] – his colleague, Abū al-Rubb,[229] estimated six months – to discuss and finalize the matter. Wafāʾ al-Aʿraj of the Ministry of Women's Affairs[230] voiced the opinion that the process toward a new family law would take more time, perhaps two years. Abū Ḥayyah held the opinion, that the meeting on November 20 was difficult because of the religious participants. Being a member of WCLAC and therefore of a famous women's rights organization, he voted for a general rethinking of family law matters. He expected the next meetings to be even more difficult, actually he said they would become a "battlefield" (*maʿraka*). Mūsā of the Ministry of Justice,[231] conceding that the meeting had been chaotic (*harj wa-marj*), argued that it went beyond the frame of the topic because of the nondiscernment of the discussants to the aim. Criticizing the new conceptualization of engagement proposed by the women's organizations, he admitted that the law had to be changed as society changed and described the law as a mirror of society but that this change was not acceptable. Asked whether law also could be ahead of society he said cautiously "only very slightly."

Abū al-Rubb of the Ministry of Justice[232] confirmed that the debate had been fierce in the meeting of November 20, 2013. According to her, the first articles discussed in the meeting did not constitute a legal problem but she considered the implementation (*taṭbīq*) difficult, i.e., Palestinian society would not accept engagement without the signature on the marriage contract. Sexual

225 Rīm Abū al-Rubb, interview on December 2, 2013.
226 ʿAbdalrazzāq Mūsā, interviews on November 24, 2013 and December 2, 2013.
227 Ashraf Abū Ḥayyah (Ashraf Abu Hayyeh), interview on November 30, 2013.
228 ʿAbdalrazzāq Mūsā, interview on November 24, 2013.
229 Rīm Abū al-Rubb, interview on December 2, 2013.
230 Wafāʾ al-Aʿraj, interview on November 24, 2013.
231 ʿAbdalrazzāq Mūsā, interview on November 24, 2013.
232 Rīm Abū al-Rubb, interview on December 2, 2013.

relations before marriage are not allowed in Islam, she argued. Al-Aʿraj[233] of the Ministry of Women's Affairs predicted the SCHC would play an important role in the process of creating a new Palestinian family law but the Ministry of Women's Affairs would also have a say in it. She explained that the personal status law has to be based in Islam. She thought the meeting was successful and the articles finally debated would remain as in the Draft.

ʿAlī al-Sarṭāwī had been Minister of Justice for a short time in 2007, nominated by Hamas.[234] He had been present in the meeting of the Sharia establishment on November 2, 2013, in al-Quds University as well and made it clear in an interview with me[235] that "we all" (*kullunā*) agreed that the *Qāḍī al-Quḍāt*'s Draft had to be the basis for the discussion in the *Muqāṭaʿa*. The Draft that had been presented by the women's organizations was, he criticized, not acceptable from a legal point of view. It was a sample of thoughts they wanted, but it had no form and contained many problems. In his opinion, the women's organizations focused on women only, but the focus should be on the family – there are also children and men, he argued. For example, the women's organization eliminated the marriage guardian. According to the old law, she could marry without a guardian but the father should have the right, when she is under eighteen, to interfere in case he was afraid that there was no suitability (*kafāʾa*)[236] between her and the groom. He also explained that "we" in law try to bind the age to the lowest possible. The women's organizations want a marriage age of eighteen, but if society does not agree to this, there would be problems, he argued. When they marry their daughters at a lower age this would become an illegal relation. If a child is born, should it be a child of an illegal relation (*zināʾ*), he asked me provocatively? To preserve *kafāʾa* and the guardian's

233 Wafāʾ Al-Aʿraj, interview on November 24, 2013.

234 See https://de.wikipedia.org/wiki/Regierung_der_Pal%C3%A4stinensischen_Autonomiebeh%C3%B6rde_vom_M%C3%A4rz_2007, accessed May 1, 2019.

235 ʿAlī al-Sarṭāwī, December 3, 2013.

236 *Kafāʾa* in law is suitability of man and woman with regard to, e.g., lineage, social status, economic position, etc. See Welchman 2000: 128–129. In the applicable law, i.e., JLPS 1976 Article 7 rules that the marriage of a woman who is not eighteen years old will be prevented if her fiancé is more than twenty years older than she is, unless the judge verifies her consent. Articles 9–12 rule who the *walī* is, normally the closest agnate. Article 20 of the JLPS states that in this code the "suitability" is reduced to the financial aspect of the husband's ability to pay the dower. With regard to the question whether a woman who reached puberty has to take a *walī* or not (according to Abū Ḥanīfa she is not obliged, other Hanafis differ), Article 13 provides that a woman who was wedded before (*thayyib*: non-virgin, deflowered woman) does not need a *walī* and this points to the fact that a woman marrying for the first time does actually need a *walī*, according to Welchman 2000: 155–156.

rights was, according to him, more important than a development of the law toward international standards. Tackling the question of sexuality, he asked me if sexual relations between men and women under the age of eighteen were prohibited in Western countries. When I answered in the negative, he showed his disgust and outlined the irrationality in this: People younger than eighteen are allowed to have sexual relations but not to marry. "Our society" does not allow sexual relations out of marriage, he explained.[237] Asked about his opinion of the first session and how long it would take to pass a Palestinian family law, he said that he did not care how much time it took, but that there would be in the end eventually a Palestinian law that is acceptable to the whole society. He expected the future discussion to become more objective.

The meeting of November 20, 2013, was not continued in the following years. Randa al-Sinyūra, head of WCLAC, confirmed in 2017 that there had been no meetings after November 2013 and explained that her organization was under pressure to put the process of discussing a new personal status law on hold because the discussion would otherwise be based on the Supreme Judge's Draft.[238]

This process reflected the aim and willingness of the government not only to have such a law but also to discuss it beforehand with different actors in society. And it centralized the discussions and brought different experts together who presented different approaches and opinions with regard to a future Palestinian family law. This can be seen as a process of streamlining the iterations in society and to include the opponents and different perspectives in the discussions. Civil society was represented mostly, but not exclusively, by women on the one side and the Sharia establishment was represented, in both meetings in al-Quds University and in the *Muqāṭaʿa*, only by males. The process was steered by Ḥasan al-ʿŪrī in preselecting the participants and choosing the Supreme Judge's Draft as basis of discussion, as *marjaʿiyya*. This influenced the discussions from the beginning and gave the women's organizations a difficult starting position for their arguments in favor of gender equality. The Sharia establishment present was not very openminded with regard to women's rights either.

In my interview with him on October 13, 2014, Ḥasan al-ʿŪrī explained that usually the draft law (*mashrūʿ*)[239] is prepared in the different ministries

237 I heard this many times from different persons with different backgrounds in the West Bank. Rīm Abū al-Rubb, for example, confirmed it.

238 Randa al-Sinyūra, interview on November 27, 2017.

239 He says *mashrūʿ* whereas the drafts of the Personal Status Law which circulated were called *miswaddāt*.

whereby experts are included in the discussion. In the presidential office normally no research is done whether a law is necessary or needed. When the ministries have prepared a draft law, it is sent to the cabinet and discussed. The cabinet consents to it or not and may give a recommendation to the president. Before the draft becomes a law, Ḥasan al-ʿŪrī and his colleagues have to examine it. Maybe there are faults in the text, maybe he sees a contradiction to other laws or to the BL. In this case, he hands it back to the cabinet. After it has been examined and found to be good, he gives it to the president who will sign it. Then it will be prepared for publication in the Legislation and Advisory Bureau and published in the Official Gazette (*jarīda rasmiyya*). Sometimes drafts never become law. He gave as an example the draft law for health insurance, which was finished completely but could not be enacted for political reasons as it would have excluded the Palestinians in East Jerusalem because they are under the Israeli health system, and the Palestinians in the refugee camps whom UNRWA serves.

Personal Status Law is different from other draft laws, he explained and the president had given him the order to form the committee[240] after the women's organizations had presented different drafts and he had taken up the responsibility for this process. He had selected the members of this committee because they were experts.[241] The members of this committee did not and cannot represent all of Palestinian society, he explained, but the idea was to select those who could help to build this new law. He could have formed a committee of only lawyers. Or the SCHC could have submitted a draft to the cabinet without discussion in this committee, he said. But the president had wanted to include more perspectives and this is why he invited lawyers from the Sharia establishment, the women's organizations, and the universities.[242] He admitted that he with his training in law was not a specialist in Islamic jurisprudence and that for the preparation of the draft of PSL such specialists in Islamic law were needed. All the participants invited were considered a kind of advisory board, the results of their discussion were not seen as binding, not for the cabinet and not for the president: "We will examine it again," he said, but it would serve as basis of the discussion. He described his role in this process as the "final examiner" (*al-mudaqqiq al-akhīr*).

The government, finally, bears responsibility for placing the topic at the top of the agenda and for drawing up the schedule and inviting the different

240 He speaks of the National Committee of the Family Law (NCFL, *al-Lajna al-Waṭaniyya li-Qānūn al-Usra*).

241 He called it a "committee of experts" (*lajnat al-khubarāʾ*).

242 Here he perhaps wanted to point to GUPW, which belongs to the Fatah of PLO.

experts and actors in Palestinian society. It should, as Ḥasan al-ʿŪrī stated himself, "bell the cat." This happened with the initiation of this process. However, after November 20, 2013, no other meetings followed. During my visits to the West Bank in the following years, I tried to find out whether any follow-up sessions had taken place, but was always informed that there had been none. In my meeting with Ḥasan al-ʿŪrī, four years later, in November 2017,[243] he first had no recollections of our interview of 2013 and generally about this committee and the meeting in the *Muqāṭaʿa* in November of 2013. Only after his assistant, al-Hindāwī, confirmed my story and the history of this session on the Draft, al-ʿŪrī finally recalled our meeting four years prior and admitted that the Palestinian family law was by the end of 2017 no longer at the top of the agenda.

This changed shortly after when Palestine had to submit the first report on CEDAW and a Palestinian delegation travelled to Geneva in July 2018 and came back with the obligation to submit a new report reflecting substantial progress toward a Palestinian family law – or an amendment of the existing laws – as soon as 2020. In this context,[244] another committee was created, named the LHC, the Legislation Harmonization Committee/*Lajnat Muwāʾamat al-Tashrīʿāt,* with the task of harmonizing international and national legislation. In a way, the LHC can be considered the continuation of the NCFL. ʿUmar ʿIwaḍallāh, Director of the Department of Multilateral Relations of the Ministry of Foreign Affairs, confirmed in an interview in spring 2019 that the LHC is working as a committee that is constituted again from different actors without the right to vote. But he had no idea when the new personal status law itself would be ready,[245] and even knew nothing about the previous committee.

243 Ḥasan al-ʿŪrī, interview on November 28, 2017.

244 See chapters 7 and 8.

245 ʿUmar ʿIwaḍallāh, interview on April 7, 2019.

CHAPTER 3

The Actors

Dale Eickelman and Jon Anderson pointed twenty years ago to the emergence of a new "sense of public" in the Muslim states shaped by contests "over the authoritative use of the symbolic language of Islam."[1] They also hinted at the global context of these debates.[2] This is observable in Palestine and reflected especially in the media in an open and controversial debate about legal topics. Three groups can be observed to take active part in this new public: the state, not only with its legislation but also with its representatives taking public positions to state policy; second, civil society, especially with regard to the topic of women's and human rights; and third, the Sharia establishment consisting of Sharia judges and scholars of Islamic law as already outlined in the second chapter. These groups, as neatly separable they seem at first glance, overlap. Several individuals belonged to more than one group, as, e.g., the Sharia judges who in the iterations often acted and argued as Muslim scholars explaining Islamic law but at the same time officially were representatives of the state. Some individuals belonged to different groups of actors during the time of the debate or had belonged to them during their lives and professional careers. As will become obvious, not all three groups were visible or publicly announced their position during different stages of the iterations in the same ways.[3] Furthermore, whereas the general political attitudes toward *khulʿ* reform and the influence of international law surely differed between the groups, the groups of actors themselves were, of course, far from homogeneous. Different representatives had different and nuanced opinions of the topic. The language of Islamic law was, however, seen as a common frame used or at least acknowledged by all actors and activists in the field.[4] In this chapter, I will describe these three groups and their most important representatives, especially the ones with whom interviews were conducted.

1 Eickelman and Anderson 1999: 1.

2 Eickelman and Anderson 1999: 1.

3 To balance this, interviews were conducted with representatives of all groups.

4 See chapter 1.1.3.

 | DOI:10.1163/9789004442313_004

3.1 State

Whereas there is a discussion about the question of whether Palestine can be called a "state," since 1994, all structures and organs belonging to a state have been created in Ramallah and in Gaza since 2007: the parliament, which in the West Bank is not working but is in Gaza; the ministries; and the administration.[5] The Palestinian Legislative Council (PLC) is the legislative organ, as explained, and in the realm of family law the Sharia Court High Council (SCHC) laid claim to drawing up the draft law, as outlined earlier. The intrinsic interest of the State of Palestine and the unity government between 2014 and 2019 had been the control of the process of legislation in the difficult situation in which there was no parliament in Ramallah but a parliament sitting in Gaza under Hamas control. But it failed early in 2019.

The interest to steer the process of legislation and to also influence the iterations had been voiced by Ḥasan al-ʿŪrī in the clarity needed when he coined in the interview the claim of the state to "bell the cat."[6] Ḥasan al-ʿŪrī, LLM, Legal Advisor at the President's Office, was appointed in 2010. He received a BA in law from the University of Alexandria and a Master's degree from al-Quds University and was one of the founders of the Palestinian Bar Association.[7] In the process of drafting the family law, he played an important role between 2012 and 2013, as outlined, because he had created the NCFL (National Committee of the Family Law/*al-Lajna al-Waṭaniyya li-l-Qānūn al-Usra*), selected its members, and organized and supervised the meeting in November 2013. I had the chance to conduct two interviews with him, in 2014 and 2017, in which he received me in his office in the *Muqāṭaʿa* and took much time to talk with me about legislation in general, his role in this process, and legislation with regard to the family law. He considered himself a jurist and not a *faqīh*, a Muslim scholar, and was well aware that he had to rely on the competence and knowledge of the Sharia establishment with regard to family law, a statement that again shows that there is a division acknowledged by all jurists between "Muslim" jurists and what can be called more "secular" jurists.

Family law is special and the Legislation and Advisory Bureau, which is normally concerned with drafting the law, does not have this duty with regard to family law. This task was given originally to the NCFL, then claimed by the SCHC, as described, and later given to the LHC. In my interview with

5 As the main research was on the West Bank, this information is restricted to the West Bank government, its ministers etc. Gaza will be examined in chapter 9.

6 See chapter 1.

7 Ḥasan al-ʿŪrī, interviews on October 13, 2014, and November 28, 2017.

Īmān ʿAbdalḥamīd,[8] head of the Legislation and Advisory Bureau, I focused on the question of whether she had already received the signed international treaties as CEDAW to prepare them for the publication in the Official Gazette and whether other laws were presently in her office – for example, the Family Protection Law against Violence. This, as she stated, was not the case in April 2019.

Different ministries were, of course, involved in the process of iterations: the Ministry of Justice, the Ministry of Women's Affairs (MoWA), the Ministry of Foreign Affairs insofar as international treaties are concerned such as CEDAW (Convention on the Elimination of All Forms of Discrimination against Women). Not many official statements of the ministries can be traced with regard to *khulʿ* in the media, but in the second phase of the iterations, which focused on the question of how international law can be integrated into national law, representatives of the Ministry of Foreign Affairs publicly took a position and were more often present in the media.[9]

The Ministers of Justice from 2012 to 2014 were ʿAlī Muhannā; from 2014 to 2015, Salīm al-Saqā; and from 2015, ʿAlī Abū Diyāk.[10] Rīm Abū al-Rubb, Legal Advisor in the Ministry of Justice in 2013, who later moved to the Legislation and Advisory Bureau (LAB) where I met her again in 2019, and ʿAbdalrazzāq Mūsā, also Legal Advisor at the Ministry of Justice had both participated in the meeting of November 2013 and both confirmed to me the important role of Sharia as the basis of Islamic law and outlined to me how they both based their legal arguments on Sharia albeit they differed in their interpretation of the holy law.

The Minister of Women's Affairs from 2010 to 2013 was Rabīḥa Dhiyāb, a member of the Fatah nicknamed "Iron Woman." She died in April 2016 and was given a funeral with military ceremony.[11] Rabīḥa Dhiyāb[12] confirmed in her interview with me that the process of developing a Palestinian family law, for which she saw her Ministry also responsible, is a process that should include the whole society. She did not deny her origins in the women's movement, in which she had been active before becoming a minister, and pointed

8 Īmān ʿAbdalḥamīd, interview on April 8, 2019.

9 See chapter 8.

10 I did not conduct interviews with these ministers and therefore will not go into detail about personal developments and educational backgrounds. None of them has, to the best of my knowledge, contributed much to the question of a Palestinian family law in official statements. Therefore, I concentrate on those persons in the ministries who were – as described in chapter 2.2.3 – involved in the process of discussing and developing a draft law and with whom I conducted interviews.

11 Maannews, April 23, 2016.

12 Rabīḥa Dhiyāb, interview on November 20, 2013.

to its power and decisive role in Palestine. Her legal advisor Wafāʾ al-Aʿraj had been present at the meeting in November 2013 in the *Muqāṭaʿa* and was, in contrast, convinced that the Supreme Judge would play an important role in legislating family law. An interview was also held with Shirīn Abū Rubb, Director of International Relations of the Ministry of Women's Affairs (MoWA).[13]

In 2014, Dr. Hayfāʾ al-Āghā became Minister for Women's Affairs (2014–2019) in the unity government between Hamas and Fatah.[14] Born in Khan Younis, Gaza, she holds a PhD from Oklahoma State University (1978) in education. In a media interview, she strongly supported women's agency, stressing that it was one of the challenges for Palestinian women to eliminate the stereotypical image of women as mere housewives. Women in Palestine had already started to compete with men in the political arena and fight to bring about international protection for themselves in view of Israeli aggression, she said.[15] When I finally had the chance to have an interview with her in the spring of 2019,[16] she showed great interest in more gender equality in the interpretation of Islamic law and revealed a high degree of personal piety in combination with an interest in promoting women's rights. She stated that she tried constantly to modify and change the law and pointed to the Family Protection Law against Violence (*Qānūn Ḥimāyat al-Usra min al-ʿUnf*), which she described at the time of the interview as "almost finished." She regretted that she had not been able to speed up the process but hoped it would be presented to the cabinet soon.

The Minister of Foreign Affairs in Palestine between 2012 and 2019 was Riyāḍ al-Mālikī. ʿUmar ʿIwaḍallāh, Director of the Department of Multilateral Relations of the Ministry of Foreign Affairs, was part of the Palestinian delegation that went to Geneva in July 2018 and also took part in the public discussions about the harmonization of international law with national law.[17] In the spring of 2019, he was responsible for the LHC (Legislation Harmonization Committee, *Lajnat Muwāʾamat al-Tashrīʿāt*), which, as argued above, can be regarded as the follow-up of the NCFL (National Committee of the Family Law) implemented by al-ʿŪrī between 2010 and 2013. The LHC has the aim to conceptualize a new Palestinian family law that would be in harmony with

13 Shirīn Abū Rubb, interview on November 25, 2017.

14 Abou Jalal, February 11, 2016. Asked what inspired her to become a minister, she answered that the unity government did not represent the views of a specific political party, and as a nonpartisan she accepted the appointment (Abou Jalal, February 11, 2016).

15 Abou Jalal, February 11, 2016.

16 Dr. Hayfāʾ al-Āghā, interview on April 9, 2019; shortly after this a new women's minister named Āmād Ḥamad was appointed.

17 See chapters 7 and 8. ʿUmar ʿIwaḍallāh, interview on April 7, 2019.

international regulations, especially CEDAW. ʿIwaḍallāh is, like al-ʿŪrī, a jurist who looks at the law from a more secular point of view.

Generally, jurists trained in law but not specifically in Sharia often work among the representatives of the ministries and different organs. This influences their arguments and position as well as their view of how Palestine should handle family law and their interpretation of the provisions of the Basic Law (BL). Whereas al-ʿŪrī, as stated above, admitted that he did not understand much of Sharia and personally did not know how Sharia could be modernized, ʿIwaḍallāh in the Ministry of Foreign Affairs, who oversees the LHC and steers the harmonization process between national and international law in the second phase of the iterations, went into a detailed discussion with Sharia Judge Ṣumūd al-Ḍamīrī about which fields of law should be revised first and how this could and should happen.[18] ʿIwaḍallāh announced that there might be a presidential decree – something very new in the realm of family law – in the matter of harmonizing the marriage ages, which are different in the different religious laws and between Gaza and the West Bank. Al-Ḍamīrī, who was present in this meeting, immediately suggested other topics that women need to have regulated but ʿIwaḍallāh did not react to this.

As stated above, these categories of actors are not always neatly separated. Whereas many jurists had an education and training in law, others, such as Rīm Abū al-Rubb working in the Ministry of Justice, had quite outspoken and well-founded opinions with regard to Islamic law. Dhiyāb, the former Minister of MoWA was rooted in civil society.

3.2 Civil Society

Whereas it is easy to define who belongs to the state and the state apparatus, e.g., the representatives of the ministries and the official state bodies, and the judges, it is more difficult to define what "civil society" is. In summary, it can be said that civil society represents the interests of citizens or groups of citizens against the state, mostly in forms of nongovernmental organizations (NGOs). With regard to Palestinian NGOs,[19] there is common agreement that Palestine – the West Bank as well as Gaza – has an active civil society with

18 ʿUmar ʿIwaḍallāh, interviews on April 7 and 8, 2019. Judge al-Ḍamīrī had arranged this interview for me – for which I would like to thank her – and she was present during the talk.

19 For an overview, see the PNGO (Palestinian Non-Governmental Organizations Netword/ *shabakat al-munaẓẓamāt al-ahliyya al-filasṭīniyya*, see English: http://www.pngo.net/; Arabic: http://www.pngo.net/?lang=ar, accessed September 15, 2018.

many organizations taking part in public debates.[20] Unlike the state that is confined to the Area A, civil society organizations are active also in the Areas B and C. NGOs are active in Gaza, too, but not many of the organizations are present in both areas at the same time.

Civil society is a concept that has first been defined in the context of Western political culture and it has been widely used to explain the social and political upheavals in Eastern Europe in the 1980s. There are many definitions, but normally civil society is understood to comprise those organizations that occupy the space between "the individual" and "the state", that initiate and continue debates in the public sphere. These organizations represent individual interests and societal interests outside formal state structures. Membership is voluntary, they are autonomous and independent of state influence, and have an organizational potential that distinguishes them from purely individual relationships like lobbying structures or family structures. Single actors may be regarded as representatives of civil society, if they have a public voice.[21] This public sphere, the space of civil society, is generally seen as opposed to the political-administrative power sphere.[22] Aurel Croissant, Hans-Joachim Lauth, and Wolfgang Merkel add as tasks of civil society institutions or individuals: protection of individuals against the state; mediation between the political and the non-political sphere, a function of socialization; and building a social community and communication network.[23] Holger Albrecht correctly points out that civil society is an empirical fact, i.e., it exists but it is also an analytical concept for the explanation of the structure and functioning of society. It has to be seen, despite the division between the social and the political sphere in theoretical thinking, very much in connection with the state. In the end, the state creates the legal and institutional framework and sets the rules thus deciding the radius of action civil society actors have.[24] According to Albrecht, democracy cannot exist without civil society, whereas in an authoritarian system, it becomes an opposition force.[25] This statement is very general and needs to be nuanced, as it leaves these questions open: can civil society be considered a kind of opposition in democratic states, too, and does the mere existence of a vibrant and critical civil society reflect a certain openness in an authoritarian regime? Derived from European history, civil society is a disputed concept,

20 Muslih 1995; Welchman 2003; Jad 2004; Hammami 2006; Kuttab 2009; Gerster 2011; Shaʿbān 2016; Zughayr 2017; for Gaza, see Roy 2011.

21 Albrecht 2005: 118–120.

22 Lubenow 2012: 62–64.

23 Croissant, Lauth, and Merkel 2000: 9–14.

24 Albrecht 2005: 120.

25 Albrecht 2005: 120.

and its application to Middle Eastern societies has been problematized.[26] The normative dimension of the concept, i.e., the idea that the development of a vibrant civil society will lead to more democracy, a connection that is sometimes seen as an automatic process, has to be challenged. The term is used by many international donors to strengthen what they see as a rudimentary democracy and to implement democratic structures. Others see no proof for this claim,[27] and surely there is no automatic connection. This, however, is not the topic of this research.

As outlined already, Seyla Benhabib's concept of iterations presupposes an active civil society that initiates and stimulates those public iterations.[28] But what exactly is the civil society's position in Palestine? How strong and powerful is it in opposition to the government, and did its position and role change during the period of 2012 to 2018? How independent is a representative of the Palestinian society? With regard to Palestine, the most important and active groups and organizations concerned with the drafting of a new family law and with women's rights issues that are active in the politics of gender equality are:

1. Women's Centre for Legal Aid and Counselling (WCLAC)[29]
2. Women's Affairs Technical Committee (WATC)[30]

---

26 Albrecht 2005: 118–119. As this discussion is not dealt with here, mention has to be made of Hamzawy (2003) who follows the normative discussions about a civil society in Arab states. His article shows that the concept has been not only deployed on an empirical level in the Arab Middle East but also developed further and adapted to the Middle Eastern context on a theoretical level.

27 Albrecht 2005: 118.

28 Benhabib 2004.

29 *Markaz al-Marʾa li-l-Irshād al-qānūnī wa-l-Ijtimāʿī*. See http://www.wclac.org/, accessed March 14, 2019. WCLAC is one of the oldest and most prominent women's rights organizations in Palestine. Lynn Welchman has published with WCLAC (1999), which has an international reputation and funding. Many reports sponsored by international donors can be found on its website. According to the website, WCLAC "is an independent Palestinian, not-for-profit, non-governmental organisation that seeks to develop a democratic Palestinian society based on the principles of gender equality and social justice. Established in Jerusalem in 1991, the organisation has special consultative status with the UN Economic and Social Council (ECOSOC). By forging a feminist vision based on equality and social justice, WCLAC plays a prominent role in addressing gender-based violence in Palestinian society in both the public and private spheres. As a leading defender of women's rights in Palestine, WCLAC is proud of its uncompromising commitment to provide legal aid, social counselling and protection services to women in an environment where human rights abuses are rampant and women's issues are regularly overlooked." WCLAC undertakes this through monitoring, documentation, and advocacy at the local and international levels; providing social and legal services to women victims of violence and those whose human rights have been violated; undertaking advocacy, training, and legal reform programs that ensure gender equality.

30 *Ṭāqim Shuʾūn al-Marʾa*, http://www.watcpal.org/, accessed July 10, 2019. According to the article of Hussein 2015, the WATC was established in 1992 as a coalition of women's grassroots committees. It strives to empower women socio-politically in accordance with,

3. Al-Haq[31]
4. Musawa[32]
5. General Union of Palestinian Women (GUPW)[33]

---

among others, international rights. Their aim is to eliminate all forms of discrimination, they have a paper and a weekly radio program. They explicitly renounce violence and intolerance. They argue that Palestinian women are marginalized and "one strategy is to reinforce a secular discourse, promote and protect pluralism, and apply the rule of law to all concerned" (Hussein 2015: 127).

31 *Al-Ḥaqq*, see http://www.alhaq.org/, accessed March 14, 2019. Al-Haq is, according to its website "an independent Palestinian non-governmental human rights organisation based in Ramallah, West Bank. Established in 1979 to protect and promote human rights and the rule of law in the Occupied Palestinian Territory (OPT), the organisation has special consultative status with the United Nations Economic and Social Council. Al-Haq documents violations of the individual and collective rights of Palestinians in the OPT, irrespective of the identity of the perpetrator, and seeks to end such breaches by way of advocacy before national and international mechanisms and by holding the violators accountable. The organisation conducts research; prepares reports, studies, and interventions on breaches of international human rights and humanitarian law in the OPT; and undertakes advocacy before local, regional and international bodies. Al-Haq also cooperates with Palestinian civil society organisations and governmental institutions in order to ensure that international human rights standards are reflected in Palestinian law and policies." Al-Haq is the West Bank affiliate of the International Commission of Jurists – Geneva, and is a member of the Euro-Mediterranean Human Rights Network (EMHRN), the World Organisation against Torture (OMCT), the International Federation for Human Rights (FIDH), Habitat International Coalition (HIC), and the Palestinian NGO Network (PNGO).

32 *Al-Musāwāh*, http://www.musawa.ps/, accessed March 14, 2019. According to its website, Musawa is "[t]he Palestinian Center for the Independence of the Judiciary and the Legal Profession, a neutral, non-partisan and independent Palestinian civil society organization based in Ramallah and Gaza, Palestine. Established in 2002 by lawyers, former judges and human rights activists, MUSAWA is dedicated to defending the independence of the judiciary and the legal profession through leading a watchdog role in monitoring the performance of the pillars of justice in Palestine."

33 *Al-Ittiḥād al-ʿĀmm li-l-Marʾa al-Filasṭīniyya* is part of the PLO and therefore not a civil society organization in the narrow sense of the definition, see http://gupw-lb.org/, accessed on March 14, 2019, for the Lebanon branch. However, I included it for my research as the GUPW was very active with regard to the drafting of a new family law and in discussing the influence of international law. I could not find a link for the West Bank branch, however, GUPW is active on Facebook, see https://www.facebook.com/pg/gupw.palestine/about/?ref=page_internal, accessed March 14, 2019. The mission of the GUPW is fivefold: (1) to mobilize Palestinian women to act on behalf of the Palestinian people, particularly in the fight against Israeli occupation; (2) to raise women's political awareness and participation in both internal Palestinian politics and the greater international arena; (3) to promote gender equality within Palestinian legal and political processes; (4) to increase women's participation in the economy; and (5) to provide literacy, cultural, and health programs that benefit Palestinian women. After the Oslo Accords (1993), the GUPW openly worked to elect women to serve in the Palestinian Authority, to write gender equality into Palestinian law and to establish new social programs. In the twenty-first century, the union successfully promoted and trained female candidates for a variety of political positions. In addition, a number of GUPW humanitarian

6. Women's Studies Centre (WSC)[34]
7. Center for Women's Legal Research and Consulting (CWLRC)[35] in Gaza

At an empirical level, the existence of a vibrant civil society in Palestine, enjoying legal status and considerable influence, is undeniable. This is the point of departure of this research, whereas discussions about the analytical concept and the normative role with regard to developing democracy are not a topic.

In Palestine in 2000, a law with regard to the "Charitable Associations and Civil Society Organizations" was passed.[36] According to Article 1, Palestinian citizens have the right to exercise social, cultural, professional and scientific activity in freedom, including the right to establish and run associations and community organizations in conformity with the provision of this law. The Ministry

projects provide health and welfare services to needy Palestinian families. There are seminars on health, political rights, and Palestinian culture, and some run vocational training centers for women (Leitz 2017). I interviewed Nihāya Muḥammad, at that time vice president of the GUPW on November 24, 2013. See also Encyclopedia Palestina (2018): https://www.palestinapedia.net/%d8%a7%d9%84%d8%a7%d8%aa%d8%ad%d8%a7%d8%af-%d8%a7%d9%84%d8%b9%d8%a7%d9%85-%d9%84%d9%84%d9%85%d8%b1%d8%a3%d8%a9-%d8%a7%d9%84%d9%81%d9%84%d8%b3%d8%b7%d9%8a%d9%86%d9%8a%d8%a9/he.

34 *Markaz al-Dirāsāt al-Nisawiyya*, see http://www.wsc-pal.org, accessed on March 14, 2019. The Women's Studies Centre is according to its website a secular, dependent ([*sic*!] It surely must be independent), feminist non-governmental organization. It is active in protecting and advocating for human rights and women's rights; in enhancing the gender equality; and in supporting women's rights as an integral part of human rights. Since its establishment in 1989, the center has worked on various programs to empower women and build female capacities for the purpose of determining and standing up for their rights. The center has struggled – along with the Palestinian feminist movement – to institutionalize a development strategy within Palestinian society that inherently adopts the main principle of complete gender equality. To this end, the center has been carrying out its institutional mandate in an effort to reform the traditional social, economic, political, and legal structures to include the integration of women in all the development initiatives as participants and beneficiaries.

35 *Markaz al-Abḥāth wa-l-Istishārāt al-Qānūniyya li-l-Mar'a*, Ghazza, see www.cwlrc.ps/en/about, accessed March 14, 2019. This organization is active in Gaza and therefore will be referred to in chapter 9. Some general information can be drawn from this website too: the CWLRC is "an independent non-profit center established in Gaza in 2005 upon the initiative of a group of Palestinian lawyers and civil society activates who believe in the importance of enhancing women's social and legal rights through providing legal consultation training and research to achieve equality, justice and thereafter democracy in Palestinian society." CWLRC even gives its registration number. For vision and mission, it outlines: "Center for Women's Legal Research and Consulting (CWLRC) works to formulate the legal and social vision for women as the main partner to men in building the Palestinian society on the basis of democracy. Also, CWLRC develop and empower the legal and social status of women to achieve their rights in all aspects of life."

36 1/2000 Qānūn bi-Sha'n Jamʿīyāt al-Khayriyya wa-l-Hay'āt al-Ahliyya, see Muqtafi.

of Justice is the reference. The ICNL (International Center for Not-for-Profit Law), an independent global supervisor of civil society activities in the world, describes Palestine as "an exceptional case" and states that "Palestine's unique history has in many ways proved conducive to the development of a vibrant and active civil society, by both regional and global standards."[37] This reflects the "normative" understanding of civil society, but also points to an empirical fact: there are many – often internationally financed – organizations active in Palestine. By 1994, when the Palestinian Authority (PA) was created, NGOs active in the region already had a long history of providing many essential social services. After coming into power, the PA attempted to assert heavy-handed control over NGOs. Relations between the PA and Palestinian NGOs declined precipitously.[38] When the PA produced a draft NGO law modeled on the highly restrictive Egyptian law, the reaction of Palestinian NGOs was swift and well-organized. After a protracted struggle between the PA and the Palestinian civil society sector, the NGOs won what has been termed "a near total victory." The abovementioned NGO law, finally passed in 2000, was for many years the most liberal and least restrictive NGO law in the Middle East.[39]

The continuing effects of Israeli occupation and the political problems the PA had to deal with are described by ICNL and others as resulting in the uneven and arbitrary application of the Palestinian NGO law and indeed a decline in the rule of law generally. The split between Fatah and Hamas affected civil society, too. Arbitrary punitive acts, including the forced dissolution of NGOs or replacement of their boards, have reportedly been undertaken against Hamas-affiliated NGOs in the West Bank and against Fatah affiliated NGOs in the Gaza Strip, but they could not destroy civil society as such.[40] In 2017, a new law on cybercrime in the West Bank, issued by President Abbas aroused angry reactions in civil society because it regulated online transactions, media websites, and social networking websites, and prescribed fines for individuals who use such venues to promote ideas that "violate the public order and morals" or incite hatred.[41] It was argued by civil society representatives that the law narrowed civil and political rights.[42] After this critique, amendments were made, but international players such as Human Rights Watch still demanded that Palestine bring the law in line with its international legal obligations.[43]

37 ICNL, July 12, 2017.
38 ICNL, July 12, 2017.
39 ICNL, July 12, 2017; Johnson 2004a: 123.
40 ICNL, July 12, 2017.
41 ICNL, July 12, 2017; Abu Amer, December 6, 2017.
42 Al-Haq, August 3, 2017.
43 Human Rights Watch, December 20, 2017.

This incident again proves the alertness and vigilance as well as powerful position of Palestinian civil society.[44]

The EU Country Roadmap distinguished between different levels of civil society and attested Palestine a vibrant civil society at the grassroots level. At the second tier of civil society, in which organizations have a more formal status and a higher institutional structure, it was stated that civil society existed in all sectors, from scientific and technological research up to women's and human rights, democracy, peace building, etc. The third level comprises coalitions of organizations focusing on a sector, a geographical area, or a campaign. The fourth-level organizations consist, according to this definition, of general aggregations of civil society organizations such as national civil society platforms.[45] It is criticized in the EU Country Roadmap, that platforms, i.e., fourth-level civil society organizations, suffer from a lack of resources, such as adequate permanent staff and limited engagement in member organizations.[46] The report sees a danger on this level that when organizations adopt service providers as reference models, there is a risk that the organization will focus on its own sustainability and less on "common interests and needs."[47] The report also states for the last years a scarcity of foreign funding.[48] A further problem mentioned by the report is the separation between Gaza and West Bank, which means that there is no civil society that operates in both the West Bank and Gaza.[49] The exact number of international civil society organizations operating in Palestine is not known.[50]

The role and obligation of Palestinian civil society is judged differently. Asmaa al-Ghoul, a journalist, accuses civil society and nongovernmental organizations to have failed to end the political problem of the schism.[51] She discusses different voices with regard to the question of the role these institutions should play, giving these organizations, nota bene, not an empirical but above all, a normative task and connecting them to the high expectations of "democratizing society." Amjad Shawa, director of the Palestinian NGO network[52] in

44 See also chapter 7.3 in which the role of civil society organizations in the debates around CEDAW is analyzed.
45 European Union Mission, July 3, 2014: 7–9.
46 European Union Mission, July 3, 2014: 9.
47 European Union Mission, July 3, 2014: 9.
48 European Union Mission, July 3, 2014: 9–10.
49 European Union Mission, July 3, 2014: 11.
50 European Union Mission, July 3, 2014: 11.
51 Al-Ghoul, October 21, 2016.
52 See http://www.pngo.net/, accessed March 2, 2019.

the Gaza Strip, argues that such an expectation would be too much for civil society, it would be beyond their capacity, given the weakness of the state and situation of occupation.[53] Atif Abu Saif, a novelist and writer, argues that despite the great effort made by NGOs, there is no progress, for two reasons: the international funding for many civil society organizations, which is not controlled by national partners, and thus not based on local development policies, and the elitist nature of Palestinian civil society.[54] ʿUmar Shaʿbān, an economist, analyses the relation between civil society and the state.[55] He praises the fact that the government, at a certain point, gave in to the demands of civil society and arranged local elections. For him, this "harmony" between civil society and state is a laudable example. He sees the powerful position of civil society as an indicator for modernity. Civil society, in his view, is a control mechanism of the state and government as well as a counterweight to the monopoly of powerful economic companies. Furthermore, he states, Palestinian civil society was critical of the political developments and especially the occupation and the "cursed split," meaning the split between Hamas and Fatah, and actively tried to deal with its consequences. He points to the fact that civil society is active in the whole territory of Palestine, also in C-Areas, where the PA has no political control. In the end, contradicting his own demand that civil society should be and is actually (on a normative and empirical level), a counterweight to politics and the state, he demands that the state should fund civil society so that it is no longer dependent on international donors who want to realize their own agenda in Palestine.[56]

Helga Baumgarten and Karin Gerster, focusing in their research on the financial basis of the NGOs, found that 80 percent of the budget of Palestinian NGOs is funded by external donors, mainly from the United States and the EU.[57] Before the backdrop of a dramatic economic decline in Palestine due to the situation of occupation in which the unemployment rate in Palestine rose in 2010 to 23 percent (15 percent in the West Bank and 39 percent in Gaza), the

53 Al-Ghoul, October 21, 2016.
54 Al-Ghoul, October 21, 2016.
55 Shaʿbān, August 16, 2016.
56 Shaʿbān, August 16, 2016. He refers to the German example, obviously meaning organizations in Germany founded by political parties, such as the Friedrich-Ebert-Foundation connected to the Social Democratic Party, the Konrad-Adenauer-Foundation connected to the Christian Democratic Party, and Heinrich-Böll-Foundation connected to Die Grünen etc. These foundations are active in many countries of the world, including Palestine.
57 Baumgarten and Gerster 2011: 1.

Palestinian NGOs provided around 10 percent of the job offers.[58] According to Baumgarten and Gerster 90 percent of the NGO employees were found to have an academic background, 57.5 percent were female and 42.5 percent were male.[59] Baumgarten and Gerster argue convincingly that many jobs in Palestine are thus created by externally funded NGOs, making job creation a powerful tool of the NGOs in an economically difficult situation.[60] A special social class emerges that has the knowledge of how to get international funding.[61] Still, one can object, this does not mean these organizations confine themselves, automatically and in each case, to the aims and objectives of the donors, or that they have no room to maneuver or develop their own agendas they deem fitting for the Palestinian context.

A group of mainly US-based and some Palestine scholars, however, argues like this and takes a highly critical, if not outstandingly negative, position toward civil society in general and women's organizations in Palestine in particular. They regard the financial dependency of the NGOs in Palestine as a problem, because it allegedly allows the direct influence of international law and international concepts to permeate societies and creates what is sometimes called Western "imperial" influence in the region.[62] This position is not plausible with regard to the civil society organizations that deal with gender topics and human rights laws and that took part in the iterations about the family law. As will become obvious from this study, the representatives of these organizations struggled to bridge the gap of human rights and gender equality laws on the one side and traditional perceptions of the role of men and women on the other side, trying to find solutions and compromises in the interest of women who according to the applicable law do not have an equal position to men.

58 Baumgarten and Gerster 2011: 2.

59 Baumgarten and Gerster 2011: 3.

60 Baumgarten and Gerster 2011: 6.

61 Baumgarten and Gerster 2011: 10–11.

62 This "NGOization" of civil society means that a former grassroots movement became allegedly more and more detached from Palestinian society, see Kuttab 2008; 2009; Jad 2004; Hammami 2006. It is argued that the NGOs are not representing Palestinian interests any more. Arguing in this way, these scholars are in line with the arguments of conservative representatives of the Sharia establishment who consider gender equality as alien to Palestinian society and against the tradition of Palestine and as something imposed by "the West." Kuttab 2008 goes one step further with her outright rejection of what she calls "imperialist" influence. Her arguments are based on conspiracy theories and cannot be taken seriously.

3.3 Sharia Establishment

The fact that a twofold judiciary exists in Palestine – both in the West Bank and Gaza – with what can be referred to as a "religious judiciary" (*al-qaḍāʾ al-dīnī*) and a "normal judiciary" (*al-qaḍāʾ al-ʿādī*) might seem surprising given the secular conceptualization of the PLO. Actually, Palestine's secular aspect of history is an exception in the region and is connected to the more secular history of the PLO, which began as a national liberation movement.

The Sharia establishment comprises, first of all, the staff and members of this powerful body and part of the state judicial system. Those judges are civil servants of the State of Palestine, and are thus simultaneously representatives of the state. But besides their jurisdictional obligations, many of them engaged in the legal debates together with Supreme Judge Yūsuf Idʿīs on how a new Palestinian family law should look. They acted in these iterations less as civil servants and more as Muslim scholars. Other scholars, mostly professors of (Islamic) law of different universities also belong to this category of the Sharia establishment. This was demonstrated in the November 2, 2013, meeting at al-Quds University (chapter 2.2.2.2). The meeting of this "Study Day" was organized by Ḥamza Dhīb of al-Quds University and more scholars than Sharia judges attended it and it reflects the powerful position of the "Sharia establishment" consisting of independent but religious scholars (*fuqahāʾ*, sg. *faqīh*) besides lawyers. As outlined above, this body denied the National Committee for the Family Law (NCFL) – of which it was originally a part – the right to draw up a draft of a family law and argued that only the SCHC should have this right. It was a clever step to have this meeting in what could be called an "Islamic public sphere," since no jurist without an Islamic background was present, even female Sharia judges were not invited. The published statements and recommendations of this body cannot claim any legally binding force, since they lack legal justification. They are, at the end of the day, only the personal opinions of a group of scholars. Still, these "recommendations" proved to be an influential statement and influenced the process of further iterations, as described.[63] Therefore, the Sharia establishment is more than just the Sharia judges of Palestine and their associate scholars. It seems to be well organized and networked. It reserves for itself the right to partake in iterations about law, especially family law, and also the right to define the authoritative interpretation of Sharia. The Sharia establishment and especially the Sharia courts are quite popular in Palestine, as Rema Hammami and Penny Johnson show in their survey. Sharia courts had gained appreciation and support in 2013 in

63 See chapter 2.2.2.2.

comparison to an earlier survey in 2003.[64] This powerful position is reflected in the Supreme Judge Maḥmūd al-Habbāsh's very outspoken statement and claim that Sharia is above anything, especially above international law.[65]

With regard to the Sharia establishment, interviews were held with the Supreme Judges Yūsuf Idʿīs – whose lecture I observed in Birzeit University – and Maḥmūd al-Habbāsh, but also with the Gaza Judge Ḥasan al-Jūjū[66] and Judge Tawfīq Abū al-Hāshim[67] and the female judges Khulūd al-Faqīh, Asmahān al-Waḥīdī, and Ṣumūd al-Ḍamīrī. Representatives of the Sharia establishment, among them lawyers and scholars were very prominent in the media.[68] Access to Sharia scholars in the Sharia faculties proved not to be easy with the exception of Professor ʿAlī al-Sarṭāwī of Nablus University.[69] Whereas there seem to have been no women serving as professors at the Sharia faculties in Palestine in 2013, there were at the date of this study three, later four, female judges in the Sharia Courts, who shall be dealt with below.

3.3.1 *Women as Sharia Judges*

In 2009, the first two female Sharia court judges in Palestine, Khulūd al-Faqīh in Birzeit/Ramallah and Asmahān al-Waḥīdī in Ḥalḥūl/Hebron,[70] were nominated by the Supreme Judge at that time, *Shaykh* Taysīr al-Tamīmī, and appointed by President Mahmud Abbas. These appointments and the appointment of a female Head of Prosecution in Family Law Matters, Judge Ṣumūd al-Ḍamīrī in 2010, were surrounded by heated and controversial debates whether women should have the right to serve as judges in the Sharia courts.[71] In 2019, there was a fourth female judge, Sīrīn ʿAynbūsī; as well as the first female marriage officer (*ma'dhūn*), Taḥrīr Ḥamād;[72] by that time the heated debates of the early days

64 Johnson and Hammami 2013: 4, 66; it is not clear what the option given that "the society should vote" means.

65 Judge Maḥmūd al-Habbāsh, interview on December 9, 2017.

66 For the special situation of Gaza, see chapter 9.

67 Judge Tawfīq Abū al-Hāshim, interview on December 6, 2017.

68 See chapter 6.3.

69 ʿAlī al-Sarṭāwī, Professor al-Nablus University, interview on December 3, 2013. He not only invited me to his home but also gave me the chance to have a long and detailed interview with him, in which I could gain a valuabe insight into his position. I want to thank him for this interview at this point. As he had also been a part of the NCFL, this interview was very revealing for me representing a conservative position with regard to gender roles.

70 In 2019, she had been moved to Bethlehem.

71 In many regards this debate was similar to the debate in Germany at the beginning of the twentieth century about women being appointed as judges, see Schultz 2017: especially 25–26.

72 I only conducted interviews with the three female judges; I did not have the opportunity to meet Sīrīn ʿAynbūsī and Taḥrīr Ḥamād.

had died down because people obviously had become used to female judges in Sharia courts. In "normal" courts, there had been female judges much earlier.

The critique of the nomination of female judges focused on an alleged inability of these women to act as judges because of their emotionality and many other reasons.[73] Al-Tamīmī defended his nomination of female judges saying that there was no obstacle in Sharia and Islamic *fiqh*,[74] and that the Hanafis being the official school of law in Palestine had long since agreed upon, that at least in family law[75] women may become judges. He added that ʿUmar b. al-Khaṭṭāb (ruled 634–644 CE) had appointed Shifāʾ Umm ʿAbdallāh,[76] a woman, as head of the market police (*wilāyat al-ḥisba*), an office that he argued is "more serious" than the office of a judge in family matters.[77]

How did the female judges deal with the publicly voiced opinion that they were not able to serve in their position? What was their reaction to the stereotypes they were confronted with when appointed? Given what can be called a legislative power of the Sharia judiciary, a second aspect in my interviews with these women concerned their position toward a new Palestinian family law and the role of the Sharia establishment in drawing it up.

The three judges shared several characteristics. On the personal level: all three are married and have children, and all three considered it important to emphasize this fact either in the interviews they gave in the media or to me. Actually, they show that working as a judge despite having children and a family is a highly esteemed value for them. All report their families and husbands supported them and they had worked hard to get to their current positions. All three have university degrees in law, mostly also in Sharia. All had worked as lawyers before they passed the exam for Sharia judges and became judges.

3.3.2 *Al-Faqīh, al-Waḥīdī, and al-Ḍamīrī*

Al-Faqīh worked as a lawyer and law advisor for eight years with the women's organization WCLAC,[78] gaining much experience in this field. She is called a

73 Rajūb 2009; Amīn 2009. The Sharia lawyer ʿAbdalḥamīd Ismaʿīl described women as influenced by their nature (*ṭabīʿa*) and their shyness (*istiḥyāʾuhā*) to speak out in legal affairs belonging to the realm of family law, which is the essence of the work of the Sharia court. Rajūb 2009.

74 Shāyib 2009.

75 Sharq al-Awsaṭ, al- 2009.

76 Reference seems to be made to Shifāʾ bint ʿAbdallāh, see https://ar.wikipedia.org/wiki/%D8%A7%D9%84%D8%B4%D9%81%D8%A7%D8%A1_%D8%A8%D9%86%D8%AA_%D8%B9%D8%A8%D8%AF_%D8%A7%D9%84%D9%84%D9%87, accessed August 26, 2017.

77 Rajūb 2009.

78 Khulūd Muḥammad Aḥmad al-Faqīh, interview on December 19, 2013.

"defender of women rights"[79] and her ties with these organizations and civil society were obviously still strong at the time of the interview. She receives a lot of publicity and was ranked tenth among the one hundred most powerful Muslim women in 2012.[80] She can be described as having a strong and tough personality, being outspoken, assertive with clear goals and opinions.

Al-Waḥīdī was nominated together with al-Faqīh.[81] In an interview I conducted, she remained reluctant to give explicit answers and sometimes answered evasively. She argued strongly in favor of preserving tradition in society. She can be described as cautious and reserved, at least when talking to me, a European woman – and eager to make clear that traditions and also traditional gender roles such as the role of the guardian in marriage are important in Palestine and have to be respected. In her ideas of the roles and duties of genders she is surely more conservative than her two colleagues.

Al-Ḍamīrī[82] has been a judge since 2010 and Chief Prosecutor of Personal Status Law/*Raʾīs Niyāba al-Aḥwāl al-Shakhṣiyya*. She has a different relationship to the secular civil society in Palestine than al-Faqīh because she was responsible for affairs of civil society when she worked in the Ministries of Interior and Justice. She is often seen on television talkshows and in the media as an expert in *fiqh* and family law. She can be described as a self-confident, tough, outspoken, and frank woman, reflective with regard to the role of Islamic law, open in her discussion and very interested in contact with colleagues in other Arab states as well as in exchanging ideas with jurists from other countries, e.g., in Europe.

3.3.3 *Striving for Gender Justice and Professionality – Tasks and Challenges of the Three Female Judges*

The women judges were confronted with various stereotypes, but all three women agreed that their appointments conform with Sharia law. Al-Faqīh succeeded in spreading her "door-opening" narrative. According to this narrative, as a defense attorney,[83] she experienced what it meant to be an oppressed

79 Salam 2009.

80 Wonews 2012; Waṭan 2016; see also her articles in Wikipedia: https://ar.wikipedia.org/w/index.php?title=%D8%AE%D9%84%D9%88%D8%AF_%D9%81%D9%82%D9%8A%D9%87&oldid=38246894, accessed October 7, 2019.
For the much shorter English version see: https://en.wikipedia.org/w/index.php?title=Kholoud_Faqih&oldid=890981432, accessed October 7, 2019.

81 Shāyib 2009; Salam 2009; Asmahān Yūsuf al-Waḥīdī, interview on November 28, 2013.

82 Ṣumūd Al-Ḍamīrī, interview on November 11, 2013, and June 26, 2018; Lahamag 2011.

83 Wonews 2012; Melhem 2015; Khulūd Faqīh in: Wikipedia, see fn. 80; Baʿlūsha 2013.

woman.[84] Seeing that there were no women judges, she decided to become a Sharia judge herself[85] and presented her idea to the Supreme Judge Taysīr al-Tamīmī in 2004. According to her, he was shocked at first but then supported her.[86]

All three judges agreed in the interviews that women are generally the weaker party in court and that they can speak more freely about their problems, especially about sensitive topics of marriage and sexuality in front of a woman judge than a male judge. Al-Waḥīdī felt obliged to add that even when she and al-Faqīh felt as women and mothers nearer to female litigants, they always gave judgments based on the law,[87] indicating her high degree of professionalism as a judge. All three women judges stressed justice (*ʿadāla*) as their leading maxim, especially gender justice. Perhaps al-Faqīh was the most outspoken of them. She said that women are created with "complete capacity" (*kāmil al-ahliyya*) – meaning the ability to act – and explained the disapproval of female judges by male colleagues simply as the male's wish not to give up his social and economic privileges.[88] The case of a female litigant, who walked into her office in Birzeit and immediately turned back, saying she did not want to be judged by a woman, is for al-Faqīh simply evidence of the woman's conservative social upbringing. Customs and traditions are the reason for this attitude and nothing else.[89] Al-Waḥīdī made a good point in a media report responding to the argument that a female judge may be biased with regard to her emotionality (*bi-sabab ʿāṭifatihā*), saying: "This is not substantiated as long as … we strive for justice irrespective of whose advantage." She added a nice little (gender) touch, saying that al-Faqīh's and her appointment meant that: "Reason beats emotion" (*al-ʿaql yataghallab ʿalā al-ʿāṭifa*). With this statement she cleverly twisted the misogynistic male/rational – female/emotional dichotomy confirming that women's jurisdiction and especially her and Khulūd's appointments are reasonable.[90]

Al-Tamīmī's political argument – Palestinian women should be strengthened – is turned by all three women into an argument of direct empowerment: Each of them used their appointment to recommend women to apply for high qualification jobs.

84 Tatar 2015.

85 Tatar 2015.

86 Wonews 2012; Melhem 2015.

87 Sharq al-Awsaṭ, al- 2009.

88 Melhem 2015; Nakhkhāl 2015; Tatar 2015; Khulūd Faqīh in: Wikipedia, see fn. 80.

89 Wonews 2012; Khulūd al-Faqīh, interview on December 19, 2013; similar: Baʿlūsha 2013; Melhem 2015; Nakhkhāl 2015.

90 Sharq al-Awsaṭ, al- 2009.

With regard to legislation, all agreed that there should be a new Palestinian family law. Al-Waḥīdī was less outspoken, but al-Faqīh and al-Ḍamīrī were more explicit regarding the problem of custody (*ḥaḍāna*), which they see as a pressing problem in need of reform. Al-Faqīh seemed to have been involved in the debate about a new law when she was working at WCLAC. She was critical of the Supreme Judge's 2013 Draft of the Palestinian Family Law, which was authored by the *Qāḍī al-Quḍāt* and "his men."[91] Al-Waḥīdī answered the question on the evaluation of this Draft evasively and argued that she as a judge only has to apply the law. However, she obviously belonged, together with al-Ḍamīrī, to a committee preparing a draft for a new Personal Status Law not in Palestine, but in Israel,[92] an information if true which would indicate her interest and activity in legislative questions. Al-Ḍamīrī, on the other hand, had no reservation on this matter and has expressed her opinion openly in different contexts: not only in the interview with me, but also, e.g., in the TV program called *Lāzim Naḥkī* (April 2013). She is in favor of a new Palestinian Family Law, being, of course, well aware of the difficulties caused by the political situation and the fact that the parliament in Ramallah currently does not meet. She has outspoken ideas how the Islamic law can be developed toward more rights for women.[93]

Summarizing the different professional views of the three women al-Faqīh can perhaps be seen as the most outspoken supporter of gender equality and the strategic orientation of the new law toward international law, whereas al-Waḥīdī seems more traditional and conservative, arguing that traditions had to be respected. Al-Ḍamīrī is a defender of the Sharia-based law, but with a strong focus on gender equality reforms in the framework of Islamic law. As long as there was no parliament, she among the female judges was the clearest supporter of the role of the *Dīwān* as a quasi-legislative organ.

It is evident, that the female judges shared certain positions, but had very independent professional opinions in other fields: They shared a clear conviction that women can become Sharia judges and that there are no obstacles in this respect in Islamic law. None of them reacted to provocative gestures and remarks on their personal unsuitability for their office, but all of them were resolute in their statements that they would apply the law equally to men and women. Their approach was highly pragmatic: Women are neither better nor worse than men, they are not different from men before the law, but in a still very much patriarchal society like the Palestinian society, female judges

91 Khulūd al-Faqīh, interview on December 19, 2013.

92 Akhbār Maḥalliyya 2015.

93 Damiri 2018.

can contribute to balancing out the disadvantages of women. Women speak more freely in front of a woman judge. However, in the end, the judgment has to be given irrespectively of who files the claim simply according to law and justice. They all saw it as their duty, to strive for what they call justice. But none of them ever suggested that male judges handed down unjust judgments with regard to women. The three judges, therefore, showed a highly pragmatic and professional approach to their task despite the difficult social surrounding critical of their abilities. Gendered perceptions of the judiciary did not play a role in their professional self-perception. However, it became evident that they had different opinions how to interpret Islamic law and adapt it to the reality of the twenty-first century, ranging between safeguarding tradition and promoting gender equality.

CHAPTER 4

Khulʿ: The New Ruling of 2012 and Its Context

4.1 Uses of the Past: Sources of *khulʿ* and the Case of Egypt

Islamic marriage and inheritance belong, in classical law, to the patriarchal type and in modern legislation this basic characteristic has been modified but not fundamentally changed.[1] In agreement with Léon Buskens I use this term to signify "a model of family life in which senior men are entitled to a dominant position over subordinate women and children."[2] The husband is head of the family; he represents his family in public and controls his wife's body and behavior while having prerogatives such as polygyny and repudiation rights. In addition, men have the right to guardianship, and inherit twice as much as a woman may. Money and sexuality are tightly connected. Dower is the property of the wife[3] and the woman can "refuse access to herself till the husband pays the dower" according to Abū Ḥanīfa (d. 767).[4] In the Egyptian Family Rights Law (EFRL) Article 38, it is written that "as soon as the marriage is concluded in a rightful manner, the dowry and alimony shall be incumbent."[5] Article 37 of the Jordanian Law of Personal Status (JLPS) states that

> The wife, after the receipt of her advance dowry, must obey and reside in the legal house of the husband and move with him to any place the husband wants even if it were outside the Kingdom [of Jordan], on condition that he be trustworthy for her and that the contract document does not entail a stipulation requiring otherwise. Should the wife refrain from obedience, her right to the alimony shall be revoked.[6]

1 Schneider 2019.

2 Buskens 2003: 75, fn. 5.

3 The JLPS deals extensively with the dower throughout twenty-two articles (Articles 44–65). According to Article 61, the dower is the wife's property; she shall not be obliged to prepare the trousseau from it. In the case of divorce (*ṭalāq*) before consummation, the wife is only entitled to half the dower (Article 48). The JLPS explicitly refers to the possibility of deferral of payment of the dower (Articles 45, 46). The legal texts can be found in Muqtafi.

4 IR II 51/60. IR= Ibn Rushd's reference is given at first in the Arabic text and then in the English translation.

5 See similar JLPS Article 35.

6 JLPS Article 37.

 DOI:10.1163/9789004442313_005

Thus, after having taken the dower, during marriage, and while receiving maintenance (*nafaqa*), the woman is obliged not only to have sex with her husband, but also to obey him in more general issues of marital life, such as live with him in his house and accompany him on travels.[7] If she does not obey, the husband is allowed to stop paying maintenance. This is regulated in the JLPS Articles 37 and 69, and 81 (for divorce) and in Article 66 of the EFRL. Property separation, being a special Islamic flavor of patriarchal family structure, may not be taken as an expression of gender equality, as is sometimes argued.[8] The basic relation is what Nadia Sonneveld appropriately calls the "maintenance-obedience relation," which featured prominently in the Egyptian debate in 2000 about the introduction of the new *khulʿ* law. Women's alleged irrationality was often presented in this debate, according to Sonneveld's research, as the main reason behind the requirement that women should obey their husbands.[9]

Ibn Rushd (d. 1198) (IR) argued that maintenance (*nafaqa*) is either seen as a countervalue of sexual utilization (*istimtāʿ*, lit. enjoyment) or as compensation for the fact that the wife is confined (*maḥbūsa*, lit. captive).[10] This relationship based on money in exchange for the obligation of sexual service and obedience is still reflected in present-day Palestine: when the couple goes to court to register the marriage, the marriage officer (*maʾdhūn*) informs the woman of the obligation of obedience (*ḍarūrat al-ṭāʿa*) and the husband-to-be of the necessity of maintenance (*ḍarūrat al-infāq*).[11]

4.1.1 Khulʿ *in Classical Law and the Reform in Egypt in 2000*

In general, *khulʿ* as redemption is one of the better known and perhaps also most practiced forms of divorce in Islamic law. The root *kh-l-ʿ* means "to take off" (clothes). Hendrik Denker classifies the terms *khulʿ* and *mukhālaʿa* as

7 JLPS Article 37 according to which the woman has to follow her husband when he moves to another city; EFRL Article 40, according to which she has to accompany him on travels; obedience is explicitly mentioned, see JLPS Article 47, which rules that if the wife consents to the postponement of the dower or the accessories for a defined term, she shall not have the right to refrain from obedience.

8 See, e.g., Moors 1999.

9 Sonneveld 2012: 15. Some scholars argue that the frequency of *khulʿ* cases in Ottoman court records reflects women's strong position in the family and society (Sonbol 1995; Zantout 2006) but Sonneveld argues that these conclusions should be "viewed with care," as court records do not reflect the reality of gender relations outside the court, see Sonneveld 2012: 31–32.

10 IR II 54/63.

11 Abū Ṭaʿīma June 23, 2013. See the video link at the end of the article, at around 02:00 to 02:20, accessed September 9, 2017.

synonyms[12] both meaning the legal institute (*Rechtsinstitut*) and being related to "taking off" (*khalaʿa*) the marriage bond. It refers to Quran 2:187 where a husband and wife are described as each other's vestment, *khulʿ* and refers metaphorically to the end of this close and intimate relationship. *Mubāraʾa* is another synonym for *khulʿ*. *Bariʾa* means "to be or become free," and *mubāraʾa* refers to the contract by which the woman is set free from her marital bonds. It can be best translated as "dissolution of marriage by agreement with mutual renunciation of any financial obligations" whereas *ṣulḥ* in this context means "reconciliation, compromise." It refers to the aspect of *khulʿ*, according to which the husband renounces his marital rights and receives the woman's dower. *Fidāʾ* is the price the woman has to pay for her "redemption" (*iftidāʾ*). The term is used in Quran 2:229 where the wife's redemption from the husband is generally accepted.[13] The Sunna contains one *ḥadīth* with its different variants that is always quoted in legal and political debate to substantiate *khulʿ*. Thābit b. Qays's wife is reported to have approached the Prophet wanting a separation from her husband. It was granted after she returned her dower, a garden, to her husband.

Denker identifies four main characteristics depicting the differences in the variations of the *ḥadīth* some of which served, could have served, or could still serve as starting points for a (re)interpretation:

1. The woman's name, when given, is either Ḥabība or Jamīla, but most often she is only called Thābit b. Qays's wife.[14]
2. She describes her motivation for a separation in different ways depending on the variation of the *ḥadīth*. She either describes her husband as a man of good character and religion but she hates unbelief (*kufr*).[15] With this she implicitly says that she cannot remain an obedient wife to him; or she describes him as ugly and repugnant to her especially when he wants to have intercourse with her. In another version, he is said to be brutal and even hit her.
3. Often the garden is named as her dower and the Prophet wants her to return it to her husband. Sometimes the variations include money or whatever else she received from her husband.

12 Denker 2004: 134, fn. 16.

13 Denker 2004: 135.

14 This fact does not influence the jurist's discussion. It is interesting only from the point of view of source critique and the question of a possible historicity of this person.

15 Here *kufr* does not mean "unbelief" in the normal sense, see Wehr 1976, but that she did not want to transgress God's limits, referring to the *ḥudūd*, the Quranic punishments for illegitimate sexual relation.

4. At the end of the *ḥadīth,* the husband is either recommended (*irshādī*) to take her money, garden, or other dower, or it is phrased as the Prophet's order, in which case the husband must obey (*ījābī*/compulsary). In one version of Ibn Māja the husband's consent is not even seen necessary.

Denker distinguishes thus three different possible forms of separation described in the variants of the *ḥadīth*

a) the consent of the husband is necessary;
b) the Prophet orders the husband to divorce her;
c) the Prophet himself separates her from the husband.[16]

Only according to a) the husband's consent is deemed necessary, but according to b) and/or c) this is not the case. A difference could also be seen, Denker argues, in whether or not the Prophet acted qua office (as a judge of the Muslim community) or qua person. If acting qua person, the husband could at least theoretically oppose the Prophet's order, whereas he would not have this option when the Prophet acted qua office.[17] Denker concludes from this textual evidence that the husband's consent to *khulʿ* cannot be seen as an absolute precondition. But consensus among the scholars of all schools for the past more than thousand years went in a different direction. According to all schools, both the husband's and the wife's consent is deemed necessary. This narrow interpretation is surprising given the often-praised interpretative flexibility of Islamic jurisprudence, as it denies from the beginning a right to women that men had in the patriarchal society, i.e., the right to a divorce, and therefore again fits into the picture of a patriarchal interpretation of the law despite a possible legitimization of such a right for women, at least according to one version of the *ḥadīth*. There is, furthermore, consensus that both the husband and the wife have to have a legal status that allows *khulʿ* and that the term *khulʿ* or one of its derivations has to be used, and, finally, that the woman has to pay a redemption sum.[18] The most substantial reform of *khulʿ* law with regard to enhancing women's rights in the Arab countries was law 1/2000 of Egypt, introducing a new version of judicial *khulʿ*, in which the husband's consent was no longer necessary. Like in Palestine, in Egypt the law was preceded and accompanied by a controversial debate in society. Arguments in favor of and against this reform were exchanged in a debate where both sides claimed compatibility with Sharia.[19]

16 Denker 2004: 137–139.
17 Denker 2004: 139.
18 Denker 2004: 140–141.
19 Denker 2004: 174; Sonnneveld 2012: 56.

But also questions of cultural authenticity, modernization, and changing notions of manhood and womanhood were at stake in Egypt, Sonneveld argues in her research.[20] The argument that women had no right to separation in Islam was generally rejected.[21] Whereas a man's right to repudiation (*ṭalāq*) was emphasized, it was weighed against a woman's right to *khulʿ*. As he has this right, the woman has to have a right to separation, too, some argued and connected it to the principle of voluntariness of the marriage.[22] Another argument with regard to reciprocity was that as women knew in the case of non-obedience they could be given *ṭalāq*, men would now know that if they maltreated their wives, they could be given *khulʿ*.[23] A reason for a necessary reform was also seen in the difficulty of divorce for women generally and in cases of *taṭlīq li-l-ḍarar* (separation because of damage), because those procedures took years in Egyptian courts and were unpredictable regarding their outcome for Egyptian women.[24] With this new law women were given the right to decide freely to end an unhappy marriage – a right seen by some as a woman's right endowed upon her by God.

Critics of the reform, on the other hand, argued that this new version of *khulʿ* would endanger the family and Egyptian society because the rate of divorce would increase. Sonneveld has collected different arguments used in this debate: Women would spontaneously take the first opportunity to give their husbands *khulʿ* because women are emotional persons, who have moodswings and act irrationally. Women could now blackmail their husbands. Abuse was deemed possible also from the husband's side according to Sonneveld's research, since the husband could be enticed to provoke his wife's *khulʿ* through maltreatment and thus be freed from the obligation to give her the whole dower, which would be obligatory in the case of repudiation (*ṭalāq*).[25] *Khulʿ* has often been criticized in Egypt as a special law for wealthy women because only rich women could afford to forfeit their financial rights.[26] According to Sonneveld's research, fear was spread in newspapers that women would use *khulʿ* to get rid of their husbands and to marry a rich and more handsome man.[27] Her research revealed, however, that poor women also filed this form of

20 Sonneveld 2012: 4.
21 Denker 2004: 177; Sonneveld 2012: 2.
22 Denker 2004: 175.
23 Denker 2004: 175.
24 Denker 2004: 174.
25 Denker 2004: 189.
26 Denker 2004: 188–189; Sonneveld 2012: 3.
27 Sonneveld 2012: 7.

divorce in the courts and that most women in court uttered that they did not want to be married ever again.[28]

Before the law was adopted by the parliament in January 2000, there had been, according to Denker, long discussions between representatives of the Ministry of Justice and experts from different groups since 1991. In December 1999, President Mubarak presented the draft law to the public and then it was approved by Muḥammad Ṭanṭāwī, *Shaykh* of al-Azhar, and other representatives of the religious establishment.[29] The debate on the draft law in parliament was fierce, albeit short.[30] The draft law was accompanied by other reforms of the divorce law, e.g., the obligation of the husband to inform his wife about a *ṭalāq*.[31] *Khulʿ* based on mutual consent, the "classical version" remained effective in Egypt and was as before possible without court procedure; the separation of the couple and the husband's *ṭalāq* was simply registered.[32]

The new variation of *khulʿ* without the husband's consent contained the following points and steps of procedure:

1. the woman files a claim for a judicial *khulʿ*;
2. she returns the dower and waives all other legal rights;
3. the court organizes an arbitration procedure in two phases consulting arbiters from the families of the partners; if this arbitration procedure fails, separation takes place;
4. the woman has to declare in court that for her, the continuation of marriage is impossible.[33]

Khulʿ will then have the legal effect of irrevocable repudiation (*ṭalāq bāʾin*) with no appeal possible.[34] The main difference scholars saw in the modern law was the change from the husband's (necessary) consent and the private setting in which consensual *khulʿ* normally took place moved to a courtroom and a judge's decision. This decision was viewed as requiring a new competence of the judges, which was regarded as the "real *ijtihād*" in the matter, as Denker shows.[35]

28 Sonneveld 2012: 7, 84, 87ff.
29 Denker 2004: 168.
30 Denker 2004: 169.
31 EFRL Article 21.
32 Denker 2004: 173.
33 Denker 2004: 173.
34 Denker 2004: 173–174.
35 Denker 2004: 174. See also the same argument for Jordan: Engelcke 2017a: 25–26. Here the Islamists argued that it was an unwanted increase of state interference and stressed that *khulʿ* could be performed without a judge.

With regard to the "uses of the past" the question would arise whether the Prophet's order to Thābit was compulsory (*ījābī*) or recommended (*irshādī*)? Or did the Prophet himself execute the judgment? Denker argues, that in the media and in the public these questions were discussed in a way in which

> the research did not refer much to the wording of the sources. Instead of taking into consideration the different variants of the tradition and the different possible interpretations and to discuss them, the authors took the easy way out. They stated that the sources either "explicitly" claim the husband's consent or vice versa, that this explicity is not necessary.[36]

Denker's analysis of the Egyptian debate is revealing: The participants in the iteration took "the easy way out," they obviously did not bother to refer to the texts to take a close look and present their new interpretation based on this close new analysis to the public. A thorough discussion of the variations of the *ḥadīth* did not take place at all, not on the formal level with regard to the transfer of the *ḥadīth*, the *isnād*, the chain of transmitters, or on the level of content or text of the *ḥadīth*, the *matn*. At the same time, whereas it is often stated that all schools of law require the husband's consent, a modern codification prescribing something completely different was not excluded generally, Denker argues, but it was not deemed appropriate. Denker concluded that "the reference to tradition of the schools of law has changed."[37] Arguments were based less on the tradition of the schools of law and derived more directly from the sources, i.e., Quran and Sunna, but not in a diligent and exhausting way, as he stresses.

Whereas in other forms of judicial separations, the woman needs a reason to file a claim such as the husband's non-payment of maintenance, the husband's absence for a long time, his imprisonment, or his maltreatment,[38] this is not the case with *khulʿ*. This is perhaps the most important difference compared to other forms of divorce. She only has to state that she is afraid of not keeping God's limits – a phrase she has to repeat in court or confirm when petitioning for *khulʿ* in Palestine, too. It is connected to Quran 2:229: "unless the couple fear they may not maintain God's bounds."[39] The reasons why she is afraid can be subjectively individual and are not taken into consideration

36 Denker 2004: 176.
37 Denker 2004: 176.
38 Denker 2004: 156–167.
39 See Quran, translation of Arberry. If nothing else is indicated, Quranic verses are quoted according to the translation of Arberry.

by the court. Furthermore, in contrast to classical law, the Egyptian legislature did not allow a redemption sum higher than the original dower (Egyptian Arabic: *ṣadāq*).[40] In the Egyptian debate, it was demanded by some that presents given before marriage (*hadīya*) and gold, which is normally given to the fiancée (*shabka*), should be returned, but this demand was not integrated into the legal regulation.[41]

Normally, the right to *ḥaḍāna* (child custody) is not allowed to be waived, but here too, several groups in Egyptian society took another position. Some demanded compensation for the husband parallel to special maintenance (*nafaqat al-mutʿa*) to which women have a right in modern law in case they become repudiated without reason.[42] Finally, the Egyptian law does not explain whether *khulʿ* is a *faskh* (dissolution) of the marriage or *ṭalāq*.[43]

4.2 Legal Regulation in Palestine

The history of family law and especially divorce in Palestine is dealt with in Tucker's work, which has been mentioned in the introduction. According to her results, the Ottoman muftis and judges[44] of the dominant Hanafi school generally accepted a more flexible approach to divorce than taken by their Shafii and Hanbali colleagues. They helped women get judgments from representatives of these other schools of law,[45] allowing them to preside over these cases[46] and granting women anullments when the husband was absent, which was explicitly against the Hanafi law. *Khulʿ* could be used only based on the husband's agreement, but it was a means by which a woman could initiate a divorce. It seems that *khulʿ* was often registered and many women brought the *khulʿ* case to court.[47] Normally the woman waived the deferred dower and all the costs of her support during her waiting period.[48] The courts also supported the position that *khulʿ* divorce was final.[49] The records thus show that women

40 Denker 2004: 179.
41 Denker 2004: 181–182.
42 Denker 2004: 184–186.
43 Denker 2004: 195.
44 Tucker 1998: 180.
45 Tucker 1998: 180.
46 Tucker 1998: 83–84. For the modern approach to this "forum shopping," which, however, seems here to have been initiated by the judges themselves, see Shahar 2013 for present-day Jerusalem.
47 Tucker 1998: 95–100.
48 Tucker 1998: 98.
49 Tucker 1998: 100.

did know about *khulʿ* and used it.[50] The question is, of course, what percentage of women turned to the court in comparison to men, and how many divorces, *ṭalāq* but also *khulʿ*, took place out of court. Tucker cautiously describes the muftis and judges in this era as "guardians of the status quo";[51] they represented what she calls an "old boys network," which tried with flexibility and creativity to solve legal questions and help women with their legal demands within the framework of Islamic law as long as the general gender hierarchy was not impacted.[52] Tucker does not at all suggest that seventeenth- and eighteenth-century Palestine and Syria represent a lost paradise of equity.[53] However, the judges seem to have had a certain agency and to have used it to the advantage of women.[54] Tucker confronts this with the modern situation where states have taken over and argues: "Codified law cannot, by definition, be flexible and fluid law. Legal codes no longer offer a variety of possible interpretations; rather they work to standardize cases and minimize the element of judicial subjectivity."[55] In an earlier article titled "Revisiting Reform: Woman and the Ottoman Law of Family Rights 1917,"[56] Tucker argues that the 1917 law was rooted in legal practices and concluded that in terms of women's rights such as marital support and female-initiated divorce, the codified law did not introduce any reforms but reflected the absence of a strategy to select what might be empowering for women. She concluded that the result, i.e., the codification, was "not a gain" for women.[57] Yitzhak Reiter criticized that Tucker referred to Articles 122, 126, and 127 of the law, which dealt with the option of annulment of a marriage on the grounds of the husband's absence or desertion, overlooking one of the more important innovative articles of the law, Article 130. Reiter, focusing on the use of this article made by Israeli Sharia judges, argues that this article was special insofar as it extended the grounds for divorce and provided couples with a mechanism to dissolve marriages by means of a declaration of "dispute and discord" in case such discord existed between them. This article gave jurists and especially judges the leeway to adapt it to the changing social norms of each Muslim community.[58] It was this solution that was also laid down in the ruling 59/2012 by Yūsuf Idʿīs – and it becomes obvious that

50 Tucker 1998: 99.
51 Tucker 1998: 183.
52 Tucker 1998: 184.
53 Tucker 1998: 184.
54 Tucker 1998: 184.
55 Tucker 1998: 184.
56 Tucker 1996.
57 Tucker 1996: 16.
58 Reiter 2009: 16.

research comparing the jurisdiction of the Sharia courts in Palestine and Israel is a desideratum.[59]

As young women in Palestine usually signed their marriage contract at the engagement, it makes sense to take a look at the legal regulation of engagements. In the JLPS[60] and the EFRL,[61] it is stated explicitly that marriage "shall not be concluded by betrothal" or by promise of marriage. The JLPS adds that neither the recitation of the Surat al-Fātiḥa nor the receipt of anything on account of the dower (*ayy shayʾ ʿalā ḥisāb al-mahr*) nor the acceptance of a gift constitutes a marriage. It states in Article 4 that both the fiancé and fiancée shall be entitled to desist from the betrothal. This is also endorsed in Article 3 of the EFRL where it is stated that if one of the spouses abstains or dies, the dower may be redeemed and other things given as gifts shall be subject to the provisions of the gift. Both laws thus draw a clear distinction between engagement and marriage and emphasize that an engagement can be ended without further legal mechanism, let alone a divorce. According to JLPS Article 14 and EFRL Article 21 marriage shall be concluded with an offer and acceptance of the suitors or their representatives.

Talāq is regulated in the JLPS in Articles 83–101, *khulʿ* in Articles 102–112. In the EFRL, separation in general and *ṭalāq* in particular are regulated by Articles 67–102. The EFRL does not deal with *khulʿ* in a specific paragraph, thus, Lynn Welchman argues, by default the classical Hanafi rules are left intact, as will be outlined in detail in chapter 9.[62] *Khulʿ* is mentioned in Article 76 as an irrevocable divorce and in Article 100, where it is part of the procedure of the judicial divorce of "dispute and discord" regulated in JLPS Article 132. *Khulʿ* divorce is recognized by all schools of law.

Ṭalāq, however, is in the husband's hand.[63] Both the law in the West Bank and Gaza follow standard patterns and sometimes classical law, Welchman argues,[64] in discounting *ṭalāq* by a man in various physical or mental states. For example, divorce of an inebriated, astounded, coerced, imbecilic, or unconscious person has no legal effect.[65] Both the JLPS and EFRL include restrictions based on the intention of the husband, in the case of "hidden expressions," of *ṭalāq*. The formula must intend to actually mean *ṭalāq*. A *ṭalāq* suspended on a

59 Some aspects are covered in the book edited by Nijmi Edres and Irene Schneider, see Edres, Lindbekk, and Schneider 2018.
60 JLPS Article 3.
61 EFRL Article 2.
62 Welchman 1999: 161.
63 JLPS Articles 83–84; EFRL Articles 67–68.
64 Welchman 1999: 145.
65 JLPS Article 88; EFRL Article 69.

condition is not valid if its real intention is to get someone (meaning the wife) to do or stop doing something.[66]

In classical law, the husband has the right to three *ṭalāqs*, which he can pronounce anywhere and at any time. Divorce is either revocable (*rajʿī*) or irrevocable (*bāʾin*). Revocable divorce is the *ṭalāq* pronounced by the husband for the first and second but not third time, whereas irrevocable divorce occurs in the case of the third *ṭalāq*, the divorce that precedes the consummation of marriage and divorce in the case of *khulʿ*.[67] The legally most approved form is a single revocable *ṭalāq* (*rajʿī*), which is followed by a waiting period (*ʿidda*) of three months or in case of pregnancy until the child is born. The husband should not repudiate her during her menstruation. During the waiting period, the husband has to pay maintenance and he can at any time revoke this *ṭalāq* and take the wife back into his marital bed. Her consent is not required. If he does so, the marriage continues. If the waiting period expires, the *ṭalāq* becomes final, and in this case, the couple would have to sign a new contract if they want to be together again. If the marriage ends in this way, it is called "lesser finality" (*baynūna ṣughrā*), which occurs only after the first and second *ṭalāq*. After the third *ṭalāq*, the marriage is ended by the so-called *baynūna kubrā* (greater finality) and here the husband cannot take back the wife until the wife has married another man and has consummated marriage with him and, of course, been divorced from him.[68] A method to restrict *ṭalāq* in modern times is to limit the options to a single revocable *ṭalāq*. Here JLPS and EFRL are roughly identical, providing that *ṭalāq*, accompanied by a number in word or sign, gives rise to one *ṭalāq* only.[69]

Rajʿa, the husband's right to take back his wife without her consent, is possible only in the revocable divorce[70] and it brings the woman into a situation of absolute dependency without any option to act, as just described. She has to wait and see whether her husband is ready to take her back or not.[71] In Gaza, it is possible for the husband to stipulate in the marriage contract that the

66 JLPS Articles 89, 95; EFRL Articles 70, 75.

67 JLPS Article 94; EFRL Article 76.

68 See JLPS Article 100; EFRL Articles 82–83; see also Welchman: 2000: 324–325; Nasir 2002: 106–115; s. 112,

69 See Welchman 1999: 145–146; JLPS Article 90; EFRL Article 74.

70 JLPS Article 97; EFRL Article 78.

71 JLPS Article 97; EFRL Article 79. In 1979, a regulation was issued by the Supreme Judge in Amman and sent to the heads of the Sharia Courts of Appeal in Jerusalem and Amman for distribution to the judges. The regulation instructed the judges not to register the incidence of the third of three *ṭalāqs* until the relevant court papers had been sent to and approved by the *Qāḍī al-Quḍāt*, for this see Welchman 1999: 148.

marriage will have a definite duration. Such a clause is considered to be valid.[72] Delegation of divorce to the woman is possible. The husband can delegate his right to *ṭalāq* to a third party and/or to his wife, but this must be fixed in writing.[73] The husband has to register the divorce within fifteen days otherwise he incurs a penalty. The court must notify the wife within one week from its registration if she is not present.[74] In the EFRL, no time is given; Article 77 states only, that a husband who divorces his wife shall notify the judge thereof.

Over the course of the twentieth century, efforts have been made in various Arab and Muslim states to restrict the wide power of the man's extrajudicial *ṭalāq*. Some countries, e.g., Iran, went as far as to abolish extrajudicial divorce.[75] Jordanian law follows what Welchman calls a "less ambitious pattern" by restricting the incidence of *ṭalāq* under certain circumstances related to the husband's physical and mental states and the formula of *ṭalāq* employed; by imposing procedural and administrative registration requirements backed up by penal sanctions for noncompliance in criminal law; and by allowing for extra financial obligations to be placed upon the husband in the event of *ṭalāq*.[76] The EFRL includes the first type of restriction, but does not explicitly refer to criminal penalties for nonregistration and has no provision for compensation for arbitrary *ṭalāq*.[77] But even if the JLPS does impose penalty upon nonregistration, it does not go so far as to connect *ṭalāq* to the court room and subject it to several procedural arrangements, e.g., to a process of reconciliation as in the case of *khulʿ*. As such, the JLPS and EFRL can still be seen very near to premodern law and as domains of almost unrestricted rights of men regarding divorce. Or, as the *Qāḍī al-Quḍāt*, Yūsuf Idʿīs, used to repeat in his class: "*al-ṭalāq fī yad al-rajul*/*ṭalāq* is in the husband's hand," i.e., not in the hand of the judge let alone in the wife's hand.

Khulʿ is not regulated explicitly in the Ottoman Law of Family Rights (OLFR) of 1917 which was in force in the area in Ottoman and British Mandate time but it is regulated in Qadrī Bāshā's codification of family law of 1875.[78] In this

72 EFRL Article 71, "divorce in future".

73 JLPS Article 87; EFRL Article 70 states that "[d]ivorce that is associated with a recognized condition shall be valid unless it is intended to force [the wife] to do something or leave her husband."

74 JLPS Article 101.

75 Schneider 2014: 74.

76 Welchman 1999: 145; Schneider 2014: 63–75.

77 Arbitrary *ṭalāq* is the husband's *ṭalāq* without reason given. He has the right to *ṭalāq* at any time, but in this case the woman can claim compensation, according to several personal status laws. See Welchman 2007: 21.

78 *Khulʿ* is mentioned in the OLFR of 1917 in Article 130 under the rubric of the divorce on "dispute and discord." For Qadrī Bāshā's codification: see Qadrī Bāshā 2007: 96–101. See

codification only consensual *khulʿ* is dealt with and Article 278 states that *khulʿ* is not dependent on a court decision.[79] Different articles deal with the question of how to proceed when *khulʿ* takes place before consummation and according to Article 281, the wife cannot demand the deferred part of the dower or maintenance if *khulʿ* took place before consummation and was initiated by the man.[80]

Mukhālaʿa/khulʿ is regulated in the JLPS Articles 102–112. *Khulʿ* terminates the marriage in a final way (*bāʾin*), although the wife still has to go through the waiting period (*ʿidda*), which is given with one menstruation cycle. Unlike unilateral *ṭalāq*, *mukhālaʿa* in the JLPS of 1976 requires the consent of both spouses and both can file the claim. In JLPS, the husband must fulfill the normal conditions of competence and the woman must be contracted to him in a legal marriage.[81] It is seen as a precedent condition for *mukhālaʿa* to be valid so that the husband would be eligible to effect the separation (*ṭalāq*) and the wife would be subject to it.[82] Welchman explained that there is no explicit mentioning of necessary mutual consent of husband and wife, but it is contextually clear that the man is seen as the active part and the wife's consent is needed. Either she, or a person duly delegated to act for her, must be present when the man utters the *ṭalāq* in the context of *khulʿ* in order to respond with the *ibrāʾ*, the renunciation of the financial rights in exchange for the divorce. Welchman writes:

> Technically, *khul'* divorces can be concluded outside court, but in practice, while the arrangements are negotiated outside court, the formal divorce by *khulʿ* is nearly always pronounced in court and registered immediately. In the West Bank and Gaza Strip, the husband is under no obligation to consent to pronounce his *talaq* in a *khul'*. A *khul'* divorce is thus dependent on mutual consent, and it can be proposed by either of the parties to the other.[83]

In the event the compensation is void, the divorce shall take effect in a recoverable manner.[84] This provision explicitly states that *khulʿ* is an alternative word

also Ebert 2010: 96–102. For Article 130 as used by the Israeli Sharia courts, see Reiter 2009. In Gaza, reference was made to these articles, see chapter 9.

79 Ebert 2010: 97.

80 Ebert 2010: 98.

81 JLPS Article 102; Welchman 2000: 347–348.

82 JLPS Article 102 (a).

83 Welchman 1999: 137.

84 JLPS Article 102 (c).

for *mukhālaʿa*. According to JLPS Article 103, each party shall be entitled to revoke the offer in the *mukhālaʿa* prior to the acceptance of the other. If the woman is under the age of legal majority, *khulʿ* is not valid unless her legal guardian gives his consent.[85] In Jordanian and Palestinian practice, *khulʿ* is concluded by a single final *ṭalāq* pronounced by the husband in exchange for the wife's renunciation (*ibrāʾ*) of some of her financial rights against him, primarily the dower and maintenance. If direct exchange is not explicity stated then the *ṭalāq* falls as a single *ṭalāq* accompanied by a voluntary waiving of rights by the wife, according to Welchman's research.[86] If the parties declare a denial of the compensation, *khulʿ* shall be "as good as a mere divorce and a pronouncement of recoverable divorce shall take effect with it."[87]

It is stipulated "that which is legally valid to be committed to, shall be fit to be a compensation in the Khulʿ."[88] In the event the parties agree on property rather than the dower, it shall be imperative to hand it over, but the parties are absolved of each right pertaining to the dower and the matrimonial alimony.[89] If there is no designation by the parties, each one of them shall be absolved of the rights of the other.[90]

There was some discussion as to whether the wife could renounce more than the husband had actually given her by way of dower and so on – that is, whether the divorce was valid if the "renunciation" became a "compensation" divorce, whereby the wife renounces her rights and in addition pays the husband a sum of money on top.[91] All four schools hold that such a divorce is valid, although disapproved.[92] Welchman argues that in contrast to Abū Ḥanīfa's view the JLPS states: "The alimony of the legally prescribed waiting period shall not abate unless it is explicitly provided for under the contract of *Mukhalaʿah*."[93]

JLPS Article 132 (EFRL Article 97) regulates separation (*tafrīq*) because of "dispute and discord" (*al-nizāʿ wa-l-shiqāq*). According to this article, a husband or a wife may petition for this kind of divorce. However, the woman has to prove the damage "in word or in deed, whereby the continuance of marital life

85 JLPS Article 102 (b).
86 Welchman 2000: 346.
87 JLPS Article 107.
88 JLPS Article 104.
89 JLPS Article 105.
90 JLPS Article 106.
91 Quoted in Welchman 2000: 348.
92 Welchman 2000: 348.
93 Welchman 2000: 349; JLPS Article 108. The regulations in the EFRL are in detail discussed in chapter 9.

is impossible with such damage."[94] If the woman can prove that the damage[95] was caused by the husband, the judge shall exert his effort to reach reconciliation. In case of reconciliation not being tenable, he shall refer the matter to arbiters. The husband as a claimant is not obliged to prove the damage but that he "proves the existence of the dispute and discord."[96] The procedure following the husband's claim is the same as for the woman. Under the JLPS, if arbiters find the wrongdoing is on the side of the wife – as well as the husband – they decide that the separation is for the compensation "they deem appropriate."[97] In case the wife requested the separation herself and the judgment on any compensation is issued against her, she must secure a payment prior to the two arbiters' decision.[98]

Judicial separation furthermore is possible because of the wife's claim – which she has to prove – with regard to

- failure of the man to pay maintenance (JLPS Article 127; EFRL Article 92);
- absence or emigration (JLPS Articles 123–128, 131; EFRL Article 93–95);
- *īlāʾ*[99] (JLPS Article 51);
- imprisonment (JLPS Article 130; EFRL Article 96);
- (physical) deficiencies (JLPS Articles 113–116; EFRL Articles 84–89).

4.2.1 Khulʿ *in the Neighboring States*

The Palestinian *taʿmīm* cannot be understood without developments in the surrounding countries, which, at the same time, contributed to Palestine's legal history. References to the laws in Egypt and Jordan were sometimes made in the Palestinian iterations but more rarely than one would have expected and often not explicitly.[100] Whereas the Egyptian law has already been dealt with, the law 82/2001 in Jordan followed its example and the development in Jordan as well as in Egypt surely did not go unwatched in Palestine. In Article 126 of the Jordanian Law of 2001, wives were given the right to ask for *khulʿ* without the husband's consent.[101] The 2010 law regulates *khulʿ* in Articles 102–113 and

94 JLPS Article 132.
95 Article 132 (a).
96 Article 132 (b).
97 Article 132 (f).
98 JLPS Article 132 (g).
99 *Īlāʾ*: divorce following the husband's vow and its fulfillment through abstinence from sexual intercourse with her. There is no regulation in the EFRL that again leaves the classical Hanafi law applicable.
100 See, e.g., the Supreme Judge in his class on *khulʿ* (October 31, 2013), see 5.3.2. He pointed to his regulation as something "new" but admitted that people could have heard about the ruling in Egypt and Jordan through the media.
101 Engelcke 2017a: 23.

regulates *khulʿ* based on consent.[102] Under the category of "judicial separation," *iftidāʾ* (redemption) is mentioned in Article 114 and actually concerns redemption before consummation in case the woman wants the separation and the husband does not. Then, there will be, just as in the Palestinian *taʿmīm*, a procedure of arbitration followed by a court judgment. The new term was, as Engelcke argues, a result of a compromise between the Sharia establishment and women's groups.[103] As in the *taʿmīm* in Palestine, women with regard to separation based on "dispute and discord" do not have to prove harm any longer but the decision is left to the judge.[104]

4.3 Analysis of *taʿmīm* 59/2012

In the West Bank, the *taʿmīm* was mainly presented as a result of internal social and legal debates. In the following paragraphs, the *taʿmīm*'s text will be analyzed with regard to the following questions:

1. Why was the reform seen to be necessary and which arguments were in favor or against the reform?
2. Which "uses of the past" were made?
3. Which terminology was used?
4. Why may *khulʿ* against the husband's will be given only before consummation of marriage?
5. What does this "ruling" mean – which relation to "legislation" does it bear?

The underlying questions concern the legal and the gender aspect of the *taʿmīm*: What does the *taʿmīm* mean for the (re)construction of gender relations? Is an approach toward gender equality observable? Does it keep the promise of the Supreme Judge: more rights for women? Or does it reify the existing gender hierarchy? And, with regard to the legal aspect: what are the legal consequences and changes in comparison to the existing regulations of *khulʿ* in the JLPS?

4.3.1 *Explanatory Text of the Dīwān*

On September 1, 2012, ruling Number 59 (*taʿmīm*) was issued by the Sharia Court High Council (SCHC) with regard to what was called the "judicial *khulʿ*"

102 JLPS Article 102. There was a new family status law in 2019 that could not be taken into consideration.

103 Engelcke 2017a: 24; Goudarzi-Gereke 2018: 59.

104 JLPS 2010, Article 126; Engelcke 2017a: 24–25.

(*khulʿ qaḍāʾī*).[105] The same *taʿmīm* also comprised two further legal regulations with regard to the separation due to "dispute and discord" (*tafrīq li-l-nizāʿ wa-l-shiqāq*) as regulated before in the applicable JLPS Article 132 and attendance and hosting (*al-mushāhada wa-l-istiḍāfa*) of minors as regulated in Article 163 of the JLPS.[106]

The full text of the *taʿmīm* is not found in either the Muqtafi database of Birzeit University or on the website of the *Dīwān*.[107] There is only a short explanatory text on the *Dīwān*'s website with regard to the new ruling under the heading "Ruling to Act according to Judicial *Khulʿ*, to See [Children] and With Regard to What Is Publicly Known About Dispute and Discord" (*Taʿmīm al-ʿAmal bi-l-Khulʿ al-Qaḍāʾī wa-l-Mushāhada wa-Shuhrat*[108] *al-Nizāʿ wa-l-Shiqāq*). The short explanatory text can be summarized as follows:

105 Polfus's article "Fiqh Arguments for the Palestinian Khulʿ Divorce (before Consummation)" (2014) refers to the regulation of 2012 and a 2008 draft law, which I could not find; she seems not to have known about the 2010 Draft Law in Palestine. She refers to *khulʿ* as a generic term (Polfus 2014: 55) arguing that there is "no agreement of the literature reviewed for this study" about what constitutes a *khulʿ* (Polfus 2014: 53). Referring to a "generic term" of *khulʿ*, she should have consulted classical *fiqh* and/or relied on the definition of the JLPS but does neither. She invents a terminology that does not exist in the ruling when she speaks of *khulʿ ṭalāq* (Polfus 2014: 57, fn. 18) and *khulʿ tafrīq* (Polfus 2014: 61). In both cases the transliteration is mine, Polfus gives no standard transliteration of the Arabic terms. Her transliteration is inconsistent and strange (*qabel id-dukhul/qabl id-dukhul*; Polfus 2014: 50, 52). Her text contains errors, e.g., when she states "Muslim marriage does not contain an engagement period" (Polfus 2014: 51) and "the fact that the Palestinian khul is limited to the time before consummation of the marriage" (Polfus 2014: 53), which ignores the text of the JLPS and the existence of consensual *khulʿ*.

106 The same changes were also discussed in Jordan. See Engelcke 2017a: 24–25.

107 I received it during a workshop the Supreme Judge gave at Birzeit University in November 2013. See the website of the SCHC: http://www.kudah.pna.ps/ar_page.aspx?id=PS9BpGa2088146082aPS9BpG, accessed on October 2, 2018. Another link is given at the bottom of the page, which, however, leads only to the Supreme Judge's letter, not to the whole *taʿmīm*: http://www.kudah.pna.ps/userfiles/file/%D8%A7%D9%84%D8%AE%D9%84%D8%B9(1).jpg accessed on October 2, 2018. I was not able to find the *taʿmīm* on the SCHC website.

108 The term *shuhra*, "what is publicly known" is a synonym of *ishtihār/intishār*, meaning "to be widespread, common, public." It means in this context that the wife and husband's dispute is public, known. The wife will say that the dispute is known (*intashara*) by everybody around them. The judge then asks the husband. If he agrees, the judge will not ask the wife to bring evidence. But if he does not confirm this, she has to convince him (*tathabbut al-sulṭa al-taqdīriyya*). With regard to this convincing there is a new *taʿmīm* on how to use different tools, e.g., reports from the police etc., which, however, was not at my disposal. I thank Judge Ṣumūd al-Ḍamīrī for this explanation (May 4, 2019).

1. The idea of *khulʿ* is taken from the Islamic Sharia and the aim is the release (*takhlīṣ*) of the woman from the man without (the husband's right) to take her back (*rajʿa*) except with her agreement and with a new contract.
2. The law ([sic] *qānūn*) gives a woman who has entered the marriage contract the choice of dissolution (*faskh*) of her contract if there is no mutual understanding with the partner during the time between the contract agreement and "consummation in the situation of privacy."
3. The law stipulates the necessity to look into each claim of *khulʿ* presented to the court and to strive for priority of a solution based on mutual consent before referring to the judicial *khulʿ* when otherwise no solution is possible.
4. The issuing of the law (*iqrār al-qānūn*) came because of the spread of the phenomenon of young men blackmailing young women who wanted a dissolution of the marriage contract before legal privacy. And it came as a result of an existing injustice against young women who were oppressed and exploited.
5. Claims of "dispute and discord" in the two past decades remained stuck in the Sharia courts for years without the judge having the chance to substantiate these cases.

The short text on the website of the SCHC, obviously designed to inform interested persons who quickly want to check on the content of the new ruling, already answers some of the questions above. The reform was justified to give women "release" (*takhlīṣ*) (1); because young women were "blackmailed" (4); because there was an injustice done to them (4); and because cases of "dispute and discord"-divorce remained stuck in the Sharia courts, sometimes for years (5). There is a general reference to the classical law, because *khulʿ* is "taken from the Islamic Sharia" (1), but this "use of the past" is not spelled out in detail in this text, but – as will be outlined below – in the text of the *taʿmīm* itself. The advantage of this kind of *khulʿ* is seen not only in "release" but also in the non-application of *rajʿa* (1). *Rajʿa*, the husband's prerogative to take back his wife after first and second repudiation, is normally connected to repudiation (*ṭalāq*) but is no legal concequence of *khulʿ*.[109] *Rajʿa* is one of the most gender unequal regulations in Islamic law, preserved in the personal status codes, which over the course of the waiting period (*ʿidda*) leaves the woman completely dependent on the husband's good will. He can decide to take her back

109 Only in JLPS Article 107 it is stated: "In case the parties to the Mukhala'ah declare a denial of the compensation, the Mukhala'ah shall be as good as a mere divorce and a pronouncement of recoverable divorce [*ṭalqatan rajʿiyyatan*] shall take effect with it."

or not. Only he can decide whether, how, and when he will do this – through words or deeds.[110] The fact that *khulʿ* comes without *rajʿa* is made even more prominent in the phrase following "except with her consent" (1). Thus, great emphasis is placed in this short text upon woman's consent, action, and power to initiate or decide.

Legally interesting and new is paragraph 2 because it gives a legal regulation to the special time after the signature of the contract, but before consummation and privacy, which had not been regulated specifically in the laws before. According to law, both – marriage contract and consummation – happen at roughly the same time. The *taʿmīm* is self-evidently called a "law" (2, 3, 4).

The keyword and title of this short text is *khulʿ qaḍāʾī* meaning "judicial *khulʿ*." This nomenclature distinguishes this kind of separation from repudiation (*ṭalāq*) and *khulʿ* in JLPS that are private actions of the husband or husband and wife in the case of *khulʿ*, which only need to be registered ex post facto.

4.3.2 *The Taʿmīm*[111]

Under the heading of the "State of Palestine" (*Dawlat Filasṭīniyya*), the first page contains a letter signed by the *Qāḍī al-Quḍāt*, Yūsuf Idʿīs, to Sharia judges. It informs the judges and advises them to implement this ruling.[112] In this letter, it is stated that based on the meeting of the SCHC (*al-Majlis al-Aʿlā li-l-Qaḍāʾ al-Sharʿī*) and the Sharia High Court (*Hayʾat al-Maḥkam al-ʿUlyā al-Sharʿiyya*) and the two Appellate Courts (*Hayʾatay Maḥkamat al-Istiʾnāf al-Sharʿiyya*) of Jerusalem and Nablus on August 27, 2012, and the Periodic Meeting of the Sharia judges at the seat of the *Dīwān* of the Supreme Judge on August 30, 2012, in Ramallah, the judges have to apply the judicial *khulʿ* from September 1, 2012, onward, together with the other rulings with regard to separation due to "dispute and discord" and attendance and hosting minors.[113]

The second and third pages, which are not to be found on the website refer to the rulings of separation and hosting. With regard to separation due to "dispute and discord," the relevant Article 132 of the JLPS is quoted and it is explained that marital strife damages the wife as well as the children. The Hanafi school of law cannot heal this whereas the Maliki school of law allows the woman to petition for separation, a right given to her in Ottoman family law. However,

---

110 See JLPS Article 93.

111 What follows is a summary with some quotations.

112 This is the document to be found on the website: http://www.kudah.pna.ps/userfiles/file/%D8%A7%D9%84%D8%AE%D9%84%D8%B9(1).jpg, accessed on December 17, 2018.

113 *Taʿmīm* 59/2012: 1.

as the partners, according to Article 132, have to prove this damage, and as it is difficult to prove marital strife that normally takes place in the privacy of the home, it was decided in this ruling to leave sufficient space for the conviction (*qināʿa*) of the judge and to give him discretion (*al-sulṭa al-taqdīriyya*) to help women get divorced. Page three, dealing with attendance and hosting of children, has no direct relevance to the *khulʿ* ruling.[114]

From page four to the end,[115] the new ruling is explained under the title "judicial *khulʿ*." The explanation of this ruling is obviously longer than the explanation of the other two rulings, encompassing more than three and a half pages.[116] In addition, it contains the request for the separation of *khulʿ* before consummation,[117] proceedings of the claim,[118] jurisdictional principles to be followed before a judgment of separation according to *khulʿ* can be given,[119] and a form for the wife to complete.[120]

It is argued[121] that there is no disagreement among Muslim scholars about the legality of *khulʿ*. *Khulʿ* is known in the Quran (Quran 2:229 is quoted) and in the Sunna of the Prophet as well as in consensus (*ijmāʿ*) and reason (*maʿqūl*). The tradition of Thābit b. Qays's wife in the version of Bukhārī is given as evidence, according to which she hates unbelief (*kufr*) in Islam, wanting divorce even if her husband is a man of "good character and religion." According to this version, the wife agreed to return the garden to her husband Thābit and the Prophet ordered Thābit to take it and divorce her (*wa-ṭalliqhā taṭlīqat*). The scholars all agree that the fear of both the husband and the wife to keep God's limits (*ḥudūd Allāh*) is important, and as a necessity, there has to be an aversion toward the husband (*karāhiyya shadīda li-l-zawj*). It is as if she would think badly of the companionship of her husband. Or, in case of discord (*shiqāq*), that she has an aversion to him because of his bad character and religion; or that she is harmed by the breach of some of his rights. It is rational (*maʿqūl*), the *taʿmīm* argues, that *ṭalāq* is in principle (*fī al-aṣl*) in the man's hand. A woman can be released from her husband on several grounds, but she

114 *Taʿmīm* 59/2012: 2–3

115 *Taʿmīm* 59/2012: 4–10. The pages were not numbered, so the pagination is mine.

116 *Taʿmīm* 59/2012: 4–7.

117 *Taʿmīm* 59/2012: 7–8.

118 *Taʿmīm* 59/2012: 8–9.

119 *Taʿmīm* 59/2012: 9. The Law of the Procedure for Sharia Courts 31/1959 Article 3 (4) is cited here as the legal text, from which the local competence (*al-ṣalāḥiyya al-makāniyya*) of the court is deduced.

120 *Taʿmīm* 59/2012: 10.

121 *Taʿmīm* 59/2012: 4.

does not have the right to *ṭalāq*. She can offer him a sum of money so that she gets her freedom (*ḥurriyyat*) from the marriage bond (*qayd al-nikāḥ*).

Islam has made *ṭalāq* the exclusive right of the man, the ruling argues,[122] which he can apply at any time. Islam gave the woman the right to *khulʿ* so that she can protect herself from the damage of intimacy with her husband (*ḍarar al-muʿāshara*). This being her right, the text goes on, is founded on the mere fact that she is a party to the marital contract. Basically, there is a difference between two kinds of *khulʿ*: the first kind is based on mutual consent (*khulʿ riḍāʾī*) and the second, judiciary *khulʿ* (*khulʿ qaḍāʾī*), was the subject of severe discussions.

Then the *taʿmīm* refers to the Maliki school of law;[123] the Malikis do allow divorce of the couple based on *khulʿ* even without consent of the wife. According to Mālik two arbiters are responsible to find out whether or not reconciliation (*ṣulḥ*) of the couple is possible. If not, both arbiters separate them. The *taʿmīm* concludes from this that the Maliki school of law allows that only after two arbiters have tried reconciliation and failed, *khulʿ* may be granted, the judge "confirms what the arbiters have decided upon even if it is *khulʿ*."[124]

Some modern scholars argued that *khulʿ* without the husband's consent is possible and this argument is well founded because it takes into account that the woman, after stressing that she cannot stay with the husband and she has an aversion (*karāha*) to continue marital life with him, redeems herself. The justifications for this opinion are:

1. That judicial *khulʿ* without the husband's agreement shapes the similarity of rights and duties of man and woman (*yujassid al-mumāthala fī al-ḥuqūq wa-l-wājibāt bayna al-rajul wa-l-marʾa*) and is implied by the Quran (2:228): "Women have such honourable rights as obligations."[125] *Ṭalāq* is binding (*mulzam*) for the man and the woman alike. The woman's opinion is not heard. And so *khulʿ* does not rest on the agreement (*riḍā*) of the husband and he does not have to give the *ṭalāq* after he took the compensation (*badal*).

122 *Taʿmīm* 59/2012: 5.

123 See Reiter 2009: 17, referring to Article 130 of the OFRL of 1917 according to which in the case of "dispute and discord," the judge has to nominate the arbiters and decide based on their opinion. Reiter argues that this article is based on the approach of Maliki scholars. See also chapter 9 with regard to the EFRL.

124 Interestingly, the text makes a shift from the two arbiters separating the couple to the judge confirming "what the arbiters have decided upon." It is in accordance with OFRL Article 130, see previous footnote.

125 The verse goes on: "but their men have a degree above them", see Quran.

2. Quran 2:229[126] proves that the husband may not retain (*imsāk*) her with the aim of damaging her: "then honourable retention or setting free kindly."[127]
3. When *khulʿ* consists in the basis of agreement of the husband and with his divorce (*taṭlīq*) then his authority ends thereof as a solution of the crises of the marriage.
4. The opinion is not correct that the woman should be incapable of exerting her right to *khulʿ* by virtue of her human capability. Therefore, her right was added to the husband's right because he is [generally] more powerful to exert it. Otherwise, it would be a challenge to her power to limit any harm done to her and to her right to express this harm. The question could arise about the value of being asked for her opinion when concluding the marriage and the condition of her consent.

In what follows, "judicial *khulʿ*" is defined as *khulʿ* before consummation or privacy, and it is defined as a lawsuit the woman files against her husband in case she disgusts him (*baghiḍathu*), has an aversion to him (*karihathu*), or is afraid that she is incapable of keeping God's limits and staying in the marriage. She returns what she or her guardian has taken, i.e., the dower given during the contract-making, what the husband had paid at the expenses of the dower (*mā dafaʿa ʿalā ḥisāb al-mahr*), the presents still existing she took, and what the husband provided for the marriage (*mā anfaqa al-zawj min ajl al-zawāj*).

Therefore, according to what the *taʿmīm* labels "law" (*qānūnan*), the separation (*tafrīq*)[128] by *khulʿ* is stipulated in the cases of aversion (*karāha*) and when the woman is afraid not to be able to keep God's limits, that she redeems herself (*an taftadiya*) with the dower and with what he paid, and the presents, when they still exist after the two arbiters were not able to reconcile the spouses.

The court only rules, this is again made explicit, after the arbiters have spoken and after there was an attempt to reconcile in a time not exceeding three months. The court rules[129] about the dissolution (*faskh*) of the contract of the spouses after ensuring the return of the payment of dower, and maintenance the wife had received. If the spouses disagree with regard to what the husband had spent and the presents, the arbiters have to deal with this.

---

126 *Taʿmīm* 59/2012: 6.

127 See Quran.

128 In my text of the ruling *tafrīq* (separation) is crossed out and replaced by "through dissolution of the contract" (*bi-faskh al-ʿaqd*) in handwriting.

129 *Taʿmīm* 59/2012: 7.

There is disagreement between the scholars whether it is a separation by dissolution (*faskh*) or repudiation (*ṭalāq*). Whereas the majority considers it a *ṭalāq*, in the *taʿmīm* the opinions of Ibn Taymiyya (d.1328) and Ibn Qayyim (d. 1350) are followed. According to them it is dissolution and no repudiation. The proof is that the Prophet ordered the woman to observe the *ʿidda* (waiting period) for one menstruation cycle only. Al-Khiṭābī says that this is the strongest proof, because if it were repudiation, it would not be only one menstruation cycle. Furthermore, God said in the Quran (2:229):

> Divorce is twice; then honourable retention or setting free kindly. It is not lawful for you to take of what you have given them unless the couple fear they may not maintain God's bounds; if you fear they may not maintain God's bounds, it is no fault in them for her to redeem herself. Those are God's bounds; do not transgress them. Whosoever transgresses the bounds of God – those are the evildoers.[130]

It goes on in Quran 2:230:

> If he divorces her finally, she shall not be lawful to him after that, until she marries another husband. If he divorces her, then it is no fault in them to return to each other, if they suppose that they will maintain God's bounds. Those are God's bounds; He makes them clear unto a people that have knowledge.[131]

God explains that divorce is twice and then mentions redemption. Then God mentions (2:230) that when the husband repudiates her she "shall not be lawful to him after that, until she marries another husband." The argument adopted in the *taʿmīm*'s text is as follows: if the redemption (*al-iftidāʾ*) were *ṭalāq*, then the *ṭalāq* that makes her lawful to him and which is only after her marriage to another husband, would be the fourth *ṭalāq*. But from the Quranic text – "divorce is twice" – it becomes obvious that the *ṭalāq* is finished after the third pronounciation. This confirms that *khulʿ* is not identical with *ṭalāq*. Reference for this argument is made to Ibn ʿAbbās (d. 688), an important, early traditionist.

130 The whole verse is not quoted in the text; only parts of it are included to make the argument, see Quran.

131 See Quran.

The regulation of claim with regard to *khulʿ* separation before consummation (*lāʾiḥat daʿwā tafrīq li-l-khulʿ qabla al-dukhūl*) follows,[132] describing the proceedures (*ijrāʾāt*):

1. the claim of the plaintiff and statement that she did not have marital sex or privacy; the number and date of her marriage contract;
2. the plaintiff's date of birth;
3. the amount and version of the dower (prompt/deferred);
4. the plaintiff's statement that she cannot continue conjugal life with her husband and is afraid not to keep God's limits;
5. that she is ready to return dower etc.;
6. that the husband did not accept *khulʿ* on the basis of mutual consent;
7. the claim itself.

The steps taken by the court are: invitation of the court, presence of the two parties, questioning the plaintiff, and so forth. The required stages before the court can give the judgment of separation, especially the reconciliation process, are regulated. The complaint of *khulʿ* is said to be different from the complaint of separation based on "dispute and discord," because the wife does not have to speak of her harm; she has only to state that there is disgust, and that she is afraid not to keep the limits of God. The court cannot proceed with the complaint of *khulʿ* without the clearance of the Office of Control and Family Reconciliation (*Dāʾirat al-Irshād wa-l-Iṣlāḥ al-Usari*), which lays out the impossibility of a mutual agreement on *khulʿ*. At the end of the file there is a form[133] that the woman who wants to file a *khulʿ* suit has to fill in.

4.3.3 *Analysis*

In the text of the *taʿmīm*, the JLPS and its already existing regulation of *khulʿ* based on mutual consent is not even mentioned.[134] The text is a purely Islamic legal justification of *khulʿ*, its two versions, the new judicial one and the old one based on consent, as if no legislation existed and as if this ruling, about to be applied at the Sharia courts, would not in fact amend or at least considerably broaden the existing law. Not only is the existing law not mentioned, but at one point the ruling itself is called a "law," in Arabic *qānūn*. After defining the judicial *khulʿ* as a *khulʿ* before privacy and first marital intercourse, it is stated: "Therefore according to law (*qānūnan*) the separation (*tafrīq*) by *khulʿ* can be provided for." General legislative processes in Palestine are also

132 *Taʿmīm* 59/2012: 7–8.

133 *Taʿmīm* 59/2012: 10.

134 This is not the case in the rulings regarding *nizāʿ wa-shiqāq* and "hosting," the other two topics of the *taʿmīm*. In both rulings the relating articles of the JLPS are mentioned.

not mentioned in the *taʿmīm*. Whereas presidential decrees always contain a conditional clause, stating that this decree will be submitted to the Palestinian Legislative Council (PLC) in its first session – meaning after the reopening of the parliament – such a formulation and procedure is obviously not foreseen here.

Many arguments presented in the *taʿmīm* are similar to those in the debates in Egypt and Jordan.[135] "Uses of the past" dominate the discourse. *Khulʿ* is constructed as a religious right anchored in the Quran and Sunna, the new version of judicial *khulʿ* is "well-founded" in Islamic legal thinking. However, as in Egypt there is no intensive analysis of the *ḥadīth* and its variations. The cited *ḥadīth* is the version in Bukhārī. Other variants are not mentioned or referred to.[136] There is no analysis of the *isnād*, i.e., the chain of transmitters having passed this *ḥadīth* from one generation of transmitters to the next. There is also no analysis of the content of the *ḥadīth*, nor of its variants, which, as Denker had shown convincingly, could have served as starting point for a new interpretation with regard to the main question, i.e., whether the husband's consent is necessary or not.[137] On the contrary, the SCHC seems to shy away from a deep and detailed hermeneutical analysis that would lead to a new interpretation of the *ḥadīth*. There is no claim of and no indication for *ijtihād* (independent legal opinion) in the sense of "making effort" or "reasoning to develop a new legal opinion."[138]

Just as there is no reference to the applicable law in general, there is also no reference to Article 183 of JLPS, which would make reference to the Hanafi school of jurisprudence necessary in regard to what is not mentioned in the JLPS. Instead, reference is made to the Maliki school of law. Scholars quoted are Mālik (d. 795) with regard to *khulʿ* and his school and the procedure as well as the Hanbalis Ibn Taimiyya (d. 1328) and Ibn Qayyim (al-Jawziyya) (d. 1350) with regard to the question, whether this kind of *khulʿ* should be categorized as *ṭalāq* or simply as a dissolution of the marriage (*faskh*). The reason that *khulʿ* cannot be *ṭalāq* but must be *faskh* is that otherwise the Quran would have mentioned four instead of three *ṭalāqs*. Thus, the ruling defines the judicial *khulʿ* as dissolution (*faskh*).

The reference to the Malikis[139] concerns the general permissibility of *khulʿ* and the role of the arbiters, which is very wide in Maliki law as they can

135 Denker 2004; Engelcke 2017a.

136 *Taʿmīm* 59/2012:4.

137 Denker 2004: 176.

138 But it was often categorized as an *ijtihād*, e.g., by the Gaza judge Ḥasan al-Jūjū (*Lāzim Naḥkī* 2013) and Hasan al-ʿŪrī, interview on October 13, 2014.

139 *Taʿmīm* 59/2012: 5; see Reiter 2009: 17.

separate the couple. Since Palestine is a Hanafi country, this might be based on earlier discussions of Article 130 of the OFRL of 1917, which dealt with "dispute and discord" and only marginally included *khulʿ*. But Article 130 of the OFRL is not mentioned in the *taʿmīm*'s text. The reference to the Maliki school, too, is not central for the argument because according to the Maliki school, the arbiters could separate the couple but according to the *taʿmīm* it is the court and the judge's obligation to separate the couple.[140]

In contrast to these arguments, all "uses of the past," another line of argumentation that could have led to the conceptualization of "gender equality" is the statement that judicial *khulʿ* without the husband's agreement shapes the "similarity" of rights and duties of man and woman.[141] This terminology is interesting and central. Judicial *khulʿ* is considered a woman's right – obviously seen to be "similar" to the male's right to *ṭalāq* and rooted in what is referred to as the "basis of her human capability." Thus, *ṭalāq* and *khulʿ* are constructed as counterterms with a gendered meaning. The authors of the *taʿmīm* stressed that freedom and voluntariness of the woman to enter into marriage would not be respected if she would not also have the right to *khulʿ*, to end the marriage. This "similarity" of rights is labeled *mumāthala* – and not *musāwāh*, which would have been the term for gender equality in the Arabic version of CEDAW.[142] *Mumāthala* is taken from Quran 2:228.[143] It is this "similarity" that establishes a woman's right to *khulʿ* as a counterweight to men's *ṭalāq*. *Mumāthala* can thus be regarded as the religious counterterm to *musāwāh* in CEDAW.[144] The fact that it is mentioned in the *taʿmīm* is important and could have served as a starting point to "translate" international law into the national framework of Islamic law, taking the case of *khulʿ* as a starting point. But this seems not to have been the intention because, first, the text of the *taʿmīm* is, as stated above, not accessible to the public, only a short summary is available that does not refer to the term "similarity." Furthermore, it was not mentioned in the Draft Law of 2013.[145] Third, in the Communiqué (November 2, 2013)[146] of the study day, the Sharia establishment rejected the concept of what they called "absolute equality" (*musāwāh muṭlaqa*), which they labeled an "unjust claim." Instead of defining an Islamic version of gender equality, i.e., *mumāthala*, they

140 See Reiter 2009: 17.

141 *Taʿmīm* 59/2012: 5.

142 See the Arabic version as one of the official versions: http://www.un.org/womenwatch/daw/cedaw/cedaw.htm, accessed October 12, 2018, see esp. Articles 2 (a) and 16 (1).

143 *Taʿmīm* 59/2012: 5.

144 See the use of this term in the Gaza draft law of *khulʿ*, which is very different, chapter 9.

145 See chapter 2.

146 See chapter 2.2.2.

returned to what they called "Islamic justice" deeply rooted in the traditional "money-obedience relation."

The reason the right to *khulʿ* is given to a woman only before consummation is not discussed in the *taʿmīm*, only in the short text on the website is the social problem referred to.

The keyword "judicial *khulʿ*" is, on the other hand, often used to distinguish it from *khulʿ* based on mutual consent and thus becomes well established. This is, according to Reinhart Koselleck's definition, a composed term and therefore a further development of a generic term. Adding a specifying attribute is a well-known strategy in history of *Begriffsgeschichte*. In a penultimate stage, the semantic development of a term that has gone through a long development and before it "collapses," becomes overloaded to the extent that in order to remain functional and meaningful as a generic term at all, it has to be followed by specifying attributes. When the language community gets annoyed with attaching attributes to the term in order to allow for terminological precision and diversity, the next and "final" state, that of "terminological consolidation," will be reached.[147] Whereas *khulʿ* in the JLPS is *khulʿ* and *mukhālaʿa*, now *khulʿ* is defined as "judicial' *khulʿ*" and the "classical" *khulʿ* in the JLPS becomes *al-khulʿ al-riḍāʾī* (*khulʿ* based on mutual consent). Only the first type of *khulʿ*, the judicial one, is dealt with in the ruling, whereas this last type is merely mentioned. A next step would be to rename it. This happened and it became *iftidāʾ* later in the 2013 Draft of the Supreme Judge.

All these references are to classical Islamic jurisprudence but not to modern debates on *khulʿ*, neither to Jordan nor to Egypt, even when it is obvious that Jordan went through a parallel discussion and had a parallel legislative process, including the reform of "dispute and discord" and regulating that the woman did not have to provide proof of harm, rather the judge had to verify her claim; furthermore, the 2010 Law also renamed judicial *khulʿ iftidāʾ*.[148] The reader of this ruling gets the impression of a completely independent legal process with the result of a new form of *khulʿ*.

Turid Smith Polfus argued that the ruling (which she called a "decree") is not for women as citizens but for women as *homo religiosus*.[149] This is true insofar as the arguments are kept completely on the level of Islamic jurisprudence. However, the classical as well as the modern laws have never been regarded as

147 See Guth 2011: 155.

148 It was mentioned in Article 104 of the Draft Law of 2013 as a separation before consummation of marriage and JLPS of 2010 Article 114. See Engelcke 2017a: 22–26, see especially 24, 25.

149 Polfus 2014: 49, 76; she uses the term like this in the Latin masculine form.

completely "religious laws," which Baber Johansen has convincingly shown,[150] but they always integrated profane aspects. And, second, the ruling was sent to the Sharia court judges and is applied by them. The Sharia courts belong to the state court system of the State of Palestine. Every Muslim citizen has to use this court system in family law matters, Christians may use it. Therefore, even if the argument is based purely on Islamic jurisprudence, the ruling became, in fact, part of state legislation and therefore applicable to women as citizens.

4.3.4 *What Are the Legal Consequences of This Ruling and What Does It Mean for the (Re)construction of Gender Relations?*

On the legal basis, *khulʿ* becomes "judicial *khulʿ*," a dissolution (*faskh*), and therefore, a new category of separation that belongs to judicial divorces is created. With the application of this *taʿmīm* in the Sharia court the law has been factually amended in different points:

- classical *khulʿ* – which was always considered *ṭalāq* – receives a new interpretation, allowing women redemption, but only before privacy and consummation; it is now judicial separation;
- the clearly drawn line between engagement and marriage as anchored in JLPS is abolished and the distinction between engagement and marriage becomes blurred;
- a new ratio is introduced, according to which women have a right to *khulʿ* as a counterbalance to the man's prerogative of *ṭalāq*; giving her this right is not called "equality," which would fit into the terminology of international law, but "similarity"; gender equality is not an objective of this regulation;
- women gain easier and quicker access to divorce together with the new ruling of the separation based on "dispute and discord" (*nizāʿ wa-shiqāq*) without the burden of proof, again as counterbalance to the husband's right to *ṭalāq*;
- gender hierarchy is, however, not endangered because the woman does not control access to divorce as a man does who can pronounce *ṭalāq* wherever and whenever he wants, instead control is in the hands of the judge who takes the finding of the arbiters into account.

As outlined above, according to Article 14 of the JLPS, marriage shall be concluded with an offer and acceptance of the suitors or their representatives, it is not concluded by betrothal, recitation of the Surat al-Fātiḥa, etc. as stated in Article 3 of the JLPS. Consummation and privacy (*khalwa*) are not mentioned here or in other articles as a constitutive condition of marriage. A void (*bāṭil*) marriage (according to Article 41), regardless of consummation does not

150 See Johansen 1999.

denote a legal status in itself. An irregular marriage (*fāsid*) without consummation also has no status in itself, according to Article 42, but if consummation has occurred the dower and the waiting period are incumbent in case of divorce. Thus, these different forms of incomplete marriages exist, but are not explicitly connected to consummation. If repudiation (*ṭalāq*) occurs before valid consummation of marriage, half of the defined dower is incumbent.[151] This points to the fact that consummation matters financially. But how does it matter? In the event separation occurs upon a request from the wife because of a deficiency or ailment in the husband, or the guardian's request of separation because of unfitness, and such was prior to sexual intercourse and valid consummation of marriage, the whole of the dower shall abate.[152] In case the contract was dissolved (*fusikha*) prior to sexual intercourse and consummation of marriage, the husband shall be entitled to recover the dower he paid.[153] The reason may be that it is the woman's wish to get this separation. This is corroborated in the next article: if the husband wants the separation (*ṭalāq* or other form), he owes the woman half of the dower.[154] Again the person wanting the separation has to renounce financial rights. This is also the rationale of *khulʿ*: the wife wants the separation and pays him back the dower. It is evident that consummation has financial consequences in the case of divorce and in combination with either the husband's or the wife's wish. Generally, the woman has the right to deny the husband access to her body before she has received the dower.[155] This right lapses with the consummation. Does it mean that with the new *taʿmīm* the woman's right to divorce (against the husband's wish) is also forfeited with consummation?[156]

In drawing the line for judicial *khulʿ* at the consummation of the marriage and especially in connecting the first sexual act to the woman's wish to get a divorce and the husband's refusal to repudiate her, the *taʿmīm* contradicts the JLPS according to which only offer and acceptance conclude a marriage[157] and

151 JLPS Article 48.
152 JLPS Article 49.
153 JLPS Article 50.
154 JLPS Article 51.
155 Yassari 2014: 39–41; Schneider 2016b: 66–68.
156 Yassari 2014: 39–41, see also 48–49, 52–53. Yassari has dealt extensively with the question if the Islamic marriage contract is a sale; it is surely, she is correct, not a simple sale. However, it has certain features that come very close to a sale, for example, the woman's right to decline access to her body before she receives the dower. This "sale" is, of course, between the husband and her and not between the husband and her father; see Schneider 2016b: 66–69.
157 JLPS Article 14.

engagement is non-binding.[158] The Palestinian custom that combines engagement with the signing of the marriage contract provided the occasion for the new regulation. Custom thus became de facto legislation. The *taʿmīm* does not abolish, but reaffirms this traditionally defined space of "engagement-cum-marriage." It gives women in this situation the right to get a *khul*ʿ divorce against the husband's wishes. But there is no rationality for this: even if it is argued – an argument which came up very often – that women are emotional and quick to abuse this right, there is no reason why this should be different before or after first intercourse in the marriage. The often-cited argument, divorce with children is much more difficult, might have more substance. But it can only make sense if one automatically equates having intercourse with pregnancy and having children.[159] Besides, nowhere in Islamic law does the fact of having offspring influence the right of divorce for women and, of course, also for men. Only the inability to conceive a child, i.e., infertility, could be a reason for a man to grant a divorce to a woman and for a woman to apply for separation from her husband.

An existing custom was legitimized and an absurd construction was transformed into a ruling, and is now even called a "law." One might argue that the ruling came about as a solution for women in a difficult situation created by the traditional, still patriarchal Palestinian society. Because families did not want their daughters to go out with their fiancés, afraid "something" (i.e., sex and pregnancy) would happen, young women were forced to sign the contract at the engagement party. They then became trapped, whereas their partners had no problem getting engaged again and even marrying a second, third, and fourth wife.

This situation was not new. Welchman stated that in the 1990s, 90 percent of marriages that were terminated were ended by *ṭalāq* (repudiation) or *khul*ʿ[160] and 25 percent of all divorces happened before consummation.[161] She explained the rate of divorce before consummation with the "engagement" period, which lasted for a long time and obviously gave the couple a chance to see that they did not want to stay together. In case *ṭalāq* happened before consummation, the woman would receive half the dower (or hand back one half) whereas in case of *khul*ʿ, she renounces the dower that is due. For the men, to give *ṭalāq* would be more disadvantageous compared to being separated by *khul*ʿ. In Nablus, Annelies Moors tracked a rise in the proportion of

158 JLPS Article 3.

159 The absence of modern devices like contraceptives in such debates is striking.

160 Welchman 1999: 135.

161 Welchman 1999: 151.

*khul*ʿ divorces before consummation from 17 percent in the Jordanian period to 38 percent in 1976 and up to 54 percent in the mid-1980s. She identified this as a mainly urban phenomenon partly attributable to longer engagement periods and increased contact between the couple in the city areas. If nothing else, she argued, these proportions suggested that in the case of divorce before consummation the general feeling in society as reflected in the records of divorces is that the couples have not really established mutual rights and duties toward each other.[162]

In the end, women did not gain much: the decision is still not in their hands because the judge decides after an arbitration procedure. They still have to sign a paper that "nothing happened," i.e., no privacy (*khalwa*) and no penetration, allowing the court to control their bodies and their sexuality. The Palestinian tradition requiring the couple to sign a contract at the time of the engagement is confirmed and legitimized. Since the introduction of the *taʿmīm* in 2012, the importance of "consummation" – the couple's first sexual intercourse – in public awareness is increased, though it is not mentioned in the JLPS. There is sustained pressure on the couple to "behave" even with a contract until the official "night of penetration" (*laylat al-dukhla*). All in all it is the female not the male body that is under increased legal and social control.

On August 30, 2012, the Supreme Judge held a press conference in Ramallah with other judges from the court sitting in attendance. He announced the changes introduced by the *taʿmīm*. Limiting the financial consideration in *khul*ʿ to the dower, Judge Idʿīs criticized men for often asking too much, saying: "These women are investment projects for men, open to extortion at any time."[163] A few months after the new *khul*ʿ ruling was issued, a headline in *Gulf News*, a newspaper published in the United Arab Emirates complained that the divorce rate in Palestine was very high, half of the marriages in the West Bank were said to have been broken up before the wedding night. This was attributed to the new ruling. In the same article, Yūsuf Idʿīs is quoted as saying the divorce rate in the West Bank is the "lowest in recent history."[164]

For 2017, the Central Bureau of Statistics gave the following information for Palestine including Gaza: 47,218 marriages were registered in 2017[165] and 8,568 divorces, i.e., roughly one-sixth of the marriages. 3,863 divorces took place before consummation and 3,599 after consummation.[166] Thus, slightly more

162 Moors 1995: 145 and 145, fn. 24.

163 Johnson and Hammami 2013: 17.

164 Johnson and Hammami 2013: 39.

165 See http://www.pcbs.gov.ps/Portals/_Rainbow/Documents/VS-2017-04e.htm, accessed October 18, 2018.

166 See http://www.pcbs.gov.ps/Portals/_Rainbow/Documents/VS-2016-11e.htm, accessed October 18, 2018. The file "Crude Divorce Rate in Palestine by Governorate 1997–2017"

marriages ended before consummation than after consummation, whereas 1,106 divorces were revocable divorces.[167]

TABLE 4.1 Registered divorces [*sic*] cases in Palestine by type and governorate, 2017

Governorate	Type of divorce			
	Divorce before consummation of marriage	**Divorce after consummation of marriage (Al-Ba'in)**	**Revocable divorce**	**Total**
Palestine	3.863	3.599	1.106	8.568
West Bank	2.499	2.287	540	5.326
Jenin	379	234	75	688
Tubas and Northern Valleys	84	26	19	129
Tulkarm	230	190	42	462
Nablus	457	285	115	857
Qalqiliya	126	99	24	249
Salfit	98	55	19	172
Ramallah & Al-Bireh	231	426	73	730
Jericho & Al Aghwar	2	98	7	107
Jerusalem	283	327	25	635
Bethlehem	75	135	44	254
Hebron	534	412	97	1.043
Gaza Strip	1.364	1.312	566	3.242
North Gaza	300	204	97	601
Gaza	501	483	216	1.200
Deir Al-Balah	187	191	70	488
Khan Yunis	210	273	97	580
Rafah	166	161	86	413

shows a slight increase in the number (of all) divorces, see http://www.pcbs.gov.ps/Portals/_Rainbow/Documents/VS-2017-07e.htm, accessed on November 23, 2018.

167 See Palestinian Central Bureau of Statistics, http://www.pcbs.gov.ps/Portals/_Rainbow/Documents/VS-2017-09e.htm, accessed May 2, 2019.

4.4 The *Qāḍī al-Quḍāt* as a Quasi-Legislator?

The critical positions of Judge Ḥasan al-Jūjū in Gaza and the Legal Advisor of the President, Ḥasan al-ʿŪrī with regard to the *taʿmīm* will be dealt with in detail. Al-ʿŪrī criticized it as a secular jurist of constitutional law and al-Jūjū as a Muslim scholar, but both demanded that such a ruling pass through legislative channels.

Another high-ranking religious voice was that of the former Supreme Judge, Taysīr al-Tamīmī.[168] He adopted a critical stance on a range of different issues. Calling the *taʿmīm* an abuse of Sharia and the law, and an oppression of legislative power, he argued that the rule of law and independence of the judiciary are important values, that according to Article 47 of the BL the PLC is the legislative body and according to Article 63 the cabinet is the executive power, and that according to Article 97 the judicial power is independent. There are several forms of laws, first the BL, then a decree (*al-qarār bi-qūwat al-qānūn*) of the president, who is able to issue decrees in cases of necessity, such as when there are no parliamentary sessions. Furthermore, he may issue a presidential ordinance (*al-marsūm al-raʾīsī*) in restricted cases seen as a threat to the security of the Palestinian people. According to the Law of the Formation of the Sharia Courts of 19/1972, applicable in Palestine, there is a text about the formation of the SCHC, but no reference to legislation and lawmaking of this institution. The same is true for the presidential decree that established SCHC. Al-Tamīmī added that *ijtihād* of judges and their interpretation of the legal texts are not binding for any judge.[169] The former Supreme Judge then asked if the new law, calling it a "law" (*qānūn*) or sometimes an "alleged law" (*al-qānūn al-mazʿūm*), would allow a woman divorced in this way to be "permitted" to the new husband referring to the classical Islamic definition of marriage?[170] He also asked how the different courts, e.g., the Sharia Court of Appeal and

---

168 Tamīmī (September 6, 2012).

169 Article 150 of the Law of the Procedure for Sharia Courts 31/1959 provides that where there are contrasting Appeal Court rulings on the matters in question, or where it seems appropriate to issue a judgment contrary to all previous judgments, the court considering the case shall be a panel of five rather than the usual three judges. The judicial exercise of *ijtihād* in Jordan is thus carefully regulated, as Welchman outlined (2000: 35).

170 According to Islamic classical law and also to JLPS Article 2, marriage is a contract between a man and a woman "who is legally permisssible to him" (*imrāʾa taḥillu lahu sharʿan*). Thus, the objective of al-Tamīmī's argument is that in case the divorce would not be legal because it goes against the BL, the woman would still be married and would not be permissible to the new husband. According to classical Islamic law, she would be committing *zināʾ*, illegitimate sexual intercourse, punishable by stoning. Even if these punishments are not included any longer in the applicable Jordanian Penal Law, this

the Sharia High Court, would deal with this ruling. How would the Supreme Constitutional Court (SCC) decide, if it was approached in the matter? Is it allowed to decide on the constitutionality of a piece of legislation issued by a body that is not responsible for legislation? He pointed to the JLPS and argued that no change of the legal regulation in Articles 102–112 is necessary – thereby ignoring the legal and social question at the bottom of the whole case and the fact, that the legal regulation comprises *khulʿ* based on mutual agreement only – and finally, he criticized the "law" for ignoring Article 183 of the JLPS, which would, if at all, have only permitted Idʿīs to go to the preferable (*rājiḥ*) opinion of the Hanafis and nothing else.[171]

What procedure was taken to enact this *taʿmīm*? In an interview per email, I asked Asem Khalil, Professor of Constitutional and International Law at Birzeit University, whether a *taʿmīm* can be accepted as "law." He wrote: "There is no way to explain the introduction of new rule of law by ta'mim based on civil law legal culture, as the court, and Qadi Qudat has no legislative power."[172] In his opinion, the reason for this could perhaps be found in common law tradition.

Whereas normally the introduction of the judicial *khulʿ* was connected in the public perception to a social custom – young women signing the marriage contract with the engagement and then being trapped – the media reported the special case of a former political prisoner, Kifāḥ Kayyāl, who had been set free and lived in Israel. She seems to have been the first woman to receive a divorce based on the *taʿmīm* 59/2012 on April 22, 2013.[173] She had been in an "inbetween" situation, which in her case lasted for more than twenty years, because she had been married to Samīr Qinṭār, another political prisoner in an Israeli jail since 1992. Qinṭār went to Lebanon in 2008 where he married another woman and had a baby but denied divorce to Kifāh Kayyāl.[174] She filed a claim and received the *khulʿ* before-consummation divorce in the West Bank, despite the fact that she lives in Acre, Israel. The case attracted a lot of media attention in Palestine and Lebanon because of this political background[175] and led the Supreme Judge to his indignant reaction, which will be described in the next chapter.

---

is the argument that lurks behind al-Tamīmī's critique of the new regulation and could be dangerous for women having been divorced this way. For penal law, see Peters 2005.

171 Tamīmī (September 6, 2012).

172 Email, January 14, 2015.

173 Johnson and Hammami 2013: 18.

174 Maannews, December 13, 2012b; Alwatanvoice, November 6, 2012; Alarabiya, April 24, 2013.

175 AlMadina, May 1, 2013.

Kayyāl's lawyer ʿImād ʿAwwād stated[176] that Kayyāl's *khulʿ* separation was decided by the court, calling her claim ransoming (*al-iftidāʾ*) and describing it correctly, as in the *taʿmīm*, as dissolution (*faskh*) of the marriage contract. ʿAwwād then explained that:

> the judgment can be appealed (*qābil al-istiʾnāf*) and demurrer of the plaintiff's claims can be made. It is a judgment after appeal (*huwa ḥukm tābiʿ li-l-istiʾnāf*), in other words: the court submits it to the Court of Appeal and it becomes automatically a rule of the law (*bi-ḥukm qānūn*).[177]

The lawyer refers to Article 28 of what he calls a "Law of the Sharia Courts", but he obviously means the Law of the Procedure for Sharia Courts" (*Qānūn Uṣūl al-Muḥākamāt al-Sharʿiyya*) 31/1959, Article 138.[178] This article states that if the primary courts refer judgments of personal status affairs (all of which are connected to the right of God) to the Court of Appeal thirty days after the judgment was given and none of the plaintiffs files an appeal in this time, the Court of Appeal decides on the matter of these judgments (*faṣalat al-maḥkama fī mauwdūʿihā*). This is also the procedure that Idʿīs described in his lecture but without mentioning the law and the article.[179] Still, the law does not speak of "judicial precedent," a term used by the Supreme Judge and not of "judgment of the law" (*ḥukm al-qānūn*) as does ʿAwwād. But it could be, as Khalil suggested, connected to the common law concept of precedent, and it is possible that turning the *taʿmīm* into a law was thought to be legal with this procedure. The procedure initiated by the Supreme Judge seems thus to have been justified as a "judicial precedent" by common law practices, a colonial heritage of the Palestinian legal system.

176 Alarabiya, April 24, 2013.

177 Alarabiya, April 24, 2013.

178 Alarabiya, April 24, 2013. I thank Judge al-Ḍamīrī for this reference; see also Muqtafi.

179 See chapter 5. Judge al-Ḍamīrī described this article as creating "precedents" (*sawābiq qaḍāʾiyya*).

CHAPTER 5

Khulʿ in University Teaching

5.1 Birzeit University as Part of the Palestinian Public Sphere

Universities have been regarded as part of the public sphere and a "link between the university and the public sphere should come as no surprise,"[1] as Diana Ambrozas argues, stating that university is not a single public sphere, but an intersection of different publics,[2] and that it is one of the "many publics where both particular and general interests may be constituted and contested through an expanded conception of rational discussion."[3] These intersecting publics are reflected in the different departments of the university, which she sees, in contradiction to Jürgen Habermas, not in decline, but as a place where political debates can and still do take place. Looking at North American universities, she points to examples of feminist movements or the New Right parties that were both politically active at universities. Consequently, university is for her a privileged site "for political action and political alliances to handle larger issues."[4]

> Still, the university is a special kind of public, one which remains privileged with respect to both knowledge and power. If it no longer has a monopoly of knowledge it retains a certain oligopoly. Its function of transmitting technical and cultural capital to future generations helps maintain existing hierarchies of power and knowledge for the upper and middle classes. Nonetheless, its simultaneous function of forming a critical political awareness can serve to challenge these same oligopolies.[5]

That universities are a part of the public sphere is even more true for Palestinian universities, which have been described as a "dynamic force across Palestinian communities" enabling Palestinians to "define and articulate a Palestinian national identity."[6] They quickly responded according to Christa Bruhn to the promise of Oslo by moving "from resistance to reconstruction," as one official

1 Ambrozas 1998: 4.
2 Ambrozas 1998: 6.
3 Ambrozas 1998: 6.
4 Ambrozas 1998: 6.
5 Ambrozas 1998: 5.
6 Bruhn 2006: 1125.

 DOI:10.1163/9789004442313_006

from the Palestinian Ministry of Higher Education put it.[7] However, in the later 2000s, the ongoing crises and the non-implementation of a Palestinian state led also to a crisis of the universities:

> The escalation of the conflict since the outbreak of the second Intifada in September 2000 has had a severe impact on Palestinian universities. Palestinian universities have faced many challenges during the past three decades since their inception, but their current state is best described as in crisis. Israel has officially closed some universities for extended periods, whereas others have at times been effectively closed.[8]

The Supreme Judge taught the course on "Personal Status Law" in the winter semester of 2013 as a representative of the Sharia establishment at BZU, which does not have a Sharia Faculty.[9] BZU is located near Ramallah in the West Bank on the outskirts of the village of Birzeit. Founded in 1924 originally as elementary school for girls by the educator Nabīhat Nāṣir (d. 1951), it became a university in the 1970s.[10] In 1976, Birzeit University awarded the first bachelor's degrees in eight disciplines, among them Arabic literature and Middle East Studies but not yet law.[11] Between 1992 and 1995, graduate programs in law, gender studies, and international studies were launched.[12] In 2018, according to the university website, BZU offered in nine faculties 111 academic programs, 32 Master programs, 75 bachelor programs, 1 PhD program, 2 diploma programs, and 1 program for foreign students. The number of students in 2018 was 14,506; 62.4 percent were female.[13] Out of the nine faculties, the faculty of Law and Public Administration[14] was in 2018 fourth largest after the Faculty of

7 Bruhn 2006: 1133.

8 Bruhn 2006: 1136.

9 Other universities, e.g., al-Quds University in Jerusalem, Abu Dis, Hebron and Nablus Universities, do have Sharia Faculties.

10 See http://www.birzeit.edu/en/about/history/chronology, accessed March 13, 2019; Wikipedia: Birzeit University, see https://en.wikipedia.org/wiki/Birzeit_University, accessed March 13, 2019.

11 See http://www.birzeit.edu/en/about/history/chronology, accessed March 13, 2019.

12 http://www.birzeit.edu/en/about/history/chronology, accessed March 13, 2019.

13 See: https://www.birzeit.edu/en/about/facts, accessed March 13, 2019. At another website the number is 13,963. See https://www.birzeit.edu/en/community-affairs, accessed March 12, 2019.

14 http://www.birzeit.edu/en/study/faculties/law-public-administration, accessed March 12, 2019.

Arts, the Faculty of Business and Economics, and the Faculty of Engineering and Technology. It had 1,158 female and 584 male students.[15]

The history of the university has been much influenced by politics. In 1980, Israel issued a military order under the mandate of the Israeli military governor enabling him to control the registration of students and the staff recruitment processes. The university launched a national campaign against this military order, which forced Israel to abandon its implementation.[16] Under the occupation, BZU was closed down at different times[17] followed by a "right-to-education" campaign.[18] The campus of BZU can be described as highly politicized: discussions take place, students often gather in front of the buildings to protest against actions of the occupying power and more generally for political reasons, there are information desks of different political groups and student demonstrations. Like other universities in the West Bank, BZU is often closed down for a couple of days due to protests of some kind.[19] "Community Affairs" play an important role and the university's community engagement, for example, helping the farmers harvesting olives. BZU is engaging "in a wide range of disciplines, including continuing education, community and public health, media, legislative reforms, gender, water and environmental issues, and others."[20] At the same time, BZU presents itself as an "enlightened environment that celebrates freedom of thought and expression, embraces democratic practices and dialogue, and provokes excellence and creativity."[21]

The course the Supreme Judge taught at BZU was given at the Faculty of Law and Administration. One slogan of this faculty is "Providing the Public Domain with Qualified Professionals."[22] The course belonged to the Bachelor program of the Faculty whose mission and aims at that level are defined as follows:

15 In 2018, there were 446 full-time faculty members teaching at the university with a percentage of females of 31.4 percent, among them 59 percent have a PhD. See https://www.birzeit.edu/en/about/facts, accessed March 12, 2019.

16 See https://www.birzeit.edu/en/about/history/education-under-occupation, accessed March 12, 2019.

17 See https://www.birzeit.edu/en/about/history/education-under-occupation/closures-history, accessed March 12, 2019.

18 See https://www.birzeit.edu/en/right2edu, accessed March 12, 2019.

19 For the political role of Palestinian universities, see Bruhn 2006.

20 See https://www.birzeit.edu/en/community-affairs, accessed August 3, 2019.

21 See https://www.birzeit.edu/en/about/life-at-bzu, accessed March 12, 2019; see also Bruhn 2006.

22 See https://www.birzeit.edu/en/study/faculties/law-public-administration, accessed March 12, 2019.

> The program's mission is to develop legal education in Palestine and provide it with unique scientific research leading to the preparation of a legal staff conversant scientifically and practically, and equipped with the skills and values needed to practice legal actions and expertise legal methodology which contributes in raising the level of various legal professions which offers services to the Palestinian community, as well as developing and strengthen relationships with justice institutions and law faculties in Palestine and abroad, beside preparing students to pursue their graduate studies [*sic*].[23]

The goals are outlined as follows:
- Develop legal education including interactive teaching techniques, working in groups, developing student's critical analysis skills aiming to create a generation of creative graduates with creative abilities who are able to innovate, compete, and have the ability and power to contribute in the attainment of the development objectives for Palestine.
- Enhance scientific research skills through writing legal researches (*sic*) according to the proper legal methodology.
- Qualify students with the minimum legal skills in order to have qualified students to practice the law and legal consulting. Also equipping them with creative skills such as creative thinking, analyzing, criticizing and elicitation.
- Build student's personalities in a way that enables them to compete, have the ability and power to contribute in finding creative solutions to important problems in the Palestinian society, and achieve development objectives.[24]

Both the mission and the goals are clearly more practice-oriented in the bachelor program and less ambitious than in the master's program,[25] but they still aim to "enhance scientific research skills" to equip students with "creative thinking, analyzing, criticizing and elicitation" and to "build students' personalities to enable them to contribute in [*sic*] finding creative solutions" to the problems in Palestinian society. Students with a BA in Law from BZU are to have "research skills" and minimum legal skills to "practice law and legal consulting."

Whereas "mission" and "aims" outline the general academic approach, the description of the syllabus in the modul of "Personal Status Law" (modul number JURI 238 *Qānūn al-Aḥwāl al-Shakhṣiyya* 1)[26] covers the following topics:

23 See https://www.birzeit.edu/en/study/programs/law-0, accessed March 12, 2019.
24 See https://www.birzeit.edu/en/study/programs/law-0, accessed March 13, 2019.
25 See https://www.birzeit.edu/en/study/programs/law-0, accessed March 13, 2019.
26 See https://www.birzeit.edu/en/study/programs/law-0, accessed March 12, 2019.

engagement, marriage, guardianship in marriage, suitability (*kafāʾa*), disobedience (*nushūz*), *ṭalāq*, waiting period (*ʿidda*), *khulʿ*, judicial divorce; maintenance of relatives, application by the court. It is only in the syllabus that the Islamic legal background of this course becomes evident because Islamic legal terms such as *ṭalāq* and *khulʿ* are used.

5.2 Approaches to Academic Teaching

The Supreme Judge of West Bank/Palestine, Yūsuf Idʿīs, was trained in Sharia and taught at BZU, because there was no chair in the Law Department who could have taught this topic.[27] For the students, this course was required because all future judges (especially the judges at Sharia courts in the West Bank and Gaza) and future lawyers are obliged to possess knowledge of this branch of law and must be able to apply its principles thoroughly. To understand how the Personal Status Law, more accurately the applicable Jordanian law, was taught, both the textbook representing the syllabus (5.4) as well as the actual teaching process (5.3) and their interrelatedness will be taken into account. In general, the Supreme Judge stuck very closely to the textbook but the *khulʿ* lesson was an exception to this.

There is to the best of my knowledge no research available on university teaching in Palestine. Research dealing with teaching in schools will have to serve as a starting point for developing a methodological approach to academic teaching, keeping in mind the difference with regard to university teaching. For example, basic education is obligatory, university courses are not; content and methods are, of course, different and adapted to the age of the students and the aims of the courses. University teaching aims to be an introduction to scientific and theoretical approaches, methods and contents, and especially to critical thinking as outlined above based on the mission and goals of BZU. On the other hand, students depend on their professors for evaluation and grades. In schools as in universities, certain contents, skills and knowledge are taught based on special didactics. The question is how to raise the students' interest in the topic. Matthias Proske and Wolfgang Meseth have described teaching as a special form of communication with a high degree of communicative dynamic, the students' obligation to be present, the asymmetric roles of teachers and students, and the teachers' obligation to give marks to the

27 In 2018, Ṣumūd al-Ḍamīrī taught this class, and on April 8, 2019, I had the opportunity to attend one of her classes.

students[28] – a description this general is applicable to both school teaching and university teaching. Some of the results of the research with regard to (European) school teaching can thus be used for the present approach. Bernhard Schär and Vera Sperisen[29] point to the difficult position of (school) teachers who – according to the curriculum – have to teach an authoritative interpretation of the syllabus and at the same time have to develop independent patterns of interpretation with the students, again an aspect that is true for high school students as well as university students. The BA program of the Department of Law required interactive teaching techniques, working in groups, developing student's critical analysis skills and aiming to create a generation of creative graduates as outlined above. However, the judge's way of teaching was more the classical style of a lecture: the teacher faces the students and gives a lecture; the students, who are expected to have read the required chapter of the textbook, answer his questions.

Whereas there were no work groups and students did not give presentations, interesting debates took place – sometimes only among the students and sometimes the Supreme Judge was asked questions and he willingly engaged in the dialogue. At certain points the communication intensified. Proske and Meseth define such "communicative intensivation" as passages in which it becomes obvious that the syllabus is really a topic and not only communicated via formal questions, where the participation of students and the teacher becomes observable and is more than a cognitive reproduction of knowledge.[30]

Of course, there can be no doubt about the asymmetric roles of professor – i.e., in this case *Qāḍī al-Quḍāt* – and students due to the professor's advanced knowledge and obligation to grade students' tests. This last point is not one that will be researched here. Instead, as part of the social iteration about the new *khulʿ* ruling, the "high degree of communicative dynamic" that developed in this lecture is put into focus in the present study. Some selected sequences of questions and answers and the students' discussions and reactions in the classes to the Supreme Judge's narrative will be presented and the role of the Supreme Judge as a teacher steering the teaching process will be analyzed. An important topic often dealt with in the research, especially related to high school teaching, is judging the "quality" of the teaching, but again this aspect cannot be dealt with here.

To sum up, the focus is on the Supreme Judge's construction of law and gender, his "uses of the past," and on the way he explained the developments

28 Proske and Meseth 2006: 129.
29 Schär and Sperisen 2011.
30 Proske and Meseth 2006: 134.

toward the implementation of the *khul*ʿ ruling to the students; analyzing the communicative processes in the class with the students will give some clue of how students reacted to these topics and reveal at least to a certain extent their perception of it.[31] To do this, a modification of Ignas Kalpokas's approach, which focuses on the teaching process at schools, is used.[32] Being present in class means, he argues, that the researcher can only analyze the communication in the class, he or she cannot say anything about the process of acquirement, about what the students think about the content of what they learn, let alone what they know afterwards or apply later after becoming, in our case, lawyers or judges. Keeping this in mind, Kalpokas suggested first to analyze the teaching material, and then, in a second step, to sit in the class and listen. Analyzing the tapes and looking at the transcripts and analyzing the sequence of the class should constitute the subsequent steps. However, as the teaching of the Supreme Judge deviated significantly from the textbook in the *khul*ʿ lecture, in presenting the class on October 31, 2013, I will proceed in reverse order. In the first section (5.3), the teaching process of October 31, 2013, will be analyzed, focusing on the Supreme Judge's narrative about how this ruling came about, but also on the communicative process his narrative evoked. In the following section (5.4), the relevant chapter of the textbook will be analyzed, which reflects the "normal" syllabus based on the version of *khul*ʿ anchored in the law.[33]

31 Proske and Meseth stress the unpredictable behavior of acquirement or contingency of high school (Germany: "Gymnasium") students dealing with classes that aim to communicate to them not only historical knowledge and critical evaluation of historical sources but also moral values. This is especially the case when high school students are confronted with the story of Nazi Germany and the perspective of Jewish victims. See Proske and Meseth 2006: 141, 146, 151.

32 Kalpokas 2012.

33 Although the *Qāḍī al-Quḍāt'* represented the religious establishment, there was no "religious climate" as has been described for some schools in Egypt by Muhammad Faour. According to his results, the Arabic-language textbooks in Egypt advocated piety and religious obervance even when key civic concepts, including freedom, social justice, and equality of citizens, are found together with religious concepts in the same course. He even speaks of the "hidden curriculum" to describe the impact of many Islamist teachers on students (Faour 2012: 6–7). Surely, the topic in the *Qāḍī al-Quḍāt*'s teaching was religious, i.e., Islamic law. But the way the *Qāḍī al-Quḍāt* dealt with it was practical – how to argue in the context of law, which verses to take to develop the law further, etc. The female students covered their hair but were otherwise dressed in a modern and fashionable way with tight-fitting jeans and t-shirts, make-up and trendy scarves. Most of the young women who did not wear a scarf seem to have been Christians. They numbered around five to six and the *Qāḍī al-Quḍāt* had informed me that he had five Christian female students in his class.

5.3 Class on *khulʿ* on October 31, 2013

5.3.1 *The* Qāḍī's *Teaching Style*[34]

The PSL classes took place on Tuesdays and Thursdays, from 8:00am to 9:00am, in the building of the Education Faculty of BZU. The classroom was big enough for around forty students. The *Qāḍī* normally entered, installed himself and started the class by taking attendance. After checking the names, the *Qāḍī* started teaching. Some students arrived after he started teaching, carrying their coffee, saying "hello" with no acknowledgement of their tardiness. He normally nodded at me, and in the second session, on October 24, he pointed to me, gave my name and profession to the students but did not give me the chance to present myself. Throughout the rest of the course, he more or less ignored me depending on his mood. Between twenty-five and twenty-eight students participated in the class, the great majority of them female and only three to five males who sat in the back in one corner. This reflects the fact that more female than male students are registered in the Faculty of Law.

The *Qāḍī* stuck normally to the form and contents of the textbook. He would introduce the topic of that session at the beginning of class and usually asked the students for the definition of a term or legal concept from Islamic law that he wanted to examine. Normally one or several of the students responded quickly, showing that they were prepared. He would repeat the correct definition loudly and present the topics as they were presented in the textbook, inserting here and there his experiences at court and concentrating on aspects that seemed of special importance to him or he thought were important for the students to know. The legal text of the Jordanian Law of Personal Status (JLPS) did not play a prominent role. I did not see students carrying it with them or referring to it in class. They had only the textbook – which will be introduced later – on their desks.

During the class, the *Qāḍī* had an engaged style of teaching and talking, which reflected his interest in the topic. He was always ready to answer

34 *Shaykh* Idʿīs was very helpful and openminded toward my research when I first met him and roughly outlined my interest in the legal discourses in Palestine to him. From the beginning he allowed me to sit in his classes and record the lectures and discourses with the students. He also gave me an interview addressing his teaching method as well as answering questions concerning *khulʿ* and gave me a copy of the *taʿmīm* in one of his workshops at Birzeit University. I selected the first courses on PSL, which took place on Tuesdays and Thursdays, 8:00am to 9:00am. There were other courses from 12:30 pm to 1:30pm scheduled for different groups of students, which more or less dealt with the same topic. I visited and recorded seven of these classes in which the *Qāḍī* dealt with family law, on October 24, 31, November 12, 14, 21, 26 and December 3. He also gave a class on inheritance, which I did not attend.

questions and clearly liked to get the chance to explain a matter, to give his opinion and to get into an argument. Sometimes he postponed questions of the students but almost always came back to them later without having to be reminded. If he arrived in the morning tired or with what seemed to be a bad mood, his face brightened up when he was asked questions by the students or when he felt the students' interest in the matter. If students had more detailed inquiries or the same student asked further questions, unsatisfied with the answers, the judge took time to explain and justify his position. His voice would become more imperative and louder, and at the same time, the students also became louder. In some cases, he asked the students for their opinion and let them discuss, albeit not for a long time. He closely monitored the discussion, always intervening when he thought it went too far or when he was convinced that everything had been said or he ran out of time. There were also times he tried to prepare the students for their future positions as lawyers or judges, giving them good advice for their professional futures in a more personal way. His teaching style could be described as serious and concentrated on the topic, but with a touch of humor. He loved to crack jokes and sometimes he exaggerated his description of a certain case or legal problem to get a laugh from the students. He clearly had immense knowledge of Islamic jurisprudence as well as of the law, and demonstrated his interest in reforming the law, finding solutions to socio-legal problems and helping vulnerable groups, in this case women. Put briefly, one could feel that he enjoyed being a teacher as well as a scholar of Islamic law who loved to engage in discussions about legal matters. On the other hand, he strictly kept to his schedule and tightly monitored upcoming discussions and often finished them with an authoritative statement. He expected the students to already have a certain knowledge of Islamic principles and rules as well as of the verses of the Quran. When he started to quote a Quran verse most students joined in and mumbled the verse together with him. The same was true with regard to general rules such as *lā ḍarar wa-lā ḍirār* (do not inflict injury nor repay one injury with another). The *Qāḍī al-Quḍāt* sometimes interrupted his lecture to ask his students, generally or individually, for definitions or a summary of a part of the textbook or to read aloud from the text and summarize it. Often at the end of the class, he asked one student to come to the blackboard to jot down what he then dictated as the settings of a court case that the students noted as a case to discuss as homework.

Students asked questions or made comments without raising their hands, mostly by calling *Ustādh* (Professor) and even interrupting when he was in a middle of an explanation or a sentence. He did not criticize this behavior. He simply either stopped to let them ask the question or he continued, raising his voice. So they often repeated their questions until he answered. It happened that many students wanted to ask questions or give explanations at the same time, so that a babble of voices arose in the room and the sound level rose quite considerably, and it was impossible to understand what the Supreme Judge said or what the students were asking. Sometimes students started discussing among themselves without listening to the Supreme Judge anymore. Order was restored when the *Qāḍī* raised his voice and called or even shouted at them, "girls, girls, youth, youth" (*yā ṣabāya, yā ṣabāya*), or addressing one or two students by name.

5.3.2 *Lecture on* khulʿ *on October 31, 2013*

As already mentioned, the class on October 31 was a special one because the Supreme Judge concentrated on the new ruling with regard to *khulʿ* and summarized the "classical" consensual *khulʿ* and referred only briefly to the textbook. This seemed justified as he had to train future lawyers and judges of civil as well as Sharia courts, who would have to know this ruling, which was not dealt with in the textbook (see 5.4). His lecture will be analyzed with regard to the following questions:

1. Which reasons did he give for the necessity of the reform? Why before consummation of the marriage only? And which gender concepts were inherent in this reform?
2. How did he use the past? Which terminology did he use?
3. How did he justify the legality of the ruling?
4. How did the Supreme Judge present his own role in the whole process?

After summarizing the session[35] the analysis will consider the above questions in combination with a selection of "reconstructive sequence analysis" as suggested by Proske and Meseth,[36] i.e., citations from the recordings including references to atmosphere, feelings uttered by students, and so on. Attention will be paid not only to what the *Qāḍī* said but also how he said it and how the students reacted, as well as their questions, arguments and their behavior, such as laughing, talking among themselves, and so forth.

At the beginning of this lecture, the Supreme Judge returned tests. He asked the students whether the questions had been easy or difficult. Some of them answered that they were "easy" but a female student complained that she had never taken a test in which memorizing dates was required, or questions about the development of the law. The Supreme Judge answered that he wanted them to know the content of the textbook and complained that some students

35 Summary and analysis are separated in order to reproduce the line of arguments of the Supreme Judge.

36 Proske and Meseth 2006: 134–135.

did not even know the title of the book after finishing the semester. They had to know the history of the personal status law in Palestine. Returning the exam papers and the discussion took less than a quarter of an hour. Then he began with a definition of *khulʿ* as "taking off vestment" taken from Quran 2:187: "your wives – they are a vestment for you, and you are a vestment for them." It followed a reference to the articles of the JLPS, according to which *khulʿ*/*mukhālaʿa* is based only on mutual consent. The main part of the session, more than half an hour, was taken up by the *Qāḍī al-Quḍāt*'s narrative of the reasons for the necessity for a new *khulʿ* ruling, its development and a discussion of it, its enactment in 2012 and his own role in this process of quasi-legislation. At the end, he summarized shortly some legal aspects of *khulʿ*, the terminology, conditions for the application, and the financial aspects of this kind of divorce.

5.3.2.1 Which Reasons Did the Supreme Judge Give for the Necessity of the Reform? Why before Consummation of the Marriage Only? And Which Gender Concepts Were Inherent in This Reform?

The Supreme Judge started with the definition of *khulʿ* in language and as a legal term connected to Quran 2:187 and continued to step, brushing aside a student's question with regard to *tafwīḍ* (authorization),[37] immediately in medias res with the social reason for the new ruling. Describing society as a product of cultural barrenness (*al-ʿaqm al-thaqāfī*),[38] he pointed briefly to the JLPS which regulates *khulʿ* based on mutual agreement (*al-khulʿ al-riḍāʾī*) in Articles 100–112.[39] This kind of divorce, he explained, is also called "repudiation based on general release" (*ṭalāq muqābil ibrāʾ ʿāmm*). He then connected this to the situation in Palestine:

> *Qāḍī*:
> Now we have a very principal problem in Palestine. It happens that many young men – you see, girls! (*yā ṣabāya*) – deceive girls by means of shape and appearance (*bi-l-shakl aw bi-l-maẓhar*). It seems that he [now singular] is well-situated, good looking and charming. Then he rushes with the procedures of the marriage … Now, disagreement becomes evident and it becomes clear that he is not a husband who is wanted or suitable and arguments between her and him start in order to give her *ṭalāq* or *khulʿ*,

37 The question referred to the authorization of women with regard to repudiation (*ṭalāq*), which can be stipulated in the contract and is possible according to law.

38 He perhaps meant the unsatisfactory situation in which many young women find themselves – anticipating his discussion of "masculine society."

39 Actually, it starts with JLPS Article 102 until 112.

> but he refuses. Perhaps he demands 20,000 or 30,000 [Jordanian Dinars, JD] and perhaps he provokes her with certain threats like "I will leave you [in this inbetween position] until you become white-haired (*tashībī*)" or "I will marry a second wife (*atazawwaj*) and we will see who can divorce you from me" or "I will marry you using force (*bi-l-quwwa*)." The fate of many young women depends on reasons like these sayings and they experience indescribable harm (*ḍarar kabīr jiddan lā yuṣaf*) as a result of this deceit and young men beguiling young women. And there are actually young men who marry other women and the young women remain inbetween (*muʿallaqāt*).

He claimed to have seen many cases like this in what he called his "field visits" (*khilāl ziyārātī al-maydāniyya*).[40] One was a woman of "inbetween" status (*muʿallaqa*) because the husband left her. One was confronted with a husband's demand of 30,000 JD, one with 5,000 JD – all the same story, the *Qāḍī al-Quḍāt* commented angrily. "Either she paid or she did not get divorced." The husbands took "revenge." He continued in his normal joking style that the husbands would lie with regard to the presents given: when the fiancé-husband would take his finacée out for a shawarma sandwich, he would afterwards claim the equivalent of four or five slaughtered muttons. Students enjoyed the humorous retelling of the fiancé's behavior and laughed at this. But despite his jokes, the *Qāḍī al-Quḍāt* was very serious in his critique of the behavior of these young men toward the young women and he regarded what the latter were experiencing, due to lack of applicable rulings, as injustice.

As reason for this the *Qāḍī al-Quḍāt* described Palestinian society as a "masculine society" (*mujtamaʿ dhukūrī*) in which men were used to hearing that only a woman can be divorced (*al-muṭallaqa*). He quoted the saying: "The divorced [woman] comes and goes" and regretted that the people were not ready to say: "The divorced man comes and goes." Men would instead say: "How can you talk about me with this word [divorced]?" Stressing over and over that this special group of young women were exposed to injury (*ḍarar*) by the young men's behavior, he explained that he wanted to find a legal healing and to find something new, but something that was acceptable to the public – an aspect he repeated several times.[41] To stop this injustice and harm done to these young women, he decided to refer to the Islamic principle of *lā ḍarar wa-lā ḍirār* (do not inflict injury nor repay one injury with another).[42]

---

40 With this he obviously referred to his experience in the Sharia courts.

41 He normally called the public "the street."

42 For the exact legal argumentation, see below p. 158.

When a female student asked for the first time, "Professor, *khul*ʿ is only before consummation, correct?" He confirmed this and said he would come back to the matter later. Ten minutes later, he tackled the subject again, explaining that women before privacy (*khalwa*) and consummation suffered most, because they could not marry and have children.[43] Pointing to the women after privacy and consummation who would need judicial divorce, he explained

> *Qāḍī*:
> *Shar*ʿ and law (*al-shar*ʿ *wa-l-qānūn*) gave us, the judges, [the right] to regulate *khul*ʿ. But why did we not apply *khul*ʿ for women after the first marital sex? We did not want to destroy (*nudammir*) families!

A student added, supporting his narrative: "She is exaggerating," confirming that a woman would abuse this right to destroy the family and the Supreme Judge referring to this continued:

> Maybe the woman will use *khul*ʿ for bigger and less important [reasons]. She might say, for example [to her husband]: I want a new dress and in case he would not buy it, [she would] give him the *khul*ʿ (*qad taqūmu bi-l-khul*ʿ) [...] and the matter becomes unbearable (*fa-yuṣbiḥu al-amr lā yuṭāq*)!

And:

> There are women who actually experience injury – why should they not use their right? There are women who experience injury and others who are ungrateful; they want to use *khul*ʿ just because it exists.

*Khul*ʿ, however, means repayment and the *Qāḍī al-Quḍāt* then mentioned another reason for not allowing *khul*ʿ in Palestine after the first marital intercourse, namely to save women from the financial loss they would experience when approaching the court for a divorce based on *khul*ʿ. Women, he explained to the students, would have to give up their dower or pay a substantial sum to the husband. He did not consider it just for women who had worked for a long time in a factory or on the fields and were married for many years that they then should have to pay for the dissolution of the marriage. To avoid this, a married woman – after consummation – should go to the court and get a divorce for

43 The argument which comes up in the media, see chapter 6 that not having children makes the dissolution of the marriage easier is only mentioned but not discussed in his lecture.

"marital dispute and discord" (*tafrīq li-l-nizāʿ wa-l-shiqāq*).[44] In this case – as in the case when the husband repudiates her – she would keep her dower. As she needed to prove her case according to JLPS Article 132, the procedure was simplified in the same *taʿmīm*. Such a ruling was already given in the Ottoman law, he explained to the students, where it was regulated that if the judge saw that there was "dispute and discord," he could separate the couple.[45] But in the JLPS of 1976 this had been changed to the disadvantage of women and divorce was made more difficult for women because she had to prove "dispute and discord." He asked the students: "where do you think a husband and wife would quarrel?" All responded: "In the house," and the *Qāḍī al-Quḍāt* confirmed this. Who could be witness to this? He answered his own rhetorical question: The woman would have no witness and the husband would swear[46] and this would be the end of the claim. The husband would say to her: "Did I not tell you that I am stronger than you?" Cases remained in court for a long time. This is why he (he said: "I") gave the judge discretionary power (*al-sulṭa al-taqdīriyya*) with regard to the divorce of "dispute and discord." This conversation was followed by the reminder to the students that "the law is the law" and that all judges, be they male or female, are obliged to give verdicts on this basis.

After having outlined the second part of his ruling concerning "dipute and discord," he went on to explain why this combination of *khulʿ* before consummation and easing the procedure in "dispute and discord" made sense and why it was in women's interest as they would save their money.

> *Qāḍī*:
> There are many women who want *khulʿ*. I asked them: "What is better for you [change into feminine singular] as a woman: Do you want to get repudiated and take your rights [i.e., the dower] or do you want to get divorced and pay?" She took an hour to explain, then she decided: *khulʿ*. [I asked her] Why? She said: "So I can show him that I gave him the *khulʿ*" (*innanī anā khalaʿtuhu*).

At this point the students started to laugh. Again, the Supreme Judge repeated the woman's last words "I want to show him that I can give him the *khulʿ*." He had changed into a jesting tone. What seemed at the beginning a general

44 See JLPS Article 132.

45 OLFR Article 130.

46 According to procedural law the defendant can swear that the claim is not true if there is no proof – according to classical law, witnesses – and would be freed of the charge. The applicable law is the *Majallat*, which regulates this in Article 76, see Welchman 2000: 22.

question to several women, turned out to be his dispute with one woman only. He explained that this saying had been uttered in the context of a lawsuit. The woman said that she divorced her husband using the term of *khul*ʿ whereas the husband said that he divorced her, using the wording of *ṭalāq*. Despite the fact that the man was not present in the court hearing, they continued to accuse one another and the matter escalated, the *Qāḍī al-Quḍāt* complained, and the search for a legal solution became a fundamental political issue because the husband was in Lebanon. Media played an important role not only in pouring oil onto the fire of the Palestinian debate but also in involving different countries.[47] The matter was even, as the *Qāḍī al-Quḍāt* mentioned nodding at me, dealt with in a German journal.[48] It developed into a "political crisis" between the two countries, i.e., Palestine and Lebanon. In his usual exaggerating and joking way he stated that it could have even possibly developed into a nuclear war. He connected to this a critique of the media without, however, denying the fact that the media had the right to be present at what was a public court session.

At this point in the lecture, the students started to discuss more and more among themselves without paying attention to the *Qāḍī al-Quḍāt*. The level of noise rose substantially and it became impossible to understand what he said. He called a female student by her name and asked her to be quiet. The students continued to discuss and laugh for a time. A little later when the hubbub had died down a female student asked: "Professor, do we in Palestine not apply *khul*ʿ after consummation?"

> The *Qāḍī* answered, a bit annoyed because he actually had explained this before:
> Not after intercourse, no. When we applied it before consummation it caused a political matter engaging Palestine and Lebanon.
> He went on:
> How could I apply it [for cases] after consummation? How many Tunesian, Moroccan, Algerian, Saudi women are there in Palestine? And this would all have been with us [meaning it would become a problem] – now we limited ourselves to [*khul*ʿ] before consummation.

47 Idʿīs obviously referred here to the Kayyāl/Qinṭār divorce based on *khul*ʿ, see above pp. 137–138. Whereas she filed the petition in November 2012 (see Maannews, December 13, 2012b), the decision was taken on April 22, 2013, see Alarabiya April 24, 2013. This media report is titled: "The Wife of the Prisoner Samīr al-Qinṭār Divorces Him (*takhlaʿuhu*) in Court."

48 The *Qāḍī* gave me the article in the following session. It is half a page in a German journal published in Arabic called AlMadina, of May 1, 2013.

5.3.2.1.1 *Analysis*

Whereas the Supreme Judge had a relaxed style of talking to the students, he was very clear and serious in several points that were obviously important to him – as they justified his introduction of judicial *khulʿ*: his obligation to help young women through legal means, to criticize what he considered unacceptable behavior of the young men, to protect women, and to find a solution in Islamic law to this problem. He cited the social situation as the main reason for the necessity of a new ruling of *khulʿ* separation and his knowledge of this necessity was a result of his experience at court. Describing the young men's behavior as "revenge" and "blackmailing," he used a language that shows his severe critique of what he labeled the "masculine society." Such clear words are surprising for a Muslim Supreme Judge.

In his whole lecture he did not deal in detail with the legal regulation of the topic. His references to the JLPS were few and short. Nor did he bring the text of the *taʿmīm* to read and discuss it with the students in detail. Instead, he focused his endeavors to find a "legal healing" in the form of a divorce. The way he did this was amusing and a vivid description of "law in context," i.e., the socio-legal and political situation he described as both reason and obligation for him to find a solution. Strife occurred and many men pressured the women by threatening to deny them the repudiation they wanted using different scenarios for their threats: to marry a second wife,[49] to leave her in this "inbetween" position, until she becomes old and her hair turns white, or even to "take her by force." The Supreme Judge was well aware and communicated this to the students that those young men were in the legally stronger position than the women they were engaged to and that they abused this position to maltreate their fiancées. His disapproval was outspoken. Forcing women to pay high sums in order to regain their freedom was for him "blackmailing." One can describe this as a subjectively sincere attitude toward gender topics and what can be called a protective position toward women and especially young women marrying for the first time. At the same time, he did not discuss other possible legal solutions. He did not mention the legal consequences of a *ṭalāq* before consummation, according to which a man would have to pay half of the amount of the dower to the woman.[50] Nor did he mention that in case women wanted this *ṭalāq* before consummation, the whole of the dower "shall

49 JLPS Article 28 allows polygyny: it states that a man who has four wives shall be prohibited from concluding a marriage contract with another – fifth – wife before he divorces one of them and her waiting period expires. This implicitly allows the marriage of up to four wives.

50 JLPS Article 48.

abate."[51] More importantly, he did not touch upon the question of why people considered it necessary to sign the contract at this early stage of the relationship and thus seemed to respect this Palestinian custom to sign the marriage contract with the engagement, instead of just celebrating the engagement and wait with the signing of the contract till the real wedding. Such an approach would have solved all legal problems, and marriage and engagement would have remained as neatly separated as they are in the law.

What did all this reveal about the Supreme Judge's concept of gender rights and gender roles? When looked at chronologically, the *Qāḍī* introduced various arguments at different points of his narrative. He conceded from the beginning that Palestinian society is still a "masculine society" and he criticized this. He then argued that the Sharia judges did not give women the right to *khulʿ* after consummation because they, the judges, did not want to "destroy families." The fear that the right of women to *khulʿ* also after the first marital intercourse would destroy the family was an often-used argument in the Egyptian debate, too, and can be seen as an implicit reference to the concept of *fitna*, literally "sedition, disorder," allegedly caused by women.[52] The Supreme Judge's example of a woman divorcing her husband just because he refused to buy her a dress was surely fictitious and can be counted as an example of his humorous and exaggerating style. Implicitly, however, and in the subtext, it was based on the assumption of female emotionality and male rationality that leads to disorder in society.[53] Women, being emotional, cannot resist temptations with regard to shopping and would, if given, use the tool of *khulʿ* as a threat to the husband. If he was poor and simply did not have the financial means, the message is, she would divorce him and thus put the family and the whole of the social fabric in danger. The argument is again given in a joking way and he surely was aware that his argument did not make much sense, because the woman, divorcing her husband in this situation would not only not get the dress but also lose her maintenance as well as the dower. However, Idʿīs here focused on an alleged female emotionality and unability to control this emotionality.

But why should women before consummation act differently than women after consummation? Maybe the students thought like this too, because when

51 JLPS Article 49. Article 49 mentions that the wife requests separation due to a deficiency or ailment in the husband etc.

52 For Egypt see Sonneveld 2012: 53–54, 182 etc.; see Schneider 2014: 21.

53 In his class on October 24, 2013, he explained with regard to Quran 4:34 that men are stronger in reflection and patience than women, even if he had to admit that some women have stronger reflection than some men. He connected this emotionality of women and rationality of men to the men's right to *ṭalāq*.

the Supreme Judge quoted this example of female behavior, unrest was noticeable among the students even if no outspoken questions were asked, no critique of his opinion was uttered. Surely, it would have been possible to openly challenge him and confront him with critique or at least critical questions concerning his arguments. Surely, the Supreme Judge would have answered to this because he presented himself in the class as a person being very much in favor of and enjoying a legal discussion, whereas he seemed more than once annoyed by the noisy talk of the students among themselves. However, none of the students dared to challenge the *Qāḍī al-Quḍāt*'s argument.

He moved on in his narrative to the financial side of marriage and argued that women would financially benefit more, if they made use of other forms of separation. This is why, he explained to the students, he reformed divorce for "dispute and discord" by taking the burden of proof from the woman. The combination of these two rulings makes sense, even if the question arises why he did not refer to this kind of separation to protect young women before consummation and help them out of the marriage bond. The question of why the right to *khulʿ* after consummation should not be given to her had been asked or at least referred to twice by the students. When giving the summary of his discussion with "women," in the plural in the beginning, which turned out to have been the conversation with one woman, again an interesting subtext is revealed. Asked why she wanted it, she "needed hours," he mockingly reported, only to state that "she wanted" to give a *khulʿ*. The subtext in this case is: whereas men have the right to repudiate a woman, they have it in their hands to grant a divorce whenever and wherever they want – without any reason – a woman demanding the same unrestricted right needs "much time to explain," meaning she is slow to voice her wish to be the powerful one, who gives the divorce. In the way he told it, he consciously or unconsciously ridiculed her wish to have equal rights to a man.

It is not only the woman's wish to be the one who decides that is ridiculed but also her alleged female irrationality that prevented her from understanding what is financially good for her: to get a proper repudiation and keep the dower. The implicit message is women need (needless to say: male) guidance and protection both emotionally and in questions like their own financial benefits. At this point, again students first laughed but then started to talk among themselves. They might have laughed because the way the Supreme Judge tells the story sounds funny at first glance but reveals later the socially allegedly unacceptable wish of this woman to be "in charge," i.e., to give divorce. But again: why should this be unacceptable especially because – as we will see later – the Supreme Judge himself labeled this new kind of divorce as "equality."

The *Qāḍī al-Quḍāt* now explained that this dispute actually happened in a court case and it is here where he refers to Kayyāl's *khulʿ* divorce, without, however, giving her name. His argument is that the matter became political, the media interfered, and in the end, he could not have given *khulʿ* after consummation exactly because of this political dimension. Kayyāl's case is revealing because it shows, as quoted above, in a drastic way the helplessness of Palestinian women and her dependence on the male with regard to divorce. It is at this point that the students started again to discuss among themselves. One reason might be that the case was well known in the Palestinian public and they felt pity for this woman.[54] Another reason may be that they were surprised by the extent of female dependency and subordination to the husband's will. On the other hand, the *Qāḍī al-Quḍāt*'s narrative of the emergence of the *taʿmīm* and the reason why it should have been restricted only to marriages before consummation may not have been altogether clear. In the media,[55] it had been reported that the Supreme Judge started to discuss the matter at the beginning of 2012. The ruling was issued August 20, 2012. Kayyāl filed her claim in November 2012 and the decision was given in April 2013. So how could this case have been the reason for connecting the ruling to marriages only before consummation?

Be this as it may, one can draw the cautious conclusion that the students started to talk among themselves in situations when the (dependent) position of women was discussed or their right to equality was ridiculed.

5.3.2.2 How Did He Use the Past? Which Terminology Did He Use?

The *Qāḍī al-Quḍāt* started with the definition of *khulʿ* in language and terminology (*fī al-lugha wa-l-iṣṭilāḥ*): linguistically (*lughatan*), *khulʿ* means "taking off vestment" (*izāla*), and as a term (*iṣṭilāḥan*), it is the "spouses taking off the vestments from the other" with separation (*tafrīq* or *ṭalāq*). This he connected to Quran 2:187, of which he only quoted the second part: "(It has been made permissible for you the night preceding fasting to go to your wives [for sexual relations]). 'They are a vestment for you, and you are a vestment for them.'"

Before going into detail of the socio-legal background of the new ruling he mentioned that *khulʿ* in the JLPS is based on mutual agreement. He said that *khulʿ* was perhaps known from the news or television broadcasts from Egypt or Jordan, in what was his only hint to the legislation in the neighboring countries, but he wanted to create something new. He explained his thoughts about

54 Johnson and Hammami 2013: 18.

55 See chapter 6.

how he could bring *khulʿ* in a revised version to the Palestinian population, to the public on the "street" as he put it several times. Asked by a student how *khulʿ* could be expressed in classical legal terms, he defined it as "*ṭalāq* based on general redemption (*ṭalāq muqābil ibrāʾ ʿāmm*)."

He summarized the development of the iteration, which he, according to his narrative, had initiated, and eventually led to the *taʿmīm*. When he had talked about it for six or seven months, people started to approach him. He did not make it easy for himself but he always stayed in connection to the people of Palestine to find out what they thought about it: "What is the reply of the street? First of all, I work with the street, with the nation, here are educated people, there are lawyers, politicians, common people … I started to think, to study, to research how I could deal with this topic."

He then collected the other Sharia judges to discuss the matter with them. Article 183 of JLPS, which states that Hanafi jurisprudence has to be used in cases where a legal matter is not regulated in the law, was taken into consideration but refuted because it did not help. He explained to the students that the Hanafis say nothing about the several different forms of separation. "They have no kind of judicial separation [which can be used by women] (*lā ʿindahum ayy nawʿ tafrīqʾ*)." He thus went back to the principal of lifting injury based on the rule *lā ḍarar wa-lā ḍirār* (do not inflict injury nor repay one injury with another). He explained the application of this rule to his students: if a problem occurs, the path of lesser evil has to be taken or the way that inflicts the least damage. Taking the example of a ship in distress at sea, this principle would require jettisoning cargo overboard in order to save human lives. When he had done all the research and heard back from the people in the public, he gathered the judges and provoked them: "Either you convince me or I convince you!"

Is *khulʿ* contained in Sharia? With this rhetorical question he – according to his narrative – opened the discussion with the Sharia judges. Of course, all had to agree. But only *khulʿ* based on mutual agreement, of course, was seen to be in the Sharia so far. He said, he would give them proof that judicial *khulʿ* was also possible. Basically, he argued that Quran 2:229 speaks of three times *ṭalāq* and in between mentions *khulʿ*. The verse speaks in addition to *ṭalāq* of the possibility for husband and wife to agree on separation through redemption of the woman, if both fear that they cannot keep God's limits. The verse reads as follows:

> Divorce is twice; then honourable retention or setting free kindly. It is not lawful for you to take of what you have given them unless the couple fears, they may not maintain God's bounds; if you fear they may not

> maintain God's bounds, it is no fault in them for her to redeem herself. Those are God's bounds; do not transgress them. Whosoever transgresses the bounds of God – those are the evildoers.
>
> If he divorces her finally, she shall not be lawful to him after that, until she marries another husband.[56]

As it is obvious – he argued – "the husband has three *ṭalāqs*, the mentioning of the redemption cannot be *ṭalāq* but must be a special separation." Otherwise, the verse would mention *ṭalāq* four times.[57]

With regard to the Prophet's *ḥadīth* on Thābit b. Qays's wife approaching the Prophet, he stated that "there are scholars" who consider the Prophet's order as a judgment (*ḥukm*) when he said (to the husband): "take the garden [i.e., dower] and give her *ṭalāq* (*ṭalliqhā taṭlīqa*)." He stressed that it should be kept in mind, that an "order creates an obligation (*wujūb*) and becomes a decision of the judge to the citizen."

Besides or even despite these "uses of the past," this rooting in the holy texts and classical law, the *Qāḍī al-Quḍāt* was confronted with what he called "masculine society" and the harsh critique of its male representatives. From the beginning, the Supreme Judge stated many times that the public on the "street" had difficulty with the term "divorced" in the passive voice,[58] that masculine society and specifically the men did not agree with being called "divorced." Men seemed to be afraid to be labeled *makhlūʿ*, for example, that the house of a divorced man would be marked as the "house of the divorced" (*dār al-makhlūʿ*) and people would refer to it as the "house of the divorced [man]." Men called in the passive voice "divorced" would ask: "How can this word be used?" (*Kayfa tuqālu hādhihi l-kalima*)? One citizen allegedly complained that Idʿīs wanted the woman to be able to "divorce us" (*an takhlaʿanā*); again another one was quoted by the Supreme Judge saying: "With God, I will give her *khulʿ* before she gives it to me!" (*wa-llāhi akhlaʿu raqabatahā qabla an takhlaʿanī*).[59] A student commented that in this case neither of them should be called "like this."

The *Qāḍī* started to declare publicly and repeated over and over again, in his lecture and in public, that *khulʿ* is a "good, clean and nice word" (*kalima ṭayyiba wa-naẓīfa wa-jamīla*). In the end, young men rushed to the court to initiate the

---

56 See Quran. The Supreme Judge neither quoted the full Quranic text nor did he go into details of interpretation.

57 The same argument is used in the *taʿmīm*, see 4.3 as well as in the textbook, see 5.4.

58 See many times in the debates, see especially chapter 6.

59 *Raqaba* "neck" is used in classical Arabic as pars pro toto for the whole person. See Lane 1863. According to Ghada Issa, my Palestinian assistant, it is used in this expression commonly today in Palestine as a threat.

separation to be quicker than their not-yet-wives. At this point of his narrative a student interrupted: "only not to be named *makhlūʿ*," now ridiculing the men's behavior.

Defining *khulʿ* the Supreme Judge stated:

> *Khulʿ* [may] occur through a certain indirect expression (*al-khulʿ yaṣīr bi-ayy alfāẓ kināʾiyya*), through *khulʿ* or *iftidāʾ*. We tried to ease the men's anger because, regrettably, the media poured oil onto the fire.

In the media men had asked him: "*Shaykh*, do you [really] want us to be called divorced (*makhlūʿ*)?"[60]

The use of the verb *khalaʿa* in the passive voice was seen in the media as an "attack on our [the men's] dignity" (*al-imsās bi-karāmatinā*). The Supreme Judge reacted to this, according to his now very lively narrative in complete incomprehension: "Why should it be an attack on your dignity? It is a nice and good word!"

But then, the Supreme Judge explained, he and his colleagues relented in order to soothe the men's anger and called it in court a "claim of redemption" (*iftidāʾ*) according to the Quran 2:229 thus making it easier for the men to accept this legal solution.[61]

Dealing with the rationale (*ḥikma*) of this ruling, he argued that Islam gave the husband the right to unilaterally repudiate his wife (*ṭalāq*) and obliged him to pay. So the Islamic Sharia gave the wife the right to *khulʿ* connected with payment.

He concluded: "This is equality (*musāwāh*) between man and woman and it is the principal rational (*al-ḥikma al-asāsiyya*)."

Toward the end of the class, a young woman asked: "Professor, the one giving *khulʿ* is the woman (*al-khāliʿ hiya al-marʾa*) because the man has the right to give *ṭalāq* (*li-anna al-rajul min ḥaqqihi an yuṭalliqa*)?"

The judge responded:

> The one giving *khulʿ* [is] *mukhāliʿa*,[62] past participle (*ism mafʿūl*). We don't say *khāliʿa* (the women is giving *khulʿ*) but [we say] *imraʾa mukhāliʿa*, because some biased persons tried to fish in troubled waters and tried to

60 *Sic*, in singular.

61 In *taʿmīm* 59/2012, I could not find this term "claim of redemption" (*daʿwā al-iftidāʾ*), but it is in the Draft Law of 2013. Article 104 calls it "divorce of redemption" (*tafrīq li-l-iftidāʾ*).

62 The Supreme Judge is actually using the participle active of the III. form *fāʿala* whereas the student used the participle active of the I. form *faʿala*: *khāliʿa*. Also see the next footnote.

abuse the word "woman giving *khulʿ*" (*imraʾa khāliʿa*) [saying] she took off her shame (*khalaʿat al-ḥayāʾ*) and wandered around in the streets here and there. Have you heard this word? Some tried to abuse the word *khāliʿa* and we said: no, she is a woman using *khulʿ* (*imraʾat mukhāliʿa*) and the word *mukhāliʿa* is taken from "partner in business" (*mushārika*)[63] [because] she redeems herself with the property and gives it to him. Therefore, it is not correct that we say *imrāʾat khāliʿa*, this word has been rejected (*marfūḍa*).

5.3.2.2.1 *Analysis*

The Supreme Judge based his argument and his reaction to these discussions "in the street" on "uses of the past." On the one hand, he was satisfied, having initiated a public iteration since he considered these arguments to be a response from the people as well as an encouragement to go on with his reflections to find an Islamic solution to the problem. On the other hand, he held against it, defended classical terms as *khulʿ* in new versions, in the passive voice *makhlūʿ* waiting for the reaction of the people before he started his intellectual work on *khulʿ*. The legal definition the Supreme Judge gave to the students for *khulʿ* was: "Repudiation (*ṭalāq*) based on general redemption (*ibrāʾ ʿāmm*) is *khulʿ*. It is the meaning of *khulʿ*. It means that the woman redeems (*an taftadiya*) herself, in that she pays an amount of money to the husband to retain repudiation by him." This definition of the traditional *khulʿ* based on mutual consent contains several legal aspects: the classical *khulʿ* based on mutual agreement is *ṭalāq* whereas, as he argued later, the new judicial *khulʿ* is dissolution of marriage, i.e., *faskh*. And it is general "redemption" (*ibrāʾ*) with which the woman redeems herself (*iftadat*). From this definition it seems that both terms, *ibrāʾ* and *iftidāʾ*, are synonyms.

The Supreme Judge made "uses of the past" based on the Quran and Sunna: Quran 2:229 was taken as a basis to argue that if *khulʿ* would be *ṭalāq* there would be four *ṭalāq*s in the Quranic text – which cannot be. It is the same argument that had been used in the *taʿmīm*, and again it is not clear why this argument could be used to introduce a new kind of *khulʿ* against the husband's will, because the text of 2:229 refers to the couple in the dual form "unless the couple fears" (*illā an yakhāfā*) and then continues to address in the dual form

63 The Supreme Judge perhaps had in mind that grammatically the III. form *fāʿala* often expresses the same action as the I. form (*faʿala*), but the action is directed to someone. The dictionary of Wehr gives for the I. form (*khalaʿa*): "to take off" (garment) and "to divorce" ones wife and for the III. form (*khālaʿa*) it gives the meaning "to divorce one's wife" (in both cases it is added: "in return for a compensation to be paid by her). The dictionary considers it thus as male actions in the I. as well as in the III. form.

men and women equally. This would hint at consensual redemption but not to the permission for women to redeem themselves against the husband's wish. The reference to the *ḥadīth* is more convincing as he argued that scholars consider the Prophet's order as a judgment and an order as an obligation for the judges. There is still a kind of contradiction to what he had said before, because in the way he quoted the *ḥadīth* the husband had to give *ṭalāq* to his wife on the order of the Prophet and it is not the Prophet who gives the separation. All in all, the "uses of the past" are not detailed and again superficial and without an in-depth analysis of the texts with no introduction for the students to use this source critically. Denker's conclusion – participants of the iteration in Egypt took the "easy way out" by roughly referring to Quran and Sunna but not going through a painstaking analysis of the texts – can be confirmed in the Palestinian context, too, at least with regard to the text of the *taʿmīm* and his lecture in Birzeit.[64]

To "translate" the talk of society into Islamic language, the Supreme Judge tried to shift the social debate and redirect it so that his ruling could be put in force. At first, the Supreme Judge had to deal with males who did not want to be called "divorced" in the passive voice, as the male gender was seen as connected to the active voice – men divorce and do not get divorced whereas the female gender was seen connected to the passive voice. This argument concerned divorce in this debate and is normally used for the sexual act, and it is connected, of course, to gender hierarchy in the Quran: men stand above women (4:34). Men protested against being called "divorced" in the passive voice and even felt their dignity was violated[65] and thus the Supreme Judge relabeled it *iftidāʾ*, which has a Quranic root – even if it did not justify *khulʿ* against the husband's wish. This term *iftidāʾ* is used in the Draft Law of 2013, Article 104, but actually not in the *taʿmīm* 59/2012. It also appears, as mentioned before, in the Jordanian law.[66] This shift in the discussion seems to have soothed the angry male spirits.

A second debate regarded the agency of women as reflected in language. Here the Supreme Judge answered a student's question regarding the terminology of a "divorcing" woman (*khāliʿa*). It was not *khāliʿa*, because this term had become abused, he explained, for being shameless or roaming the streets. Thus, the Supreme Judge wanted to change *khāliʿa* to *mukhāliʿa* – which is

64 Denker 2004: 176.

65 Fāṭima ʿĀshūr, attorney from Gaza, even repeated several times that in most Arabic societies, a man does not accept the passive act of being divorced (*makhlūʿ*) and "abandoned" (*matrūk*) by his wife but that he is the one who rejects, abandons, and gives repudiation (*Lāzim Naḥkī* April 30, 2013), see also 6.3.

66 Goudarzi-Gereke 2018: 61.

taken from the same root but expresses the aspect of "taking action against someone". He did this, as he said, to stop the evil talk about women divorcing men. This neologism, however, seems, to the best of my knowledge, not to have been taken up in society and had no follow up in the legal texts.

The Supreme Judge does not quote international law at all, but his statement that giving women the right to this version of *khulʿ* "can be called equality (*musāwāh*) between men and women" must be interpreted as an allusion to Articles 2 and 16 of CEDAW. However, in the *taʿmīm* another term had been introduced with the potential to stimulate the process of "translating the global into the local," which is not mentioned here: "similarity" (*mumāthala*).[67] The version of *khulʿ* the *Qāḍī al-Quḍāt* created and defended here as "equality" did not give both genders the same access to divorce. Men could give *ṭalāq* at any time and were not obliged to go to court whereas women had to go to court and needed a mediation procedure, before the judge would decide.[68] The ruling was restricted to marriages before consummation. Still, one could suspect that the Supreme Judge used this assertion on purpose, as a subtext referring to the debate with women's organizations, to suggest that his ruling effected gender equality or at least enhanced women's rights as prescribed by CEDAW. In both cases, i.e., with "similarity" (*mumāthala*) and "woman giving *khulʿ*" (*mukhāliʿa* instead of *khāliʿa*), new terms, neologisms, were created that were partly linguistically connected to the existing expressions (*mukhāliʿa*) and partly connected to the Quran (*mumāthala*). None of them were successful in the end in the iterations, and they were not used by the public or referred to in any other legal text, exept Gaza.[69] Concerning the "woman giving *khulʿ*," the Supreme Judge's explanation was triggered by a student's question. As before with the ruling as such he wanted to show in his lecture that he protected women, helped them against male aggressions and even, on the linguistic level went so far to invent new terms, trying to twist the discourse towards a more positive perception of women "giving *khulʿ*."

Again and again, the Supreme Judge did his best, from his perspective as a Muslim scholar, to refashion an Islamic legal term: *Khulʿ* is a "nice and good word" etc., but he could not bend it completely in the direction he wanted. Social feelings, or to be more exact, patriarchal prejudices, were still too strong

---

67 See chapter 4.3.

68 Sonneveld quotes in her research a report from Human Rights Watch of 2004 with regard to the necessity of reconciliation in the *khulʿ* separation but not when the husband gives *ṭalāq*: "Taken to its logical conclusion, the troubling implication of the court requirement that women, and only women, attempt to reconcile with their spouses is that only women are capable of destroying the family," quoted in Sonneveld 2012: 102.

69 See chapter 9.

to accept men being called *makhlūʿ* in the passive voice, even against the voice of a very well-respected *Qāḍī al-Quḍāt*. The Supreme Judge was fighting against the men who felt their dignity was violated by being called "divorced" (*makhlūʿ*). At the same time, he was eager not to create the impression that he steered this discussion: he initiated it and accompanied it intellectually but he always waited for feedback from society and listened to it – even adapting the terminology.

All in all, and especially with regard to the term *khulʿ*, a sophisticated development can be observed on the linguistic level, focusing on the "linguistic, legal, cultural, and political repetitions-in-transformation."[70] In the end, the new term "judicial *khulʿ*" was established and widely used as well as *iftidāʾ*, which at some points replaced *khulʿ*.

The iterational process and especially the debate about "active-passive" is parallel to what happened in Egypt, according to Sonneveld's analysis of cartoons in Egypt, published in connection to the new *khulʿ* law in 2000:

> All cartoons communicated the same message: once women were given the right to unilateral divorce, society would be turned upside down. Husbands whose wives divorced them through *khulʿ* were sarcastically labeled *makhlūʿ*, a term deriving from the same verb as *khulʿ*. In the context of women's unilateral divorce rights, *makhluʿ* was used to refer to husbands whose wives had gotten rid of them in much the same way one pulls out a bad tooth.[71]

5.3.2.3 How Did He Justify the Legality of the Ruling?

The Supreme Judge proudly announced that he already developed seven "laws" (*waḍaʿtu sabʿata qawānīn*)[72] – among them a ruling (*taʿmīm*) with regard to *takhāruj*.[73]

He expressed to the students that in the beginning, he was not convinced that his judicial colleagues would follow. This was more due to personal than purely scientific reasons, as he was afraid, they would perhaps say yes but then change their minds because of personal reservations they had against him

70 Benhabib 2004: 180.

71 Sonneveld 2012: 64. This also can be observed for the Jordanian case, see Goudarzi-Gereke 2018: 61.

72 Obviously, he speaks of regulations (*taʿmīmāt*) calling them "laws" as if they were laws.

73 The *taʿmīm* with regard to *takhāruj* (waiving of shares of inheritance) regulated the registration of the inheritance four months after the death of the deceased at the earliest, see Wafa, May 13, 2011. The *taʿmīm* is not on the website of the SCHC, see 2.1.2.

since he, as a Supreme Judge, might have made decisions that offended some of them, for example, sending them to a small court.

After the successful discussion with his colleagues, described above, he decided to take his colleagues to a press conference where photos were taken – a remark humorously made that caused laughter among the students. He touched briefly on the critique of the lawyers, mentioning Article 183 that requires observance of the predominant opinion of the Hanafi school. But he was not very detailed about the discussion with lawyers and other jurists.

He did not, in addition, describe in detail the process used to enforce the *taʿmīm*. He proposed to his fellow judges that the first *khulʿ* case should be decided very quickly and they should

> then submit it to the Appeals Court (*Maḥkama al-Istiʾnāf*) to validate it without considering. Why? Because every judgment looked at and validated by the Appeals Court becomes a judicial precedent (*sābiqa qaḍāʾiyya*). The Constitutional Court is not allowed to overrule it under any condition.

He challenged the lawyers, saying he wanted to apply this ruling on *khulʿ* and whoever was against it should go to the Constitutional Court. It was submitted to the Appeals Court within one month and it was accepted. And the lawyers could not do anything, he announced triumphantly: "It became judicial precedent and nobody can abolish *khulʿ* because it became law (*fa-lā yastaṭīʿ ayy aḥad an yubaṭṭilu al-khulʿ li-annahu aṣbaḥa qānūnan*)." So, he concluded, "We were successful in this matter (*najaḥnā fī hādhā al-mawḍūʿ*), meaning we got a law (*yaʿnī kasabnā qānūnan*)."

5.3.2.3.1 *Analysis*

Stating that he had already issued different "laws" and thus describing the existing *taʿmīmāt*[74] as laws as well as the present *taʿmīm* must be called a blurring of the boundary between the state's right to issue laws and the issuing of rulings (*taʿmīmāt*) of the SCHC. The Supreme Judge neither brought the text of the *taʿmīm* to class nor did he read with the students the text of the JLPS nor did he discuss with them the fact that according to the BL every law has to go through parliament or at least it has to be issued as a presidential decree. Instead, he shared with the students his enthusiasm about the new ruling that improved women's position in a situation without parliament and without a president who would have been ready to amend the law based on a presidential decree.

74 Those *taʿmīmāt* cannot, as the one about *khulʿ* be found on the website of the SCHC.

Yūsuf Idʿīs made all efforts to legalize this new *khulʿ* ruling and explained the procedure in several steps: he developed the new ruling, discussed it with his colleagues (the Sharia judges), presented it to the public, and wrote a letter to encourage all judges to apply it. After a first decision in the *khulʿ* case, the matter went to the Appeals Court, being validated and being thus promoted to be not only a legal precedent but a "law." He was obviously proud not only that he could initiate this process so quickly, that the matter went through the Appeals Court and that "we got a law," but also that he had discussed it with "the street" as well as with the necessary experts, the Sharia establishment.

What does this procedure mean? The *Qāḍī al-Quḍāt* presented it as judicial precedent legitimized via the Appeal Court[75] but strictly speaking, it means that the Sharia judiciary took over legislative competence. Idʿīs' predecessor, al-Tamīmī, had criticized this harshly, as outlined above, he had pointed to the inconsistency of this procedure and mentioned that all three powers, the legislative, executive, and judicial have to be kept separate, that legislation has to be in the hands of the legislative branch, i.e., the parliament.[76] He had outlined that the Law of the Formation of the Sharia Courts of 19/1972 does not bear evidence to legislation and lawmaking of the judiciary. He had added that *ijtihādāt* of judges and their interpretation of the legal texts are not binding on any judge. Still, this seems to be the way the *taʿmīm* became enforced. It is the narrative the *Qāḍī al-Quḍāt* presented to his students.

5.3.2.4 How Did the Supreme Judge Present His Own Role in the Whole Process?

The *Qāḍī al-Quḍāt* presented the development of the *taʿmīm* not only as a law – thus laying claim to legislation – but also very much as a personal success story. Dealing with the "law in context" and less with the legal background, he referred to the social debate and the way he developed his thoughts, thus giving the students insight into the Palestinian iterations from the point of view of the Supreme Judge.

At the beginning of his class, he defined politics as the supervision of the wellbeing (*maṣlaḥa*) and management of society. Describing himself as being in an important position and responsible, he explained that he felt obliged to think about a solution to this problem and a "legal and *sharʿī* healing" (*ʿilāj qānūnī wa-sharʿī*). He described the Palestinian public space first as reluctant and than going into discussion with him about this form of divorce and also

75 See chapter 4.4.

76 See chapter 4.4.

about the appropriate terminology, pointing again and again to the importance of the "street," as he called Palestinian society. If there would have been an uncontrollable rage, he assured the students, he would not have dealt further with the matter.

5.3.2.4.1 *Analysis*

In a way, he created a quasi-democratic public space that discussed his suggestions. In a second stage of the development of this iteration, when society started to respond to his ideas and suggestions, the media took over, as he dramatically described it. Whereas he welcomed the reaction of the Palestinian people, their questions and suggestions, and whereas he also outlined and appreciated the importance of the role of the media in society, he also criticized the fact that they "poured oil onto the fire" and described their behavior as leading to a crisis. He complained especially that he was constantly followed by the media, they called him day and night, and still, when he gave interviews, he was misunderstood and misquoted in some of the media. He criticized this because it lead to the aforementioned politicization of the case of Kifāḥ Kayyāl.

He painted a picture of himself starting this process of iteration on purpose and with an actual reason; it was a social problem on the ground but it was difficult to control the process and its outcome. He emphasized in his lecture the important role of other judges of the Sharia judiciary who discussed the matter with him, and hinted at the discussion with other lawyers and jurists but never went into the details of the critique of his proceedings. He presented himself as an initiator and as an important player of this jurisgenerative iteration. He described himself acting in different roles, as a judge and a civil servant of the state, and – besides teaching at BZU – as a traditional Muslim scholar, a *faqīh*, a scholar using independent legal opinion (*ijtihād*) in the best interests of society.

Applying Seyla Benhabib's concept of iteration to the Supreme Judge's narrative, one could say that not only he was the starting point and initiator of this de facto jurisgenerative iteration, but also the intellectual center. How much was he steering the iteration? His claim that he would not have gone on with the matter if there had been serious resistance in society can well be believed. He was sensitive to the public and tried to understand their responses. His defense of the "good" word *khulʿ* comes from a religious point of view and is revealing with regard to his position in society. Despite being a highly respected scholar, he could not convince all of his fellow citizens and could not completely steer them in the direction he thought would be useful. He had to give in and rename *khulʿ* to *iftidāʾ* in the Draft Law of 2013, if not in the *taʿmīm* where it remained as "judicial *khulʿ*" still clearly distinguishable from the "classical" version.

Going one step further, it can be stated that he described himself in the whole process as not only the person who recognized necessary social changes and – resulting from this – necessary legal changes, but also the one who saw himself invested with power to push it through. Thus, he saw himself as, and perhaps was, the symbol and core of the iteration process, but he was – or at least presented himself – also as the juridical key to the solution and as a remedy for a social problem on the ground. It was necessary for him to construct his position separately from the "legislature" – the state – in spite of being head of the *Dīwān*, i.e., part of the legal system of this state. He argued that he had to explore the legislator's preparedness to follow his ideas for a change.

That he was well aware of his different roles can be shown by a distinction he made in one of his other classes. He stated that the judge only judges on the basis of the outer appearance (*bi-ẓāhir*), but religion is based on what is inside (*bāṭin*).[77] In another lecture, he hinted at the existence of *mujtahids* in modern times.[78]

Even if he exaggerated his role in what can be called his personal success-narrative in the lecture, there is no doubt that as a jurist in Islamic law, a teacher at Birzeit University, as the signee of the *taʿmīm* and the letter to the judges he was at that time an influential but also widely respected player in Palestinian iterations around the topic. Thus, he might be called a factual legislator as "his" ruling was applied afterward in the courts. The combination of his different roles gave him a powerful position in West Bank society, which can be called "political" and which also transgressed the limits of the separation of the three powers. At the same time, his ruling found much consent and approval especially among the affected women and women's organizations but also from the Sharia establishment.[79]

What about the role of the students in this lecture? They did ask some questions, but not as many and not as critical as one might have expected. Instead, they started very often to talk among themselves. This was obviously always the case when they either did not understand the context – as might have been with regard to the Kayyāl case – but also at points where they were

---

77 Class notes, October 24, 2013.

78 Class notes, November 14, 2013.

79 His successor in the position of the *Qāḍī al-Quḍāt* acted very differently, and by the end of 2018, he had made some public statements about women that got him into serious trouble with the women's organizations, see chapter 8.

confronted with the Supreme Judge's clear position with regard to gender relations. Sometimes they just laughed because of the exaggerated way the Supreme Judge described certain points, e.g, when he stated that young men invite the women to one shawarma sandwich and then reclaim the value of several slaughtered muttons. Here it seems that they supported his critique. At another point, when he made fun of the woman – who perhaps was Kayyāl – who claimed the right to give *khulʿ*, they laughed first because of the funny way he described the situation, her taking a lot of time and then still demanding this right. But soon afterward, they started to reflect and talked among themselves: What did it mean? It is possible that gender roles and how they were talked about by the Supreme Judge evoked students' criticism but this never turned into a real discussion, queries and a deeper debate in the classroom and only sometimes cautious questions were asked.

5.4 Textbook of the Supreme Judge's Class: Past or Present?

Why are textbooks important?[80] John Issitt defined textbooks as a fuzzy category[81] but as useful sources, even goldmines.[82] They are being produced for practical considerations[83] and extensively used.[84] Students of the Supreme Judge's course were required to buy the textbook in a little shop on campus, prepare the lessons, and know the contents of the chapter that would be discussed in the next class. They used the textbook extensively in class even reading parts of the chapter aloud and commenting on the text. The students, of course, used the textbook for preparation for the exams.

Textbooks summarize knowledge, according to Issitt's definition of this genre, and present it in a handy version, laying a definitional claim to the knowledge they contain – they assert that "this is certain knowledge and this is the knowledge you [the student of law] need"[85] and thus reveal underlying patterns of the construction of knowledge in a certain discipline, time, and context. What is in the textbook and therefore part of the examination can be regarded as the essence of knowledge in a disciplinary field.

For Issitt, the "textbook is furthermore the vehicle for the transmission of authorized dogma. In its role as an essential site of learning, the textbook is

80 This section is a revised version of my article, see Schneider 2018b.
81 Issitt 2004: 685.
82 Issitt 2004: 684, 686.
83 Issitt 2004: 687.
84 Issitt 2004: 683.
85 Issitt 2004: 685.

a key mechanism for the production and reproduction of ideas."[86] Textbooks contain, according to him, "a focused educational program in text allied to a scheme of work."[87] They are based on a "mix of sources" and include "dominant ideas and social values."[88] The function of textbooks in university teaching is a hitherto ignored topic. Monique Cardinal investigated teaching in the area of Islamic legal theory (*uṣūl al-fiqh*) in contemporary Arab universities – comparing Tunisia, Morocco, Egypt, Syria, and Jordan.[89] She observed that judges, court officials, and lawyers were no longer required to know the substantive law of Islamic legal tradition, since they apply foreign-inspired modern law. Islamic legal theory is taught in a simplified and reformulated manner. Thus, she argued, legal theory remains a subject of interest, albeit "on a highly reduced scale," often taught in the form of a one-semester course.[90] The classics of Islamic legal theory have, according to her, gradually been superseded by modern textbooks, and the level of understanding of classical *uṣūl* texts has dropped. The professors she interviewed doubted that their undergraduates could adequately read and understand classical *fiqh* texts.[91] As a consequence, classical works on Islamic legal theory were taught mostly as excerpts alongside or in contemporary textbooks.[92] Cardinal described this process as a breakdown of the classical tradition of education,[93] which she, however, did not research. Neither did she go into detail or look at the way in which one special topic is dealt with, let alone the level of *Begriffsgeschichte* nor did she attend classes but relied on interviews with the professors.

The title of the textbook used in the Supreme Judge's class is in Arabic and English (whereas the content is in Arabic only):

> Birzeit University [in Arabic and English]: Faculty of Law and Public Administration Discipline of Law (in Arabic) [here phone number and website of the university are given]: Lectures of the Curriculum of the

86 Issitt 2004: 688.
87 Issitt 2004: 685.
88 Issitt 2004: 685.
89 Cardinal 2005.
90 Cardinal 2005: 224–225.
91 Cardinal 2005: 240.
92 Cardinal 2005: 241.
93 See Cardinal 2005: 225, where she is well aware that the issue at hand is not nor should it be the question of whether or not modern manuals are better than their classical counterparts, but to understand how and why the modern manuals, designed for a new purpose in a new context, have come to differ from the classics. In her conclusion she sees a "devastating" effect of the importation of Western law on the integrity of Islamic legal theory as a discipline (Cardinal 2005: 269).

PSL [all in Arabic: *Muḥāḍarāt Masāq Qānūn al-Aḥwāl al-Shakhṣiyya*] (Personal Status Law 338). First semester 2013–2014.[94]

The first pages of the *Muḥāḍarāt* outline the syllabus and include a chronologically ordered list of topics to be taught in the semester. The author of the first part dealing with the definition of PSL and quotations from different PSL texts in history is not mentioned. For the remaining chapters, two authors are named: ʿUmar al-Ashqar and Maḥmūd al-Sarṭāwī. As the textbook is composed of several texts copied from different books or publications, there is a new additional pagination added in handwriting to the folios. It starts with folio 1 and ends with folio 226. Each folio comprises two pages; which are referred to as "a" and "b." From folio 2 to folio 9 the legal development of Palestine is dealt with, including the applicable Jordanian laws and Christian laws, personal status law, folio 130–266 deal with the Christian family laws of the different churches.

The focus in the following pages will be on *mukhālaʿa*[95] written by ʿUmar al-Ashqar.[96] As the textbook does not mention the new ruling of 2012 – but could have done so because it was produced in 2013 – the contents of this chapter of the textbook will be analyzed with regard to questions falling broadly into two categories: (1) how the Islamic past was used in the textbook and (2) which gender roles were discussed and reflected. In detail these questions are:

1. Is the Islamic past used in the textbook? And, if so, how?
   a. Which legal terms are used: Islamic terms, the terms of the JLPS? How, especially, is the term *khulʿ* defined? Are parallel terms and counterterms given?
   b. Which sources are used? JLPS? Islamic sources?
   c. Which other Arab PSLs are quoted?
2. What are the gender roles discussed and reflected in the book?
   a. How are gender relations (re)constructed: on the basis of equality or of gender hierarchy?
   b. As a result, is a new, modern version of gender relations proposed or is the classical gender concept, what Sonneveld calls the "maintenance-obedience relation"[97] repeated?

Based on the results of these two sets of questions the basic question will be answered: ultimately, what is, to quote Issitt,[98] the "certain knowledge" that

94 It is referred to as *Muḥāḍarāt* (lit. "Lectures") 2013–2014.

95 *Muḥāḍarāt* 2013–2014: 78b–86a.

96 The chapter seems to be taken from his book *Al-Wāḍiḥ fī Sharḥ Qānūn al-Aḥwāl al-Shakhṣiyya al-Urdunnī*, Beirut 2001.

97 Sonneveld 2012.

98 Issitt 2004.

students are expected to gain and should reproduce in the exams according to this textbook? Moreover – also quoting Issitt – what are the "authorized dogmas" conveyed in this text with regard to gender and with regard to the "uses of the past"? In the end, law students are trained on the basis of these texts to enter the judicial system, either as judges or defense lawyers or to contribute to reforming the law as scholars.

The close reading of the textbook will again be guided by the research questions given above and by Koselleck's *Begriffsgeschichte*.[99] The synchronic analysis focuses, as before, on the meaning of *khulʿ*, as well as parallel concepts that help to define the main terms,[100] e.g., *mubāraʾa* (divorce by mutual consent) and *iftidāʾ* (redemption), which have all been discussed already with regard to the *taʿmīm* and in the context of teaching. Furthermore, counterconcepts[101] help to co-constitute the semantics of a given concept. The analysis of the counterconcepts will focus on an *ikhtilāf* (diversity [of opinions]) dealing with the question of whether *khulʿ* is *faskh* (dissolution of marriage) or *ṭalāq* (repudiation).

According to Koselleck, there are three categories of terms: (1) terms that have persisted and contain empirical validity; (2) terms and concepts whose content has changed so radically that, despite the existence of the same wording, the meanings are barely comparable and can be recovered only historically; and (3) neologisms.[102] Finally, it will be discussed to which of these categories the new version of *khulʿ* belongs.

Chapter 16 of the textbook, titled *al-mukhālaʿa* starts with a linguistic and terminological definition[103] and the wordings[104] and continues with the "rationale" of the legislation.[105] Then, different indicators for the legality of *khulʿ* are given[106] and the question of whether *khulʿ* is *ṭalāq* (repudiation) or *faskh* (dissolution) is discussed including an appreciation of this difference.[107] Then the question is discussed what should be ruled when the husband treats his wife

99 Koselleck 2004: 76–92. Terms such as *khulʿ* have to be analyzed synchronically and diachronically under the aspect of how the past is used by the authors of the textbook. This does not comprise a thorough analysis of classical *fiqh* texts and the historical development of this concept, which is not possible in this context. For Egypt, see Denker 2004.

100 Koselleck 2004: 87–88.

101 Koselleck 2004: 88.

102 Koselleck 2004: 83.

103 *Muḥāḍarāt* 2013–2014: 1. *Taʿrīf al-Khulʿ fī al-Lugha wa-l-Iṣṭilāḥ*: 78b.

104 *Muḥāḍarāt* 2013–2014: 2. *Alfāẓ al-Khulʿ*: 78b–79a.

105 *Muḥāḍarāt* 2013–2014: 3. *Ḥikmat Tashrīʿ al-Khulʿ*: 79a.

106 *Muḥāḍarāt* 2013–2014: 4. *Adillat Mashrūʿiyyat al-Khulʿ*: 79b.

107 *Muḥāḍarāt* 2013–2014: 5. *Hal al-Khulʿ Faskh aw ṭalāq*?: 80a–b; 6. *Thamarat al-Khilāf wa-fāʾidatuhu*: 81a–b.

badly.[108] Up to this point in the chapter, the JLPS is not even mentioned, the framing is purely Islamic law. The next paragraph discusses the topic of who is allowed to give *khulʿ*.[109] Here, for the first time the JLPS, Article 102, is quoted. Then, detailed regulations of *khulʿ* are given[110] and financial regulations are discussed, which are not the main focus of this study.[111]

5.4.1 *Is the Islamic Past Used in the Textbook? And, If So, How?*

The text starts with a classical linguistic and then terminological definition of *khulʿ* in the first paragraph.[112] *Khulʿ* linguistically is defined, as usually, as taking off vestment. As a term (*iṣṭilāḥ*), it is defined as "the man separating from his wife on the basis of the money she pays to him." This is directly and diachronically connected to Quran 2:187, the so-called *libās*-verse: "they are a vestment (*libās*) for you, and you are a vestment for them."[113]

This definition is in accordance to the Supreme Judge's definition given in class. The "wordings" (*alfāẓ*) of *khulʿ* are connected to the discussion of the scholars of the classical schools of law and their use of the particular wordings[114] (*al-alfāẓ bi-ʿaynihā*). Different expressions with which the term was connected are given. This paragraph is diachronic insofar as it deals with the term in the history of Islamic law and gives at the same time the broad range of parallel concepts of that time. The Hanafis connect it to sale (*al-bayʿ wa-l-shirāʾ*), to *mubāraʾa* (dissolution of marriage by agreement with mutual renunciation of any financial obligations) and *ṭalāq* (repudiation), the Malikis to *khulʿ*, *al-fidāʾ* (redemption), *al-ṣulḥ* (reconciliation) and *mubāraʾa*, the Hanbalis to *ṭalāq*, *faskh* (dissolution) and *mufādāt* (redemptions). These parallel concepts are not explained and only some of them are discussed further in the text, e.g., *faskh* in the discussion of whether *khulʿ* is *faskh* and not *ṭalāq*. In the third paragraph,[115] the "rationale of legislation" is pointed out. Reference is again made to Quran 4:20, and the argument, which will be discussed further in the second part, is offered that whereas men have the right to *ṭalāq*, women have the right to *khulʿ*, an argument that had also been used in the *taʿmīm* and in the Supreme Judge's teaching. It seems to indicate that both genders are on equal

108 *Muḥāḍarāt* 2013–2014: 7. *Idhā kāna Sūʾ al-ʿIshra min Qibal al-Zawj*: 81a–b.

109 *Muḥāḍarāt* 2013–2014: 8. *Ṣifat man taṣiḥḥu mukhālaʿatuhu*: 81b–82a.

110 *Muḥāḍarāt* 2013–2014: 9. *Al-khulʿ min al-Ajnabī*: 82b.

111 *Muḥāḍarāt* 2013–2014: chapters 10–19: 82b–86a.

112 *Muḥāḍarāt* 2013–2014: 78b.

113 See https://www.islamawakened.com/quran/2/187/default.htm, accessed November 15, 2018.

114 *Muḥāḍarāt* 2013–2014: 78b–79a.

115 *Muḥāḍarāt* 2013–2014: 79a.

footing, but this is not the case as will be outlined. It is interesting to see that despite the title "rationale of legislation," and despite the mentioning of *tashrīʿ* (legislation), the JLPS is not cited in this paragraph and the EFRL is never cited.

It can be stated (1.a) that the terms used are classical Islamic terms and that those terms are at the beginning of the paragraph discussed only in the context of their classical use. There is no reference whatsoever to the terminology of the JLPS (Articles 102–112), in which *khulʿ* and *mukhālaʿa* are used interchangeably. The way the sources are quoted (1.b) is equally conventional, starting[116] with the most prestigious text, the Quran (2:229 and 4:19), continuing with *ḥadīth*, followed by the *ijmāʿ*, the consensus of the schools of law. Reference is made only to the Sunni school of law, never to the Shiite. This reflects a certain tradition in Palestinian legal teaching to exclude the Shiite school of law from the common legacy. Scholars of the early time before the establishment of the schools are quoted, for example, Ibn ʿAbbās, Ṭāwūs, Zuhrī, Shaʿbī, Ibn Musayyib, and others.

In the *Muḥāḍarāt*, the *ḥadīth* is represented first in one version, which is quoted without the source. In addition, the text of a conversation between the Prophet and Thābit's wife follows. According to this text, the first *khulʿ* was again as usual the *mukhālaʿa* of Thābit b. Qays's wife, who complained to the Prophet that she was afraid not to keep her husband's right.[117] The Prophet ordered her separation (*amara al-rasūl bi-taṭliqihā*) after she had returned the garden her husband had given her as dower. A version of this *ḥadīth* in Bukhārī based on Ibn ʿAbbās follows, in which the woman is quoted directly approaching the Prophet: "Oh Prophet, I don't blame Thābit b. Qays for his character (*khulq*) or religion (*dīn*), but I hate unbelief in Islam (*akrahu al-kufr fī al-Islām*)." The Prophet asked if she can give back the garden, she answers in the affirmative. The Prophet said (obviously to her husband): "Take the garden and divorce her (*khudh al-ḥadīqa wa-ṭalliqhā taṭlīqa*)." Thus the second version is only quoted for conveying the direct speech between the Prophet and Thābit's wife. No attention is paid to differing legal aspects of the case. The many existing variations are again ignored as well as their wide range of different possible interpretations, which Denker had analyzed so meticulously. Later in the text, the *ḥadīth* is again used as a reference point to introduce more detailed regulations with regard to the waiting period – shorter for *khulʿ*, only one menstruation cycle, than in normal *ṭalāq*, three cycles.[118] After quoting the *ḥadīth*,

116 *Muḥāḍarāt* 2013–2014: 79b.

117 *Muḥāḍarāt* 2013–2014: 79b.

118 *Muḥāḍarāt* 2013–2014: 80b.

it is explained to the students that almost all scholars, with one exception, accept *khulʿ*.

Denker's analysis of the Egyptian debate is again confirmed for the Palestinian textbook, too: the *ḥadīth* is quoted only in one version and not interpreted in detail. In addition, other personal status laws in the Arab world, modern interpretations of Islamic law, Western law, let alone international law, are not referred to (1.c). In the first seven paragraphs of the chapter, one looks for the JLPS in vain. It is only in paragraph 8, which deals with the question of who is allowed to give *khulʿ*, that the JLPS is mentioned and Article 102 is quoted: "(a) It shall be a condition precedent for mukhala'ah to be valid that the husband be eligible for the effecting of the divorce and that the wife be subject to it."

Additional information, described as "valid," is given and reference is made to Article 83 according to which the husband must be eligible for divorce and Article 88 specifying that "a divorce by the inebriated, astounded, coerced, imbecile and unconscious man shall not take effect." Article 83 mentions in the Arabic text that the man has to be *mukallaf*, obligated to observe the precepts of religion. In the *Muḥāḍarāt* this is qualified further as *bāligh* (of age) and *ʿāqil* (reasonable), thus interpreting or explaining the text of the law, the framing always being Islamic law. Not only are the sources completely "classical," but the acts are also classified according to the *aḥkām khamsa*, i.e., the five classic categories ranging between "obligatory" (*wājib*) and "forbidden" (*ḥarām*), of evaluation of all rules and acts as well as persons. There is no discussion about different possible legal consequences this could have or has in the frame of legislation. Instead the discussion is based again completely on Islamic jurisprudence focusing on the issue, whether a husband who was mistreating (*nāshiz*) his wife[119] should be allowed to take money from her.[120] The Hanafis reject this notion and call it *makrūh* (reprehensible), and according to Ibn ʿĀbidīn, it is even *ḥarām* (forbidden), referring to Quran 4:20. Ibn Qutayba called it a consensus (*ijmāʿ*), he should only take the money in case the disobedience (*nushūz*) is from her side.[121] Such a behavior from the husband would be against the text,

119 Wehr (1976) translates the noun *nushūz*, adjective *nāshiz*, as "violation of marital duties on the part of either husband or wife." However, as these duties are different and gendered so is the meaning of *nushūz* with regard to man and woman. Wehr thus continues: "For women it means normally recalcitrance of the woman towards her husband, for the husband it means brutal treatment of the wife."

120 *Muḥāḍarāt* 2013–2014: 81a–81b.

121 In this case *nushūz*, the noun, has to be translated as "disobedience" as women are concerned.

quoted is Quran 4:20. The whole discussion, however, does not bear reference to the text of the JLPS.[122]

In the *Muḥāḍarāt*, the question of whether *khulʿ* is repudiation (*ṭalāq*) or dissolution (*faskh*) is dealt with and this is framed as a (traditional) *ikhtilāf* (diversity of opinions).[123] The students learn that a group of scholars consider *khulʿ* to be irrevocable repudiation (*ṭalāq bāʾin*), regardless of whether the term *ṭalāq* or *khulʿ* is used. Among those named as scholars adopting this position are Mālik, Saʿīd b. al-Musayyib, Ḥasan, ʿAṭāʾ and others as well as the "people of the personal opinion" (*aṣḥāb al-raʾy*) thus mostly scholars of the time before the schools were established. A second opinion considers *khulʿ* to be the dissolution (*faskh*) of the marriage. This opinion is attributed, among others, to Ibn ʿAbbās, Isḥāq b. Rāhwayh, and Aḥmad b. Ḥanbal; it is one of the sayings of Shāfiʿī. ʿUmar al-Ashqar, the author of this chapter, summarized: "Most scholars whom I have looked at, make it *faskh*,[124] if not, the word *ṭalāq* is given." Only when clearly connected to the wording of *ṭalāq* is it *ṭalāq*. It is then argued that *Shaykh* al-Islām, meaning Ibn Taymiyya, in his "Legal Opinions on Women" (*Fatāwā al-Nisāʾ*) always considers it a dissolution (*faskh*), with or without the word *ṭalāq* with reference to Ibn ʿAbbās and Ibn Ḥanbal. To substantiate this view one page of evidence (*adilla*) follows in favor of *khulʿ* being a dissolution whereas less evidence is provided for the opposite position. As evidence for it being *faskh* Quran 2:229–230 is quoted, which also had been dealt with in the *taʿmīm*.[125]

It is argued, again similar to the argument used in the *taʿmīm* and in the Supreme Judge's class, that this Quranic text comprises two separations (*taṭlīqatayn*), *khulʿ* and then another separation (*taṭlīq*), and if *khulʿ* were *ṭalāq* it would be the fourth. This argument is attributed to Ibn ʿAbbās, whose interpretation is presented as being the preferred one. In the *taʿmīm* and in the Supreme Judge's class, the same argument had been used to deliver a proof for the "judicial *khulʿ*" against the husband's wish. But it does not prove anything beyond the fact that there is, besides *ṭalāq*, another form of consensual separation.

122 Until now there has been no mentioning of the JLPS. In Article 102 of the JLPS, *ṭalāq* is only mentioned in one place: the husband might be eligible to effect the divorce (*ṭalāq*) and the wife is subject to it. Besides this very general reference to *ṭalāq*, neither the term *ṭalāq* nor the term *faskh* are mentioned in the JLPS in the paragraphs that deal with *khulʿ*.

123 *Muḥāḍarāt* 2013–2014: 80a.

124 *Muḥāḍarāt* 2013–2014: 80a.

125 See https://www.islamawakened.com/quran/2/229/default.htm and https://www.islamawakened.com/quran/2/230/default.htm, both accessed on November 15, 2018.

A discussion about the waiting period (*ʿidda*) follows,[126] which is only one menstruation cycle in *khulʿ* but three menstruation cycles with *ṭalāq*. This is taken again from the *ḥadīth* in which the Prophet advised Thābit b. Qays's wife to wait one menstruation cycle. Reference is made to the collection of Abū Dāwūd and al-Tirmidhī. This, again, is taken as a strong argument for *khulʿ* not being repudiation (*ṭalāq*) but *faskh*, followed by the argument that *khulʿ* can take place during menstruation, which is not allowed for repudiation (*ṭalāq*).

With all these peculiarities, it is evident that *ṭalāq* is constructed as a counterconcept to *khulʿ*, differing in certain important points: there are three *ṭalāq*s but only one *khulʿ* in the Quran. *Khulʿ* has a shorter waiting period; it can take place during menstruation. It is seen as the "clear wording" (*al-qawl al-thābit*) established by the Companions of the Prophet.

This diversity of opinions is then summarized under the heading "Profit and Usefulness of the Diversity."[127] But what is all this good for? There is no clue whatsoever as to why this and only this "diversity of opinions" is quoted here, and what use it should have for the students. Diversity being an important feature of Islamic law (*ikhtilāf*) has always been considered a reflection of the plurality of interpretations in the Sharia. But here it is given with a clear bias to support the position that *khulʿ* is dissolution of marriage and not repudiation. The interpretation (in this case of Quran 2:229 and 2:230) is not critically discussed but premade. There is no guidance or encouragement for the students to develop their own positions, not even to weigh the two opinions. It therefore can serve as a good example of what Issitt calls the "transmission of authorized dogma,"[128] offering the students a bite sized summary of knowledge to be reproduced in the examination instead of stimulating critical debates or an approach to critical source interpretation in the sense of Islamic jurisprudence (*ijtihād*). The question of whether the chain of transmitters (*isnād*) is sound, and the transmitters could have met each other, as well as the question whether the text is clear, i.e. classical methodological approaches to *ḥadīth* critique are not even mentioned. Still less debated is how these sources could and should be applied in a modern nation-state and whether a modern interpretation would make sense and could be applied to solve social problems such as women who cannot get a separation from their husbands without having to bring proof.

126 *Muḥāḍarāt* 2013–2014: 80b.
127 *Muḥāḍarāt* 2013–2014: 81a.
128 Issitt 2004: 685

Thus, three important results emerge:

- Perhaps the most interesting finding is that despite the explicit mention of "PSL" in the name of the class and the fact that the students are supposed to be trained in modern codified family law, the JLPS does not play a prominent role in the text.
- There is no in-depth introduction in Islamic jurisprudence (*fiqh*) and its reasoning, either. One might expect that the textbook, *fiqh*-oriented as it is, aims to train the students in classical critical *fiqh* thinking, i.e., *ijtihād*, stimulating discussions etc., but this is not the case.
- The text goes deep into the past, summarizing different definitions and parallel concepts such as *mubāra'a* and others, which, however, are not spelled out. Again, they are not put into dialogue with the present legal situation.

A more general discussion with counterconcepts, (*ṭalāq* in this case) by its definition must be also rooted in the past. *Khulʿ* obviously belongs to the terms that are persistent according to Koselleck's definition.[129]

5.4.2 *What Are the Gender Roles Discussed and Reflected in the Textbook?*

In the *Muḥāḍarāt* there seems to be an inherent tension or ambiguity between gender equality and hierarchic gender arguments and positions. At the beginning,[130] Quran 2:187 – the "vestment" verse and the idea that both spouses are garments to each other – is quoted. This verse could have opened a possible road to gender equality interpretations and is often referred to as such in debates.[131] But in analyzing the textbook, it becomes evident that this is not the chosen approach. Second, the argument that each of the spouses, male or female, has to pay for breaking up a marriage is another interesting argument that also could have served as a starting point to develop gender equal legal regulations or at least of equal access to divorce for both genders.

Under the heading *ḥikmat tashrīʿ al-khulʿ* (rationale for the legislation),[132] it is stated that because God gave the husband the right of repudiation (*ṭalāq*) if he detests his wife and obliges him to pay (4:20), the woman has the right to redeem herself if she detests her husband. This seems to imply gender equality, at least to a certain degree. The medieval scholar Ibn Rushd (d. 1198), i.e., the "past," is quoted to corroborate this statement: Redemption (*fidāʾ*) of the woman is, according to him, in exchange for the right to repudiation being in

129 Koselleck 2004.

130 *Muḥāḍarāt* 2013–2014: 78a.

131 See *Lāzim Naḥkī* 2013.

132 *Muḥāḍarāt* 2013–2014: 79a.

the husband's hand.[133] Because the repudiation was put into the man's hand if he despises (*faraka*, literally, to rub) the woman, *khulʿ* was put into the woman's hand if she despises (*farakat*) the husband. This is an interesting piece of evidence of "uses of the past" in debating male and female rights to divorce and recognizing rights for both spouses. Is it proof of gender equality in the twelfth century? It is certainly an interesting point made by Ibn Rushd, but he does not, of course, refer to the term "equality," let alone "gender equality," but instead points to one specific situation, in which the husband and/or wife hate/despise each other and should equally have the opportunity to get out of this situation.[134]

Rajʿa, the husband's right to take back his wife during the waiting-period after the first and second repudiation is then dealt with,[135] as was the case in the short text announcing the *taʿmīm* on the website of the SCHC.[136] As *rajʿa*, leaving the woman subject completely to the husband's arbitrariness, is not allowed to him in a *khulʿ*-divorce, the mentioning in the textbook as well as on the website of the SCHC could be a hint of women's more powerful position in this version of divorce and their broader access to agency.

The points mentioned, i.e., the non-existence of the husband's right to take her back (*rajʿa*), the stress on the "vestment" verse as well as the economic argument that whoever wants to break up the marriage has to pay could be classified as attempts to introduce, in an indirect way, gender equality arguments. Again, this is not outlined and students are not given a clue as to how such gender equality or at least more agency for women could be achieved.

There is another line of arguments running against this and focusing on gender inequality. Instead of sticking to the "vestment" metaphor as a possible starting point for an argument in favor of gender equality, *khulʿ* is defined as "the husband's divorce of his wife on the basis of money she spends." The wording is as follows: "If the woman redeems herself (*iftadat*) from her

133 Ibn Rushd II: 68/81: "Yet, the juristic reasoning is that *fidāʾ* (price to be paid for redemption) grants a woman something equivalent to what is possessed by the man, namely (the right to) divorce. A man possesses repudiation when he pressures (*faraka*) a woman, while a woman possesses *khulʿ* when she wants to pressure a man (her husband)." To translate *faraka* as "to pressure" is perhaps nearer to the linguistic meaning of *faraka*, lit. "to rub." I translated it here as "to despise." The Arabic text in the textbook is in the quotation of Ibn Rushd in (nearly complete) accordance with the Arabic edition of Ibn Rushd.

134 It is not possible in this context to follow up Ibn Rushd's construction of gender relations, even though it would be a challenging and highly interesting topic. We have to confine ourselves to the way in which the past is used in present jurisprudence and therefore how arguments from classical Islamic jurisprudence are inserted into present debates.

135 *Muḥāḍarāt* 2013–2014: 79b.

136 See chapter 4.3.

husband by giving him money (*māl*), so that he can divorce her (*li-yubīnahā minhu*), and he responds to her [positively], then she is divorced from him."[137] Several points in this definition reflect a gender hierarchy with the male on top: the initiative rests with her, but he has to consent; she pays, he divorces her; there is no court involvement mentioned. This is the classical definition of *khulʿ* based on mutual consent. In two decisive points the man has the last word in this traditional *khulʿ* based on "mutual consent": to agree, and to carry out the repudiation. The consent is mutual but he plays an active part.

A further argument reinforces this impression of gender inequality, the text comments: "It is not just (*laysa min al-ʿadl*) that the woman gets rid of the marital bond after he spent money for her without him being the cause for the divorce."[138] This argument is in the text connected to Ibn Rushd's "gender equal" explanation of *khulʿ* as being the right of the women against male repudiation. What might at first glance give the impression of a certain degree of equality turns out to be none. It ignores that whereas the man can divorce his wife at will – even if she gave him no reason for doing so – for the woman, the same act on her side is now evaluated as "unjust." Here, the problems of qualification, of evaluating the act of the woman, of justice and, in the end, of a gendered concept of marriage in a broader range intersect.

The problem lies in the unequal gendered basis of the marriage: the husband pays and gains the right to have sexual relations with the wife and she has to obey after she takes the dower. Her right to refuse sexual relations with the husband lapses after she has taken the dower. Money and especially the dower can be considered a kind of entrance fee for sexual relations. A relationship simply based on payment for intercourse would be unproblematic: the wife could decide to end the sexual relationship and give back the dower, not of course the maintenance (*nafaqa*), because she has already had sexual relations with the husband and maintenance could be seen as the payment for the sexual relations she had with him during marriage. But the relationship is not one based on money for intercourse. Besides the economic aspect, the woman's obligation to obey, the concept of *ṭāʿa* (obedience) is of central importance. Once she takes the dower and agrees to the sexual relations, she cannot step back, she has to obey.[139] Denying her husband sexual relations is not a financial affair, but a violation of her duty of obedience. Not fulfilling the sexual needs of the husband is disobedience (*nushūz*). This can by no means

137 *Muḥāḍarāt* 2013–2014: 78b.

138 *Muḥāḍarāt* 2013–2014: 79a.

139 See Shaham 2018 with regard to the *bayt al-ṭāʿa*, but the articles on *ṭāʿa* in the Encyclopedia of Islam and of Quran do not deal with female obligation to *ṭāʿa*.

be described as a relationship of equality but is in accordance with the "money for obedience and sex" principle of the Islamic marriage. It therefore makes sense to broaden the term "maintenance-obedience" into "money-obedience" thus including the "entrance fee," i.e., the dower, as establishing this fundamental relation. Also, it obviously does not count that a woman deciding at a certain point in her marriage that she does not want to be married anymore did actually obey for many years and that she is only now changing her mind, as the example of Thābit's wife shows. She has to choose other options for a separation to save her dower, she has to show that he infringed her right to maintenance, presence and reproduction.

In the *Muḥāḍarāt* another reasoning is added. The woman's decision to step out of the marriage, which is described by Ibn Rushd as something that might occur to either one of the spouses, is now connected to another Quranic verse, Quran 2:229.[140] This verse mentions the fear that both cannot keep God's limits. The verbs are given in the dual form, relating to a husband and a wife thus indicating equal rights or at least mutual agreement to end the marital relationship. But what do the exegetes make out of it? Ibn ʿAbbās, Mālik and others interpret the inability to keep God's limits (*iqāmat ḥudūd Allāh*) as the wife's "disdain (*istikhfāf*) of the husband's right and her disobedience (*sūʾ ṭāʿa*) towards him."[141] Given the gender equality in the Quranic text, this is an openly misogynic twist in the exegesis for two reasons: the Quranic text refers to both genders, but the commentators focus only on the woman; the Quranic text speaks of the fear of not keeping God's limits, but the commentators speak of the wife's disobedience. It stands in opposition to the "vestment" verse quoted at the beginning, which somehow and very generally could have been associated with a more egalitarian approach to the gender roles. The Quran is trumped by the Quran in this textbook, to the disadvantage of women.

Again, Denker's result is corroborated.[142] There is no in-depth analysis of this verse; on the contrary, the interpretation presented to the students is not evident but misogynistic and ignores the Quranic text. At the same time, it is not explicit. No other possible interpretations are alluded to. Students are confronted with a problematic interpretation that they are not equipped to critically examine. The authors of this twenty-first-century textbook take what Denker calls the "easy way out" on the road to misogyny and leave the students behind without any tools to reject such a misogynist interpretation.

---

140 *Muḥāḍarāt* 2013–2014: 79b.
141 *Muḥāḍarāt* 2013–2014: 79b.
142 Denker 2004.

To summarize, the gender relation constructed here in the context of *khulʿ*, despite a certain ambiguity in the text that became obvious, for example, in the "vestment" verse, is the classical one: both spouses have to agree, not much agency is left for the woman. If the husband does not agree, but the woman wants the divorce, in this case the husband's right is stronger, no divorce takes place, and the wife is branded a disobedient wife. The argument that economic aspects should regulate the marital relationship – the one who pays can get out of the marriage – does not override the basic inequality. If money for sexual relations were to be the basis of the marital relationship, then women could buy themselves out of the marriage. But the relationship is more complicated because obedience plays a central role. The "vestment" verse as well as the economic argument of equality are not developed further but trumped by a misogynistic interpretation of 2:229.

5.4.2.1 Comparison of Text and Teaching

The analysis of the *Muḥāḍarāt* on personal status law reveals interesting results. First, the framing and structure of the chapter is completely classical, starting with the definition at the beginning and continuing with the sources, the "uses of the past": Quran, Sunna, and consensus (*ijmāʿ*) are referred to and not, as one would expect, stipulation and analysis of the relevant articles of the JLPS, let alone the EFRL, which is applicable in Gaza. "Certain knowledge," as Issitt calls it,[143] is given in the form of ready-made definitions, selective quotations from the classical sources, and therefore a selective "use of the past," which is partly misogynic, is made. Authorized dogmas are presented in the same way, as was shown with the example of the "diversity of opinions" on the question of whether *khulʿ* is a dissolution of the marriage or a repudiation. So, what are the underlying ideas[144] of this chapter?

First, the idea regarding the general methodological training of the students lends itself more to what can be called "training for imitation" (*taqlīd*) the counterterm of *ijtihād*,[145] even though these two contrary concepts are not mentioned in this chapter. The chapter obviously did not have the aim of training students in classical Islamic methodology or in critical thinking. Neither an in-depth analysis of the Quranic verses with different interpretations nor of the important *khulʿ-ḥadīth* are found in the text. In the case of Quran 2:229,

143 Issitt 2004: 685.

144 Issitt 2004: 688.

145 *Taqlīd* is the counterterm of *ijtihād*. Whereas *ijtihād* means the efforts made to find a new interpretation from the texts, *taqlīd* means to adhere to something.

even an obviously problematic and male-biased interpretation is presented without offering the students room for reflection.

With regard to the second aspect, the construction of gender relations, a certain ambiguity is revealed. Either the "vestment" verse or the idea that whichever spouse wants the divorce has to pay could have served as starting points to develop arguments in favor of more gender equality in this legal realm. Again, this did not happen and the cautious approaches were overruled by a highly misogynistic interpretation of Quran 2:229, which considers the woman's "right" to redemption as a violation of the man's right to obedience.

If looked at in depth: the result is still gender inequality. Neither with regard to legal methodology nor with regard to gender concepts – an important topic in the debate about the construction of a modern society and the concept of a Palestinian Family Law to come – do students get a clue as to how to approach this difficult and complex topic in a highly developing and vibrant modern society such as Palestine. More explicitly, they are not given the tools to connect this classical debate to the legal situation of women, family, sexuality, or gender roles in the West Bank in the twenty-first century and develop a more gender equal approach to the interpretation of the sources. According to this textbook, the authorized dogma is methodological: to use the past uncritically and, with regard to gender relations, to accept classical misogynistic interpretation.

How does this compare to the Supreme Judge's teaching? Neither the textbook nor the Supreme Judge in his teaching refer much to the law, if at all, only to the JLPS and not to the EFRL; in both cases, the framing is clearly Islamic law and in both cases there is no training in critical thinking or *ijtihād*. It must be conceded, however, that the Supreme Judge, if asked, would have been ready to introduce the students to more aspects of Islamic legal reasoning. Like the textbook, he was not very detailed in his "uses of the past" and it is strange that he used the same argument with regard to the "four *ṭalāq*s" for his justification of the introduction of his *khul*ʿ ruling as the textbook does with regard to *khul*ʿ being separation (*faskh*). There are, however, differences: the misogynistic interpretation of the Quran is not taken up by the Supreme Judge in his arguments. Just the opposite, he not only criticized "masculine society" or, more specifically male behavior toward young women, but outspokenly declared it as his aim to help vulnerable women. Of course, this lecture was special, as he dealt with the implementation of the or better "his" new ruling in this session. But generally, in his teaching he was eager to give not only the Islamic legal regulations but examples from his practice, to show the students how applied law works. Law is put into its socio-legal context, social problems are discussed and the Supreme Judge presented his solution for this problem – which was, perhaps not surprisingly, a Sharia solution and did not refer to the JLPS – very much as his personal success story. In the end, he connected it to a deep insight into the functioning of the family law system in Palestine. He applied classical legal thinking to the present situation and showed the students a way to adapt the classical concept of *khulʿ* to modernity, to "translate" it into the realm of Palestinian society of the twenty-first century, by finding a "Palestinian" solution that satisfied the needs and calmed the prevailing debates. *Khulʿ* is made possible for women against the husband's will, but only in marriages before consummation. It can be called "*khulʿ* Palestinian style,"[146] which, however, ignores the constitutional requirements for enacting a law. Last, but not least, this difference between the analysis of the text and the analysis of the teaching process reveals an interesting discrepancy between these two approaches and shows, that understanding "teaching" as a process always has to take into consideration both sides: the textbook and the actual teaching process.[147]

146 However, this form of *khulʿ* is not confined to Palestine, it was discussed in Jordan too. See Goudarzi-Gereke 2018.

147 For the sake of comprehensiveness and if this research was about university teaching only and not about the analysis of legal iterations in the Palestinian public, it would, of course, have been necessary to include in-depth interviews with the Supreme Judge as a teacher (my focus in the interview with him was on his role as "quasi-legislator") and with the students about how they experienced the teaching process.

CHAPTER 6

Khulʿ in Iterations

On April 30, 2013, the television program *Lāzim Naḥkī* (We have to talk) about *khulʿ* was broadcast on Palestinian television.[1] The host, Jumān Qunayṣ,[2] a graduate in media sciences from Birzeit University, started the program with the following statement:

> There exists a repudiated woman (*muṭallaqa*) and another "inbetween" woman (*muʿallaqa*). In both cases, the man is the acting person (*al-rajul huwa al-fāʿil*). He repudiates the woman or leaves her "inbetween." But we want to hear from a man who is divorced (*makhlūʿ*). The actor (*al-fāʿil*) in this case is the woman. Yes, she is the one who divorces (*takhlaʿu*) the man. *Khulʿ* means that a woman asks for separation in exchange for a financial compensation that she pays to him. This is now applied in Palestine. Women benefit from it only before actual marriage (*al-zawāj al-fiʿlī*). *Khulʿ* and what is in favor or against it is our topic today on *Lāzim Naḥkī*.[3]

With this introduction, she directly tackled the central aspect of the *khulʿ* iteration, the terminology, mentioning the two main counterterms: *ṭalāq* as a man's privilege and *khulʿ* as a means for the woman to get divorced and focusing on the active-passive tension in the terminology, which, as the Supreme Judge had confirmed, had caused so much controversy in (male) Palestinian society.[4]

---

1 *Lāzim Naḥkī*, April 30, 2013.

2 Jumān Qunayṣ, interview on November 7 and 27, 2013, holds a master's degree in Media sciences from Birzeit University. She prepared and presented several issues of the progam *Lāzim Naḥkī* for Palestinian television. I had two interviews with her. In the first one, we talked about the important topics of iterations in the West Bank. She confirmed that at that time it was *khulʿ* as well as honor crimes. In the second, much shorter, interview I asked her about the *khulʿ* program of *Lāzim Naḥkī*.

3 *Lāzim Naḥkī*, April 30, 2013.

4 This chapter deals with *khulʿ* but also with debates about family law and its different drafts in a larger context in roughly the first phase iterations. However, later interviews with representatives of civil society, the state, and the Sharia establishment were also included when they dealt with these topics. Despite a clearly recognizable shift of the discourse around 2014 and later toward debates around international law, *khulʿ* but especially the more general topic of

 | DOI:10.1163/9789004442313_007

Qunayṣ used the gendered language consciously: "We want to hear of a man who is divorced" she said challengingly. "Yes, she is the one who divorces the man" using the verbal form of the second person feminine, which in Arabic is different from the form used for a man (*takhlaʿu* instead of *yakhlaʿu*) and thus stressing the woman's agency. *Khulʿ* was discussed widely in the media before and after the issuing of the *taʿmīm*. Whereas, for example, on *Ḥārisāt Nārinā* (Custodians of our fire) on April 9, 2017, four years later,[5] the topic discussed was more generally the "Family Law",[6] the issue of the TV magazine *Lāzim Naḥkī* on April 30, 2013, focused exclusively on the new ruling.

Lāzim Naḥkī gives a good example of how different experts discussed the ruling. By the time of the broadcasting, the new ruling had been in force for seven months, so first conclusions from its application could be drawn and were drawn in the program. Whereas the guests in the studio were experts from the Sharia establishment as well as legal experts, short visual sequences captured the opinion of a sample of women and men in the streets of Ramallah and a voice of a young woman going through a *khulʿ* procedure. A short glance is cast at Gaza and the discussion there. Legal and Islamic legal discussion of the topic was underpinned with reports from the courtroom and a Sharia judge explaining the ruling and a staff member of the court demonstrating the necessary steps when filing a *khulʿ* claim. Several boards containing information about the legal background in Palestine informed the public about the new ruling. *Lāzim Naḥkī* along with other television talk shows gave valuable insight into the iteration in the Palestinian public and how it shaped mainstream thinking in the Palestinian public about the topic. The title "We have to talk" already reflects concentration on socially relevant topics.[7] Media in Palestine are very active with regard to political-social and legal topics. Dale Eickelman and Jon Anderson have pointed in 1999 to the important role of the media in an emerging Muslim public sphere that exists at the intersection

a Palestinian Family Law remained a topic even after 2014, see e.g. *Ḥārisāt Nārinā*, April 9, 2017. These parts of the debates were also included in this chapter.

5 *Ḥārisāt Nārinā*, April 9, 2017.

6 Here, as a representative of civil society, Ṣabāḥ Salāma, Coordinator of the Palestinian Non-Governmental Organisation against Domestic Violence against Women al-Muntada had been invited and her counterpart on the Sharia side was Al-Ḍamīrī, see chapter 8.

7 Asked, how she had selected the topics and planned the *Lāzim Naḥkī* issue on *khulʿ* on April 30, 2013, Qunayṣ explained that she acted in close cooperation with the editor and selected with him the specialists known to the public for their knowledge on the topic. She considered it an especially important experience to go to the Sharia court in Ramallah and interview the legal staff as well as a young woman in the middle of a *khulʿ* procedure. People in the street were selected randomly, the aim was, Qunayṣ outlined, to show how much or how little the people knew about the ruling after being in force for seven months.

of religious, political, and social life: "Facilitated by the proliferation of media in the modern world, the Muslim public can challenge or limit state and conventional religious authorities and contribute to the creation of civil society."[8] They also point to a new development of what gets into circulation and who introduces new ideas: "The proliferation of actors able to assert a public role leads to a fragmentation of authority, and it increases the number of persons involved in creating and sustaining a religious-civil public sphere."[9]

This is reflected in Palestinian media with lively discussions and programs on law and women's rights. The experts present in the studio on *Lāzim Naḥkī*[10] were: Arīj ʿAwda, a Sharia lawyer (Sharia *mustashāra qānūniyya*) from Ramallah/al-Bireh, and member of the civil society organization Women's Technical Affairs Committee/*Hayʾa Idariyya fī Ṭāqim Shuʾūn al-Marʾa*; Ṣumūd al-Ḍamīrī, Sharia Judge and Head of Prosecution in Family Matters; and Dr. Ikrām al-Qaysī, the lawyer of the Sharia Court. All of them welcomed this new ruling. Judge Farūq ʿAdīlī and Judge Khitām Abū Arjīla, Head of Office of Control and Family Reconciliation (*Qism al-Irshād al-Usarī*)[11] of the Sharia Court of Ramallah who were not present in the studio but interviewed in the Sharia Court, explained in detail the procedure to the audience, whereas Ḥasan al-Jūjū, Chief of the Gaza SCHC and Gaza lawyer Fāṭima ʿĀshūr described the situation in Gaza as they saw it. Al-Ḍamīrī had the final word arguing that in cases of young women being in the situation described, *khulʿ* was the solution. Qunayṣ finished in the lead-out of the program a shade provocatively: "Dear husbands, if you approve injustice to your wife – be prepared, you may become divorced (*mukhlūʿ*)."[12]

This chapter discusses the iterations according to the different actors, i.e., civil society, the state, and the Sharia establishment. As in the previous chapters, the statements of these three groups of actors were analyzed according to the following questions:

- Why was the reform of the family law generally and with regard to *khulʿ* seen as necessary; and what reasons were given in favor of or against the reform?
- Which "uses of the past" were made? Which terminology was used?
- Why was *khulʿ* against the husband's will given only before consummation of marriage? Which gender concepts were negotiated?
- What does this ruling (*taʿmīm*) mean? How does it compare to legislation?

8 Eickelman and Anderson 1999: 1; see also Masud 2005.

9 Eickelman and Anderson 1999: 14.

10 *Lāzim Naḥkī*, April 30, 2013.

11 This is a short name of the office of "Control and Family Reconciliation" (*Dāʾirat al-Irshād wa-l-Iṣlāḥ al-Usarī*).

12 *Lāzim Naḥkī*, April 30, 2013.

6.1 Civil Society

6.1.1 *What Does Palestinian Society Think about* khulʿ?

What do people "in the street," whom civil society claims to represent, think about the new ruling? A short sequence from *Lāzim Naḥkī*[13] – randomly selected people in the streets of Ramallah were asked three questions – gives an interesting albeit not representative insight into the way the topic of *khulʿ* was publicly perceived and talked about; second, a survey conducted by Rema Hammami and Penny Johnson in 2013 that focused less on the new ruling and more generally on people's opinions about marriage and divorce including *khulʿ* is used here to tackle this question.

At the beginning of *Lāzim Naḥkī*, eight people, men and women, were selected in the streets of Ramallah and asked three questions:

1. Question: Are you in favor of or against a woman's right to *khulʿ*?
   A[14] (young woman): Surely, I am for this issue.
   B (elderly man): I am with both sides.
   C (young woman): It should be fifty-fifty.
   D (elderly woman): I am against *ṭalāq*.
   E (elderly man): No, surely, only for the man.
   F (young man): Surely not.
   G (elderly man): I am very supportive of complete equality (*al-musāwāh al-kāmila*) between a man and a woman.
2. Question: When the woman is treated unjustly, should she be able to ask for *khulʿ*?
   D: If she is treated unjustly she should have the right to leave him.
   G: She has the right if she has reasonable reasons.
   B: When the woman is treated unjustly, then she should have the right to divorce her husband (*tuṭalliq zawjahā*), if not, then not.
   E: She should go to the judge and he should say something about it.
3. Question: What does religion say with regard to *khulʿ*?
   H (man, middle aged): According to Sharia it is the right of the wife to go to the judge and tell him that she does not want to go on living with her husband. The judge will ask her "why" and she will answer that she

13 *Lāzim Naḥkī*, April 30, 2013.

14 Because the names of the persons interviewed are not known, letters are given and gender and age are provided to distinguish them. The order of the persons reflects the order they were asked the first question. For the second and third questions, the persons reappear in chronological order of the program.

> has very strong excuses (*mubarrirāt*) and she has the chance to tell them to the judge.
> E: With regard to the new law (*al-qānūn*) that the Palestinian Authority issued or the Palestinian judiciary, it is a *khulʿ* law, it is before consummation (*al-zawāj*) and after the contract was made and it is unobjectionable (*lā ghubāra ʿalayhi*).

Quite probably all interviewees, A through H, were asked all the questions but afterward a selection seems to have been made and only some of the answers were chosen to be shown on the program. Furthermore, incomplete answers might have been presented to the audience. The analysis can only proceed on what was in the end shown in the program and therefore might not give the real position of the persons asked.

Whereas the first and the third question are general questions about the right of *khulʿ* and the position of religion, the second question is tricky, as *khulʿ* separation, strictly speaking, does not need to be substantiated by evidence of unjust treatment of the woman. The woman only has to say in front of the judge – and this is underpinned by a short clip from the Egyptian film *Lawyer of Khulʿ* (*muḥāmī al-khul*)[15] on *Lāzim Naḥkī* – "I am afraid I cannot keep God's limits (*ḥudūd*)."[16] In case the woman experiences damage, she can file a claim with regard to "dispute and discord," a way of divorce made more accessible in *taʿmīm* 59/2012, too. ʿAwda[17] in the television studio, referring to the interviewees' answers to this question commented that the husband can repudiate his wife with or without reason, being unjust or being treated unjustly.

Two points become evident from these short interviews with women and men in the streets. First, not everyone responded directly to the question. And second, the knowledge about the exact ruling and its legal meaning seems not to have been very profound. More men were asked than women. For the first question, four men and three women were asked. Two of the women were in favor of the woman's right to *khulʿ*, the third was generally "against *ṭalāq*."

15 Sonneveld (2012: 68–69) analyzed this film in her book: The main character, Rasha, has hired the lawyer Badr for her "frivolous" *khulʿ*. She wanted a divorce because her husband snored. She then fell in love with the lawyer and accompanied him to his village where she provoked a scandal when putting on her bikini and swimming in the Nile. Sonneveld describes the intention of this film as follows: "Instead of presenting a female as defender of the nation, the film seems to depict the opposite, namely the Westernized Egyptian woman as embodying the threat that *khulʿ* poses to the Egyptian nation." Sonneveld 2012: 69.

16 This is a reference to Quran 2:229.

17 *Lāzim Naḥkī*, April 30, 2013.

Whereas the answers of A, B, and C (two women and a man) to the first question could be understood as being in favor of rights for both sides, E and F seem to be critical. Both are men. One is an elderly man, the other a very young man. The elderly man added: "only for the man" – which is explicitly directed against the woman's right. The young man (F) commented "surely not," which could refer to the first part of the question (are you in favor of?) or to the second part (are you against?). Neither in the question, nor in the answers, the already existing form of *khulʿ* based on mutual consent,[18] in which the woman has the right to claim separation but only with the husband's consent, is referred to. The answer of D, an elderly woman, who is against *ṭalāq*, has no bearing on the question. But her statement can perhaps be understood as a general expression of critique of the male's prerogative in divorce. D's answer to the second question makes it clear that she is convinced that the woman who is treated unjustly must have the right to divorce. D, G, B, and E are asked the second question, out of whom only D is a woman. The answer to the third question is given only by two men (H, E) and not by a woman. One of them, H, had not been in the sample of the first and second question.

Concerning the second question, should the woman be able to use *khulʿ* if treated unjustly, the answers of the elderly woman (D) as well as of three men are shown. The elderly woman (D) said that if the woman is treated unjustly, she should have the right to leave him. But her view is in accordance with the already existing law.[19] G, who in the first question voted generally and perhaps as a political statement for complete gender equality, now wanted to give the woman the right to *khulʿ* only if she has "reasonable reasons" (*asbāb maʿqūla*). This would be gender unequal in the Palestinian context on two grounds: first, because men have the right to divorce women without reasons, whenever and wherever they want; second, women have to go to court and navigate a special procedure that is not necessary for men who repudiate their wives. B, a man, interestingly said that she should give him the *ṭalāq* (*tuṭalliq zawjahā*) when she is unjustly treated. Taking the terminology seriously, this would mean giving a woman the male prerogative of repudiation (*ṭalāq*). This is possible according to the law[20] and can be inserted as a stipulation into the marriage contract, but again is dependent on man's consent. This legal information is not given here. How did he mean it, then? It may be a lack of knowledge with regard to legal terminology but is, nevertheless, interesting before the background of the sensitive reaction of many males when called "separated by *khulʿ* (*makhlūʿ*)."

18 JLPS Article 102.

19 JLPS Article 132 on "dispute and discord."

20 JLPS Article 87.

B made it very clear that only if she is mistreated should she have this right. E voted for the court decision in this case but did not take into consideration the procedure of such a claim.

With regard to the third question both answers show that the persons did know the procedure in the case of *khulʿ* a bit more in detail. H, a middle aged man, who appeared for the first time in the sample, is right in the first part of his explanation: the woman has the right to go to the judge and ask him for separation because she does not want to continue her life with her husband. But then he thinks that she has to give "strong excuses" in her support, which she has the chance to convey to the judge. This is not correct as she simply has to state that she is afraid she cannot keep God's limits. The procedure of reconciliation, necessary according to law and also anchored in the Sharia, is ignored. E, the elderly man, who had answered the first question by saying that only the man and not the woman has a right to *khulʿ*, now has no objection against the new *khulʿ* ruling and he knows that it is confined to the time before consummation. But he misinterprets it as a "law" (*qānūn*) issued by the Palestinian Authority or by the judiciary, whereas it was actually issued by the Sharia Court High Council (SCHC). ʿAwda in the studio again felt obliged to correct this view.[21]

This short sequence of questions and answers can be seen to serve the viewers, on the one hand, as a check of their own knowledge about the matter, which is then corrected by the information following in the program. On the other hand, it might be cautiously interpreted as giving a rough impression of what is known and not known about *khulʿ* in the Palestinian public.

But how can these voices of the women and men in the streets of Ramallah be interpreted? Their answers are to a certain extent unclear and only tentative conclusions can be drawn from them. This might be due to the fact that the questions, too, were not focused on the new aspects of the ruling, as outlined above.

This small sample seems to indicate that women as well as some men would be in favor of the *khulʿ* ruling seeing it as gender equality. The "50–50" expression points in this direction. Only men (E, perhaps F) explicitly rejected the new ruling. E answered the first question in the negative as he was against a woman's right to *khulʿ* but seems to have had no objection to this special version of *khulʿ* before consummation according to his third answer. There is also general agreement among all the interviewees that in the case of unjust treatment – which however has nothing to do with *khulʿ* – the woman should

21 *Lāzim Naḥkī*, April 30, 2013.

have the right to leave. Such a divorce is in accordance with existing law.[22] The crucial questions are: under which conditions can such a divorce happen and how can the woman prove her case? It was exactly at this point that the Supreme Judge had introduced his additional ruling for "marital dispute and discord" in the 59/2012 *taʿmīm* and made women's access to this divorce easier since they did not have to prove their case anymore. His argument had been that women should not lose their money, i.e., the dower. Neither the money question nor the question why this kind of divorce can only happen before consummation nor the aspect of the husband's consent, which was no longer necessary, had been touched upon in these interviews.

The difficulty to pin down people's information and knowledge and their exact opinion as reflected in these short interviews is to a certain degree also obvious in the scientific survey done by the Women's Institute of the BZU in 2000 and 2013.[23] In 2000, Hammami asked respondents about their reactions to the then recent law on divorce enacted in Egypt, which included the new *khulʿ*.[24] She outlined that the questions were not dependent on the respondents' actual knowledge of the Egyptian reform (i.e., divorce against the husband's will before and after consummation) but focused on the economic side, i.e., whether the asked persons saw a "law enabling women to divorce by waiving their financial rights as a positive innovation they would support in Palestine."[25] Only one-third of the respondents in 2000 supported the enactment of such a law (37 percent of women, 32 percent of men), the lowest support for such a law was among Gaza males, the highest among Jerusalem females. Other statistics include: 71 percent of women were in favor of women's rights to divorce generally, but 44 percent did not want women to lose their property rights.[26] Generally women were more supportive of their right to divorce than men were, with an approximately 10 percent gender gap.[27] The question focused on the financial aspect – the loss of money – reinforcing or at least playing with the cliché that *khulʿ* is a prerogative for rich women.[28] It did not focus on *khulʿ* as a chance for women to get out of an unhappy marriage

22 JLPS Article 132.

23 Hammami 2004; Johnson and Hammami 2013; reference to the methodology of 2003 is broader than for 2013, see Johnson and Hammami 2013: 24.

24 Hammami 2004.

25 Hammami 2004: 141–142.

26 Hammami 2004: 141–142.

27 Hammami 2004: 142.

28 Sonneveld 2012: 7, 84, 87ff; Sonneveld's results reveal that this was not the case: women were just eager to get out of marriage.

against the husband's will and thus on *khulʿ* as a counterterm to repudiation (*ṭalāq*) as a purely male prerogative.

On a general level, there was in the year 2000 as well as in 2013 support for a reform of family law. Over 80 percent of male and female respondents in 2000 and 2013 believed that family law should change to meet new needs in Palestinian society; 83 percent supported a new unified family law, but here numbers vary between the West Bank (87 percent) and Gaza (76 percent).[29] More than half of women and a quarter of men wanted the reform to expand women's rights. Johnson and Hammami show that this constitutes a decline from two-thirds of women in 2000 to only half in 2013 and from one-third of men in 2000 to one-quarter in 2013.[30] With regard to divorce and *khulʿ* in Palestine after the issuing of the ruling Johnson and Hammami refer to the press conference the Supreme Judge gave on August 30, 2012, in which he announced the changes in the *taʿmīm*. In their opinion the "new and positive changes in divorce proceedings" were triggered by a public event and the public's reaction to it: the murder of a woman in Bethlehem in August 2012 who had struggled to get a divorce from her abusive husband for a long time without success. He had slashed her throat when she was shopping in a Bethlehem market.[31] This caused an outcry in Palestinian society and discussion that fueled and sped up the process of issuing the *taʿmīm*. The ruling however had been in preparation since the beginning of 2012.[32]

The 2013 survey asked concrete questions about reasons that could be in the opinion of the asked persons acceptable for divorce. If the husband is a collaborator, for example, a very high percentage of women and men agree that women should get a divorce (both round 95 percent). This can be explained by the political situation in Palestine. There is also a high degree of acceptance on reasons for divorce such as mental illness, sexual disease and abuse, which are already regulated in JLPS and EFRL. If the husband has abandoned the family – in which case divorce is accepted according to the JLPS Article 128 – 79 percent of women and 77 percent of men supported this right to divorce in comparison to 58 percent of the women in 2000 and 50 percent of men. That there should be a right to divorce for women when the husband physically abuses children is supported by 59 percent of women and 49 percent of men, when he marries a second wife by 36 percent of women and only 18 percent

29 Johnson and Hammami 2013: 3.
30 Johnson and Hammami 2013: 4.
31 Johnson and Hammami 2013: 18.
32 See p. 55, 227.

of men.[33] The numbers show an increased awareness for women's rights to divorce in comparison to 2000, which lags behind the applicable law. With only 18 percent of men supporting the wife's right to divorce if the husband marries a second wife, polygyny seems still strongly rooted in Palestinian society even if it is often stated that there are very few polygynious marriages.[34]

Asked whether women and men should have equal rights to divorce or women should have no right for divorce under any circumstances, 61 percent of the West Bank males and 57 percent of the West Bank females were in favor of equal rights; in Gaza, 52 percent of males and 65 percent of females were in favor of equal rights. This number is interesting as more men than women support equal rights generally in this legal realm and in response to this very general question. But no divorce for women under any circumstances was supported by 11 percent of West Bank males (and 17 percent of Gaza males) and 11 percent of West Bank females (18 percent of Gaza females),[35] which is still a significant number.[36] Johnson and Hammami argued that there existed both a trend toward greater openness to women's rights and an increase in polarization with a substantial polarized minority.[37] However, the analysis of the numbers seems to be more complicated with regard to *khulʿ*.

Support for women-initiated divorce – *khulʿ* in the 2013 survey – was asked with the following question: "Do you support or oppose women's right to divorce, *khulʿ*, if she waives her financial rights?" The aspects of the husband's consent and the woman's agency were thus not mentioned explicitly[38] and were not the central aspects in the debate. In response, 43 percent of the women supported the woman's right as formulated in this queston and 35 percent of men;[39] 51 percent of the women and 66 percent of the men answered with

33 Johnson and Hammami 2013: 41.

34 That polygyny rarely exists is a common argument I encountered in many Muslim states. It is normally substantiated with reference to the financial burden the husband has to shoulder taking a second wife, i.e., her dower and maintenance. Wives have to be dealt with equally. However, this is the legal requirement that not all men meet. In the 1990s, the percentage of polygyny was around 4.5 percent, see Welchman 2004: 99–101. The Palestinian Multiple Indicator Cluster Survey (2014) cites 4 percent.

35 Johnson and Hammami 2013: 42.

36 Johnson and Hammami 2013: 42. This answer could be influenced by a high percentage of Christians asked in this survey as the Christian churches do not recognize divorce or only recognize it in exceptional cases. However, Johnson and Hammami state that 99 percent of the respondents were Muslims, see Johnson and Hammami 2013: 3.

37 Johnson and Hammami 2013: 8.

38 Johnson and Hammami 2013: 43–44 state this themselves.

39 These are the total numbers for the West Bank, Gaza and Jerusalem. The question of how the sample was composed is dealt with for the 2000 sample but regrettably not for the 2013 sample, as far as I can see. Johnson and Hammami 2013: 24–25.

"no,"[40] which is a high percentage and shows much reservation against this specific form of divorce or perhaps gender equal divorce in general. Another question asked was "Why do you oppose women's right to divorce *khul*ʿ if she waives her financial rights?" Here 28 percent of men and 55 percent of women chose the answer "because women should not give up financial rights" and 54 percent of men and 43 percent of women answered that they opposed it because it "enables women to divorce."[41] The answers to this second question confirm a conservative position toward gender equality and a woman's right to divorce, but conflict with the response that 61 percent of males and 57 percent of women support gender equal rights to divorce. It seems that people were more ready to support general statements on "equality" without concrete implications than support concrete solutions enclosing or leading to gender equality in terms of divorce. The numbers can be read as a confirmation of the fact that the cautious steps taken by Yūsuf Idʿīs to introduce judicial *khul*ʿ only partly, i.e., before consummation of marriage, were based on his correct interpretation of public opinion, according to which even a significant number of women, 43 percent, were reluctant to demand for themselves full and equal rights to divorce. It also confirms that the "equality" discussion, the question how gender equality should be spelled out in the Palestinian context, and how *musāwaḥ*, the Arabic term for equality, should be "translated" into concrete rights for women in Palestine had not yet arrived in Palestine. This was also reflected in the highly superficial scholarly discourse on *khul*ʿ being "equality" for women as a compensation for the man's right to *ṭalāq*. Whereas the Supreme Judge had argued in his lecture that judicial *khul*ʿ established "equality,"[42] the Sharia establishment in its meeting of November 2, 2013, at Al-Quds University had rejected "equality" as an "unjust claim" and reaffirmed the "money-obedience" model of marriage. International law, let alone CEDAW, which anchors "equality" in Articles 2 and 16, is not referred to at all at this point of the iterations.[43]

According to another interesting finding with regard to the "agents of reform" in Palestinian society, Johnson and Hammami saw in 2013 a decline in support for the democratic role of society, dropping from 33 percent in 2000 to 27 percent in 2013, as well as a decline in support for presidential decrees (from 12 percent to 7 percent) accompanied by a substantial rise in support for Sharia Court judges (from 26 percent in 2000 to 35 percent in 2013)

40 Johnson and Hammami 2013: 43.
41 Johnson and Hammami 2013: 43.
42 See chapter 5.3.
43 See chapter 2.2.2.

and for the Palestinian Legislative Council from 17 percent to 20 percent.[44] "The highest growth has been for the position that Sharia' [*sic*] Court judges are the legitimate authorities for reform of family law though still a minority position," they state.[45] One could conclude from this that the choice of who should reform the law shifted to the religious authorities, more exactly to the Sharia Court judges and thus toward religious conservativism.[46] Hammami and Johnson however interprete this as a "practical solution" as the PLC did not work as a unified body, as there were two contending presidents, "putting reform in the hands of Shari'a Court judges, who have proven themselves at times responsive to emerging crises and needs in society" made sense.[47] If this result is correct, it is important because, as it came after the *taʿmīm* was issued, it would again support ex post the Supreme Judge's approach of taking the reform into his hand by issuing *taʿmīmāt*.

Balqīṣ Ḥarbī,[48] a young woman, contributed her personal perspective as a concerned person and reported about the procedure in her *khulʿ* lawsuit. The *Lāzim Naḥkī* team met her at the court. Her uncle had been opposed to her giving an interview to the program,[49] but the judge asked her if she was ready for the interview and she agreed. The uncle's reluctance may have been caused by the problem divorced women still face in Palestinian society, so that he perhaps was afraid to make her case of *khulʿ* public. Balqīṣ Ḥarbī, however, decided differently. She had been engaged to a young man from Jordan but wanted to separate, she reported. He denied her, left her "engaged," went to Jordan and married another woman. She was trapped in this situation for one year, and her only solution was *khulʿ*. The matter was still in process at the time of her interview. She pointed to many differences she and her fiancé had in their thinking and customs. Asked whether it was a problem for her that financial obligations for her arose from *khulʿ*, she laughed and answered in the negative. He did not give her anything. She explicitly recommended this kind of separation to all young women in the same situation, emphasizing that there are "girls who marry and girls who divorce," stressing that divorce has to

44 Johnson and Hammami 2013: 4, 66; it is not clear to me what the option given that "the society should vote" means and exactly which parliament is meant, as the one in Ramallah did not meet.

45 Johnson and Hammami 2013: 4.

46 Johnson and Hammami 2013: 4; 67 see no acute regional differences between West Bank and Gaza; however, Gaza had an operating parliament, the West Bank did not.

47 Johnson and Hammami 2013: 4.

48 *Lāzim Naḥkī*, April 30, 2013.

49 Qunayṣ, interview on November 27, 2013.

be considered something normal. It was important to her to mention that this kind of separation was anchored in the Quran thus legitimizing it religiously.

Women's organizations[50] – as representatives of civil society – are traditionally very strong in the West Bank, also in Gaza with the organizations listed above. All have been prominent and highly visible players on the political scene in the last twenty years or so. Mutaz Qafisheh (Hebron University) even considered them to have the leading role in the process whereas he described the state as inactive in the discussion about family law.[51] All representatives of the organizations welcomed the *khulʿ* ruling and sometimes even claimed to have steered the iteration process. There was discussion whether or not the ruling could have gone farther in this direction, i.e., to allow *khulʿ* after consummation. The mainstream opinion among the organizations of civil society was that Idʿīs tried to help women but with regard to a new Palestinian family law, gender equality should be introduced.

6.1.2 *Why Was the Reform of the Family Law Generally and with Regard to* khulʿ *Seen as Necessary; and What Reasons Were Given in Favor of or against the Reform?*

Qunayṣ[52] explained that the signing of the marriage contract at the time of the engagement was a relatively new development in Palestinian society[53] because people had become more religious. After having the contract, the couple could be closer, meaning, for example, that the woman could show him her hair. She also said that "privacy" (*khalwa*) was possible, but had to concede, when I asked, that religious people did not allow "real" privacy before the wedding party with the marriage night (*laylat al-dukhla*). The couple could go to a café or to a restaurant or visit the family. But the family would not allow the couple to stay away overnight, adding: "Women and girls are very firm on this,

50 For the organizations, see chapter 3, the most important and active ones in the debates were Women's Centre for Legal Aid and Counselling (WCLAC), Women's Affairs Technical Committee (WATC), Al-Haq, Musawa, General Union of Palestinian Women (GUPW), Women's Studies Centre (WSC), and Center for Women's Legal Research and Consulting in Gaza (CWLRC).

51 Mutaz Qafisheh, interview on December 25, 2017; see also Shaʿwān Jabārīn, al-Haq, interview on November 29, 2017. Different newspapers were also consulted in their electronic versions, among them: Maannews: https://www.maannews.net/, accessed December 21, 2018. The names of the news agencies are quoted in English because I approached the links in English, but the Arabic transcription is also added; Safa: http://safa.ps/, accessed December 21, 2018; Watan: https://www.watan.ps/ar/, accessed December 21, 2018; Samanews: http://samanews.ps/ar/, accessed December 21, 2018.

52 Jumān Qunayṣ, interview on November 27, 2013.

53 See also the analysis of CWLRC for Gaza, chapter 9.

in general." It is left to the groom to find out on the wedding night whether the bride is still virgin or not. Qunayṣ confirmed that if the husband found his wife was not a virgin in the wedding night, there would be a problem for the woman. Virginity is considered important in Palestinian society, and is related to the custom that sexual relations outside marriage are not accepted, at least not openly.[54]

Discussion about the reform had started in January 2012 when the Supreme Judge announced a special committee of the SCHC starting to work to find a solution for separation for women.[55] At that point and since then, the social need and the social situation with regard to marriage and engagement continued to be discussed. Muḥammad Naʿīm Faraḥāt, professor of Sociology, based his explanation for the increase in the divorce rate before consummation on a number of factors. The most important factor was, according to him, the widening of social intercourse between young women and men, which previously used to be within the Sharia framework of the contract before the wedding feast. The possibility of spending time together before the wedding allowed, he argued, a deeper knowledge of one another that could lead to the discovery of unwanted attributes resulting in "frequencies to choose." Young couples hesitated to choose their final partner and were uncertain. Other factors responsible for the increase of divorce included, according to his research: high marriage requirements, interference, and meddling by people close to the couple, and costly requirements for the agreed dower. Economic reasons related to life expenses as well as cultural reasons were important because there was a remarkable change in the concept of marriage among young people and the fact that society became more understanding about the reluctance of the youth toward marriage. Faraḥāt considered this a possible influence from the West. With regard to polygyny, Faraḥāt explained that the "laws of the market" ruled over the area of marriage, meaning that too many unmarried women in society raised the social acceptability for polygamous marriages.[56] There was an increasing number of women married to Israeli (Arab) men as second wives.

In an article titled "*Khulʿ* … Soon in Palestine,"[57] two reports of women eagerly awaiting (*bi-fārigh al-ṣabr*) the *khulʿ* separation were presented. In one

54 Jumān Qunayṣ, interview on November 27, 2013.

55 Maannews, January 14, 2012; see also paltoday, January 19, 2012, according to which there had been a press conference the day before with the official announcement of *khulʿ*.

56 Maannews, January 14, 2012; see also paltoday, January 19, 2012.

57 See Raya of February 18, 2012. Raya is not a Palestinian newspaper but a daily Arabic newspaper published in Qatar. It reported on the social background in Palestine, the blackmailing of young woman, and quoted the Supreme Judge with his wish to help young women at a very early stage of the debate. In the beginning the report stated that the

case, the woman's father spoke for his daughter. Abū Bāsil, sixty years old, a father of a young woman who was waiting for the new law, explained his daughter's problem: A man proposed to his daughter and after signing the marriage contract, she discovered undesirable traits in his personality. When it turned out that he had lied to her and her family with regard to his education, it was like "the straw that broke the camel's back" (*al-shaʿra allatī qaṣamat ẓahr al-baʿīr*). Still he refused separation. Perhaps, Abū Bāsil added, it would not have been a problem if he had not lied to them, but "what is built on something void is void" (*mā buniya ʿalā bāṭil fa-huwa bāṭil*). The second case concerned a woman named Mahā who also was waiting for the new ruling in Gaza. She had been engaged to her cousin for three years and from the beginning she was not happy with her engagement. When he postponed the wedding and went to Libya, claiming he would get an excellent job there and come back to take her to Libya, she did not believe him anymore. She wanted to end this marriage, but had to wait for him to come back and divorce her.

There was a concern that the new *khulʿ* ruling could potentially be abused by women. Like in Egypt, it was feared that it would increase the rate of divorce.[58] The feminist activist Nāhid Abū Ṭaʿīma argued that this objection reflected the traditional view that women would be unable to make serious decisions if they were given the right.[59] However, Abū Ṭaʿīma was critical of the *khulʿ* ruling in other Arab states because only rich women, she argued, would be able to return their dowers.[60] Muḥammad Ṣabrī, a thirty-year-old government employee from Ramallah criticized the law and said that the ruling "has serious gaps as it enables the woman to get *khulʿ* without a reason." He said, "I think that *khulʿ* affects the status of men and will bring even more troubles to them."[61] The university student Wāʾil ʿAbdallaṭīf, from Hebron thought that the law would allow women to misuse it. He said: "The woman reacts and decides spontaneously far from deep reflection like the man; this can lead to an increase in separation cases and troubles between families."[62]

---

discussion comes as a warning to every young man who does not represent the "brave knight" (*al-fāris al-humām*) in his fiancée's eyes; that today a woman can use weapons granted to her by law. For the ruling, different terms are used throughout the article such as *taʿmīm*, *qarār* and *qānūn*.

58 Alhourriah, October 6, 2012.

59 Alhourriah, October 6, 2012. It had been an argument of the Supreme Judge in his class, too, when asked why *khulʿ* was not applicable after consummation, see chapter 5.3.

60 Alhourriah, October 6, 2012. This is not confirmed by Sonneveld's research on Egypt, see Sonneveld 2012: 83–103.

61 Qashṭa 2013.

62 Qashṭa 2013.

Others supported the law, such as Nā'il Abū 'Aysh, a master's student at Al-Najāh University in Nablus. He defended the law and said: "I think it is a young woman's right to determine her future when she finds that her future husband cannot guarantee her a dignified life." Abū 'Aysh, married with a child, thought that the law would reduce divorce after marriage with all its greater dangers for the crumbling of the family.[63]

On a more general level, the necessity of reforming the Palestinian Family Law is always hinted to by representatives of the state, of civil society, and the Sharia establishment.[64] But how should it look? The topic had been discussed in the meeting in the Muqāṭa'a in November 2013.[65] There had been in the past voices in civil society calling for the separation of religion and state, suggesting the adoption of a civil code.[66] Sāmā 'Awayḍa,[67] Head of WSC, was, according to her own statement, involved in the process of proposing legislation with regard to family law and the penal law before 2013, but had not been present at the meeting in the *Muqāṭa'a* in November 2013. She and her organization opted for a civil personal status law for Muslims and Christians, based on international law and gender equality. She spoke out against the idea of reforming Islamic law, because it would not apply to the Christians.[68] This approach was supported not only by WCLAC (Women's Centre for Legal Aid and Counselling)[69] but also by WATC (Women's Affairs Technical Committee)[70] and al-Haq.[71] Qafisheh, Professor of Law at Hebron University argued in an interview,[72] that there could be a parallel civil law. In 2013, the additional option of civil marriage was supported by 18 percent of the West Bank population and 15 percent of the Gaza population.[73] Asem Khalil had described this idea of having a

63 Qashṭa 2013.

64 Alhourriah, October 6, 2012. See *Lāzim Naḥkī*, April 30, 2013, in the contributions of 'Awda, al-Qaysī, al-Ḍamīrī; see also *Ḥārisāt Nārinā*, April 9, 2017; Tawfīq Abū al-Hāshim, interview on December 6, 2017; 'Adarrāziq, interview on November 24, 2014; Rīm Abū al-Rubb, interview on December 2, 2013; Mahā Abū Dayyah, interview on November 30, 2013; Nihāya Muḥammad, interview on November 24, 2013. See also chapter 9 for the discussion of Gaza.

65 See 2.2.3.

66 Khalil 2009a: 25, see 2.1.1.

67 Sāmā 'Awayḍa, Head of WSC, interview on November 16, 2013.

68 Sāmā 'Awayḍa, interview on November 16, 2013.

69 See Randa al-Sinyūra, Head of WCLAC, interview on November 27, 2017.

70 Surayda Ḥusaynī, General Director of WATC, interview on December 7, 2017.

71 Sha'wān Jabārīn, al-Haq, interview on November 29, 2017; see also Ibrāhīm Barghūṭī of Musāwāh, interview on February 28, 2018.

72 Mutaz Qafisheh, interview on December 25, 2017; see also Qafisheh 2018.

73 Johnson and Hammami 2013: 37.

parallel civil law for personal status in 2009 as a minority position.[74] It was also no option for the Ministry of Justice in my interviews in 2013.[75] Thus, also in 2013 but even later, as the iterations show until the end of 2018, the chance for a civil law, even if it was only conceptualized to be used parallel to the religious family law, was not high.

Nihāya Muḥammad, vice president of General Union of Palestinian Women (GUPW) had already in the meeting in the *Muqāṭaʿa* in November 2013, as outlined above, criticized the process of discussing the family law and had hoped for the 2010 Draft to become the basis for discussion.[76] Ashraf Abū Ḥayyah, a lawyer at WCLAC had argued in 2013[77] that he did not want to change the law article by article but wanted a general rethinking with regard to women's rights. Mahā Abū Dayyah (d. 2015), his boss and the head of WCLAC at that time, named the following issues as most pressing:[78] raising the marriage age; non-obligation of guardianship of marriage; and extension of rights for women with regard to custody (*ḥaḍāna*), divorce in court and sharing common property after divorce.[79] She elaborated on the general aims and strategies of WCLAC and explained[80] that divorce should be in court and both parties should have the right to initiate it. The property acccummulated during the marriage should be divided equally between men and women. But the core of the problem was, she stated explicitly, the "money-obedience" relation. She saw, however, no chance to break up this relation arguing that families will not

74 Khalil 2009a: 25.

75 Munjid ʿAbdallāh, Ministry of Justice, interview on November 14, 2013.

76 See 2.2.3.

77 Ashraf Abū Ḥayyah, interview on November 30, 2013.

78 Ashraf Abū Ḥayyah, interviews on October 21, 2013, and November 30, 2013; Mahā Abū Dayyah, interview on November 30, 2013.

79 Mahā Abū Dayyah, interview on November 30, 2013. She was the head of WCLAC, http://www.wclac.org/, accessed March 18, 2019. Born in Jerusalem and a graduate of Smith College, she completed her study of English in the United States. In 1991, together with others, she founded the Women's Centre for Legal Aid and Counselling (WCLAC), one of the most important NGOs for women's affairs in Palestine. F. Abdulhadi (2015) described it as her – and the Centre's – aim to change politics and laws. This was especially important after the establishment of the Palestinian National Authority in 1994, and after the initiation of "The Women's Rights Document" by the General Union of Palestinian Women hand-in-hand with women's centers and women's networks. The Women's Rights Document referred to the Palestinian "Declaration of Independence" and was based on many other local and international agreements. It included detailed and precise descriptions for the most important rights of Palestinian woman in all aspects, with reference to international standards and declarations, Palestinian constitutional principles, and Palestinian legislation. It linked political rights, economic and social rights, criminal law, rights of citizenship, and Personal Status Laws.

80 Mahā Abū Dayyah, interview on November 30, 2013.

give up dower because many women do not work and there is no social welfare system. Sharing property after divorce is easier to achieve than overcoming the "money-obedience" connection, she argued. One has to compromise between international law and what can be accomplished in Palestine at this point, she argued. Also polygyny cannot be abolished but it can be restricted. Her organization supports women who fight against it: "Because you need to keep negotiating." Under the present political situation, she considered it difficult to change all this. Also, not all women support her organization's position. But with regard to polygyny, the husband has to at least inform the wife. There should be a guarantee that her interest is protected, she could protect herself with a stipulation in the marriage contract. WCLAC was, Abū Dayyah stated, currently developing specific marriage forms. But there was resistence by the *ma'dhūnīn* (marriage officers). Religious courts are important: "If you can win them over, this is great." She was, on the other hand, skeptical with regard to the state and the likelihood of intervention in the matter and put more hope on the discussion process she said could change people's minds.[81] With regard to President Abbas she was not optimistic – but she thought Yūsuf Idʿīs was interested in finding a solution in favor of women.

Asked, how she wanted to influence society, she said through volunteer groups and regional coalitions it would be possible to improve personal status laws. They, as an organization, were in touch with society, workshops were organized. She rejected the accusation that WCLAC concentrated on Westernized, upper-class women, but saw the organization as a representative of grass root groups. Asked if religious women were difficult to reach, she responded that WCLAC reached some, but not the ideologically biased, Islamist women. The aim was keeping family unity, keeping resources in the family etc, mental and sociological well-being of the family, she said. Everybody would understand this language and accept these premises. They had tried different ways, until the committee, which had met on November 20, 2013, was seen as the best solution to come together and discuss the matter. However, "one should not expect to get the ultimate solution, but anything one can gain is better than nothing." She repeatedly described WCLAC's work as an ongoing struggle: "And if you don't touch the core belief system, you can reach them."[82]

Abū Dayyah can be considered a great strategic thinker and a feminist who never gave up. She died in 2015 from cancer and the more secular women's organizations lost an important activist. Her successor as head of WCLAC, Randa

81 Mahā Abū Dayyah, interview on November 30, 2013.

82 Mahā Abū Dayyah, interview on November 30, 2013.

al-Sinyūra,[83] was even more explicit in stating that WCLAC was opting for a civil personal status law, at least in addition to the religious one, to give secular citizens the possibility to choose, e.g., to make interreligious marriages easier. Coming from a Christian Orthodox background, al-Sinyūra was eager to point to the fact that discrimination against women, which she saw in the existing personal status law, also existed in Christian contexts. In the 1990s it seemed possible to pass such a civil law, now it seemed impossible, she argued. On the other hand, she was reluctant to see a chance to achieve gender equality through new interpretations of the Sharia. She pointed to the interrelatedness of penal law and family law. For the time being (November 2017), she stated that a new law against violence in the family was on the table and she was positive that it would come into force through a presidential decree soon.[84] Based on the experiences of other Arab states, especially Lebanon, all three laws – the penal law, the law against violence in the family, and the personal status law – have to be seen as a unit and the personal status law in particular was necessary.[85] She, too, considered it important to compromise: This is why WCLAC as an organization agreed to find out the most pressing legal problems and demand improvement on these points. Very similar to what Mahā Abū Dayyah had mentioned four years prior, the pressing issues in 2017 were still: the marriage age, guardianship in marriage, custody, polygyny and divorce, and equal rights to property after divorce. In 2017, al-Sinyūra was more optimistic that a compromise could be achieved with regard to the marriage age if not raising it to eighteen, at least nearer to this age; and with regard to guardianship in marriage because it was accepted in Hanafi law. With regard to polygyny, she explained they worked very hard but perhaps one could only reach a cautious limitation of this practice. She considered polygyny one of the hardest topics in negotiating women's rights and gender equality because of the economic situation. According to a survey done by WCLAC in the Jordan Valley, polygyny was on the rise. With regard to divorce al-Sinyūra, like her predecessor, opted for divorce in court only and men as well as women should have equal possibility to initiate it. Other than Abū Dayyah, who had considered it important to win over the Sharia Courts, she did not see much chance of reaching an agreement with the Sharia establishment with regard to equal rights and sharing property after a divorce. Economic reasons were, as in 2013,

83 Randa al-Sinyūra, interview on November 27, 2017. Randa al-Sinyūra holds master's degrees in human rights and sociology and has been working for different civil society organizations, she was the head of al-Haq, and in 2017, she became head of WCLAC.

84 At the end of 2017, there was much discussion and many workshops about the "Family Protection Law against Violence," but by March 2019, this law had not yet been enacted.

85 Randa al-Sinyūra, interview on November 27, 2017.

the main stumbling point. She pointed to a study of WCLAC with regard to inheritance according to which only 12 percent of women inherited in 2014 and only 4 percent inherited without losing family connections. Women were often pressured by their brothers, who would threaten not to support them in case of divorce, not to take their (Islamic) share of inheritance, i.e., half of what a male in the same position in the family inherited.[86] Since many women did not work, they would have no place to go if they got divorced.

Her colleague from MUSAWA, Ibrāhīm Barghūṭī, agreed with al-Sinyūra to postpone the matter and argued that one should start to reform other laws first.[87] Shaʿwān Jabārīn of al-Haq in November 2017 pointed to the founding of the LHC (Legislation Harmonization Committee/*Lajnat Mulāʾamat al-Tashrīʿāt*) and that his organization would be ready to work toward not only the acceptance of the international treaties but also the development of a new personal status law.[88] There should be a civil law, he argued. He saw the *taʿmīmāt* of Yūsuf Idʿīs with regard to inheritance and family law as a positive development for women's rights. According to him, the Supreme Judge, Maḥmūd al-Habbāsh, could press for a new law.

6.1.3 *Which Uses of the Past Were Made? Which Terminology Was Used?*

Quranic verses and the famous *khulʿ ḥadīth* were always present in public awareness. They were so well-known that they were rarely quoted in full but normally just alluded to and incorporated into the structure of an argument. Even if religious discourse provided the background and the Quranic verses and the *ḥadīth* were in the public awareness and in everybody's mouth and mind, representatives of civil society used openly Islamic language less then representatives of the Sharia establishment. But reference to Quran and Sunna was made, when it was seen as useful. "Blackmailing" (*ibtizāz*), originally a social or social-legal term widely used by representatives of civil society as well as of the Sharia establishment to criticize young men's behavior, was connected to Quran and ethical admonishment was religiously justified, e.g. ʿAwda gave the prosaic example of a professor of English language – thus obviously not a very young man – who had given to his fiancée private lessons in English and now retroactively wanted to get paid for these lessons at ten Jordanian Dinars per hour. She added that he surely had enjoyed these lessons commenting sourly that "the standard fell" in this matter.[89]

86 Randa al-Sinyūra, interview on November 27, 2017.
87 Ibrāhīm Barghūṭī, interview on February 28, 2018.
88 Shaʿwān Jabārīn, interview on November 29, 2017.
89 ʿAwda in *Lāzim Naḥkī*, April 30, 2013.

Muḥammad,[90] who had argued in the meeting in the *Muqāṭaʿa* in favor of a secular non-Islamic marriage definition based on equality, surprised me by quoting in the interview a tradition that went back to the second caliph, ʿUmar b. al-Khaṭṭāb (r. 634–644 CE) and wanted to take it as proof in Islamic tradition for a demand of equal property inheritance (*amwāl mushtarak*), which is not included in classical Islamic law.[91] Women had worked during their marriage as housewives, especially in villages, and therefore this demand for equal property inheritance was important, she argued. Answering my surprised question of why she quoted the ʿUmar tradition, which I had not heard in Palestine so far, she explained that religious language was necessary to reach the goal of gender equality legislation. "We want to refer to CEDAW but take the examples from Islam," she stated.[92]

Abū Dayyah, on the other hand, preferred to be explicit. Rather than using her time to learn Quran, she preferred to come to an agreement on the general principles: maintaining basic dignity and protecting rights of women. The Sharia establishment would not say "no" to these principles, she was convinced. She considered guardianship and polygyny two concepts rooted deeply in tradition that even women of the upper classes and leftist women – did not want to give up.[93] Others argued on a general level that what civil society demanded for women was not in opposition to the Sharia.[94]

The gendered active-passive legal terminology was dealt with extensively in the TV program *Lāzim Naḥkī*, after Qunayṣ had put it so prominently in the introduction.[95] When Qunayṣ posed the question how men reacted to being called divorced (*makhlūʿ*) ʿAwda answered by expressing her incomprehension about these reactions, and referring to incriminating caricatures stated "as if it would be something strange". Why would it be bad to call a man *makhlūʿ* and wonderful to call a woman *muṭallaqa* (repudiated)? It was a word rooted in religion, she stated in line with Yusūf Idʿīs's argument. Asked if making fun of the word *makhlūʿ* helped men to be more accepting of being a divorcé, ʿAwda

90 Nihāya Muḥammad, interview on November 24, 2013.

91 She referred to *kadd wa-siʿāya* (exhaust and effort), meaning the efforts women had made in the marriage to entitle them to half the marital assets in case of divorce; this has been discussed in Morocco, see startimes http://www.startimes.com/?t=21083046, accessed on June 8, 2017.

92 Nihāya Muḥammad, interview on November 24, 2013.

93 Mahā Abū Dayyah, interview on November 30, 2013. For a similar argument, see Munā al-Khalīlī of GUPW in 2018, see Abū Ṭaʿīma, December 20, 2018.

94 Ṣabāḥ Salāma, coordinator of the Platform of Palestinian Non-Governmental Organizations against Domestic Violence against Women, in *Ḥārisāt Nārinā*, April 9, 2013, and Zaynab al-Ghunaymī in Gaza see Maannews, February 15, 2017.

95 *Lāzim Naḥkī*, April 30, 2013, stated in the introduction to this chapter.

confirmed the Supreme Judge's observation[96] that after the issuing of the *taʿmīm* families agreed on private *khulʿ* settlements based on mutual consent rather than have a *khulʿ*-divorce case in the court. They just did not want to be called *makhlūʿ*.

ʿAwda made one of the rare references to the JLPS. Having watched in the studio the interviews with women and men in the streets of Ramallah she corrected the idea that *khulʿ* was already mentioned in the existing law (JLPS). This was not the case, because in the law, it was called *mukhālaʿa*, she argued.[97] She took pains to explain the difference between the existing *khulʿ* based on consent and therefore necessarily needing the husband's consent and the new "judicial *khulʿ*" in which this consent was not required, at least before consummation. *Khulʿ* based on consent (*khulʿ riḍāʾī*) is defined as "*ṭalāq* based on general redemption" (*ṭalāq muqābil ibrāʾ ʿāmm*), she outlined. She herself would not have voted for *khulʿ* after consummation to save women's financial rights.

6.1.4 *Why Was* khulʿ *against the Husband's Will Given Only before Consummation of Marriage? Which Gender Concepts Were Negotiated?*

Everybody in the television programs, but also those whom I interviewed, agreed that: first, sexual relations before or outside marriage were not acceptable at all; and second, according to Palestinian custom, only after consummation and the wedding party was the couple considered fully married. This implied, third, that sexual relations should not happen after the engagement even if there was a signed marriage contract, which would have allowed the couple to consummate the marriage.

Whereas in the JLPS consummation of the marriage only becomes important in the case of divorce, it gained a high importance in society and there seemed to be a constant fear that, when left alone, the couple would have sex in what was called "privacy" (*khalwa*), i.e., when they met alone at the house, went alone to a hotel, etc. This was de facto a restriction especially or even exclusively imposed on women because other than their betrothed they were not allowed to have another spouse. Being engaged and especially having signed a marriage contract meant that the woman socially would be frowned upon or talked about when she mingled with other young men, whereas her fiancé could go and look for a second wife.[98] Qunayṣ confirmed that virginity, the first

96 See chapter 5.

97 JLPS Article 102.

98 Nihāya Muḥammad, interview on November 24, 2013; Jumān Qunayṣ, interview on November 7, 2013. Randa al-Sinyūra, interview on November 27, 2017.

intercourse, and the female's body were important for the honor of the family, explaining that there are many families in Palestine who waited through the wedding night to see a sign of the blood of the broken hymen.[99] The important role of virginity and the fact that in the new penal code sex outside of marriage is still criminalized, she argued,[100] proved that in this case traditional approaches to sexuality and the control of a woman's body are still in force. Sāmā ʿAwayḍa stated that her organization, the WSC, had not been able to convince the legislatur to eliminate the role of virginity.[101] In this situation, *khalwa* is important. If it did not happen, then she was not considered "penetrated" (*madkhūl bihā*). To file the claim she only had to declare that there had not been a *khalwa*. There was no need for a medical examination.[102]

The focus on virginity and the act of consummating the marriage has consequences for the gender role. Women are not accepted as having full legal rights and are restricted in their social movements. They need a marriage guardian to sign their contract and have to proof their virginity in the wedding night. It is thus the female's and not the male's body that is constantly controlled and under suspicion. ʿAwayḍa from WSC in Jerusalem confirmed that women in Palestine aspire for a radical change and the law does not grant them full rights (*ḥuqūq kāmila*). She told *Safa*: "Arbitrary divorce (*ṭalāq taʿassufī*] should be abolished; yet in the situation of the absence of the responsible institutions we value the approach of the chief judge to apply this law [the *khul*ʿ ruling] as it solves one of the many problems that we presented before him; besides inheritance and other problems." She added: "Generally, the personal status law discriminates against women and the woman is subordinate to the man. This is the main reason for the failure of marriages in most cases."[103]

Randa al-Sinyūra, Head of WCLAC,[104] confirmed that the *taʿmīmāt* issued by the Supreme Judge with regard to *khul*ʿ and other topics came as a consequence of the pressure women's organizations exerted on the Sharia establishment – whereas, as outlined in chapter 5, the Supreme Judge had described them as a consequence of his "field research" and his observations in court of women

99 Jumān Qunayṣ, interview on November 7, 2013; Randa al-Sinyūra, interview on November 27, 2017.

100 According to the JPL (Jordanian Penal Law/*Qānūn al-ʿUqūbāt*) of 16/1960 Article 282 *zināʾ* is punishable for women with imprisonment between six months and two years and for the man with imprisonment between one month and one year.

101 Sāmā ʿAwayḍa, interview on November 16, 2013.

102 Nihāya Muḥammad, interview on November 24, 2013; Wafāʾ al-Aʿraj, interview on November 24, 2013.

103 Qashṭa 2013.

104 Randa al-Sinyūra, interview on November 27, 2017.

under pressure and his activity in developing a "legal healing".[105] ʿAwayḍa and al-Sinyūra, both representatives of important civil society organizations were happy with this ruling but would have wished further corrections of the law.

Other women's activists, Nāʾila ʿIyāsh of the Woman's Affairs Center of Gaza (*Markaz Shuʾūn al-Marʾa/WAC*)[106] and Salwā Ḥamdān argued, that the ruling was "defective" (*nāqiṣ*) because it curtails a woman's right and is limited to the time between the contract signing and *khalwa* and did not include women who lived a marital life and have children.[107] Ḥamdān said: "The right (*al-ḥaqq*) cannot be divided … amendment of the law is necessary to preserve the right of the Palestinian woman before and after *khalwa*."[108]

6.1.5 *What Does This Ruling* (taʿmīm) *Mean? How Does It Compare to Legislation?*

All representatives of NGOs were well aware that the rulings had been issued as *taʿmīmāt* and not according to the legal and constitutional requirements; that they were therefore not officially "law" and could be taken back at any time by the Supreme Judge.[109]

The media, however, did not do much to clarify the difference between law (*qānūn*) or ruling (*taʿmīm*) of the Sharia Judicial system and decision (*qarār*), which could have been given by the president, if he had wished to do so. Often the new ruling was referred to as a "law" or even in the same article the terminology was inconsistent. The Supreme Judge was often reported to have spoken of a "law," which may have been his wording, because he used it in the lecture, too. It may also have been a misunderstanding or deliberate misdirection of the media.[110] ʿAwda felt obliged to explain at the beginning of her interview in *Lāzim Naḥkī* that the Supreme Judge, Head of SCHS, made a "wise decision" (*qarār*) but it was, "not a law (*laysa qānūnan*), as many say."[111] However, she

105 See chapter 4.

106 See http://site.wac.ps/ar/, accessed December 18, 2018. According to the website, WAC is a non-profit knowledge-based women's organization playing an innovative and catalytic role in empowering women, advocating women's rights and gender equality in the Palestinian sustainable development process. It is located in Gaza.

107 Qashṭa 2013. In Gaza, this restriction to women before consummation was criticized and actually the draft law did not contain it, see chapter 9.

108 Qashṭa 2013.

109 Interview with Randa al-Sinyūra, November 27, 2017; Ibrāhīm Barghūṭī, interview on February 28, 2018 and others.

110 Wafa, August 30, 2012; Maannews, January 14, 2012; Paltoday, January 19, 2012; Qashṭa 2013; palpress, January 14, 2012.

111 *Lāzim Naḥkī*, April 30, 2013.

used the term *qarār*, which, according to the Article 43 of the BL, would be the term for the president's decision.

On *Lāzim Naḥkī*, five information boards prepared by Zayna Zaʿūr,[112] all bearing the title "The *Khul*ʿ Law in the Sharia Courts" (*Qānūn al-Khul*ʿ *fī al-Maḥākim al-Sharīʿa*) were presented to the audience and read out aloud. On the first board the urgency of the ruling is described as follows: "As young women were kept for several years with a marriage contract before consummation, the work with regard to the law (*qānūn*) of judicial *khul*ʿ in the West Bank was settled with a ruling of the Head of SCHC, *Shaykh* Yūsuf Idʿīs on the first of September 2012."[113] According to this information, the "law" (*qānūn*) was based on the *taʿmīm* of the Supreme Judge. This incorrect information was confirmed on the fifth board. Here one can read that the "enactment of the law" (*iṣdār al-qānūn*) happened only in the West Bank, and since the PLC does not sit, it is justified to be called a law (*wa-dūna inʿiqād al-majlis al-tashrīʿī lahu mā yubarriruhu qānūnan*). The text goes on: "The Palestinian Personal Status Law allows the SCHC (*al-Majlis al-Aʿlā li-l-Qaḍāʾ*) the issuing (*iṣdār*) of laws (*qawānīn*) to the benefit of the common welfare (*maṣlaḥa ʿāmma*). And this is what really happened."[114] Again the board delivers incorrect information. There was, at that time in April 2013 and later, nothing like a "Palestinian Personal Status Law" and also nowhere in the constitution and the laws could permission be found for the SCHC to issue laws (*iṣdār qawānīn*), not even to the benefit of the "common welfare." The role of the concept of *maṣlaḥa* in reforming Islamic law is generally well-known and often used but will not be discussed here as it has not been elaborated on in the iterations in detail.[115] On the other boards, the number of *khul*ʿ cases in different regions of the West Bank was given and it was stated that *khul*ʿ is not applied in Gaza because of the split and the non-existent legal unity in both parts "of the nation." Where did this incorrect description and categorization come from? The content of the boards may be said to reflect the way the Sharia establishment justified the issuing of the *khul*ʿ ruling and shows a conscious or unconscious blurring of the boundary between such a ruling given by the SCHC and a "real" law.

112 *Lāzim Naḥkī*, April 30, 2013, 34:05.
113 *Lāzim Naḥkī*, April 30, 2013.
114 *Lāzim Naḥkī*, April 30, 2013.
115 Opwis 2007.

6.2 The State: Palestinian Authority

To my knowledge, there was no official statement of the government with regard to the *Qāḍī al-Quḍāt*'s ruling on *khulʿ*. Taking into consideration that the ruling actually amended applicable law, the silence of the state is surprising and reflects a certain weakness of the government. The position of the state representatives thus has to be reconstructed through the interviews I conducted with them. The journal *Safa* (*Ṣafāʾ*) reported that the PA itself had worked on promoting this law, (*hādhā al-qānūn*) which is incorrect. The article stated that the "law" would be applied in the West Bank but not in Gaza because of the political split.[116]

6.2.1 *Why Was the Reform of the Family Law Generally and with Regard to* khulʿ *Seen as Necessary and What Reasons Were Given in Favor of or against the Reform?*

The representatives of the state who were interviewed were well aware of the Palestinian custom and the religious foundation of personal status law.[117] Only Ḥasan al-ʿŪrī, jurist trained in civil law and legal advisor to President Abbas since 2010,[118] did not refer to this custom but argued that as he was not a Muslim jurist (*faqīh*), he would not know what the benefit (*maṣlaḥa*) would be to have a new ruling with regard to *khulʿ* or not. Being responsible for the creation of the NCFL (National Committee of the Family Law) and the meeting of the committee on November 20, 2013,[119] he seems not to have been involved in the public discussion about young couples signing their marriage contract at the engagement ceremony and creating problems for young women with the break-up of the marriage.

Conversely, Rīm Abū al-Rubb of the Ministry of Justice[120] was cognizant of this social problem and stated that society agreed to have the contract with engagement, pointing to the fact that sex before marriage was completely forbidden in Islam, which, she argued, was anchored in the law and respected in society. She, like many others, categorized the signature of the contract with engagement as a Palestinian custom. In the Ministry of Justice, I was informed

116 Qashṭa 2013.

117 ʿAbdalrazzāq Mūsā, Ministry of Justice, interview on November 24, 2013; Wafāʾ al-Aʿraj, interview on November 24, 2013; Rabīḥa Dhiyāb, Minister of Women's Affairs, interview on November 20, 2013; Rīm Abū al-Rubb, Ministry of Justice, interview on December 2, 2013.

118 Maannews January 20, 2010; Ḥasan al-ʿŪrī, interviews on October 13, 2014, and November 28, 2017.

119 See chapter 2.2.3.

120 Rīm Abū al-Rubb, interview on December 2, 2013.

about the different drafts for a Palestinian personal status law since the year 2000 and that the latest one was by the *Qāḍī al-Quḍāt*.[121] ʿAbdalrazzāq Mūsā, who had represented the Ministry of Justice in the meeting in the *Muqāṭaʿa* on November 20, 2013, explained in my interview with him that the Supreme Judge's draft was good but needed some improvement.[122] Palestinian family law cannot be against the Sharia, he stated. Abū al-Rubb confirmed this.[123] Mūsā suggested a change with regard to *ṭalāq*: whereas the woman had to go to the lawyer after being informed about the repudiation to get help with the payment of her dower, maintenance, and with preservation of her right to child custody (*ḥaḍāna*), in future all these should be the judge's responsibility. This would ease the woman's burden, he argued. I objected that this would in actuality be a very minor improvement for women in comparison to other Muslim states that had referred all cases of divorce to the court and obliged husbands to attend the hearing and denied them the right to pronounce a legally valid *ṭalāq* in the street,[124] as it is still possible in Palestine. Mūsā answered that he did not think men and women should have equal rights in divorce and the idea that only a court can decide a divorce could not be a part of a future Palestinian family law as he saw it. The right to *ṭalāq* was in the husband's hand (*al-ṭalāq fī yad al-rajul*), he quoted the well-known statement that had the potential to end any further debate on this issue. He referred to the different physical constitutions of men and women whereby he acknowledged that women could be "leaders" (*qādāt*) but still that the physical/biological difference with regard to pregnancy and lactation would be a difference between the genders. Asked again if "equality" (*musāwāh*) generally would be possible, he answered evasively by pointing to several Islamic rights for women such as stipulatons in the marriage contract and the *khulʿ* ruling. Asked with regard to the Supreme Judge's ruling, he explained that the argument of the representatives of the women's movement in the session on November 20, 2013, was not logical: Having a certain time for the engagement in the way the women's organizations obviously wanted, would be against society and the law. Palestinian society, being a traditional society, would not accept women and men to go out together without a marriage contract. He pointed to freedom of contract, i.e., the permission to insert stipulations into the contract. Furthermore, economic factors played a role. As marriage was very expensive – he spoke of US$50,000

121 ʿAbdalrazzāq Mūsā, interview on November 24, 2013; Munjid ʿAbdallāh, interview on November 14, 2013.

122 ʿAbdalrazzāq Mūsā, interview on November 24, 2013.

123 Rīm Abū al-Rubb and ʿAbdalrazzāq Mūsā, interview on December 2, 2013.

124 See Schneider 2014: 74.

to US$60,000 "from engagement to consummation" – young men needed time to save this money.[125]

The Women's Minister, Rabīḥa Dhiyāb (2010–2013),[126] pointed to the importance of a unified Palestinian family law. Having a background in civil society, she stated that "we, the women's movement" worked hard to stress the necessity of including all parts of society in developing this new law. She mentioned the NCFL, which had been created by the president, and included representatives of the Ministry of Women's Affairs. She explained that there had been many problems and obstacles related to this law since the PA came into existence. Asked about the most important points to change, she hesitated and then referred to polygyny, stating that this is a religious right of the men, but should be used only under certain circumstances.

6.2.2 *Which Uses of the Past Were Made? Which Terminology Was Used?*

It is surprising how intensively government officials used Islamic language – and the past. The Minister of Women's Affairs, Rabīḥa Dhiyāb of Fatah felt obliged, despite her more secular background, to explain that polygyny came about in Islam as a consequence of wars in which many men died and as a result there were more women than men. She quoted a part of the Quranic verse 4:3: "marry such women as seem good to you, two, three, four."[127] She stated that this was not necessary, but in certain situations it was allowed. Customs and traditions (*ʿādāt wa-taqālīd*) allowed it to the man. She thought for polygyny men should have a good reason, e.g., an illness of the first wife. Years later, in the middle of the discussion about the harmonization of Islamic law and international law, her successor, Hayfāʾ al-Āghā, used a similar argument to incite debate about curtailing polygyny but was silenced by a member of the Sharia establishment, a lecturer of al-Quds University.[128]

Being well aware of the important role of religion as one of the sources of legislation, Dhiyāb outlined that custom even ignored Islamic law in the field of inheritance. Even if the religion gives the women the right to inherit, this is not respected in Palestinian society, she complained. Asked what could be done, her answer was that workshops and discussions with religious scholars were organized, and religious scholars talked about it from the pulpit of

125 ʿAbdalrazzāq Mūsā, interview on November 24, 2013.

126 Rabīḥa Dhiyāb, interview on November 20, 2013.

127 The whole verse is as follows: "If you fear that you will not act justly towards the orphans, marry such women as seem good to you, two, three, four; but if you fear you will not be equitable, then only one, or what your right hands own; so it is likelier you will not be partial," see Quran.

128 See chapter 8.1.

the mosques, and there was even a program on television by the Ministry of Endowments (*Wizārat al-Awqāf*). There is also cooperation of the MoWA with the Sharia Courts, and people go there and discuss questions with the judges.[129] As civil society, she considered cooperation with the Sharia establishment important but it seems, in addition, that she considered it a valuable strategy to implent Islamic law as a first step to correct the existing custom and then to go on toward gender equality.

Whereas Mūsā from the Minstry of Justice stressed that God created human beings of different [physical] constitution (*takwīn*) pointing to the man's position in Quran 4:34,[130] his colleague Abū al-Rubb argued that Sharia is the basis of the constitution and therefore had to be respected,[131] but there were different interpetations and these were all part of Sharia. Everything that fits into the frame of Sharia was permitted (*ḥalāl*) and acceptable to the Ministry of Justice, she said. In my interview with her and Mūsā, a certain tension between the two of them emerged and it became obvious that Abū al-Rubb was generally more inclined to accept interpretations in favor of women when they remained in the framework of Sharia. When Mūsā explained to me that the Islamic regulations were based on an essential difference between genders as encapsulated in *fāʿil*/active/male and *mafʿūl*/passive/female, the active being the man and, for example, making the offer of engagement – not the woman – Abū al-Rubb responded that "our lady" Khadīja, the Prophet's first wife, made the offer of engagement to the Prophet.[132] ʿMūsā had nothing to answer to this and instead started to take refuge in what perhaps can be called the "quantitative argument" explaining how many different forms of divorce before the first marital sex according to the JLPS were available for women as if this would compensate the fact that none of these divorces was equal to the man's right to repudiation. Both had no problem with the Supreme Judge's *taʿmīm* and both also supported the classical Islamic definition of marriage according to which the woman is "permitted" (*ḥalāl*) to the man.

Whereas both positions seemed to be in accordance with the Supreme Judge's ruling, al-ʿŪrī strongly criticized what he called the *Qāḍī al-*Quḍāt's use of *ijtihād* in this case and that he created judicial *khulʿ* according to his own personal disposition (*mizāj shakṣī*).[133] This position, al-ʿŪrī stressed, was not acceptable at all. It was only the *Qāḍī*'s personal opinion (*raʾy*) and he labeled

129 Rabīḥa Dhiyāb, interview on November 20, 2013.
130 ʿAbdalrazzāq Mūsā, interview on November 24, 2013.
131 Rīm Abū al-Rubb, interview on December 2, 2013.
132 Rīm Abū al-Rubb and ʿAbdalrazzāq Mūsā, interview on December 2, 2013.
133 Ḥasan al-ʿŪrī, interview on October 13, 2014.

it as wrong (*khaṭaʾ*). There cannot be an *ijtihād* in Hebron and another one in Nablus, he argued.[134] One ought to lodge an appeal against the *Qāḍī*'s ruling to the High Court (*maḥkama ʿulyā*). This he said but according to my knowledge it never happened and the Supreme Judge's ruling is still applied in the Sharia courts of Palestine which are state courts.

6.2.3 *Why Was* khulʿ *against the Husband's Will Given Only before Consummation of Marriage? Which Gender Concepts Were Negotiated?*

Asked why the new *khulʿ* ruling was confined to the time before consummation and not after consummation as in Egypt, Mūsā explained that the situation in Palestine was different from Egypt. He described Palestine as a traditional society with a different judicial system. According to the law, engagement is only a promise. But the traditional Palestinian society – again Palestine was classified like this – would not allow men and women to go out together without a marriage contract. This was the custom. Saying this he used the Arabic *ʿādāt wa-taqālīd,* sometimes also *ʿurf.* The woman has no sexual freedom, he explained. Mostly, the engagement time is not much more than a year. Engagement was important in Palestine, "for us Muslims consummation is the real marriage (*zawāj ḥaqīqī*)" and it happens with the marriage party (*ḥaflat al-ʿurs/zifāf*).[135] In the interview with Rīm Abū al-Rubb both again had different opinions on whether the ruling should be before first marital sex.[136] Mūsā argued that permitting *khulʿ* even after consummation would open the doors for women who have children to a "quick divorce" and women could make use of many other forms of separation. Abū al-Rubb interfered, saying that *khulʿ* is easier for women, referring to the judicial *khulʿ* just created but Mūsā labeled *khulʿ* before first marital sex a "reparation of damage" (*jabr al-ḍarar*), and pointed to the acceptance in society – meaning that society only accepted *khulʿ* before first marital sex. He regarded what he called the "good behavior of women" with regard to divorce as a problem and recommended more research. Abū al-Rubb, on the other hand, argued on a general legal level and endorsed any solution allowed in Sharia, not only personally but stated this for her Ministry. In the discussion with Mūsā, she seemed inclined to accept *khulʿ* not only before but also after consummation of marriage.[137] Thus the gendered

134 Arguing in this way, he obviously did not refer to the fact that the *taʿmīm* was taken by SCHS as a Sharia body and that an instruction had been sent by the Supreme Judge to all judges in the Sharia Courts to apply this ruling.

135 ʿAbdalrazzāq Mūsā, interview on November 24, 2013.

136 Rīm Abū al-Rubb, interview on December 2, 2013.

137 Rīm Abū al-Rubb and ʿAbdalrazzāq Mūsā, interview on December 2, 2013.

concepts put forward by the representatives of the state differ, but they are always very strictly framed by Islamic law and based on certain common assuptions such as the impermissibility of intercourse outside marriage.

6.2.4 *What Does This Ruling* (taʿmīm) *Mean? How Does It Compare to Legislation?*

Al-ʿŪrī regarded the *Qāḍī al-Quḍāt*'s ruling not only as an unacceptable "independent legal opinion" (*ijtihād*), as stated above, but also as "unconstitutional" (*ghayr dustūrī*).[138] He argued that in case the Sharia establishment wanted a new ruling they should suggest official amendments to the applicable law. In a modern state, the judge is bound by the law until there is a new law (*qānūn jadīd*), he argued. If religious scholars (*fuqahāʾ*) saw it necessary to have *khulʿ*, then they should create official amendments to the law. He seemed to be critical in general about the Sharia institution and criticized the creation of the department of the Personal Status Prosecution in the Sharia court system as well as the implementation of various stages of appeal in the Sharia court system as introduced by al-Tamīmī. On the other hand, Abū al-Rubb of the Ministry of Justice discussed the point freely and did not criticize the *Qāḍī al-Quḍāt* for handing down this ruling.[139] The Minister of Women's Affairs, Rabīḥa Dhiyāb even welcomed it according to one of the very rare reports in the media mentioning a participant of the state. Speaking on the occasion of a lecture about "*Khulʿ* in Palestine" at BZU on December 13, 2012, she said with regard to the motivations behind issuing this "law [*sic!*] on judicial *khulʿ*" (*qānūn al-khulʿ al-qaḍaʾī*) that it gave the woman the right to claim separation in court and had to be classified as a positive step. It gave, she went on, girls the freedom to choose their future spouse and diminish treacheries in marriage and it helped to restrict repudiation (*ṭalāq*). She considered the combination with the legal control necessary to avoid the negative consequences connected to its use, stating: "We, the Ministry for Womens's Affairs, decided that the issuing of this law (*iqrār hādhā al-qānūn*) can be seen as one of the most important steps the judicial system took. And we will pursue seriously the issuing of a Personal Status Law."[140] This comes near to a kind of official statement of a representative of the State of Palestine with regard to the *khulʿ taʿmīm* welcoming and even accepting it as a law and is in stark contrast to Ḥasan al-ʿŪrī's critical evaluation.

---

138 Ḥasan al-ʿŪrī, interview on October 13, 2014.

139 Rīm Abū al-Rubb, interview on December 2, 2013.

140 Maannews, December 13, 2012a.

6.3 Sharia Establishment

In January 2012,[141] the public discourse started with Yūsuf Idʿīs's announcement in the media of the work of the Juridical Committee of the Sharia Courts (*al-Lajna al-fiqhiyya fī al-maḥākim al-sharʿiyya*) exploring the possibility of a decision[142] of *khulʿ* for women. He gave the increasing "blackmailing" of young women as the reason:

> The most urgently studied cases at the moment were undertaken by the juristic committee of the Sharia Courts and there will be a decision in due course with regard to the possibility for the woman to divorce (*khulʿ*) her husband, and this *khulʿ* is before consummation and privacy and the decision will be under the authority of the judge.[143]

Idʿīs gave as reasons for the increase of divorce before consummation, just like in his lecture, hastiness in choosing a partner and following from this misunderstandings and disagreements. There were many young persons who started to take steps toward marriage without thinking of the future, he complained. The economic situation made it hard for young men to meet with the requirements that had been agreed upon in the marriage contract like clothing for the bride, gold, and other gifts usually given in Palestinian society.[144]

Directly after the introduction of the *taʿmīm*, universities offered workshops to train judges and lawyers. Three months after the ruling, a report appeared about a workshop the *Dīwān* of the Supreme Judge had organized in cooperation with the Faculty of Law of BZU to train Sharia Court judges, jurists, academics, and feminists simulating a court procedure.[145] The *Qāḍī al-Quḍāt* supervised the session and at the end of the training session certificates were handed out to the participants. Lawyer Ṣāliḥ Abū ʿAzza praised the law (*qānūn* [*sic!*]) and expressed his relief as a lawyer after it was issued, stating:

> The Sharia jurisdiction (*al-qaḍāʾ al-sharʿī*) is complete and not partial and since the implementation of the Palestinian Authority until now we could not change anything regarding that applied law. The efforts of the

141 Maannews, January 14, 2012; see also paltoday, January 19, 2012, according to which there had been a press conference the day before with the official announcement of *khulʿ* to come.

142 Here the term *qarār* is used which normally is used for presidential decisions.

143 Maannews, January 14, 2012; very similar report: palpress, January 14, 2012.

144 Maannews, January 14, 2012; very similar report: palpress, January 14, 2012.

145 Maannews, December 23, 2012.

> president of the SSC (*al-Maḥkama al-ʿUlyā al-Sharʿiyya*) to reduce the burden on Palestinian citizens deserve respect.... In all cases, we should differentiate between the *khul*ʿ based on mutual consent and the judicial *khul*ʿ (*khul*ʿ *qaḍāʾī*).[146]

This quotation seems to lay claim to an all-encompassing Sharia that is not reduced to family law matters and which gives it a substantial role, which is, however, not further outlined.[147] Universities and especially BZU were thus involved openly in the spreading of and training in the new ruling and cooperated intensively with the state – as the invitation of the Minister of Women's Affairs shows – as well as the Sharia establishment.

6.3.1 *Why Was the Reform of the Family Law Generally and with Regard to* khulʿ *Seen as Necessary; and What Reasons Were Given in Favor of or against the Reform?*

All experts asked in *Lāzim Naḥkī*, being members of the Sharia establishment, agreed that the Palestinian custom of signing the marriage contract with the engagement was the origin of the legal problem leaving young women as "in-betweeners," and they criticized the young men's behavior of "blackmailing" these young "inbetween" women.[148] Ṣumūd al-Ḍamīrī confirmed that the new ruling was handed down because the blackmailing had to be stopped.[149] In a television program, al-Ḍamīrī gave more explicit numbers. There had been dozens of young girls between the ages of twenty and twenty-two who after several years still did not have a judicial divorce[150] and this was confirmed by the Sharia Lawyer al-Qaysī.[151] In this critique, civil society and Sharia establishment are in accordance. The general social necessity of the *khul*ʿ *taʿmīm* was confirmed by the Sharia establishment[152] and reference was made to the social

146 Qashṭa 2013.

147 See similar Ṭuwāfisha 2014.

148 See also Judge Asmahān al-Waḥīdī, interview on November 28, 2013; *Ḥārisāt Nārinā*, April 9, 2017. See also ʿAwda and al-Qaysī in *Lāzim Naḥkī*, April 30, 2013. In general, divorce for women is still seen as negative, and divorced women are frowned upon, see Maannews, January 14, 2012; Arīj ʿAwda, *Lāzim Naḥkī*, April 30, 2013.

149 *Lāzim Naḥkī*, April 30, 2013.

150 *Ḥārisāt Nārinā*, April 9, 2017.

151 *Lāzim Naḥkī*, April 30, 2013.

152 Alhourriah, October 6, 2012; Maannews, January 14, 2012; *Lāzim Naḥkī*, April 30, 2013, in nearly all interviews. Ṣumūd al-Ḍamīrī mentioned that the waiting period could be up to five years, see *Lāzim Naḥkī*, April 30, 2013. See also ʿAwda and al-Qaysī, both in *Lāzim Naḥkī*, April 30, 2013; Tawfīq Abū al-Hāshim, interview on December 6, 2017; ʿAlī al-Sarṭāwī, interview on December 3, 2013.

situation, especially by the judges who argued that they were acquainted with this situation through their "field experience."[153]

Al-Sarṭāwī, professor at the University of Nablus, seemed to accept this custom in Palestinian society. As a participant of the meeting of the Sharia establishment on November 2, 2013, and of the group who met on November 20, 2013, at the *Muqāṭaʿa*, and like his colleague Mūsā in the Ministry of Justice, he opposed the suggestion of the women's organizations to have a preparatory contract (*ʿaqd ibtidāʾī*) or a "probationary period" (*fatra tajribiyya*) for the engagement period and insisted that another husband should know from the beginning that there had been a marriage before, even if it was not consumated. With regard to engagement, he advised the couple to come together, sit, not only look at each other, but also talk and find "harmony in thinking" (*insijām fikri*).[154] Sharia judge Ḥātim al-Bīṭāwī criticized that the ruling had been drawn up in a hurry. He explained that the law of *khulʿ* had already been enacted in Sharia courts for many years, referring to *khulʿ* based on mutual agreement, and added:

> We support changes and reforms as long as they are in the branches (*furūʿ*) and do not touch upon the principles (*uṣūl*). In our situation, we are in great need to reform some issues, especially in the personal status law. However, I object to those calls demanding to touch upon the principles of Sharia. General rules should be followed and we should also take new developments into consideration and that is necessary in those issues in which we can apply *ijtihād*.[155]

According to him, the new law came about because of the oppression women were subjected to, but the responsible persons should have been more patient before activating the law (*qānūn* [*sic!*]) in order to give more time to study it and to recognize the problematic points and fully overcome them.[156] There was serious concern that in a situation where actual legislation is not possible, but a social problem is pressing, urgent measures had to be taken.[157]

---

153 Al-ʿAwda, al-Qaysī, al-Ḍamīrī in *Lāzim Naḥkī*, April 30, 2013; e.g., Tawfīq Abū al-Hāshim, interview on December 6, 2017; the representatives of the women's organizations pointed to their experience with women who complain about the lengthy court process of a separation initiated by them, e.g. Nihāya Muḥammad, interview on November 24, 2013, etc.

154 ʿAlī al-Sarṭāwī, interview on December 3, 2013.

155 Qashṭa 2013.

156 Qashṭa 2013.

157 Al-Ḍamīrī, *Lāzim Naḥkī*, April 30, 2013.

6.3.2 *Which Uses of the Past Were Made? Which Terminology Was Used?*

Of course the "uses of the past" are the core business of the Sharia establishment. "We use the past every day in our life," al-Ḍamīrī explained to me.[158] In his announcement on the *khul*ʿ ruling, the Supreme Judge explained that *khul*ʿ is a right for the woman; it is an old right going back to the time of the Prophet.[159] The judge of the Sharia High Court, Tawfīq Abū al-Hāshim, member of the committee working on the *taʿmīm*, explained that as times change, society changes, and the position of women changes. Therefore, the old JLPS of 1976 was no longer suitable. When a pressing need was seen, they decided under the direction of the Supreme Judge to change it, because in Islamic jurisprudence, one can always find different opinions of the scholars and they can be used for adapting the law to modernity. For the new situation, a different opinion was issued. He defended the reform of the law and its adaptation to changing times and circumstances.[160]

The rooting of *khul*ʿ in the Quran and Sunna was always pointed to by their representatives. The by now well-known Quranic verses as well as the *ḥadīth* concerning Thābit b. Qays's wife were generally quoted, for example, by Judge ʿAdīlī on *Lāzim Naḥkī*.[161] He started as usual with the explanation that *khul*ʿ is redemption (*iftidāʾ*) and is anchored in the Quran verse: "If you fear they may not maintain God's bounds, it is no fault in them for her to redeem herself" (2:229). He added the normal proof from *ḥadīth* and explained the procedure that should follow when a woman comes to court and wants a *khul*ʿ divorce, also in cases when the husband was not present and did not attend the sessions at court. The procedure takes, according to him, around four to five months. If the husband was not present – this was the case foreseen in the whole discussion, because he had left his not-yet-real wife and gone to another country or even married another wife – the judgment would be given in his absence and a copy sent to him. Mentioned were the woman's fear of *kufr*[162] in Islam, the Prophet's ruling that she should give back the dower and consequently he – the husband – should grant her a divorce.[163]

158 Interview with her on June 26, 2018 in Göttingen during her visit to Göttingen university.

159 Paltoday, January 19, 2012.

160 Tawfīq Abū al-Hāshim, interview on December 6, 2017. Still, Abū al-Hāshim would stick to the traditional gender perception that women are "lenient" and men are more rational, but pointing to, among others, Germany's Chancellor Angela Merkel, he would concede that there are "strong" women and "lenient" men.

161 Judge ʿAdīlī in *Lāzim Naḥkī*, April 30, 2013.

162 *Kufr* is normally translated as "unbelief," but here it means the woman's conviction that she could not follow God's limits.

163 See al-Ḍamīrī and ʿAdīlī in *Lāzim Naḥkī*, April 30, 2013.

The ruling was negatively and positively described as *ijtihād*.[164] Al-Ḍamīrī mentioned the *taʿmīm* and stated:

> Therefore, all the above shows a clear implementation of *ijtihād fiqhī* in terms of personal status and provides real legal guarantees for women based on justified clear *sharīʿa* rules that were carefully examined in order to realize the aim of the legislature; achieving the *maqāṣid* (intentions) by exercising *ijtihad*.[165]

Who is permitted to issue an *ijtihād*?[166] The Sharia establishment obviously claimed the right to *ijtihād* – but there were critical voices among the scholars themselves as Ḥasan al-Jūjū and al-Tamīmī,[167] the former Supreme Judge. Both were in this case in accordance with[168] Ḥasan al-ʿŪrī of the presidential Bureau. The Supreme Judge himself was cautious in naming "his" ruling *ijtihād* but considered *ijtihād* within the realm of his scientific work; his colleagues, as the quotations shows, on the other hand, were clear in classifying the ruling as *ijtihād*.[169]

Whereas according to the Supreme Judge's narrative, he had convinced all his judges, Abū al-Hāshim spoke of a general agreement and of a "majority" who supported the new ruling, because there was no obstacle seen (*māniʿ*) with regard to this reform.[170]

The new *khulʿ* was often classified as *maṣlaḥa*, a benefit for young girls and therefore for society.[171] The Sharia lawyer (and women's activist) ʿAwda referred to it saying that the concept of *khulʿ* is not for money in return, it is a lawsuit (*daʿwā*) called *iftidāʾ*, a redemption lawsuit, which meant that the woman redeemed herself with whatever he gave her. If he gave her ten thousand, then she gives back the same amount but not double. It is not an investment, she explained.[172] Al-Ḍamīrī confirmed the report of Fāṭima ʿĀshūr, lawyer of

164 This was criticized by Ḥasan al-Jūjū, *Lāzim Naḥkī*, April 30, 2013; but positively confirmed by Tawfiq Abū al-Hāshim, interview on December 6, 2017, and Damiri 2018: 111–112, and by her in *Ḥārisāt Nārinā*, April 9, 2017.

165 Damiri 2018: 112.

166 This highly interesting question cannot be dealt with in this research.

167 See 4.4.

168 *Lāzim Naḥkī*, April 30, 2013.

169 See chapter 5; see also Abū al-Hāshim, who had been on the committee drawing up the *taʿmīm* and who confirmed explicitly in his interview with me on December 6, 2017, that it was *ijtihād*.

170 Tawfiq Abū al-Hāshim, interview on December 6, 2017.

171 Paltoday, January 19, 2012.

172 *Lāzim Naḥkī*, April 30, 2013.

Gaza, that the word *khul*ʿ is sometimes not liked and was thus changed to *iftidā*ʾ (*ustubdila bi-iftidā*ʾ), as has already been outlined in the analysis of the Supreme Judge's lecture.[173]

One additional aspect of a "use of the past," which broadened the debate about the Palestinian "customs and traditions," is to be found in a legal opinion (*fatwā*) issued in 2015 by the "House of the *Fatwā*" (*Dār al-Iftā*ʾ). It contained the answer to the question asked by an unknown person: "What is the difference between engagement, the contract, and consummation? And which Sharia rules result from this?"[174] Despite the *taʿmīm*, thus, in 2015 still a need was felt in society to understand the interrelatedness between engagement, marriage, and consummation on which the *khul*ʿ ruling of 2012 was based. The *fatwā* is not referring explicitly to the *taʿmım* 59/2012 but deals with the underlying social problem – even without mentioning it outright – of marriage contracts made at the engagement, and comes to a new and surprising explanation.

The *fatwā* 123/2015, signed by *Muftī Shaykh* Muḥammad Saʿī Ṣalāḥ, defines and explains the legal institutes of engagement and marriage and first sexual intercourse. As a *fatwā*, a legal opinion, it is not bound to the applicable law but can and does draw heavily on Islamic law. It first defines marriage as the beginning of family life and as a pillar of the society and of the Muslim community (*umma*), whereas engagement (*khiṭba*), coming first, is only an offer in which the man asks for the girl's hand. In accordance with the law the *fatwā* defines engagement as a non-binding promise for both sides. During the time of engagement, the woman may have no other fiancé. Needless to say – and this statement is actually missing in the text – the man, of course, can. With regard to engagement a *ḥadīth* is quoted, according to which the Prophet reminded men not to ask for the hand of a woman who is already engaged. From the engagement, no legal obligations (*aḥkām sharʿiyya*) follow, not inheritance, maintenance, or any form of dower (*mahr*) or add-ons (*tawābiʿ*).

Having outlined these legal basics correctly and in accordance with the applicable law the *fatwā* goes into the practical application and draws on Islamic law outlining how the matter should be dealt with. It is evident that the Palestinian custom to sign the marriage contract at the engagement ceremony is known to the author of the *fatwā* but he does not mention it directly. According to him it is strictly forbidden (*yuḥarram*) for the engaged couple to spend time together in privacy, because they are like strangers (*ajānib*) to each other. Engagement does not allow the man to "jump and wander around"

173 *Lāzim Naḥkī*, April 30, 2013, 45:11; see chapter 5.

174 Ṣalāḥ 2015.

(*yaṣlu wa-yajūlu*), "roam around and be cheerful" (*yasraḥu wa-yamraḥu*) – or, more concretely, visit his fiancée alone at her house. The fiancé is not even allowed to shake the woman's hand. The fiancée is not allowed to show her attractions or charms, use cosmetics, or take off her scarf. The restrictions put on the engaged couple leave no doubt that, according to what the *Muftī* defines as "Islamic law," not much room is left for the couple to learn about each other during the engagement period, let alone to communicate freely with each other.

The marriage contract is then described as a document based on mutual agreement and the next step after the engagement, but nothing is mentioned here about the time of the signature. It thus ignores the practice in Palestine that created such problems. But it is outlined that – as stipulated in the law – a guardian (*walī*) is necessary as well as two witnesses. After signing the contract, both spouses inherit from each other. A dower is paid (*mahr*) and each one is "permitted" to the other. However, and here the *Muftī* deviates from the applicable law according to which the contract is already the permission for consummation, the man having signed a contract is still not yet allowed to be with the woman alone without "announcement and presentation" (*ishhār wa-iẓhār*). "Great evils" and danger to society and family will arise in this case. The introduction of *ishhār wa-izhār* as an important if not indispensable necessity before consummation at this point is legally new and a special example of a "use of the past" adding it to the Palestinian iteration about family law and to the debates about *khulʿ* before consummation. It belongs not to the Palestinian-Hanafi legal context but is rooted again, as so much in the debates about *khulʿ*, in the Maliki school where "announcement and presentation" are mostly used instead of witnesses.[175] However, the text had pointed to the necessity of witnesses before when dealing with the marriage contract.

After outlining the legal consequences of repudiation (*ṭalāq*) before consummation,[176] it becomes evident what is meant by "announcement and presentation": from privacy (*khalwa*), the *Muftī* warns pregnancy might result, and in case the contractor dies – to whom will the child belong? Who will be the father? This is a difficult fate for women, he warns. This argument does not

175 Ibn Zahra 1970: 52: Note of Judge al-Ḍamīrī (June 3, 2019): it is normally not used in Palestine, just in case of "custom-marriage", i.e., not registered marriage could it be accepted.

176 The *fatwā* explains that when there is *ṭalāq* after the contract and before consummation, half of the prompt and deferred dower (*mahr muʿajjal* and *muʾajjal*) has to be paid to the woman as well as half of the dower add-ons. In this case, there is no waiting period (*ʿidda*), it is a minor irrevocable *ṭalāq* (*bāʾin baynūna ṣughrā*), and she is not allowed to him except with a new contract and dower (*mahr*).

meet the reality on the ground: the matter discussed in Palestinian society was not about the husband dying, which might happen, but the matter was about a bad habit of young men leaving their fiancées with a marriage contract as "inbetween" women. The *Muftī* ignores this social reality completely. One could argue that he has the right to do so as the social custom of signing the marriage contract with engagement and young men leaving young women after this is not included in the question put forward to him. He does worry about the consequence of privacy from which pregnancy could result, the possible sexual relation which might happen: "We [*sic!*] look after our [*sic!*] girls and do not allow the contractor[177] to be alone with the woman with whom he has a contract (*maʿqūda*) without the company of an immediate family member (*dhī raḥm muḥarram*)." Thus: "When privacy (*khalwa*) happens, it is necessary at once to have announcement (*ishhār*) of both spouses."

His argumentation contains a nice example of "othering" when he says "we look after our girls," "we" referring to the scholars but in a broader sense, to men. Women are "ours" in what seems to be understood as a kind of ownership and responsibility but certainly no expression of gender equality. The *Muftī* states that a contract alone is not enough. After having slept with each other, the husband and wife have to step out on the street and tell the neighbors that they had sex. Legally, one more step not mentioned in the applicable law and not discussed so far in the iterations in Palestine is inserted: the announcement of the marriage. It has according to the *Muftī*'s opinion to happen despite the fact that there were two witnesses present when the contract was signed. Consummation, "enjoyment" (*istimtāʿ*) comes and here the *Muftī* points to Quran (30:20).[178]

This *fatwā* not only gives strict guidelines for the engaged couple on how to behave after having signed the contract but before "announcement," it also puts the act of consummation into public focus. Sexual experiences even with a marriage contract are not permitted. Against this *fatwā*, the applicable law seems unconstrained and liberal because it protects every couple that has a contract – irrespective of when and where the marital sex may have happened and it guarantees the legality of children resulting from this marriage. According to the *fatwā*, children begotten in such a situation without "announcement" are considered illegitimate children. The *fatwā* thus not only contradicts the

177 Also in these cases the active/passive terms are used: the contractor/*ʿāqid* and the contracted (*maʿqūda*). Fiancé and financée are referred to as *khāṭib* and *makhṭūba*, which again represents the active/passive dichotomy.

178 "And of His signs is that He created for you, of yourselves, spouses, that you might repose in them, and He has set between you love and mercy. Surely in that are signs for a people who consider."

applicable law but reflects the spirit of a very conservative and rigid sexual morality that threatens women if they have an unplanned pregancy.

In contrast to this, Idʿīs had always stressed in his reasonings and arguments his aim to help women in a difficult situation. He had, it is true, in the first part of his narrative, assumed that women would misuse the ruling in case it was extended to the time after consummation, but then conceded that there had been a hot social debate with Palestinian men, too, who refused to be called "divorced" in the passive voice – and who wanted to preserve the "active men/ passive women" dichotomy; he even admitted that Palestine's society was "masculine" and he had criticized male behavior violating women's rights.[179] Both, the *taʿmīm* and the *fatwā* have one thing in common: they legalize the "customs and traditions" that prohibited sex before the wedding party.

Another tradition and custom besides forbidding sex before marriage (or better even: in marriage) makes it absolutely impossible for the man to accept the idea that he is the passive object (*mafʿūl bihi*), not the acting one (*fāʿil*).[180] The Supreme Judge had dealt with this topic and uttered his incomprehension, and Jumān Qunayṣ had provoked the male audience in her introduction to *Lāzim Naḥkī* on April 30, 2012. The West Bank lawyer Ikrām al-Qaysī confirmed in this program that in an "Eastern" society, the husband would not accept a divorce (*ṭalāq*) initiated by a woman, and that there is a vehement rejection of this idea among them. Gaza lawyer Fāṭima ʿĀshūr described the "traditional masculine thinking" (*al-ʿaqliyya al-dhukūriyya al-taqlidiyya*) as the biggest obstacle and confirmed the observation that men would not accept the passive term. She repeated several times that in any society and most Arab societies, a man does not accept being called divorced (*makhlūʿ*), or being "left" (*matrūk*) or rejected. He is the one who rejects, leaves, and gives repudiation (*huwa man yarfuḍu wa-yatruku wa-yuṭalliqu*).[181] In court, when he hears that she will divorce him, he will give her the repudiation first, she reported from her experience. The men's refusal to be called "divorced," "separated" in the passive voice was emphasized by the female experts in *Lāzim Naḥkī*.[182] Judge Tawfīq Abū al-Hāshim was more reluctant.[183] Asked whether there is a fear of men being called "divorced" in the passive voice, he answered: "maybe" (*qad yakūnu*) and then pointed generally to traditions (*taqālīd wa-ʿādāt*). Again different opinions among the Sharia scholars become visible and among the

179 See chapter 5.

180 *Lāzim Naḥkī*, April 30, 2013.

181 *Lāzim Naḥkī*, April 30, 2013.

182 Ṣumūd al-Damīrī, Ikrām al-Qaysī and Fāṭima ʿĀshūr, see *Lāzim Naḥkī*, April 30, 2013.

183 Tawfīq Abū al-Hāshim, interview on December 6, 2017.

more conservative Muslim scholars are al-Sarṭāwī, who referred to the Quran and the Prophet and explained that there was no doubt that the Draft of the Supreme Judge was based on these two sources and would serve as the basis for a general discussion of a new Palestinian Family Law[184] as well as Judge Waḥīdī who fought for maintaining the marriage guardian.[185] When discussing with her the question of whether a marriage guardian (*walī*) should be mandatory for the woman when signing the contract, or to let the future husband and wife sign the contract themselves, al-Waḥīdī was against a woman signing her own contract. She, too, referred to the "traditional" (*muḥāfiẓ*) and Eastern society where respect for the family is important in Palestine and compared it to the unfavorable behavior in the West – at least as she imagined it. She considered it important that the father or a guardian accompany the bride to the court for signing the contract. Where should she go in case of difficulties in her marriage and in case of a divorce? She had to go to her father! When asked about the woman's freedom and agency in her own life, she just repeated her arguments. Asked whether this could not be seen as an expression of a patriarchal society, she rejected this and insisted that there has to be a guardian out of respect (*iḥtirām*), ignoring that according to the Hanafi school of law an adult woman can sign her marriage contract on her own.

6.3.3 *Why Was* khulʿ *against the Husband's Will Given Only before Consummation of Marriage? Which Gender Concepts Were Negotiated?*

Two arguments for *khul*ʿ before consummation were advanced among the Sharia establishment, which at least partly had been uttered by Yūsuf Idʿīs in his lecture: there were no children and therefore no complicated family issues to be decided upon; and women after consummation were better off with a separation based on "dispute and discord," because in this case they would keep their dower.[186] The two rulings were seen as mutually supportive.[187] On *Lāzim Naḥkī*, al-Ḍamīrī argued that for both *khul*ʿ after consummation and also before consummation there are legal principles and Sharia principles. As a solution for the problem outside of the legislative framework, the Sharia judges decided to settle for *khul*ʿ before consummation as "a first step".[188] On the

184 ʿAlī al-Sarṭāwī, interview on December 3, 2013.

185 Asmahān al-Waḥīdī, interview on November 28, 2013.

186 Ikrām al-Qaysī in *Lāzim Naḥkī*, April 30, 2013; Asmahān al-Waḥīdī, interview on November 28, 2013.

187 Paltoday, January 19, 2012; see also *Lāzim Naḥkī*, April 30, 2013; Asmahān al-Waḥīdī, interview on November 28, 2013.

188 *Lāzim Naḥkī*, April 30, 2013.

television program *Ḥārisāt Nārinā*,[189] al-Ḍamīrī agreed wholeheartedly that *khulʿ* would also be possible after consummation, quoting the Prophet's decision and stating that it "is allowed (*ḥalāl*), it is clear in the Sunna."[190] Al-Qaysī confirmed that many girls had awaited this ruling eagerly and explained that before consummation (she even said: before "marriage" [*zawāj*]), there are no children, there are only few social relations that make a separation easier,[191] and a divorce based on "dispute and discord" gives her her legal rights, i.e., the dower. Judge al-Faqīh, on the other hand, argued, that all women should be included as women after consummation were more oppressed and needed *khulʿ* equally.[192] Al-Sarṭāwī argued that in Egypt repudiation had been in the man's hands and the woman could not apply for *ṭalāq* before the court.[193] But in the JLPS of 1976, there are many opportunities for the woman to apply for separation through the court, for example, with regard to "dispute and discord," he explained, using the popular "quantitative argument." With regard to the burden of proof on the woman, he answered that every claim in court needed proof. But under the new Jordanian law, the woman could go to court and the judge would separate the spouses. Asked whether there should be some balance to the unrestricted man's right to repudiation, he replied with the question: "Is there any law on earth which can force the husband to stay with his wife?"[194]

6.3.4 *What Does This Ruling Mean? How Does It Compare to Legislation?*

The fact that in the media there was a lack of awareness that the ruling (*taʿmīm*) was not a law (*qānūn*) has been outlined above. In a report it was correctly outlined that the ruling did not come as a *fatwā*, a legal opinion, but then mistakenly stated that it was issued as "law" (*qānūn*) from the center (*ṣulb*)

189 Ṣumūd al-Ḍamīrī, April 9, 2017.

190 *Ḥārisāt Nārinā*, April 9, 2017.

191 *Lāzim Naḥkī*, April 30, 2013; also Tawfīq Abū al-Hāshim, interview on December 6, 2017; Asmahān al-Waḥīdī, interview on November 28, 2013.

192 Khulūd al-Faqīh, interview on December 19, 2013.

193 ʿAlī al-Sarṭāwī, interview on December 3, 2013. This is not correct. In the year 2000, different forms of judicial divorce were possible according to law, e.g., when the husband was absent, etc., see Denker 2004: 156–167.

194 ʿAlī al-Sarṭāwī, interview on December 3, 2013. We got in an argument about this when I outlined German divorce law – both parties can ask for divorce at court and both have to spend one year separated, then the divorce judgment will be issued. He asked: "Can German legislation force the man not to divorce his wife?" When I explained that there is only divorce in court, he again reformulated his question: "Can the judge prevent the man from repudiating his wife?" I tried to explain that there is no repudiation of the wife by the man but equal access to divorce but he remained convinced that "*ṭalāq* is in the man's hand" (*al-ṭalāq fī yad al-rajul*) and should remain in the man's hand.

of Islamic Sharia.[195] The media normally quoted the Sharia establishment – and not representatives of the state – in this regard. About the mechanism to ratify this "law" (*qānūn*), Idʿīs is quoted in the media to have said: "In case this decision (*qarār*) is taken …, it will be valid immediately after the issuing of this ruling (*taʿmīm*) and circulation of that note to all the Sharia Courts by the President of the *Majlis*, and that is because the Palestinian Legislative Council does not meet."[196] This is in contradiction to what he told his students in the class according to which it had to be validated by the Appeals Court and then became a law.[197]

In a report from August 2012, Idʿīs announced the new *khulʿ* "law" (*qānūn al-khulʿ*) and said that it came after preparation and an eight-month discussion with the people after which they had not rejected it.[198] The president of the Sharia Bar Association, ʿAlī Shuqayrāt, explained that Sharia was encompassing and not partial (*kullī wa-laysa juzʾiyyan*).[199] He hinted at the efforts of the President of the Supreme Sharia Court and explained that he aimed to lighten the burden on the Palestinian citizens. Sharia judge Khulūd al-Faqīh, on the other hand, considered the ruling illegal because it should have come as a presidential decree, an opinion which, as she confirmed, she had communicated to the Supreme Judge.[200]

The lack of parliamentary meeting was often used as an excuse. Al-Ḍamīrī was clear in *Lāzim Naḥkī* that it was not a law and also not an amendment of the law, "we do not legislate" (*naḥnu lā namlik*)[201] she stated twice, but the Council has 'interpreted' (*fassara*) the article in the JLPS to make it easier for the citizens."[202] Judge al-Waḥīdī spoke of the *taʿmīm* and was well aware that this is not a law,[203] whereas Judge al-Faqīh stated that she did not have cases of this ruling in her court in Birzeit.[204] Tawfīq Abū al-Hāshim, a judge of the HSC, confirmed, that this matter had been debated and the "normal" way via

195 Alhourriah, October 6, 2012.
196 Maannews, January 14, 2012.
197 See chapter 5.3.
198 Wafa, August 30, 2012.
199 Wafa, August 30, 2012; see also Ṣāliḥ Abū ʿAzza's similar statement Qashṭa 2013.
200 Khulūd al-Faqīh, interview on December 19, 2013.
201 *Lāzim Naḥkī*, April 30, 2013. Literally, it means "we do not own." The meaning, as she explained to me, is "to own the right of legislation." Ṣumūd al-Ḍamīrī, May 4, 2019. There was awareness among the SCHC that they are not a legislative body; but at the same time, a solution to the pressing social problem had to be found.
202 *Lāzim Naḥkī*, April 30, 2013.
203 Asmahān al-Waḥīdi, interview on November 28, 2013.
204 Khulūd al-Faqīh, interview on December 19, 2013.

legislation had not been possible. Also a decision (*qarār*) of the president was not seen as probable.[205]

Al-Ḍamīrī spoke of a difficult "application" (*tanfīdh*) of the rulings, using the term *qarārāt,* and she saw no possibility of enforcing them in Gaza. The Head of HSCC of Gaza, Ḥasan al-Jūjū criticized, as outlined already, the West Bank *ijtihād*.[206] Asked for her position on what al-Jūjū had said, al-Ḍamīrī answered "We don't want to continue the separation … we want a formal procedure of legislation, but for now, there are many *taʿmīmāt* and they are part of the legislative activity (*ʿamaliyya tashrīʿiyya*). The Jordanian Law of 1976 is not sufficient, it is not appropriate for Palestine. There is an urgent need for reform."[207]

6.4 Conclusion

Iterations are not grasped easily. The topic was only dealt with in one survey,[208] which did not make the *taʿmīm* a topic of the questions asked and focused more on the financial aspect and the general question of women's divorce and less on the question of a woman's agency and her right to divorce against the husband's wishes. It revealed that Palestinians are in favor of changing the law and this law in family matters is seen to be based on Islamic law. Generally, gender equality is supported but when it comes to details, the regulation of the divorce law, for example, gender equality is not much supported in society. Instead of the official institutions foreseen in the constitution, i.e., the parliament and in certain cases presidential decrees, Sharia courts have high repudiation rates and are seen as the decisive body to reform the law.

Not in this survey or in other places was the basis of classical Islamic marriage, the "money-obedience" relationship, questioned. It was not mentioned in public discussions and civil society representatives – being well aware of the issue and its implication of gender inequality – hastened to reassure society that the payment of the dower and the obligation of maintenance could not be touched in Palestinian society. The reason was seen in the economic situation. The survey of 2013 confirmed this concern for women's financial security and the numbers for 2018 speak for themselves: women's participation rate in the labor force increased from 10 percent in 2001 to 19 percent in 2018 but with a considerable gap between the income of women and men.

205 Tawfīq Abū al-Hāshim, interview on December 6, 2017.
206 *Lāzim Naḥkī*, April 30, 2013.
207 *Lāzim Naḥkī*, April 30, 2013.
208 Johnson and Hammami 2013.

The unemployment rate of women was 47 percent compared to 22 percent of males; 65 percent of females between the ages of fifteen and twenty-nine were unemployed in 2018.[209]

When questioned in the street, it seemed that women and men did not have profound knowledge about the new ruling. Information in the media and television talk shows, which not only reflected but also shaped public opinion, was quite comprehensive but not always accurate. In the media reports and television talk shows with regard to *khulʿ*, representatives of the Sharia establishment dominated. They were seen as the preferable experts from the field to be invited to the studio. The non-presence of the state in the public sphere on this matter can be interpreted as an eloquent silence: the weak state, which had tried in vain to gain control over these legislative debates and had created the National Committee of the Family Law (NCFL) to push forward the process of drafting a family law, had to give this space to civil society and the Sharia establishment in the end. Whereas Ḥasan al-ʿŪrī's idea had been that the state should take the lead in this process, to "bell the cat," in fact, the state stepped out of the process after the failure of the meeting in November 2013.[210] The process came to a halt.

There are common opinions that became mainstream thinking through the process. Generally, all agreed that there should be a new Palestinian family law; this has also been corroborated in the 2013 survey. But for political reasons, the split, and because there was no parliament sitting in Ramallah, there was no way to bring this into existence in the legally prescribed way by the BL. Women's organizations criticized the president for not taking matters into his own hands and issuing a presidential decree. In 2012/13, nobody expected this to happen and public opinion had shifted away from the president to the Sharia Courts for pushing forward the family law.

The iterations revealed several basic assumptions as well as taboo topics that were not touched upon. The majority of the voices of civil society and the Sharia establishment acknowledged that there was a social problem – young

209 The average daily wage for females was 84.6 NIS compared to 119.6 NIS for men, see Press Release, 7 March 2018.

210 In the second phase of the iterations LHC, the Legislation Harmonization Committee (*Lajnat muwāʾamat al-tashrīʿāt*), was established as a de facto follow-up of the earlier committee; in spring 2019, different information was available. According to the Ministry of Foreign Affairs (ʿUmar ʿIwaḍallāh, interview on April 7, 2019) the committee was constituted; according to an interview with civil society representatives (Munā al-Khalīlī, April 8, 2019), the committee was just in preparation and civil society so far had no idea how to proceed.

women left "inbetween" and being maltreated by young men[211] – which had to be solved and the majority welcomed and supported the 2012 *taʿmīm* even if some would have wished that it went further and give the right of *khulʿ* to women after consummation of marriage whereas others feared that women would abuse this right. This was also confirmed to a certain degree by the survey according to which only 32 percent of the men and 37 percent of women supported "women's right to divorce *khulʿ*."[212] Still, this support in public opinion cannot be labeled substantially.

That law can be changed, even if it is "God's law," was thus taken for granted. The Islamic framing of the iterations was or had to be accepted by all participants of the iterations and confirmed by the survey. As Johnson and Hammami state: the "overall framework ... remained situated in Islamic *sharīʿa*."[213] Dörthe Engelcke comes to the same conclusion with regard to the Jordanian discussions about *khulʿ*. She writes, "In Jordan, the debate over *khulʿ* demonstrates the extent to which women activists accept the religious framework in order to advance their demands."[214] She argues that the women only succeed when they explicitly acknowledge the *orthodoxy* of the field.[215]

Reference to international law – in contrast to the second phase of the iterations – was not made and the *khulʿ* ruling was discussed as an Islamic solution to an internal Palestinian problem. Another important point that was not touched on was the custom out of which the ruling had emerged: it was always stated with a shrugging of shoulders that this was a Palestinian "custom and tradition" but no one demanded an end to this "custom and tradition" or campaigned for a clear separation between engagement and marriage as foreseen in the law. The same was true with regard to the "masculine" or patriarchal society. It was stated, but taken for granted, by the female experts on *Lāzim Naḥkī* as well as by the Supreme Judge in his lecture. Predominant sexual morality tied sexual relations to marriage only and connected it to the requirement of having legal offspring. Descent in the sense of a legally confirmed descent of a child and fear of pregnancy was used in the *fatwā* as the main reason to restrict the movement of young men and women and to forbid them to have sex with each other even after they had signed the marriage contract. Children born out

211 Regrettably, the Johnson and Hammami survey of 2013 did not ask this question.

212 Johnson and Hammami 2013: 43. The exact number for the West Bank – not Gaza and Jerusalem – were: 34 percent of men and 41 percent of women being in favor of "woman's right to divorce," wording that did not refer explicitly to the woman's right against the man's wishes.

213 Johnson and Hammami 2013: 3.

214 Engelcke 2017a: 22–23.

215 *Orthodoxy* in the Bourdieuian sense, as counterterm to *doxa*, see Engelcke 2017a: 23.

of wedlock were considered a threat to society. Contraceptives as a solution were not discussed. On the contrary, the classical concept of a *walad al-zināʾ* (child resulting from an illicit sexual relation) lurked everywhere especially in the *fatwā* but was never mentioned explicitly. The tight relations between family law, construction of gender roles and penal law – even if the applicable penal law is influenced by French law and no longer by classical Islamic law – cannot be denied. There was some dissent about restricting the judicial *khulʿ* to marriages before consummation but the fighters for the "Egyptian version" were soothed with reference to the now easier divorce for women after consummation with regard to "dispute and discord." With regard to the labeling of the *taʿmīm*, the media did not do much to differentiate between ruling, law, and decision. This can be seen as part of the more journalistic and less legal style in the media. Blurring the boundary between "ruling" and "law" became evident in the information boards in *Lāzim Naḥkī*, which established a narrative according to which the "ruling" was a "law," a "Palestinian Personal Status Law" allowed the SCHC the issuing of "laws" to the benefit of the common welfare.[216] This, of course, is the perception and the point of view of the Sharia establishment,[217] which it thus successfully spread in the media and introduced into mainstream thinking.

216 *Lāzim Naḥkī*, April 30, 2013.

217 It must be noted here that not all representatives of the Sharia establishment went so far. The Supreme Judge never spoke of an existing Palestinian family law – but he sometimes called his *taʿmīm* a "law." Al-Ḍamīrī, on the other hand, took much effort to explain that the SCHC was well aware that the amendment should have gone through the parliament but she saw it as a pragmatic solution for a burning social problem in a politically difficult situation without parliament.

CHAPTER 7

CEDAW and Palestine

On April 2, 2014, the "State of Palestine" [*sic!*][1] deposited with the Secretary-General its instruments of accession to a number of international treaties. These included seven of the nine core human rights treaties plus one of the substantive protocols, as follows:[2]

- The International Covenant on Civil and Political Rights (ICCPR)
- The International Covenant on Economic, Social and Cultural Rights (ICESCR)
- The Convention on the Elimination of All Forms of Discrimination against Women (CEDAW)
- The Convention on the Rights of Persons with Disabilities (CRPD)
- The International Convention on the Elimination of All Forms of Racial Discrimination (CERD)
- The Convention against Torture and Other Cruel, Inhuman or Degrading Treatment or Punishment (CAT)
- The Convention on the Rights of the Child (CRC)
- The Optional Protocol to the Convention on the Rights of the Child on the Involvement of Children in Armed Conflict (CRC-OPAC)

On the United Nations website, this step by the State of Palestine was welcomed with the following words:

> This accession to seven core human rights treaties and a key protocol is a significant step towards enhancing the promotion and protection of human rights in Palestine. It is notable in a region with a high number of

1 See https://www.ohchr.org/EN/NewsEvents/Pages/DisplayNews.aspx?NewsID=14556&LangID=E, accessed January 22, 2019. The UN always speaks of the "State of Palestine" even if the status of Palestine is not yet clear.

2 All UN references dealt with in this chapter can be found on the UN website, see https://tbinternet.ohchr.org/_layouts/treatybodyexternal/SessionDetails1.aspx?SessionID=1171&Lang=en, accessed January 4, 2019. On this page, all documents of all states that reported in the time between July 3 and July 12, 2018, are accessible. Under the heading "State of Palestine," of July 11, 2018, the official documents as well as the shadow reports (7.3), the speech of the Minister of Women's Affairs (7.4), a list of the participants and the final report (see 7.4) can be found. For easier access, it was decided to list all these reports under the heading of "CEDAW" – i.e., the initial "State Report," the "Questions and Issues" of the Committee and again the "Replies" of the State of Palestine (both 7.2). Only the Shadow Reports (7.3) were named under the heading of the civil society organizations that had edited it.

 | DOI:10.1163/9789004442313_008

> reservations to human rights treaties, that Palestine is acceding to eight human rights treaties without making a single reservation.[3]

In his article "Without Reservation: Reforming Palestinian Family Laws in Light of CEDAW" (2018), Mutaz Qafisheh, Professor of Law at Hebron University, noticed Palestine was the only Arab state that joined this treaty without reservation and asked:

> What does that mean? Is Palestine willing to apply CEDAW domestically and to ensure the equality between sexes? If so, can Palestine enforce this treaty taking into account centuries-long traditions that discriminate against women, notwithstanding the conservative nature of local communities and the rise of Islamist renaissance across the Middle East?[4]

The two articles on which most reservations were made were Article 2 of CEDAW and Article 16.[5]

---

3 See https://www.ohchr.org/EN/NewsEvents/Pages/DisplayNews.aspx?NewsID=14556&LangID=E, accessed January 22, 2019.

4 Qafisheh 2018: 29.

5 See http://www.un.org/womenwatch/daw/cedaw/, accessed January 21, 2019. Article 2 reads as follows:
States Parties condemn discrimination against women in all its forms, agree to pursue by all appropriate means and without delay a policy of eliminating discrimination against women and, to this end, undertake:
(a) To embody the principle of the equality of men and women in their national constitutions or other appropriate legislation if not yet incorporated therein and to ensure, through law and other appropriate means, the practical realization of this principle;
(b) To adopt appropriate legislative and other measures, including sanctions where appropriate, prohibiting all discrimination against women;
(c) To establish legal protection of the rights of women on an equal basis with men and to ensure through competent national tribunals and other public institutions the effective protection of women against any act of discrimination;
(d) To refrain from engaging in any act or practice of discrimination against women and to ensure that public authorities and institutions shall act in conformity with this obligation;
(e) To take all appropriate measures to eliminate discrimination against women by any person, organization or enterprise;
(f) To take all appropriate measures, including legislation, to modify or abolish existing laws, regulations, customs and practices which constitute discrimination against women;
(g) To repeal all national penal provisions which constitute discrimination against women.
Article 16 reads as follows:
1. States Parties shall take all appropriate measures to eliminate discrimination against women in all matters relating to marriage and family relations and in particular shall ensure, on a basis of equality of men and women:
(a) The same right to enter into marriage;

Whereas gender equality is anchored in the Palestinian Basic Law (BL) in Article 9, Palestinians declared that they shall be equal before the law and the judiciary, without distinction based upon race, sex, color, religion, political views, or disabilities; the applicable Jordanian Law of Personal Status (JLPS) and Egyptian Family Rights Law (EFRL), however, do not follow this proposition. Qafisheh, without pointing directly to the 2012 *khulʿ* ruling, argued generally with regard to divorce that vesting the primary power of divorce with men and depriving women of it, clearly violates a number of CEDAW's stipulations.[6] To be reformed in light of international standards, he demanded that the law should either give equal rights to men and women or limit divorce to decisions that cannot be exercised by the individual will of any spouse but rather through formal court verdicts.[7] Conditions that might be inserted into the marriage contract and would give women an equal right to divorce could provide a solution, Qafisheh argued, but are not practical because marriage officers who conduct marriage contracts do not draw the attention of the bride and groom to this possibility.[8] Generally, he concluded that Palestine should contemplate filing a reservation on Article 16 if it would prefer to maintain the status quo. He questioned if it is still possible for Palestine to do so since it signed the CEDAW without reservations. Furthermore, filing reservations might be problematic, because they might be considered "incompatible with the object and

(b) The same right freely to choose a spouse and to enter into marriage only with their free and full consent;
(c) The same rights and responsibilities during marriage and at its dissolution;
(d) The same rights and responsibilities as parents, irrespective of their marital status, in matters relating to their children; in all cases the interests of the children shall be paramount;
(e) The same rights to decide freely and responsibly on the number and spacing of their children and to have access to the information, education and means to enable them to exercise these rights;
(f) The same rights and responsibilities with regard to guardianship, wardship, trusteeship and adoption of children, or similar institutions where these concepts exist in national legislation; in all cases the interests of the children shall be paramount;
(g) The same personal rights as husband and wife, including the right to choose a family name, a profession and an occupation;
(h) The same rights for both spouses in respect of the ownership, acquisition, management, administration, enjoyment and disposition of property, whether free of charge or for a valuable consideration.

2. The betrothal and the marriage of a child shall have no legal effect, and all necessary action, including legislation, shall be taken to specify a minimum age for marriage and to make the registration of marriages in an official registry compulsory.

6 Qafisheh 2018: 40.

7 Qafisheh 2018: 40.

8 Qafisheh 2018: 40.

purpose of the present Convention," based on Article 28 (2).[9] Qafisheh quoted the position of the body that monitors the implementation of the Convention by States Parties that

> reservations to Article 16, whether lodged for national, traditional, religious or cultural reasons, are incompatible with the Convention and therefore impermissible and should be reviewed and modified or withdrawn.... Hence, the most likely option available for Palestine is to implement CEDAW and change domestic legislation, policies and practices accordingly.[10]

Is this option likely against a strong conservative Sharia establishment headed by Maḥmūd al-Habbāsh, the new conservative Supreme Judge since 2014? From the viewpoint of international law, Palestine with its signature agreed to a process of monitoring, which is equal for all states. It has to report on the implementation of the international contracts and was invited to Geneva on July 11, 2018, and answered critical questions in this regard.[11]

International law and especially international covenants claim universality but, as Sally Merry outlined, this did not mean that the implementation was simply imposed by "the West" on the state parties who signed the convention. Merry distinguishes different forms of global cultural flows that take place across and within global and local spaces. One is the "transnational consensus building" process that comprises the "global production of documents and resolutions that define human rights and social justice," i.e., the major treaties, conventions, etc:

> In this process, representatives of states and civil society negotiate a consensus across differences in ideology, politics, and cultural practices. This requires a protracted and often excruciating debate about wording and sentence structure, but the result is a *document legitimated by its unified transnational support*.[12]

The fact that representatives of different states take part in the development of international treaties, conventions etc., and therefore influence this process

9 Qafisheh 2018: 44.

10 Qafisheh 2018: 44.

11 All relevant documents in English and Arabic can be found at https://tbinternet.ohchr.org/_layouts/treatybodyexternal/SessionDetails1.aspx?SessionID=1171&Lang=en, accessed July 2, 2018.

12 Merry 2006: 19, emphasis added.

themselves is often forgotten.[13] These conventions are seen as mere outcomes of the claim of a law which is "Western" and "imperial" and therefore not in accordance with a country's own "authentic" culture. This argument seems to be simplistic and based on an essentialist notion of cultures that have their own "authentic" features and that these have to be respected. A non-essentialist conception of the difficult term of "culture" surely is, according to Merry, more adequate to understand the social debates in the Muslim world.[14] Cultures are "hybrid and porous and ... the pervasive struggle over cultural values within

13 Even civil society organizations contribute to this process from their point of view, see chapter 7.3. It seems that here lies one of the main misunderstandings in some of the recent feminist literature, as is reflected, for example, in the writings of Lila Abu-Lughod. Regarding the Arab Human Development Report 2005, Abu-Lughod harshly criticizes the "pathologizing" of the Middle East in what she describes as painting a negative picture of women's rights and lives there and painting the backwardness of the region (Abu-Lughod 2009: 98). She fears that the report focusing on the Arab world could be appropriated in negative ways in creating a dichotomy of modern – traditional and in seeing with respect to gender-roles "the" Islamic culture as a culture of gender inequality (Abu-Lughod 2009: 85). This can be regarded as a real problem because it would put the blame squarely on an essentialist notion of an "Islamic" or "Arab" culture as "anti-modern." Going a step further, however, she criticizes the transnationalism of international concepts expressed in a language – a particular "international" or "transnational" dialect that frames rights and transports certain assumptions and politics, the experiences of the "urban professional middle class" – which, as she argues, intersects with liberal feminism but which she sees highly critically (Abu-Lughod 2009: 83, 98). Abu-Lughod blames the three "keys to women's empowerment" dealt with in the report: education, employment, and individual rights as imposed by a hegemonic Western discourse (Abu-Lughod 2009: 98). Pointing to herselfas an anthropologist working with a small rural group of women in Egypt of the 1970s and 1980s (Abu-Lughod 2009: 88, 90), she seems to overlook the most powerful and surely not specifically Arabic structure suppressing women, the patriarchal system. Is the fact that women have more difficulties not so much in getting education but gaining access to the employment market really so overestimated? Or is it a consequence of a patriarchal society controlling access to the really profitable market? Describing empowering structures of women in a given traditional society does not mean that one should turn a blind eye to the unequal gender structure of this society and legal system. Arguing in favor of "collective" instead of "individual" rights, and pointing to the important role of family in the Arab world, she overlooks that it is exactly this family structure that hinders women from having equal access to the public and politics and getting the same rights in family law. Her article gives the impression that gender equality is not a right women should strive for. Taking up and defending this argument (Abu-Lughod 2009: 89), she draws on a well-known cultural essentialism brought in by Asian states in 1993 with the claim that human rights failed to incorporate communal values – itself, as Merry outlined, an Orientalist notion of a "communitarian East" with communal values, and an "individualistic West" (Merry 2006: 14).

14 Merry 2006: 9.

local communities are competitions over power."[15] They are not contained within stable borders but "are open to new ideas and permeable to influences from other cultural systems."[16] As has been outline before: within an Arab society such as Palestine, there are conservative, traditional, and more secular approaches side by side, reflecting the broad variety of opinions in a pluralistic society.

It has to be kept in mind that cultural discourses "legitimate or challenge authority and justify relations of power."[17] One of the features most often used by states to defend their "cultural authenticity" is patriarchy and patriarchal power:

> Women's rights are often opposed by those who claim to defend culture. Challenging women's subordinate position in the family or the workplace threatens to disrupt a wide range of patriarchal privileges … Thinking of culture as a national essence provides governments with an excuse not to intervene more energetically to protect human rights since they can defend their resistance as the protection of the national identity.[18]

The most important, or at least most focused, cultural flow is "localization of transnational knowledge," which happens by national and local actors who "participate in transnational events and bring home what they learn."[19]

So the crucial question is how is international law transferred into the national legal contexts of states? When jurists deal with the implementation of international covenants into the national legal context they often speak of the "migration" of the concept of (human) rights,[20] thereby concentrating on the process of "travelling" or "coming to" the nation state. In their book *The Power of Human Rights*, Thomas Risse and Kathryn Sikkink (1999) investigated the general conditions under which international norms are implemented in states. They argued that international human rights norms challenged state rule over society and national sovereignty, were well institutionalized in international regimes and organizations, and were contested and competed with other principled ideas.[21] They furthermore argued that the diffusion of international norms in the area of human rights depended crucially on the establishment

15 Merry 2006: 9.
16 Merry 2006: 11.
17 Merry 2006: 11.
18 Merry 2006: 14.
19 Merry 2006: 20.
20 Baer 2011.
21 Risse and Sikkink 1999: 4.

and the sustainability of networks among domestic and transnational actors, especially NGOs (nongovernmental organizations) and INGOs (international NGOs) that manage to link up with international regimes to "alert Western public opinion and Western government."[22] They challenge norm-violating governments by creating a transnational structure to pressure such regimes "from above" and "from below." Risse and Sikkink called the process by which international norms were internalized and implemented domestically a process of "socialization"[23] and used a "spiral model" to illustrate this. This spiral model had the following stages:

1. repression: the state represses human rights activities;
2. denial: the repressive state denies the validity of human rights norms;
3. tactical concessions: the state makes tactical concessions to the human rights network, which reduce its room for maneuver against human rights;
4. prescriptive status: the state accepts international norms, ratifies treaties and institutionalizes norms domestically;
5. rule-consistent behavior: this is what will prevail in the end.[24]

In stage 1, domestic-societal opposition is too weak or too oppressed to present a significant challenge to the government. In stage 2, the norm-violating state is put on the international agenda of human rights networks. This serves to raise the level of international public attention toward the "target state." If this continues and escalates, the norm-violating state seeks cosmetic changes to pacify international criticism in stage 3. Stage 4 sees the actors regularly refer to human rights norms to describe and comment on their own behavior and that of others. It is a necessary step toward, but not identical with the next stage, stage 5: rule-consistent behavior. Governments might accept the validity of human rights norms, but still continue to torture prisoners or detain people without trial, etc.[25]

Where in this model could Palestine be located? Despite the harsh criticism of civil society,[26] a complete repression of human rights activities is not happening in the West Bank and Gaza, and stage 2 in which the state denies the

---

22 Risse and Sikkink 1999: 5. However, it is not so much the "Western" public that is alerted, but the international public, because the resistance to international conventions is monitored by the UN itself and the UN committees, e.g. the CEDAW Committee are not "Western" but composed of experts from different national, ethnical, religious backgrounds.

23 Risse and Sikkink 1999: 5.

24 Risse and Sikkink 1999: 20.

25 Risse and Sikkink 1999: 19–35.

26 See chapter 7.3.

validity of human rights norms is overcome. Tactical concessions belong to the past, Palestine is already at stage 4 where it has signed the treaties. But 4 is a crucial stage – at least for Palestine. Abbas has signed the treaties without reservations but they are not yet published in the Official Gazette. This comes along with a judgment of the SCC of November 2017 according to which international law is above national law but still the situation has not moved to the point where the state has "institutionalized norms domestically." It is somewhere stuck on stage 4, because this "institutionalization" in the "domestic area" is a problematic process; here the devil is in the details. This model[27] was developed by the authors as a "theory of the stages and mechanisms through which international norms can effect changes in behavior"[28] and the authors did not assume an evolutionary or automatic progression. Instead they suggested that regimes might return to oppression after some tactical concessions in stage 3 when international pressures had decreased. States might not care about transnational and international opposition to their behavior.[29] They argued that countries that resist are not economically weak per se, but do not care about their international image.[30] This, however, is not the case for Palestine. Palestine's government eagerly wants to become a full member of the international community, but first, it wants to be a recognized state. To reach this goal compliance with international law seems a reasonable way. It cannot be denied that this might have been one of the reasons why President Abbas signed so many international human rights instruments and why he signed them without any reservation going against the practice of all the other Muslim states. Furthermore, Risse and Sikkink are well aware – as can be seen in the quotation above – that international human rights norms "compete with other principled ideas"[31] but they do not elaborate on this. But this is the nub of the problem: a conservative interpretation of the religious texts will always be in sharp contrast to the contents of CEDAW. To put it bluntly: international norms compete with a traditional interpretation of Sharia. Their "traveling" and "arrival" triggers a national iteration in which different parts of the society take part and different actors have different interests. Merry states: "In order for human rights ideas to be effective, they need to be translated into local terms and situated within local contexts of power and meaning. They need, in other words, to be remade in the vernacular. How does this happen?"[32]

27 Risse and Sikkink 1999: 18
28 Risse and Sikkink 1999: 2.
29 Risse and Sikkink 1999: 34.
30 See Schneider 2015 for the special situation in Iran, which has not signed CEDAW so far.
31 Risse and Sikkink 1999: 4.
32 Merry 2006: 1.

The question that arises is how the regulations of international law are exactly integrated into national legislation, or, with regard to Palestine, how the discussion about the CEDAW and the connected concepts and terminology of gender-equality continue after the signature and after the official delegation had been questioned in Geneva in July 2018, and where this all leads.

The internal discussions before and after the Palestinian delegation's journey to Geneva are analyzed[33] along with civil society's Shadow Reports.[34] NGOs are the main actors in this flow, and meetings such as the one scheduled for Palestine on July 11, 2018, before the CEDAW Committee were an important channel for the international community to learn more about the implementation of international law in the country. That means that these actors introduced the debate to the CEDAW Committee but that afterward it must be taken up by local actors.[35] If this takes place, we can speak of the occurance of a "translation" process in a Palestinian political and social setting, as outlined in the introduction. Where does Palestine stand in this field at the end of 2018? The process can be followed by looking at the iterations and different voices in Palestine around the report the state of Palestine had to submit, the Shadow Reports of the different civil society organizations and the Sharia establishment.

How does this "translation" function in Muslim nation-states? It is a crucial question with controversial answers. Abdullahi An-Na'im, dealing with what he calls the "cross-cultural perspective on human rights"[36] rightly argues that people "are more likely to observe normative propositions if they believe them to be sanctioned by their own cultural traditions," so that the observance of human rights standards can be improved by enhancing the cultural legitimacy of those standards.[37] This seems to be roughly in accordance with what has been described as a process of "translation" as defined by Merry and is the focus of this chapter. But how can this "cultural legitimacy" be achieved? What does it look like in detail? Taking the example of what is called "cruel, inhumane or degrading treatment or punishment" in international conventions An-Na'im consciously selected one highly controversial topic between Islamic law and the approach of Muslim countries and international law, because of the

33 This will be done in chapter 8.

34 Chapter 7.3.

35 As outlined in chapter 8, the debate started in Palestine before July 2018 in preparation for the delegation's travel to Geneva. This can be seen as a reflection of the wish of the State of Palestine to be prepared for this important meeting together with important societal players.

36 An-Na'im 1992: 20.

37 An-Na'im 1992: 20.

different forms of punishable offences and punishments such as the Quranic punishments (*ḥudūd*, lit. "limits"). *Ḥudūd*, rooted in Quran and Sunna including, for example, a hundred lashes for *zinā'* (illicit sexual relations) contradict modern concepts of punishment and are seen as "cruel." So are punishments for homicide, which are punishable by *qiṣāṣ* (retaliation) in the sense of "an eye for an eye" and *ta'zīr*, which are punishments that are in the power of the judge or ruler and contradict the modern concept of *nulla poene sine lege*.[38] Arguing that Sharia regulations have been "displaced" by secular criminal law in many but not all Muslim countries, he adds:

> Muslim political leaders and scholars may debate whether general social, economic, and political conditions are appropriate for the immediate application of Shari'a, or whether there should be a preparatory stage before the reintroduction of Shari'a where it has been displaced by secular law. None of them would dispute, at least openly and publicly, that the application of Shari'a criminal law would be a high priority, if not an immediate reality.[39]

As the majority of modern Muslim states have abolished Islamic penal law and introduced modern penal codes, An-Na'im does not adequately substantiate this argument when stating this in his article. In general, he considers cultural dialogue helpful, for – again like Merry – he argues that cultures are not closed entities.[40] But he also considers it unrealistic to expect this approach of implementation of international law to achieve total agreement on the interpretation and application of standards, whether of treatment or punishment or any other human right.[41] This leaves the crucial question asked above by Qafisheh: how far can international conventions be restricted through "cultural" interpretations? An-Na'im concludes that the standard itself should be the product of internal discourse and cross-cultural dialogue. "I believe that in the final analysis, the interpretation and practical application of the protection against cruel, inhuman, or degrading treatment or punishment in the context of a particular society should be determined by the moral standards of that society."[42] He argues that there are legitimate ways of influencing and informing the moral standards of a society, but he considers it unacceptable

38 An-Na'im 1992: 33; Peters 2005: 175–181.
39 An-Na'im 1992: 34.
40 An-Na'im 1992: 36.
41 An-Na'im 1992: 38.
42 An-Na'im 1992: 37.

to "dictate" to a society.[43] But again: where is the line to be drawn? How much room is left for what was named "translation" or "translation process"? At which point does it contradict the idea of international law? This interpretation of An-Na'im becomes problematic and essentialist when he argues at the end of his article that "a North American" may think that a short term of imprisonment is the appropriate punishment for theft, whereas "a Muslim" might feel that the amputation of the hand is appropriate "under certain conditions and after satisfying strict safeguards."[44] Here An-Na'im is personalizing ("a Muslim") and essentializing cultures as if they were in the age of globalization – or ever before – neatly separable and monolithic and ignores that there are, first, controversial debates in Muslim societies and nation states and second, that international law itself is a discoursive product of many, not only the "Western" countries. He seems to be inclined to accept this kind of punishment, which is not any more existent in most of the penal codes in the Middle East and which is controversially debated among intellectuals in the Muslim countries.[45]

A more pragmatic and equality-oriented approach is suggested by Shaheen Sardar Ali with the "policy of small steps" for the area of gender relations, the question of equality of genders and the question of how to change a society based on patriarchal rules. Arguing that the regulations in family law in the Muslim states differ widely, she conceptualizes an "Operative Islamic Law," which represents the special blend of legal regulations based on constitutional, customary, and Islamic regulations in regional versions.[46] Thus, she argues that the multiplicity of norms affecting women's human rights in Muslim jurisdictions renders it extremely difficult to sketch with any degree of accuracy the fine details of the Operative Islamic Law on the subject.[47] It thrives in a "plural legal system" and the socio-economic and political circumstances prevailing within a country also play a crucial role.[48] With regard to international law she argues:

> The emergence of this "operative" Islamic law has also been influenced by international human rights instruments and there is strong evidence that it has played an important role in developing an outward-looking

43 An-Na'im 1992: 37.
44 An-Na'im 1992: 38.
45 See the explanations of Peters 2005: 181–185.
46 Ali 2000: 7–8, see also 172: "Thus, an 'operative' Islamic law emerges based on constitutional, religious and 'secular' law but heavily conditioned by customary practices of a particular jurisdiction."
47 Ali 2000: 187.
48 Ali 2000: 188.

> approach to human rights positions taken by governments as well as human rights activists in the country.[49]

Other than an-Na'im, she considers the use of international standards on human rights an important dimension of the Operative Islamic Law and hints at the importance of checking if the official positions of the Muslim states match their rhetoric.[50] Her approach thus seems to leave less leeway for thwarting standards of international law.

In what follows, the State of Palestine's report – as well as the reports of the civil society – will be analyzed at first, and then the processes following the journey of the Palestinian delegation to Geneva in July 2018 and the iterations that evolved around it.

7.1 CEDAW State Report of Palestine, March 10, 2017

In 2005, Palestine adopted the convention with a cabinet decision. In 2009, Palestine ratified the Convention with a unilateral declaration contained in Presidential Decree No. 19 of 2009. On April 1, 2014, less than a year and a half after Palestine was granted observer status by the United Nations, Palestine acceded to the Convention without reservations. In the Report of Palestine, this is seen as a "concrete expression of political will and a qualitative step forward in national efforts to protect the rights of Palestinian women, rid national laws and policies of provisions that discriminate against women, and combat de facto discrimination in all areas."[51] Palestine's first report to CEDAW, which was received by the CEDAW Committee on March 10, 2017, comprised seventy-one pages discussing the articles of CEDAW one by one.[52] The report pointed to the fact that it was prepared by a joint committee composed of the relevant government agencies and civil society institutions.[53] It had been presented to government agencies and civil society institutions "at intensive workshops and consultations that covered all its aspects and provided opportunities to discuss it prior to adoption of the final version and submission to the Committee on

49 Ali 2000: 191.

50 Ali 2000: 191.

51 CEDAW Report 2017: 5.

52 See: https://tbinternet.ohchr.org/_layouts/treatybodyexternal/Download.aspx?symbolno=CEDAW%2fC%2fPSE%2f1&Lang=en, accessed January 3, 2019. It will be quoted in what follows as CEDAW Report in the English version, but important terms are given in Arabic.

53 CEDAW Report 2017: 3.

the Elimination of Discrimination against Women."[54] The State of Palestine was eager to show that this Report was based on approval of and consent within society. However, civil society organizations submitted their own partly critical Shadow Reports, which will be analyzed below. The delegation was headed by Dr. Hayfāʾ al-Āghā (transcribed in the UN documents as Dr. Hayfaa Alaga), Minister of Women's Affairs, and Dr. ʿUmar ʿIwaḍallāh (Omar A. H. Awad Ala), Head of UN Department at the Multilateral Affairs Sector, Ministry of Foreign Affairs and Expatriates. As a representative of the Sharia establishment, Ṣumūd al-Ḍamīrī was part of the delegation.[55]

The State of Palestine stressed in the beginning and throughout the Report, as a political framework, the special and difficult situation for women and girls under Israel's occupation.[56] Israel's occupation is, for example, made responsible for the inability to exercise rights of Palestinian citizenship.[57] This special situation of Palestine was taken up in the final report of the CEDAW Committee, and it was acknowledged that the occupation "poses severe challenges for the State party in fully implementing its obligations under the Convention," recalling that Israel as the occupying power is not "absolved of its obligations under international humanitarian law and international human rights law."[58]

In the following, the Report itself as well as the "Issues and Questions" to which the CEDAW Committee reacted and also the "Replies" of the State of Palestine will be analyzed under three aspects and questions:

1. How is the "state of the art" described, i.e., the existing family law and to what extent it complies with international law, especially with regard to divorce but also focusing on what the Report sees as important points of compliance and divergence.
2. What are the resulting problems of drafting and issuing a new Palestinian law and which body is responsible for it?
3. How are international conventions, especially CEDAW, actually "translated" into Palestinian law, and if they are not, which future options are open?

With regard to the (legal) "state of the art" (1) the Report acknowledged that the current legislation in force in Palestine did not provide for an explicit definition

54 CEDAW Report 2017: 3.

55 See CEDAW List of Delegation 2018, https://tbinternet.ohchr.org/_layouts/treatybodyexternal/Download.aspx?symbolno=INT%2fCEDAW%2fLOP%2fPSE%2f31337&Lang=en, accessed January 10, 2019. Regrettably, this list is only given in English and the English transcription of the Arabic names is incorrect. Ṣumūd al-Ḍamīrī is listed as Abusaa.

56 CEDAW Report 2017: see for example 3, 5, 9, 12, 19, 31, etc.

57 CEDAW Report 2017: 31–32.

58 CEDAW July 25, 2018: 3.

of "discrimination" as required by Article 1 of the Convention. Reference is made to the Palestinian Declaration of Independence of 1988 and to the preamble as well as Article 9 of the BL that prohibit discrimination. Article 9 guarantees the equality of all Palestinians before the law and the judiciary.[59] Efforts to realize women's rights and gender equality are made across various sectors and by a number of national mechanisms established for that purpose, the Report stated. The Palestinian National Development Plan 2014–2016 had been adopted for "State-building to Sovereignty, which makes greater protection for Palestinian women a national priority."[60]

There is, however, one major contradiction in the Report. It is stated that women possess full legal capacity in all laws:

> 311. As a rule, there is nothing in the laws in force to prevent women from possessing legal capacity to carry out legal procedures on an equal footing with men. However, there are some exceptions. Like men, women in Palestine are considered to have full legal capacity at the age of 18, regardless of social status, with respect both to eligibility to act and eligibility to take on obligations. Women have the same legal capacity as men to carry out civil and commercial transactions on behalf of themselves and others. That includes signing contracts or managing property, businesses or companies. Women have full capacity to impose and take on obligations, and to conclude credit and real estate contracts under the same terms as men.[61]

This is in contradiction to what the Report itself mentions with regard to family law, referring to Article 16 of the Convention. Different applicable laws are mentioned as well as common features of Muslim and Christian legal regulations, such as marriage takes place between a man and a woman, the woman's consent is always necessary and that sexual relations between men and women outside marriage are not allowed.[62] Here the most important regulations in marriage and divorce are summarized[63] and restrictions of women's legal capacity become evident. Among those restrictions, the legal need for a marriage guardian (*walī*) is named, which discloses a fundamental inequality of the sexes with regard to marriage. Different marriage ages in JLPS and

59 CEDAW Report 2017: 5.
60 CEDAW Report 2017: 6.
61 CEDAW Report 2017: 63.
62 CEDAW Report 2017: 66.
63 CEDAW Report 2017: 66–69.

EFRL and among the different Christian churches, always below eighteen, are mentioned.[64] It is stated that a woman has no free movement because she is required to stay with her husband.[65] The restrictions to choose a husband for the woman are named, e.g., the man's right to marry a woman of another religion whereas women do not have the same right.[66] Personal status laws in force are described as enshrining traditional roles for the various members of a family. While the man is the head of the family and has guardianship and decision-making authority, the woman is supposed to be obedient and take care of the home. "The marital relationship is based on reciprocity of rights and obligations (*tabāduliyya fī al-ḥuqūq wa-l-wājibāt*) rather than equality."[67]

This cautious formulation of the fundamental inequality as "reciprocity" is striking but the inequalities are expressed. Polygyny is stated as the man's prerogative.[68] The obligation to inform the first wife in case the husband wants to marry a second woman is mentioned, apparently as a sort of compensation to this gender unequal legal right of Palestinian men.[69] However, it is not made explicit, that this is only a *taʿmīm* and not anchored in the applicable law. With regard to divorce, the husband has the right to end the marriage "of his own free will for any reason" and that there are two ways of divorce, revocable, in which the husband has the right to take her back, and irrevocable. It is explained that in principle the woman cannot get a divorce on her own, she has to go to court.[70] Among the different forms of divorce the Supreme Judge's ruling of 2012, i.e., judicial *khulʿ* is specifically mentioned:

> A wife may seek a court-ordered dissolution of the marriage if she has not yet consummated the marriage or been alone in complete seclusion with her husband. She may do so even without his consent by suing for dissolution of the marriage before a sharia court, on condition that she feels a revulsion against her husband that prevents her from consummating the marriage and embarking on married life, and that she pay a sum of money that she herself guarantees. That is in accordance with Circular No. 59 (2012) issued by the Office of the Chief Qadi.[71]

64 CEDAW Report 2017: 66–71.
65 CEDAW Report 2017: 64.
66 CEDAW Report 2017: 67.
67 CEDAW Report 2017: 67.
68 CEDAW Report 2017: 67.
69 CEDAW Report 2017: 67.
70 CEDAW Report 2017: 69.
71 CEDAW Report 2017: 69.

A Supreme Judge's "Circular," meaning the 59/2012 *taʿmīm*, is taken as an example of a legal ruling women can benefit from to some extent in the framework of the given law, but it is not made explicit that the "Circular" did not pass the parliament and thus is not based on the constitution, and it can be withdrawn at any moment by the Supreme Judge.

Custody is dealt with together with the regulation that women lose the right to custody (*ḥaḍāna*) if they remarry.[72] And with regard to inheritance, the Supreme Judge's ruling is mentioned, which is intended to eliminate certain social attitudes, customs, and traditions that pressure women to sign over their inheritances to their brothers after the death of the father or mother. It prohibits the registration of any inheritance arrangement between sisters and brothers with Sharia courts until four months after the death, after a thorough accounting has been made of all the heritable assets, signed by all the heirs and certified by the relevant local agency.[73] Under the title "challenges," the Israeli occupation is named as the main obstacle and only a short article is dedicated to the fact that Palestinian women suffer from home grown problems, too: "Palestinian women also suffer from inherited customs and traditions that assign them subordinate status and focus on their reproductive role. Palestine has also inherited legislation that is prejudicial to certain women's rights, particularly as regards penal provisions and personal status."[74]

Using the adjective "inherited" for customs and traditions evokes the impression of something which has been there for a long time and cannot be extinguished easily. Interestingly, the Report, after dealing with the special protection of motherhood,[75] points to stereotypical roles of women and describes Palestinian society as a patriarchal culture among other patriarchal cultures. "In the home: Palestinian descriptive studies show that the roles that women are traditionally expected to perform usually involve obedience, care, running the household and getting things done, whereas men are typically associated with headship of the household and decision-making."[76]

Those discriminatory practices that target women as women are described as if they were so entrenched in social traditions and customs that they became invisible and are not reflected upon.[77] The role of religion and religious law reifying these practices in establishing traditional gender roles is only cautiously hinted at:

72 CEDAW Report 2017: 70.
73 CEDAW Report 2017: 71. The term is *takhāruj* (waiving shares of inheritance), see p. 164 fn. 73.
74 CEDAW Report 2017: 13.
75 CEDAW Report 2017: 17.
76 CEDAW Report 2017: 18.
77 CEDAW Report 2017: 18.

> Counter-efforts to reinforce stereotypical, traditional roles and entrench a culture of women's subordination take various forms. They include calls to hold on to certain interpretations of religious teachings and reject demands to eliminate discrimination against women as Western cultural imports that violate customs and traditions.[78]

The topic of women and violence is dealt with extensively[79] and so is the role of women in the public space and politics.[80] With regard to female judges, the women in Sharia courts are mentioned, and it becomes evident that the increase in the number of women in the judiciary since 2008 was very moderate, but with a great change in Sharia courts, where in 2009, women were allowed to be judges for the first time.[81] The national judicial system, which has jurisdiction over issues relating to the Convention, is described as "an additional safeguard that strengthens the protection of women and gender equality."[82] Article 30 (1) of the BL is quoted giving the "sacrosanct" right to litigation to all citizens and guaranteeing every Palestinian the "right of recourse to his natural judge, and that litigation procedures shall be regulated by law to ensure prompt settlement of cases."[83] Women are equal before courts but not in Sharia courts where their testimonies are valued at only half of a male's testimony.[84] With regard to the Sharia courts, it is stated:

> The sharia courts and ecclesiastical courts have the authority to rule on cases involving personal status and marital disputes that relate to marriage contracts, including divorce, separation, alimony, child support and custody. *Unfortunately, rulings are often made on the basis of personal status codes that are still discriminatory against women.* Each sharia court has a family counselling unit that tries to strengthen family bonds and resolve disputes between spouses. Such units help to minimize marital disputes and divorce. Periodic workshops are held to discuss and develop standard operating procedures for those units, with sharia judges in attendance.[85]

78 CEDAW Report 2017: 18.
79 CEDAW Report 2017: 18–22.
80 CEDAW Report 2017: 25–30.
81 CEDAW Report 2017: 28.
82 CEDAW Report 2017: 7.
83 CEDAW Report 2017: 7.
84 CEDAW Report 2017: 64.
85 CEDAW Report 2017: 8, emphasis added.

Again, the choice of the adverb "unfortunately" evokes the impression of something the government of the State of Palestine regrets but cannot or does not want to change. It conceals the fact that the State of Palestine is responsible for its legislation and also conceals the long history and vibrant activities that have taken place to change this legislation since the PA came into existence.

The State Report admitted freely that women's participation in the public sphere or as civil servants, in the judiciary, etc. falls "short of minimum international standards."[86] The reasons given again are "customs and traditions" and a "patriarchal mindset." Religion and law are not mentioned.[87] "Equal citizenship" was explained to depend on Article 7 of the BL, which stipulated that this matter has to be regulated by law. However, it cannot be regulated as long as Palestine is under occupation.[88] Thus, besides the one major contradiction with regard to women's legal capacity, the Report described more or less accurately the existing legal discrimination of women. Two aspects are remarkable: there is no mention at all of all the long, intensive, and controversial iterations in Palestine since the 1990s to change the personal status law, and second, the role of religion and religious law is downplayed.

With regard to the second set of questions, i.e., how the problems of drafting and issuing a new Palestinian law are tackled and which body is the relevant one for this (2), the State Report describes the system and a bundle of measures taken. It mentions that the Palestinian government has "adopted a number of national policies that commit it to transparency, accountability and respect for human rights" and names the Palestinian National Development Plan 2014–2016 as the most important measure, which includes state-building to sovereignty, and would then create greater protection for Palestinian women, in a step called a "national priority." This plan will also have "finalizing reviews of legislation in force to ensure the integration of women's rights."[89] The Report also states that not much time has elapsed since Palestine's accession to the Convention.[90] As an important step, a presidential decree with regard to "honour" crimes was mentioned. The Report states: "Legislative development in Palestine, and in particular the work being done on draft laws to incorporate international human rights standards, including women's rights, demonstrates our national political will to eliminate legal and de facto discrimination against women and achieve gender equality."[91]

86 CEDAW Report 2017: 29.
87 CEDAW Report 2017: 29.
88 CEDAW Report 2017: 31f.
89 CEDAW Report 2017: 6.
90 CEDAW Report 2017: 13.
91 CEDAW Report 2017: 13.

Referring to Article 3 of CEDAW, "General Measures and Policies," Palestine outlines that it adopts the "National Policy Agenda 2017–2022" (*Ajinda al-Siyāsāt al-Waṭaniyya li-l-Aʿwām al-Sitta al-Qādima* 2017–2022),[92] which is

> based upon three pillars, namely, the path to independence, reforming and improving the quality of services, and sustainable development. Specific national priorities and policies will be implemented to that end. Priority areas include strengthening gender equality, empowering women and girls, eliminating all forms of discrimination and violence against them, and eliminating all obstacles to their full participation in social and economic development and public life. In that connection, the 2017–2022 Cross-Sectoral National Gender Strategy: Promote Gender Equality and Equity, which has been ratified by the Council of Ministers, is organized around five strategic objectives, namely, halving the incidence of all forms of violence against Palestinian women; increasing women's participation in governmental and non-governmental decision-making positions that have the greatest impact on the lives of men and women so that no fewer than 10 per cent of those positions are filled by women; integrating gender equality and equity and the empowerment of women into official institutions; promoting women's participation in the economic sector; and improving the quality of life of poor and marginalized families.[93]

The Ministry of Women's Affairs (MoWA), created in 2003, is named and given importance:

> The Ministry's effort towards the adoption of measures to enhance gender equality include the following: proposing and drafting laws and amendments; setting forth economic, cultural, social and media strategies to promote women's equality and raise awareness of women's rights across sectors; institutionalizing gender diversity within ministries and within the relevant institutions in the principal sectors; promoting national consolidation and coordination of efforts among major institutions; and promoting dialogue towards a consensus on priorities for action on women's issues.[94]

---

92 CEDAW Report 2017: 13–14, Arabic version p. 15.

93 CEDAW Report 2017: 14–15.

94 CEDAW Report 2017: 6.

Thus, "proposing and drafting laws and amendments" belong, according to the Report, to the MoWA's "effort." Interestingly, the word "effort" and not "obligation" is used. There is no hint about the influence of the Sharia establishment, and the fact that the Draft Law, discussed in November 2013 by the NCFL, the National Committee of the Family Law, had finally been developed and presented by the SCHC under supervision of the Supreme Judge and that the Sharia establishment explicitly claimed the right to prepare such a Draft. Representatives of the MoWA and the Ministry of Justice had in 2013 confirmed that with regard to Article 4 of the BL, drafting the law in family matters would be the right of the SCHC.

Nongovernmental organizations are mentioned and their activities acknowledged in the Report not only for working to support and empower women but also for taking part in discussions about amending legislation to promote women's rights and ensure their exercise in practice.[95] Concerning the status of draft laws different "plans" and "committees" are mentioned containing intentions but no concrete initiatives are given. This reflects again the fact that the strategy of the NCFL has collapsed.

With regard to the implementation of international law (3) the State of Palestine declares that its accession to CEDAW without reservations "means that Palestine has declared its recognition at the highest political level of the definition of gender discrimination contained in those instruments and its commitment to taking all measures necessary to prohibit such discrimination in all its forms."[96]

Article 10 of the BL is given as proof that "basic human rights and liberties shall be protected and respected" and that Palestine shall work without delay to become a member of international declarations and covenants.[97] The BL is quoted in the Report often with reference to equal rights of all citizens of Palestine, as well as equal access to the judiciary, etc.[98] But nowhere is the problematic Article 4 that deals with the Sharia quoted or discussed.

In May 2014, immediately after the accession to the Convention, the president formed a Standing National Ministerial Committee for Follow-up on the Accession of the State of Palestine to International Treaties and Instruments (*al-Lajna al-Waṭaniyya [al-Wizāriyya] al-Dā'ima li-Mutāba'a Filasṭīn ilā al-Mu'āhadāt wa-l-Mawāthīq al-Dawliyya*) with a subcommittee of experts that

95 CEDAW Report 2017: 7.
96 CEDAW Report 2017: 4.
97 CEDAW Report 2017: 4, 71.
98 CEDAW Report 2017: 4, 5, 7, 9, 25, 28, 31, 35, 54, 63, 64.

prepared the reports as well as reviewed the legislation and proposed amendments to the legislation.[99]

7.2 List of Issues and Questions Relating to the Report by the State of Palestine to the CEDAW Committee, November 30, 2017,[100] and Replies to Questions (List of Issues), February 19, 2018[101]

On November 30, 2017, the Committee on the Elimination of Discrimination against Women raised some questions and issues in response to the Report of the State of Palestine focusing on selected problems.[102] The State of Palestine replied on February 19, 2018. These Issues and Questions are grouped together with their replies and presented in the following analysis.

With regard to the first aspect, the "state of the art" (1), the State of Palestine is asked under the heading of "stereotypes" to "provide information on measures taken to develop a comprehensive policy to change social and cultural patterns that lead to stereotyping and the reinforcement of traditional roles of women and men in the family and in society, in particular targeting gender socialization practices that promote men as breadwinners and women as caregivers."[103] Palestine promised in its reply to promote "awareness-raising campaigns." It also maintained that gender has been mainstreamed into curricula in order to change the stereotype of the role of women.[104] More importantly, the CEDAW Committee targeted the above-mentioned contradiction in the report and asked the State of Palestine to ensure that there are no "exceptions" to the rule and that "nothing in its laws restricts women's legal capacity."[105] In reply, the State of Palestine referred to the original report[106] that had provided a detailed account of the legal capacity of women. It promised that all legal provisions that are discriminatory against women will be reviewed and brought into line

99 CEDAW Report 2017: 4–5.

100 It is quoted in what follows as CEDAW List of Issues and Questions 2017. https://tbinternet.ohchr.org/_layouts/treatybodyexternal/Download.aspx?symbolno=CEDAW%2fC%2fPSE%2fQ%2f1&Lang=en, accessed January 7, 2019.

101 See https://tbinternet.ohchr.org/_layouts/treatybodyexternal/Download.aspx?symbolno=CEDAW%2fC%2fPSE%2fQ%2f1%2fAdd.1&Lang=en, accessed January 7, 2019.

102 Mentioned here are topics related to family law, its legislation and the integration of international law.

103 CEDAW List of Issues and Questions 2017: 3.

104 CEDAW Replies 2018: 9.

105 CEDAW List of Issues and Questions 2017: 7.

106 CEDAW Report 2017: 63–64.

with the Convention.[107] The CEDAW Committee asked the State of Palestine to provide information on legislative and other measures taken to revise discriminatory provisions, including:

a) The provision that considers a woman subsidiary to her husband when he files for bankruptcy (para. 312);
b) The evidentiary rule that considers the testimony of a man to be equivalent to that of two women;
c) The provision that invalidates a woman's right to custody when she remarries a man who is not a close relative of the child (para. 345);
d) The restriction on women with regard to marrying non-Muslim men (para. 330);
e) The provision that grants legal capacity to a male guardian to contract marriages on behalf of his female relatives and to decide to annul a marriage irrespective of the married woman's consent;
f) The provision that grants men the unilateral right to divorce.[108]

Palestine promised with regard to points a through f that the testimony matter and the custody question will be taken up in the new Personal Status Law.[109] The harmonization and standardization of the different marriage ages in the West Bank, Gaza and Jerusalem, as well as in the different religious communities, which the CEDAW Committee also requested, is not seen as a problem because in Palestine a social consensus exists to harmonize it and fix a higher marriage age.[110] At the same time, the State of Palestine also stated frankly that there were points in which an adaption to non-discrimination according to CEDAW seems not possible for the time being. Those issues concerned marriage between a Muslim woman and a non-Muslim man. With regard to the marriage guardian no reform plan was announced, only Palestine's current legal regulation was repeated: "The guardian may not annul the marriage by withholding consent for it. However, the guardian may dispute the husband's financial competence."[111] This avoids the question of why a marriage guardian should be necessary at all. There were two legal points that were obviously considered not adaptable to CEDAW at all on which Palestine commented that "no steps have been taken," meaning that no steps could be taken, at least not at that time. These points concerned the man's *ṭalāq* and his right to marry a non-Muslim woman.[112] Thus several topics such as

107 CEDAW Replies 2018: 24.
108 CEDAW List of Issues and Questions 2017: 7–8.
109 CEDAW Replies 2018: 24–25.
110 CEDAW List of Issues and Questions 2017: 8; CEDAW Replies 2018: 25.
111 CEDAW Replies 2018: 24.
112 CEDAW Replies 2018: 24–25.

the marriage guardian and, still more so, divorce and polygyny were implicitly admitted as problems for the time being. But there is reference made to the future personal status law.[113]

With regard to the second aspect, the drafting and issuing of a new Palestinian law and the question of the responsible body (2), Palestine was asked under the heading "legislative, policy framework and harmonization of laws" to provide "information on measures taken to develop legal frameworks to govern women's rights, to repeal archaic laws that do not conform to the provisions of the Convention and to address the discrimination against women and girls under personal status laws with regard to marriage, divorce, custody of children and inheritance."[114] Second, in light of the reconciliation between Fatah and Hamas and the establishment of a LHC, Legislation Harmonization Committee in 2017, Palestine was asked to provide information on steps being taken to harmonize laws and policies in the Gaza Strip and the West Bank and about measures needed to re-establish a unified legislative body, i.e., the parliament.[115]

The answer of the State of Palestine with regard to these questions was as follows:

> *The Personal Status Code is part of the 2018 legislative review*. In addition, the sharia justice system is working to promote independent reasoning (*ijtihad*) in the absence of a binding provision, in a manner consistent with the Arab and Islamic commitment enshrined in the 2004 Arab Charter on Human Rights, which was adopted under the aegis of the League of Arab States and is based on the 1990 Cairo Declaration on Human Rights. No amendment has been made with regard to inheritance. However, the transfer of assets must take place four months after the death in order to ensure that nobody takes advantage of the woman's grief. With regard to marriage and divorce, measures have been taken to ensure that, if the husband wishes to marry again or to divorce, he must notify the wife formally through the courts and register the process formally. The best interests of the child are taken into consideration when awarding custody.[116]

113 CEDAW Replies 2018: 24.
114 CEDAW List of Issues and Questions 2017: 1–2.
115 CEDAW List of Issues and Questions 2017: 2.
116 CEDAW Replies 2018: 3, emphasis added.

The first statement of the reply creates the impression that the Palestinian Personal Status Code is on its way and that it will be anchored in Sharia is not said explicitly in the reply but becomes evident from the statement that the Sharia justice system is working to promote independent reasoning (*ijtihād*). How does this connect to the statement that drafting the family law is a matter of the Ministry of Women's Affairs? And how does this relate to the fact that the "Replies" stipulated that there were sensible areas of law, e.g., polygyny?

The 2017–2022 Cross-Sectoral National Gender Strategy (*al-Istrātījiyya al-Waṭaniyya ʿabra al-Qiṭāʿiyya li-Taʿzīz al-Musāwāh wa-l-ʿAdāla bayna al-Jinsayn wa-Tamkīn al-Marʾa* 2017–2022) is mentioned in the Replies. Palestine made it explicit that it understood the need to harmonize the laws in force in the West Bank, Gaza and Jerusalem. In this context an already existing consensus "among Palestinians" is stressed regarding the need to raise the age when people are allowed to marry, which is not uniform, not in the Muslim legislation in Gaza and the West Bank nor in the different Christian churches and not among the religious communities.[117]

The LHC is, according to the Replies, currently looking into measures to repeal legislation that discriminates against women. With regard to the CEDAW Committee's exhortation to take measures to re-establish a legislative body,[118] the State of Palestine postponed this harmonization process stating:

> Once the reconciliation is complete, the priority step will be to hold legislative elections for the Palestinian Legislative Council with a view to working towards harmonizing the legislation in force in the West Bank, including occupied Jerusalem, and the Gaza Strip, and to adopting legislation for the State of Palestine that is consistent with international conventions.[119]

Asked by the CEDAW Committee to "clarify the hierarchy between statutory law and the Sharia, their respective scope and any provisions governing their coexistence" and to explain whether decisions rendered by Sharia and ecclesiastical courts were subject to appeal in civil courts[120] the State of Palestine declared:

117 CEDAW Replies 2018: 4.
118 CEDAW List of Issues and Questions 2017: 2.
119 CEDAW Replies 2018: 4.
120 CEDAW List of Issues and Questions 2017: 2.

> In accordance with *Article 4* of the Palestinian Basic Law, the Islamic sharia is *a* primary source of legislation, as opposed to *the* [only] primary source of legislation. *Palestinian law also draws on other sources. Accordingly, the legislation based on the Islamic sharia has the same status as civil law, and does not have priority.* In the absence of a legal provision, the courts apply the prevailing rule from the school of Abu Hanifah, which is the most moderate interpretation of the sharia.[121]

This explanation is interesting because it explicitly poses Islamic Sharia on the same level as civil law. It "does not have priority." Reference is made only to the BL, not to the SCC judgment. But why is it first stated that Palestinian law also draws on sources other than the Sharia but then mentioned that "in the absence of a legal provision, the courts apply the prevailing rule from the school of Abu Hanifah"? The explanation, that it "is the most moderate interpretation of the sharia" does not hold, because this is not the case – as the Supreme Judge himself stated when dealing with *khulʿ* (divorce). The sentence could be read as a statement of intent to preserve this recourse to the Hanafi school of law as it is given in the JLPS, Article 183, to strengthen Islamic law as a counterweight to the "other sources."

The State of Palestine also outlined that, as "sharia and ecclesiastical courts are independent of the civil courts, appeals against their decisions are filed before the sharia and ecclesiastical courts of appeal, and subsequently before the sharia or ecclesiastical supreme courts."[122] The number of female judges (in civil courts) is given and it is promised to raise it[123] and thus to ease women's access to justice.[124] It is stated that women have full rights to access Sharia courts.[125]

Obviously, the State of Palestine remained very general if not evasive in its answers, but it made the statement that Sharia is "a primary" source of legislation without going into any detail, such as constitutional debates of the jurists.

With regard to the third aspect, the "translation" of international law on the level of legislation (3) the CEDAW Committee wanted to know "the steps taken *to integrate into national legislation the provisions of the Convention*, in particular a definition of discrimination against women that is in line with article 1 of the Convention." The state should report on the status of the Convention

121 CEDAW Replies 2018: 5, emphasis added.
122 CEDAW Replies 2018: 5.
123 CEDAW Replies 2018: 9.
124 CEDAW List of Issues and Questions 2017: 2.
125 CEDAW Report 2017: 2; Replies 2018: 5.

in the state's legal system and indicate whether the state envisaged publishing the Convention in the Official Gazette.[126] The State of Palestine explained in its answer to these questions that a request for interpretation had been sent to the SCC, the responsible body, to outline the steps to be taken to integrate into national legislation the provisions of the Convention:

> The request for interpretation asks for a definition of the nature of the Basic Law of the State of Palestine with regard to the incorporation of international law into domestic law; whether the legal system is monist, dualist or hybrid; what party is responsible for enforcing international conventions and incorporating them into the domestic legal system; and what is the legal standing of international conventions in relation to other legislation. For those purposes, it requests interpretation of article 10 of the Palestinian Basic Law. Decision No. 4 (2017) of the Supreme Constitutional Court provides that international conventions are superior to local legislation, as consistent with the national, religious and cultural identity of the Palestinian people.[127]

The definition of discrimination set forth in the Convention on the Elimination of All Forms of Discrimination against Women was adopted, according to the State of Palestine, in the draft decree/law concerning protection of the family from violence.[128] The conventions would be published in the Palestinian Official Gazette once their standing and the mechanism for their enforcement were defined by the competent authority. Once the conventions are published in the Official Gazette, any judge would have the right to cite and invoke their provisions when issuing a judgment.[129] The LHC is mentioned again as an important committee working on the harmonization of international with national law.[130] Palestine was also asked to report about any progress made with respect to the ratification of the Optional Protocol of CEDAW.[131] The quite evasive answer was that accession to the Optional Protocol to the Convention was viewed "favourably."[132]

126 CEDAW List of Issues and Questions 2017: 1, emphasis added.
127 CEDAW Replies 2018: 2.
128 CEDAW Replies 2018: 2.
129 CEDAW Replies 2018: 2.
130 CEDAW Replies 2018: 2.
131 CEDAW List of Issues and Questions 2017: 8.
132 CEDAW Replies 2018: 25.

The most important points are the announcement or promise that the family draft law was in process ("part of the 2018 legislative review"[133]); the hint to its basis in Sharia but that Sharia would not be the only basis; the promise that the harmonizing committee would take up its work. As of the end of 2018, no officially published result appeared.

7.3 Shadow Reports by Civil Society Organizations

Palestine's strong civil society used the chance to submit reports to the CEDAW Committee, the so-called Shadow Reports, which added their perspective to the State Report – which had claimed to be based on partial contribution from civil society organizations. According to a general statement in a press release of the CEDAW Committee meeting with civil society organizations of Palestine, New Zealand and Turkmenistan on the afternoon of July 9, 2018, the civil society's critique of the State of Palestine's policy with regard to CEDAW and women's rights was harsh and fundamental. From the perspective of civil society, the State of Palestine had failed to introduce an integrated legal system; to regulate legally gender-based discrimination and create laws against violence against women and girls; it had, furthermore, failed to adopt policies to change traditional attitudes and modify social and cultural patterns. The personal status law continued to discriminate against women in divorce, inheritance, and child custody. Child marriage remained a significant problem and was especially mentioned in the protocol of this meeting.[134] The CEDAW Women Coalition, composed of forty-three Palestinian organizations, stressed that discrimination against women need not be dealt with in only one piece of legislation, such as the family law, but required the harmonization of all laws to ensure equality, and this must be enshrined in the constitution.[135] Reports of civil society organizations can be found on the website of CEDAW beside the documents provided by the state and documents provided by the CEDAW Committee. They were issued by ICHR,[136] a state-created human rights

133 CEDAW Replies 2018: 3.

134 CEDAW Discusses with Civil Society Organizations, July 9, 2018, see https://www.un.org/unispal/document/cedaw-discusses-with-civil-society-organizations-the-situation-of-women-in-state-of-palestine-press-release-excerpts/, accessed on January 9, 2018.

135 CEDAW Discusses with Civil Society Organizations, July 9, 2018.

136 See ICHR (without date [2017]) and ICHR (2018). ICHR (Independent Commission of Human Rights; *al-Hay'a al-Mustaqilla li-Ḥuqūq al-Insān*) has a special status as it is a state-created human rights organization that was, according to its website, created through a presidential decree. Its duties and responsibilities are: "to follow-up and ensure

organization; GUPW (General Union of Palestinian Women);[137] al-Haq,[138] an independent Palestinian NGO; a coalition of Human Rights Watch/WCLAC/ Equality Now,[139] a mixture of national (WCLAC) and international NGOs; Musawa,[140] a transregional Muslim civil society organization, and WCLAC/ Equality Now/Muntada, again a combination this time of two Palestinian NGOs and one international NGO.[141]

that different Palestinian laws, by-laws and regulations, and the work of various departments, agencies and institutions of the State of Palestine and the Palestine Liberation Organization meet the requirements for safeguarding human rights." The decree entrusted ICHR with the drafting of its statutes in a manner that would ensure its independence and effectiveness. Most of the non-governmental organizations have two papers in the CEDAW sample: one initial with comments on the State Report of Palestine and one for the session in July. Often both reports are more or less equal.

137 There is a report of GUPW of 2017 named "Report on the Status of Women and Girls in the State of Palestine," see: https://tbinternet.ohchr.org/Treaties/CEDAW/Shared%20Documents/PSE/INT_CEDAW_NGO_PSE_29031_E.pdf, accessed January 9, 2019. However, even if it is under the title of GUPW, it is made explicit on page 2 that different organizations contributed to this report, among them WATC and also WCLAC. There is a second report by GUPW in 2018 named "Leaving No One Behind," see: https://tbinternet.ohchr.org/Treaties/CEDAW/Shared%20Documents/PSE/INT_CEDAW_NGO_PSE_31720_E.pdf, accessed January 9, 2019.

138 See al-Haq, June 2018: https://tbinternet.ohchr.org/_layouts/treatybodyexternal/Download.aspx?symbolno=INT%2fCEDAW%2fNGO%2fPSE%2f31670&Lang=en, accessed January 8, 2019.

139 All three organizations – one of them Palestinian (WCLAC) and two global organizations: Human Rights Watch and Equality Now have two papers from June 2018 and July 9, 2018. Human Rights Watch, see https://www.hrw.org/de, accessed January 7, 2019; and Equality Now, see https://www.equalitynow.org/, accessed January 7, 2019. Human Rights Watch is, according to its own website, a nonprofit, nongovernmental human rights organization made up of roughly four hundred staff members around the globe. Its staff consists of human rights professionals including country experts, lawyers, journalists, and academics of diverse backgrounds and nationalities. Established in 1978, Human Rights Watch is widely accepted for its accurate fact-finding, impartial reporting, effective use of media, and targeted advocacy, often in partnership with local human rights groups, see https://www.hrw.org/about, accessed January 9, 2019. Equality Now is a global network of lawyers, partners and supporters and its mission, according to its website, is to achieve legal and systematic change that addresses violence and discrimination against women and girls, see https://www.equalitynow.org/our_mission, accessed January 7, 2019.

140 See http://www.musawah.org/, accessed January 7, 2019; for the report for CEDAW, see: https://tbinternet.ohchr.org/_layouts/treatybodyexternal/Download.aspx?symbolno=INT%2fCEDAW%2fNGO%2fPSE%2f31669&Lang=en, accessed January 8, 2019.

141 Al-Muntada submitted the report together with others: WCLAC/Equality Now/Muntada (October 2017). https://tbinternet.ohchr.org/_layouts/treatybodyexternal/Download.aspx?symbolno=INT%2fCEDAW%2fNGO%2fPSE%2f29167&Lang=en, accessed January 8, 2019.

As stated already in the press release, the most important critique made by the civil society organizations concerned the fact that there was no adequate legislation. The old legislation was still in force and the State of Palestine had not introduced new legislation.[142] ICHR, albeit a state-created human rights organization, was among the most outspoken critics of the State of Palestine and therefore here serves as an example for the strongest arguments against the Palestinian State Report. It enumerated several important and fundamental shortcomings and failures of the State Report. Thus, the State of Palestine had failed to cover relevant issues, for example, to explain the government's inability to implement human rights treaties in Gaza and Area C and to explain the lack of a legal framework to incorporate international treaties into the Palestinian legal system:[143]

> This means, the report has ignored to make explicit reference to the non-obligatory nature of the human rights treaties, including CEDAW, for all official and non-official bodies in the State of Palestine due to the non-existence of a legal framework that would regulate the merger of these treaties in the national legal system. They have not also been published in Palestine's *Official Gazette* of [*sic!*] and have been officially disseminated.[144]

This leads to noncommitment of the judiciary to enforce these treaties. ICHR quoted a judge of the Jerusalem Appeal Court saying that CEDAW is non-obligatory law.[145] Furthermore, the State Report had failed to spell out if the government had taken any measures to implement the treaties.

There are also a number of restrictions and exceptions to the freedom and rights guaranteed in the BL. The BL guaranteed the most important rights and basic freedoms. However, there are ambiguities that lead to general restrictions and exceptions that are difficult to identify or control. These include, for example, phrases like "within the law" and "taking into account the provisions of the law."[146] A number of laws were still in effect that were not in accordance with the BL.[147] The law-making bodies had failed to draw up legislation in ac-

142 Al-Haq, June 2018: 4; GUPW 2018: 17; GUPW 2017: 4; Human Rights Watch/ WCLAC/Equality Now 2018: 1ff; WCLAC/Equality Now/Muntada, October 2017: 3; Musawah, July 2018: 3.

143 ICHR [2017]: 1–2; ICHR 2018: 3.

144 ICHR [2017]: 2.

145 ICHR [2017]: 2.

146 ICHR [2017]: 3.

147 ICHR [2017]: 3.

cordance with the treaties[148] and to introduce an integrated legal system that could reduce discrimination between the two sexes as a means to eliminate all violence.[149] Above all and of utmost importance, the report complained that there were "*no signs of the presence of an official will to change these laws* in the foreseeable future."[150]

ICHR also accused the State of Palestine of exerting violence against its citizens, especially women.[151] The state's report failed to produce important numbers to indicate the government's interest in women's development and social status and in preparing development and anti-violence plans. There was no information about whether the state had taken action to modify social and cultural patterns.[152] Also, the state's report did not provide a diagnosis of the influence of the political division on women and girls.[153] In addition, there was not enough funding for women's projects: "The Ministry of Women's [Affairs'] budget is the lowest, in comparison with other ministries, and its running costs take the lion's share."[154]

ICHR requested the CEDAW Committee to oblige the state to increase the budget. The MoWA's budget is limited to one program, everything else is funded by international donors, it argued.[155] Participation of women in the public sphere is still "substandard."[156] Furthermore, the Report failed to mention minority women, such as the Samaritan women who are marginalized, as well as women in refugee camps, in rural areas,[157] and women with disabilities.[158] Women's fatalities due to medical negligence were documented by ICHR but ignored by the state and no measures followed.[159] ICHR provided new numbers, for example, with regard to unemployment, which had since 2015 – the numbers given in the State Report – gone up for women from 34 percent in 2015 to 50 percent in 2017.[160]

148 ICHR [2017]: 3.
149 ICHR [2017]: 3–4.
150 ICHR [2017]: 4, emphasis added; ICHR 2018: 7 with regard to CEDAW, there are no conferences etc. organized by the government to promote CEDAW.
151 ICHR [2017]: 4–5; see also WCLAC/Equality Now/Muntada, October 2017: 11.
152 ICHR [2017]: 5.
153 ICHR 2018: 6.
154 ICHR [2017]: 6; see also ICHR 2018: 5.
155 ICHR 2018: 5–6.
156 ICHR 2018: 6.
157 ICHR [2017]: 6.
158 ICHR 2018: 4–5.
159 ICHR [2017]: 7.
160 ICHR [2017]: 8.

All civil society reports agreed that the applicable family law discriminates against women and girls.[161] The GUPW argued that the Israeli occupation must be held responsible for violence and discrimination against women as well as neoliberal economical politics.[162] The ICHR report,[163] on the other hand, stated that violence against women was the outcome of imbalances in power relations existing between women and men and because of inequality in Palestinian society. The ICHR reaffirmed that violence is one of the decisive social mechanisms that are imposed on women and that their position in society is subordinate to men. Clearer than in the State Report, Al-Haq stated that the PA does not have effective power outside Area A[164] and that overall plural legislation is to be found. It also complained that the "state of emergency" announced in 2007 still existed, which is contrary to the BL.

The GUPW criticized the fact that men and women do not have equal rights in marriage and the applicable laws in Palestine do not consider the wife's full legal capacity.[165] In its original report of 2017, GUPW hinted to several issues in family law, commenting that divorce is an especially thorny issue,[166] a flagrant violation of women's rights, because the personal status law provides that men have absolute power to divorce their wives; but if women want a divorce, they must invest a lot of time. The GUPW pointed to the Supreme Judge's decision allowing the wife to initiate the divorce herself by waiving her financial rights, i.e., *khulʿ*, and explained that this ruling is not applicable in Gaza because of the reality of the political division. Divorce is possible for Christians in extremely limited cases. Human Rights Watch/WCLAC/Equality Now declared that the husband's rights to polygamy and divorce are both an infringement of women's rights.[167]

Al-Haq and ICHR mentioned the judgment of the SCC of November 17, 2017, which is interpreted as an affirmation that international law stands above national law.[168] The Al-Haq report argued that consistency with the "national, religious and cultural identity of the Arab Palestinian people," could be interpreted as a general reservation in violation of the Convention, the Basic Law,

161 Al-Haq, June 2018: 4–5; GUPW 2018: 18; Human Rights Watch/ WCLAC/Equality Now, June 2018: 3–7; ICHR [2017]: 4; see also Human Rights Watch and WCLAC, July 9, 2018.

162 GUPW 2018: 5, 7.

163 ICHR [2017]: 3.

164 Al-Haq, June 2018: 1–2; see also ICHR [2017]: 1.

165 GUPW 2017: 21.

166 GUPW 2017: 23–24; see also WCLAC/Equality Now/Muntada, October 2017: 5–6.

167 Human Rights Watch/WCLAC/Equality Now 2018: 3; see also WCLAC/Equality Now/ Muntada, October 2017: 6.

168 Al-Haq, June 2018: 2; ICHR 2018: 8.

and the 2006 Law on the Supreme Constitutional Court.[169] The judgment of March 12, 2018, according to which the enforcement of international treaties would have to be approved domestically was also harshly criticized by Al-Haq, because the "general reservation" in the judgment of November 17, 2017, was reiterated. Al-Haq criticized the fact that the SCC was created by a decision by the president on April 26, 2016, thus questioning its legitimacy.[170] Al-Haq as well as ICHR warned that the human rights situation was currently deteriorating and that this was due to not only the occupation but also to the ongoing internal divide as well as the non-functioning of the parliament, which caused the executive to monopolize the executive and legislative branch. The executive was additionally accused of placing restrictions on the actions of civil society. "Transparency and public dialogue are largely absent in the law and policy-making processes."[171] Intransparency was also responsible, Al-Haq and ICHR maintained, for the absence of accountability and redress for victims in the judiciary.[172] Whereas GUPW criticized, among others, the judges who viewed women from a patriarchal point of view,[173] Al-Haq and ICHR accused the state as well as the clerics of not having amended the old family laws in the West Bank and Gaza.

Lesbians, gays, and transgender people face discrimination.[174] GUPW hinted at the problem of tribal committees that reinforce patriarchal structures.[175] And Al-Haq mentioned and criticized the Supreme Judge's statement that Sharia takes precedence over international conventions[176] and voiced its concern about it. Al-Haq also referred to the discussion on the interpretation of the constitution, especially Article 4 (2) of the BL according to which the principles of Islamic Sharia "shall be a principal source of legislation,"[177] going into the details of the discussion and correcting the Supreme Judge, noting that there was a difference between the terms "principles of Islamic Sharia" (i.e., the general, conclusively proved and established principles) and the term

169 Al-Haq, June 2018: 2; ICHR 2018: 8. This is in accordance with the interpretation of the jurists of BZU, see chapter 2.1.3.

170 Al-Haq, June 2018: 3.

171 Al-Haq, June 2018: 3.

172 Al-Haq, June 2018: 3; ICHR [2017]: 4–5.

173 GUPW 2018: 17.

174 Human Rights Watch/WCLAC/Equality Now, June 2018: 10. It is only here, as far as I can see, that reference is made to these groups.

175 GUPW 2018: 19.

176 Al-Haq, June 2018: 5–6.

177 See https://www.palestinianbasiclaw.org/basic-law/2003-amended-basic-law, accessed September 26, 2018, see also Muqtafi.

"Islamic Sharia" that al-Habbāsh had used.[178] The Legislation Harmonization Committee (LHC) was described to have been established by a decision of the Council of Ministers and it mostly, al-Haq complained, comprised government bodies.[179] The recommendations given by al-Haq are: to define discrimination,[180] to amend and change legislation, or to enact a new personal status law.[181]

Musawah, the international NGO, recommended that Palestine should involve all stake holders in the process of preparing the family law and consider progressive personal status law as found in Morocco, Algeria, and Turkey.[182] The GUPW recommended conducting special surveys and gathering statistics.[183] For all civil society organizations, it was important to press for ratification of the Optional Protocol of CEDAW[184] and to publish the ratification of CEDAW.[185] Human Rights Watch/WCLAC/Equality Now also demanded that the CEDAW Committee should be allowed to conduct an exceptional review after two years instead of the standard four-year periodic review "in order to allow for monitoring of the drafting and enactment of the Family Protection Law against Violence."[186] The Committee followed this suggestion. A civil family rights law was demanded by some civil society organizations.[187]

Whereas the ICHR and the other civil society organizations criticized the state of Palestine from a secular perspective, pushing for a civil law and ignoring more or less the tension with Sharia, the transregional organization Musawah provided a very critical position toward the Palestinian law from an outspoken Islamic point of view. Musawah[188] (*musāwāh*, equality) has an outspoken Islamic feminist agenda.[189] Its report on Palestine is very detailed and

178 Al-Haq, June 2018: 6.

179 Al-Haq, June 2018: 5.

180 Al-Haq, June 2018: 10–11.

181 Al-Haq, June 2018: 10–11; GUPW 2017: 29; Human Rights Watch/WCLAC/Equality Now, June 2018: 12; WCLAC/Equality Now/Muntada, October 2017: 11; Musawah, July 2018: 10.

182 Musawah, July 2018: 10.

183 GUPW 2017: 29.

184 GUPW 2017: 29; Human Rights Watch/WCLAC/Equality Now, June 2018: 11; ICHR 2018: 3.

185 GUPW 2017: 29; Human Rights Watch/ WCLAC/Equality Now, June 2018: 11; ICHR 2018: 3; WCLAC/Equality Now/Muntada, October 2017: 11.

186 Human Rights Watch/WCLAC/Equality Now, June 2018: 12.

187 WCLAC/Equality Now/Muntada, October 2017: 11.

188 Not to be mixed up with the Palestinian NGO of this name, see http://www.musawa.ps/about/about-us.html, accessed January 8, 2019.

189 According to its website, Musawah is a global movement for equality and justice in the Muslim family. It was launched at a gathering in February 2009 in Kuala Lumpur, Malaysia, attended by over 250 women and men from some fifty countries around the globe. Musawah considers itself pluralistic and inclusive, bringing together from around

connected with comparative research about the status of legislation in thirty-one Muslim countries.[190] It gave detailed recommendations on how to amend the law within an Islamic framework. Musawah argued that egalitarian laws based on the Quran are possible. Amendments and laws introduced in the name of Sharia must reflect equality, justice, love, compassion, and mutual respect.[191] *Fiqh* is a human product and therefore changeable. *Maṣlaḥa* (welfare) and *istiḥsān* (choosing the best opinion) are appropriate instruments to achieve those goals. Despite equality of the sexes being anchored in the Palestinian BL, Article 10, the laws still reflect the concept of "maintenance-for-obedience" in Palestine.[192] Musawah argued:

> This provides for a marital framework based on "reciprocal" or "complementary" rights (as opposed to "equal" rights) between the two spouses, whereby in return for maintenance and protection from her husband, a wife is expected to "obey" him. Thus personal rights of married women in the West Bank and Gaza Strip are significantly restricted and women lose their rights in situations where they are considered to be "disobedient" (*nusyuz*).[193]

The idea of complementarity of rights is a manifestation of male authority (*qiwāma*) and guardianship (*wilāya*) and plays a central role in justifying the patriarchal model. Legislation in Palestine should guarantee that men and women have equal rights, Musawah stressed.[194] Musawah was thus unique in openly challenging the "maintenance-for-obedience" principle from an Islamic point of view and claiming that equality is anchored in the Quran. Musawah also criticized the fact that women still needed a guardian (*walī*) for marriage: Women could become judges or representatives or assume high-level decision-making positions, but they could not stand for themselves when it came to the right to enter into marriage whereas in countries like Afghanistan and Bahrain (Shia), Egypt, Iraq and others, the consent of the *walī* was not necessary.[195] The Quran, according to Musawah, promoted monogamy and thus polygamy

the world NGOs, activists, scholars, legal practitioners, policymakers and women and men from grassroots organizations, see http://www.musawah.org/about-musawah, accessed January 8, 2019.

190 Musawah, July 2018: 3.

191 Musawah, July 2018: 6.

192 Musawah, July 2018: 7.

193 Musawah, July 2018: 7.

194 Musawah, July 2018: 9.

195 Musawah, July 2018: 10, 13.

should be abolished.[196] Musawah criticized the fact that men and women in Palestine had no equal rights to divorce.[197] With regard to *khulʿ*, Musawah only addressed the legal text in the West Bank and did not mention the *taʿmīm* of 2012. For Gaza, Musawah stated that women could petition for *khulʿ* and the judge might decide on it.[198] According to women's rights groups, challenges include: women being dissuaded from divorce in order not to lose their children; long delays in court; the ability to divorce outside the court system, and the existence of negative stereotypes of women divorcing their husbands. Musawah considered it cruel and unjust to allow men to divorce their wives, the unilateral right of men contradicted the Quran 2:229 ("either hold together on equitable terms (*maʿruf*) or separate with kindness (*ihsan*)"[199]) and 4:35.[200] The proceedings for arbitration and mediation place both spouses on equal footing, the organization argued.[201] It recommended equal access to divorce, abolishing the unilateral rights of the husband; having all divorces in court; clarifying procedure and timeline; and setting guidelines for *khulʿ* based on the request by the wife and payment of a sum. Musawah pointed to positive developments in the Muslim world such as in Tunisia and Turkey, where unilateral repudiation has been abolished, and to countries such as Algeria, Mauretania, Bangladesh and others where divorce can only take place in court.[202]

7.4 The Palestinian Delegation in Geneva, July 2018

The above-mentioned statements of the civil society were partly written at the end of 2017 and submitted together with the State Report. Some of the same organizations submitted further papers in June/July 2018 in direct preparation for the meeting with the CEDAW Committee bringing up mostly the same but sometimes different aspects. The hearing for Palestine was scheduled for July 11. Relevant documents in this context are: a speech by Dr. Hayfāʾ al-Āghā, the

196 Musawah, July 2018: 19.
197 Musawah, July 2018: 20.
198 Musawah, July 2018: 23.
199 Musawah, July 2018: 24. Arberry: 2:229: Divorce is twice; then honorable retention or setting free kindly, see https://www.islamawakened.com/quran/2/229/default.htm, accessed January 8, 2019.
200 Arberry: Quran 4:35 "And if you fear a breach between the two, bring forth an arbiter from his people and from her people an arbiter, if they desire to set things right"; see https://www.islamawakened.com/quran/4/35/default.htm, accessed January 15, 2019.
201 Musawah, July 2018: 24.
202 Musawah, July 2018: 25.

Minister of Women's Affairs,[203] as well as summaries of the morning (1614th) and afternoon (1615th) meetings of the CEDAW Committee with the representatives of the delegation of the State of Palestine[204] and the final observations.[205]

In her speech, the Minister introduced the members of her delegation and hinted at the difficult situation of Palestine because of the occupation. She pointed then to Article 9 of the BL in which gender equality is anchored,[206] admitting that some legislation needed revision, affirming the obligation of the State of Palestine to abolish these laws. She pointed to the accession of Palestine to CEDAW without reservations,[207] stressing that the state works toward enforcement.[208] She referred to the important cooperation between the state bodies and civil society in this respect,[209] stating that on the local level the way in which international conventions were integrated into Palestinian legislation had to be made clear. She mentioned the judgment of the SCC of November 2017 and that for the reason of this judgment the LHC had been created. As one example of its work, she pointed to the draft of the Family Protection Law against Violence.[210] On March 5, 2018, a "Technical Committee for the Systematic Review of Legislation Controlling Personal and Civil Status" had been created for the family law (*Lajna fanniyya li-murājaʿat manẓūma al-tashrīʿāt al-nāẓima li-l-aḥwāl al-shakhṣiyya wa-l-madaniyya*). This Committee started its work in July 2018 with representatives of the ministries and the GUPW. It was formed to present recommendations to the cabinet.[211] Also

203 See CEDAW Documents concerning Palestine under the title "introductory statement." Dr. Agha's talk is given under the title "Kalimat dawlat Filasṭīn tulqīhā d. Hayfāʾ al-Āghā," see https://tbinternet.ohchr.org/_layouts/treatybodyexternal/Download.aspx?symbolno=INT%2fCEDAW%2fSTA%2fPSE%2f31734&Lang=en, accessed January 9, 2018.

204 CEDAW Summary record of the 1614th meeting, July 11, 10:00 am–1:00 pm, see https://tbinternet.ohchr.org/_layouts/treatybodyexternal/Download.aspx?symbolno=CEDAW%2fC%2fSR.1614&Lang=en, accessed January 15, 2019 and CEDAW Summary record of the 1615th meeting, July 11, 3:00 pm –5:10 pm, see https://tbinternet.ohchr.org/_layouts/treatybodyexternal/Download.aspx?symbolno=CEDAW%2fC%2fSR.1615&Lang=en, accessed January 15, 2019.

205 CEDAW, July 25, 2018; "Concluding Observations," see https://tbinternet.ohchr.org/_layouts/treatybodyexternal/Download.aspx?symbolno=CEDAW%2fC%2fPSE%2fCO%2f1&Lang=en, accessed January 9, 2019.

206 Āghā 2018: 4.

207 Āghā 2018: 4.

208 Āghā 2018: 5.

209 Āghā 2018: 5.

210 Āghā 2018: 7. On April 8, 2019, I had an interview with Imān ʿAbdalḥamīd, Head of the Legislation and Advisory Bureau, and she confirmed that to this date none of the international treaties had arrived in her office to be prepared for publication in the *Gazette*.

211 Āghā 2018: 8.

Agenda 2030 is mentioned, which contained gender equality as one of its aims.[212] Having been criticized for relying on outdated statistics, the Minister presented some new numbers on women's percentages in the labor market[213] before returning to the critique of Israel in the end.[214]

The Minister's speech was political, focusing on the international context, and she pinpointed the occupation as the main obstacle to solve. She named a few challenges and announced steps to be taken to tackle them; she specifically mentioned many agendas and committees. There was not much of substance she could contribute. In accordance with the whole report, she avoided mentioning the important role of Islam and Sharia in the BL, the patriarchal society, traditions and customs discriminating against women and the fact that the government in Ramallah did not have any influence on Area C and Gaza. She tried her best to create the impression that the legislation is completely in the state's hand, not mentioning the claim of the SCHC to draw up the draft law in family law matters. She surely did not refer to the "split" between religious (mostly conservative) scholars and the women's movement, let alone the need for a new gender equal interpretation of the Islamic law defended by some as solution of this aporia.

In the two CEDAW Summary Records of the 1614th and 1615th meetings,[215] concrete legal problems such as inequality in divorce laws and so forth were again not touched upon and the role of the Sharia Judiciary was only mentioned briefly.[216] The questions focused on a possible new constitution and what measures had been taken, "including through the use of presidential decrees," to develop a comprehensive legal framework.[217] This question was answered, surprisingly, by ʿIwaḍallāh outlining that the "government had managed to put in place a parliament and the Palestinian Central National Council had been given the power to give laws."[218] What did he mean by that? There

212 Āghā 2018: 9.

213 Āghā 2018: 10. According to these numbers, the percentage of women working is 19 percent in the first quarter of 2018. In the Ministry of Foreign Affairs and abroad, the percentage is 40 percent.

214 Āghā 2018: 10–11.

215 The minister, al-Āghā, is quoted as saying that the SCC's rule, i.e., that the convention prevailed over domestic legislation, had been adopted by the parliament. CEDAW Summary record 1614: 3.

216 CEDAW Summary record 1614: 4; CEDAW Summary record 1615: 8. In both cases, Palestinian members of the delegation pointed to the role of Sharia. In 1615: 8, one can read that the "dialogue would be held with religious institutions and civil society organizations with a view to amending family laws."

217 CEDAW Summary record 1614: 3.

218 CEDAW Summary record 1614: 4.

was, to the best of my knowledge, no parliament in Ramallah, whereas the Gaza Parliament under Hamas control surely was not what he referred to here. The work of the LHC was mentioned several times[219] and ʿIwaḍallāh also rejected the argument, that the SCC had made factual reservations on international law.[220]

In the final report,[221] the Committee welcomed the fact that Palestine had signed many international conventions but urged Palestine to take all measures to urgently convene a parliament.[222] Taking the fact of the occupation into consideration, the Committee regretted that the split between Hamas and Fatah had not yet been solved[223] and pointed to the different forms of legislation that are problematic for women and girls. It urged Palestine to: "Adopt, without delay, national legislation that includes a comprehensive definition of discrimination against women covering all prohibited grounds of discrimination and encompassing direct and indirect discrimination in both the public and private spheres."[224]

The Committee voiced its concern about the fact that the Convention had not yet been published and about the de facto reservations in the judgment of the SCC. The Committee was further concerned about the absence of a timeframe for acceding to the Optional Protocol, notwithstanding the state's declared commitment to do so.[225] The situation did not, the Committee argued, absolve the state from taking concrete steps, which indicated the Committee's slight frustration with the State of Palestine, since it had made many declarations, made announcements, and created committees without, as it seems, concrete steps taken to move the matter forward. With regard to the harmonizing process, the Committee again showed concern about the absence of a timeframe.[226] It advised the state to allocate more funds to the MoWA.[227] It should adopt a comprehensive strategy to eliminate discriminatory stereotypes,[228] from textbooks as well, since these could still be found in many Palestinian textbooks. The Commission thus ruled that the state should

219 CEDAW Summary record 1614: 4.

220 CEDAW Summary record 1614: 4.

221 CEDAW, July 25, 2018, "Concluding Observations," see https://tbinternet.ohchr.org/_layouts/treatybodyexternal/Download.aspx?symbolno=CEDAW%2fC%2fPSE%2fCO%2f1&Lang=en, accessed January 9, 2019.

222 CEDAW July 25, 2018: 3.

223 CEDAW July 25, 2018: 3.

224 CEDAW July 25, 2018: 3.

225 CEDAW July 25, 2018: 4.

226 CEDAW July 25, 2018: 4.

227 CEDAW July 25, 2018: 7.

228 CEDAW July 25, 2018: 8.

"continue to review textbooks in order to eliminate the negative image of women and girls with regard to their roles in the family and in society, and ensure a positive reflection of that image."[229]

It should also give priority to enact the Family Protection Law against Violence.[230] With regard to family law, the Committee recommended that the state should:

(a) Review all personal status laws with a view to repealing or amending all provisions that discriminate against women and girls, in particular those relating to marriage, divorce, inheritance and the legal capacity of women, and in that regard, address family status matters by taking into account the best practices of countries with similar cultural backgrounds.
(b) Adopt a law that provides for an alternative legal regime to govern civil marriage in the State party.[231]

Palestine was asked to provide a new report within two years.[232] This short period of time, i.e., 2020, had been demanded by parts of civil society,[233] and it may reflect the Committee's doubts that all the steps that the State of Palestine had promised were actually "on the way."

229 CEDAW July 25, 2018: 8.
230 CEDAW July 25, 2018: 8.
231 CEDAW July 25, 2018: 15.
232 CEDAW July 25, 2018: 16.
233 Human Rights Watch/WCLAC/Equality Now, June 2018: 12.

CHAPTER 8

CEDAW in Iterations

8.1 Palestine Discusses: How Can International Law and Sharia Be Harmonized?

On December 9, 2018, the Platform of Palestinian Nongovernmental Organizations against Domestic Violence against Women, al-Muntada (*Muntadā al-Munaẓẓamāt al-Ahliyya al-Filasṭīniyya li-Munāhaḍat al-ʿUnf ḍidda al-Marʾa*), launched a severe verbal attack against the Supreme Judge, Dr. Maḥmūd al-Habbāsh, in the *Wattan* news agency.[1] Al-Muntada condemned his televised opinion that violence against women as a means of "education and disciplinary punishment" (*tarbiya wa-taʾdīb*) was acceptable and pointed out that twenty-two women had been violently killed in 2018. Those killings were, as the statement expressed, not all attributable to Israel, but also to "customs and traditions" (*ʿadāt wa-taqālīd*). It stressed the fact that this proclamation had come shortly after Palestine's ratification of the Optional Protocol[2] to CEDAW and four years after the ratification of CEDAW itself. Violence against women, al-Muntada explained, was against not only the Basic Law but also several other laws. It argued that the Supreme Judge's statement came as a "positive push" (*dafʿa ījābiyya*) and a whitewash (*tajmīl*) for violent social customs against women, dressing them in a religious garment. Al-Habbāsh's statement also violated the basal respect all monotheistic religions bear toward women. Al-Muntada strictly rejected any justification of using violence against women and demanded the immediate adoption of the Family Protection Law against Violence. It also demanded that the Supreme Judge's statement should be withdrawn, and in future, the media should endeavor to oppose all forms of violence against women.

What happened?[3] By the end of 2018, the Supreme Judge had provoked harsh criticism with his opinion, namely placing Sharia above any other law,

---

1 Wattan [*Waṭan*], December 9, 2018.

2 Apparently, the Palestinian delegation in Geneva in July 2018 stated the President was ready to sign the Optional Protocol of CEDAW, see also chapter 7.2. The State of Palestine accessed the Optional Protocol of CEDAW on April 10, 2019, see https://treaties.un.org/Pages/ViewDetails.aspx?src=TREATY&mtdsg_no=IV-8-b&chapter=4&lang=en, accessed September 19, 2019.

3 In this chapter, I rely mainly on TV programs. However, as I had a chance to return to Palestine in the spring of 2019 and to interview individuals I had not been able to meet before – e.g., the women's minister Hayfāʾ al-Āghā. I include these interviews here, even when they were

 | DOI:10.1163/9789004442313_009

and with his very conservative and provocative idea about family life as the one quoted above. He had successfully brought himself into opposition with the women's movement. Unlike Yūsuf Idʿīs, who might have favored classical gender roles but was ready to talk to civil society and think about reforming the law in favor of women, al-Habbāsh presented himself as a hardliner without willingness to dialogue. Permitting violence against women just after the Palestinian delegation had returned from its visit to Geneva on July 11, 2018, can be understood as an outright provocation, not only against women's organizations but also against the state of Palestine and the influence of international law and its anti-discriminatory policies. State and civil society reacted with outrage. Whereas iterations from 2012 to 2014 were dominated by the Sharia establishment and focused on its issuing law-like rulings like the one concerning the new interpretation of the *khulʿ*, enjoying much public support, especially among women and women's organization, iterations since 2014 and especially around 2017 and 2018 shifted. The Sharia establishment, mainly represented now by the Supreme Judge al-Habbāsh, took a conservative and obstinate position and provoked harsh criticism. The State of Palestine, having signed CEDAW in 2014, was obliged in 2017/18 to produce its first report (chapter 7), and the Shadow Reports by civil society organizations demonstrated, as outlined in chapter 7, impressively not only the power of civil society in Palestine but also the strength of the more secular forces in Palestinian society. As a whole, the iteration now shifted to the role of international law against Sharia and in connection to this to the question of whether one should have two sets of laws, a civil one and a religious one, or one law that could be brought into harmony with international standards. Palestine faced the obligation to make a serious decision, which, in any case, would influence the internal legal structure for the years and decades to come. The signature under the international contracts obliged compliance; and this was of utmost importance for Palestine in its weak international position. How would Palestine be perceived in the West and by international organizations, especially the UN, which Palestine so much wanted to join? The situation was precarious. There were two old statutes – the JLPS in the West Bank and the EFRL in Gaza – both incompatible with the signed international statutes. There were two parts of Palestine between which no reconciliation seemed possible for the time being. The visit to Geneva had been successful in the sense that it had created an

conducted after the end of my official research period, 2012–2018. They all concerned the developments especially since 2014 and the first trip of the Palestinian delegation to Geneva and the question of how the necessary harmonization of the national laws could be brought about.

international awareness of the State of Palestine's wish to fight against discrimination against women, and there had been an increased public awareness in Palestine of the tension between the old applicable laws and women's rights in international law. Vehement iterations had started in the West Bank and will be analyzed with regard to two aspects: Who were the participants and what was their position with regard to international law? This last question was explicitly tackled in a series of reports in *Wattan* from June 21 to June 30, 2018, that is even before the travel of the Palestinian delegation to Geneva, which bear the title: "Palestine discusses interpretations of the Sharia which can be harmonized with 'CEDAW' and the split between the scholars of religions and politicians becomes wider."[4] This first report was followed by two other reports from June 25 and 30, 2018. The second one reflected the position of women's organizations; the third the position of the ICHR represented by its head, Ammar al-Dwaik (ʿAmmār [al-] Duwayk).[5] This series of reports in *Wattan* reflect the important role of the media in bringing together the different sides in these iterations, but it also dealt precisely with the core problem, i.e., the discussion about the (im)possibility of harmonizing international and national-Islamic law and the way this could be done. Its conclusion was that there is a "split" (*sharkh*) between scholars of religion and politicians. Reports by civil society representatives took up this metaphor and spoke of a split between civil society, i.e., women's organizations, and scholars of religion.

The report in *Wattan* of June 21, 2018, started with the story of a woman who suffered from the applicable laws. She had been mistreated and beaten by her husband. He had married his second wife while still married to her, and threw her out of their family home with her seven children. Although she had helped to build their family home, she was left with neither a home nor compensation; in addition, the husband denied maintenance for the daughters who decided to stay with their mother after the divorce. The woman had to spend more than a year in court to get at least some of her rights. Rīmā Shamāsana, law expert of WCLAC explained that these discriminations, e.g., polygyny, divorce against her will, having to fight in court for more than a year to get her rights, not getting half of the property gained during marriage, and cutting the maintenance for the daughters because they chose to live with the mother, were in compliance with the applicable law but against CEDAW. The woman complained about injustice and called the applicable law "unjust."

4 Wattan, June 21, 2018.

5 ICHR had also provided a very critical Shadow Report for CEDAW. See https://www.linkedin.com/in/ammar-al-dwaik-81749374, accessed January 5, 2019. For the organization, see http://www.ichr.ps/en, accessed January 5, 2019.

According to the host of this TV program, Nazār Ḥabash, there were many women in similar situations. He introduced the audience[6] to international law and the most important facts about CEDAW, outlined the centrality of Article 16 of CEDAW and the steps the State of Palestine had taken so far to introduce this convention. The CEDAW Committee's central requirements for Palestine were quoted in writing:

> Please provide information on measures taken to develop legal frameworks to govern women's rights, to repeal archaic laws that do not conform to the provisions of the Convention and to address the discrimination against women and girls under personal status laws with regard to marriage, divorce, custody of children and inheritance.[7]

The State of Palestine's answer was shown, which stipulates that the Islamic Sharia is, according to BL Article 4, *a* primary source of legislation as opposed to *the* primary source of legislation and that Palestinian law also draws on other sources. Ḥabash drew the conclusion that the main problem Palestine was confronted with after the signature was the application of Article 16 of CEDAW, because the applicable law in the West Bank contradicted it. What would be the solution? The experts he consulted voiced different opinions: Randa al-Sinyūra of WCLAC was, as WCLAC always had been, in favor of drawing up a civil law[8] and criticized that "we are afraid to touch" personal status law because it is anchored in Sharia regulations; Maḥmūd al-Habbāsh, the *Qāḍī al-Quḍāt*, conceded that "we are ready to harmonize the law with international law under the condition that the principles of Sharia are not violated." What he meant by this was that Sharia is above international law, and he also said it explicitly later in the debates. *Shaykh* Muṣṭafā al-Ṭawīl, head of Sharia High Court, already identified a contradiction: "This convention is in some parts against the Islamic Sharia, especially [in the] matter of equality (*musāwāh*) of man and woman in inheritance,"[9] pointing to the nub of the problem.

Asked whether Palestine is heading for a new interpretation of the Sharia, al-Habbāsh's reply was very general without dealing with such important questions as which parts of family law could be reformed or what a new interpretation could look like or how women as the vulnerable part of the society could

6 There is a video and a written report, I draw on both of them; see Wattan, June 21, 2018.

7 CEDAW List of Issues and Questions 2017: 1–2.

8 In the interview with him, ʿUmar ʿIwaḍallāh of the Ministry of Foreign Affairs opted personally – not as representative of his Ministry – for a civil law: ʿUmar ʿIwaḍallāh, interview on April 7, 2019.

9 Wattan, June 21, 2018.

be better protected. On the other hand, he did not demonstrate any openness to discuss the matter with the society at large, with the state, and with women's organizations but his claim to have the right to guide the discussions became evident. On a general level, he stressed that all "that is allowed is what God allows and all that is prohibited is what God prohibits (*al-ḥalāl mā aḥallahu Allāh, wa-l-ḥarām mā ḥarramahu Allāḥ*)" and left no doubt that Sharia is above law (*fawqa al-qānūn*) and above any political obligation or any obligations of the law or international contracts, stating: "We will not accept any contradiction to what God has legislated (*mā sharraʿahu Allāh*)."[10]

When he was confronted with ʿUmar ʿIwaḍallāh's statement,[11]as a representative of the Ministry of Foreign Affairs, saying: "International conventions are above national law,"[12] the Supreme Judge reacted vehemently and emotionally: "No, no, we absolutely reject this! (*lā, lā, naḥnu narfuḍu dhālika rafḍan qāṭiʿan*!)."[13] ʿIwaḍallāh took the liberty of pointing in the interview to the rank of the *Qāḍī al-Quḍāt* as a minister below the president who decided to sign the international conventions. He is also not the head of the SCC, he stated, and described him as a "dignitary" in Palestine. "Our decisions are usually not taken by one person," he added.[14] He was clear that all legislation that is not in harmony with international law has to be amended: "The decision of the Constitutional Court was clear about this."[15] International law stands against backward ideals and customs that are not in accordance with any religion, and that he saw no conflict between CEDAW and Islamic Sharia. This international convention, he argued, aimed to fight discrimination against women, and he could not imagine that any religion in the world would be in favor of discriminating against women.

Other than in 2012–2014, state and Sharia establishment thus had become involved into a very controversial and highly polarized discussion, which, however, remained mostly on a general level and did not tackle the concrete problems on the ground: marriage age, divorce, child care, and the central question: how to "translate" "equality" into the Palestinian legal context.

Whereas the State of Palestine in its answer to CEDAW outlined that Palestinian law also draws on sources other than the Sharia, the Supreme Judge started a dispute about the interpretation of the constitution, arguing:

10 Wattan, June 21, 2018.
11 In the text his name is given as ʿUmar ʿIwaḍ, not ʿIwaḍallāh.
12 Wattan, June 21, 2018.
13 See https://www.youtube.com/watch?v=wcwPM9tqYVE, June 21, 2018, around minute 01:32.
14 ʿUmar ʿIwaḍallāh, interview on April 7, 2019.
15 Wattan, June 21, 2018.

> The first article of the Basic Law or from the constitution states that the Islamic Sharia is the religion of the land and state[16] and that it is the [*sic!*] principle source (*al-maṣdar al-asāsī*) of legislation. How can it be the principal source of legislation and how can I implement laws which contradict it? We cannot accept this and it is not possible for the Palestinian leadership or the president or the parliament (*al-Majlis al-Tashrīʿī*) and not for the Palestinian people to accept this.[17]

This triggered a strong reaction of jurists both from the state and civil society. Al-Habbāsh was obviously wrong when quoting the "first article," which does not say anything about the Sharia, as well as in his interpretation of the BL. ʿIwaḍallāh rejected his statement and corrected the Supreme Judge's quotation from the Basic Law saying that the Sharia is *one* of the foundations (*usus*) of the Palestinian laws: "Our law is not Sharia," he stressed, "but Sharia is *one* of the sources (*iḥdā al-maṣādir*)." ʿIṣām ʿĀbidīn, expert in constitutional law and member of the NGO al-Haq, referred to Article 4 (2) of the BL, not, as the Supreme Judge had claimed, Article 1, which states that the "principles of the Islamic Sharia are *a* main source (*maṣdar raʾīsī*) of the legislation." Like ʿIwaḍallāh, he explained that it is not the only source for legislation. In addition, he continued his argument, the constitution is clear about the "principles (*mabādiʾ*) of the Islamic Sharia" and not the "rules" (*aḥkām*), and there is a big difference between "principles" and "rules."[18] As examples for those "principles," he named the principle of "justice" (*ʿadāla*), the principle "not to inflict injury nor repay one injury with another" (*lā ḍarar wa-lā ḍirār*), the principles of "safeguarding life and property" (*ḥifẓ al-nafs wa-l-māl*) or the principle that there is "no coercing in religion" (*lā ikrāh fī al-dīn*), all taken from Quran or Islamic law. As ʿIwaḍallāh, he expressed his firm belief that these principles do not contradict international law. To avoid difficulties, one should be precise with the texts of the constitution, he recommended, attacking the Supreme Judge, who had not quoted the text of the BL correctly.

The Supreme Judge was supported by a representative of the Sharia establishment Jihād al-Kaswānī, lecturer of the Faculty of Law of Al-Quds University (Jerusalem, Abu Dis), who intervened in this discussion about the

---

16 He should have referred to Article 4 (1) and (2):
Islam is the official religion in Palestine. Respect for the sanctity of all other divine religions shall be maintained.
The principles of Islamic *Shariʿa* shall be a principal source of legislation.

17 Wattan, June 21, 2018.

18 For the same argument, see also ʿAmmār al-Duwayk, Head of ICHR (Wattan, June 30, 2018).

interpretation of the constitution and the question of principles and rules. He connected these "principles" of the constitution to "rules" arguing there are "decisive" rules (*aḥkām qaṭʿiyya*) that are not changeable, but "presumptive rules" (*aḥkām ẓanniyya*) that can be interpreted according to time and space. ʿĀbidīn rejected this argument stating, as mentioned above, that the word *ahkām* (rules) did not occur in any of the articles of the constitution.

The clash over the interpretation of the constitution remained unsolved. With regard to the family law-question, Nazār Ḥabash, the host, outlined two possible solutions: a civil law or a new interpretation of the Sharia. Whereas the women's organization, especially Al-Sinyūra as head of WCLAC were quoted to favor civil law, the position of the Ministry of Women's Affairs was more oriented toward harmonization and reached out to the Sharia establishment to discuss the matter and to find a compromise. The Minister of Women's Affairs Hayfāʾ al-Āghā agreed that the law had to be modernized. She pointed to the Family Protection Law against Violence, which would hopefully come soon, and a labor law, which was in process,[19] mentioning also the Legislation Harmonization Committee (LHC),[20] which had, as she stated, already made good progress. Sūnā Niṣār, Head of Women's Legal Affairs in the MoWA, suggested that one should go back to the texts and interprete them anew, stating that she worked together with the civil society organizations as well as with religious scholars and that many of them had good ideas for women's rights.[21] Al-Āghā and Niṣār both pointed to the problem that a woman's testimony is still considered only half of the testimony of a man (Quran 2:283). Whereas al-Āghā argued that in the Quran this would refer only to debt and commercial transactions, Niṣār, calling it "one of the most prominent problems" outlined the consequences for women working in the government and administration, more exactly for female Sharia judges and marriage officers: How can a woman, whose testimony is only worth half of man's testimony as a female judge or marriage officer testify to a marriage contract when their own testimony is deficient?

19 Hayfāʾ Al-Āghā, interview on April 9, 2019. Her assistant Sūnā Niṣār was present and outlined the state of affairs of the labor law. Al-Āghā complained that processes with regard to legislation are slow and that she wanted them to be quicker but could not influence the process.

20 She did not give the name, but it is clear from the context that she meant this committee.

21 At this point in the report, Ḥabash, the journalist, interfered and explained that these suggestions were rejected by the Supreme Judge. Al-Habbāsh is then shown sitting opposite Ḥabash saying: "We reject this unequivocally."

Her boss, Minister al-Āghā, took up an even more sensitive topic, pointing to Quran 4:3,[22] the polygyny verse, and the dire need for a new interpretation. This verse would not mean that the "door is wide open" for men, she warned, because God said: "but if you fear you will not be equitable, then only one." She argued that "if you fear you will not act just[ly]," it would be as if God wanted to say to the husband take only one. Generally, she was convinced that one could find solutions with a deeper reading of the texts. In my interview with her, she outlined that she would not extend consideration to abolishing polygyny because it was God's law. But it could be restricted. She also supported the obligation to inform the first wife, who should have the option to get divorced.[23]

This was a very civilized approach and a cautious attempt to start a debate about limiting polygyny, which had been restricted in other countries for a long time and in Tunisia even been abolished half a century ago.[24] Her reaching out to the Sharia establishment and suggesting a new – for Palestine – interpretation was nevertheless rejected by the already mentioned lecturer of Al-Quds University al-Kaswānī.[25] He made it clear that there are forbidden things or sacred topics (*al-muḥarramāt*) that cannot be touched upon; they are at the "heart of the Palestinian people." One of these, al-Kaswānī maintained, was polygyny: "Because polygyny is a principle (*aṣl*) in Sharia." It is unacceptable to touch those "sacred matters" (*muqaddasāt*), he warned. His choice of the religiously highly loaded term – *muḥarramāt* related to *ḥarām* (absolutely forbidden) and *muqaddasāt* – showed that he would not permit any further discussion about this with the Ministry of Women's Affairs.

Others did not go into the harmonization debate but were more concerned with the international perspective. Ashraf Abū Ḥayyah, lawyer of the al-Haq organization at this time, warned that if Palestine did not fulfill its obligations this would influence Palestine's reputation in the world.[26] ʿIwaḍallāh, who stated in the interview with him that "we believe in the mechanisms of international law,"[27] said it would be embarrassing for Palestine not to be against the discrimination against women on the international level.[28] But the member of the central committee of Fatah Nāṣir al-Qadwa stated that the international conventions put obligations on Palestine "we cannot fulfil." If so many conventions are signed at one time, he argued, it needs examination by the

22 Wattan, June 21, 2018.
23 Hayfāʾ Al-Āghā, interview on April 9, 2019.
24 Schneider 2014: 63–75.
25 Wattan, June 21, 2018.
26 Wattan, June 21, 2018.
27 ʿUmar ʿIwaḍallāh, interview on April 7, 2019.
28 Wattan, June 21, 2018.

legislative body and deep study because there is the obligation to harmonize them with the existing law.[29]

At this point Ḥabash, the host, explained to the audience that Palestine is under time pressure to reform the laws so that they are in harmony with international conventions before the Palestinian delegation heads to Geneva in July. He mentioned several amendments. In March 2018, the cabinet had decided to abolish the exemption of a rapist from penalty in case he married the victim.[30] A mother was now allowed to obtain a passport and to open a bank account for her minor children, and she gained the right to change their schools.[31] But all this was not considered sufficient by him and the thorny issues of family law had to be tackled. Ḥabash's conclusion at the end of this first part of this reportage was thus not encouraging. The changes mentioned were not at all enough, the whole family law would have to be changed, he said.[32] There should be a discussion about new interpretations of the Sharia to harmonize it with CEDAW and "translate" it into a personal status law. But it is precisely this matter that brings about the split between scholars of religion and politicians; a split that becomes wider because there are topics in the debate that are considered by some "religious taboos."[33] This can be read as a critique of al-Kaswānīs rude rejection of Al-Āghā's invitation to the discussion and as a hidden critique of the irreconcilability of the Sharia establishment, which was not ready to discuss certain topics as, e.g., polygyny simply by labeling them as taboo topics choosing the religious term *muḥarramāt*. Civil society had offered a compromise in opting for a civil law in addition to a family law based on Islamic law and the MoWA had offered talks to compromise on new interpretations. The offers had been rejected outright by the Sharia establishment, and the offer of an additional civil law seems not to have caused any reaction. Irreconcilable differences had appeared with regard to the position of the Sharia generally and its role in the constitution. But there was also no willingness to discuss detailed questions such as polygamy.

The first follow-up report[34] was the outcome of a meeting of the women's movement convened specifically because of the report in *Wattan* of June 21. The women thanked the media generally and *Wattan* especially for the role they played in initiating social discourse and concentrated on the aspect of international law, gender equality and the question how to amend or reform

29 Wattan, June 21, 2018.
30 See Article 308 of the JPL of 1960.
31 Wattan, March 5, 2018.
32 Wattan, June 21, 2018.
33 Wattan, June 21, 2018.
34 Wattan, June 25, 2018.

the law. All of them made it clear that the personal status law was outdated and had to be renewed. Ṣabāḥ Salāma, member of al-Muntada, explained that her organization had lobbied for a new personal status law for years now. Rīma Kitāna Nizāl, member of the Secretariat of the GUPW and member of the "Coalition for the Convention of CEDAW" (*I'tilāf Ittifāqiyya Sīdāw*), explained that they discussed the discrepancies between the applicable law and CEDAW and that they would launch a press campaign to amend this law. The first step would be to mobilize the citizens and inform them about the existing law and also to present the draft law that had been prepared by the women's organizations some time before.[35] The second step would be to form a coalition across different parties and organizations to stand up together for an amendment of the law on the basis of the woman's freedom, equal rights and dignity. To outline the intolerability of the legal position of women, Nizāl pointed – similar to Niṣār in the MoWA – to women working in the government, referring to female ministers[36] – who make decisions on the national level and enter into important contracts but with regard to marriage would need a marriage guardian themselves.

The second follow-up report contained an interview with al-Duwayk,[37] head of ICHR, exclusively. He argued that the creation of a new personal status law was necessary because Palestine signed the international convention but that it also was a "big challenge" (*taḥaddin kabīr*) and a sensitive topic (*mawḍūʿ ḥassāsī*). Among the most important and pressing problems he named the marriage age, saying "we are in favor of raising the marriage age," but also polygyny, which he described clearly as a violation of CEDAW and discrimination against women. He mentioned divorce, which according to CEDAW must be accessible equally for men and women and took great pains to explain that CEDAW claims equal rights for men and women, also in inheritance laws. To achieve the necessary harmonization, he believed in a pragmatic solution, the result of a discussion between religious scholars and legal scholars. Based on such a discussion he hoped the "split" could be eliminated and the contradictions solved. There should be *ijtihād* from inside Sharia to solve the sensitive topics in which contradiction is seen between international law and Sharia. Similar to al-Āghā, the Minister of Women's Affairs, he argued that Sharia was wide enough to adapt new interpretations, and he pointed to the experiences in other Arab

35 In an interview on April 8, 2019, Munā al-Khalīlī, General Secretary of GUPW explained that all the women's organizations now were about to get together, and distribute the tasks to be prepared for the mission of working on a new family law; see also Maannews December 19, 2018.

36 One form is in the plural: *wazīrāt*, i.e., female ministers, but then in the singular.

37 Wattan, June 30, 2018.

and Muslim countries like Turkey, Malaysia, and Tunisia.[38] But where were the Sharia representatives in this debate? While outlining the potential of Sharia to be developed and adapted to international standards of equality, al-Duwayk criticized that there were still reservations among the scholars and a still "masculine thinking" (*ʿaqliyya dhukūriyya*), a "non-openness" of thinking. Debate was necessary, as the state is obliged to harmonize the laws with international law. But what happened so far was judged by him to be only "superficial talk" (*ḥadīth saṭḥī*). There had to be a "serious, deep and open debate" (*ḥiwār jaddī wa-muʿammaq wa-ṣarīḥ*). On the one hand, he obviously aimed to calm down the conflicts and the "split" that had become visible in the first report, but on the other hand, he seemed eager to trigger a more objective and result-oriented in-depth debate and to build bridges between the positions of the religious scholars and politics.

Confronted by the Supreme Judge's opinion that Islamic Sharia is "the principal source" for legislation in Palestine and stands above international conventions, however, he supported the position of the jurists, and, pointing to Article 4 (2), as ʿĀbidīn argued, the "principles of the Islamic Sharia are *a* main source (*maṣdar raʾīsī*) of the legislation," not *the* source of legislation. He also explained that there is certainly a difference between "Sharia" and "principles of Sharia." It means that the legislator has to take these "principles" into consideration – all arguments that had been put on the table by others before but without success. However, whereas ʿIwaḍallāh had stated generally that international law is above national legislation and that the SCC had made this clear, al-Duwayk commented on the two judgments of the SCC. The first had argued that international law is generally above national law and could be applied directly without publishing it in the Official Gazette; the second judgment had stated, differently from the first one,[39] that international law has to be published and that legislation has to be harmonized with it, and that this harmonization means harmonization with "national, religious and cultural identity." He conceded that this meant the SCC put de facto reservations on the international conventions. But this cannot be, al-Duwayk argued, as the SCC cannot put reservations on international conventions, only the state can. In the end, there has to be a debate, there has to be a choice of priorities. As the Palestinians signed the conventions without reservations, they have to define the priorities. The lawyers have signed to many international conventions.

38 The selection of countries with more progressive gender policies, such as Turkey and Tunisia, reflects his inclination toward a gender equal interpretation of Sharia, Turkey actually having abolished Islamic law a long time ago.

39 See 2.1.3.

With regard to personal status, "we are in favor of the amendment and harmonization of all laws including the personal status law," but there has to be a debate, and "cultural sensitivity" has to be taken into account. There must be the possibility of gradual advance (*tadarruj*). Demanding a serious debate and openness, ʿAmmār al-Duwayk's subtext is clear: a solution has to be found, the real debate has not yet started, Sharia can be developed toward gender equality, but it means openness and willingness from all sides, to give up "masculine thinking," to enter into a result-oriented debate. His contribution can be understood as an attempt to connect to different positions in the legal iterations, to build bridges between the controversial positions as reflected in the first part of the reportage, but also to make clear there had to be an amendment of the law in light of international standards of women's rights. Again, his voice was not heard by the important players in the iteration and the respronsible persons in the Sharia establishment.

8.2 Developments through the End of 2018

On October 5, three months after the delegation had returned from Geneva, GUPW published excerpts from the National Workshop for the Coalition of the Personal Status Law (*Iʾtilāf Qānūn al-Aḥwāl al-Shakhṣiyya*).[40] Intiṣār al-Wazīr, Head of GUPW, pressed for a unified personal status law in Palestine not only to honor the Palestinian women's fight but also because in the present political situation – she referred to the policy of US President Donald Trump[41] – she saw it as necessary to have this law soon, she described it as an urgent task of the Coalition. The coordinator of the Coalition Haytham ʿArār supported this task, complaining about not only the plurality of applicable laws but also their rootedness in the patriarchal system (*al-niẓām al-abawī*) and the primacy of the masculine gender (*al-awlawiyya al-dhukūriyya*). She pointed to the problem of the marriage age, which is below eighteen, and the marriage guardian, who could in certain cases, when the woman is a widow and has no other close male relative, also be the son of the bride. She concluded from this that the woman has no legal capacity (*ahliyya*). Al-Sinyūra of WCLAC pointed to the urgency to publish the accession to CEDAW in the Official Gazette.[42]

40 See GUPW October 5, 2018.

41 The US President had in 2018 moved the US embassy from Tel Aviv to Jerusalem and, despite promising a solution of the Palestine-Israel Question, had done nothing to solve the conflict, see *The Guardian*, January 1, 2019.

42 GUPW October 5, 2018.

The debate was fueled by two issues. First, the idea was aired to add reservations to the international conventions retroactively.[43] It is unclear where and when exactly this talk originated, but by the end of 2018, it was widely discussed in Palestine. In an interview with him in April 2019, ʿIwaḍallāh admitted that there had been a discussion but stated that there had never been a serious push toward this because it would not be possible, he outlined in an interview with me.[44] And second, there was the talk of the *Qāḍī al-Quḍāt*. Al-Habbāsh, on a Palestinian television program on December 1, 2018,[45] mentioned in the beginning of this chapter, in which he defended, based on the Quran, a light "educational beating of women." In the program "Violence against Women: The Position of Islam" the host, after welcoming his "permanent guest" Dr. Maḥmūd al-Habbāsh, introduced the topic saying that some men base their actions on a "misconception" (*mafhūm khāṭiʾ*) of the phrase "beat them" in Quran 4:34 and asked al-Habbāsh for an interpretation, obviously hoping for a clarification that such "misconceptions" would be corrected.[46] But al-Habbāsh used the opportunity to explain that the verse is an indisputable order (*amr musallam bihi*), is the holy text and a "holy order" (*amr muqaddas*). It deals with female (mis)behavior, and it is a gradual advance (*tadarruj*) to chastise a woman's wrong behavior. Who are these men who are allowed to beat women in order to admonish them? Whereas normally the discussion around this verse focuses on the husband's right to beat his wife,[47] he outlined that the group of men being permitted to beat women is broader and includes beside the husband also the father, the brother, society and last, but not least, the governing authority (*al-sulṭa al-ḥākimiyya*). To "banish them to their couches" is especially reserved for husbands, of course, but the other two options are open to these other categories of men, too.[48] Asking whether non-hurtful, "educational

---

43 At the end of 2017, several of my interviewees indicated that there should have been reservations made when Palestine acceded to CEDAW and now these reservations had to be made belatedly.

44 ʿUmar ʿIwaḍallāh, interview on April 7, 2019.

45 Āfāq, December 1, 2018.

46 The whole verse, parts of which are quoted during the interview by al-Habbāsh, is in Arberry's translation as follows: "Men are the managers of the affairs of women for that God has preferred in bounty one of them over another, and for that they have expended of their property. Righteous women are therefore obedient, guarding the secret for God's guarding. And those you fear may be rebellious admonish; banish them to their couches, and beat them. If they then obey you, look not for any way against them; God is All-high, All-great." For the translation of "men are managers" see fn. 188, chapter 2.

47 Schneider 2014: 46–55.

48 *Wa-hjurūhunna* has been translated differently, not only "banish them to their couches" as Arberry does, but also "forsake them in the bed." For other translations, see https://www.islamawakened.com/quran/4/34/default.htm, accessed January 22, 2019.

beating" is a means to correct behavior, the Supreme Judge mentions that there is perhaps disagreement about the beating and the host comments: "That means the form or forms of violence." Al-Ḥabbāsh then felt obliged to define violence (*ʿunf*), which he understood not only as physical violence but also, for example, psychological or verbal violence. It is a transgression of a special limit and "educational beating" (*ḍarb taʾdībī muʾaddib*) differs from a violent beating (*ḍarb ʿanīf*). Women reading the verse should know that in case of *nushūz*, i.e., in case they do not obey they risk punishment. When the host asked why a woman should not be allowed to also beat her husband, the Supreme Judge answered with an explanation of a general difference between men and women saying that women were more sensitive and that this was even a "kind of preference" (*nawʿ al-tafḍīl*) for her gender.[49] Generally – he obviously meant: for men – it is allowed to beat a man as anchored in Quran 24:2 where it is said the "fornicatress and the fornicator – scourge each one of them a hundred stripes." The host asked what a woman should do who is beaten by her husband and does not dare to speak out. The Supreme Judge than explained that any man beating a woman without reason does something forbidden (*ḥarām*), meaning, of course, that beating with a reason as he had defined before, i.e., for educational reasons, is allowed. And he made this again clear when stressing that a disobedient woman (*al-marʾa al-nāshiz*) can be beaten. A woman having to endure "not-rational" beating, however, has a choice. She can endure it and hope it becomes better or turn to her family. He recommends that she should endure it first and see if the husband's behavior improves.[50] In the end, he connected all this with general advice to respect women as mothers and wives, i.e., in their sexual and reproductive function. His message was clear: generally hitting women is allowed; in marriage, a man can beat the woman, not the other way round; and women who are beaten should first be patient and give men the chance to regret their behavior.

The interview had been conducted at a time in which other sides – politicians and civil society – had, as described above, reached out to get an idea of how to harmonize international with national law, in a situation in which Palestine was under pressure to prepare for the second report for CEDAW in 2020 and before the backdrop of a Family Protection Law against Violence, which had been drafted in 2017 and praised highly by the civil society as well as in the political realm but had not yet been put into force. His speech caused a stir, as described in the beginning of this chapter, and was criticized harshly

49 Āfāq, December 1, 2018.
50 Āfāq, December 1, 2018.

in the Palestinian public, whereas there was, to the best of my knowledge, no public support for him. It was even classified as "hate speech."

As an answer to the *Qāḍī al-Quḍāt*'s provocative statements and to discuss at the same time the circulation of the idea to add reservations to the already signed conventions, Nāhid Abū Ṭaʿīma invited Munā al-Khalīlī, Coordinator of the "Coalition of CEDAW" and member of the General Secretary of GUPW, and ʿIṣām ʿĀbidīn, legal advisor to Al-Haq, onto a television program called "Critique of Hate Speech (*khiṭāb karāhiyya*) and the Intention of the Government to Make Reservations on International Conventions,"[51] bringing together these two developments in the iterations around international law and women's rights. Under her sway, the two legal experts tackled the two problems in an atmosphere of surprise and anger about this development. Abu Ṭaʿıma, the host, posed the decisive question at the beginning: "Does the state have two speeches, a religious and a political speech?" From her questions and comments it became obvious that she, herself, was worried about the development and supported the women's organizations' point of view: "Shouldn't we raise [our] voice in a different way?" she asked al-Khalīlī and pointed to twenty-five years of fighting for women's rights. What was the position of the invited guests with regard to possible reservations at that time, i.e., four years after CEDAW had been signed, and what was their position with regard to the *Qāḍī al-Quḍāt*'s hate speech? Was there a relation seen between these two topics?

With regard to possible reservations, both guests in the program voiced more than once their surprise about the addition of reservations at such a late stage. They complained about the lack of transparency, lamenting that the situation was not clear and no information had been given by the government and the ministries. There had obviously been a paper from a ministry about this, but it was not published.[52] ʿĀbidīn held the opinion that filing reservations at that time made no sense at all and would result in a loss of international respect for Palestine. The problem was not only the reservations, but an "emptying of the contents of the conventions," which should instead be implemented.[53] Just signing international conventions was not enough, they have to be put in force, he argued and outlined that for a state under occupation like Palestine, it would give a bad impression to fight for the right of self-determination but not to respect human rights.[54] Complaining that none of the drafts, e.g., the

51 Abū Ṭaʿīma, December 20, 2018.
52 Abū Ṭaʿīma, December 20, 2018.
53 Abū Ṭaʿīma, December 20, 2018.
54 Abū Ṭaʿīma, December 20, 2018.

penal law draft, had been made ready for enactment,[55] ʿĀbidīn saw in this development a missing political aim behind the enforcement of these international conventions. For him, the discussion of inserting reservations at that time was absurd, and he suspected that policy had buckled before the voices against international law. He also hinted to different positions in the different ministries and representatives of the government but but did not elaborate on this point.

Al-Khalīlī also uttered her surprise about this development four years after the accession to CEDAW and presented the point of view of the GUPW, which was similar to ʿĀbidīn's opinion: it was not right to discuss reservations at that time, because Palestine wanted to become a part of the community of nations.[56] The women's organizations planned to meet with the president and discuss the matter with him and with the different parties who should outline their positions in the matter. She also pointed to the obligation of Palestine to submit a second report in the near future, i.e., 2020.[57] She argued that the accession to CEDAW had been a success of the women's movement in Palestine[58] but was disappointed with the state and its representatives. During the previous two weeks there had been attacks on the women's movement and on CEDAW but no support of the state representatives, she complained. The Women's Affairs minister had promised a press release with regard to the Family Protection Law against Violence, but this did not come. Despite all these developments she was still ready to see the signature of CEDAW generally as a positive and important step, and she also had not yet lost all hope that there would be a good end, i.e., no reservations would be added to the signature.[59] When Abū Ṭaʿīma hinted at obstruction and delay in the issuing of these laws, al-Khalīlī pointed to the LHC as a possible solution. Abū Ṭaʿīma, the host, forgot for a moment her position as a host and became impatient at this point exclaiming emotionally: "They don't want to harmonize, Professor Munā!" referring obviously to the Sharia establishment. Al-Khalīlī agreed with this but was not yet ready to give up hope: "Yes, but we have to push it in this direction!"[60]

With regard to the second topic of the program, the Supreme Judge's speech, both guests in the program condemned it unequivocally. ʿĀbidīn attacked the Supreme Judge, criticizing his aim to make his office an institution

55 Abū Ṭaʿīma, December 20, 2018.
56 Abū Ṭaʿīma, December 20, 2018.
57 Abū Ṭaʿīma, December 20, 2018.
58 Abū Ṭaʿīma, December 20, 2018.
59 Abū Ṭaʿīma, December 20, 2018.
60 Abū Ṭaʿīma, December 20, 2018.

of the executive.[61] This absolute power of the Supreme Judge undermined the independence of the judiciary and the principle of the separation of powers, he warned.[62] Referring to the interview, he reproached the Supreme Judge that beating is prohibited not only by international law, i.e., CEDAW, but also by Article 132 of the JLPS, which gives a woman the right to divorce when she is damaged.[63] Al-Khalīlī, too, regretted the development and voiced her incapacity to understand it, rejecting outright what she had always rejected, as she stated, the "religious talk."[64]

Abū Ṭaʿīma asked for a connection between the two topics of her program – the impending reservations and the hate speech. When al-Khalīlī talked about the resistance some people had against CEDAW and asked whether the government would insert the reservations for this reason, Abū Ṭaʿīma became more outspoken and connected the two topics herself, arguing that the hate speech made evident who is against women's rights. "Which should be the steps taken?" she asked, pointing to twenty-five years "and all the work we spent" in fighting violence against women. Al-Khalīlī answered that it is the president who governs the country, there was a government responsible for politics, there are politics and strategies and international obligations Palestine has to fulfill. She thus obviously regarded al-Habbāsh's interview as something that should not be taken too seriously, hoping that the government would step in. At this point ʿĀbidīn added an observation, as he had heard an interview with a judge from the HSC voicing publicly: "We have obtained a letter and we will put the reservations we want into CEDAW." He took this as proof – and saw a connection of the two topics here – that politics sided with the Sharia establishment. Abū Ṭaʿīma confirmed this connection and, accusing the *Qāḍī al-Quḍāt* of being against human rights and even allowing the hitting of women, she blamed him for claiming the responsibility to make the law and added "all these things are connected: the hate speech, challenging the whole system as well as international law."

The program was not very clearly structured, there were repetitions and in the end there was no clear answer to the question asked in the beginning whether the state would have "two speeches." But there was a connection identified between the Supreme Judge's hate speech and the idea to add reservations to CEDAW retroactively leading to a slowdown of the process of implementing the international covenants. Whereas al-Khalīlī had more confidence

61 Abū Ṭaʿīma, December 20, 2018.

62 Abū Ṭaʿīma, December 20, 2018.

63 Abū Ṭaʿīma, December 20, 2018.

64 Abū Ṭaʿīma, December 20, 2018.

in the state and its policy, in the "political speech," the other two, including the host, considered the "religious speech" obviously as powerful. They saw a great influence of the conservative part of the Sharia establishment on the policy of Palestine. What al-Duwayk had tried so hard to opt for, a "serious, deep and open debate" (*ḥiwār jaddī wa-muʿammaq wa-ṣarīḥ*), which, according to him, had not yet started, seemed now impossible. In 2017, and more so in 2018, the Sharia establishment, which had previously been strong in defending "women's rights" under Idʿīs and in suggesting concrete improvements of the law, more or less fell back to a position of issuing general statements – that Sharia is above international law – and defending gender inequality such as the position taken by al-Kaswānī, who outlined "taboo topics," the *muḥarramāt*, sacred topics, and the Supreme Judge with his support of "educational beating" of women.

It seems the Sharia establishment fought with all means against a "harmonization": indirectly and behind the scenes, pressing for reservations to be added to the conventions, while in public debate, its representatives tried to block a thorough discussion about a possible new interpretation of the problematic legal regulations and stuck to what al-Duwayk had called "superficial talk." There had been many promises of the delegation of the State of Palestine in the CEDAW meeting, as reflected in the reports, as well as clear requests of the Committee: for instance, to adopt, "without delay" national legislation that would end discrimination against women; to publish the text of the Convention and make clear that the SSC's judgment did not actually contain reservations; to sign the Optional Protocol; to allocate more funds to the Ministry of Women's Affairs; and to adopt a comprehensive strategy to eliminate discriminatory stereotypes.[65] None of these requests had been finalized by the end of 2019.[66]

8.2.1 *Summary*

The debates in the second phase of the iterations (2014–2018) substantially differed from the debates in the first phase (2012–2014) under the following aspects. First, the visibility and active participation of the actors were different. This time representatives of the state played a more active role and sometimes even took the leading role in the media. Lawyers and especially constitutional lawyers voiced their interpretation of the BL and put it against the interpretation of the Sharia establishment. All of them agreed that after signing, Palestine had to fulfill the obligations arising from it and that signing was an important

65 CEDAW July 25, 2018: 7–8.

66 The State of Palestine had, however, ratified the Optional Protocol as stated above in fn. 2 of this chapter.

step on the way to becoming internationally regarded as a state. There was a common aim of lawyers and civil society organizations to fight discrimination against women and a concern to protect the international reputation of Palestine. Still nothing moved ahead.

The women's minister, al-Āghā, suggested cautiously a new (for Palestine) interpretation to curtail polygyny, ʿIwaḍallāh of the Ministry of Foreign Affairs voiced his opinion that no religion could be in favor of discrimination against women. In the discussion with Judge Ṣumūd al-Ḍamīrī[67] he admitted that exchange between religious and legal scholars was necessary and regretted that he could not "clone" al-Ḍamīrī thus praising her invaluable knowledge in Islamic law in connection with the wish to improve women's rights according to international standards and find a way to implement reforms in compliance with Islamic jurisprudence. He was aware of the necessity to find and connect to persons who had the necessary knowledge, like her, of Islamic legal terminology and classical law, who are able to make "uses of the past" and use this knowledge to improve the situation of women. And who, like Judge al-Ḍamīrī, know from court experience which are the most pressing articles in the laws that need reform. On the other side, all representatives of the state, but also the just-mentioned Judge al-Ḍamīrī as a Sharia scholar and representative of the Sharia courts, were clear in that the signature on international documents had consequences for the national legislation and that inserting reservations at this point was no longer possible. Al-Ḍamīrī had accompanied the Palestinian delegation to Geneva and generally has much experience in working with colleagues from other Arab and European countries and thus is well acquainted with the international discourse. Persons such as the Supreme Judge, al-Habbāsh – but also Yūsuf Idʿīs – never before left the circle of Arab countries and do not speak English. Their knowledge of the international perception of Palestine is thus limited.

The LHC had been created[68] and ʿIwaḍallāh informed me in my interview with him that it was under the supervision of his ministry, the Ministry of Foreign Affairs, together with the Ministry of Justice and the main aim was to

---

67 ʿUmar ʿIwaḍallāh, interview on April 7, 2019. Al-Ḍamīrī introduced me to ʿIwaḍallāh. She also arranged the interviews with Dr. al-Āghā and Munā al-Khalīlī and Īmān ʿAbdalḥamīd of the Legislation and Advisory Bureau and she was present during these interviews. I am grateful to her for arranging this for me.

68 In the interview with him on April 7, 2019, ʿUmar ʿIwaḍallāh admitted, that the creation of this committee was not yet completed and that it had not yet started its work. His assistant ʿAbīr ʿAbdalḥaqq, who was also present, commented that the process would be difficult because of the "mentality of the judges" who thought that CEDAW was against Islamic law.

harmonize the "two big laws": the penal code and the personal status law. The target was what he called a "comprehensive vision" of the laws of the state of Palestine. The heritage of the "old" laws is not accepted anymore, there has to be a new unified law. He also stated that the accession to the international laws gave the opportunity to harmonize the existent laws. "It is a big challenge, but it is an opportunity," he said.[69]

International pressure, as argued by Risse and Sikkink (1999),[70] was important insofar as the perception of Palestine was used by the civil society but also state representatives to promote the implementation of international covenants, especially CEDAW, a procedure that had been started with an act of the president – the signature of a whole bundle of conventions – and state representatives travelling to Geneva to defend their policy "at home." The representatives of the state who travelled to Geneva would have to bear the responsibility to the international community that the obligations resulting from these signatures would be fulfilled. They were under enormous pressure, as the CEDAW Committee had given them only until 2020, to do their job. Whereas they were supported by the civil society, the Sharia establishment or at least important representatives of it reacted negatively. The relation between state and Sharia establishment in this matter ranged between outward clashes, cautious attempts to take first steps in the direction of harmonization in combination with offers how the Islamic law could be reformed. Clashes ocurred between jurists and the Sharia establishment, as was indicated in the title of the TV program of *Wattan*, where especially ʿIwaḍallāh (Ministry of Foreign Affairs) but also ʿĀbidīn, a member of civil society, harshly criticized the *Qāḍī al-Quḍāt* for his misinterpretation of the Basic Law. Cautious attempts to take a step toward what was considered the Sharia establishment's very own task, the interpretation of Sharia, were made by al-Āghā when she suggested a new understanding of polygyny. Her thoughtful arguments were rejected brusquely by a representative of the Sharia establishment, al-Kaswānī, who on a general level had admitted that Islamic jurisprudence can change in time and space but who was very clear that there are topics that cannot be touched, "sacred topics," such as polygyny. These matters Ḥabash, the host, called correctly and in accordance with Foucault's analysis of discourse matters of religious "taboos" and marked them as the reason why the split between religious scholars and politicians became wider. Thus, what could be debated and what could not be debated was decided at least at this point by the Sharia establishment. The exchange between a state representative – a minister after all – and a

69 ʿUmar ʿIwaḍallāh, interview on April 7, 2019.

70 See chapter 7.

lecturer of a university reflects perhaps even better than the *Qāḍī al-Quḍāt*'s odd permission to beat disobedient women the strength and self-perception of the Sharia establishment, their claim to the monopoly of defining and dealing with "taboo" matters and deciding what could be discussed and what could not be discussed.

The Sharia establishment can be seen as the great counter-party of the state in this phase of the iterations. The role of the *Qāḍī al-Quḍāt* was especially clear: he was not against harmonization with international law but Sharia is above law, he stated.[71] He was supported in the TV program of June 21, 2018, by Judge Muṣṭafā al-Ṭawīl, head of Sharia High Court, and Jihād al-Kaswānī, lecturer at Al-Quds University. Judge al-Ḍamīrī approached the matter from a different angle being convinced not only that there has to be a harmonization and reform from within Sharia, but also that it is possible to go ahead with cautious steps, taking into consideration the need of the women in Palestine suggesting the areas this could reach and outlining the means.[72]

Civil society and especially the lawyers in civil society, on the other hand, considered the signing of the conventions as an opportunity to press for a new family law – after the discussions of 2013 had become dormant. They were very present in the public, opting, as al-Sinyūra, for a civil law if necessary in addition, and they did not tire of pointing to the many existing inequalities in law and how these were in violent breach of international law.

With regard, second, to the content of the debates, a major difference to the first phase of 2012–2014 was voiced by al-Duwayk: the debate was and remained "superficial talk" (*ḥadīth saṭḥī*) and did not go into depth. It was a general clash of statements – that Sharia was above international law, international conventions after having been signed needed to be adapted, harmonization was necessary – but *how* this could be achieved was not talked about. The "two speeches," the religious and political, did not come together. Other than in the *khulʿ* discussion there was no terminological debate. The important and central term would have been of course "equality" (*musāwāh*). A possible Islamic counterterm, which had already been used in the 59/2012 *taʿmīm*, was *mumāthala* (similarity), which referenced the Quran. But these words were not debated or filled with content. *Khulʿ*, being defined even in its castrated version of *khulʿ* before consummation, had been established as a counter-term to men's *ṭalāq* and thus served as a starting point for the discussion – as it was in Gaza.[73] This discussion, however, was not taken up. Responsibility can

71 See also Maḥmūd al-Habbāsh, interview on December 9, 2017.

72 Al-Ḍamīrī/Damiri 2018.

73 See chapter 9.

be given to the *Qāḍī al-Quḍāt*, whose talk remained on the general level, who did not admit openly that there should be changes with regard to women's rights and almost never mentioned concrete topics – e.g., the marriage age or *khulʿ* – to start with. In short, he did not make a substantial contribution to harmonize Sharia with women's rights. Al-Kaswānī, too, confined himself to reject al-Āghā's offer for dialogue. The discussion about subsequent reservations was surely fueled by this powerful intervention of the Sharia establishment, but it had died down in spring 2019, because to apply reservations after signing is at least a difficult process, if possible at all. But, as already stated, the process of discussing, drafting and enacting a new Palestinian family law had been blocked, too.

CHAPTER 9

Khulʿ and International Law in Gaza

The Gaza Strip has approximately 1.5 million inhabitants in an area of 360 square kilometres and is thus one of the most densely populated areas in the world. More than 75 percent of its population is registered as refugees with UNRWA.[1] The demographics in Gaza, particularly in relation to women, are, according to Sarah Adamczyk, "unique and at times paradoxical." Women in Gaza are very well educated but only 8 percent of them work.[2] More than 40 percent of women marry at the age of eighteen or younger. About half of the population is under fifteen years old.[3] The political situation affects the quality of living of the population. Israel's 2008–2009 military campaign against Gaza, for example,[4] caused women a lot of harm. Codenamed "Operation Cast Lead" and lasting from December 27, 2008, through January 18, 2009, it resulted in the deaths of 1,414 Palestinians in Gaza, including 118 women and 355 children, and an estimated 107,330 individuals were displaced. Eighty-three percent of these fatalities were civilians. A joint UNRWA and UNDP survey in August 2009 found 3,540 homes completely destroyed during the offensive, 2,870 sustained major damage, and 52,900 sustained minor damage. Nearly 800 women were widowed, many of whom then faced one or more personal status legal issues as a result.[5] Adamczyk's research concluded that widows in Gaza often find it difficult to live on their own, either due to financial or social constraints, and may be pressured to return to their family homes or remarry. Widows may also face manipulation and intimidation from their husband's families, including threats regarding custody of the children. This may be particularly so in the

1 Adamczyk 2011: 8.

2 Adamczyk 2011: 8.

3 Adamczyk 2011: 8.

4 There were two other operations in 2012 and in 2014 which had similar effects on Gaza's economy and infrastructure; for the later developments, see Human Rights Watch 2018.

5 Divorce, according to Berger (May 22, 2017), used to be rare in Gaza, but then became a topic of frequent public concern and was seen as an indicator of how bad Gaza's humanitarian and sociopolitical crises had become. For earlier and more detailed research, see Welchman 1999: 135–199. According to Al-Waheidi (June 4, 2017), a Gaza dating site represented a very new development in matchmaking: special dating sites organize mostly polygamous marriages often for widows of "martyrs." If the widow's deceased husband was affiliated with a political party, it is reported that this party might intervene and pressure the woman to marry a man from the same group. She will often agree because she is struggling financially, and the group would pay her a salary.

 | DOI:10.1163/9789004442313_010

wake of a military offensive where widows and orphans may receive (or may be perceived as receiving) increased international aid and martyr's payments from the Hamas government. Another indirect consequence of "Cast Lead" was increased rates of gender-based violence observed in Gaza. In a UNIFEM survey undertaken in March 2009, 70 percent of respondents in Rafah and 61 percent in Khan Younis noted increases in domestic violence in the months after the conflict.[6] The social and legal situation for women is thus very difficult in Gaza and surely more difficult than in the West Bank.

On the political level, Hamas had after the 2006 elections formed a majority in the PLC, and tensions had erupted between Hamas and Fatah culminating in the Hamas military takeover of the Gaza Strip on June 14, 2007.[7] Following Hamas's seizing of control, Israel imposed a full blockade of Gaza.[8] The blockade has severely hindered the economy and freedom of movement in Gaza.[9] Since then, Hamas has exercised control and functioned as the government in Gaza, which Nathan Brown would characterize as authoritarian because the "political system is completely bereft of any mechanisms of accountability."[10] Directly after Hamas's military takeover, a great part of the employees of the PA went on strike and, at least initially, the judiciary in Gaza ceased functioning. In November 2007, the authorities began appointing new judges and officials to replace those on strike. In January 2008, the Palestinian Bar Association, fearing that its members in Gaza would lose their jobs or simply be replaced, formally suspended the strike.[11] Soon after the split, Brown observed that Hamas began to take more forceful action against NGOs that were affiliated with Fatah. The organizations with high domestic and international profiles were particularly willing and able to resist governmental influence "with the result that several human rights and other organizations with a strongly critical stance have continued unscathed."[12] This is applicable to CWLRC (Center for Women's Legal Research and Consulting/*Markaz al-Abḥāth wa-l-Istishārāt al-Qānūniyya wa-l-Ḥimāya*) led by Zaynab al-Ghunaymī who plays a leading role in the iterations in Gaza around women's rights and family law and especially in the attempt to establish a *khulʿ* regulation.

6 Adamczyk 2011: 13–14.
7 Adamczyk 2011: 12.
8 Adamczyk 2011: 13.
9 Adamczyk 2011: 13.
10 Brown 2012: 1.
11 Adamczyk 2011: 13
12 Brown 2012: 7.

The Gaza government, Brown writes, "most fully resembles a state, at least in rudimentary terms, in the legal arena."[13] It has a "fully functional if imperfect judicial structure and improvised system that can draft a modest amount of narrow legislation."[14] But because of the division, it remains incomplete and has induced Hamas largely to postpone any Islamizing agenda. For 2012, Brown could work out that Hamas' first improvised structures in the legal system now work and litigants returned to court, whereas the originally established ad hoc conciliation committees became less active.[15] Nearly all of the Sharia court system judges in Gaza, who boycotted the courts when Hamas took power in 2007, were subsequently replaced with justices more sympathetic to the Hamas government.[16] The lack of continuity following the boycott and subsequent replacement of the previous judges under the PA and restrictions from the ongoing blockade of the Gaza Strip by the Israeli and Egyptian governments largely prevented, for example, judges' traveling abroad for rule of law training.[17] The blockade has also imposed severe financial burdens on the judges in the Sharia Court system. Salaries for judges have been reduced by an estimated 50 percent since the imposition of the blockade in 2007. Meanwhile, many of the previous Sharia court judges and officials who served under the PA have continued to receive their regular salaries from the Ramallah-based PA government while continuing their strike. While specific details are not available to Adamczyk, it is unlikely, she argues, that the Sharia court fees and taxes are sufficient on their own to guarantee the budget for the Sharia judiciary and it is likely that what funds are collected are supplemented through external sources and Islamic charities.[18]

Brown highlighted in 2012 three outstanding legal issues that the Gaza government has not been able to solve, which do not seem to have changed much by the time of this study. First, there is no clearly legitimate way to make law – but here the West Bank is in a similar situation. In the West Bank, as described, the president may issue decrees but does not do so in family matters. Instead, the *Qāḍī al-Quḍāt* stepped in and issued rulings, especially with regard to *khul*ʿ in 2012. In Gaza, the *Dīwān al-Fatwā wa-l-Tashrī*ʿ (Legislation and Advisory Bureau) and the cabinet continue to develop legislative proposals and submit them to the rump parliament that meets in Gaza every two weeks in the

13 Brown 2012: 10.
14 Brown 2012: 10.
15 Brown 2012: 10.
16 Adamczyk 2011: 25.
17 Brown 2012: 10–11.
18 Adamczyk 2011: 25.

presence of the *Kutlat*.[19] All non-Hamas members boycott it, according to Brown, Hamas members in the West Bank are barred from entering the parliament's meeting place in Ramallah, and large numbers of Hamas deputies are in Israeli prisons. But the Gaza-based deputies from Hamas do meet and claim that they hold proxies from jailed deputies as well as consult Hamas deputies in the West Bank by telephone. Such devices allow them, Brown shows, to assert that they have a quorum and to get majority votes. Until 2009, the year that Gaza regards President Abbas's term to have expired, the Gaza Parliament would submit laws to President Abbas, who ignored them. A constitutional provision inserted because of former President Yassir Arafat's refusal to act on parliamentary legislation allows a law to go into effect if the president fails to respond. Gaza used this tool, as Brown describes it, to declare laws enacted and published them in its version of the Official Gazette – here again parallel versions exist because the West Bank has its own version of its Gazette. Since 2009, Gaza has regarded the president's office as vacant, so presidential inaction is a given and laws go directly into effect.[20] This leads, second, to a deepening of the split and any law or regulation passed by the Gaza government is ignored in the West Bank and Gaza "returns the courtesy."[21] Lawsuits issued in Gaza are not recognized in the West Bank, but Gaza courts have enforced some West Bank judgments.

Brown states:

> Any legal enactment taken by either government drives the two entities further apart. Since the division is deeply unpopular among Palestinians – and the general sentiment among all but the most partisan seems to be that Fatah and Hamas fail to reconcile because they prioritize the interests of their movements over the national cause – extensive legislation is politically unpalatable. Thus, with a small and still-inexperienced staff and a constitutionally dubious set of procedures for making law, Gaza, like Ramallah, has generally curbed its legislative appetites in favor of the technical and necessary.[22]

---

19 Brown 2012: 11; *Kutlat al-taghyīr wa-l-iṣlāḥ*, the "Change and Reform Bloc" was the name of the list under which Hamas took part in the elections in 2006. Under this name it supervises the parliament sessions; see Wikipedia (Arabic): https://ar.wikipedia.org/wiki/%D9%83%D8%AA%D9%84%D8%A9_%D8%A7%D9%84%D8%AA%D8%BA%D9%8A%D9%8A%D8%B1_%D9%88%D8%A7%D9%84%D8%A5%D8%B5%D9%84%D8%A7%D8%AD, accessed February 8, 2019.

20 Brown 2012: 11.

21 Brown 2012: 11.

22 Brown 2012: 12.

A third point mentioned by Brown is that Hamas, an Islamist movement that is able to rule alone in the Strip, had to postpone any efforts at Islamizing the Palestinian legal order. Any step in this direction would bring "international condemnation and, more importantly, domestic grumbling."[23] Brown sees a sign for this in the postponement of a new criminal code that would be based on Islamic law and the reluctance of every official he contacted to even speak about this topic.[24]

The power struggle also effects the position of the Sharia judiciary. According to the website Ḥasan al-Jūjū is the Head of the Gaza HSCC (the Higher Sharia Court Council/*Raʾīs al-Majlis al-Aʿlā li-l-Qaḍāʾ al-Sharʿī*), which corresponds to the SCHC, the Sharia Court High Council in Ramallah.[25] On February 19, 2008, the *al-Aqṣāʾ*, a Gaza newspaper, reported that President Abbas had deposed al-Jūjū as Head of the Sharia Appeal Court (*Maḥkamat al-Istiʾnāf al-Sharʿiyya*) based on a decree of the SCHC.[26] Abbas referred to the BL and the Law of the Sharia Courts of 1973. Al-Jūjū called this decree "political" and not conforming to the law – like many other decrees Abbas issued. The BL did not give Abbas the right to depose the Head of the Gaza HSCC and did not give him the final mandate over the Sharia judiciary, he argued, and the 1973 Law of the Sharia Courts was not even applicable in Gaza. He announced that he would go on with his work.[27] An answer followed only two days later in the newspaper and online media *Wafāʾ*.[28] The Supreme Judge in the West Bank, at that time Taysīr al-Tamīmī, rejected the interference of the Executive Force of Ḥamas into the Sharia Court system stating that the SCHC deposed al-Jūjū with Decision (*qarār*) 8/2008 issued on February 11, 2008, because of his "forceful seizure of the *Dīwān Qāḍī al-Quḍāt* (*istīlāʾihi ʿalā Dīwān Qāḍī al-Quḍāt bi-l-qūwa*)." Al-Jūjū

23 Brown 2012: 12.

24 Brown 2012: 12.

25 Here as in many other areas parallel structures have been built up. There are two Sharia Court High Councils, for Gaza, see http://www.ljc.gov.ps/, accessed April 1, 2019. The Gaza version is named in Arabic *al-Majlis al-Aʿlā li-l-Qaḍāʾ al-Sharʿī*, which is translated into English as Higher Sharia Court Council (HSCC). Ḥasan al-Jūjū is named *Raʾīs al-Majlis al-Aʿlā li-l-Qaḍāʾ al-Sharʿī*/Head of Higher Sharia Court Council. On the Ramallah website, the representation is somehow different and it is presented as: *Dīwān Qāḍī al-Quḍāt*/Supreme Judge Department, here one of the bodies is *al-Majlis al-Aʿlā li-l-Qaḍāʾ al-Sharʿī*. The English version here (different from Gaza) is Sharia Court High Council (SCHC), see www.kudah.pna.ps, accessed October 19, 2017. See also 2.1.2.

26 *Alaqsavoice*, February 19, 2008.

27 *Alaqsavoice*, February 19, 2008.

28 *Wafa*, February 20, 2008; here the correct date is given, whereas in *Alaqsavoice*, February 19, 2008, it was stated erroneously that the decision was based on an order of the SCHC of December 11 instead of February 11, 2008.

had issued decisions to depose employees and to replace others, all of which was against the rules of the Islamic Sharia, the SCHC in Ramallah argued, against the BL, and against the independence of the judiciary. This action thus especially hurt the unity of the state and reaffirmed the split between the two parts of the homeland. Al-Jūjū was seen to have no mandate (*wilāya*) over the Sharia courts in Gaza, nor over their judges or their employees.The principle of the independence of the judiciary is a principle agreed upon by all schools of law (*al-madhāhib al-fiqhiyya*) in Islamic Sharia, the Ramallah-SCHC went on, as well as in all constitutions of the world and the only person responsible is the president.[29] To call the principle of the "independence of the judiciary" a "principle agreed upon by all schools of law" is a nice example of an anachronistic "use of the past" as it roots the modern concept of separation of powers in classical Islamic law.[30] The whole affair gives insight into the power struggle between the West Bank and the Gaza judiciary and the claim of the West Bank branch to be the legitimate representative of the Sharia judiciary in Palestine with the *Qāḍī al-Quḍāt*/Supreme Judge at its top.

When in 2012 the Supreme Judge and Head of the SCHC of the West Bank, Yūsuf Idʿīs, issued the ruling with regard to *khulʿ* divorce, giving women the right to divorce against the husband's will and therefore broadening women's access to divorce, at least before consummation, Judge al-Jūjū denied in an interview in Lāzim Naḥkī the legitimacy of this ruling, as already outlined. *Khulʿ*, he said, was applicable in Gaza in the version of *khulʿ* based on mutual consent, which could be agreed upon out of court as "reconciliation based on money with *ṭalāq* with a minor irrevocable divorce" (*muṣālaḥatan ʿalā māl bi-ṭalāq bāʾin baynūna ṣughrā*). It was applicable before and after consummation. What is applicable now in the West Bank, he continued, is *khulʿ* before consummation when the woman turns to the court and the judge desides to grant her request for a divorce. He stated: "This is an *ijtihād* that our brethren in the West Bank decided upon. But we want that this *ijtihād* goes through legislative channels (*ʿabra al-qanawāt al-tashrīʿiyya*)."[31] He reiterated that women could file a petition to get a divorce (*tafrīq*) if they were victims of damage.[32]

---

29 *Wafa*, February 20, 2008.

30 The position of the classical judiciary can in a certain way be called independent because the ruler could – at least in theory – not interfere in the jurisdiction of the judges. On the other hand, he had the right to appoint and depose judges at will – and in fact, there always seems to have been a parallel jurisdiction controlled by the ruler/state. See Schneider 1990; 1993.

31 *Lazim Naḥkī*, April 30, 2013.

32 He seems to refer to Article 97 of the EFRL, which will be dealt with later.

Arguing like this, he ignored the fact that exactly because of the split between Hamas and Fatah, there was no official legislative channel for all of Palestine to easily use.[33] Second, he ignored the fact that the West Bank ruling went further than anything regulated in the EFRL of 1954 and the JLPS of 1976, because it allowed divorce against the husband's will before consummation and made divorce for women based on "dispute and discord" after consummation easier. Third, he did not see any social necessity for such a ruling in Gaza. For this he was criticized by Judge Ṣumūd al-Ḍamīrī in the same television program. Al-Ḍamīrī claimed that the version based on mutual consent had always been available but that this was not a solution to the social problem of young women being left by their fiancés.[34] The Gaza lawyer Fāṭima ʿĀshūr in the same program had been taken by surprise with the question of *khul*ʿ.[35] She denied its application and use. It is not applied at all in Gaza, she stated with great emphasis (*ghayr muṭabbaq muṭlaqan*) and nobody talks about it, neither lawyers nor the people.

Not long after the West Bank ruling had been issued in September 2012, there had been a heated debate in the media, and among women's organizations in Gaza, with the aim of pressuring the Gaza government to reform the law on *khul*ʿ in Gaza. Women's organizations complained that there was no *khul*ʿ law and no legal regulation of *khul*ʿ in Gaza and demanded that the need be addressed. Women's agency was at the center of the debate: women should have the right to divorce.[36] No such regulation has been issued to date in Gaza (February 2019).[37] There was even a draft law regulating *khul*ʿ but instead, al-Jūjū issued a *taʿmīm* in 2016[38] that gave men the right to apply for divorce based on "dispute and discord" (*al-nizāʿ wa-l-shiqāq*) – a form of divorce that originally could be initiated by women only in Gaza.[39]

Sharia representatives and organs such as the *Majlis al-Aʿlā li-l-Qaḍāʾ al-Sharʿī* and the Sharia High Court – organs that exist in parallel in Gaza and Ramallah – and Muslim scholars play an important role in socio-legal iterations in Gaza as well as in the West Bank. Is their role decisive for the different

33 Schneider 2016b: 47–49.

34 *Lazim Naḥkī*, April 30, 2013.

35 *Lazim Naḥkī*, April 30, 2013. She said that she started to look for a *khul*ʿ regulation and later found several articles – obviously she refers to the regulation in Qadrī Bāshā, see fn. 52.

36 Othman 2015.

37 See the website http://www.ljc.gov.ps/index.php?option=com_content&view=article&id=32&Itemid=53, accessed February 8, 2019.

38 *Taʿmīm* 08/2016, see also 07/2016. See the website of the *Dīwān al-Qaḍāʾ al-Sharʿī*: www.ljc.gov.ps/images/court2016.pdf, accessed September 15, 2017.

39 EFRL Articles 97–107.

development of the *khulʿ* ruling in both parts of Palestine? Which differences and which common features in iterations about *khulʿ* and international law can be observed in the West Bank and Gaza?

There is a difference in legislation because Gaza has another applicable family law, the EFRL of 1954. Ḥasan al-Jūjū is head of the HSCC even if he does not bear the title of *Qāḍī al-Quḍāt* – a title left to the West Bank representative – but he is still a strong and influential jurist in the Gaza Sharia establishment. There is, as will be outlined below, a strong and very professional civil society fighting for women's rights. Whereas all social actors in Palestine – West Bank and Gaza – say they want to end the split and create one common Palestinian family law, there are today to the best of my knowledge, no common activities to achieve such a goal. How much influence will the jurists of Gaza have, how much input will the Gaza judiciary add to shaping the future judiciary of Palestine? Who "bells the cat" in Gaza?

These questions seemed to gain importance in light of political developments. On June 2, 2014, a unity government was sworn in, consisting of persons "whom Abbas has said would be politically unaffiliated."[40] Prime Minister Rāmī Ḥamdallāh, a former university president, led what was called by the *New York Times* a largely technocratic administration, made up of lawyers, business men and academics, all of whom were politically independent but had the approval of both Fatah and Hamas.[41] The members of the government took the oath of office in a televised ceremony in Ramallah. A number of ministers from the Hamas-run Gaza Strip, who were denied entry to the West Bank by Israel, were sworn in by teleconference.[42] In the fall of 2017, Hamas made the declaration to step back from government and hand over power to Fatah in Gaza.[43] The end of the political split, and therefore a political unification, elections and a parliament seemed possible in the near future. This development, however, turned out to be short-lived. On January 29, 2019, the Palestinian government resigned partly because reconciliation between Gaza and West Bank was not reached and the reconciliation project was considered to have made little progress.[44] On April 13, 2019, a new cabinet was sworn in with new Prime Minister Muḥammad Ashtiya, a development that was seen as a blow to faltering reconciliation efforts with Hamas. Still, upon presenting the

40 Kershner, January 29, 2019.

41 Kershner, January 29, 2019.

42 Khoury and Hass, June 2, 2014.

43 See *Haaretz*, September 20, 2017.

44 Kershner, January 29, 2019.

new government to Abbas, Ashtiya said that he will act to promote Palestinian unity and help prepare for parliament elections.[45]

How did representatives of the Sharia establishment and the civil society structure their arguments around the *khulʿ* debate and refer to the debates in the West Bank? And what were the gender models they strived to implement? How did Yūsuf Idʿīs (until 2014), Maḥmūd al-Habbāsh (since 2014) in the West Bank and Ḥasan al-Jūjū in Gaza, all heads of the *Majlis al-Aʿlā li-l-Qaḍāʾ al-Sharʿī* as representatives of the Sharia establishments but also counterparts anchored in two rival governments, act?[46] What was the state of the art in discussing and debating international law, CEDAW, and women's rights in Gaza? In the first section of this chapter, the legal setting of Gaza is dealt with and the situation of legislation in the realm of family law with focus on *khulʿ* and "dispute and discord" is laid out (9.1). In the next section (9.2), the *khulʿ* Draft Law as described in the Position Paper of the parliament and two rulings issued by al-Jūjū in 2016 as an answer to the ongoing discussions and pressure of the women's organizations regarding divorce are presented and discussed;[47] a short comparison with the legal situation in the West Bank (9.3) serves as background for the analysis of the heated debate between the Sharia establishment and civil society in Gaza in 2017 (9.4). The chapter ends with a conclusion (9.5).

9.1 The Legal Background of Gaza

Judicial divorce on grounds of "dispute and discord" (*nizāʿ wa-shiqāq*) in the applicable law in Gaza is closely connected to *khulʿ*. It represents, according to Lynn Welchman, "a limited adoption of Maliki rules on this area of divorce law, and was first made part of the applicable family law in the West Bank area in the OLFR of 1917."[48] The phrase "dispute and discord" refers to severe abuse by either one or both parties to the extent that marital life cannot possibly continue. If the judge failed to reconcile the spouses, he transferred the matter to two arbiters, who in turn exerted pressure toward reconciliation. If this arbitration process fails, the spouses would be separated by the judge on the

45 Khoury, April 13, 2019.

46 I could travel to Gaza in 2019 only for a day and a half, April 10–11. However, I was very lucky to have the chance to conduct interviews with Ḥasan al-Jūjū (April 10, 2019); Member of Parliament Hudā Naʿīm (April 10, 2019) and Zaynab al-Ghunaymī (April 10 and 11, 2019), representative of the civil society. My thanks go to Zaynab al-Ghunaymī, who is very well-connected and helped me to ask my questions.

47 *Taʿmīm* 07/2016 and *taʿmīm* 08/2016.

48 Welchman 2000: 367; Ebert 2010.

recommendation of the arbiters, with each spouse paying or forfeiting financial dues in proportion to the relative amount of blame attributed to them by the arbiters. The original text in the OLFR Article 130 permitted either spouse to apply for judicial divorce on grounds of *nizāʿ wa-shiqāq*. The Jordanian Law of Family Rights of 1951 restricted it to the wife only. Article 132 of the JLPS of 1976 returned to the original position by allowing either spouse to make such an application.[49] Under the Jordanian Law of Family Rights of 1951, Welchman argued, it had theoretically been possible for the wife to deliberately cause problems within the marriage until the husband unilaterally divorced her to save himself and his family from further embarrassment. In this case, the husband would have to pay his wife all her remaining financial rights. Under the terms of the JLPS, however, the husband may have recourse to the court in such a situation, and if he can establish the abuse by his wife, may obtain judicial divorce with the wife forfeiting an amount of her remaining financial rights in proportion to the blame attributed to her by the arbiters. In Welchman's case material in Palestinian courts under the JLPS of 1976 in 1985, only one was submitted by a man. The explanatory memorandum to the JLPS had justified the extension to the husband of the right to seek separation on grounds of *nizāʿ wa-shiqāq* by reason of the equality it afforded to the spouses as well as referring to the original position of the OLFR.[50]

According to the EFRL of 1954 applicable in Gaza, Article 97 reads as follows:

> Article 97: Separation of the wife by divorce due to dispute and discord
>
> In the event *the wife claims* that her husband caused damage [*iḍrār*] to her in a manner with which the continuance of the marital life has become impossible amongst the like of her [*sic!*, arab. *bayna amthālihā*], she may request separation from the judge. Thenceforth, the judge shall separate her by divorce in case the damage [*ḍarar*] is proven and he is incapable of reconciling them. If the request was first rejected, then the complaint was repeated and the damage was not demonstrated, the judge shall dispatch two arbiters and shall rule in the manner expounded under Articles 98, 99, 100, 101 and 102.[51]

Articles 98, 99, 101 and 102 deal with terms, conditions, and obligations of the arbiters, disagreement between them and the reporting of the arbiters' decision to the judge. Other than in the JLPS, according to EFRL Article 97, only

---

49 Welchman 2000: 367–368.

50 Welchman 2000: 368.

51 EFRL 1954, emphasis added.

the woman can request separation. The idea of a separation based on mutual consent is not to be found explicitly in the text of EFRL but left to the OLFR by default.[52] But *khulʿ* is mentioned in Article 100:

> Article 100: Arbiters' incapability of reconciliation between the spouses
>
> If the two arbiters are incapable of reconciliation and if the wrongdoing is on the part of the husband or on the part of both of them or if the situation was unidentifiable, they shall decide on the separation between them by one pronouncement of irrevocable divorce. *In the event the wrongdoing is on the part of the wife, they shall decide to submit her to Mukhala'ah* [divorce in return for a monetary compensation to be paid by the wife to the husband] for the whole of the dowry or for a portion thereof.[53]

Khulʿ or *mukhālaʿa* is thus regulated in the EFRL as an effect of a divorce due to "dispute and discord" and the related proceeding of reconciliation of the spouses.[54] This is what women's organizations referred to when they criticized the fact that there is no separate *khulʿ* law and not even an article in the applicable law that would enable a husband and wife to file a *khulʿ* claim, let alone a version of *khulʿ* that would allow a woman – if only before consummation of marriage – to redeem herself from her husband.[55] The woman has to ei-

52 OLRF 1917 deals with *nizāʿ wa-shiqāq* in Article 130. It has more or less the same regulation as the EFRL 100, but both spouses can file the claim. Welchman 1999: 161; see also Anderson 1951: 285–286. Furthermore, *khulʿ* is dealt with in Articles 273–297 in the codification of Qadrī Bāshā (ca. 1875): 96–101, see Ebert 2010: 96–102. Sometimes, e.g., Fāṭima ʿĀshūr in *Lāsim Naḥkī*, April 30, 2013, and Naʿīm: 2013: 2, reference to these articles seems to have been made without giving the name of the codification of Qadrī Bāshā but only generally to an "Ottoman law." Only consensual *khulʿ* is regulated. In Article 283, the case of *khulʿ* before consummation is mentioned. See also p. 115 fn. 78.

53 EFRL 1954, emphasis added.

54 See Reiter 2009: 17, referring to Article 130 of the OFRL of 1917 according to which in the case of "dispute and discord," the judge has to nominate the arbiters and decide based on their opinion. In this article, *khulʿ* is quoted in case the arbiters come to the decision that the divorce is the woman's fault and that she should repay her dower. This solution obviously was integrated into Article 100 of the EFRL of 1954. Reiter argues that Article 130 of the OFRL is based on the approach of Maliki scholars and some Shafii scholars according to which the arbitrators in matrimonial disputes are empowered to dissolve the marriage themselves, even if they do not have prior authorization by the spouses to take such action. The shift in Article 130 of the OFRL is made toward the decision of the judge and not the arbiters.

55 There is a *khulʿ*-before-consummation case described by Shehada in the time of her research in Gaza. A husband wanted to bring his wife, with whom he had not yet consummated the marriage, but to whom he had paid at least a part of the dower, to his house,

ther find an agreement with her husband – as Ḥasan al-Jūjū mentioned in the television program *Lāzim Naḥkī* of April 30, 2013 – or go through "dispute and discord" and prove "damage." If she cannot prove her case, she has to wait for the second round. On the one hand, this procedure secures the woman's right to get the dower, whenever the husband is found guilty or as the wrongdoer in the marriage. But on the other hand, divorce is not easily accessible for her, and if she cannot prove the "damage," she has to go through the process twice. It has been reported that, like in the West Bank, women had to wait sometimes for years – fifteen years was mentioned in Gaza – to get a divorce based on "dispute and discord."[56]

Ḥasan al-Jūjū's criticism of his West Bank brethren created the impression that the government in Gaza would approach legal problems only through "legislative channels," which could be taken as a reason not to reform the law through rulings by the HSCC. However, the website of the HSCC of Gaza is full of *taʿmīmāt*, even more than the West Bank website.[57]

---

using the legal term of the "house of obedience" (*bayt al-ṭāʿa*). He gave as a reason that she did not want to stay married to him but he wanted to persuade her to look at the apartment he had prepared for her, complaining that she "humiliated my *rujūla* (masculinity)." However, the judge explained to him that a virgin cannot be brought to the "house of obedience." There is not yet an existing marriage in which she could be in opposition to him. In the end, the woman was divorced in exchange for redemption (*ibrāʾ*), the normal term in a *khulʿ* case, see Welchman 2000: 166 fn. 15. But Shehada did not categorize it as a *khulʿ* case or discuss on what basis the separation happened. It would have been important to know the exact claim the husband had used in court (to bring her to the "house of obedience"?). Also, did the *khulʿ*, because she was divorced in exchange for redemption, happen in privacy? This is possible in Gaza and the West Bank or before the judge in court. Was it called *khulʿ* or *ṭalāq muqābil ibrāʾ ʿāmm* (divorce against complete redemption)? Regrettably, Shehada does not provide these important details and terms (Shehada 2005: 203–204). Instead she takes this case as an example of a "less conservative procedure" of the judge (Shehada 2005: 202) and speculates that the judge used "our customs and traditions" as an excuse not to force her into the "house of obedience." But in this case the mentioning of redemption *ibrāʾ* (Shehada 2005: 204) would not fit. The case also cannot be taken as proof for a "mainstream approach" in *fiqh* that does not favor the use of force to bring women to the "house of obedience" (Shehada 2005: 204) because the decisive fact in this matter seems to be that there had not been consummation. Also, she misinterpreted as *khutba* (engagement) the timespan between signing the contract and the actual consummation (Shehada 2005: 203), ignoring that there was already a marriage contract. For these reasons, her general results that Gaza judges are more flexible and "act as protectors" of women (Shehada 2005: 323) needs to be challenged. In addition, it would be useful to take a closer look at and conduct a deeper analysis of the cases taking into consideration Islamic legal history as well as the applicable law.

56 Othman 2015.

57 See http://www.ljc.gov.ps/index.php?option=com_content&view=article&id=32&Itemid=53, accessed January 30, 2019. The website is structured better than its counterpart in

With regard to prior history of the *khulʿ* iteration in Gaza, two rulings have to be looked at: *taʿmīm* 33/2009 and *taʿmīm* 09/2012.

- In *taʿmīm* 33/2009, Article 97 is quoted and it states that this article gives the woman the right to file a suit in case she cannot continue the marriage because of damage (*ḍarar*). The term "damage" is explained as harm done to her by word and deed and in cases where this damage is proved and the judge cannot mediate between the spouses, the judge can grant her request for divorce with a minor irrevocable divorce. In case her claim is rejected and she wants to resubmit, reference is made to Article 97, saying: "If the request was first rejected, then the complaint was repeated and the damage was not demonstrated, the judge shall dispatch two arbiters and shall rule in the manner expounded under Articles 98, 99, 100, 101 and 102." The *taʿmīm* thus only explains what repetition means: the ongoing marital dispute and the husband's damaging of her. And that in this case, the *qāḍī* can proceed according to Articles 98 to 102. This *taʿmīm* thus only clarifies what "damage" means exactly and explains or clarifies the law's wording, "the complaint was repeated."
- *Taʿmīm* 09/2012 (with reference to 33/2009) clarifies and amends the law's text in saying that the wife *may* resubmit her claim if she has new "causes and facts" (*asbāb wa-waqāʾiʿ jadīda*), but if not, it requires her to *to wait for six months* before resubmitting the claim. This requirement is new and had not been mentioned in the text of the law.

Khulʿ is, to summarize, not separately mentioned in the EFRL as a paragraph in its own right leaving by default the classical version of *khulʿ* in force. *Mukhālaʿa* in the EFRL has become part of the procedure of "dispute and discord," and a woman will have to pay back her dower in case she is found to be the wrongdoer. When she files a claim she cannot be sure about the outcome because if the arbiters find her guilty of wrongdoing, the claim she herself filed with regard to "dispute and discord" to get out of an unhappy marriage will turn into a claim against herself and endanger her financial assets. This, one could argue, is not in accordance with the traditional idea of *khulʿ* in which both spouses agree to separate, and women need not give a reason but must pay back the dower. It can be seen as an interesting version of how to codify classical *khulʿ* already in OLFR Article 130 by integrating it into another form of divorce. Generally, it was argued – and this was a main reason to reform the JLPS of 1976 through

Ramallah, because all the *taʿmīmāt* can be found easily on it with the whole text, which is not the case on the Ramallah website. An in-depth comparison of what has been regulated – how and what the differences and similarities might be between Ramallah and Gaza – would be of utmost interest but cannot be undertaken here.

the West Bank *taʿmīm* on *khulʿ* and "dispute and discord" in 2012 – that proof in those matters concerning "damage" is extremely difficult because "damage" is mostly done to women in the marital house without witnesses. Yūsuf Idʿīs's 2012 *taʿmīm* took this into consideration and spared women at the same time the obligation to provide proof of damage with regard to "dispute and discord" and put the matter into the hands of the judge.[58]

Ḥasan al-Jūjū explained on *Lāzim Naḥkī* on April 30, 2013, that the woman is the person who has been hurt (*maḥjūra*) but with this legal regulation in Gaza her dignity (*karāma*) would be preserved. The reference to a wife's "dignity" evokes the impression that the Gaza version of divorce is more in favor of women and protects them more than the West Bank *taʿmīm*. Women's groups and especially Zaynab al-Ghunaymī and the Center for Women's Legal Research and Consulting (CWLRC) in Gaza contradicted him vehemently in this representation, pointing out that easy and quick divorces for women in Gaza courts were nonexistent.[59]

9.1.1 *Associated Social Debates*

CWLRC,[60] one of the main actors of women's rights in Gaza had already in 2012 published a paper titled "Legal Document: Towards Justice and Fairness for the Woman in the Family Rights" (*Wathīqa Ḥuqūqiyya: Naḥw al-ʿAdāla wa-l-Inṣāf li-l-Marʾa fī al-Ḥuqūq al-ʿĀʾiliyya*).[61] In it, the Center developed many suggestions for amendments to the applicable law in Gaza. It dealt with divorce and especially the question of *khulʿ* in great detail, identifying the same problem as in the West Bank: young men and women sign the marriage contract at the beginning of their engagement, which "traps" the young women and the young men exploit this situation. Was this *Wathīqa* not known to Ḥasan al-Jūjū and Fāṭima ʿĀshūr when they delivered their statements in the West Bank TV program on April 30, 2013? The legal document (*Wathīqa Ḥuqūqiyya*) shows a high degree of professionalism and legal knowledge not only in the description of the social reality and the summary of the legal regulations in the applicable laws but also in suggested ways to heal this situation. It argues that Article 9 of the BL of 2003 guaranteed the equality of all citizens before the law and the judiciary

58 However, this process is not without problems, too; see chapter 4, fn. 108. The woman has to convince the judge that her husband does not support her argument and her dispute with him is well-known in the family and neighborhood.

59 Maannews, February 15, 2017.

60 See www.cwlrc.ps/en/about, accessed July 7, 2017.

61 The project of which this publication was an outcome was financed by the German Heinrich-Böll-Foundation and was titled "Towards a Better Future for Youth in regards to Marriage and Divorce," see CWLRC, June 4, 2013.

and non-discrimination of women and that the applicable law of 1954 was outdated and in contradiction to the BL and therefore had to be amended.[62] It argued that the divorce rate in Gaza in 2011 was as high as 17 percent, out of which 40 percent happened in marriages of young men and women who had a contract, but before the actual consummation of the marriage. Despite the fact that consummation did not occur, these couples were legally married, the *Wathīqa* stressed, and divorce had to take place according to the applicable law to give women their freedom. The *Wathīqa* laid out in detail the legal conditions of engagement and marriage under the heading "Engagement and Marriage Contract before Consummation" carefully differentiating between engagement as a "promise of marriage," not a contract and the marriage with contract. Engagement, it was stated, can be solved from both sides. The document outlines that for more than three decades in society the "marriage contract before consummation is considered to be engagement" (*iʿtibār ʿaqd al-zawāj qabl al-dukhūl ʿalā annahu khiṭba*), thus confirming Jumān Qunayṣ's assessment that such a custom developed during the last decades, and lays out the differences in the legal definition.[63] Families do not allow continuous relations between the engaged couple without an official contract. The time before the contract is just for both families to come to know each other, a time in which it is not possible for the engaged couple to meet on a regular basis. They should only see each other once or twice for some limited talk, which would not reveal their real "nature." This resulted in the custom of considering the time before the wedding ceremony (*marāsim al-zifāf*) and consummation (*dukhūl*) as the "engagement" despite the existence of the contract.[64] If there is no consent, the contract has to be solved legally according to Articles 67–102 of EFRL. As the husband has the main say in this, it happens, the *Wathīqa* explains, that he denied her the *ṭalāq* despite the dissent between them. His motive, according to the *Wathīqa*, may be revenge because she rejected him, or he wanted to take revenge on her family or to force her to give up her financial rights despite the fact that he was the reason for her wish to separate. This results in damage (*iḍrār*) for the girl, it was argued, because she would be called "divorced" in official documents and socially she would then be in a difficult situation, because it would take a long time to get the divorce in court and

62 CWLRC, July 8, 2013.
63 CWLRC, July 8, 2013.
64 CWLRC, July 8, 2013.

she would lose her financial rights.[65] The recommendations given refer in the *Wathīqa* to divorce before consummation.[66]

This analysis confirmed not only that in Gaza and in the West Bank the same socio-legal problem existed on the ground and people here and there contracted marriage contracts in anticipation, but also that a high percentage of legally married, but de facto engaged couples found out before the consummation that they did not match and wanted a divorce. Thus, contrary to what al-Jūjū and Fāṭima ʿĀshūr said on *Lāzim Naḥkī*,[67] there must have already been social awareness of this problem resulting in detailed deliberations by civil society in Gaza, obviously at the same time as discussions were going on in the West Bank. Gaza civil society's West Bank counterpart developed concepts to deal with this problem, which are very detailed and sophisticated. There seems to be one main difference from the West Bank iteration. In Gaza, the initiative seems to have come from civil society and not from the HSCC. Zaynab al-Ghunaymi confirmed this in my interview with her.[68] The *Wathīqa* not only analyzed the social and legal situation but also aimed to heal this legal situation and had "the aim to amend the personal status law with regard to the conditions of engagement and marriage."[69] The CWLRC's suggestions were developed to get a just solution, protect the rights of young women regarding Sharia regulations (*al-qawāʿid al-sharʿiyya*), the law and the constitution. It was argued that the aim was to have a sound and healthy family but if there was no understanding between the partners, the easiest way was to separate before the wedding ceremony. But it should only happen in a way that respects the rights of both, de facto fiancé and fiancée, because they are legally married. The document quoted Quran 2:229 and 2:231 to point to the necessity of a just procedure. CWLRC asked the bodies of the Sharia jurisdiction or the parliament or the executive power to quickly take measures to preserve the rights of the young women. They demanded that both partners – in the case of having a contract but not having consummated the marriage – should have the chance of dissolution (*faskh*) of the contract if either one of them did not want to continue the marriage. If the husband wished to cancel the contract, he should bear the financial consequences. There would be no refunding of the paid dower and presents. The woman, on the other hand, wanting to cancel

65 CWLRC, July 8, 2013.

66 CWLRC, July 8, 2013: 5. In a newer publication, work on establishing a new law that is in line with provisions of the Basic Law and CEDAW, and includes forms for ending marital relations is seen as necessary, see Moghrabi and Hassouna 2016: 55.

67 *Lāzim Naḥkī*, April 30, 2013.

68 Zaynab al-Ghunaymi, interview on April 11, 2019.

69 CWLRC, July 8, 2013.

the contract would have to pay back what she received and return the presents. In certain cases, the divorce should not be considered a dissolution (*faskh*) of marriage, e.g., in case of his sterility, a lasting or contagious illness; or if he took drugs or was guilty of immoral behavior (*irtikāb al-fāḥisha*), mistreatment or injury of the woman or – interestingly – if he intended (*thubūt nīya*) to harm her by marrying another woman during litigation.[70] The *Wathīqa* thus not only gave a clear analysis but also developed sophisticated legal solutions for these complicated and special situations of a "marriage-engagement." In the West Bank, women's organizations had developed the idea of a special engagement time but had not been able to convince the Sharia lawyers how this could be put into a legal regulation.

On July 29, 2013, the head of CWLRC, al-Ghunaymī invited Judge al-Jūjū officially for August 22, 2013, to participate in a discussion on the topic "Legal Amendment to End the Marriage Contract before Consummation," which was financed by the German Heinrich-Böll-Foundation. Other participants were experts from different ministries, the parliament, and the legal sector. Following this round of discussion, Ḥasan al-Jūjū announced in the media on August 22, 2013,[71] an amendment (*taʿdīl*) of the law with regard to *khulʿ* by the end of the next year (i.e., 2014). Now he explained that the HSCC wanted the "judicial *khulʿ*" as well as *iftidāʾ* because the legal regulation was restricted to the agreement of both spouses. *Iftidāʾ* was defined by him as the woman's redemption on the basis of her dower. Asked what the content of the document reportedly signed with CWLRC was, he stated: "We are in agreement with any substantial amendment of the personal status law to come to a law that combines the contemporary (*muʿāṣira*) with the authentic (*iṣāla*)."[72] He added that the Palestinian split is hindering this goal, but expressed his aim to facilitate women's position and to support Palestinian women and end the injustice (*ẓulm*) done to them and end their suffering. With regard to the divorce before or after consummation he said that more research was needed.[73]

On November 13, 2013, there was a final conference of CWLRC with Ḥasan al-Jūjū and Saʿīd Abū al-Jabīn, Judge of the High Sharia Court in Gaza (*al-Maḥkama al-ʿUlyā al-Sharʿiyya*) according to which it was again corroborated that *khulʿ* should be possible for the woman without the husband's agreement. In these cases the woman could file a claim at the court.[74] In addition,

70 CWLRC, July 8, 2013: 5.

71 See Alwatanvoice, August 22, 2013; see also Abū Ṭaqiyya 2013, a media report published on October 31, 2013.

72 Alwatanvoice, August 22, 2013.

73 Alwatanvoice, August 22, 2013.

74 See CWLRC, November 13, 2013; See also Maannews, February 15, 2017.

CWLRC had announced in a paper[75] that the HSCC in Gaza had agreed to the requests of the CWLRC made in the aforementioned *Wathīqa* to make repudiation (*ṭalāq*) before consummation easier and at the same time to not change the marital status and the name on the identity card. In November 2013, the media reported on a workshop that had been organized by the Committee of Education and Social Issues (*Lajnat al-Tarbiyat wa-l-Qaḍāyā al-Ijtimāʿiyya*) in the PLC about the "*khulʿ* law" [*sic!*] (*qānūn al-khulʿ*),[76] which recommended introducing "judicial *khulʿ*." Member of the Gaza Parliament Hudā Naʿīm[77] was reported to be in favor of such a regulation, because of the great number of women being in the "inbetween status" and waiting for a divorce. It was stated, that the PLC would look at the suggestions of the workshop as well as on the submission of a draft of a *khulʿ* law at the earliest convenience.[78]

However, two years later nothing had happened. In a report from April 13, 2015, in *Al-Monitor*, Mohammad Othman stated that *khulʿ* was still a topic in Gaza, but still not regulated.[79] Sharia courts in Gaza sought to find a balance when it came to the right to file for divorce, so as to change the traditional concept that the sole eligibility to divorce comes from the husband. Ḥasan al-Jūjū was quoted as saying that the Islamic faith advocated partnership between spouses. Both individuals have a say in their marriage because marriage can only be consensual. "When marriage ends, it should also be consensual," he told *Al-Monitor* in what can perhaps be best described as wishful thinking in the realm of marital strife. He did mention that there were plans to "compensate women for any arbitrary divorce,"[80] and he added:

> Although Islamic Sharia gave men the right to divorce however and whenever they want, restrictions were imposed on this right. Women also have the right in some cases to divorce. The man cannot, for example, divorce his wife arbitrarily. We seek to have a law that compensates women for any arbitrary divorce.[81]

---

75 I thank CWLRC and especially Zaynab al-Ghunaymī for the paper I received in March 2018. It, however, does not have a date and is not available on the website of CWLRC.

76 Paltimesnet, November 3, 2013.

77 For her see http://www.plc.ps/ar/home/page_deputy/128, accessed February 8, 2019.

78 Pal24.net, November 4, 2013; Paltimesnet, November 3, 2013; she confirmed this in my interview with her. Hudā Naʿīm, interview on April 10, 2019.

79 Othman 2015.

80 Othman 2015.

81 Othman 2015.

Perhaps this was thought as a consolation for women who were still confronted with the man's nearly unrestricted right of repudiation anchored in the EFRL, Articles 67 and 68. But the statement was beside the point because it did not help women in cases when the husband *did not want* to divorce her. Al-Jūjū ignored the fact that many women had been waiting, sometimes for many years, to get a divorce.[82] He argued that "law must be amended by the legislative council" and now criticized the CWRLC concept for a *khulʿ* regulation on the grounds that if passed as a law, "it would serve high-income women only."[83] What had happened to the *khulʿ* discussion and the solution which seemed within reach?

9.2 A Failed Draft Law in 2013 and the Issuing of Two *taʿmīmāt* in 2016

The puzzle was solved when I had the chance to travel to Gaza and have interviews with Ḥasan al-Jūjū, Zaynab al-Ghunaymī, and Hudā Naʿīm on April 10 and 11, 2019. All three, representatives of the state (the Hamas government, Hudā Naʿīm), the Sharia establishment (Ḥasan al-Jūjū), and civil society (Zaynab al-Ghunaymī), are connected to each other. They speak directly to each other and they stated that they appreciated each other despite their different points of view, positions, interests, and educational and professional backgrounds. Zaynab al-Ghunaymī took me to the office of Ḥasan al-Jūjū and we spoke for about an hour.[84] After this, we went to the Gaza Parliament, the office of Hudā Naʿīm and spoke there for around an hour.

9.2.1 *A Failed Draft Law in 2013*

The result, which all three confirmed independently,[85] was: a *khulʿ* law had been drawn up, it was actually a draft for a law and not a *taʿmīm*, it had been submitted to the Gaza PLC, and that the Gaza PLC had passed it. This last part was due to Hudā Naʿīm's efforts to promote women's rights. Then, all of them

82 Othman 2015.

83 Othman 2015.

84 Whereas the Hamas government imposed headscarves on its employees, in the state administration al-Ghunaymī does not wear a scarf, as many of her staff and many women in the women's organizations I met. She considered it important to preserve this freedom for women to decide themselves whether they want to cover their hair. I was therefore asked not to bring a scarf to my visit to the Sharia Court and the Parliament in Gaza.

85 The interviews took all place on April 10, 2019. In addition, I met al-Ghunaymī again on April 11, 2019. Al-Ghunaymī prepared the meeting with al-Jūjū and afterwards with Naʿīm. Owing to this field research, I must revise my prior analysis of the situation in Gaza given in Schneider 2018a.

confirmed, the unity government was formed, and as this law was a Gaza law, it was not put on the agenda for legislation of the new government sworn in in June 2014.

The Draft Law is mentioned in a document bearing the title "Position of the Parliament with Regard to the *Khulʿ* Law and the Self-Redemption of the Woman" (*Mawqif al-Majlis al-Tashrīʿī min Qānūn al-Khulʿ wa-Iftidāʾ al-Marʾa li-Nafsihā*), prepared by Hudā Naʿīm, dated November 13, 2013. It[86] contains a summary of the discussion of the workshop of November 2013, an introduction, definition of *khulʿ*, reasons for reviewing the law, the legal regulations, comments from the parliament, efforts of the parliament, and results and recommendations. *Khulʿ* is defined as "*ṭalāq* based on redemption."[87] As reasons for the review, many pending proceedings in the courts are given. The fact is mentioned that women in Gaza cannot file a claim with regard to *khulʿ*, that many women are left inbetween (*muʿallaqāt*), and that the new law should serve women before consummation and privacy as solution if they do not want to finalize the marriage. The terminological debate in this document is revealing and covers up for what is missing in the West Bank. It is argued that from the perspective of the "principle of the similarity of rights and duties that Islam recognizes" (*mabdaʾ al-mumāthala fī al-ḥuqūq wa-al-wājibāt alladhī aqarrahu al-Islām*) and to prevent damage to the women, the Palestinian legislator was obliged to think about how to activate *khulʿ*.[88] The central "Islamic" term for equality, *mumāthala*, is mentioned as a principle and connected to rights and duties contained in Islam. It is clarified that the existing law does not give women the possibility to file a claim with regard to *khulʿ*, the law does not differentiate between *khulʿ* before and after consummation and the waiting period (*ʿidda*) is not defined.[89] The parliamentary Committee of Education and Social Affairs (*Lajnat al-Tarbiya wa-l-Qaḍāyā al-Ijtimāʿiyya*) had thus initiated the review of this law together with CWLRC, organized a conference on November 2, 2013, in which there had been agreement about the necessity of amending the regulations with regard to *khulʿ* and to have a judicial *khulʿ*.[90] From this text it could be concluded that the parliamentary committee, not the women's organization, had initiated the whole debate. Be this as it may, the important part of this Draft with regard to the research questions is to be found under the heading "Position of the Parliament with Regard to *Khulʿ* in

86 The document does not hint at the fact that it was prepared for the Parliament in Gaza.
87 Naʿīm 2013: 1.
88 Naʿīm 2013: 2.
89 Naʿīm 2013: 2.
90 Naʿīm 2013: 3.

Light of the Draft Law of Personal Status" (*Mawqif al-Majlis al-Tashrīʿī min al-Khulʿ fī Ḍawʾ Mashrūʿ Qānūn al-Aḥwāl al-Shakhṣiyya*)[91] because it gives a clue as to how the Draft Law conceptualizes *khulʿ* and what the position of the Parliament is in this matter. The important new regulations approved by the Gaza Parliament are given:

1. The Draft Law recognizes the woman's right to redeem herself with compensation (*ḥaqq al-marʾa fī iftidāʾ nafsihā bi-ʿiwaḍ*).
2. The Draft Law recognizes the wife's right to *khulʿ* before consummation and after consummation.
3. According to the Draft Law, *khulʿ* is connected to a compensation the wife has to give to the husband.
4. The Draft Law recognizes the wife's right to petition for *khulʿ* in court (*ṭalab al-khulʿ qaḍāʾiyyan*) when the husband refuses *khulʿ* based on mutual consent.
5. The Draft Law gives the judge the discretionary power (*al-salṭa al-taqdīriyya*) to issue a judgment with regard to *khulʿ* after being convinced of the impossibility to continue the conjugal community.
6. The Draft Law takes as its basis the amount the spouses agreed upon of *khulʿ* settlement to be paid by the woman. If they do not agree, the judge sets the value of the substitute of the equivalent of the dower and he prohibits the exchange of *khulʿ* for the wife's renunciation of the children's custody or their maintenance.
7. The Draft Law obliges the husband who gives *khulʿ* (*mukhāliʿ*) to pay maintenance and housing for the waiting period (*ʿidda*). The husband will not be released without having listed this in the *khulʿ* contract (*ʿaqd al-mukhālaʿa*).[92]

Under the heading of "results," it is again stressed that the Palestinian legislature gives women the right "to redeem themselves" (*iftidāʾ nafsihā* [*khulʿ*])."[93] The right of the spouses to mutually agree on *khulʿ* remains intact and now an interesting futher paragraph for the legal perspective of iterations follows:

> The [Gaza] Parliament wants to enact laws that follow the necessities of individuals, come from the middle of the society and in this frame the Parliament adopts the idea to recognize (*iqrār*) an amendment to the personal status law that recognizes the wife's right to file for *khulʿ* at Sharia Court even if the husband rejects this including laying the foundation

91 Naʿīm 2013: 3–4.

92 Naʿīm 2013: 3–4.

93 Naʿīm 2013: 4.

> (*takrīs*) for *her right to the dissolution of the marriage which* CEDAW *guarantees to her and all the international standards* (*maʿāyīr*) *in connection with this*. Often the regulations of the law are in harmony with the parameters (*muḥaddadāt*) and basic principles (*al-mabādīʾ al-asāsiyya*) described above.[94]

With this Draft Law, Gaza went several decisive steps further than the West Bank and reformed *khulʿ* law in a way that would not have been expected from the Hamas government. The reform of *khulʿ* was, first, not prepared as a judicial ruling (*taʿmīm*) but as a real amendment of the applicable law, as a draft law. Ḥasan al-Jūjū did stick to what he said in the television program of *Lāzim Naḥkī*,[95] namely that he preferred to regulate such an *ijtihād* through legislative channels. Second, legally it went further because *khulʿ* would be possible according to this law before and after consummation of the marriage. It thus came close to or was even congruent with the Egyptian law of 2000. Al-Ghunaymī confirmed my impression about this when I asked her in my interview with her.[96] And third, surprisingly, CEDAW and therefore international law is mentioned explicitly and the new regulation is put into relation to international law and women's rights resulting from international law. Hudā Naʿīm explained that this new regulation of *khulʿ* did give women the right to divorce and that it was in accordance with Islamic Sharia which promotes justice (*ʿadāla*) to women.[97] Earlier in the text, the term "similarity" (*mumāthala*) had been used as a term and it had been outlined and argued that there can be harmony between both Islamic and international law. Now it is confirmed that the aim of this law is to lay "the foundation for her right to the dissolution of the marriage which CEDAW guarantees to her and all the international standards in connection with this." *Mumāthala* as a possible "translation" of *musāwāḥ* (equality) had been used as a term in the 59/2012 *taʿmīm* (see 4.3) but it had not played a substantial role in West Bank iterations afterward. Here it does play a prominent role and appears under the paragraph that gives the reasons why the *khulʿ* law should be looked at again.[98] It is connected to the "results" outlined by the legislature.[99] Thus, here an important first step to a

94 Naʿīm 2013: 4, emphasis added. Some recommendations were followed, e.g., to define whether *khulʿ* should be final or appeal should be possible, regulations on giving back the dower to the husband, whether this kind of divorce can be made by proxy, etc.

95 *Lāzim Naḥkī*, April 30, 2013.

96 Zaynab al-Ghunaymī, interview on April 11, 2019.

97 Hudā Naʿīm, telephone interview on June 14, 2020.

98 Naʿīm 2013: 2.

99 Naʿīm 2013: 4.

"translation" of international law into the national legislation is taken. This happens, to repeat it, ironically in the Gaza Parliament, which is presided by the Islamist movement of Hamas.

It is evident that these points – the legal regulation of *khul*ʿ before and after consummation, the insertion of international law, the proposed harmony with international law – had all been carefully prepared by al-Jūjū, Naʿīm, and al-Ghunaymī. All of them had worked together, taken part in the workshop, discussed and then put together a detailed new regulation, which was then submitted to the Gaza Parliament. That it was accepted by the Gaza Parliament surely is the consequence of the efforts of Hudā Naʿīm, a young and very active female member of the Gaza PLC whose interest is in preserving and promoting women's rights.

However, the law was never implemented. As the representatives of state, Sharia establishment and civil society unanimously confirmed,[100] this was due to political developments, the creation of a unity government in which Gaza took part and in which it would not have been possible to put a law into force that had been developed in Gaza and approved by the Gaza Parliament. Whatever the exact fate of the Draft Law may be, it disappeared into a drawer unnoticed or even ignored by jurists of the West Bank and the unity government between 2014 until the beginning of 2019 when the unity government crashed. There was no regulation and the women's organizations went on to complain and push for a new law. Instead, two *taʿmīmāt* were issued in Gaza.

9.2.2 *Two New taʿmīmāt*

These two new *taʿmīmāt* were in a way the jurisgenerative consequence of these iterations and the political ignorance or even reluctance in Gaza and the West Bank to enact the aforementioned law. They were not at all, however, what the women's organizations had hoped for even when al-Jūjū tried to sell it as a success to women:

Taʿmīmāts 07/2016 and 08/2016 were both issued in February 2016. Their content briefly is as follows:

- *Taʿmīm* 07/2016 exempts in Article 1 a woman whose marriage has not yet been consummated and who did not have privacy from keeping the period of six months for (re)submitting the claim without new causes and facts. It refers in Article 2 to *taʿmīm* 09/2012, issued on May 29, 2012. *Taʿmīm* 07/2016 actually cancels the regulation of *taʿmīm* 09/2012, which had introduced a six-month period for repeating the complaint and goes back to the original

100 Ḥasan al-Jūjū, interview on April 10, 2019; Hudā Naʿīm, interview on April 10, 2019; Zaynab al-Ghunaymī, interview on April 11, 2019.

text of the law *but only for women before consummation*. Now women whose marriage is not consummated could repeat their complaint, also in the case that they had no new facts and reasons, without having to wait six months.

– *Taʿmīm* 08/2016 regulated in Article 1 that the husband has, like the wife, the right to claim separation in the case of "dispute and discord" between him and his wife when he claims that she damages him (*iḍrāruhā bihi*) in word or act and when he does not see himself fit to continue the marriage because of this damage. Article 2 regulates: When the husband proves this "dispute and discord" the judge will take pains to reconcile the spouses. If there is no reconciliation, he sets a time not less than a month hoping for improvement and when the husband still holds up his claim after this time and there is no reconciliation the judge transmits the case to the two arbiters. According to Article 3 the court will proceed after the transmission of the claim to the two arbiters as laid down in Articles 98, 99, 100, 101 and 102 of the EFRL.

This regulation could at first glance be regarded as a step toward gender equal legislation, because now the husband, as the wife, has the right to claim divorce based on "dispute and discord," as was the case before in the OLFR of 1917.[101] Such a regulation is also in accordance with the JLPS regulation of *khulʿ*[102] and "dispute and discord."[103] But the alleged argument of gender equality falls short because first there is still no access for women directly to *khulʿ* in Gaza,[104] and second, the husband still has the general right to *ṭalāq*[105] in addition to his new right to sue his wife based on *nizāʿ wa-shiqāq*. It belongs to the absurdities of this legal development that al-Jūjū, who had been in principle critical with regard to the *taʿmīmāt*, issued *taʿmīmāt* only to reverse them later, now easing the situation a bit but not really for women in cases of unconsummated marriages. In the interview, he argued that under the JLPS, men also have the right to sue for such a claim.[106]

9.3 Comparison between the West Bank and Gaza

The agency in Gaza is thus still on the side of men; women cannot file *khulʿ* claims. The just-described new regulation giving men an additional right to

101 See fn. 52

102 Articles 102, 103.

103 Article 132.

104 As in the West Bank in Articles 102f. of the JLPS.

105 Articles 67 and 68 of EFRL.

106 Ḥasan al-Jūjū, interview on April 10, 2019.

file for "dispute and discord" (*nizāʿ wa-shiqāq*) might even be preferable for the husband, because in cases where the arbiters find the wife "guilty," she will have to pay back her dower or at least a part of it, according to the degree she is found guilty of breaking up the marriage. Thus, the husband's position is improved by two points. His access to a divorce is broadened and he can gain financial advantages. As few women have professions and jobs in a traditional and poor society like Gaza, the decision of the Gaza judiciary matters and makes women more financially dependent on their husbands. An end of the basic "money-obedience" relation is not in sight, not in the West Bank nor in Gaza but a comparison between the legal regulation in the West Bank and Gaza reveals remarkable differences between the two parts of Palestine. The following table shows the greater agency and options regarding divorce for women in the West Bank:

TABLE 9.1 Comparison West Bank and Gaza

	West Bank	**Gaza**
1.	*Khulʿ* can be initiated by both the husband and the wife and is based on mutual consent (JLPS Articles 102–112).	*Khulʿ* is not mentioned in the EFRL as an independent form of separation but only as part of the procedure in "dispute and discord" (EFRL Article 100) when the arbiters decide that the wife should undergo *khulʿ* because the wrongdoing is on her side. Classical *khulʿ* is applicable by default.
2.	*Khulʿ taʿmīm* (59/2012): redemption before consummation against the husband's will is possible.	There is no such regulation.
3.	"Dispute and discord" can be claimed by both spouses (Article 132 JLPS with proof).	"Dispute and discord" can be claimed by the woman (Article 97 EFRL). This right is given to the man too in *taʿmīm* 08/2016.
4.	"Dispute and discord" without proof (*taʿmim* 59/2012) is possible for the woman. The judge decides.	No such regulation. In "dispute and discord" proof is necessary (Article 100); resubmission is possible. According to *taʿmīm* 09/2012, this term is six months in cases where there are no new facts; according to *taʿmīm* 07/2016 the six-month term was cancelled for women before consummation.

The Draft Law not enacted because of the unification of the government in June 2014 would of course have been a decisive step forward in gender equal legislation in Gaza and, if enacted by the unification government, even for all of Palestine. Because it gave also women after consummation the right to petition for *khulʿ*, this law would have been preferable for women. The additional regulation of *nizāʿ wa-shiqāq* in the West Bank, which was announced to ease women's access to divorce after consummation, was also not without problems. It was ruled in *taʿmīm* 59/2012 that women do not need proof to get divorced in cases of "dispute and discord" (*nizāʿ wa-shiqāq*) and it gave "discretionary power" (*al-sulṭa al-taqdiriyya*) to the judge to decide. But in the time after 2012, debates arose in the West Bank, as already outlined, that women's petition for divorce could not be accepted without further verification. It was argued that the woman should convince the judge about *shuhra*, i.e. that her conflict with her husband was publicly known and her husband should confirm this. If not, other ways to convince the judge would be necessary – and again women were de facto in the position to have to prove their claim for being damaged by their husbands.[107]

9.4 Standing Up for a New *Khulʿ* Law in Gaza: The Civil Society Debate in Gaza 2012 to 2017

Women's organizations protested vehemently against the two rulings. Why should men get, on top of the full and only very marginally restricted right to repudiation, the right to claim divorce under "dispute and discord," whereas women as the vulnerable part of society had to wait for years – up to fifteen years, some said – to be granted a divorce by the court based on "dispute and discord"? And why should men and not women be strengthened in the battle of the sexes, in which women did not have the same rights to initiate divorce, contrary to international law? Before and after the Draft Law was drawn up there had been a controversial debate in society similar to the one in the West Bank in context with the 59/2012 *taʿmīm*. In the media a woman named Umm Anas, "Mother of Anas" strongly supported a new *khulʿ* regulation, because it reduced the suffering for women,[108] whereas Umm Muḥammad was afraid it would endanger the leadership of the man in society. If at all, *khulʿ* should be introduced with great restrictions, so that women would not abuse

107 See chapter 4, fn. 108.
108 Abū Ṭaqiyya 2013.

it, she argued.[109] Critical comments came from civil and Sharia lawyer Iṣlāḥ Ḥusniyya, who explained that many women who wanted a divorce, instead tolerated unhappy marriages[110] to protect their homes. Only "when serious problems occur and women reach a stalemate, they file for divorce," she said.

> Most women have to stay due to financial and familial conditions. Many sacrifice so that they may stay with their children. In addition, financial status does not allow [some] women to divorce by khula [*khulʿ*]. This is why they do not opt for this option.[111]

Dunyā al-Amal Ismāʿīl, a writer, feminist activist, and head of Gaza's Creative Women Association, confirmed this and said that *khulʿ* in Gaza has helped women who can pay back their husbands for the dower and gifts. However, financially underprivileged women cannot benefit from this kind of divorce, she argued and added: "Even elite women in Gaza have to watch out for social traditions that prevent them from opting for divorce by khula [*sic!*]." Adding the perspective that *khulʿ* is a possibility only for wealthy women, she continued: "These traditions apply to them as much as they apply to normal women. Fear of how their behavior might be religiously interpreted may also constitute an impediment."[112] Ismāʿīl said social acceptance of *khulʿ* could lead many women to embrace this option, but fearing the stigma of divorce, women have second thoughts when considering it. For divorce by *khulʿ* to be effective, women would need an open social culture.[113] Abū Ṣuhayb, whose profession is not stated in the article, supported the announced introduction of *khulʿ* seeing it also as a means to solve the grief of women in the "inbetween" situation, who wanted to get divorced but faced intimidation by men. However, he felt obliged to express some worries and warnings: "*Khulʿ* would make the man feel humiliated in his society, but it is suitable to reclaim women's stolen rights; hence, there should be rules that control the situation."[114]

The president of *Iftāʾ* committee at the Islamic University of Gaza, Māhir Al-Sūsī, clarified that *khulʿ*, obviously meaning the "judicial *khulʿ*," had been debated among scholars. There is, according to him, weak evidence in favor of this *khulʿ*. The injustice should be stopped, but without any pressure put on the

109 Abū Ṭaqiyya 2013.

110 See www.al-monitor.com/pulse/originals/2015/03/gaza-hamas-conservative-rise-of-poly gamy.html, accessed July 22, 2018.

111 Othman 2015.

112 Othman 2015.

113 Othman 2015.

114 Abū Ṭaqiyya 2013.

husband. He warned women from using it in trivial situations as a way to pressure the husband and to blackmail him. If misused, *khulʿ* would lead to harm for society; thus, it should be used wisely in order to get its benefits. There should be an adequate juridical supervision that would not leave the decision solely to the woman. He added that a *khulʿ* law would limit injustice toward women, but thought it would increase problems for men.[115] All these statements show that in Gaza as well as in the West Bank objections were raised against what was considered to be a too far reaching right for women to divorce.

Civil society had lobbied hard to get a regulation similar or even better for women in Gaza than in the West Bank; they had succeeded in drafting a law that went further than the regulation in the West Bank. In the end, only the above-mentioned two rulings were issued in 2016.[116] So what happened after the issuing of the two rulings? Did the women's organizations react positively to *taʿmīm* 07/2016 in which women prior to consummation were spared the six-month term for resubmitting the claim? The answer is, of course, "no," given the active and critical as well as professional women's movement, especially CWLRC in Gaza. The reactions varied between surprise and outrage; al-Jūjū was heavily attacked from different sides. Giving the husband the right to request a divorce (judicial divorce; *taṭlīq*) was criticized, as stated above, and seen as being "against the principle of equality and non-discrimination."[117] CWLRC called this ruling even "unconstitutional," stating that the applicable law in Gaza already gives the husband the unrestricted right to divorce whenever and however he wants, and that "there is no need for the right to file the suit for *ṭalāq*, whereas the woman only has the legal right to file the claim for separation (*tafrīq*) for specific reasons, among them 'dispute and discord,' because she does not have the same right as the husband."[118] CWLRC warned that this ruling would encourage husbands to file suits against the women whereas the women would bear the burden of "dispute and discord" to get a divorce in which their financial rights are waived. It regarded this ruling as an attack on women's rights.[119]

The women's organizations again vehemently opted for a *khulʿ* law or at least for a regulation of *khulʿ*. The director of CWLRC, Zaynab al-Ghunaymī, went on to complain publicly that there is still no special *khulʿ* law in Gaza

115 Abū Ṭaqiyya 2013.
116 Dūḥān 2016.
117 Dūḥān 2016
118 Dūḥān 2016.
119 Dūḥān 2016.

and that the only form of *khulʿ* is consensual *khulʿ*[120] and was supported by Hudā Naʿīm.[121]

In a meeting that was organized by CWLRC in 2017,[122] which included lawyers, representatives from women's organizations, the media, representatives of the Sharia establishment, and the PLC, Iṣlāḥ Ḥasaniyya pressured in vain to achieve a decision with regard to *khulʿ* and to abolish the abovementioned ruling demanding a Palestinian law and uniform legislation as well as unification of the organization of the Palestinian Sharia jurisdiction. CWLRC and others, such as the lawyer Suʿād al-Mashnī, demanded that women under pressure from their husbands should have the right to file a claim for *khulʿ*.[123] The same discussion that had been there before continued after the failure of the Draft Law.

By others, *taʿmīm* 08/2016 was considered the healing of a special legal problem: the husband as victim and violated person (*al-ḍaḥīya aw-al-muʿannaf*).[124] This argument provoked much surprise and resistance. It was considered "strange" (*gharīb*) for Palestinian society that a husband should not be the strong one but the victim and vulnerable part of the marriage.[125] Ayman Ḥammād, judge at the Sharia court of Rafaḥ, explained that in February 2016 for the first time a man submitted a claim for divorce based on "dispute and discord" and described it as a new matter.[126] Saʿīd Abū al-Jabīn tried to explain that the reasons behind the ruling (*taʿmīm*), with regard to the husband's right to claim divorce based on "dispute and discord" against the wife, i.e., *taʿmīm* 08/2016, were the many cases of insults by women toward their husbands. Even cases of women beating their husbands in the court had been observed, it was said. Not women but men, and especially husbands, as victims and violated persons, beame the focus of the legal and social debate.[127]

Why did this new narrative emerge in a still patriarchal society in which gender equality was not implemented, both on the legal and on the social level? What could be the reason behind it? Surely, it cannot be ruled out that in a society so much affected by violence like Gaza, women also acquire violent traits. But statistics spoke against this: Al-Jabīn had to admit, that only eleven

120 Dūḥān 2016.

121 Pal24.net, November 4, 2013; Paltimes, November 3, 2013. Hudā Naʿīm, interview on April 10, 2019.

122 CWLRC, March 1, 2017.

123 Dūḥān 2016.

124 Dūḥān 2016.

125 Dūḥān 2016

126 Dūḥān 2016

127 CWLRC, March 1, 2017.

cases had been filed by men in 2016 whereas 205 had been filed by women. He felt obliged to explain that this regulation was different from the regulation for women in so far as there was no possibility of resubmission and in cases where the women's right was confirmed, she would get all the rights, just as if she had been divorced normally by repudiation.[128]

In February 2017, a discussion took place on the Palestinian television program *Maan* between Ḥasan al-Jūjū and Zaynab al-Ghunaymī, which brought all these debates together and included an audience that asked critical questions. The discussion took place in the beginning between al-Jūjū and al-Ghunaymī but was later opened to the audience in the studio.[129] It focused on two topics: the *khulʿ* question and its current (non-)regulation in Gaza, and more generally, on the question of how a future Palestinian family law would or should look, touching upon the status and role of international law and its sensitive core and kernel, gender equality. With regard to the *khulʿ* question, al-Ghunaymī stated that "we" – meaning women's organizations more generally and explicitly her organization – had demanded the "judicial *khulʿ*" and had cooperated with al-Jūjū and had made suggestions. There is a difference, she explained, between divorced based on "dispute and discord" – obviously pointing to Article 100 of the EFRL – and *khulʿ*. Rejecting al-Jūjū's claim, she denied that *khulʿ* was given in the courts: "There is a problem for women getting divorce against the husband's will," she said. She attacked al-Jūjū for ignoring this problem of women whose cases are stuck in the court and who need help to get a divorce. She pointed out, that even *khulʿ* based on agreement of the spouses is not registered as *khulʿ* in Gaza but as "repudiation of minor irrevocable divorce" (*ṭalāq banūna ṣughrā*). In reality, there are women who need help, she argued. Al-Jūjū answered many points evasively and often countered very vehemently. Whereas he had criticized in the television program *Lāzim Naḥkī* of April 30, 2013, the *khulʿ* ruling of his West Bank brethren before consummation and pointed to the existence of *khulʿ* before and after consummation in Gaza, ignoring that in Gaza only *khulʿ* based on consent could be practiced,[130] he now conceded that there were two forms of *khulʿ*, one before and one after consummation. This form of judicial *khulʿ* had established itself in the public perception by then. He stated that there is a version of *khulʿ* that is used when

128 CWLRC, March 1, 2017.

129 Maannews, February 15, 2017; the discussion took place in a studio with guests. The film available gives the impression that cuts were made so that sometimes passages of the discussion seem to be missing. The conversation between al-Ghunaymī and al-Jūjū in the beginning was controversial and sometimes turned emotional. They interrupted each other several times. Often they did not finish their sentences or complete their arguments.

130 *Lāzim Naḥkī*, April 30, 2013.

marriage cannot be continued and because of harm done, stating "in truth *khulʿ* is applied in a legal manner (*bi-shakl qānūnī*) during a claim (*al-daʿwā*)." With this he referred to the existing regulation in the EFRL (without mentioning it explicitly), Article 100, which was not a *khulʿ* regulation but the article concerning divorce based on *nizāʿwa-shiqāq*. Where there was a regulation in the EFRL, it would have to be applied first and not the regulation in the OLFR, because the EFRL is newer, he argued, and had preference. He thus, in a way, denied the solution he had found and supported together with al-Ghunaymī and Naʿīm and fell back behind his support of the Draft Law, which all three had submitted to the Gaza Parliament. He did admit at some point that "we" had wanted to widen the space for *khulʿ* divorce with the proposal put forward by al-Ghunaymī and her organization but left the reasons why this failed unexplained.

After a very intensive and controversial verbal clash between al-Ghunaymī and al-Jūjū, the audience was allowed to ask questions. These questions turned out to be quite critical with regard to the non-regulation of *khulʿ* in Gaza and targeted especially al-Jūjū. Women expressed their anger about the suffering of women generally and the nonexistence of "welfare" (*maṣlaḥa*) because women had to bring proof and needed years in court to get a divorce specially. A man named Kārim stood up and spoke out against *khulʿ* only for virgins – the West Bank solution – because it would discriminate against the rest of the women who could not resort to *khulʿ*. He referred to the well-known *ḥadīth* of Thābit b. Qays's wife, arguing that *khulʿ* is not connected to the consent of the husband and there is no need for two arbiters, because the Prophet's question is: "Do you give him back his garden?" and when she responded positively, he gave her the repudiation.[131] Kārim concluded that as the husband has the right to repudiation (*ṭalāq*) without giving reasons, the woman has the right to *khulʿ* without giving reasons "else we do have cucumber and Armenian cucumber in the matter", meaning: else we have no equality in the matter.[132] This can be read as an offer to the Muslim jurist al-Jūjū to engage in discussion about a possible new interpretation of this *ḥadīth* but al-Jūjū did not take up this argument in his answer and did not react explicitly to this suggested interpretation, missing the chance to review or even outline his position toward *khulʿ* with regard to "uses of the past." Referring to the order "give him back his garden," he only said that this could not be applied without looking at the custom and the

131 He says *ṭallaqhā,* which would mean he, the Prophet, gave her the *ṭalāq*.

132 "Else we have cucumber and Armenian cucumber in the matter" (*illā iḏā kāna ʿindanā khiyār wa-faqūs*) means idiomatically "not having equality" because the vegetables are different. I thank Ghada Issa for explaining this Palestinian proverb to me.

surrounding conditions of the society at that time. He could have used Kārim's explanation for a scholarly introduction into the exegesis of this *ḥadīth* but did not do that, either. With regard to the general topic of family law, Kārim outlined his understanding of equality further: "The question on the table is, when we want to talk about the personal status law: how do we understand family? How do we understand the relation between the sides in the family? Is it a relation of equality (*musāwāh*) or a relation of despotism (*istibdād*)?"[133] He used the word "*musāwāh*" deliberately at this point obviously to provoke al-Jūjū and to receive an answer. Taking the example of his daughter's marriage contract he did not want to sign but was eventually forced by the judge to sign together with his daugher, he criticized women's missing rights.[134] With regard to the general problem of a new Palestinian law and how it should look, Kārim noted that the parliament had issued 126 laws between 1996 and 2006 and that President Abbas had issued something like 170 laws and the *Kutlat al-Taghyīr wa-l-Iṣlāḥ*, the Hamas government since 2007, had issued 57 laws – but none of these laws was a family law. He concluded that the issuing of a new Palestinian family law was not a priority for any of the named governments.

Al-Jūjū answered again using subterfuges, pointing several times, especially at the end, to the difficult situation because of the political split. He criticized Gaza and the West Bank for issuing different *taʿmīmāt*. He publicly pleaded for joint *taʿmīmāt*: "Let's issue common *taʿmīm* (*fa-l nuṣdir taʿmīm mushtarak*)!" for the "welfare of the Palestinian people" (*min ajl al-maṣlaḥat al-shaʿb al-filasṭīnī*). "I am not your enemy, I am your brother," he stated – a statement that perhaps may indicate that his harsh critique of the West Bank *taʿmīm* as given in *Lāzim Naḥkī*[135] was based on his feeling that he had been ignored in this matter.[136] Taking refuge to politics, he avoided getting into an Islamic legal discussion, and thus he did not respond clearly to Kārim. Maybe this was a result of his not being successful in implementing a law to which he had consented. But he went on to complain that he could not skip a text of the Quran and Sunna, which are the two main sources among the sources for the legislation in family law matters. His *taʿmīmāt*, he assured, were all based on the holy text and the application to the reality (*al-wāqiʿ*), "but if there is no text I cannot come up with another text because the law can only be amended by law and new legislation which has to go through the parliament."[137] Where was *ijtihād*?

---

133 Maannews, February 15, 2017.

134 See Welchman 2003: 151–163.

135 *Lāzim Naḥkī*, April 30, 2013.

136 In the interview with me on April 10, 2019, he confirmed that there is no communication between his West Bank colleagues and him.

137 Maannews, February 15, 2017.

Where the scholarly self-confidence to be able to think out of the legal box and develop new regulations based on Islamic law?

When the host asked for the "point of reference" (*marjaʿiyya*) for the new law, first Zaynab al-Ghunaymī and then Ḥasan al-Jūjū both gave longer explications. Al-Ghunaymī, pointing to the president's signing of CEDAW without any reservations, stated that the future state of Palestine would have to fulfill the obligations resulting from this Convention. She pointed to the BL, which also refers to international law. She then stated: "Concepts of human rights are the same concepts which exist in the Islamic Sharia that require that there is justice among the people and that there is justice and equality."[138] She continued: "The point of reference of the laws is, yes, the Basic Law, a source of legislation is the Islamic Sharia."[139] She added at the end: "We want a Palestinian society based on justice and equality." This statement can be understood as an offer to al-Jūjū to combine human rights and international law with Islamic law that he did not take up: Islam and human rights match; it is no problem to combine them, and justice and equality should be the guiding line.

Al-Jūjū's answer to this question, touching upon the centrality of a future legal positioning in Palestine is to a certain extent similar to the position of his colleague Maḥmūd al-Habbāsh in the West Bank as he outlined it in the media, but more reflected and detailed. Al-Jūjū did not take up the two keywords "justice and equality" thrown into the discussion by al-Ghunaymī, but started a scholarly outline of his position in the language of Islamic jurisprudence. He explained that Islamic Sharia has different sources: those that are agreed upon (*muttaffaq ʿalayhi*) and those that are disputed (*mukhtlaf fīhi*). The object (*manāṭ*) of these sources (*maṣādir*) is the realization of the welfare (*maṣlaḥa*) of the people in this world and the next world. The agreed upon sources are the Quran, Sunna, consensus and analogy. The disputed ones are, among others: custom (*ʿurf*) and welfare (*maṣlaḥa*) to which he referred in his talk. He then mentioned the concept of decisive and presumptive (*qaṭʿī* and *ẓannī*)[140] texts. His example for decisive texts, where no interpretation is possible, was inheritance, quoting Quran 33:36:[141] "Can I give according to the law to male the portion of a female? Never!"[142] Thus excluding women from an

138 Maannews, February 15, 2017.

139 Maannews, February 15. 2017.

140 See for his position in the 1990s around the Model Parliament, Welchman 2003: 49.

141 "It is not for any believer, man or woman, when God and His Messenger have decreed a matter, to have the choice in the affair. Whosoever disobeys God and His Messenger has gone astray into manifest error."

142 Al-Jūjū had proposed some basic approaches for the new law. At the time of the Model Parliament in the 1990s, there were two principles he considered unchangeable:

equal share in inheritance he felt obliged to add that these texts, which cannot be interpreted, are few and we have a "wide door" open for interpreting the texts according to the welfare of the people. The legislature can choose among the texts the preferred opinion (*al-ra'y al-marjūḥ*)[143] with regard to the welfare of the people. He continued: "We are in favor of CEDAW as long as it does not allow forbidden things and forbids allowed things (*naḥnu maʿa īttifāqiyyat Sīdāw mā dāmat lā tuḥillu ḥarāman wa-lā tuḥarrim ḥalālan*)."[144]

This echoes what Maḥmūd al-Habbāsh had said in the West Bank but is connected with a reference to the flexibility of Sharia and the priority of the well-being of the people. It is based on outlining the methodological approach to the sources according to which the few decisive texts have to be respected, however, these few texts seem to be the ones debated hotly by women's activists. He went on to explain that he was confident that there "were scholars as well as legislators" being conscious and able to produce an *ijtihād* that combines modernity and authenticity for the welfare of the people. Having said this, he stated explicitly that he himself saw no "problem" with regard to repudiation (*ṭalāq*), marriage and inheritance. "Islam is not in contradiction with human rights but came to confirm human rights," he said and quoted another verse of the Quran (17:70)[145] to support his opinion. His explanations left the audience with a certain degree of contrariness and inconsistency – would it be possible to develop Islamic law toward gender equality? Obviously not in the realm of inheritance law – but where then?

Again, it was Kārim who put his finger on the weak spot and pointed to an important aspect al-Jūjū had left out of his argument: the human interpretation of divine law. He would be careful to speak of the personal status law as taken from Islamic Sharia and not from the sphere of Islamic jurisprudence, he argued. The example of how he equally shared an inheritance with his sister, which he explained, offered a pragmatic solution for the sharing of an inheritance, and al-Jūjū in his answer to him consented to it. Kārim summarized: "Islamic Sharia is not against equality but the Islamic reasoning (*ʿaql*) is what refutes equality."[146] This statement again would have had the potential to provoke a scholarly answer from al-Jūjū but once again he did not react to this.

inheritance and the men's *qiwāma*, whereas he offered a "balanced account of what could be done and how," see Shehada 2005: 40; Welchman 2003: 17.

143 He argues that preferring surpassed (*marjūḥ*) opinion over preferable (*rājiḥ*) opinion in a school of law is possible when it is for the people's welfare.

144 Maannews, February 15, 2017.

145 "We have honoured the Children of Adam and carried them on land and sea, and provided them with good things, and preferred them greatly over many of those We created."

146 Maannews, February 15, 2017.

Al-Ghunaymī, normally combat-ready and outspoken without any fear about hiding her views, either, reacted with a certain tameness to al-Jūjū's comments on inheritance expressing her expectation that there would be a solution for a legal text. Al-Jūjū then conceded that he would be in favor of raising the marriage age to eighteen. Some discussion developed around a remark made by someone from the auditorium who told a story about a young woman who killed her husband because she had been forced to marry him. Al-Jūjū now again felt obliged to object immediately, stating that the legal regulation would not have allowed her to get married against her will. At this point, al-Ghunaymī delivered an important statement:

> The most important point in the discussion is, who has the right to decide about the mandate[147] on behalf of the woman and what is beneficial for her and what is not beneficial for her? … I do not talk just about marriage but about all the regulations of the law with regard to marriage and its dissolution, … the *ṭalāq* for example.[148]

With this she touched upon the central point of the discussion, the question of what has been called the *marjaʿiyya*, the point of reference or principle described as either Islamic law or intenational law. Al-Ghunaymī added the pivotal and decisive aspect to this discussion: "who decides … what is beneficial to her [the woman]." In the West Bank, Idʿīs had presented himself as the women's spokesman, as the one who not only recognized their problem (to get out of the marriage/engagement) and developed a solution (*khulʿ* before consummation) but also the one who could actually implement this solution. However, he had faced much opposition by men who were afraid to lose their dignity when being labeled "divorced."

On the tv program, al-Jūjū angrily interrupted al-Ghunaymī when she asked: "Who has the right to decide?" and he replied: "She herself decides," but he was still referring to the concrete case that she cannot be married against her will. He added: "Bring me a girl whom the judge forces to marry against her will after she declared she does not want the marriage" as if al-Ghunaymī had insulted the Gaza Sharia courts. But al-Ghunaymī went on to explain what she meant. In the end, both talked at the same time and about different topics. Al-Jūjū pointed to the male prerogative of *ṭalāq* whereas al-Ghunaymī wanted equal access for women with regard to divorce. At this point al-Jūjū repeated,

147 She used the word *niyāba* and not the Islamic term *wilāya*, which one would have expected here.

148 Maannews, February 15, 2017.

as he did in his interview in 2015,[149] his opinion that "there is no doubt that *ṭalāq* should occur by mutual consent." But *ṭalāq* according to the law, here he is clear, is in the man's hands: "Is the action of *ṭalāq* dependent on the consent of the wife? No."[150]

The program ended with al-Jūjū pointing again to the well-known situation of separation that hinders the development of a new law and al-Ghunaymī, pointing to the necessity of a new and unified law, spoke of the necessary welfare of the people. There had been partially a critical exchange of opinions, but it had not developed into a constructive debate on how matters could be initiated and brought forward.

9.5 Conclusion

What was the same in the West Bank and Gaza and what was different with regard to the iterations, the jurisgenerative processes, and the role of the actors? First and foremost: despite the negative position Ḥasan al-Jūjū took with regard to the West Bank *taʿmīm* and his and Fāṭima ʿĀshūr's argument on the television program *Lāzim Naḥkī* in April 2013[151] that *khulʿ* was already regulated in Gaza and that there was no need to discuss it, the two problems that were the incentives for the West Bank ruling existed in Gaza as well. There was a high percentage of women wanting divorce before they had consummated the marriage and many cases of divorce were stuck in the Sharia courts for many years making women suffer. The CWLRC report, which dated from 2012,[152] confirmed this, and not only highlighted the legal situation but also suggested detailed and well-thought-out solutions.

The legal situations in Gaza and the West Bank are different insofar as the EFRL does not contain articles regulating *khulʿ*. It does mention *khulʿ* only in Article 100 as one possible consequence when the woman files a claim of *nizāʿ wa-shiqāq*. This leaves the "classical" consensual *khulʿ* by default in force. Whereas *taʿmīm* 59/2012 gave women in the West Bank the right to *khulʿ* before consummation without having to prove their case, women in Gaza still do not have access to this kind of divorce (May 2019). Can it be said that the Sharia establishment and especially the SCHC are stronger in the West Bank than in

149 Othman 2015.

150 Maannews, February 15, 2017.

151 *Lāzim Naḥkī*, April 30, 2013.

152 There had been an earlier and more detailed version of the report from 2012 that disappeared from the website in May 2019; I used one from July 2013.

Gaza? Certainly, the discussion in Gaza was initiated by civil society, specifically by the CWLRC. Al-Jūjū, who had issued many *taʿmīmāt*, did not want to regulate *khulʿ* with a *taʿmīm*. He insisted that such a far-reaching regulation would have to go through the legislative channels required by the BL. He failed and issued instead a ruling giving men the additional right to file a claim according to "dispute and discord" in addition to their already existing right to unlimited *ṭalāq*.

This new *taʿmīm* can be considered problematic from the perspective of gender equality. Whereas general gender equal access to "dispute and discord" divorce[153] must be welcomed and exists also in the JLPS, Ḥasan al-Jūjū's ruling in this context gains a special flavor for men in Gaza because of the connection to *mukhālaʿa* in Article 100 of EFRL and the chance for men to get a "cheap divorce" in addition to their unrestricted right to *ṭalāq*.[154] It was not the idea that whoever wants to divorce has to pay – men with *ṭalāq* and women with *khulʿ* – but whoever is guilty of the break-up of the marriage or whoever is considered by the arbiters as "guilty" has to pay. This gives the arbiters a central power. The idea of *khulʿ*, which in classical law was considered separation based on mutual consent and connected with the obligation of the woman to pay back her dower, was never based on any consideration of condition or even guilt. This new *taʿmīm* thus de facto cut woman's agency in this version of the codified *khulʿ* down to the ground and her access to a form of divorce not connected to a specific reason is nonexistent. Women gained nothing comparable with the right to avoid the six-month period when resubmitting their claim, but only in cases when the marriage had not been consummated. Such a regulation surely cannot be called generous and was hardly even mentioned in public debates.

The debate in Gaza was fueled by the introduction of a new concept in the iterations: the idea that the husband could be considered the victim and the violated one in marriage.[155] Introducing such a figure was considered strange and new for Palestinian society, partly because a patriarchal society does not consider men weak or even victims per se, partly because there was an awareness that where there was not yet equality in the law the concept of a man as a victim might be a misinterpretation of the real power structure in society.[156] This was the point of view of the women's organizations who perceived it as a misinterpretation of the law, which should first be amended toward gender

153 EFRL Article 100.

154 In Article 132 (c) of JLPS, it is also regulated that the arbiters decided on the percentage of "wrongdoing" and give their decision on the appropriate compensation "not less than the dowry."

155 Dūḥān 2016.

156 Dūḥān 2016.

equality. It was seen as a reification of the gender hierarchy. It is evident that the debate in Gaza is as controversial as in the West Bank and that legal regulation is slightly better in the West Bank with regard to women's agency in divorce. But this is only one side of the story.

There is another side of the story or another more surprising perspective of the legal iterations in Gaza. Civil society, the state, and the Sharia establishment cooperated in Gaza in an unexpectedly effective and constructive manner to write a draft law for *khulʿ* that went much further than the West Bank *taʿmīm* 59/2012. It not only included the women's right to *khulʿ* against the husband's wish before and after consummation, but it was a draft law and not only a ruling of the HSCC. Thus, a Hamas-controlled parliament accepted a draft law that, would it have been put into force, would have given women in Palestine the opportunity for the first time to file for divorce against the husband's will, both before and after consummation of the marriage. Even more surprising was the Position Paper of the Parliament stating that women should be given this right because it was considered their right according to international law. The women's convention, CEDAW, was mentioned in the Position Paper of the Hamas-led parliament.[157] Mentioning the central term of *mumāthala* in the Position Paper authored by Hudā Naʿīm reflected a first and important intellectual and political step toward a harmonization of international law with national law. As outlined, this term, which was also mentioned in *taʿmīm* 59/2012 in the West Bank but got lost in the discussion, has the potential to fuel the process of "translating" international law into national law. On a general level, it could spell out what "equality" (*musāwāh*) as laid down in Articles 2 and 16 of CEDAW means exactly in the Palestinian context. In this context, it meant a draft law that connected Palestine to the much praised Egyptian law of *khulʿ* of 2000 and the Jordanian Law of 2010 and brought it a decisive step nearer to a gender equal approach to divorce.

How did it come about? It was the result of a concerted effort of civil society with a strong Zaynab al-Ghunaymī, the state with the courageous member of the Gaza Parliament Hudā Naʿīm, and the scholar of Islamic law, Ḥasan al-Jūjū who was willing to discuss the legal regulation in detail and give it his blessing. All three actors have, as outlined above, tight relations with each other. They regularly meet and discuss issues. They explained to me that they belong to a common "network,"[158] but have different points of view in many matters. This is illustrated in the highly controversial television debate between

157 Naʿīm 2013: 4.

158 Hudā Naʿīm, interview on April 10, 2019. Zaynab al-Ghunaymī was present, too.

al-Ghunaymī and al-Jūjū in February 2017.[159] Naʿīm's Position Paper of 2013 contains the most important points of the CWLRC report but goes further in granting women, even after consummation, the right to *khulʿ* against the husband's will. Needless to say, this was one of the arguments of al-Ghunaymī.[160] Without the final agreement of al-Jūjū, however, it could not have been presented to Parliament. Without a political environment that was positive toward Naʿīm pushing it forward, it would not have been accepted by the Gaza Parliament.

There was, thus, the chance for Gazan women to have not only a legal regulation from the HSCC but a real amendment of the law. It all came to a halt, as all three told me in unison in the interviews, because of the establishment of the new unity government in June 2014. Once again Palestine and more specifically Palestinian women suffered from the internal political developments and strife. This is regrettable because the unity government officially had the aim of unifying the country, and it eventually had to resign in April 2019.

Did the Draft Law just fall into oblivion and vanish? After so much debate and discussion, this would be surprising. Implementing this Draft Law would have helped enhance gender equality and it would have helped women in Gaza and the West Bank towards more agency – although still not completely equal – with regard to divorce. It would have helped on the international level to show that Palestine was eager to implement CEDAW regulations. Why did it not happen? Given the fact that all parties paid lipservice to the wish to have a single Palestinian family law, there are several possible answers that remain speculative.

On a political level – and this surely is true on a level of legislation or legal debates – there is a high degree of distrust between Fatah and Hamas and distorted perceptions. There seems even to be hardly any cooperation between women's organizations in the West Bank and Gaza and what is done by the other side is seen with reservation. There was no chance to overcome this distrust and enact the Draft Law on *khulʿ* for the sake of all women in Palestine. It might even be true that there was not much knowledge about this Draft Law on the Fatah side of the administration or on the civil society side in the West Bank. With regard to the Sharia establishment, the claim that the West Bank SCHC is trying to control the Sharia system in Gaza has been described above taking the example of al-Jūjū's deposition from his position as a judge in the Gaza Appeals Court through the SCHC.

---

159 Maannews, February 15, 2017.

160 Zaynab al-Ghunaymī, interview on April 11, 2019.

But going one step further, one could speculate that there might have been the perception that such a draft law could not be accepted from a Hamas-led government, even when it concerned a draft law and not a political act. What Ḥasan al-Jūjū had requested and hoped for did not happen: cooperation among the legal institutions in Gaza and the West Bank for the benefit of the Palestinian people.

It is true that al-Jūjū on a general level was in favor of CEDAW, as long as it "does not allow forbidden things" etc.,[161] as does Maḥmūd al-Habbāsh. Both judges have conservative positions with regard to inheritance and the man's right to *ṭalāq*. However, unlike al-Habbāsh, al-Jūjū was ready to be present on a television program in 2017 together with Al-Ghunaymī who did not make his life easy with her gnawing questions and her insistence on taking into account the suffering of women in the Gaza legal system. Al-Ghunaymī had cleverly made it clear that, in her opinion, human rights and Islamic law do not contradict each other and that solutions are available. She reminded all participants in this program that the most important point in the discussion was that women should decide about what was beneficial for them and what was not.

This combination of mutual openness among the three persons representing each one of the main actors in the legal iterations in Gaza, despite very different opinions of how the law should look, could have served as a starting point for a thorough "translation" of international law into national law, of which first steps could be found in the Position Paper of the Gaza Parliament. But political conditions did not allow it.

161 Maannews, February 15, 2017.

CHAPTER 10

Conclusions

This study strived to break new ground and has brought to light new results in mainly four research areas. First, by observing legal iterations and the connected construction of gender roles in a Muslim state for a period of more than seven years (2012–2018), the question was asked why these iterations partly lead to "jurisgenerative" results and partly failed to do so. The aim was to understand how these iterations developed in Palestinian society and "who belled the cat," i.e., who steered these iterations successfully and how some discourses became dominant while others did not. Research so far had most often considered only short-term developments leading to reforms,[1] ignoring long-term developments and discourses that ended without success.

Second, the research combined the analysis of the dominant discourses in these iterations between 2012 and 2018 – *khulʿ* in the first phase (2012–2014) and the question of how international law can be brought into harmony with national law in the second phase (2014–2018) – on the socio-legal level with an in-depth linguistic analysis based on Koselleck's *Begriffsgeschichte* and the approach of "translating from the global to the local." This linguistic analysis proved essential in understanding the shifts in these iterations as well as the social power struggle behind these shifts.[2] In the case of *khulʿ*, there was a successful legal reinterpretation of this kind of divorce, named "judicial *khulʿ*" or even "redemption" (*iftidāʾ*) and a legal implementation in the courts in the West Bank whereas no such process could be observed for the second phase, the harmonization of international and national law. "Equality" (*musāwāh*) as the central term was mentioned but not discussed at the level of legal terminology and a possible neologism, "similarity" (*mumāthala*) was only established in Gaza. In 2020 (summer), no "harmonized" family law draft has found its way to the table of the Ramallah government. Both topics – *khulʿ* and international law – were not selected randomly but had actually dominated the discourse between 2012–2014 and 2014–2018. This approach, i.e., to take the

1 See Buskens 2003; Moors 2003; Schneider 2016b.

2 Welchman 2000 and 2004; Johnson 2004b focused on the long-term development in the transitional period in Palestine, especially on the Model Parliament created by – at that time – a strong civil society; neither of them, however, took the linguistic aspect into consideration. Both researched the whole range of family law topics. Merry 2006 points to the necessity to research those processes of translating "into the vernacular" but has not the regional focus of the Middle east. For the bulk of the Muslim states, this research still remains to be done.

 | DOI:10.1163/9789004442313_011

iterations in the choice of their topics and in the way these topics are spoken about socially and linguistically serious, revealed much about Palestinian society and the main actors contributing to these debates. Palestinian society is struggling for its legal identity. The lens of *khulʿ* and "international law versus Sharia" allowed it to gain a deeper understanding of the Palestinian society and its position toward law and legal reform and the different ways gender was constructed by different actors. I argue that to include the linguistic level and to integrate *Begriffsgeschichte* as well as the approach of "translation" as linguistic "repetitions-in-transformation" are indispensable prerequisites to understanding the power struggle about the authoritative definition of gender roles in Palestine.[3]

Third, the concentration on university teaching as part of iterations, especially when combined with an analysis of the textbook and the actual teaching process has revealed a deeper understanding of intellectual discourses in Palestine in a section of the public sphere, i.e., the universities, which has been ignored so far. It is still a surprisingly underresearched area taking into consideration that it is in universities that the future elite – in this case future lawyers, judges, and scholars – are trained. The question, whether they are well-enough equipped with the existing education to take up the task of harmonizing international law with national law based on Islamic legal terminology must be seriously asked.

Fourth, because of the political situation especially since 2007, there has been more research on the West Bank than on Gaza and research most often concentrated on one area or the other but was not combined and compared as is done in this book.

Seyla Benhabib defined iterations as "complex processes of public argument, deliberation and exchange."[4] These take place in Palestine in legal matters and – regardless of the (non)democratic character of the (not/not yet) State of Palestine – a controversial and open public discussion can be observed. Media played a highly important and surprisingly independent role in transporting these iterations into the public sphere, providing a platform to contradictory opinions, such as the highly contested Supreme Judge's view from December 2018 that beating women lightly for educational reasons is God's law and thus sacrosanct, as well as the harsh reactions of the women's organization to this, which even included the demand not to allow such a humiliating opinion to be officially aired. There was a common commitment of all actors and political factions to want to have a unified Palestinian family law

3 Benhabib 2004: 180.

4 Benhabib 2004: 19; Benhabib 2010: 6.

instead of the applicable old and outdated JLPS and EFRL. Representatives of Fatah in Ramallah stated it as did representatives in Gaza, civil society members as well as Sharia establishment members and representatives of the state. Still, as I finish this book there is no draft law on the table. Why is this the case?

This general question leads us back to the research questions formulated in the introduction: Who can influence or steer these iterations in a certain direction? What is the role of Islamic law, is it a *doxa*? How and when do iterations turn "jurisgenerative"? With regard to the linguistic level the questions asked were: What are the terms, the counterterms and key concepts, which are used in these iterations? Are the terms equally applicable for men and women or do they reveal a gendered meaning, i.e., a meaning that is different for men and women? How are they (re)interpreted? How is the Islamic past "used" and transferred to the present? How is international law "translated" into national law and the national debate on law? And finally: Why was all this considered a "wasps' nest" nobody wanted to touch? A closer look at the iterations reveals a first answer. In the first phase, from 2012 to 2014 discussions focused[5] on a new form of *khulʿ* that should help young women desperately wanting divorce before consummation of the marriage. Whereas the Supreme Judge took a leading role and can be said to have steered the discussions or at least to have influenced them significantly, the civil society claimed also to have exerted pressure in the matter on the Sharia establishment and agreed with *taʿmīm* 59/2012, even praised it. Thus, this iteration and its result cannot be labeled a "demagogic processes of manipulation or authoritarian indoctrination" of the Palestinian society.[6] Yūsuf Idʿīs may have actually "belled the cat" in this situation but he did not impose the topic on the society.

Legally the new ruling can be described as a blurring of the boundary between marriage and engagement and as a legal reification and even a legalization of a Palestinian custom: signing the marriage contract with the engagement to be on the safe side if "something happens." The *taʿmīm* (chapter 4.3) and the *fatwā* of 2015 (chapter 6.3) redefined "engagement," drawing heavily on Maliki "uses of the past" and putting moral pressure on the young couple to "behave" and keep their distance. Not the contract, but the official announcement of the consummation now became central in the *fatwā*. It goes without saying that the reality might look very different and young couples in

5 Another topic debated in the area of law in the public at that time was so-called honor killings. This topic is officially connected to the area of penal law and being connected to the question of whether the perpetrator might get a reduction of his punishment (Welchman and Hossain 2005) has of course close ties to the discussion about family law, because in both debates gender hierarchies are at stake and women are in vulnerable positions.

6 Benhabib 2010: 6.

Palestine as anywhere else in the world did evade these rules and will evade them. But these strict rules are validated by Islamic legal and normative order and are wanted and respected by the society and the families. The question is whether the creation of such a legally problematic construction as *khulʿ* before consummation made sense, as it contravenes the regulations in the old applicable Jordanian and Egyptian laws (JLPS and EFRL) and contradicts Islamic law. The aim of all the regulations is to keep engagement and marriage neatly separated and to allow the bride and bridegroom to part without further legal implications if problems between them arise. While it is true the targeted group of young women gained agency in this special situation of "engagement-cum-marriage" before consummation, gender hierarchy was never touched upon. Soon men took over again and used the new ruling to their benefit, either by repudiating women (*ṭalāq*) or, what seems to have happened more often,[7] by giving their consent to the old version of "consensual *khulʿ*" (*khulʿ riḍāʾī*) thus avoiding going to court. Control of the woman's body remained with the not-yet husband and the family or was transferred to the court but did not go to the women themselves. Sexuality outside of marriage remained strictly forbidden on the grounds of controlling the descent, which de facto still means control over the woman's body, never over the man's.

Taʿmīm 59/2012 did not make much sense legally but did so socially because it helped a specific group of young women and because it gave the Supreme Judge the opportunity to strongly criticize the young men's indecent behavior, to rebuke what he called Palestinian "masculine society" and this aspect of Palestinian custom. Whereas de facto he reaffirmed a custom and integrated it into an Islamic reasoning based on *ijtihād*, he strengthened his prominent position as the highest religious authority in Palestine and his right to take the lead in not only religio-legal but also social discourses. This first phase of the iterations can be said to have ended jurisgeneratively with the issuing of *taʿmīm* 59/2012 and the introduction in the courts in the West Bank. In Gaza, the same iterations can be observed but they led to different results: a draft law that went further than the *taʿmīm* but was not put into force in the end.

Terminological debates start, this is one main observation, when the matter is discussed in society intensively and deeply. In the first phase of the iteration (2012–2014), the fight for the correct term, the "judicial *khulʿ*" was intense and controversial and happening in the public sphere. "Uses of the past" were common among people in the street, on television, and in intellectual discussion.

7 Here empirical research would be necessary that would have to start not at the courts but with families because as was reported, many couples did not go to court but agreed upon the classical *khulʿ* out of the courtroom.

The Quran was quoted, the relevant *ḥadīth* was mentioned at every occasion, the rootedness of this ruling in the religious law stressed even by those in civil society who opted for a civil law. Men fought against being labeled "divorced," whereas Idʿīs defended the "beautiful" word *khulʿ*. In the end, he agreed to change the term to "redemption" (*iftidāʾ*) to soothe them. Different terminologies were thrown into the discussion, e.g., in the case of the active participles of the root *kh-l-ʿ* – *khāliʿa/mukhāliʿa* – to find an acceptable expression for women's new agency. In the television program *Lāzim Naḥkī* (April 30, 2013), the host Jumān Qunayṣ tackled the gendered language consciously and provoked men: "Dear husbands, if you approve injustice to your wife, be prepared, you may become divorced (*makhlūʿ*)."[8] The term *khulʿ* was defined further in the West Bank through adjectives added to it: the traditional version had to be labeled "consensual *khulʿ*" to differentiate it from the new "judicial *khulʿ*." Counterterms were put forward, here especially "repudiation" (*ṭalāq*). *Khulʿ* remained generally a "traditional concept" in the Koselleckian sense and retained an empirical validity as a kind of divorce in exchange for money – the new elements being that the divorce is now attached to a court procedure and can, at least before consummation, be achieved against the husband's will. Surprising or perhaps revealing is that according to at least one reading of the *ḥadīth*, this interpretation (against the husband's will) could have been used 1,400 years ago – but was not and was still much debated in 2012. It will be interesting to see whether the term *khulʿ* will be replaced by "redemption" (*iftidāʾ*) in a future Palestinian family law as it was in the 2010 legislation in Jordan.

In Gaza, conversely, civil society and the Sharia establishment had in a concerted effort prepared a *khulʿ* law that was actually a draft law, not only a *taʿmīm*, and thus went formally and with regard to the legal regulation beyond the West Bank *taʿmīm* 59/2012. It allowed women the redemption before and after consummation and thus can be compared to the Egyption version of the law issued in 2000 and highly praised for giving women for the first time in the Middle East the right to divorce against the husband's will without having to give a reason. In a Gaza Parliament Position Paper, this was justified with Sharia but reference was made to international law. The Gaza citizen who stood up in the television program and expressed his incomprehension about why his daughter should not sign her marriage contract herself[9] shows the critical potential in Gaza society as well as the anger about the slow development

8 *Lāzim Naḥkī*, April 30, 2013; it would be interesting to look now, several years later, at the use of the active-passive dichotomy in the legal language.

9 Maannews, February 15, 2017.

of women's rights. In this case, it was the father wanting more rights for the daughter. He was stopped by the judge defending the applicable law.

In the second phase (2014–2018), the discourse in the West Bank but also in Gaza shifted to a more general discussion about the way international law should have to be integrated into national legislation. A title of a television program in the West Bank reflected this very precisely: "Palestine Discusses Interpretations of the Sharia which can be Harmonized with CEDAW … and the Split between the Scholars of Religion and Politicians Becomes Wider."[10] It tackled the core and kernel of the problem. The persons interviewed took controversial positions – from the *Qāḍī al-Quḍāt* al-Habbāsh saying: "Any contradiction to what God has legislated (*mā sharraʿahu Allāh*) we will not accept," to ʿIwaḍallāh of the Ministry of Foreign Affairs, responsible for international treaties, who argued that international law is against backward ideals and customs that are not in accordance with any religion.[11] In the different Shadow Reports, civil society referred to international law, stressing the fact that Abbas had signed the treaties, especially CEDAW without reservations thus obliging the State of Palestine to harmonize the existing laws with international standards.

The Report of the State of Palestine delivered to the CEDAW Committee contained a polished picture of the legal situation, partly accusing the Israeli occupation and the "suffering from inherited customs and traditions" to be the cause for the non-existence of a Palestinian law,[12] partly integrating the SCHC *taʿmīmāt* as amendments as if they were part of the legislation thereby modestly hiding the fact that in the twenty-five years since the creation of the Palestinian Authority, fifteen years of which there had existed a working parliament, no progress has been made toward a Palestinian family law. Needless to say, the Report had been drawn up with the help of the West Bank Sharia establishment and the civil society, but Gaza scholars or activists do not seem to have played a role in it. The progressive Gaza Draft Law reforming *khulʿ* was put away in a drawer and forgotten.

The Report was strangely silent about the role of religious law as anchored in Article 4 of the Basic Law and the de facto powerful position of the Sharia establishment, especially the SCHC. When asked by the CEDAW Committee the Report gave an evasive answer that did not point to the central task standing in front of the door: to harmonize religious law with international legislation, a task that could not be achieved against the *Qāḍī al-Quḍāt* at the top of the Sharia establishment. Both state and civil society might have been guided

10 Wattan, June 21, 25 and 30, 2018.

11 Wattan, June 21, 2018.

12 CEDAW Report 2017: 13.

by the wish to present a modern, secular Palestine to the international community, which is only held back from giving women full equal rights because of the occupation and – in the perspective of the civil society – by what they regarded as a non-democratic government. Both underestimated the important position and role of the Sharia establishment and especially the role of the Supreme Judge, who, since 2014, is Maḥmūd al-Habbāsh.

The only strong, convincing and very self-confident report arguing in favor of gender equality from an Islamic point of view came from a transregional NGO, the Malaysian Musawah. Musawah raised its voice and argued that egalitarian laws based on the Quran are possible in Palestine.[13] Is it pure accident that such an Islamic voice could make itself heard independent from the national Sharia establishment? What does this mean for the role of Islamic law in the Palestinian iterations and its being a *doxa*? In a certain sense, Islamic legal regulations were taken for granted in the first part of the debate; but even here – and much more so in the second phase when international law was discussed and the question raised of how it could be harmonized with Islamic law – Sharia was never seen as something unchangeable, just existent, i.e., a *doxa*. It may have been considered "taken for granted" but was never "unaware of the very question of legitimacy."[14] It can be better described as a "dominant repertoire" in discussions of personal status, but not as a *doxa*.[15]

Despite "harmonizing the law with international law" being an often-heard phrase in the second phase of the iterations and besides the often-announced aim to use *ijtihād* as a method to achieve this goal, the central questions remained unanswered: how could international law be "translated" from the global to the local, into the "vernacular"?[16] And who would be the right person or body to lead the process, especially given the fact of a very conservative head of the Sharia Judiciary who was unlikely to move in this direction?

With regard to the first part of the question – how – it can be assumed that, as the whole framing of the discourse in Palestine as in many Muslim states is Islamic, international law has to be "translated" not only into national legal terms but also into Islamic terms with regard to family law. The concept of "equality" (*musāwāh*) as the central concept to define gender relations in CEDAW could have served as starting point to become the linguistic focus on the stage of "translating the global into the local." Idʿīs's argued in his lecture

13 Chapter 7.3.
14 Bourdieu 1972: 168.
15 Welchman 2003: 69, see also Engelcke 2017a: 33 who speaks of "orthodoxy" for the Jordanian context.
16 Merry 2006: 1.

at Birzeit University that giving women the right to *khulʿ* against the husband's wishes could be seen as "equality" (*musāwāḥ*). However, in the meeting at al-Quds University in early 2013, in which he also was present, the Sharia establishment not only demanded the exclusive right of the SCHC to draft a family law but also attacked the draft drawn up by the National Committee of the Family Law (NCFL) of which it had itself been a party on many points, calling "equality" an "unjust claim." This reveals the Supreme Judge's use of "equality" in his lecture as merely cosmetic and reflects a conservative approach with regard to gender equality in the Sharia establishment in the West Bank. Another, competing term taken from the Quran, *mumāthala* (similarity) of rights was used in *taʿmīm* 59/2012 but not discussed further, and also, to the best of my knowledge, not developed further.

Again Gaza reveals a different picture. The new *khulʿ* Draft Law gave women the right to *khulʿ* against the husband's wishes before and after consummation. It was, in addition, connected to the "principle of the similarity (*mumāthala*) of rights and duties which Islam recognizes," those rights, in turn, were connected to CEDAW and international law. It is here, in the Position Paper of the Gaza Parliament controlled by Hamas that "translation" from international law to the national and Islamic context began and *mumāthala* was introduced and defined as an Islamic version of "equality," which at least with regard to *khulʿ* went further than the West Bank ruling. Given the political background of an Islamist government, this achievement for women's rights seems even more surprising. It even might be said that Gaza in this legal area of redefining "equality" "belled the cat." All the more regrettable that it was not implemented by the Ramallah-led unity government that ruled from 2014 to 2019.

In the public discussion in Gaza,[17] reference was even made to the legal term *musāwāh*, and for inequality, the charming metaphor for men's and women's right of "[normal] cucumber and Armenian cucumber" was used. Even if this metaphor for inequality does not replace an in-depth legal discussion about the central term of equality, it does show that "political repetitions-in-transformation" did happen in the Gazan public sphere.[18] Whereas in the West Bank, the debates remained too general and less focused on concrete topics, and did not approach "translating" equality into an Islamic context.[19]

As a result, it can be stated that substantial shifts toward jurisgenerative acts take place only after the debate has gone through an intensive phase of

17 Maannews, February 15, 2017.

18 Benhabib 2004: 180.

19 As exceptions see scientific articles of Qafisheh 2018 and Damiri 2018.

in-depth linguistic discussion and "repetitions-in-transformation." This is at least one important requirement. But it is, of course, not sufficient.

To translate "equality" on a general level and more in detail to make new suggestions to harmonize national law with international law, competence in Islamic law and especially developing Islamic legal thinking further, i.e., *ijtihād*, is needed. At this point, the decisive role of the universities comes in: other than at universities, where should training and education in classical Islamic law, its sources, its manifold interpretations, and its methodological approaches for reforming it take place? The chapter on university teaching showed that in this special course on personal status law in the winter of 2013/14 at Birzeit University neither in the textbook nor in the actual teaching process was a foundation laid for a thorough training of students. An introduction into a critical use of *ijtihād* was not included. This may be true for this course but not for others; universities with Sharia faculties must be included in the research. Analyzing university teaching and education for law students in these fields is only at its inception and this study hopes to stimulate further work in this area.[20]

For the time being, the other part of the question, who could take up the leading position in such a debate, has to be tackled. It is the position of the *Qāḍī al-Quḍāt* that is regarded as central for the initiation of these iterations. This was confirmed in many interviews with representatives of the state and the Sharia establishment. The civil society representatives viewed the matter differently and claimed for themselves the right to draw up draft laws in family law as they had claimed the right to have recognized the underlying social problem and to have developed strategies for its solution. In a way, this is not ultimately decidable and may well have been a process of mutual interference. In Gaza, the initiative certainly came from civil society. Whereas the Sharia establishment observed the legal and social problems of women from the point of the view of judges, in civil society many lawyers are active who had to wrestle with the same problem from the woman's point of view.[21]

20 My research focused on BZU, which has no Sharia Faculty. This is why personal status law, based on Islamic law, was taught by the Supreme Judge as a visiting professor in 2013. In 2019, Ṣumūd al-Ḍamīrī taught it. Thus, the approaches of the Sharia faculties in other Palestinian universities still could be an interesting research area. However, the communique (*bayān*) presented by the majority of scholars and some judges as result of the "day of study" at Al-Quds University, see 2.2.2, reflected a very conservative position of Islamic law, which was not oriented toward gender equality at all. At several points where I tried to make contact to Sharia scholars in universities in Palestine, I was not successful.

21 Here reference can be made to Engelcke's research on Jordan: "The SJD [Supreme Judge Department] was able to impose the terms of debate, to shape the development of family law, and to reserve the religious foundation of the law." Engelcke 2017a: 33. It has to

The *Qāḍī al-Quḍāt* may not be the only one. The Women's Affairs minister, Hayfā' al-Āghā, was, according to the state report to CEDAW, the one who should take a leading position in developing the family law. This is actually what Ḥasan al-ʿŪrī was referring to when he proposed "to bell the cat": he saw it as the state's obligation to initiate a discussion process and to decide in the end what the law should look like. Al-Āghā's position in the iterations was weak. When she tried very cautiously and gently to criticize polygyny, she was immediately rebuked by a (male) lecturer from al-Quds University, al-Kaswānī, arguing that there are forbidden things (*al-muḥarramāt*), i.e., topics that cannot be touched upon in Palestinian society suggesting that polygyny is one.[22] This again hints to the great power and influence of the Sharia establishment and here especially of the scholars in Islamic law at the universities. As Islamic law is adaptable and, as in other Arab and Muslim states, reforms in many areas have been made – see Egypt for *khulʿ* in 2000 – this cannot be a question of the study of Islamic jurisprudence alone. It simply reflects a very patriarchal position of those scholars and judges who do not wish to give up their right to interprete the texts in a conservative and gender hierarchial manner. There are, on the other side, persons in the Sharia establishment who are trained in and concentrating on traditional gender stereotypes and also wish to overcome them and opt for an interpretation of Sharia that is more directed toward gender equality. Ṣumūd al-Ḍamīrī,[23] Judge of the Court of Appeals and Head of Prosecution and thus in a high position in the Sharia establishment,[24] is such a person. She actively opted for a new *ijtihād* in those matters concerning women and generally showed her preparedness to think about reforming the applicable law toward international standards without giving up the core and kernel of Islamic law. In Gaza, the well-functioning cooperation between the representatives of state, civil society and Sharia establishment led to substantial suggestions to revise the law, which was accepted by the Gaza Parliament.

This is connected to the question not only *who* has the knowledge to speak but also *who can speak louder than others and silence other voices*. It is about what Foucault considered so important: the power that is intrinsically connected to all discourses. The debate about the harmonization of international and national law started in the summer of 2018, even before the delegation had visited Geneva. Certainly there are reasons outside of society, especially political

---

be kept in mind, however, that the Sharia establishment and also the Supreme Judge Department is not a homogeneous body.

22 See Abū Ṭaʿīma, December 20, 2018.

23 Damiri 2018.

24 See for more information, Nilesat, March 24, 2019.

reasons, why bringing forward a draft law is difficult. But a new Palestinian family law would have helped to raise international awareness of Palestine's gender policy. Or to put it in the words of ʿIṣām ʿĀbidīn: for a state under occupation like Palestine, it gives a bad impression to fight for the right of self-determination but not to respect human rights.[25]

It might not seem too farfetched to recognize the cause of this gridlock in the person of Maḥmūd al-Habbāsh, the Supreme Judge since 2014. He succeeded in redirecting the discourse and drawing all media attention in December 2018[26] to his statement that light hitting of women for educational purposes does not pose a problem from the perspective of Islamic law. This can be considered a well-placed and successful provocation because it de facto immediately distracted the discussion from the necessity to harmonize national law with international law and the question of how to do this and forced civil society to start again defending at a very basic level – which in Palestine had been overcome long time ago – a woman's right not to be beaten and killed; to make clear that violence against women is forbidden and that hitting is violence. The Supreme Judge had to be reminded that he had transgressed even the applicable laws[27] of 1976 and 1954, because both family laws allow women who were injured to go to court and get a divorce. The State of Palestine – and the government in Ramallah – added to this situation the factual ignorance of a detailed draft law in Gaza and an indecisiveness and lethargy with regard to the international treaties.[28] After signing the CEDAW, and still by April 2019, the signing had not been announced in the Official Gazette.[29]

This leads us back to the question of who influences the iterations, when do iterations turn "jurisgenerative" and who will "bell the cat"? And how is all this connected to the linguistic aspect of these iterations? Several answers can be given to this: in the West Bank, it is not the state but the Sharia establishment that can be seen as the powerful player who can either stimulate a discussion – as in the case with the *khulʿ* ruling – or block it as al-Habbāsh did; it can do this on a social and on a linguistic level. The Sharia establishment in the West Bank thus took a constructive as well as a destructive role. Civil society

25 Abū Ṭaʿīma, December 20, 2018.

26 *Āfāq*, December 1, 2018.

27 JLPS Article 182; EFRL Article 97.

28 Alwatanvoice, December 4, 2017. Not even the Family Protection Law against Violence, on the table and much discussed since late 2017, had a chance to be enacted as law by the president.

29 On April 8, 2019, I had an interview with Imān ʿAbdalḥamīd, Head of the Legislation Advisory Bureau, and she confirmed that to this date none of the international treaties had arrived in her office to be prepared for publication in the Gazette.

interfered and representatives of the women's organizations did their best, for example, by blocking the process of drafting the law when they saw it would lead to a conservative Islamic version. They tried to gain ground when Abbas signed CEDAW and the Palestinian delegation went to Geneva. But so far they have not been as strong as the Sharia establishment.

President Abbas might not have been willing or able to step into this "wasps' nest" of family law knowing how highly contested it is between these two players. He may have decided to sign the international treaties in 2014, hoping to kill two birds with one stone: raising international acceptance and respect for Palestine, which as a Muslim state decided to not only join international conventions but also to sign them without reservations, and, second, creating a strong obligation in Palestine to harmonize the existing laws with international law. However, as long as he does not take matters into his own hands – to "bell the cat," to quote that saying again – and issue a decree of family law, there is a danger that his expectations will be unfulfilled or that the process might even backfire. It is here that the internal power struggle about the "right" version of a Palestinian family law started.

In Gaza, as explained, the cooperation between the three representatives of state, civil society and Sharia establishment led to a draft law, strictly based on Islamic principles, which, had it been implemented, would have helped women whose divorce cases were stuck for several years in court. The woman would have been the one, as al-Ghunaymī put it, "who decides … what is beneficial to her."[30] This central aspect to reform the divorce process and the Palestinian family law got lost in the political developments at the end of 2018. That the Gaza law failed was in this special case – as all three agreed – not the fault of the Gaza state but the fault of the Ramallah-based unity government.

Ḥasan al-ʿŪrī's wish that the State of Palestine should be the one to "bell the cat" and initiate legislation has in the area of family law – the stronghold of Sharia – not been realized so far. There seems to have been a strong reluctance of the government, especially on the part of the president, to put together a law and enforce it via presidential decree. Whereas fifteen years earlier there had been hope that this weakness of the state would or could lead to "opportunities for gender-aware reform,"[31] in 2019, it seems obvious that the Sharia establishment in the West Bank stepped in and blocked such debates. This is a development that Engelcke also noted with regard to the 2010 family law reform in Jordan.[32]

30 Maannews, February 15, 2017.
31 Johnson 2004b: 161.
32 Engelcke 2017a.

The legal development is, of course, dependent on political developments. In 2019, *Haaretz* published a poll titled "42 percent of Israelis Back West Bank Annexation including Two-State Supporters,"[33] reporting that only a third of the Israeli population (34 percent) still supported the two-state solution.[34] Different versions are seen as possible. The two-state solution – "two states for two peoples" – means the establishment of an independent and demilitarized Palestinian state in the West Bank and Gaza; the confederation modelled on the European Union in which each state would have its own government and legislative bodies but certain areas like water management, the environment, and natural resources would be jointly administered. The one-state solution ranges between the vision of an exclusively Jewish or Palestinian state or the vision of one democratic state. It includes various forms of Israeli annexation, some provide citizenship and voting rights for the Palestinian and some do not.[35]

Still, if Palestine has the option of forming a state of its own, neither its political order nor the family law-gender conceptions would diverge much from those in the neighboring states, such as Egypt, Jordan, or Israel. Taking Muhammad Khalid Masud's definition of a public sphere in a Muslim country as a starting point, religion will play a role[36] and a "social construction of the Sharia"[37] will take place. It will have its own "Palestinian" flavor as described in this book. Much will depend on the position of the Sharia establishment. Al-Habbāsh was reinstated as the Supreme Judge after a cabinet shuffle in spring 2019. However, the Sharia establishment is not confined to the Supreme Judge, nor is it a monolith. The question is whether representatives of the Sharia establishment, other than the Supreme Judge, can divert the iterations in another direction and open the debates toward a harmonization between national and international law. In this situation, the appointment of women as judges and ministers has proven decisive. After the first wave of oppositions against their nominations died down, new questions were put on the table revealing serious inconsistencies and contradictions in the Palestinian public: How could a woman, who was not even allowed to sign her own marriage contract, act as a minister and make decisions on national political issues? How could a female judge or marriage officer in a Sharia court testify to a marriage

33 Kraft, March 25, 2019.

34 Kraft, March 25, 2019.

35 Maltz, March 24, 2019

36 Masud 2005: 155–156.

37 Masud 2005: 158. For very short descriptions of these debates in Pakistan, see for the family law reform 1961–1971, Masud: 2005: 169–171; followed by a process of "Islamization of laws" between 1979 and 1985, see Masud 2005: 171–175.

contract while her own testimony as a woman is legally deficient? It is typical for the open and controversial public in Palestine that these questions are asked and traditional positions are challenged. Despite all social difficulties, despite a still "masculine society" and despite a weak government, it seems not imaginable that women who gained high positions in the Palestinian society can be dislodged from these positions. In front of the international community, Palestine showed that gender equality is a target it will go on to pursue. Much will depend on the position of civil society and whether it can consolidate its position and press for reforms aimed at gender equality – surely in an Islamic framing. It will also depend on how much the weak, almost non-existent Palestinian state, which showed its readiness to engage for gender equality when Abbas signed CEDAW, will be able to balance both players, Sharia establishment and civil society, and initiate a real iterative process in the framework of the LHC, the Legislation Harmonization Committee, to bring about a Palestinian family law acceptable to the the society as a whole.

Above all, however, one hopes that one or another version of a state becomes a reality for Palestine and that it is modeled in such a way that Palestinians can decide what their state should look like and which legal instruments and methods should be used to develop and implement new laws.

References

Abdo, Nahla (1999): "Gender and Politics under the Palestinian Authority." *Journal of Palestine Studies* 28, pp. 38–51.

Abdulhadi, Faiha (February 17, 2015): "Maha Abu Dayyeh: A Life of Dedication." *The Feminist Wire*, see: http://www.thefeministwire.com/2015/02/maha-abu-dayyeh/ (accessed June 8, 2017).

Abdulhadi, Rabab (1998): "The Palestinian Women's Autonomous Movement." *Gender and Society* 12, pp. 649–673.

Abou Jalal, Rasha (February 11, 2016): "How One Palestinian Minister is Empowering Women." *Al-Monitor*, see: https://www.al-monitor.com/pulse/originals/2016/02/palestinian-women-affairs-minister-empower.html (accessed February 7, 2018).

Abu Amer, Ahmad (December 6, 2017): "Cybercrime Law Draws Mixed Reactions among Palestinians." *Al-Monitor*, see: https://www.al-monitor.com/pulse/ru/contents/articles/originals/2017/07/palestine-cybercrime-law-opposition-government.html (accessed January 31, 2018).

Abu Hayyeh, Ashraf (2011): *The Experience of Personal Status Law Reform in the Occupied Palestinian Territory*. Ramallah: WCLAC.

Abu-Lughod, Lila (2009): "Dialects of Women's Empowerment: The International Circuitry of the Arab Human Development Report 2005." *IJMES* 41, pp. 83–103.

Abusada, Mkhaimar (2010): "Islam versus Secularism in Palestine: Hamas vs. Fatah." Conference Paper, prepared for "The Transformation of Palestine: Palestine and the Palestinians 60 Years after the 'Nakba'", March 2010. Heinrich Böll Stiftung, Berlin, see: https://www.boell.de/en/2010/03/12/islam-versus-secularism-palestine-hamas-vs-fatah (accessed April 30, 2019).

Abū Ṭaʿīma, Nāhid (June 23, 2013): "Taḥqīq ṣuḥufī – ʿabāʾat al-raʾīs wa-l-maḥākim al-sharʿiyya." *Maannews* [*Maʿan*], see: http://maannews.net/Content.aspx?id=607478 (accessed September 9, 2017).

Abū Ṭaʿīma, Nāhid (December 20, 2018): "Al-ḥaqq la-mīn [sic! i.e., li-man] intiqādāt ḥawla khiṭāb al-karāhiyya wa-raghbat al-ḥukūma bi-l-taḥaffuẓ ʿalā al-ittifāqiyyāt al-dawliyya." *Maannews* [*Maʿan*], see: https://www.youtube.com/watch?v=UibVpize6jM (accessed January 18, 2019).

Abū Ṭāqiyya, Āṣāl (October 31, 2013): "'Qānūn al-Khul'' ... Riḍan ḥadhir wa-khashya min sūʾ istikhdāmihi." *Alray* [*al-raʾy*], see: https://alray.ps/ar/post/112194/قانون-الخلع--رضا-حذر-وخشيةٌ-من-سوء-استخدامه (accessed December 10, 2018).

Adamczyk, Sarah (2011): *The Shariʿa Courts and Personal Status Law in Gaza*. Norwegian Refuge Council, see: https://www.nrc.no/globalassets/pdf/reports/the-sharia-courts-and-personal-status-laws-in-the-gaza-strip.pdf (accessed February 9, 2019).

Āfāq (December 1, 2018): "Al-ʿunf ḍidda al-marʾa wa-mawqif al-Islām minhu." See: https://www.youtube.com/watch?v=OZDL9Uq6FoU&t=0s&list=WL&index=15 (accessed January 22, 2019).

Āghā, Hayfāʾ al- (2018): "Kalimat dawlat Filasṭīn tulqīhā d. Hayfāʾ al-Āghā." See: https://tbinternet.ohchr.org/_layouts/treatybodyexternal/Download.aspx?symbolno=INT%2fCEDAW%2fSTA%2fPSE%2f31734&Lang=en (accessed January 9, 2018).

Akhbār maḥalliyya (November 10, 2015): "Nisāʾ wa-Āfāq taṭraḥ miswaddat taʿdīl li-qānūn qarār ḥuqūq al-ʿāʾila al-ʿuthmānī." *Panet*, see: http://www.panet.co.il/article/1119202 (accessed August 30, 2017).

Alaqsavoice [idhāʿat ṣawt al-Aqṣā] (February 19, 2008): "Iqṣāʾ jadīd … ʿAbbās yuqīl raʾīs maḥkamat al-istiʾnāf al-sharʿiyya bi-Ghazza." See: http://alaqsavoice.ps/news/details/13626 (accessed April 1, 2019).

Alarabiya [al-ʿarabiyya] (April 24, 2013): "Zawjat asīr ḥizb Allāh Samīr al-Quntār takhlaʿuhu fī al-maḥkama." See: https://www.alarabiya.net/ar/arab-and-world/2013/04/23/زوجة-أسير-حزب-الله-قنطار-تخلعه-في-المحكمة.html (accessed January 30, 2019).

Al-Botmeh, Reem (2012): *A Review of Palestinian Legislation from a Women's Rights Perspective*. N.p.: UNDP: Rule of Law and Access to Justice Program.

Albrecht, Holger (2005): "Zivilgesellschaft und der Vordere Orient: Das Prinzip Hoffnung und die Grenzen eines Sozialwissenschaftlichen Konzepts." *Zivilgesellschaft* (eds. Joachim Betz and Wolfgang Hein), pp. 118–143. Wiesbaden: VS Verl. für Sozialwissenschaften.

Al-Ghoul, Asmaa (October 21, 2016): "Are NGOs in Palestine up to the Challenge?" *Al-Monitor*, see: http://www.al-monitor.com/pulse/en/originals/2016/10/palestine-civil-society-institutions-fail-hamas-fatah.html (accessed January 31, 2018).

Al-Haq (December 27, 2016): "Al-Haq Expresses Concern about the Internal Palestinian Political Situation." See: https://medium.com/@AlHaq.EN/al-haq-expresses-concern-about-the-internal-palestinian-political-situation-a5846f4d21ca (accessed January 18, 2018).

Al-Haq (August 3, 2017): "Letters Sent to UN Special Rapporteur on Palestines Cyber Crimes Law." See: http://www.alhaq.org/advocacy/topics/palestinian-violations/1131-letters-sent-to-un-special-rapporteur-on-palestines-cyber-crimes-law (accessed January 31, 2018).

Al-Haq (June 2018): "Al-Haq Submission to the Committee on the Elimination of Discrimination against Women in the First Periodic Review. The State of Palestine, 70th Session." See: https://tbinternet.ohchr.org/_layouts/treatybodyexternal/Download.aspx?symbolno=INT%2fCEDAW%2fNGO%2fPSE%2f31670&Lang=en (accessed January 8, 2019).

Alhourriah [*al-ḥurriyya*] (October 6, 2012): "Iqrār al-khulʿ fī Filasṭīn lam yaʾti bi-fatwā al-sharʿiyya bal ijtihād li-murāʿāt ḥuqūq al-marʾa." See: http://www.alhourriah.ps/ar/?page=det&id=16200 (accessed July 15, 2017).

Ali, Shaheen S. (2000): *Gender and Human Rights in Islam and International Law*. The Hague: Kluwer Law International.

AlMadina (May 1, 2013): "Maḥkama sharʿiyya filasṭīniyya tuqirru bi-ʿkhulʿ'." *AlMadina*, see: http://almadina.de/pdf/2013-05.pdf (accessed April 30, 2019).

Al-Muqtafī, Palestinian Legal and Judicial System. See: muqtafi.birzeit.edu/en (accessed December 28, 2017).

Al-Waheidi, Majd (June 4, 2017): "Gaza Dating Site Matches Widows to Men seeking 2nd (or 3rd) Wife." *New York Times*, see: https://www.nytimes.com/2017/06/04/world/middleeast/gaza-palestinians-hamas-wesal-polygamy.html?mcubz=0 (accessed September 27, 2017).

Alwatanvoice [*Dunyā al-waṭan*] (November 6, 2012): "Zawjat Samīr al-Qunṭār tarfaʿ ḍiddahu qaḍīyat 'al-khulʿ… shāhid bi-l-ṣuwar'." See: http://www.alwatanvoice.com/arabic/news/2012/11/06/331678.html (accessed January 30, 2019).

Alwatanvoice [*Dunyā al-waṭan*] (August 22, 2013): "Taṭbīq al-khulʿ fī Gazza qarīban." See: https://m.alwatanvoice.com/show/427715.html (accessed July 7, 2017).

Alwatanvoice [*Dunyā al-waṭan*] (December 4, 2017): "Muntadā al-munaẓẓamāt al-ahliyya yuṭālib bi-iqrār qānūn ḥimāyat al-usra min al-ʿunf." See: https://www.alwatanvoice.com/arabic/news/2017/12/04/1104358.html (accessed March 23, 2019).

Amīn: [Shabakat amīn al-aʿlamiyya] (October 11, 2009): "Filasṭīn taḥṣul ʿalā al-asbaqiyya: awwal qāḍiya fī al-maḥākim al-sharʿiyya tataḥaddath ʿan tajribatihā." See: http://blog.amin.org/hibalama/2009/10/11/فلسطين-تحصل-على-الأسبقية-أول-قاضية-في-ا/ (accessed August 28, 2017).

Ambrozas, Diana (1998): "The University as Public Sphere." *Canadian Journal of Communication* 23 (1), see: http://cjc-online.ca/index.php/journal/article/view/1024/930 (accessed January 7, 2015).

Anderson, James Norman Dalrymple (1951): "Recent Developments in Sharīʿa Law V: The Dissolution of Marriage." *The Muslim World* 41, pp. 271–288.

Anderson, James Norman Dalrymple (1968): "The Eclipse of the Patriarchal Family in Contemporary Islamic Law." *Family Law in Asia and Africa* (ed. James Norman Dalrymple Anderson), pp. 221–234. London: Allen and Unwin.

An-Naʿim, Abdullahi A. (1992): "Toward a Cross-Cultural Approach to Defining International Standards of Human Rights: The Meaning of Cruel, Inhuman, or Degrading Treatment or Punishment." *Human Rights in Cross-Cultural Perspectives* (ed. Abdullahi A. An-Naʿim), pp. 19–43. Philadelphia: Univ. of Pennsylvania Press.

Bachmann-Medick, Doris (2009): "Introduction: The Translational Turn." *Translation Studies* 2, pp. 2–16.

Baer, Susanne (2011): "Travelling Concepts: Substantive Equality on the Road." *Tulsa Law Review* 46, pp. 59–79.

Baʿlūsha, Ḥāzim (February 23, 2013): "Khulūd al-Faqiyya [sic!] ūlā imraʾa ʿalā kursī al-qaḍāʾ al-sharʿī al-filasṭīnī." *Deutsche Welle*, see: http://www.dw.com/ar/خلود-الفقية-أولى-امرأة-على-كرسي-القضاء-الشرعي-الفلسطيني/a-16613862 (accessed August 28, 2017).

Basic Law for the Federal Republic of Germany (1949, last amended in 2014). See: https://www.gesetze-im-internet.de/englisch_gg/englisch_gg.html#p0029 (accessed March 5, 2019).

Basic Law Palestine 2003 (amended 2005). See: www.venice.coe.int/webforms/documents/default.aspx?pdffile=CDL(2009)008-e (accessed September 15, 2017).

Bauer, Thomas (2011): *Die Kultur der Ambiguität*. Berlin: Verlag der Weltreligionen.

Baumgarten, Helga, and Karin A. Gerster (2011): "Palestinian NGOs and their Cultural, Economic and Political Impact in Palestinian Society." Rosa-Luxemburg-Foundation, December 30, 2011, see: http://rosaluxemburg.ps/wp-content/uploads/2015/03/RLF_PAL_Paper.-Palestinian-NGOs2.pdf (accessed October 5, 2017).

Bayān al-khitāmī, al- (November 2, 2013): "ʿUqida fī Kulliyyat al-daʿwā wa-uṣūl al-dīn fī Jāmiʿat al-Quds, yawm dirāsī li-munāqashat miswaddat mashrūʿ qānūn al-aḥwāl al-shakhṣiyya al-muqtaraḥ min al-lajna al-waṭaniyya li-qānūn al-usra (Dhū l-ḥijja 28 1434/Tashrīn al-thānī 2, 2013)." See: http://www.feqhweb.com/vb/t17803.html (accessed September 8, 2017).

"Belling the Cat." (2019). *Wikipedia*, see: https://en.wikipedia.org/wiki/Belling_the_Cat (accessed April 1, 2019).

Belting, Julia (2008): "Empirical Methods: Expert Interviews." See: http://www.oat.ethz.ch/education/Autumn_term_08/Material_on_Empirical_Methods/Expert_Interview.pdf (accessed June 17, 2014) (site discontinued).

Benhabib, Seyla (2004): *The Rights of Others*. Cambridge: Cambridge Univ. Press.

Benhabib, Seyla (2010): "Human Rights, Sovereignty and Democratic Iterations." Keynote Lecture "Human Rights – Global Culture – International Institutions", Hannover, November 4, 2010. See: http://www.ourcommonfuture.de/fileadmin/user_upload/dateien/Reden/Benhabib.pdf (accessed December 9, 2016).

Berlinerblau, Jacques (2001): "Toward a Sociology of Heresy, Orthodoxy, and Doxa." *History of Religions* 40, pp. 327–351.

Berger, Miriam (May 22, 2017): "Divorced in Gaza because of Reality." *US News*, see: https://www.usnews.com/news/best-countries/articles/2017-05-22/conflict-feeds-rising-divorce-rates-across-gaza (accessed September 27, 2017).

Berti, Benedetta (2015): "Non-State Actors as Providers of Governance: The Hamas Government in Gaza between Effective Sovereignty, Centralized Authority, and Resistance." *Middle East Journal* 69 (1), pp. 9–31.

Bourdieu, Pierre (1972): *Outline of a Theory of Practice*. Transl. by Richard Nice. Cambridge: Cambridge Univ. Press.

Brown, Nathan (2000): "Constituting Palestine: The Effort to Write a Basic Law For The Palestinian Authority." *Middle East Journal* 54 (1), pp. 25–43.

Brown, Nathan J. (2012): *Gaza Five Years On: Hamas Settles In*. Washington, DC: The Carnegie Endowment for International Peace.

Bruhn, Christa (2006): "Higher Education as Empowerment: The Case of Palestinian Universities." *American Behavioral Scientist* 49 (8), pp. 1125–1142.

Buskens, Leon (2003): "Recent Debates on Family Law Reform in Morocco: Islamic Law as Politics in an Emerging Public Sphere." *Islamic Law and Society* 10, pp. 70–131.

Cardinal, Monique C. (2005): "Islamic Legal Theory Curriculum: Are the Classics Taught Today?" *Islamic Law and Society* 12, pp. 224–272.

CEDAW (*Convention on the Elimination of All Forms of Discrimination against Women*). See: http://www.un.org/womenwatch/daw/cedaw/cedaw.htm (accessed January 16, 2019).

CEDAW Report (date received March 10, 2017): *Committee on the Elimination of All Forms of Discrimination against Women. Consideration of Reports Submitted by State Parties under Article 18 of the Convention Pursuant to the Simplified Reporting Procedure. Initial Reports of State Parties Due in 2015. State of Palestine*. See: https://tbinternet.ohchr.org/_layouts/treatybodyexternal/Download.aspx?symbolno=CEDAW%2fC%2fPSE%2f1&Lang=en (accessed January 3, 2019).

CEDAW *List of Delegation* (2018). See: https://tbinternet.ohchr.org/_layouts/treatybodyexternal/Download.aspx?symbolno=INT%2fCEDAW%2fLOP%2fPSE%2f31337&Lang=en (accessed January 10, 2019).

CEDAW List of Issues and Questions (November 30, 2017): *List of Issues and Questions in Relation to the Initial Report of the State of Palestine*. See: https://tbinternet.ohchr.org/_layouts/treatybodyexternal/Download.aspx?symbolno=CEDAW%2fC%2fPSE%2fQ%2f1&Lang=en (accessed January 7, 2019).

CEDAW Replies (date received February 19, 2018): *Replies of the State of Palestine*. See: https://tbinternet.ohchr.org/_layouts/treatybodyexternal/Download.aspx?symbolno=CEDAW%2fC%2fPSE%2fQ%2f1%2fAdd.1&Lang=en (accessed January 7, 2019).

CEDAW *Discusses with Civil Society Organizations the Situation of Women in State of Palestine – Press Release (Excerpts)* (July 9, 2018). See: https://www.un.org/unispal/document/cedaw-discusses-with-civil-society-organizations-the-situation-of-women-in-state-of-palestine-press-release-excerpts/ (accessed January 7, 2019).

CEDAW *Summary Record of the 1614th Meeting, July 11, 10 am–1 pm*. See: https://tbinternet.ohchr.org/_layouts/treatybodyexternal/Download.aspx?symbolno=CEDAW%2fC%2fSR.1614&Lang=en (accessed January 15, 2019).

CEDAW *Summary Record of the 1615th Meeting, July 11, 3 pm–5.10 pm*. See: https://tbinternet.ohchr.org/_layouts/treatybodyexternal/Download.aspx?symbolno=CEDAW%2fC%2fSR.1615&Lang=en (accessed January 15, 2019).

CEDAW (July 11, 2018): *Info from Civil Society Organizations*. See: https://tbinternet.ohchr.org/_layouts/treatybodyexternal/SessionDetails1.aspx?SessionID=1171&Lang=en (accessed January 7, 2019).

CEDAW (July 25, 2018): *Concluding Observations on the Initial Report of the State of Palestine.* See: https://tbinternet.ohchr.org/_layouts/treatybodyexternal/Download.aspx?symbolno=CEDAW%2fC%2fPSE%2fCO%2f1&Lang=en (accessed January 9, 2019).

Chakrabarty, Dipesh (2008): *Provincializing Europe.* Princeton, NJ: Princeton Univ. Press.

Chakrabarty, Dipesh (2014): “Place and Displaced Categories, or How We Translate Ourselves into Global Histories of the Modern.” *The Trans/National Study of Culture* (ed. Doris Bachmann-Medick), pp. 53–68. Berlin: De Gruyter.

Conaghan, Joanne (2013): *Law and Gender.* Oxford: Oxford Univ. Press.

Constitutional Law Unit at Birzeit University (12/2017): “Waraqat mawqif ḥawla ḥukm al-maḥkama al-dustūriyya bi-khuṣūs makānat al-ittifāqiyyāt al-duwaliyya fī al-niẓām al-qānūnī al-filasṭīnī (Position Paper on Constitutional Court Judgment Concerning the Status of International Conventions in the Palestinian Legal System, Arabic).” *Birzeit’s Working Papers Series in Legal Studies No. 12/2017*, see: https://papers.ssrn.com/sol3/papers.cfm?abstract_id=3092514 (accessed February 21, 2018).

Croissant, Aurel, Hans-Joachim Lauth, and Wolfgang Merkel (2000): “Zivilgesellschaft und Transformation: ein Internationaler Vergleich.” *Systemwechsel 5. Zivilgesellschaft und Transformation* (ed. Wolfgang Merkel), pp. 9–49. Opladen: Leske + Budrich.

CWLRC [Center for Women’s Legal Research and Consulting/Markaz al-abḥāth wa-l-istishārāt al-qānūniyya wa-l-ḥimāya li-l-mar’a] (July 8, 2013): “Wathīqa ḥuqūqiyya ‘Naḥw al-ʿadāla wa-l-inṣāf li-l-mar’a fī al-ḥuqūq al-ʿā’iliyya’.” See: http://www.cwlrc.ps/ar/cases/”-وثيقة-حقوقية-“-نحو-العدالة-والإنصاف-للمرأة-في-الحقوق-العائلية (accessed May 8, 2019).

CWLRC (June 4, 2013): “Towards a Better Future for Youth in Regards to Marriage and Divorce.” See: http://www.cwlrc.ps/en/projects/towards-a-better-future-for-youth-in-regards-to-marriage-and-divorce (accessed February 7, 2019).

CWLRC (November 13, 2013): “Women’s Rights on Khula File Claim (Women’s Right to Divorce Her Husband) before the Shariah Courts in Gaza Strip.” See: http://www.cwlrc.ps/en/news/women’s-rights-on-khula-file-claim-(-women’s-right-to-divorce-her-husband)------------before-the-shariah-courts-in-gaza-strip (accessed July 7, 2017).

CWLRC (March 1, 2017): “Naḥw taghyīrāt munṣifa wa-ʿādila li-l-nisā’ fī qānūn al-ḥuqūq al-ʿā’iliyya.” See: http://www.cwlrc.ps/ar/news/مركز-الأبحاث-والاستشارات-القانونية-والحماية-للمراة-ينفذ-لقاء-بعنوان-“نحو-تغييرات-منصفة-وعادلة-للنساء-في-قانون-الحقوق-العائلية” (accessed September 9, 2017).

Dahīdī, Afkār al- (December 13, 2017): “Khubarā’: qarār al-maḥkama al-dustūriyya bi-sumūw al-ittifāqiyyāt al-dawliyya ghāmiḍ wa-khārij ikhtiṣāṣihā.” *24fm /akhbār 24*, see: http://www.24fm.ps/ar/news/1513164824 (accessed January 19, 2018).

Damiri, Somoud [Al-Ḍamīrī, Ṣumūd] (2018): “‘A Female Sharīʿa Judge in Palestine between Sharīʿa and Law’: Personal Experience.” *Uses of the Past: Sharīʿa and Gender in Legal Theory and Practice in Palestine and Israel* (eds. Nijmi Edres and Irene Schneider), pp. 97–117. Wiesbaden: Harrassowitz.

Denker, Hendrik (2004): "Die Wiedereinführung des ḫulʿ und die Stärkung der Frauenrechte. Eine Studie zur Reform des Personalstatusrechts im islamischen Rechtskreis am Beispiel des ägyptischen Gesetzes Nr. 1 von 2000." *Beiträge zum Islamischen Recht IV* (eds. Silvia Tellenbach and Thoralf Hanstein), pp. 125–209. Frankfurt a. M.: Lang.

Dūḥān, Muṣṭafā (May 10, 2016): "Khabar 'al-khulʿ fī Ghazza' … akthar min 2500 ḥālat khulʿ bi-l-tarāḍī sanawiyyan fī al-qiṭāʿ." *Samanews*, see: https://samanews.ps/ar/post/269725/الخلع-في-غزة-اكثر-من0-2500-حالة-خلع-بالتراضي-سنويا-في-القطاع (accessed September 9, 2017).

Dupret, Baudouin (1999): "Legal Pluralism, Normative Plurality, and the Arab World." *Legal Pluralism in the Arab World* (eds. Baudouin Dupret, Maurits Berger, and Laila Al-Zwaini), pp. 29–40. The Hague: Kluwer Law International.

Dupret, Baudouin, Maurits Berger, and Laila Al-Zwaini (1999): "Introduction." *Legal Pluralism in the Arab World* (eds. Baudouin Dupret, Maurits Berger, and Laila Al-Zwaini), pp. XI–XVIII. The Hague: Kluwer Law International.

Ebert, Hans-Georg (2010): *Die Qadrī-Pāshā-Kodifikation*. Frankfurt a.M.: Lang.

Edres, Nijmi, Monika Lindbekk, and Irene Schneider (2018): "Introduction." *Uses of the Past: Sharīʿa and Gender in Legal Theory and Practice in Palestine and Israel* (eds. Nijmi Edres and Irene Schneider), pp. 11–26. Wiesbaden: Harrassowitz.

Eickelman, Dale F. and Jon W. Anderson (1999): "Redefining Muslim Publics." *New Media in the Muslim World. The Emerging Public Sphere* (eds. Dale F. Eickelman and Jon W. Anderson), pp. 1–18. Bloomington: Indiana Univ. Press.

Encyclopedia Palestina (2018): see: https://www.palestinapedia.net/%d8%b9%d9%86-%d8%a7%d9%84%d9%85%d9%88%d8%b3%d9%88%d8%b9%d8%a9-%d8%a7%d9%84%d9%81%d9%84%d8%b3%d8%b7%d9%8a%d9%86%d9%8a%d8%a9/ (accessed December 5, 2018).

Engelcke, Dörthe (2017a): "Law-making in Jordan: Family Law Reform and the Supreme Justice Department." *Islamic Law and Society* 24, pp. 1–35.

Engelcke, Dörthe (2017b): "Jordan." *Parental Care and the Best Interests of the Child in Muslim Countries* (eds. Nadjma Yassari et al.), pp. 121–140. The Hague: T.M.C. Asser Press; Heidelberg; Berlin: Springer.

Engelcke, Dörthe (2019): *Reforming Family Law*. Cambridge: Cambridge Univ. Press.

European Union Mission (July 3, 2014): *Palestine. EU Country Roadmap for Engagement with Civil Society 2014–2016*. Jerusalem/Ramallah, see: https://eeas.europa.eu/sites/eeas/files/20140723_palestine_eu_civil_societyroadmap_en.pdf (accessed January 31, 2018).

Faour, Muhammad (2012): *The Arab World's Education Report Card*. Washington, DC: Carnegie Endowment for International Peace.

Fathi, Karim, and Ireneusz Pawel Karolewski (2015): "Civil Society in a Transcultural Comparison: Eastern Europe and the MENA Region." *The Arab Revolution of 2011* (ed. Said Amir Arjomand), pp. 217–249. Albany, NY: SUNY Press.

Foljanty, Lena (2015): "Legal Transfers as Processes of Cultural Translation: On the Consequences of a Metaphor." *Max Planck Institute for European Legal History Research Paper Series* 9, see: https://papers.ssrn.com/sol3/papers.cfm?abstract_id=2682465 (accessed February 28, 2019).

Gerster, Karin A. (2011): *Palestinian Non-Governmental Organizations*. Ramallah: Rosa-Luxemburg-Stiftung.

Gharib, Ali (December 20, 2012): "UN Adds New Name 'State of Palestine'." *The Daily Beast*, see: https://www.thedailybeast.com/un-adds-new-name-state-of-palestine (accessed September 10, 2018).

Giunchi, Elisa (2014): "From Jurists' Ijtihad to Judicial Neo-Ijtihad: Some Introductory Observations." *Adjudicating Family Law in Muslim Courts* (ed. Elisa Giunchi), pp. 1–31. Abingdon: Routledge.

Goudarzi-Gereke, Lara-Lauren (2018): "Perspectives on Palestinian Family Law: Divorce Regulations in the Qāḍī al-Quḍāt's Draft Law of 2013 in the Context of Current Legislation and Demanded Reforms." *Uses of the Past: Sharīʿa and Gender in Legal Theory and Practice in Palestine and Israel* (eds. Nijmi Edres and Irene Schneider), pp. 47–67. Wiesbaden: Harrassowitz.

GUPW (General Union of Palestinian Women/*al-Ittiḥād al-ʿĀmm li-l-Marʾa al-Filasṭīniyya*) (2017): *Report on the Status of Women and Girls in the State of Palestine*. Submitted by: the Non-Governmental Women Coalition for the Implementation of CEDAW in the Occupied State of Palestine; submitted to: The Committee on the Elimination of all Forms of Discrimination against Women-Geneva; September 2017, see: https://tbinternet.ohchr.org/_layouts/treatybodyexternal/Download.aspx?symbolno=INT%2fCEDAW%2fNGO%2fPSE%2f29031&Lang=en (accessed January 8, 2019).

GUPW (2018): *Leaving No One Behind: The Imperative of Inclusive Development in Palestine*. Report by the General Union of Palestinian Women (GUPW), the Non-Governmental Women Coalition for the Implementation of CEDAW in the Occupied State of Palestine, with support from the International Women's Rights Action Watch Asia Pacific (IWRAW AP). Compiled by Luna Saadeh, see: https://tbinternet.ohchr.org/Treaties/CEDAW/Shared%20Documents/PSE/INT_CEDAW_NGO_PSE_31720_E.pdf (accessed January 9, 2019).

GUPW (October 5, 2018): "Muqtaṭafāt min aʿmāl al-warsha al-waṭaniyya li-iʾtilāf qānūn al-aḥwāl al-shakhṣiyya." See: https://www.youtube.com/watch?v=eSauLnBzboI&t=0s&index=106&list=PLqJBmN-bsGoCRv_H_4JBgmUJMAirHJx8G&fbclid=IwAR2yA8VMpd_vFQVaB057njpex09Dbu7DEPX7wkz82afiCkN5Vvc2y69gRA0 (accessed January 16, 2018).

Guth, Stephan (2011): "From Water-Carrying Camels to Modern Story Tellers, or how 'riwāya' Came to Mean 'Novel'." *Borders and Beyond: Crossings and Transitions in Modern Arabic Literature* (eds. Kerstin Eksell and Stephan Guth), pp. 147–179. Wiesbaden: Harrassowitz.

Haaretz (September 20, 2017): "Hamas Leader Invites Abbas to Resume Control of Gaza." See: www.haaretz.com/middle-east-news/palestinians/1.813472 (accessed October 10, 2017).

Hall, Stuart (1997): "Discourse, Power and the Subject." *Representation. Cultural Representations and Signifying Practices* (ed. Stuart Hall), pp. 41–64. London: Sage.

Hammami, Rema (2004): "Attitudes towards Legal Reform of Personal Status Law in Palestine." *Women's Rights & Islamic Family Law* (ed. Lynn Welchman), pp. 125–143. London: Zed Books.

Hammami, Rema (2006): "Palestinian NGOs since Oslo: From Politics to Social Movements?" *The Struggle for Sovereignty. Palestine and Israel, 1993–2005* (eds. Joel Beinin and Rebecca Stein), pp. 84–93. Stanford, CA: Stanford Univ. Press.

Hamzawy, Amr (2003): "Normative Dimensions of Contemporary Arab Debates on Civil Society." *Civil Society in the Middle East* (ed. Amr Hamzawy), pp. 10–46. Berlin: Schiler.

Ḥārisāt nārinā (April 9, 2017): "Ḥārisāt nārinā: Qānūn al-aḥkām al-shakhṣiyya, Rāniyā Alḥamdulillāh." *Talfazyūn Filasṭīn/Palestine TV*, see: https://www.youtube.com/watch?v=rChZeOOJpe0 (accessed January 13, 2018).

Hauser-Schäublin, Brigitta (2003): "Teilnehmende Beobachtung." *Methoden und Techniken der Feldforschung* (ed. Bettina Beer), pp. 33–54. Berlin: Reimer.

Hélie-Lucas, Marie-Aimée (1994): "The Preferential Symbol for Islamic Identity: Women in Muslim Personal Laws." *Identity Politics and Women* (ed. Valentine M. Moghadam), pp. 391–407. Boulder, CO: Westview Press.

Hughes, Geoffrey (May 3, 2016): "The Emergence of 'Divorce before Consumation' as a Legal Category in Jordanian Sharia Courts #Fictions." *AllegraLab*, see: http://allegralaboratory.net/the-emergence-of-divorce-before-consummation-as-a-legal-category-in-jordanian-sharia-courts-fictions/ (accessed September 2, 2018).

Human Rights Watch (December 20, 2017): "Palestine: Reform Restrictive Cybercrime Law." See: https://www.hrw.org/news/2017/12/20/palestine-reform-restrictive-cybercrime-law (accessed January 31, 2018).

Human Rights Watch (2018): "Israel and Palestine. Events of 2018." see: https://www.hrw.org/world-report/2019/country-chapters/israel/palestine (accessed January 17, 2019).

Human Rights Watch/WCLAC/Equality Now (June 2018): *Joint Submission to the CEDAW Committee on the State of Palestine, 70th session.* See: https://tbinternet.ohchr.org/_layouts/treatybodyexternal/Download.aspx?symbolno=INT%2fCEDAW%2fNGO%2fPSE%2f31404&Lang=en (accessed January 9, 2019).

Human Rights Watch and WCLAC (July 9, 2018): *Oral Statement to the CEDAW Committee on the State of Palestine's Report, 70th session.* See: https://www.hrw.org/news/2018/07/09/wclac-and-human-rights-watch-oral-statement-cedaw-committee-state-palestines-report (accessed January 9, 2019).

Hussein, Soraida (2015): "Women's Affairs Technical Committee." *Journal of Middle East Women's Studies* 11, pp. 126–127.

Ibn Rušd (1403/1983): *Bidāyat al-muǧtahid wa-nihāyat al-muqtaṣid.* 2 vols. (ed. by ʿAbd al-Ḥalīm Muḥammad). Beirut: Dār al-Kutub al-Islāmīya.

Ibn Rušd (1994–96): *The Distinguished Jurist's Primer: A Translation of Bidāyat al-mujtahid.* 2 vols., transl. by Imran Ahzan Khan Nyazee. Reading, UK: Garnet.

Ibn Zahra, Muḥammad (1970): *Al-aḥwāl al-shakhṣiyya*, 2nd ed. Al-Qāhira: Dār al-Fikr al-ʿArabī.

ICHR (no date [2017]): *ICHR's Written Intervention on the Initial Report by the State of Palestine to CEDAW.* See: https://tbinternet.ohchr.org/_layouts/treatybodyexternal/Download.aspx?symbolno=INT%2fCEDAW%2fIFN%2fPSE%2f29030&Lang=en (accessed January 8, 2019).

ICHR (July 2018): *The Report of the Independent Commission for Human Rights (ICHR) on the Initial Report of the State of Palestine.* See: https://tbinternet.ohchr.org/_layouts/treatybodyexternal/Download.aspx?symbolno=INT%2fCEDAW%2fIFN%2fPSE%2f31344&Lang=en (accessed January 9, 2019).

ICNL (International Center for Not-For-Profit-Law) (July 12, 2017): "Civic Freedom Monitor: Palestine." See: http://www.icnl.org/research/monitor/palestine.html (accessed January 31, 2018).

Issitt, John (2004): "Reflections on the Study of Textbooks." *History of Education* 33, pp. 683–696.

Jabʿītī, ʿAnān (2012): *Taqrīr ḥawla al-qaḍāʾ al-sharʿī fī Filasṭīn: Taḥaddiyāt wa-āfāq.* Ramallah: Salsalat taqārīr 50 (aman Transparency Palestine), February 2012, see: https://www.aman-palestine.org/ar/reports-and-studies/725.html (accessed September 17, 2018).

Jad, Islah (2004): "The NGO-isation of Arab Women's Movement." *Institute of Development Studies* 35, pp. 34–42.

Johansen, Baber (1999): "Die sündige, gesunde Amme. Moral und gesetzliche Bestimmung (ḥukm) im islamischen Recht." *Contingency in a Sacred Law* (ed. Baber Johansen), pp. 172–188. Leiden: Brill.

Johnson, Penny (2004a): "Palestinian Interim Governance: State Legitimation, Legal Reform and the Shari'a." *Women's Rights and Islamic Family Law* (ed. Lynn Welchman), pp. 112–124. London: Zed Books.

Johnson, Penny (2004b): "Agents for Reform: The Women's Movement, Social Politics and Family Law Reform." *Women's Rights and Islamic Family Law* (ed. Lynn Welchman), pp. 144–163. London: Zed Books.

Johnson, Penny, and Rema Hammami (2013): *Change and Conservation: Family Law Reform in Court Practice and Public Perceptions in the Occupied Palestinian Territory. Summary and Report of 2013 Family Law Survey Findings*. Institute of Women's Studies, Birzeit University in Collaboration with AWRAD with support from UNDP, see: http://iws.birzeit.edu/sites/default/files/2016-12/Family%20Law%20Survey%20FINAL%20WEB_Penny%20and%20Rema_0.pdf (accessed July 14, 2018).

Joseph, Suad (2005): "Gender and Citizenship in Middle Eastern States." *Women and Islam: Critical concepts in Sociology, Vol. III* (ed. Haideh Moghissi), pp. 47–57. London: Routledge.

Kalpokas, Ignas (2012): "Remembering Independence, Desiring Enemies: Reflections on Nationhood in Contemporary Lithuania." *Studies of Transition States and Societies* 4 (1), pp. 16–30.

Kandiyoti, Deniz (1991): "Bargaining with Patriarchy." *The Social Construction of Gender* (eds. Judith Lorber and Susan A. Farrell), pp. 104–118. Newbury Park: Sage Publications.

Karamapress [Al-Karāma Brass] (July 2, 2015): "Āmāl Ḥamd: Nihāya Muḥammad kānat ʿunwānan musharrafan li-l-marʾa wa-l-thawra al-filasṭīniyya." See: http://www.karamapress.com/arabic/?Action=PrintNews&ID=131913 (accessed September 19, 2018).

Kershner, Isabel (January 29, 2019): "Palestinian Government Resigns with no Clear Replacement." *New York Times*, see: https://www.nytimes.com/2019/01/29/world/middleeast/palestinian-government-resigns.html?rref=collection%2Ftimestopic%2FPalestinian%20Authority&action=click&contentCollection=timestopics&region=stream&module=stream_unit&version=latest&contentPlacement=1&pgtype=collection (accessed February 5, 2019).

Khalil, Asem (2009a): "Constitutional Framework of the Future Palestinian State." Working Paper presented within the context of the Project: "The Contours of a Future State" A multi-part compendium of Palestinian Thinking Commissioned by the Institute of Law – Birzeit University.

Khalil, Asem (2009b): "Formal and Informal Justice in Palestine: Dealing with the Legacy of Tribal Law." *Études Rurales* 184, pp. 169–184.

Khalil, Asem (2012): "Constitution-Making and State-Building: Redefining the Palestinian Nation." *Constitutionalism in Islamic Countries: Between Upheaval and Continuity* (eds. R. Grote und T. Röder), pp. 583–596. Oxford: Oxford Univ. Press.

Khalil, Asem (2013): "Beyond the Written Constitution: Constitutional Crisis of, and the Institutional Deadlock in, the Palestinian Political System as Entrenched in the Basic Law." *I-con* 11, pp. 34–73.

Khalil, Asem, and Raffaella A. del Sarto (2015): "The Legal Fragmentation of Palestine-Israel and European Union Policies Promoting the Rule of Law." *Fragmented Borders, Interdependence and External Relations* (ed. Raffaella A. del Sarto), pp. 129–154. New York: Palgrave Macmillan.

Khoury, Jack (April 13, 2019): "New Palestinian Government Sworn in with Abbas Loyalist at Its Helm." *Haaretz*, see: https://www.haaretz.com/middle-east-news/palestinians/.premium-new-palestinian-government-sworn-in-with-abbas-loyalist-at-its-helm-1.7112263 (accessed April 26, 2019).

Khoury, Jack, and Amira Hass (June 2, 2014): "Palestinians Swear in Unity Government." *Haaretz*, see: https://www.haaretz.com/.premium-palestinians-swear-in-unity-government-1.5250505 (accessed April 26, 2019).

Koselleck, Reinhart (2004): *Futures Past: On the Semantics of Historical Time*. Transl., with an introd. by Keith Tribe. New York: Columbia Univ. Press.

Koselleck, Reinhart (2013): *Vergangene Zukunft: Zur Semantik geschichtlicher Zeiten*. 8th ed. Frankfurt a. M.: Suhrkamp.

Kraft, Dina (March 25, 2019): "Haaretz Poll: 42% of Israelis Back West Bank Annexation, including Two-States Supporters." *Haaretz*, see: https://www.haaretz.com/israel-news/israeli-palestinian-conflict-solutions/.premium-42-of-israelis-back-west-bank-annexation-including-two-state-supporters-1.7047313 (accessed March 26, 2019).

Krüger, Hilmar (2014): "Länderbericht Palästina." *Internationaler Rechtsverkehr in Zivil- und Handelssachen, Band VI* (eds. Reinhold Geimer and Rolf Schütze), pp. 1110–1–1110–10. Munich: Beck.

Kuttab, Eileen (2008): "Palestinian Women's Organizations: Global Cooption and Local Contradiction." *Cultural Dynamics* 20 (2), pp. 99–117.

Kuttab, Eileen (2009): "The Palestinian Women's Movement: From Resistance and Liberation to Accomodation and Globalization." *Vents d'Est, Vents d'Ouest* (ed. Christine Verschuur), pp. 101–116. Graduate Institute Publications; published as open edition book in 2016.

Laborce, Rachel, Jonathan Malcolm et.al. (2018): *2018 Conflict Risk Assessment Report. Palestinian Territories: West Bank and Gaza Strip*. [Ottawa]: The Norman Paterson School of International Affairs, Carleton University.

Lahamag [*lahā*] (March 21, 2011): "Awwal raʾīsat niyāba sharʿiyya fī Filasṭīn." See: https://www.lahamag.com/article/12226-أول_رئيسة_نيابة_شرعية_في_فلسطين_ (accessed August 30, 2017).

Lane, Edward William (1863, repr. 1984): *Arabic-English Lexicon, Vol. I and II*. Cambridge: The Islamic Texts Society.

Langenfeld, Christine (2016): "Geschlechterrollen in Ehe und Familie im Wandel der Zeit und des Rechts." *Beiträge zum islamischen Recht XI* (eds. Thoralf Hanstein and Irene Schneider), pp. 33–43. Frankfurt a. M.: PL Academic Research.

Layish, Aharon (2004): "The Transformation of the Sharīʿa from Jurists' Law to Statutory Law in the Contemporary Muslim World." *Die Welt des Islams* 44, pp. 85–113.

Lāzim naḥkī (April 30, 2013): *khulʿ*. Palestinian TV, see: https://www.youtube.com/watch?v=EXvQuK8TDU0 (accessed September 6, 2017).

Leitz, Lisa (2017): "General Union of Palestinian Women (GUPW)." *Encyclopaedia Britannica*, see: https://www.britannica.com/topic/General-Union-of-Palestinian-Women (accessed June 8, 2017).

Lubenow, Jorge Adriano (2012): "Public Sphere and Deliberative Democracy in Jürgen Habermas: Theoretical Model and Critical Discourses." *American Journal of Sociological Research* 2 (4), pp. 58–71.

Lüders, Christian (2003): "Teilnehmende Beobachtung." *Hauptbegriffe Qualitative Sozialforschung* (eds. Ralf Bohnsack, Winfried Marotzki, and Michael Meuser), pp. 151–153. Opladen: Leske + Budrich.

Maannews [*Maʿan*] (January 20, 2010): "Al-Oury Appointed Legal Advisor to Abbas." See: http://www.maannews.com/Content.aspx?id=255614 (accessed September 15, 2018).

Maannews [*Maʿan*] (January 14, 2012): "Qarīban fī Filasṭīn … Li-l-nisāʾ ḥaqq khulʿ azwājihinna fī al-maḥākim al-sharʿiyya." See: http://maannews.net/Content.aspx?id=452434 (accessed September 9, 2017).

Maannews [*Maʿan*] (February 21, 2012): "Dīwān Qāḍī al-Quḍāt yukhaṭṭiṭ li-bināʾ quṣūr ʿadliyya wa-maḥākim sharʿiyya mamlūka li-l-dawla." See: http://maannews.net/Content.aspx?id=462228 (accessed August 30, 2017).

Maannews [*Maʿan*] (December 13, 2012a): "Jāmiʿat Bīrzayt tunaẓẓim muḥāḍara ḥawla 'al-khulʿ fī Filasṭīn'." See: http://maannews.net/Content.aspx?id=547663 (accessed December 10, 2018).

Maannews [*Maʿan*] (December 13, 2012b): "Maḥkamat Ramallāh al-sharʿiyya tuqirr bi-sharʿiyyat khulʿ Kayyāl bi-Qinṭār." See: http://maannews.net/Content.aspx?id=547722 (accessed June 15, 2019).

Maannews [*Maʿan*] (December 23, 2012): "Namūdhaj li-muḥākama ṣūriyya li-daʿwā iftidāʾ 'khulʿ qaḍāʾī'." See: http://maannews.net/Content.aspx?id=550368 (accessed December 10, 2018).

Maanews [*Maʿan*] (April 23, 2016): "Palestinians Hold Funeral for Lawmaker Rabiha Diab." See: http://www.maannews.com/Content.aspx?ID=771258 (accessed September 15, 2018).

Maannews [*Maʿan*] (February 15, 2017): "Liqāʾ samāḥat raʾīs al-Majlis al-aʿlā maʿa Qanāt Maʿan ḥawla al-tashrīʿāt wa-l-qawānīyīn al-khāṣṣa bi-l-aḥwāl al-shakhṣiyya, al-ḥalqa 1." See: www.youtube.com/watch?v=V_3OVKe3eEs (accessed August 20, 2018).

Maannews [*Maʿan*] (December 19, 2018): "Ittiḥād al-marʾa yastaghrib al-tarājuʿ ʿan ittifāqiyyat al-qaḍāʾ ʿalā kāffat ashkāl al-tamyīz." See: http://www.maannews.net/Content.aspx?id=970741&fbclid=IwAR11meGAjba_x-QMMfr74ZyA8FCU7CmhyaT24KoNjTC4reS9mfnyRLynWPQ (accessed January 5, 2019).

Maltz, Judy (March 24, 2019): "Two States, One and Other Solutions to the Israeli-Palestinian Conflict." *Haaretz*, see: https://www.haaretz.com/israel-news/israeli-palestinian-conflict-solutions/.premium-explained-two-states-one-and-other-solutions-to-the-israeli-palestinian-conflict-1.7044468 (accessed March 26, 2019).

Marotzki, Winfried (2003): "Thematisches Interview." *Hauptbegriffe Qualitative Sozialforschung* (eds. Ralf Bohnsack, Winfried Marotzki, and Michael Meuser), pp. 153–154. Opladen: Leske + Budrich.

Massad, Joseph (1995): "Conceiving the Masculine: Gender and Palestinian Nationalism." *Middle East Journal* 49 (3), pp. 467–483.

Masud, Muhammad Khalid (2005): "Communicative Action and the Social Construction of Shari'a in Pakistan." *Religion, Social Practice, and Contested Hegemonies. Reconstructing the Public Sphere in Muslim Majority Societies* (eds. Armando Salvatore and Mark LeVine), pp. 155–179. New York: Palgrave Macmillan.

Melhem, Ahmed (March 22, 2015): "Palestinian Female Judges Gavel Down Taboos." *Al-Monitor*, see: http://www.al-monitor.com/pulse/en/originals/2015/03/palestine-female-judge-sharia-judiciary.html (accessed on August 25, 2017); see Arabic version: http://www.al-monitor.com/pulse/ar/originals/2015/03/palestine-female-judge-sharia-judiciary.html (accessed January 30, 2019).

Merry, Sally Engle (2006): *Human Rights & Gender Violence*. Chicago: Univ. of Chicago Press.

Milhem, Feras (2004): *The Origins and Evolution of the Palestinian Sources of Law.* Brussels: s.n.

Moghrabi, Omar, and Fayeq Ahmad Hassouna (2016): *Separation Lawsuit for Damage, Dissension and Conflict: Causes, Effects, Obstacles* (Arabic/English). CWLRC Gaza.

Monterescu, Daniel (2006): "Stranger Masculinities: Gender and Politics in a Palestinian-Israeli 'Third Space'." *Islamic Masculinities* (ed. Lahoucine Ouzgane), pp. 123–141. London: Zed Books.

Moors, Annelies (1995): *Women, Property and Islam: Palestinian Experiences, 1920–1990*, Cambridge: Cambridge Univ. Press.

Moors, Annelies (1999): "Debating Islamic Family Law: Legal Texts and Social Practices." *Social History of Women and Gender in the Modern Middle East* (eds. Margaret L. Meriwether and Judith E. Tucker), pp. 141–175. Boulder, CO: Westview Press.

Moors, Annelies (2003): "Introduction: Public Debates on Family Law Reform: Participants, Positions, and Styles of Argumentation in the 1990s." *Islamic Law and Society* 10, pp. 1–11.

Motala, Ziyad (1995): "The Promotion of National Unity and Reconciliation Act, the Constitution and International Law." *The Comparative and International Law Journal of South Africa* 28, pp. 338–362.

Muḥāḍarāt masāq qānūn al-aḥwāl al-shakhṣiyya (Personal Status Law 338). First semester 2013–2014, Birzeit University.

Muqtafī, al- s. al-Muqtafī.

Musawa (May 17, 2016): "Demanding Withdrawal of the Constitutional Court Formation. Eyes on Political Parties and Community Forces to Raise their Voices."

See: http://www.musawa.ps/post/demanding-withdrawal-of-the-constitutional-court-formation.html (accessed January 30, 2019).

Musawah (July 2018): *Thematic Report on Muslim Family law and Muslim Women's Rights in Palestine, 70th CEDAW Session*. See: https://tbinternet.ohchr.org/_layouts/treatybodyexternal/Download.aspx?symbolno=INT%2fCEDAW%2fNGO%2fPSE%2f31669&Lang=en (accessed January 8, 2019).

Muslih, Muhammad (1995): "Palestinian Civil Society." *Civil Society in the Middle East, Vol. 1* (ed. Augustus Richard Norton), pp. 243–368. Leiden: Brill.

Naʿīm, Hudā (2013): *Mawqif al-Majlis* ([*of Gaza*]) *al-tashrīʿī min qānūn al-khulʿ wa-iftidāʾ al-marʾa li-nafsihā*). (Exemplar received from Zaynab al-Ghunaymī, CWLRC.)

Nakhkhāl, Ramūz (April 5, 2015): "'Khulūd al-Faqīha': Awwal imraʾa filasṭīniyya tataqallad manṣab al-qaḍāʾ al-sharʿī." *Erem-news*, see: https://www.eremnews.com/latest-news/253811 (accessed January 30, 2019).

Nasir, Jamal (2002): *The Islamic Law of Personal Status*. The Hague: Kluwer Law International.

Nazzal, Nasouh (April 4, 2016): "Abbas Establishes Palestinian Constitutional Court." *Gulf News*, see: http://gulfnews.com/news/mena/palestine/abbas-establishes-palestinian-constitutional-court-1.1703902 (accessed January 18, 2018).

Nilesat (March 24, 2019): "Ahkām sharʿiyya: Nataʿarraf ʿalā ikhtiṣāṣ wa-mahāmm dāʾirat al-niyāba al-sharʿiyya fī manẓūmat al-qaḍāʾ al-sharʿī al-filasṭīnī." See: https://m.facebook.com/story.php?story_fbid=1015069225355863&id=393871814142277&sfnsn=mo (accessed March 29, 2019).

OCHA (2018): "Area C." *United Nations Office for the Coordination of Humanitarian Affairs. Occupied Palestinian Territory*, see: https://www.ochaopt.org/location/area-c (accessed June 13, 2020).

Opwis, Felicitas (2007): "Islamic Law and Legal Change. The Concept of Maṣlaḥa in Classical and Contemporary Islamic Legal Theory." *Sharia. Islamic Law in the Contemporary Context* (eds. Abbas Amanat and Frank Griffel), pp. 63–82. Standford, California: Stanford University Press.

Othman, Mohammad (2015): "Divorce at Gaza Comes at Steep Price." *Al-Monitor*, see: http://www.al-monitor.com/pulse/originals/2015/04/gaza-divorce-sharia-courts-khul-wealthy-women.html (accessed July 7, 2017).

Pal24.net [*Filasṭīn24*] (November 4, 2013): "Tawṣiya bi-iʿtimād "al-khulʿ al-qaḍāʾī" fī al-maḥākim al-sharʿiyya bi-Ghazza." See: https://www.pal24.net/news/15513.html (accessed February 9, 2019).

Palestinian Declaration of Independence (November 15, 1988): see: http://www.mideastweb.org/plc1988.htm (accessed March 3, 2019).

Palestinian National Charter (1968): See: http://www.palwatch.org/main.aspx?fi=640&doc_id=8210.

Palestinian Multiple Indicator Cluster Survey (2014) by: Palestinian Central Bureau of Statistics, United Nations Children's Fund and United Nations Population Fund, see: https://mics-surveys-prod.s3.amazonaws.com/MICS5/Middle%20East%20and%20North%20Africa/State%20of%20Palestine/2014/Final/State%20of%20Palestine%202014%20MICS_English.pdf (accessed June 17, 2019).

Palestinian Women and Security: A Legal Collection (2012). Geneva: Geneva Centre for the Control of the Armed Forces (DCAF); English see: https://www.dcaf.ch/sites/default/files/publications/documents/Legal_Collection_Women_EN.pdf (accessed September 23, 2019). Arabic Version see: http://www.dcaf-tunisie.org/Ar/publication/securite-des-femmes-palestiniennes-cadres-legaux-et-reglementaires/6/10029 (accessed June 16, 2020).

Press Release Palestinian Central Bureau of Statistics (March 7, 2018): Palestinian Central Bureau of Statistics issued a Press Release on the Eve of the International Women's Day on Tuesday, 08/03/2018, see: www.pcbs.gov.ps/portals/_pcbs/PressRelease/Press_En_7-3-20148-women-en.PDF (accessed June 9, 2019).

Palpress [*Wakālat Filasṭīn Brass bi-anbāʾ*] (January 14, 2012): "Al-Shaykh Idʿīs: qarīban qānūn bi-l-khulʿ fī Filasṭīn wa-imkāniyyat ilghāʾ tawābiʿ al-muhūr." See: http://www.palpress.co.uk/arabic/?Action=Details&ID=36014 (accessed December 10, 2018).

Paltimesnet [*Filasṭīn al-ʾān*] (November 3, 2013): "Tawṣiya bi-iʿtimād "al-khulʿ" fī al-maḥākim al-sharʿiyya." See: https://paltimes.net/post/51939/توصية-باعتماد-الخلع-بالمحاكم-الشرعية (accessed February 9, 2019).

Paltoday [*Filasṭīn al-yawm*] (January 19, 2012): "Al-maḥkama al-ʿulyā: Qānūn al-khulʿ sa-yuṭabbaq qarīban fī al-arāḍī al-filasṭīniyya." See: https://paltoday.ps/ar/post/128140 (accessed December 10, 2018).

Pernau, Margrit (2016): "Provincializing Concepts: The Language of Transnational History." *Comparative Studies of South Asia, Africa and the Middle East* 36, pp. 483–499.

Peteet, Julie (2005): "Icons and Militants: Mothering in the Danger Zone." *Women and Islam, Vol. III* (ed. Haideh Moghissi), pp. 104–129. London: Routledge.

Peteet, Julie, and Barbara Harlow (1991): "Gender and Political Change." *Middle East Report* 173, pp. 4–8.

Peters, Rudolph (2005): *Crime and Punishment in Islamic Law*. Cambridge: Cambridge Univ. Press.

Polfus, Turid Smith (2014): "Fiqh Arguments for the Palestinian khulʿ Divorce (before Consummation)." *Hawwa* 12, pp. 49–78.

Proske, Matthias, and Wolfgang Meseth (2006): "Nationalsozialismus und Holocaust als Themen des Geschichtsunterrichts." *Geschichtsdidaktik empirisch* (eds. Hilke Günther-Arndt and Michael Sauer), pp. 127–154. Berlin: Lit-Verlag.

Qadrī Bāshā, Muḥammad (2007): *Al-aḥkām al-sharʿiyya fī al-aḥwāl al-shakhṣiyya ʿalā madhhab Abī Ḥanīfa al-Nuʿman*, bi-ʿināyat Bassām ʿAbdalwaḥḥāb al-Jābī. Bayrūt: Dār Ibn Ḥazm, see: https://archive.org/details/a1150n/page/n3 (accessed May 2, 2019).

Qafisheh, Mutaz (2018): "Without Reservation: Reforming Palestinian Family Laws in Light of CEDAW." *Uses of the Past: Sharīʿa and Gender in Legal Theory and Practice in Palestine and Israel* (eds. Nijmi Edres and Irene Schneider), pp. 29–46. Wiesbaden: Harrassowitz.

Qashṭa, Tāmir (December 2, 2013): "'Al-khulʿ' yaṣil Filasṭīn." *Safa* [*Ṣafā*ʾ], see: http://safa.ps/post/123609/%D8%A7%D9%84%D8%AE%D9%84%D8%B9-%D9%8A%D8%B5%D9%84-%D9%81%D9%84%D8%B3%D8%B7%D9%8A%D9%86 (accessed September 7, 2017).

Qatrawi, Iyad (April 26, 2016): "Is Abbas Tightening his Grip on Power with New Constitutional Court?" *Al-Monitor*, see: https://www.al-monitor.com/pulse/originals/2016/04/palestine-abbas-decree-constitutional-court-legality.html (accessed January 18, 2018).

Quran [Qurʾān]: *The Quran Interpreted: A Translation* (1955), by Arthur John Arberry, see: https://www.islamawakened.com/index.php/qur-an/ (accessed January 22, 2019).

Rajūb, ʿIwaḍ al- (February 1, 2009): "Filasṭīniyyatāni tadkhulāni at-taʾrīkh bi- tawallīhimā al-qaḍāʾ al-sharʿī bi-l-Ḍiffa." *Al-Jazeera*, see: https://www.aljazeera.net/news/reportsandinterviews/2009/2/1/فلسطينيتان-تدخلان-التاريخ-بتوليهما (accessed August 26, 2017).

Raya [al-Rāya] (February 18, 2012): "Khulʿ ... qarīban fī Filasṭīn." See: http://www.raya.com/home/print/f6451603-4dff-4ca1-9c10-122741d17432/f2a33c3d-35bd-42dc-a744-a73d6d06cd8e (accessed June 29, 2017) (site discontinued).

Registered Divorces [*sic*] Cases (2017): *Palestinian Central Bureau of Statistics*, see: http://www.pcbs.gov.ps/Portals/_Rainbow/Documents/VS-2017-04e.htm (accessed October 18, 2018).

Risse, Thomas, and Kathryn Sikkink (1999): "The Socialization of International Human Rights Norms into Domestic Practices, Introduction." *The Power of Human Rights: International Norms and Domestic Change* (eds. Thomas Risse, Stephen C. Ropp, and Kathryn Sikkink), pp. 1–38. Cambridge: Cambridge Univ. Press.

Roy, Sara (2011): *Hamas and Civil Society in Gaza: Engaging the Islamist Social Sector*. Princeton, NJ: Princeton University Press.

Reese-Schäfer, Walter (2007): *Politisches Denken Heute*. Munich: Oldenbourg.

Reiter, Yitzhak (2009): "Judge Reform: Facilitating Divorce by Shari'a Courts in Israel." *Journal of Islamic Law and Culture* 11, pp. 13–37.

Ṣalāḥ, Muḥammad Saʿīd (2015): "Al-farq bayna al-khiṭba wa-l-ʿaqd wa-l-dukhūl." Fatwā 123. *Dār al-Iftāʾ*, see: http://www.darifta.ps/fatawa2014/showfatwa.php?subfatwa= الفرق بين الخطبة والعقد والدخول (accessed May 20, 2020).

Salam, Kawther (February 20, 2009): "Palestine, First Females Islamic Judges Inaugurated in Palestine." *Women Living under Muslim Laws*, see: http://www.wluml.org/fr/node/5082 (accessed September 13, 2017).

Schäfer, Wolf (2014): "Reconfiguring Area Studies for the Global Age." *Social Theory and Regional Studies in the Global Age* (ed. Said Amir Arjomand), pp. 145–175. Albany, NY: State Univ. of New York Press.

Schär, Bernhard, and Vera Sperisen (2011): "Zum Eigensinn von Lehrpersonen im Umgang mit Lehrbüchern." *Forschungswerkstatt Geschichtsdidaktik 09* (eds. J. Hodel und B. Ziegler), pp. 124–134. Bern: hep.

Schneider, Irene (1990): *Das Bild des Richters in der adab al-qāḍī-Literatur*. Frankfurt a.M.: Lang.

Schneider, Irene (1993): "Die Merkmale der Idealtypischen qāḍī-Justiz – Kritische Anmerkungen zu Max Webers Kategorisierung der islamischen Rechtsprechung." *Der Islam* 70, pp. 145–159.

Schneider, Irene (2007): "Freedom and Slavery in Early Islamic Time (1st/7th and 2nd/8th centuries)." *Al-Qanṭara* 28, pp. 353–382.

Schneider, Irene (2008): "Islamisches Recht zwischen Göttlicher Satzung und Temporaler Ordnung? Überlegungen zum Grenzbereich zwischen Recht und Religion." *Recht und Religion in Europa* (eds. Christine Langenfeld and Irene Schneider), pp. 138–191. Göttingen: Universitätsverlag Göttingen.

Schneider, Irene (2012): Review of Die Kultur der Ambiguität. Eine andere Geschichte des Islams by Thomas Bauer. *Der Islam* 88, pp. 439–448.

Schneider, Irene (2014): *Women in the Islamic World*. Princeton, NJ: Markus Wiener Publishers.

Schneider, Irene (2015): "Translational Turn and CEDAW: Current Gender Discourses in the Islamic Republic of Iran." *Indonesian and German Views on the Islamic Legal Discourse on Gender and Civil Rights* (eds. Fritz Schulze and Noorhaidi Hasan), pp. 133–165. Wiesbaden: Harrassowitz.

Schneider, Irene (2016a): "Polygamy and Legislation in Contemporary Iran: An Analysis of the Public Legal Discourse." *Iranian Studies* 49, pp. 657–676.

Schneider, Irene (2016b): "Recht und Geschlechterordnung: Gesellschaftliche Debatten um die ḫulʿ-Scheidung in Palästina 2012–2014." *Beiträge zum Islamischen Recht XI* (eds. Thoralf Hanstein and Irene Schneider), pp. 45–69. Frankfurt a.M.: PL Academic Research.

Schneider, Irene (2018a): "Divorce Gaza Style: Regulations and Discussions in Gaza and the West Bank (2013–2017)." *Islamisches Recht in Wissenschaft und Praxis* (eds. Hatem Elliesie, Beate Anam, and Thoralf Hanstein), pp. 177–205. Wiesbaden: Harrassowitz.

Schneider, Irene (2018b): "How is the Past Used to Construct Gender Concepts in the Present? The Example of the Textbook for the Course on Personal Status Law at Birzeit University/West Bank (Winter Semester 2013/14)." *Uses of the Past: Sharīʿa and Gender in Legal Theory and Practice in Palestine and Israel* (eds. Nijmi Edres and Irene Schneider), pp. 69–95. Wiesbaden: Harrassowitz.

Schneider, Irene (2019): "Family Law and Succession." *Routledge Handbook of Islamic Law* (eds. Khaled Abou El Fadl, Ahmad Atif Ahmad, and Said Fares Hassan), pp. 324–339. London: Routledge.

Schneider, Irene (forthcoming): "The Religious against the Secular: Othering in the Legal and Political Debates in Palestine: Debates about the Family Draft Law in 2013." *Thank God We're Not Like Them. The Global Dimensions of Religious Othering* (eds. Mark Juergensmeyer, Kathleen Moore, and Dominic Sachsenmaier). Oxford: Oxford University Press (in process).

Schultz, Ulrike (2017): "Do Female Judges Judge Differently? Empirical Realities of a Theoretical Debate." *Women Judges in the Muslim World* (eds. Nadia Sonneveld and Monika Lindbekk), pp. 23–50. Leiden: Brill.

Shaʿbān, ʿUmar (August 16, 2016): "Sharākat al-sulṭa maʿa al-mujtamaʿ al-madanī … al-intikhābāt al-baladiyya namūdhajan." *Palthink*, see: http://palthink.org/ar/?p=1319 (accessed October 5, 2017).

Shaham, Ron (2018): "Bayt al-ṭāʿa." *Encyclopedia of Islam THREE* (eds. Kate Fleet et al.); consulted online, see: http://dx-1doi-1org-1lreiydas3ac0.han.sub.uni-goettingen.de/10.1163/1573-3912_ei3_COM_22946 (accessed April 30, 2019).

Shahar, Ido (2013): "Forum Shopping between Civil and Shariʿa Courts: Maintenance Suits in Contemporary Jerusalem." *Religion in Disputes: Pervasiveness of Religious Normativity in Disputing Processes* (eds. Franz von Benda-Beckmann, Keebet von Benda-Beckmann, Martin Ramstedt, and Bertram Turner), pp. 147–164. New York: Palgrave.

Shalhoub-Kevorkian, Nadera (2010): "Palestinian Women and the Politics of Invisibility." *Peace Prints: South Asian Journal of Peacebuilding* 3, pp. 1–21.

Shalhoub-Kevorkian, Nadera (2012): "Casting Out 'Citizenship': Israel's Eviction of Palestinians." *Review of Women's Studies* 7, pp. 47–49.

Sharq al-awsaṭ, al- (Januar 30, 2009): "Awwal qāḍiya sharʿiyya li-l-Sharq al-Awsaṭ: nashʿur bi-taḥaddin kabīr wa-nasʿā li-taḥqīq ʿadāla akbar." See: http://archive.aawsat.com/details.asp?section=4&article=505005&issueno=11021#.WaWPMsZpzcs (accessed August 29, 2017).

Shasha News [*shāsha niyūz*] (April 20, 2016): "Filasṭīn: Mā hiya al-maḥkama al-dustūriyya." See: https://www.shasha.ps/news/208253.html (accessed September 18, 2018).

Shāyib, Yūsuf al- (March 2, 2009): "Asmahān al-Waḥīdī wa-Khulūd al-Faqīh … awwal qāḍiyatayn sharʿiyyatayn fī Filasṭīn." *Al-Ayyām*, see: http://www.al-ayyam.ps/ar_page.php?id=5e2d560y98751840Y5e2d560 (accessed August 29, 2017).

Shehada, Nahda (2005): *Justice without Drama*. Maastricht: Shaker.

Shehada, Nahda (2011): "Debating Islamic Family Law in Palestine." *Feminist Activism, Women's Rights, and Legal Reform* (ed. M. Sharwani), pp. 23–47. London: Zed Books.

Sonneveld, Nadia (2012): *Khul' Divorce in Egypt: Public Debates, Judicial Practices, and Everyday Life*. Cairo: The American University in Cairo Press.

Tamīmī, Taysīr al- (September 6, 2012): "Al-ʿamal bi-l-khulʿ al-qaḍāʾī fī al-maḥākim al-sharʿiyya intihāk li-l-sharīʿa wa-l-qānūn." *Alwatanvoice* [*Dunyā al-waṭan*], see: https://pulpit.alwatanvoice.com/content/print/270413.html (accessed June 13, 2020).

Tatar, Hidāyat Muḥammad al: (February 15, 2015): "Al-Qāḍī al-sharʿī al-Faqīh: Wulūj al-marʾa manṣab al-qaḍāʾal-sharʿī taḥaddin li-l-ʿādāt wa-l-taqālīd." *Ni sāʾ min ajl Filasṭīn*, see: http://www.womenfpal.com/news/2015/2/22/ القاضي-الشرعي--الفقيه---ولوجُ-المرأة-منصبَ-القضاء-الشرعي-تحدٍّ-للعادات-والتقاليد (accessed August 28, 2017).

The Guardian (January 1, 2019): "Why Trump's Middle East Peace Plan is Just a Side Show." See: https://www.theguardian.com/us-news/2019/jan/01/donald-trump-middle-east-peace-plan-israel-palestine (accessed January 22, 2019).

Tucker, Judith (1996): "Revisiting Reform: Woman and the Ottoman Law of Family Rights 1917." *Arab Studies Journal* 4 (2), pp. 4–17.

Tucker, Judith (1998): *In the House of the Law*. Berkeley: Univ. of California Press.

Ṭuwāfisha, ʿAbdalkạrīm Jabr ʿAlī (2014): *Dirāsat ʿan wāqiʿ al-maḥākim al-sharʿiyya wa-taṭawwur al-qawānīn al-maʿmūl bi-hā fī Filasṭīn*. Ishrāf: Jamāl al-Kilānī, quddimat hādhihi risāla istikmālan li-mutaṭallabāt al-ḥuṣūl ʿalā darajat al-Mājistīr fī al-fiqh wa-l-tashrīʿ bi-Kulliyyat al-dirāsāt al-ʿulyā fī Jāmiʿat al-Najāḥ al-waṭaniyya fī Nāblus, Filasṭīn, see: https://scholar.najah.edu/sites/default/files/Abdel-Karim%20Toafshh.pdf (accessed February 7, 2018).

Usher, Barbara Plett (May 15, 2018): "Jerusalem Embassy: Why Trump's Move Was Not about Peace." *BBC*, see: https://www.bbc.com/news/world-us-canada-44120428 (accessed March 2, 2019).

Vesey-Byrne, Joe (2017): "Which Countries Recognize Palestine." *Independent*, see: https://www.indy100.com/article/palestinians-recognised-which-countries-palestinian-state-statehood-recognition-balfour-declaration-8033876 (accessed September 18, 2018).

Wafa [*wafāʾ*] (February 20, 2008): "Al-majlis al-aʿlā li-l-qaḍāʾ al-sharʿī yudīn tadakhkhul Ḥamās fī ʿamal al-maḥākim al-sharʿiyya fī qiṭāʿ Ghazza." See: http://www.wafa.ps/ar_page.aspx?id=sdMHoza477235603284asdMHoz (accessed April 1, 2019).

Wafa [*wafāʾ*] (May 13, 2011): "Taʿmīm li-raʾīs Majlis al-qaḍāʾ al-aʿlā ʿan al-takhāruj al-irthī." See: http://www.wafa.ps/ar_page.aspx?id=hp09hya575879091216ahp09hy (accessed November 17, 2018).

Wafa [*wafāʾ*] (August 30, 2012): "Idʿīs yuʿlin badʾ al-ʿamal bi-qānūn al-khulʿ fī Filasṭīn." See: http://www.wafa.ps/ar_page.aspx?id=jWHDs3a606829147023ajWHDs3 (accessed December 10, 2018).

Wathīqat ḥuqūq al-mar'a al-filasṭīniyya (2008): "Charter of Women's Rights Issued by the General Union of Palestinian Women, the Ministry of Women's Affairs and Civil Society Groups." See: http://www.pal-tahrir.info/audio/files/law.pdf (accessed January 24, 2018).

Wattan [*Wikālat waṭan al-anbā'*] (March 5, 2018): "Al-Hay'a al-mustaqilla turaḥḥib bi-qarār majlis al-wuzarā' li-izālat al-tamyīz ḍidda al-mar'a." See https://www.wattan.tv/ar/news/243214.html (accessed August 20, 2019).

Wattan [*Wikālat waṭan al-anbā'*] (June 21, 2018): "Filasṭīn tabḥath 'an tafāsīr li-l-Sharī'a tansajim ma'a "Sīdāw" … wa-sharkh yattasi' bayna 'ulamā' al-dīn wa-l-siyāsa." See: https://www.youtube.com/watch?v=wcwPM9tqYVE (accessed December 21, 2018).

Wattan [*Wikālat waṭan al-anbā'*] (June 25, 2018): "Ba'd taḥqīq Waṭan … al-mu'assasāt al-niswiyya tatadā'ā li-ta'dīl qānūn al-aḥwāl al-shakhṣiyya wa-tas'ā li-iṭlāq ḥamla ḍāghiṭa." See: https://www.wattan.tv/ar/video/256784.html (accessed December 31, 2018), see also https://www.youtube.com/watch?time_continue=13&v=EvZeS3qF1p8 (accessed August 19, 2019).

Wattan [*Wikālat waṭan al-anbā'*] (June 30, 2018): "Ba'd taḥqīq Waṭan … al-hay'a al-mustaqilla: al-maṭlūb al-baḥth 'an ijtihādāt taqaddumiyya min al-sharī'a tansajim ma'a Sīdāw." See: https://www.wattan.tv/ar/tv/257258.html (accessed December 31, 2018).

Wattan [*Wikālat waṭan al-anbā'*] (December 9, 2018): "Muntadā al-munaẓẓamāt al-ahliyya li-munāhaḍat al-'unf ḍidda al-mar'a yudīn al-da'wā al-ṣarīḥa li-istikhdām al-'unf ḍidda al-mar'a." See: https://www.wattan.tv/ar/news/270827.html (accessed December 31, 2018).

WCLAC/Equality Now/Muntada (October 2017): *Pre-Session Report on Palestine for Consideration during the 68th Session of United Nation Committee on the Elimination of Discrimination against Women.* A Joint Submission by WCLAC, Equality Now, Muntada, see: https://tbinternet.ohchr.org/_layouts/treatybodyexternal/Download.aspx?symbolno=INT%2fCEDAW%2fNGO%2fPSE%2f29167&Lang=en (accessed January 9, 2019).

Wehr, Hans (1976): *A Dictionary of Modern Written Arabic.* Ed. by J. Milton Cowan. Ithaca, New York: Spoken Language Services.

Welchman, Lynn (1999): *Islamic Family Law: Text and Practice in Palestine.* Jerusalem: WCLAC.

Welchman, Lynn (2000): *Beyond the Code.* The Hague: Kluwer Law International.

Welchman, Lynn (2003): "In the Interim: Civil Society, the Shar'ī Judiciary and Palestinian Personal Status Law in the Transitional Period." *Islamic Law and Society* 34, pp. 34–69.

Welchman, Lynn (2004): "Legal Context: Shari'a Courts and Muslim Family Law in the Transitional Period." *Women's Rights and Islamic Family Law* (ed. Lynn Welchman), pp. 99–111. London: Zed Books.

Welchman, Lynn (2007): *Women and Muslim Family Laws in Arab States*. Amsterdam: Amsterdam Univ. Press.

Welchman, Lynn (2009): "Family, Gender, and Law in Jordan and Palestine." *Family, Gender, and Law in a Globalizing Middle East and South Asia* (eds. Kenneth M. Cuno and Manisha Desai), pp. 126–144. Syracuse, NY: Syracuse Univ. Press.

Welchman, Lynn, and Sara Hossain (2005): "Naming the Crime: 'Honour,' Rights and Wrongs." *Review of Women's Studies* 3, pp. 67–78.

Wikipedia: "Khulūd Faqīh." See: https://ar.wikipedia.org/w/index.php?title=%D8%AE%D9%84%D9%88%D8%AF_%D9%81%D9%82%D9%8A%D9%87&oldid=38246894 (accessed October 7, 2019). For the much shorter English version see: https://en.wikipedia.org/w/index.php?title=Kholoud_Faqih&oldid=890981432 (accessed on October 7, 2019).

"Who Will Bell the Cat?" (24 August 2015), see: https://www.youtube.com/watch?v=gz7wHiFfbRo (accessed April 1, 2019).

Wonews [*wakālat akhbār al-mar'a*] (December 20, 2012): "Al-Qāḍiya Khulūd al-Faqīh – al-mar'a al-filasṭīniyya al-waḥīda min bayn aqwā 100 imra'a 'arabiyya mu'aththira." See: http://wonews.net/ar/index.php?act=post&id=4741 (accessed August 26, 2017).

Worster, William Thomas (2009): "Law, Politics, and the Conception of the State in State Recognition Theory." *Boston University International Law Journal* 27, pp. 115–171.

Yassari, Nadjma (2014): *Die Brautgabe im Familienvermögensrecht: innerislamischer Rechtsvergleich und Integration in das deutsche Recht*. Tübingen: Mohr Siebeck.

Zughayr, Niḍā al- (2017): "'An mafhūm al-mujtama' al-madanī al-filasṭīnī." See: http://www.badil.org/ar/component/k2/item/1862-art8.html (accessed October 4, 2017).

Websites

State of Palestine/Official Institutions

Dār al-Iftā' (Ramallah): http://www.darifta.ps/.

Government: http://www.palestinecabinet.gov.ps/Website/AR/Govs/Default?ID=17.

HSCC Higher Sharia Court Council/*al-Majlis al-A'lā li-l-Qaḍā' al-Shar'ī* [Gaza]: http://www.ljc.gov.ps/; http://www.courts.gov.ps/details.aspx?id=sEugV5a60912192asEugV5.

Legislation and Advisory Bureau/*Dīwān al-Fatwā wa-l-Tashrī'*: http://www.lab.pna.ps/ar_new/index.php?p=home.

Ministry of Justice/*Wizārat al-'Adl*: http://www.moj.pna.ps/index.aspx.

MoWA Ministry of Women's Affairs/*Wizārat Shu'ūn al-Mar'a*: https://www.mowa.pna.ps/.

PA Palestinian Authority/*al-Sulṭa al-Filasṭīniyya*, see: Palestinian Government: http://palestine.dk/palestine/government/.

Palestinian Central Bureau of Statistics/*al-Jihāz al-Markazī li-l-Iḥṣā' al-Filasṭīnī*: www.pcbs.gov.ps.

Personal Status Prosecution/*Niyāba al-Aḥwāl al-Shakhṣiyya*: http://kudah.pna.ps/ar_page.aspx?id=hMCuLfa1909216518ahMCuLf.

PLC Palestinian Legislative Council/*Al-Majlis al-Tashrī'ī al-Filasṭīnī* [Gaza]: http://www.plc.ps/ar.

SCHC Sharia Court High Council/*al-Majlis al-A'lā li-l-Qaḍā' al-Shar'ī* [West Bank]: http://www.kudah.pna.ps/ar_page.aspx?id=jxY55ca1925396319ajxY55c.

Sharia High Court/*al-Maḥkama al-'Ulyā al-Shar'iyya*: http://kudah.pna.ps/ar_page.aspx?id=uZ7Giva1911120024auZ7Giv.

Supreme Judge Department/*Dīwān Qāḍī al-Quḍāt* [West Bank]: http://www.kudah.pna.ps/.

Civil Society

Al-Haq/al-Ḥaqq: http://www.alhaq.org/ (accessed January 18, 2018).

CWLRC Center for Women's Legal Research and Consulting, Gaza/*Markaz al-Abḥāth wa-l-Istishārāt al-Qānūniyya lil-Mar'a, Ghazza*: http://www.cwlrc.ps/en/ (accessed January 30, 2019).

GUPW General Union of Palestinian Women/*al-Ittiḥād al-'Āmm li-l-Mar'a al-Filasṭīniyya*: http://www.gupw.net/ [January 30, 2019 not accessible, but see: https://www.facebook.com/pg/gupw.palestine/about/?ref=page_internal).

ICHR The Independent Commission for Human Rights/*al-Hay'a al-Mustaqilla li-Ḥuqūq al-Insān*: English: http://www.ichr.ps/en; Arabic: https://ichr.ps/ar/1 (accessed January 30, 2019).

Muntada, al-: Platform of Palestinian Non-Governmental Organizations against Domestic Violence against Women/*al-Muntada*; *Muntadā al-Munaẓẓamāt al-Ahliyya al-Filasṭīniyya li-Munāhaḍat al-'Unf ḍidda al-Mar'a*): http://www.almuntada-pal.ps/ (accessed August 19, 2019).

Musawa/*Musāwāh* [Palestinian NGO]: http://www.musawa.ps/ (accessed Janauary 18, 2018).

Musawah/*Musāwāh* [International NGO]: http://www.musawah.org/ (accessed April 30, 2019).

PNGO Palestinian Non-Governmental Organizations Network/*Shabakat al-Munaẓẓamāt al-Ahliyya al-Filasṭīniyya*: English: http://www.pngo.net/; Arabic: http://www.pngo.net/?lang=ar (accessed September 15, 2018).

WAC Women's Affairs Center, Gaza/*Markas Shu'ūn al-Mar'a*: http://site.wac.ps/ar/ (accessed April 30, 2019).

WATC Women's Affairs Technical Committee/*Ṭāqim Shu'ūn al-Mar'a*: http://www.watcpal.org/ (accessed July 10, 2019).

WCLAC Women's Centre for Legal Aid and Counselling/*Markaz al-Mar'a li-l-Irshād al-Qānūnī wa-l-Ijtimāʿī*: http://www.wclac.org/ (accessed April 30, 2019).

UN

UN United Nations: http://www.un.org/en/ (accessed April 30, 2019).

CEDAW Convention on the Elimination of all Forms of Discrimination against Women. See: http://www.un.org/womenwatch/daw/cedaw/cedaw.htm (accessed January 16, 2019).

CEDAW 70 Session July 2–July 20, 2018: https://tbinternet.ohchr.org/_layouts/treatybodyexternal/SessionDetails1.aspx?SessionID=1171&Lang=en (accessed April 30, 2019).

OCHA see UN OCHA

UN OCHA oPt Office for the Coordination of Humanitarian Affairs, Occupied Palestinian Territory: https://www.ochaopt.org/page/about-us (accessed September 20, 2018).

UNHCHR United Nations High Commissioner for Human Rights: https://www.ohchr.org/EN/Pages/Home.aspx (accessed January 30, 2019).

UNRWA United Nations Relief And Works Agency For Palestinian Refugees in The Near East: https://www.unrwa.org/ (accessed May 30, 2020).

Laws

BL: Basic Law 2003, amended 2005 (*al-Qānūn al-Asāsī*), see: https://www.palestinianbasiclaw.org/basic-law/2003-amended-basic-law (accessed April 30, 2019).

EFRL: Egyptian Family Rights Law 303/1954 (*Qānūn Ḥuqūq al-ʿĀ'ila*), see Muqtafi, see also http://www.plc.gov.ps/menu_plc/arab/files/sT%C2%BD%C3%9Fnd/%C6%92Tft%C6%92Pp%20%C6%92TsT%C2%BD%C3%9Fndn%C3%AD/0/t%C6%92dfd%20%C3%91tft%20%C6%92Tp%C6%92PT%C3%AD.htm (accessed April 30, 2019).

Egyptian Law No. 1/2000 (*Khulʿ*-law): https://arbia6swerv1.wordpress.com/2011/07/05/قانون-الأحوال-الشخصية-المصري-رقم-1-لسن/ (accessed on September 19, 2019).

JLFR: Jordanian Law of Family Rights 92/1951 (*Qānūn Ḥuqūq al-ʿĀ'ila*), see Muqtafi.

JLPS: Jordanian Law of Personal Status 61/1976 (*Qānūn al-Aḥwāl al-Shakhṣiyya*), see Muqtafi.

JLPS: Jordanian Law of Personal Status 36/2010 (*Qānūn al-Aḥwāl al-Shakhṣiyya*), see: https://sjd.gov.jo/EchoBusV3.0/SystemAssets/PDFs/AR/AppliedLegislations/a7walsha5seye.pdf (accessed June 13, 2020).
JPL: Jordanian Penal Law 16/1960 (*Qānūn al-ʿUqūbāt*), see Muqtafi.
Law of the Formation of the Sharia Courts 19/1972 (*Qānūn Tashkīl al-Maḥākim al-Sharʿiyya*), see Muqtafi.
Law of the Procedure for Sharia Courts 31/1959 (*Qānūn Uṣūl al-Muḥākamāt al-Sharʿiyya*), see Muqtafi.
Law of the Procedure for Sharia Courts 12/1965 (*Qānūn Uṣūl al-Muḥākamāt al-Sharʿiyya*), see Muqtafi.
Law of Sharia Lawyers 12/1952 (*Qānūn al-Muḥāmīn al-Sharʿiyyīn*), see Muqtafi.
Law with Regard to the Charitable Associations and Civil Society Organizations 1/2000 (*Qānūn bi-Shaʾn Jamʿiyāt al-Khayriyya wa-l-Hayʾāt al-Ahliyya*), see Muqtafi.
OLFR: Ottoman Law of Family Rights 1917 (*Qānūn Ḥuqūq al-ʿĀʾila*), see Muqtafi.
Taʿmīmāt [*West Bank*]:
Taʿmīm iblāgh al-zawja 48/2011 (*Taʿmīm* with regard to inform the wife [in case of her divorce]) (2011). *Dīwān Qāḍī al-Quḍāt, West Bank*; see: http://kudah.pna.ps/userfiles/image/%D8%A7%D8%A8%D9%84%D8%A7%D8%BA%20%D8%A7%D9%84%D8%B2%D9%88%D8%AC%D8%A9%20.jpg (accessed September 8, 2017).
Taʿmīm al-khulʿ 59/2012 *Dīwān Qāḍī al-Quḍāt, West Bank*; http://www.kudah.pna.ps/ar_page.aspx?id=PS9BpGa2088146082aPS9BpG.
Taʿmīmāt [*Gaza*]:
http://www.ljc.gov.ps/index.php?option=com_content&view=article&id=32&Itemid=53 (accessed January 30, 2019).
Taʿmīm 33/2009: www.ljc.gov.ps/images/stories/pdf/2.pdf (accessed August 20, 2018).
Taʿmīm 09/2012: www.ljc.gov.ps/images/stories/final19122012.pdf (accessed August 20, 2018).
Taʿmīm 07/2016: www.ljc.gov.ps/images/court2016.pdf (accessed August 20, 2018).
Taʿmīm 08/2016: www.ljc.gov.ps/images/court2016.pdf (accessed August 20, 2018).

Terminology

ʿādāt wa-taqālīd	customs and traditions
al-qūwa al-tanfīdhiyya al-tābiʿa li-Ḥamās	*Ḥamās* Executive Force
bāʾin baynūna ṣughrā	minor irrevocable divorce
bāʾin baynūna kubrā	major irrevocable divorce
bāṭil	void
baynūna kubrā	greater finality
baynūna ṣughrā	lesser finality
ḍarar	Injury, damage, harm
daʿwā	claim, lawsuit
dhukūrī	masculine
dukhūl	consummation of marriage
fāsid	irregular
faskh	dissolution of marriage
fatwā, pl. fatāwā	legal opinion
fidāʾ	price to be paid for redemption; redemption
fiqh	jurisprudence
fitna	disorder/sedition
ḥaḍāna	child custody
ḥadīth, pl aḥādīth	saying of the Prophet/tradition referring to what the Prophet said, did and accepted
ḥalāl, opposite to *ḥarām*	(religiously) permitted
ḥarām, opposite to *ḥalāl*	(religiously absolutely) forbidden, sacred
ḥikma	rational
ḥukm, pl. aḥkām	rule; judgment
ibrāʾ	renunciation of financial rights in exchange for divorce; redemption
ʿidda	waiting period
iftidāʾ	redemption
ijmāʿ	consensus
ijtihād	independent legal opinion
inḍimām	accession (to a treaty etc.)
iqrār	acknowledgement, confession, issuing
ikhtilāf	diversity [of opinions]
ishhār wa-iẓhār	announcement and presentation
ʿiṣma	protection
isnād	chain of transmitters

kafāʾa	suitability
karāha	aversion
karāma	dignity
khalwa	privacy
khulʿ	divorce based on compensation of the husband by the wife
khulʿ qaḍāʾī	judicial *khulʿ*
khul riḍāʾī	*khulʿ* based on consent
kufr	*unbelief*
lā ḍarar wa-lā ḍirār	no infliction of injury or repaying one injury with another
libās	vestments
mafhūm	concept
maʾdhūn	marriage officer
mahr	dower
maqāṣid, sg. *maqṣad*	intentions
marjaʿiyya	point of reference, principle
marsūm	ordinance
maṣdar	source
mabdaʾ pl. *mabādiʾ*	principle
maṣlaḥa	benefit; welfare
mubāraʾa	dissolution of marriage by agreement with mutual renunciation of any financial obligations
muḥarramāt	forbidden things, sacred topics
mumāthala	similarity
musādaqa	ratification
musāwāh	equality
mustashār qānūnī	legal advisor
nafaqa	maintenance
nasab	descent
nāshiz (*relating to a man*)	mistreating
nāshiz[*a*] (*relating to a woman*)	disobedient
nizāʿ wa-shiqāq	dispute and discord
qānūn	law
qarār	decision
qawāʾid sharʿiyya	Sharia rules; technical principles of Sharia
qaṭʿī/ẓannī	decisive (proof) / presumptive
rajʿa	taking back the wife after first and second repudiation
rajʿī	revocable repudiation

ṣulḥ	reconciliation
sulṭa taqdīriyya	discretionary power
ṭāʿa	obedience
taʿdīl	amendment of the law
tafrīq	separation
takhayyur	selection (of opinions from the different schools of law)
takhāruj	waiving of shares of inheritance
ṭalāq bāʾin	irrevocable repudiation
talfīq	combination of opinions (from different schools of law)
ṭalāq	repudiation
ṭalāq muqābil ibrāʾ ʿāmm	divorce based on complete redemption
taʿmīm pl. *taʿmīmāt*	ruling
tarāḍī	mutual consent
tawābiʿ	dower add-ons
wilāya	guardianship
wujūb	obligation
zināʾ	illegal sexual relations

Index

The index lists scholars and institutions only if mentioned in the text. Footnotes are taken into consideration only as far as concepts are concerned.

Printed in the United States
By Bookmasters